W9-CTM-179

Fodor's 92 Pacific North Coast

Fodor's Travel Publications, Inc.
New York • London • Toronto

Copyright © 1992
by Fodor's Travel Publications, Inc.

ISBN 0–679–02073–X

Fodor's Pacific North Coast

Editor: Alison Hoffman
Contributors: Susan M. Bain, Tom Barr, Robert Brown, Susan Brown, Ray Chatelin, John Doerper, Tom Gaunt, Barbara Hodgin, Eve Johnson, Philip Joseph, Jeff Kuechle, Mike Miller, Marcy Pritchard, Glenn W. Sheehan, Loralee Wenger, Terri Wershler, Adam Woog
Art Director: Fabrizio La Rocca
Cartographer: David Lindroth
Illustrator: Karl Tanner
Cover Photograph: Ron Thomas/FPG International

Design: Vignelli Associates

Special Sales

MANUFACTURED IN THE UNITED STATES OF AMERICA
10 9 8 7 6 5 4 3 2

Contents

Foreword

We wish to express our gratitude to those who have helped with this guide, including Portland/Oregon Visitors Association; Oregon Historical Society; Seattle/King County News Bureau, especially Barry Anderson and David Blandford; Elvira Quarin at Tourism Vancouver; The Whistler Resort Association; Robert Brown with the Canadian Consulate General; and Hinda Simon.

While every care has been taken to ensure the accuracy of the information in this guide, the passage of time will always bring change, and consequently, the publisher cannot accept responsibility for errors that may occur.

All prices and opening times quoted here are based on information supplied to us at press time. Hours and admission fees may change, however, and the prudent traveler will avoid inconvenience by calling ahead.

Fodor's wants to hear about your travel experiences, both pleasant and unpleasant. When a hotel or restaurant fails to live up to its billing, let us know and we will investigate the complaint and revise our entries where the facts warrant it.

Send your letters to the editors of Fodor's Travel Publications, 201 E. 50th Street, New York, NY 10022.

Highlights'92 and Fodor's Choice

Highlights '92

Oregon Portland, Oregon, rang in the new decade with the opening of the **Convention Center** and the **Pioneer Place Shopping complex,** which is anchored by Saks Fifth Avenue. According to the Portland/Oregon Convention and Visitors Association, the Convention Center is the cornerstone for developing a city-center east side. The Convention Center encompasses 17 acres, and Pioneer Place covers four city blocks. There are other big city revitalization plans that loom further in the future: Over the next 5–10 years, railroad tracks and freeways along the east bank of the Willamette River will be replaced with several miles of **greenways** and **parks** for locals and tourists to enjoy. While these developments reflect the strong, growing economy throughout the state, the Columbia River Gorge and Hood River are enjoying their reputation as the sailboarding capital, and they have welcomed more than 28 new businesses over the past three years, most of which are linked to the sport.

Washington Washington's cultural scene continues to flourish, with repertories growing as quickly as the state's already solid world-class reputation for it's progressive attitude toward the arts, dance, and theater. The **Seattle Art Museum,** originally scheduled to open in December 1991, may be opening a bit behind schedule. In any case, the five-story post-modern-style building will house Asian, Native American, Oceanic, African, and pre-Columbian art.

Washington is flourishing in other ways, as well. Known as one of the most liveable cities in the country, Seattle's tourism brings much money into the state, and the strong political contingent who are determined to maintain a balance between nature and development continues to grow.

British Columbia British Columbia, Canada's third-largest province, has reason to celebrate these days. In spring 1990 the town of Duncan, on Vancouver Island, got back to basics with the opening of the **Native Heritage Centre,** an establishment devoted to the rich ethnic history of the province. Interpretive presentations and exhibits reflect the lives of the region's indigenous peoples.

Maintaining its speed in the fast lane, Vancouver prepares for the **Indy Vancouver,** part of the PPG Indy Car World Series. One of 16 international car races, the 1.7-mile circuit will run through downtown during Labour Day weekend. The city continues to make the headlines as plans for North America's largest urban development project gets underway, beginning with the former site of Vancouver's Expo 86. **International Village,** the first phase, sits adjacent to Chinatown and will be a mixture of condominiums, town houses, an office tower, hotels, parks, and commercial space. The entire project will not be completed for about 20 years.

Southeast Alaska Alaska's **tourism industry** climbed in 1990, with reports from Juneau's Convention and Visitor's Bureau that there had been more than a 16% increase in cruise travel to the city over the previous year. While Southeast Alaska enjoys the attention, it also looks forward to joining the rest of the state in a 50th-anniversary celebration in 1992 to commemorate the building of the **Alaska Highway.** Events and festivities are planned along stretches of Alaska's highway and into British Columbia.

Fodor's Choice

No two people will agree on what makes a perfect vacation, but it's fun and helpful to know what others think. We hope you'll have a chance to experience some of Fodor's Choices yourself in the Pacific North Coast. For detailed information about each entry, refer to the appropriate chapter.

Portland

Attractions   Pioneer Square Courthouse
Portland Building
Salmon Street Plaza fountain

Special Moments   Celebrations at The Rheinlander Restaurant
Saturday and Sunday Market

Restaurants   Atwaters (*Very Expensive*)
Couch Street Fish House (*Expensive*)
Digger O'Dell's Oyster Bar and Restaurant (*Moderate*)
Dan and Louis Oyster Bar and Restaurant (*Inexpensive*)

Hotels   Heathman (*Very Expensive*)
Red Lion Lloyd Center (*Expensive*)
Execulodge/Portland Airport (*Moderate*)
Best Western Fortniter Motel (*Inexpensive*)

Western Oregon

Sights   View of the Columbia River Gorge from Crown Point/
Vista House on U.S. border

Multnomah Falls from U.S. 30 and I–84
(Columbia River Gorge)

View of Haystack Rock from the beach (Cannon Beach)

Sea Lion Caves from the cliff-top (Heceta Head)

Attractions   Mission Mill Village, Salem
Shakespeare Festival Exhibit Center, Ashland
Wildlife Safari, Roseburg

Restaurants   The Bistro, Cannon Beach (*Expensive*)
The Chetco River Inn, Brookings (*Moderate*)
Nick's Italian Cafe, McMinnville (*Moderate*)
La Serre, Yachats (*Moderate*)
Kum-Yon's Coos Bay (*Inexpensive*)

Hotels   Timberline Lodge, Timberline (*Expensive*)
Chateaulin, Ashland (*Moderate–Expensive*)
The Steamboat Inn, Steamboat (*Moderate–Expensive*)
Franklin Street Bed & Breakfast, Astoria (*Moderate*)
This Olde House B&B, Coos Bay (*Moderate*)
The Whale Cove, Port Orford (*Moderate*)

Seattle

Attractions International District
Pike Place Market
Seattle Aquarium
Space Needle

Special Moments Sitting in on the "Out To Lunch" concert series
at one of Seattle's parks

Seeing Seattle at night from the Space Needle's
observation deck

Reading the hundreds of name tiles on the floor
of the Pike Place Market

Seeing Mt. Rainier looming over Puget Sound
on a clear day when "the mountain comes out"

Hotels Alexis (*Very Expensive*)
Four Seasons (*Very Expensive*)
Edgewater (*Expensive*)
Sorrento (*Expensive*)
Inn at the Market (*Moderate–Expensive*)
Meany Tower Hotel (*Inexpensive*)

Restaurants Canlis (*Very Expensive*)
Cafe Alexis (*Expensive*)
Wild Ginger (*Moderate*)
Hien Vuong (*Inexpensive*)

Washington

Scenic Travels The 23-mile loop on Highway 11, along Chuckanut Bay

A ferry ride through the San Juan Islands

Highway 101 north from Hoquiam to Quinault Lake
and west to Queets and Kalaloch

Attractions Hoodsport Winery, Hoodsport
Hovander Homestead Park, Ferndale
Northwest Trek Wildlife Park, Eatonville
Point Defiance Park, Tacoma

Hotels Inn at Langley, Langley (*Expensive*)
James House, Port Townsend (*Moderate–Expensive*)
The Castle B&B, Bellingham (*Moderate*)
Olde Glencove Hotel, Gig Harbor (*Moderate*)

Restaurants Il Fiasco, Bellingham (*Expensive–Very Expensive*)

C'est Si Bon, Port Angeles (*Expensive*)

The Shoalwater Restaurant, Seaview
(*Moderate–Expensive*)

Alice's Restaurant, Tenino (*Moderate*)

Fountain Café, Port Townsend (*Moderate*)

Tides Tavern, Gig Harbor (*Inexpensive*)

Wild Berry, Ashford (*Inexpensive*)

Vancouver

Attractions   Dr. Sun-Yat Sen Classical Garden, Chinatown

Granville Public Market, Granville Island

Museum of Anthropology, on University of British Columbia campus

Maritime Museum, Granville Island

Stanley Park Zoo

Shopping   Chinatown
Fourth Avenue (between Burrard and Balsam streets)
Pacific Centre Mall
Robson Street

Restaurants   Chartwell (*Expensive*)
Tojo's (*Expensive*)
Kirin Mandarin Restaurant (*Moderate*)
Rubina Tandoori (*Moderate*)
Szechuan Chongqing (*Inexpensive*)

Hotels   Le Meridien (*Very Expensive*)
Pan Pacific (*Very Expensive*)
Wedgewood Hotel (*Expensive*)
Georgia Hotel (*Moderate*)
West End Guest House (*Moderate*)
Sylvia Hotel (*Inexpensive*)

Coastal British Columbia

Attractions   Ann Hathaway's Cottage, Victoria
Crystal Gardens, Victoria
Pacific Undersea Garden, Victoria
Royal British Columbia Museum, Victoria

Shopping   Chinatown, Victoria
Government Street, Victoria
Market Square, Victoria

Great Outdoors   Adams River Salmon Run, Okanagan Valley
Cathedral Park, Penticton
Inside Passage
Pacific Rim National Park, Vancouver Island
Queen Charlotte Islands

Restaurants   Sooke Harbour House, Sooke (*Very Expensive*)
Larousse, Victoria (*Expensive*)
Corbett Lake Country Inn, Merritt (*Moderate*)
Old Mahle House, Nanaimo (*Moderate*)
Six-Mile House, Victoria (*Inexpensive*)

Hotels   Hotel Grand Pacific, Victoria (*Very Expensive*)
Laurel Point Inn, Victoria (*Expensive–Very Expensive*)
Lake Okanagan Resort, Kelowna (*Expensive*)

Coast Bastion Inn, Nanaimo (*Moderate–Expensive*)
Painter's Lodge, Campbell River (*Moderate–Expensive*)
Crest Motor Hotel, Prince Rupert (*Moderate*)
Lac Le Juene Resort, Kamloops (*Moderate*)
Craigmyle Guest House, Victoria (*Inexpensive–Moderate*)
Gables Country Inn and Tea House, Kelowna
(*Inexpensive*)
The Greystone Manor, Comox (*Inexpensive*)
The Roadhouse Inn, Parksville (*Inexpensive*)

Southeast Alaska

Special Moments
The howl of a train whistle near Skagway
The roll of a humpback whale in Glacier Bay
A misty morning in Sitka with bald eagles on high
The scream of a salmon reel near Ketchikan
Helicopter flightseeing over Juneau's glaciers

Activities
Rafting through an eagle sanctuary near Haines

Watching Indian totem carvers at Ketchikan

Hiking the route of the gold rush on the Chilkoot
trail near Skagway

Stopping in to the Red Dog Saloon in Juneau

Hotels
Glacier Bay Lodge, Glacier Bay National Park (*Expensive*)
Captain's Choice Motel, Haines (*Moderate–Expensive*)
Ingersoll Hotel, Ketchikan (*Moderate*)
The Prospector, Juneau (*Moderate*)
Golden North Hotel, Skagway (*Moderate*)

Restaurants
The Channel Club, Sitka (*Moderate–Expensive*)
The Summit, Juneau (*Moderate–Expensive*)
Glacier Bay Country Inn, Glacier Bay (*Moderate*)
Salmon Falls Resort, Ketchikan (*Moderate*)
The Beachcomber Inn, Petersburg (*Inexpensive*)
Gold Creek Salmon Bake, Juneau (*Inexpensive*)

Pacific North Coast

PACIFIC

ALASKA

Skagway
Haines
Juneau
Sitka
Petersburg
Wrangell
Prince
of Wales
Island
Ketchikan

CANADA
U.S.

Prince
Rupert
Sandsplit
Queen
Charlotte
Islands

Johnsons
Crossing
YUKON
Watson Lake
Cassiar

NORTHWEST TERRITORY

Great Slave
Lake

Bistcho
Lake

Fort Nelson

Williston
Lake

Babine
Lake
Smithers
Ootsa
Lake

BRITISH
COLUMBIA

Prince
George
Quesnel
Lake

Dawson
Creek

Grimshaw

ALBERTA

Lake
Claire

Lesser Slave
Lake

Bonnyville

Edmonton

Red Deer

Jasper

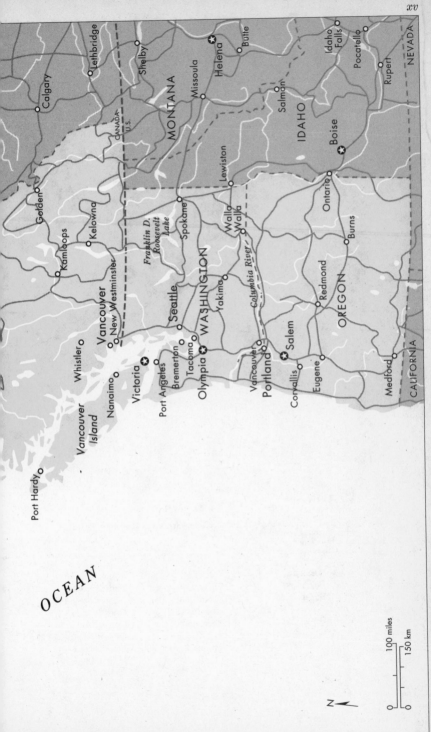

Port Hardy

Vancouver Island

Whistler

Nanaimo

Victoria

Port Angeles

Bremerton

Tacoma

Olympia

Seattle

Vancouver

New Westminster

Kamloops

Kelowna

Golden

Calgary

Lethbridge

Shelby

Helena

Butte

Missoula

MONTANA

CANADA
U.S.

Salmon

IDAHO

Idaho Falls

Pocatello

Ruperl

NEVADA

Boise

Ontario

Lewiston

Spokane

Franklin D.
Roosevelt
Lake

Walla
Walla

Yakima

WASHINGTON

Columbia River

Redmond

Burns

OREGON

Salem

Corvallis

Eugene

Medford

CALIFORNIA

Portland

Vancouver

OCEAN

N

0   100 miles

0   150 km

World Time Zones

Numbers below vertical bands relate each zone to Greenwich Mean Time (0 hrs.).
Local times frequently differ from these general indications,
as indicated by light-face numbers on map.

Introduction

By Tom Gaunt

Tom Gaunt works as editor of the magazine section of The Business Journal of Portland. *A native of the state, Tom has covered Northwest politics and culture for the past 12 years. His writing has appeared in* Pacific Northwest Magazine, OMNI, *and* The Oregon Magazine of Nature, Exploration and Science.

It was getting dark high in the Oregon Cascades as we rowed ashore at the small, isolated lake. The peaks, just wrapped in an autumn snow, were blurred by the dusk. With less than an hour of light left, we decided one of us should get back to camp quickly, unencumbered, while the other deflated the raft and carried it back the 4 miles to camp, with little chance of making it out before pitch blackness fell over the dense forest.

Maybe it was because my brother is older and has bad knees, or perhaps it was just because I was soaking wet and needed to change anyway. But I elected to be the one who walked in the dark.

Soon I was alone with the lake as a wispy fog slipped in from the upper basin; the tall firs creaked in the wind and to the east, barely visible now, three rugged peaks shrugged in the distance. I knew that my brother, rapidly moving away, was the only other human near me. Behind me were hundreds of tiny lakes like this one, all empty and quiet in their own seldom-explored basins.

I was very alone, feeling at once joyous and frightened, exalted and exhausted, both overwhelmed and completely free. I had not just *connected* with nature in some fleeting, superficial way; I had melded with it. Things of the world below the meadows, canyons, and forests simply did not exist. There were only those moments of scary wonder as I got into some dry clothes and prepared to walk through the woods in the dark.

The sensation of being alone with Nature, of being in the very cup of her hands, is something that is familiar to those who live in the Pacific Northwest. There are certainly more remote areas, but here nature can be enjoyed for what it is. Here man seems to have found his niche in the ecosystem and, more or less, stays there as pleased with his failures to conquer Nature as with his occasional, temporary successes.

To understand the people of the Pacific Northwest—and there are roughly 10 million of us in an area about the size of western Europe—one has to understand the land and the climate and how the two combine to cast its spell. For even in the cities of the Pacific Northwest, nature is never far. In Seattle, Mount Rainier and the Olympics entrance commuters stuck in traffic; in Vancouver, British Columbia, the Coast Range juts out over downtown, keeping the metropolis in line; and in Portland, city fathers have kept 4,700 acres of primitive forest lands that harbor deer, elk, and the odd bear and cougar in the hills just north of the city center. It's not a zoo, it's just there, a piece of primeval forest that

serves as a constant reminder of Nature's enduring presence here. No matter how many planes Seattle's Boeing
Corporation churns out, or how many chips come out of Oregon's high-tech Silicon Forest, or how many shares of
stock change hands in the volatile Vancouver Stock Exchange, the relationship with Nature and the wilds is not
altered. There is always this mixture of respect and love,
fear and admiration, topped off with simple awe.

These feelings come naturally when you survey the landscape—an array of shapes, colors, textures—but still there
is one sensation. To understand, look at the far corners of
this land: southern Alaska and southeastern Oregon.

Swathed in Sitka Spruce, the islands scattered below the
Alaskan mountains are like small individual worlds. Roads
and people are few. The intrepid can kayak through the inlets and fjords for days on end, catching salmon or watching
the glaciers peel majestically off into the sea, sheet by
sheet. Roughly in the middle of this region is Juneau, the
only state capital inaccessible by road. Here, it is common
for legislative aides to live in makeshift camps in the hills
above town and ski to the state's modest capitol building.
Behind the coast ranges are deep, remote river canyons and
lakes that stretch all the way east to where the mighty
Rockies dribble off into a few bumps on the tundra. Moving
south along Coastal British Columbia, the terrain is no less
steep, but the glaciers shrink back into the hanging valleys,
leaving only a few waterfalls. Other than fishing vessels
and the occasional cruise ship, this is lonely country, beautiful, but often pelted with wild rainstorms and blizzards
that blast straight across the north Pacific.

L ikewise, southeastern Oregon is solitary country. It is
a land of extremes, a high desert where it is not all uncommon, especially in the spring or fall, to find the
highest and lowest temperature reading in the lower 48
states in the same county. A 100-mile drive across the desert and scrub land is not likely to turn up another soul.
What people there are—many of them descendants of
Basque settlers a century ago—tend to their stock on the
arid plains. The land is dominated by Steens' Mountain, a
60-mile-long slab of desert floor that over the millennia
gradually tilted upward. From the west, the gain in elevation is barely noticeable at first, just a steppe rolling into
the distance. But after 30 miles of bad road, the mountain
simply breaks off into space, the Alvord Desert a gasping
5,000 feet below. And beyond, the gray horizon fades into
Nevada and Idaho.

Whether it is the cathedrallike island forests of southern
Alaska or the sagebrush-covered frontier of southeastern
Oregon, the awe is there—subtle yet omnipresent. In many
ways, the land here shapes us, mellowing and hypnotizing
us until other ways of life seem improbably complicated. I
don't know how many people I've known who come back

from visiting New York or San Francisco or some other fa-
mously bustling place and say something along the lines of
"It was very exciting, but I don't know why anyone would
go to the trouble of living there."

Go to the trouble . . . A key phrase. In the Pacific Northwest, going to the trouble is more likely the consequence of
some recreational choice. You go to the trouble of rafting a
river just for the hell of it; you go to the trouble of hiking to
the top of a butte you've never gone up before; or you go to
the trouble of taking a road in the baking deserts of eastern
Oregon and Washington just to see the mirages disappear
as you approach them.

Okay, so Pacific Northwesterners may seem a bit
flaky—carefree, perhaps—but some say this con-
tagious attitude simply comes with the land. The
Native Americans of the Pacific Northwest had it pretty
easy compared to their brethren on the Great Plains.
Whereas a family of Sioux might need to scour 100 square
miles of land to get enough food to live on, West Coast Indians only needed to dip into the river for fish or take a few
steps out of the village for game. Sure, the weather was
damp, but wood for shelter and warmth was plentiful and
the time saved gathering food went toward monumental
projects of art such as the totems of Coastal British Columbia.

Even today this plenty is obvious. While Pacific Northwest
cuisine has become popular on some menus, picking a single
cuisine here is a difficult task. Most distinctive cuisines of
the world have developed because of shortages, not boun-
ties; folks had only a few basic items and they had to be creative in cooking them up in different ways. But in the
Pacific Northwest, food is seldom a problem. The ocean and
rivers teem with scallops, crab, salmon, crayfish, sturgeon,
and everything in between. The region abounds with fresh
water. Wineries and breweries are liberally scattered
throughout the area. The Hood River and Yakima,
Okanagan, and Rogue valleys are famous for their orchards. Dairies dot the western areas and cattle graze the
eastern expanses on ranches the size of Delaware.

In the Pacific Northwest, rich is defined as living a clean
life; nature deals the bonuses. What people here compro-
mise in salaries, they are compensated for by having the opportunity to hike, fish, hunt, or just wake up every morning
with a view of a forest. Some might call this simple living,
others just call it wacky. Some examples: Portland has
twice elected as mayor a local tavern owner who bikes
around the city in lederhosen and calls out "Whoop, whoop"
at the drop of a photo opportunity. And a few years ago,
there was a strong effort, (serious does not seem to be the
right word), to make the rock n' roll classic "Louie, Louie"
the state song of Washington.

Is there some sort of pattern here? Perhaps all the rain twists great and creative minds? When Lewis and Clark arrived almost 200 years ago, the rain almost drove them crazy, and that was after only one winter! Imagine a lifetime of gray winters; you look out of your window in October at a line of dark clouds rolling in from the west and know there will be only a handful of clear days (probably below freezing) until mid-March. Northwest author Ken Kesey has blamed everything from impotence to union problems on this drizzly season. True, residents of the Pacific Northwest drink more and are more likely to commit suicide than others in the country, but it may be that the weather helps us keep a sense of the absurd and the macabre; for example, in Portland's new Oregon Convention Center the mens' rooms have etchings of Oregon waterfalls perched above the urinals.

So we're a little eccentric. But remember, when an impulse sends you ripping down an untracked ski run or landing a thrashing steelhead in a river at flood stage, the humdrum details of daily life become pretty ridiculous, like some sort of cosmic joke, and you fade back to a private place, to *your* lake beneath the peaks. Just before dark.

1 Essential Information

Before You Go

Visitor Information

For free travel information, contact the following tourism offices:

In the U.S. **Washington Tourism Development Division** (101 General Administration Bldg., Olympia, WA 98504, tel. 206/586–2088; for a *Destination Washington* travel guide, tel. 800/544–1800, ext. 2).
Oregon Tourism Division (775 Summer St. NE, Salem, OR 97310, tel. 800/543–8838 in OR or 800/547–7842 out of state).
Alaska Division of Tourism (Box E–701, Juneau, AK 99811, tel. 907/465–2010).

In Canada **Tourism British Columbia** (1117 Wharf St., Victoria, B.C. V8W 2Z2, tel. 800/663–6000).

In the U.K. For touring tips and brochures, contact the **United States Travel and Tourism Administration** (22 Sackville St., London W1X 2EA, tel. 071/439–7433), **Canadian High Commission, Tourism Division** (Canada House, Trafalgar Sq., London 5W1Y 5BJ, tel. 071/930–6857), or **Tourism British Columbia** (1 Regent St., London SW1Y 4NS, tel. 071/930–6857).

Tour Groups

Group tours pack a lot of sightseeing into a short period of time, hitting all the traditional tourist spots and some of the out-of-the-way places you might miss on your own.

Keep in mind, however, that these tours only permit you to spend as much time in any one place as the itinerary allows. If freedom and flexibility are important to you, pick up a map, decide where you want to go, plot a route, and experience the region at your own leisurely pace.

When evaluating any tour, be sure to find out: (1) exactly what expenses are included—particularly tips, taxes, service charges, side trips, meals, and entertainment; (2) the ratings of all hotels on the itinerary; (3) the cancellation policies for both you and the tour operator; and (4) if you are traveling alone, the additional cost of single, instead of double, accommodations.

Many tour companies offer reduced rates for their off-peak tours (i.e., May–June and September–October). These "shoulder season" rates can be bargains, and the weather and scenery is often just as good as in the peak summer season. Listed below is a sample of available operators and packages. For additional resources, contact your travel agent or the tourist office of the state or province you plan to visit. All may be booked through your travel agent.

General-Interest Tours **Westours** (300 Elliott Ave. W, Seattle, WA 98119, tel. 206/281–3535 or 800/426–0327) operates an extensive motorcoach tour program in Alaska and British Columbia. Itineraries are designed to coincide with the Vancouver departures and arrivals of Holland America Line cruise ships.

Princess Tours (2815 2nd Ave., Suite 400, Seattle, WA 98121, tel. 206/728–4202) offers motorcoach tours through Alaska and

British Columbia that connect with Princess Cruise Line departures from Vancouver.

Brennan Tours (1402 3rd Ave., Suite 717, Seattle, WA 98101, Seattle, WA tel. 206/622–9155 or 800/237–7249) has 9- to 12-day motorcoach tours that begin and end in Seattle and travel through Washington, British Columbia, and Alberta.

Tauck Tours (11 Wilton Rd., Westport, CT 06880, tel. 203/226–6911 or 800/468–2825) offers deluxe Canadian Rockies and West Coast packages that range in length from 8 to 15 days.

Gadabout Tours (700 E. Tahquitz Way, Palm Springs, CA 92262, tel. 619/325–5556) offers a 12-day "Pacific Ports of Call" as well a 15-day tour of Oregon and Washington.

Globus–Gateway (150 S. Los Robles Ave., Pasadena, CA 91101, tel. 818/449–0919 or 800/556–5454) takes you from San Francisco to Vancouver in nine days.

Gray Line of Seattle (720 S. Forest St., Seattle, WA 98134, tel. 206/624–5813) features two- to seven-day tours of the region, including the "Northwest Triangle" of Seattle, Vancouver, and Victoria.

Maupintour (Box 807, Lawrence, KA 66044, tel. 913/843–1211 or 800/255–4266) explores Pacific Northwest seaports in eight days.

Britons The following UK tour operators feature tour packages to the Pacific North Coast: **Canada Air Holidays** (50 Sauchiehall St., Glasgow G2 3AG, tel. 041/332–1511) makes group and individual flight arrangements to Canada in both summer and winter seasons.

Accessible Isolation Holidays (Midhurst Walk, West St., Midhurst, West Sussex, England GU29 9NF, tel. 0730/812535) offers wilderness packages to western Canada. Offerings include a kayaking package off Vancouver Island.

All Canada Travel & Holidays (All Canada House, 90 High St., Lowestoft, Suffolk NR32 1XN, tel. 0502/585825), a full-service tour company offers escorted and independent tours to Western Canada.

Countrywide Holidays Association (109 Birch Heys, Cromwell Range, Manchester, England M14 6HU, tel. 061/257–2055) has wilderness programs to British Columbia that include hiking, mountain biking, and river rafting.

Jetsave Travel Ltd. (Sussex House, London Rd., East Grinstead, West Sussex RH19 1LD, tel. 0342/328231) offers fully inclusive tour packages featuring motorcoach tours, car and motorhome rentals with set itineraries, Alaska cruises, and rail tours.

Special-Interest Tours
Cruises **The Resource Institute** (6532 Phinney Ave. N, Bldg. B, Seattle, WA 98103, tel. 206/784–6762) is a nonprofit organization that offers a series of cultural and environmental education cruises through Alaska and the Inside Passage.

Wilderness **Goway's American Adventures** (2300 Yonge St., Suite 2001, Box 2331, Toronto, Ont., Canada M4P 1E4, tel. 416/322–1034) specializes in camping tours throughout North America. Itineraries are geared primarily to 18- to 35-year-olds, but also have many open-age departures.

Package Deals for Independent Travelers

Americans **American Airlines** (tel. 800/433–7300) and **United Airlines** (tel. 800/328–6877) both offer independent fly/drive packages that start in the region's major cities.

Britons **Go Vacations** (95 High St., Burnham, Slough, Berks, England SL1 7JZ, tel. 06286/68061) books motorhome trips that originate in Vancouver and Seattle.

Air Canada (tel. 081/759–2636) offers a Flexipass that provides travel to and from any North American city served by the carrier. Passengers must be residents of the United Kingdom and purchase their passes within the commonwealth.

American Connections (7 York Way, Lancaster Rd., High Wycombe, Buckinghamshire HP12 3PY, tel. 0494/473173) offers clients a brochure of ground-only items that can be built up into a package including trans-Atlantic flights or bought as separate arrangements for independent travelers to North America.

When to Go

June through September are the most popular months to visit the Pacific North Coast because the region's mild, pleasant climate is at its best then. Summer temperatures generally range in the 70s, and rainfall is usually minimal. Nights, however, can be cool, so if you're going to enjoy the nightlife, take along a sweater or jacket.

Hotels in the major tourist destinations are often filled in July and August, so it is important to book reservations in advance.

Spring and fall are also excellent times to visit. The weather usually remains quite good, plus the prices for accommodations, transportation, and tours can be lower (and the crowds much smaller!) in the most popular destinations.

In winter, the coastal rain turns to snow in the nearby mountains, making the region a skier's dream. As such, world-class ski resorts such as British Columbia's Whistler Village are luring a growing number of winter visitors from around the world.

Climate Tempered by a warm Japan current and protected by the mountains from the extreme weather conditions found inland, the coastal regions of Oregon, Washington, British Columbia, and Southeast Alaska experience a uniformly mild climate.

Average daytime summer highs are in the 70s; winter temperatures are generally in the 40s, with snow uncommon in the lowland areas. If it does snow (usually in December or January), everything grinds to a halt—but the children love it!

The amount of rainfall in the Pacific North Coast varies greatly from one locale to another, so the area's reputation for rain is somewhat misleading. In the Pacific coastal mountains, for example, 160 inches of rain falls annually, creating temperate rain forests. In eastern Oregon, Washington, and British Columbia, near-desert conditions prevail, with rainfall as low as six inches per year.

Seattle has an average of only 36 inches of rainfall a year—less than New York, Chicago, or Miami. The wetness, however, is concentrated during the winter months, when cloudy skies and drizzly weather persist. More than 75% of Seattle's annual precipitation occurs from October through March.

The following are average daily maximum and minimum temperatures for major cities in the Pacific North Coast region.

Portland	Jan.	44F	7C	May	67F	19C	Sept.	74F	23C
		33	1		46	8		51	10
	Feb.	50F	10C	June	72F	22C	Oct.	63F	17C
		36	2		52	11		45	7
	Mar.	54F	12C	July	79F	26C	Nov.	52F	11C
		37	3		55	13		39	4
	Apr.	60F	15C	Aug.	78F	25C	Dec.	46F	8C
		41	5		55	13		35	2

Seattle	Jan.	45F	7C	May	66F	19C	Sept.	69F	20C
		35	2		47	8		52	11
	Feb.	50F	10C	June	70F	21C	Oct.	62F	16C
		37	3		52	11		47	8
	Mar.	53F	12C	July	76F	24C	Nov.	51F	10C
		38	3		56	13		40	4
	Apr.	59F	15C	Aug.	75F	24C	Dec.	47F	8C
		42	5		55	13		37	3

Vancouver	Jan.	41F	5C	May	63F	17C	Sept.	64F	18C
		32	0		46	8		50	10
	Feb.	46F	8C	June	66F	19C	Oct.	57F	14C
		34	1		52	11		43	6
	Mar.	48F	9C	July	72F	22C	Nov.	48F	9C
		36	2		55	13		37	3
	Apr.	55F	13C	Aug.	72F	22C	Dec.	45F	7C
		41	5		55	13		34	1

Juneau	Jan.	29F	-2C	May	55F	13C	Sept.	56F	13C
		18	-8		38	3		42	6
	Feb.	34F	1C	June	62F	16C	Oct.	47F	8C
		22	-6		44	7		36	2
	Mar.	38F	3C	July	64F	18C	Nov.	37F	3C
		26	-4		48	9		28	-2
	Apr.	47F	8C	Aug.	62F	17C	Dec.	32F	0C
		31	-1		46	8		23	-5

Current weather information for more than 500 cities around the world can be obtained by calling **WeatherTrak** (tel. 900/370–8725). A taped message will instruct you to dial the three-digit access code for the destination you're interested in. For a list of access codes, send a stamped, self-addressed envelope to Cities, Box 7000, Dallas, TX 75209. For further information, call 214/869–3035 or 800/247–3282.

Festivals and Seasonal Events

The Pacific North Coast comes alive each year in a burst of colorful festivities. The following is a sample of noteworthy seasonal events. For dates and more details, contact the local state or provincial tourism department.

British Columbia   **Mid-May. Vancouver Children's Festival,** the largest event of its kind in the world, presents dozens of performances in mime, puppetry, music, and theater. Tel. 604/687–7697.

Late May. Swiftsure Race Weekend draws more than 300 competitors to Victoria's harbor for an international yachting event. Tel. 604/592–2441.

Late May. Victoria Day, a national holiday, is usually celebrated throughout Canada on the penultimate weekend in May.

Late June. Canadian International Dragon Boat Festival, Vancouver is a multicultural festival featuring dragon boat races based on Chinese legend. Community and children's activities, dance, and visual arts. Tel. 604/684–5151.

Late June. Du Maurier International Jazz Festival celebrates a broad spectrum of jazz, blues, and related improvised music, with over 200 performances in 20 locations in Vancouver. Tel. 604/682–0706.

July 1. Canada Day inspires celebrations around the country in honor of Canada's birthday.

Mid-July. Harrison Festival of the Arts, in Harrison Hot Springs offers a spectrum of artistic expression with a unique blend of international, national, and regional artists and performers. Tel. 604/796–3664.

Mid-July. Vancouver Sea Festival features water-related activities, such as a wooden- and heritage-boat festival, plus a parade, fireworks, entertainment, and a carnival. Tel. 604/684–3378.

Late July. International Bathtub Race takes to the high seas, from Nanaimo to Vancouver. Tel. 604/754–8474.

Late July–early Aug. Squamish Days is the largest logging sport show in the world, featuring logger sports events, chair carving contest, street entertainment, and a parade. Tel. 604/892–9244.

Early Aug. Abbotsford International Air Show takes off with a three-day extravaganza of military and civilian flight performances and presents a large aircraft display. Tel. 604/859–9211.

Mid-Aug.–early Sept. Pacific National Exhibition, western Canada's biggest annual fair, brings top-name entertainment and a variety of displays to Vancouver. Tel. 604/253–2311.

Washington   **Early–mid-Apr. Skagit Valley Tulip Festival** showcases millions of colorful tulips and daffodils in bloom. Tel. 800/869–7107.

Mid-May. Viking Fest celebrates the Norwegian community of Poulsbo's proud heritage. Tel. 206/779–4848.

Late May. Northwest Folklife Festival lures musicians and artists to Seattle for one of the largest folk fests in the United States. Tel. 206/684–7200.

Late July. Pacific Northwest Arts and Crafts Fair in Bellevue highlights some of the best work of Northwest artists and craftsmen. Tel. 206/454–3322.

Late June–early July. Fort Vancouver Days in Vancouver is a citywide celebration with rodeo, bluegrass festival, chili cook-off, and the largest fireworks display west of the Mississippi. Tel. 206/696–7655.

Mid-July. Bite of Seattle serves up sumptuous specialties from the city's finest restaurants. Tel. 206/232–2982.

Mid-July–early Aug. Seafair, Seattle's biggest event of the year, kicks off with a torchlight parade through downtown and culminates in hydroplane races on Lake Washington. Tel. 206/728–0123.

Late Aug. Washington State International Kite Festival sends kites of all shapes and sizes flying above Long Beach. Tel. 206/642–2400.

Late Aug.–early Sept. Bumbershoot, a Seattle festival of the arts, presents more than 400 performers in music, dance, theater, comedy, and the visual and literary arts. Tel. 206/684–7200.

Early–mid-Sept. Western Washington Fair brings top entertainment, animals, food, exhibits, and rides to the town of Puyallup. Tel. 206/845–1771.

Oregon **Mid-Feb.–late Oct. Oregon Shakespearean Festival,** held annually since 1935 in Ashland, presents a repertoire of classic and contemporary plays. Tel. 800/533–1311 (in OR) or 800/547–8052 (outside OR).

Mid-May. Sandcastle Day transforms Cannon Beach into a sculpted fantasyland of fanciful castles and creatures. Tel. 503/436–2623.

Late May. Fleet of Flowers Memorial Service, which begins at Depoe Bay, scatters a mass of flowers into the ocean to commemorate those lost at sea. Tel. 503/765–2889.

Late May–mid-June. Portland Rose Festival features 24 days of diverse events, such as ski racing on nearby Mt. Hood, an air show, a hot-air-balloon classic, the Grand Floral parade, and auto racing. Tel. 503/227–2681.

Mid-June–early Sept. Peter Britt Gardens Music and Arts Festival features folk, country, bluegrass, and jazz music, as well as musical theater and dance, on the stages of Jacksonville. Tel. 800/88BRITT (outside OR) or 800/33BRITT (in OR).

Late June–early July. Oregon Bach Festival, sponsored by the University of Oregon School of Music, brings the works of the great composer to Eugene. Tel. 503/346–5666.

Early Aug. Mt. Hood Festival of Jazz brings nationally acclaimed jazz musicians to Gresham for performances in an outdoor setting. Tel. 503/666–3810.

Late Aug.–early Sept. Oregon State Fair, which is held in Salem for 11 days prior to Labor Day, hosts concerts, flea markets, horse and livestock shows, and sporting events. Tel. 503/378–3247.

Alaska **Late Mar. Seward's Day** is celebrated around the state on the last Monday in March and commemorates the signing of the 1867 treaty purchasing Alaska from Russia.

Mid-May. Little Norway Festival, a 3-day event, honors the town of Petersburg's Scandinavian heritage. Tel. 907/772–3646.

Mid-May. Southeast Alaska State Fair, which takes place in Haines, features entertainment, a timber show, workshops, contests, and agriculture, home arts, fine arts, and crafts exhibits. Tel. 907/766–2478.

June. Sitka Summer Music Festival presents internationally known musicians ranging from classical to pop in the Centennial Building. Tel. 907/747–6774.

Oct. 18. Alaska Day commemorates the formal transfer of Alaska from Russia to the United States.

Throughout 1992. Alaska Highway's Rendezvous '92 celebrates—in a variety of communities in Alaska, Yukon, and northern British Columbia—the 50th Anniversary of the 1,520-mile Alaska Highway. Tel. 907/452–8000.

What to Pack

Clothing Residents of the Pacific North Coast are generally informal by nature and wear clothing to match their disposition. During the summer, the days are warm but evenings can cool off substantially. Layered clothing is the local preference—sweatshirts, sweaters, and jackets are removed or put on as the day progresses. If you plan to explore the region's cities on foot, or if you choose to hike along mountain trails or beaches, bring comfortable walking shoes.

Dining out is usually an informal affair, although some restaurants require a jacket and tie for men and dresses for women. Residents tend to dress conservatively when going to the theater or symphony, but it's not uncommon to see some patrons wearing jeans. In other words, almost anything is acceptable for most occasions.

Passengers aboard cruise ships bound for Alaska should check with their travel agents about the dress code on board. Some vessels expect formal attire for dinner, while others do not. In all cases, you will need a waterproof coat and warm clothes if you plan to spend time on deck.

Miscellaneous It is often a good idea to pack an extra pair of eyeglasses, contact lenses, or prescription sunglasses when traveling. Also, be sure to pack any prescription medicines that you use regularly as well as any allergy medications you might need. Take along, too, a copy of any current prescription in case it needs to be refilled while you are away.

Carry-on Luggage Passengers aboard U.S. and Canadian airlines are usually limited to two carry-on bags. On U.S. carriers, bags stored under the seat must not exceed 9″ × 14″ × 22″; bags hung in a closet can be no larger than 4″ × 23″ × 45″; and bags in overhead bins must not exceed 10″ × 14″ × 36″ in total dimensions. Items exceeding these dimensions may be restricted from the cabin and sent through as checked baggage. Keep in mind that airlines adapt these rules to circumstances; on a crowded flight, you may be allowed only one carry-on bag.

In addition to two carryons, passengers may also bring aboard a handbag; an overcoat or wrap; an umbrella; a camera; a reasonable amount of reading material; an infant bag; and crutches, a cane, braces, or other prosthetic device. Infant/child safety seats can also be brought aboard if parents have purchased a ticket for the child or if there is space in the cabin.

Checked Luggage Passengers are generally allowed to check two or three pieces of luggage, none of which can exceed 62 inches (length + width + height) or weigh more than 70 pounds. Baggage allowances vary among airlines, so check with the carrier before departure.

Taking Money Abroad

To get the best exchange rate for your money, convert it into local currency at a bank or recognized currency exchange office (rather than at a hotel). It's a good idea to exchange at least a small amount of money before leaving home, because you may arrive at your destination when these offices are not open. Currency can be favorably exchanged at **Deak International** offices (630 5th Ave., New York, NY 10011, tel. 212/635–0515). Contact them for a list of their office locations.

Major credit cards and traveler's checks are widely accepted throughout the region. The most recognized traveler's checks are from American Express, Barclay's, Thomas Cook, and those issued through major commercial banks such as Citibank and Bank of America. Some banks will issue traveler's checks free to established customers, but most charge a 1% commission. Remember to take along addresses of offices where you can get refunds for lost or stolen traveler's checks.

It's a good idea to carry at least one major credit card when traveling, particularly for hotel and car rental payments, where you will probably be asked for a credit card in place of a cash deposit.

Getting Money from Home

There are at least three ways to get money from home: (1) Have it sent through a large commercial bank with a branch in the city you're visiting. The only stipulation is that you must have an account with the bank. If not, you'll have to go through your own bank and the process will be slower and more costly. (2) Have it sent through American Express. If you are a cardholder, you can cash a personal check or a counter check at an American Express office for up to $1,000. You can also receive money through an American Express Moneygram, which enables you to obtain up to $10,000 in cash—usually within 24 hours. For further information about this service, call 800/543–4080. (3) Have money sent through Western Union (tel. 800/325–6000). If you have a MasterCard or Visa, you can have money sent for any amount up to your credit limit. If not, have someone take cash or a certified cashier's check to a Western Union office. The money will be delivered to a bank in the town where you're staying. Fees vary with the amount of money sent and the location of the recipient.

Cash Machines Virtually all banks in the United States and Canada belong to a network of automatic teller machines (ATMs) that dispense cash 24 hours a day. Cards issued by Visa and MasterCard may also be used in ATMs, but the fees are usually higher than the fees on bank cards, and there is a daily interest charge on the "loan," even if monthly bills are paid on time. Each network has a toll-free number you can call to locate machines in a given city. The number for the Cirrus system, owned by Master-

Card, is 800/4–CIRRUS; the number for the Plus system, affiliated with Visa, is 800/THE–PLUS.

Currency

The United States and Canada both use the same currency denominations—dollars and cents—although each currency has a different value on the world market. In the United States the most common paper currency comes in $1, $5, $10, and $20 bills. Common notes in Canada include the $2, $5, $10, and $20 bills. (Canada recently phased out its $1 bill, replacing it with a $1 gold-colored coin, nicknamed the "loonie" by Canadians because it contains a picture of a loon on one side.) Coins in both countries come in denominations of 1¢ (penny), 5¢ (nickel), 10¢ (dime), 25¢ (quarter), and 50¢.

Traveler's checks can be purchased in either U.S. or Canadian dollars at banks and other financial institutions and are generally accepted by restaurants, hotels, and other businesses for payment of goods and services.

What It Will Cost

Prices for meals and accommodations in the Pacific North Coast are generally lower than in other major North American regions. Prices for first-class hotel rooms in major cities (Seattle, Portland, Vancouver, and Victoria) range from $80 to $150 a night, although you can still find some "value" hotel rooms for $50–$60 a night. Most hotels offer weekend packages that offer discounts up to 50%. Don't look for these special deals during the peak summer season, however, when hotels are filled nearly to capacity.

Costs outside the major cities, as a rule, are lower, but prices for rooms and meals at some of the major deluxe resorts can rival those at the best big-city hotels.

In Alaska, food costs are higher because the state has to import virtually all of its produce, as well as its manufactured goods, from the "lower" 48 states.

Compared with many other parts of the world, the Pacific North Coast is a travel bargain. The region is becoming increasingly popular with Japanese visitors, for example, who find prices for hotels, meals, and commodities to be quite a steal.

Prices in Canada are always quoted in Canadian dollars. When comparing prices with those in the United States, costs should be calculated via the current rate of exchange.

The amount of sales tax levied on goods and services varies among areas. The states of Oregon and Alaska impose no sales tax on purchased goods, although some cities will levy a tax on hotel rooms. Portland, for example, has a 9% room tax. The sales tax in Washington is 7.9%. The city of Seattle adds another 5% onto its hotel rooms. Canada's 7% Goods & Services Tax (GST) is added onto hotel bills, but will be rebated to foreign visitors. In British Columbia, consumers pay an 8% provincial tax. Where approved, an additional 2% is levied by local municipal governments.

Passports and Visas

Americans/ Citizens and permanent residents of the United States and
Canadians Canada do not require passports or visas to visit each other's
country. However, native-born citizens should carry identification showing proof of citizenship, such as a birth certificate, a
voter-registration card, or a valid passport. Naturalized citizens should carry a naturalization certificate or some other
proof of citizenship. Permanent residents of the United States
who are not U.S. citizens should carry their Alien Registration
Receipt Cards. U.S. citizens interested in visiting Canada for
more than 90 days may apply for a visa that allows them to stay
for six months. For more information, contact the Canadian
Embassy (501 Pennsylvania Ave., NW, Washington, DC
20001, tel. 202/682–1740).

Britons To enter the United States or Canada, you will need a valid, 10-
year British passport (cost £15 for a standard 32-page passport, £30 for a 94-page passport). Note that a one-year British
passport is not acceptable for entry under any circumstances.
You can obtain passport application forms from most travel
agents and major post offices, or from the **Passport Office** (Clive
House, 70 Petty France, London SW1H 9HD, tel. 071/279–
3434 or 071/279–4000).

You will not need a visa if you are staying in the United States
for less than 90 days, have a return or onward ticket on a major
airline, and complete a visa waiver form and an arrival/depar-
ture card. There are some exceptions to this, so check with your
travel agent or with the Visa Unit of the **United States Embassy**
(Visa and Immigration Dept., 5 Upper Grosvenor St., London
W1A 2JB, tel. 071/499–3443 for recorded information or 071/
499–7010). Visa applications must be made by mail. Britons are
required, however, to have a visa for the United States if they
are entering from Canada. Again, confirm requirements with
the U.S. Embassy in London.

British visitors are not required to have a visa to enter Canada.
Their stay in Canada, however, cannot exceed six months without authorization from Canadian immigration.

Customs

Customs regulations between the United States and Canada
are among the most liberal in the world. Americans may bring
home from Canada $400 in foreign goods, as long as you've been
out of the United States for at least 48 hours and you haven't
made an international trip in 30 days. Each member of the family is entitled to the same exemption regardless of age, and ex-
emptions may be pooled. Visitors to Canada who meet the
minimum age requirements of the province of entry (19 years in
British Columbia) may take in either 1.1 liters (40 ounces) of
liquor or wine or 24 12-ounce cans or bottles of beer. Visitors
over 16 may take in 50 cigars, 200 cigarettes, and one kilogram
(2.2 pounds) of manufactured tobacco. Gifts valued at less than
C$40 each can also be brought into Canada, providing they do
not contain tobacco or alcohol. Gifts valued at more than C$40
are subject to regular import duty on the excess amount.

Visitors age 21 or over can take into the United States 200 cigarettes or 50 cigars, or two kilograms of tobacco; one liter of alcohol; and duty-free gifts to a value of $100. For further

information on United States customs regulations, write to the **United States Customs Service** (1301 Constitution Ave. NW, Washington, DC 20229).

Returning to the United Kingdom, you may bring home: (1) 200 cigarettes or 100 cigarillos or 50 cigars or 250 grams of tobacco; (2) two liters of table wine with additional allowances for (a) one liter of alcohol over 22% by volume (most spirits), (b) two liters of alcohol under 22% by volume (fortified or sparking wine), or (c) two more liters of table wine; (3) 60 milliliters of perfume and 250 milliliters of toilet water; and (4) other goods up to a value of £32, but not more than 50 liters of beer or 25 lighters. For further information, contact **HM Customs and Excise** (Dorset House, Stamford St., London SE1 9PS, tel. 071/620–1313.)

Canada has very strict gun control laws. Firearms with no legitimate sporting or recreational use are not allowed into the country. This includes all handguns, automatic weapons, and any rifle or shotgun that has been modified. For further information on Canadian customs regulations, write to **Revenue Canada** (Customs and Excise, Ottawa, Ont. K1A 0L5, tel. 613/993–6220).

Traveling with Film

If your camera is new, shoot and develop a few rolls of film before leaving home. Pack some lens tissue and an extra battery for built-in light meters. Invest about $10 in a skylight filter; it will protect the lens and also reduce haze in your pictures.

Hot weather can damage film, so if you're driving in summer, don't store film in the glove compartment or on the shelf under the rear window. Put it behind the front seat on the floor, on the side opposite the exhaust pipe. Try to avoid leaving film in a parked car on sunny days.

On a plane trip, never pack unprocessed film in checked luggage. If your bags get X-rayed, you can say goodbye to your pictures. Always carry undeveloped film with you through security and ask to have it inspected by hand. It helps to keep your film in a plastic bag, ready for quick inspection. Inspectors at U.S. airports are required to honor requests for hand inspection of film.

If your film gets fogged and you want an explanation, send it to the National Association of Photographic Manufacturers (550 Mamaroneck Ave., Harrison, NY 10528). Experts will try to determine what went wrong. The service is free.

Language

English is the language predominantly spoken throughout the Pacific North Coast. It is not uncommon, however, to hear many other languages spoken on the street, both by visitors and by residents who have immigrated to the area in recent years. Partly because of the region's proximity to the Pacific Rim, the Asian influence is becoming increasingly widespread. Other ethnic groups also contribute to the populations of the region's major cities. Canada is officially a bilingual country (English and French). You will see many signs and services offered in both languages; however, little French is spoken on Canada's west coast.

Staying Healthy

There are no serious health risks associated with travel to the Pacific North Coast, and no special shots are required before visiting the area. People with heart conditions may want to check the elevations of mountain passes on highways they plan to travel. Some passes may be higher than 5,000 feet and could affect people with respiratory problems. If you have a health problem that may require prescription drugs, have your doctor write a prescription using the generic name, because brand names can vary widely. The prescription can also help to eliminate delays at border crossings.

Insurance

Health and Accident *In the U.S.* Hospital and medical services are excellent in the United States and Canada, but hospital care in particular, can be very expensive, so before leaving home, be sure and check your existing health-insurance policy to see if it covers health expenses incurred while traveling or emergency medical-evacuation services abroad. If it does not, you can purchase a supplemental policy from one of the following companies: **Carefree Travel Insurance** (Box 310, 120 Mineola Blvd., Mineola, NY 11501, tel. 516/294–0220 or 800/323–3149), **International SOS Assistance** (Box 11568, Philadelphia, PA 19116, tel. 215/244–1500 or 800/523–8930), **Travel Assistance International** (1133 15th St. NW, Suite 400, Washington, DC 20005, tel. 202/331–1609 or 800/821–2828), **Travel Guard International** (1145 Clark St., Stevens Point, WI 54481, tel. 715/345–0505 or 800/782–5151), **Wallach and Company, Inc.** (243 Church St. NW, Suite 100D, Vienna, VA 22180, tel. 703/281–9500 or 800/237–6615), **WorldCare Travel Assistance Association** (1150 South Olive St., Suite T-233, Los Angeles, CA 90015, tel. 213/749–0909 or 800/666–4993).

In the U.K. We recommend that to cover health and motoring mishaps, you insure yourself with **Europ Assistance** (252 High St., Croydon, Surrey CR0 1NF, tel. 081/680–1234). Also, travel insurance can be obtained from **Our Way Travel Ltd.** (Atlas House, Station Approach, Hayes, Kent BR2 7EQ, tel. 081/462–7746). It is wise to take out insurance to cover lost luggage (if your current homeowners' policies don't cover such loss). Trip-cancellation insurance is also a good idea. **The Association of British Insurers** (Aldermary House, 10–15 Queen St., London EC4, tel. 071/248–4477) will give you comprehensive advice on all aspects of holiday insurance and publishes a fact sheet on travel insurance, which can be obtained by sending a self-addressed envelope to ABI.

Lost Luggage On international flights, airlines are responsible for lost or damaged luggage of up to $9.07 per pound ($20 per kilo) for checked baggage, and up to $400 per passenger for unchecked baggage. On U.S. domestic flights, airlines are responsible for up to $1,250 per passenger in lost or damaged property.

If you're carrying valuables, take them with you on the plane or purchase additional insurance for lost, damaged, or stolen luggage. This type of coverage is available through travel agents or directly through various insurance companies. These policies may also include coverage for personal accidents, trip cancellation, default, and bankruptcy.

Two companies that issue luggage insurance are **Tele-Trip** (Box 31685, 3201 Farnam St., Omaha, NE 68131, tel. 800/228–9792) and **The Travelers Corporation** (Ticket and Travel Dept., 1 Tower Sq., Hartford, CT 06183, tel. 203/277–0111 or 800/243–3174).

Before you go, itemize the contents of each bag in case you need to file an insurance claim. Be certain to put your home or business address on each piece of luggage, including carry-on bags. If your luggage is lost or stolen and later recovered, the airline will deliver the luggage to your home free of charge.

Car Rentals

Renting a car can be a relatively inexpensive way to travel. If you're planning to do a lot of touring, check for rates that offer unlimited mileage. Most major car-rental firms have downtown and airport locations in main cities; some can be found in smaller towns as well. You can often rent a car in one location and return it to another in the same city without paying a penalty fee. However, if you return your car to a counter in another city, you may be hit with a hefty penalty charge.

A valid U.S., Canadian, or national driver's license is required to rent a car. An International Driving Permit is also accepted, but it must accompany a state or national license. In most cases, a major credit card is required as a security deposit for rentals. If you don't have a credit card, you may be asked to leave a large cash deposit as collateral.

When renting a vehicle, find out what the collision-damage waiver (usually an $8–$12 daily surcharge) covers and whether your personal insurance or credit card already covers damage to a rental car. If so, bring a photocopy of the benefits section along.

Taking a rental car across the U.S.–Canada border should not be a problem, especially if you keep a copy of the rental contract with you. It should bear an endorsement stating that the vehicle is permitted entry into the other country.

The following car rental companies have outlets throughout the Pacific North Coast: **Hertz** (tel. 800/654–3131), **Budget** (tel. 800/527–0700), **Avis** (tel. 800/331–1212), **National** (tel. 800/227–7368), **Thrifty** (tel. 800/367–2277), **General** (tel. 800/327–7607), **Dollar** (tel. 800/800–4000), **Agency** (tel. 800/321–1972), and **Rent-A-Wreck** (tel. 800/535–1391).

Rail Passes

For Britons, **Amtrak** (tel. 800/USA–RAIL) has USA Rail Passes that are good for unlimited coach travel throughout the United States for 45 days. The cost for these passes is: one region $189; two regions $269; whole country $339. Children (2–15) travel for half-fare. Rates may be slightly higher during peak season (late May–Sept.). The ticket must be purchased from a travel agent in the United Kingdom before departure. The offer does not apply to Americans or Canadians.

VIA Rail Canada (tel. 800/665–0200) offers a **Canrailpass** that is good for 30 days. Systemwide passes cost U.S. $427 (June 1–Sept. 30) and U.S. $287 (Oct. 1–May 31). Youth passes (age 24 and under) are U.S. $373 in peak season and U.S. $245 in the off season. Tickets may be purchased in the United States or the United Kingdom from **Compass Travel** (9 Grosvenor Gardens, London SW1W OBH, tel. 71/828–9028 or upon arrival in Canada. This offer does not apply to Canadian citizens.

Bus Passes

Greyhound offers the International Ameripass, which is good for unlimited travel throughout the United States and Canada. It is available for periods of 7, 15, and 30 days and can be purchased in the United Kingdom before you leave. Contact Greyhound International Travel (14–16 Cockspur St., London SW1Y 5BL, tel. 071/839–5591).

Student and Youth Travel

The **International Student Identity Card** (ISIC) entitles full-time students to rail passes, special fares on local transportation, student charter flights, and discounts at museums, theaters, sports events, and many other attractions. If purchased in the United States, the cost of the ISIC card gives the holder $3,000 in emergency medical insurance and a collect phone number to call in case of emergencies. Apply to the **Council on International Educational Exchange** (CIEE, 205 E. 42nd St., New York, NY 10017, tel. 212/661–1414), or in Canada, **Travel Cuts** (187 College St., Toronto, Ont. M5T 1P7, tel. 416/979–2406).

Travelers under age 26 can apply for a **Youth International Educational Exchange (YIEE) Card,** issued by the **Federation of International Youth Travel Organizations** (81 Islands Brugge, DK-2300 Copenhagen S, Denmark). It provides the same services and benefits as the ISIC card. The YIEE card is available in the United States from CIEE and in Canada from the **Canadian Hostelling Association** (CHA, 1600 James Naismith Dr., Suite 608, Gloucester, Ont. K1B 5N4, tel. 613/748–5638) or the **Canadian Hostelling Association, B.C. Region** (1515 Discovery St., Vancouver, B.C. V6R 4K5, tel. 604/224–7111).

An **International Youth Hostel Federation** (IYHF) membership card is the key to inexpensive dormitory-style accommodations at thousands of youth hostels around the world. Hostels aren't only for young travelers on a budget; many have accommodations for families. Most, however, provide separate sleeping quarters for men and women at rates of $7–$20 a night per person. IYHF memberships, valid for 12 months from the time of purchase, are available in the United States through **American Youth Hostels** (AYH, Box 37613, Washington, DC 20013, tel. 202/783–6161). The cost for a first-year membership is $25 for adults 18–54. Renewal thereafter is $15. For youths (age 17 and under) the rate is $10, and for senior citizens (age 55 and older) the rate is $15. Family membership is available for $35. National hostel associations can arrange special reductions for members, such as discounted rail fares or free bus travel.

Council Travel, a CIEE subsidiary, is the foremost U.S. student travel agency. It specializes in low-cost charters and serves as the exclusive U.S. agent for many student airfare bargains and student tours. CIEE's 80-page *Student Travel Catalogue* and "Council Charter" brochure are available free from any Council Travel office in the United States. In Seattle, the organization is located at 1314 N.E. 43rd Street, tel. 206/632–2448; in Portland, it is at 715 S.W. Morrison Street, Suite 600, 97205, tel. 503/228–1900.

The **Educational Travel Center** (438 N. Frances St., Madison, WI 53703, tel. 608/256–5551) is another travel specialist for student tours, bargain fares, and bookings.

Students who would like to work abroad should contact CIEE's **Work Abroad Department,** at the CIEE address given above. Various types of paid and voluntary work experiences can be arranged overseas for up to six months. CIEE also sponsors study programs in Europe, Latin America, Asia, and Australia, and publishes many books of interest to the student traveler. These include *Work, Study, Travel Abroad: The Whole World Handbook* and *Volunteer! The Comprehensive Guide to Voluntary Service in the United States and Abroad.*

The Information Center at the **Institute of International Education** (809 United Nations Plaza, New York, NY 10017, tel. 212/984–5413) has reference books, foreign university catalogs, study-abroad brochures, and other materials that may be consulted by students and nonstudents alike, free of charge.

Traveling with Children

Regulations about infant travel are in the process of changing. Until they do, however, if you want to be sure your infant car is secure and traveling in his or her own safety seat, you must buy a seperate ticket and bring your own infant car seat. Check with the airline in advance to be sure your seat meets the required standard. For more information, write for the booklet *Child/Infant Safety Seats Acceptable for Use in Aircraft* from the **Federal Aviation Administration** (APA–200, 800 Independence Ave., SW, Washington, DC 20591, tel. 202/267–3479).

Most large hotels offer licensed baby-sitters or referrals. Hyatt Hotels, for example, feature children's programs and activities. Resorts are more likely to provide children's services than downtown hotels, which are geared to business travelers. Contact individual hotels for specifics, as facilities vary widely.

There are many exciting activities for children throughout the Pacific North Coast. Museums designed especially for children, science centers, zoos, aquariums, and parks offer children endless opportunities to use their imaginations and burn off excess energy.

Many local organizations, such as public libraries, museums, parks and recreation departments, and YMCA/YWCAs, also have special events throughout the year for children of all ages. Check local newspaper listings for activities such as plays, storytelling, sporting events, and so forth.

The Vancouver Children's Festival, held annually in May, is the largest event of its kind in the world, with dozens of troupes presenting mime, puppetry, theatrical performances, and music.

Family Travel Times, a newsletter published 10 times a year, also offers ideas for having fun with children, although not all data is specific to the Pacific North Coast area. To order the newsletter, contact **Travel with Your Children** (80 8th Ave., New York, NY 10011, tel. 212/206–0688).

Hints for Disabled Travelers

The Information Center for Individuals with Disabilities (Ft. Point Pl., 1st floor, 27–43 Wormwood St., Boston, MA 02210, tel. 617/727–5540; TDD 617/727–5236) offers useful problem-solving assistance, including lists of travel agents who specialize in tours for the disabled.

Moss Rehabilitation Hospital Travel Information Service (1200 W. Tabor Rd., Philadelphia, PA 19141–3009, tel. 215/456–9602) provides information on tourist sights, transportation, and accommodations in destinations around the world for a nominal fee.

Barrier Free Alaska (1001-AT Boniface Pkwy., #6-M, Anchorage, AK 99501, tel. 907/338–2087) gives disabled travelers information about accessible facilities throughout the state.

Challenge Alaska (Box 110065, Anchorage, AK 99511–0065, tel. 907/563–2658) is a group that provides recreational opportunities for disabled persons. Activities include downhill and cross-country skiing, sea kayaking, canoeing, camping, fishing, swimming, dogsledding, and backpacking.

Travel Industry and Disabled Exchange (5435 Donna Ave., Tarzana, CA 91356, tel. 818/368–5648), for a $15-per-person annual membership fee, issues a quarterly newsletter and information on travel agencies and tours.

Mobility International USA (Box 3551, Eugene, OR 97403, tel. 503/343–1284) coordinates exchange programs for disabled people around the world. For a $20 annual fee, the organization offers information on accommodations and organized study programs.

Access Alaska (3710-AK Woodland Dr., Suite 900, Anchorage, AK 99517, tel. 907/248–4777) provides information and referral to disabled visitors to Alaska.

Evergreen Travel/Wings on Wheels (4114 198th SW, Lynnwood, WA 98036–5699, tel. 206/776–1184) is a well-recognized tour operator specializing in domestic and internation travel for the disabled. Group and individual trips can be arranged.

The **Canadian Paraplegic Association** (780 S.W. Marine Dr., Vancouver, B.C. V6P 5Y7, tel. 604/324–3611) provides information to the disabled traveler about touring through British Columbia. Information for the hearing impaired is available from the **Western Institute for the Deaf** (2125 W. 7th Ave., Vancouver, B.C. V6K 1X9, tel. 604/736–7391 [voice] or 736–2527 [TDD]). The annual *British Columbia Accommodation Guide* (tel. 800/663–6000) includes a list of hotel facilities for persons with disabilities.

Greyhound/Trailways (tel. 800/752–4841; TDD 800/345–3109) "Helping Hand" program will carry a disabled person and companion for the price of a single fare. You must have a doctor's certificate verifying the need for assistance.

Amtrak (tel. 800/USA–RAIL) advises that you request redcap service, special seats, or wheelchair assistance when making reservations. Not all stations are equipped to provide these services. All handicapped passengers are entitled to a 25% discount off regular coach fares. A special children's handicapped fare is also available, offering qualifying children, ages 2–12, a 50% discount on already discounted children's fares. For a free copy of *Access Amtrak*, a guide to its services for elderly and handicapped travelers, write to Amtrak (400 N. Capitol St. NW, Washington, DC 20001, tel. 800/872–7245).

VIA Rail Canada (tel. 800/665–0200) will arrange preboarding for people in wheelchairs or with other special needs if given at least 24 hours notice.

Publications Twin Peaks Press publishes several useful books: *Travel for the Disabled* ($9.95), *Directory of Travel Agencies for the Disabled* ($12.95), and *Wheelchair Vagabond* ($9.95). You can order them through your local bookstore or from the publisher (Box 129, Vancouver, WA 98666, tel. 206/694–2462). Add $2 per book for postage if you are requesting the books by mail.

Access to the World: A Travel Guide for the Handicapped, by Louise Weiss, provides general information on transportation, hotels, travel agents, tour operators, and travel organizations. It is available at your local bookstore or from Henry Holt & Co. (tel. 800/247–3912) for $12.95.

Access America: An Atlas and Guide to the National Parks for Visitors with Disabilities (National Cartographic, Box 133, Burlington, VT 05402, tel. 802/655–4321) contains detailed information about access to the 37 most-visited national parks in the United States. This award-winning book is available directly from the publisher for $44.95 plus $5 shipping.

"**Fly Rights,**" available free from the U.S. Department of Transportation (tel. 202/366–2220), offers airline service information for the handicapped.

The Easter Seal Society (521 2nd Ave. W, Seattle, WA 98119, tel. 206/281–5700) publishes *Access Seattle,* a free guide to the city's services for the handicapped.

Circling the City—A Guide to the Accessibility of Public Places In and Near Portland, Oregon is a 144-page book that is available from the Junior League (4838 S.W. Scholls Ferry Rd., Portland, OR 97225, tel. 503/297–6364). **Shared Outdoor Adventure Recreation** (SOAR, tel. 503/238–1613), another Portland organization, provides listings of recreational activities for persons with disabilities.

Hints for Older Travelers

The **American Association of Retired Persons** (AARP, 1909 K St. NW, Washington, DC 20049, tel. 202/662–4850) has two programs for independent travelers: (1) the Purchase Privilege Program, which offers discounts on hotels, airfare, car rentals, RV rentals, and sightseeing; and (2) the AARP Motoring Plan, provided by Amoco, which furnishes emergency road-service aid and trip-routing information. AARP also arranges group tours and cruises at reduced rates through **American Express Vacations** (Box 5014, Atlanta, GA 30302, tel. 800/637–6200 in GA, or 800/241–1700 outside GA). AARP members must be 50 years of age or older. Annual dues are $5 per person or per couple.

If you're planning to use an AARP or other senior-citizen identification card to obtain a reduced hotel rate, mention it at the time you make your reservation. At participating restaurants, show your card before you are seated, because discounts may be limited to certain menus, days, or hours. When renting a car be sure to ask about special promotional rates, which may offer greater savings than the available discount.

Elderhostel (75 Federal St., 3rd floor, Boston, MA 02110–1941, tel. 617/426–7788) is an innovative program for people age 60 or older. Participants live in dormitories on some 1,200 campuses around the world. Mornings are devoted to lectures and seminars; afternoons to sightseeing and field trips. The Elderhostel catalog is free for the first year, if you participate in a program, and costs $10 a year thereafter.

Saga International Holidays (120 Boylston St., Boston, MA 02116, tel. 800/343–0273) specializes in group travel for people age 60 or older. A selection of variously priced tours allows travelers to choose the package that meets their needs.

National Council of Senior Citizens (925 15th St. NW, Washington, DC 20005, tel. 202/347–8800) is a nonprofit advocacy group with about 5,000 local clubs across the country. Annual membership is $12 per person or couple. Members receive a monthly newspaper with travel information and an ID card that entitles them to reduced rates on hotels and car rentals.

Mature Outlook (6001 N. Clark St., Chicago, IL 60660, tel. 800/336–6330) is a travel club for people over age 50, offering discounts at participating hotels and motels and a bimonthly newsletter. Annual membership is $9.95 per person or couple. Instant membership is available at participating Holiday Inns.

Golden Age Passport is a free lifetime pass to all parks, monuments, and recreation areas run by the federal government. Travelers age 62 or older can pick one up at any national park that charges admission. The passport also provides a 50% discount on camping, boat launching, and parking.

September Days Club (tel. 800/241–5050) is run by the moderately priced Days Inns of America. The $12 annual membership fee for individuals or couples over 50 entitles them to reduced car-rental rates and to reductions of 15%–50% at most of the chain's 350 motels.

Greyhound/Trailways (800/752–4841; TDD 800/345–3109) offers special fares for senior citizens, subject to date and destination restrictions.

Amtrak (tel. 800/USA–RAIL) requests advance notice to provide redcap service, special seats, or wheelchair assistance at stations that are equipped to provide these services. Elderly passengers are entitled to a 25% discount on regular coach fares. There are some exceptions to these discounts; always check with Amtrak before traveling.

VIA Rail Canada (tel. 800/665–0200) offers senior citizens (60 and over) a 10% discount on basic transportation throughout its system for travel anytime and with no advance-purchase requirement. This 10% discount can also apply to off-peak reduced fares which do have advance-purchase requirements.

Publications ***The International Health Guide for Senior Citizen Travelers,*** by Dr. W. Robert Lange, MD, and ***The Senior Citizens Guide to Budget Travel in the United States and Canada,*** by Paige Palmer, are available for $4.95 and $3.95, respectively, plus $1 shipping from Pilot Books (103 Cooper St., Babylon, NY 11702, tel. 516/422–2225).

The Discount Guide for Travelers Over 55, by Caroline and Walter Weintz, lists helpful addresses, package tours, reduced-rate car rentals, and so forth, in the United States and abroad. To order, send $7.95 plus $1.50 shipping to Penguin USA/NAL (120 Woodbine St., Bergenfield, NJ 07621, tel. 800/526–0275).

"Fly Rights," a free brochure issued by the U.S. Department of Transportation (tel. 202/366–2220), provides information on airline services that are available to elderly passengers.

Further Reading

The late Bill Spiedel, one of Seattle's most colorful characters, wrote about the early history of the city in books full of lively anecdotes and legends; *Sons of the Profits* and *Doc Maynard* are two of his best. *Washingtonians, A Biographical Portrait of the State,* edited by David Brewster and David M. Buerge, is a series of essays on well-known and influential residents who have left their mark on the state. *Skookum,* by Shannon Applegate, is the history of an Oregon pioneer family.

At the Field's End, by Nicolas O'Connell, features interviews with 20 leading writers who are all closely connected to the Pacific North Coast and reflect the character of the region. *Whistlepunks and Geoducks—Oral Histories from the Pacific Northwest* by Ron Strickland is a collection of stories told by old-timers from all walks of life in Washington State. Gloria Snively's *Exploring the Seashore* offers a guide to shorebirds and intertidal plants and animals in Washington, Oregon, and British Columbia. The *Northwest Sportsman Almanac,* edited by Terry W. Sheely, provides an in-depth guide to fishing and hunting in the Pacific North Coast.

Well-known fiction writers of the region include Raymond Carver, Ursula LeGuin, Jean Auel, Ken Kesey, W. P. Kinsella, Tom Robbins, William Stafford, Walt Morey, and Norman Maclean.

Some magazines that focus on life and travel in the Pacific North Coast are *Pacific Northwest* magazine (Dexter Ave. N, Suite 101, Seattle, WA 98109, tel. 206/284–1750), *Beautiful B.C.* (929 Ellery St., Victoria, B.C. V9A 7B4, tel. 604/384–5456), *Northwest Travel* and *Oregon Coast* (Box 18000, Florence, OR 97439, tel. 503/997–8401), and *Peninsula* (901 Hwy. 101E, Box 2259, Sequim, WA 98382–2259, tel. 206/683–5421).

Arriving and Departing

From the U.S. by Plane

There are three types of flights: nonstop—no stops or changes of aircraft; direct—one or more stops but no change of aircraft; and connecting—at least one change of aircraft and possibly several stops as well.

Airports and Airlines The Pacific North Coast has three major airports: Seattle, Portland, and Vancouver. All major U.S. carriers—**Delta** (tel. 800/221–1212), **American** (tel. 800/433–7300), **Continental** (tel. 800/525–0280), **United** (tel. 800/241–6522), **US Air** (tel. 800/428–4322), **Alaska** (tel. 800/426–0333), **Northwest** (tel. 800/225–2525), and **TWA** (tel. 800/221–2000)—offer regular flights into Seattle and Portland from points throughout the United States. Nonstop flying time from New York to Seattle or Portland is approximately five hours; flights from Chicago to both Seattle and Portland are about 4–4½ hours; flights between Los Angeles and Seattle take 2½ hours.

Air Canada (tel. 800/663–8868) and **Canadian Airlines International** (tel. 800/426–7000) offer frequent service from all major Canadian cities to Vancouver. **Delta, American Airlines, Continental,** and **United** fly direct to Vancouver from various points in the United States. Flying time from New York to Vancouver is about 8 hours with connections; from Chicago to the city takes about 4½ hours nonstop; and flights from Los Angeles to Vancouver are about 3 hours nonstop.

Enjoying the Flight Unless you're flying to the United States or Canada from Europe, jet lag shouldn't be a problem. There is only a three-hour time difference between the East Coast and West Coast of the United States. Because the air on a plane is dry, it helps, while flying, to drink nonalcoholic beverages. Drinking alcohol contributes to jet lag, as does eating heavy meals. Feet swell at high altitudes, so it's a good idea to remove your shoes at the beginning of the flight. Sleepers usually prefer window seats to curl up against; those who like to move about the cabin should ask for aisle seats. Bulkhead seats (located in the front row of each cabin) have more legroom. But generally, these seats are reserved for the disabled, the elderly, or parents traveling with babies.

Discount Flights The major airlines offer a range of tickets that can vary the price of any given seat by more than 300%, depending on different conditions. As a rule, the further in advance you buy the ticket, the less expensive it is but the greater the penalty (up to 100%) for canceling.

APEX (advanced purchase) tickets on any of the major airlines carry certain restrictions. They must be bought in advance (usually 21 days); they restrict your travel, usually with a minimum stay of seven days and a maximum of 90; and they also penalize you for changes—voluntary or not—in your travel plans. But if you can work around these drawbacks (and most travelers can), they are among the best-value fares available.

Other discounted fares—up to 50% below the cost of APEX tickets—can be found through consolidators, companies that buy blocks of tickets on scheduled airlines and sell them at wholesale prices. Tickets are subject to availability, so passengers must have flexible travel schedules. Also, be aware that if you change your plans, you could lose all or most of your money. As a precaution, purchase trip-cancellation insurance. Consolidators advertise in Sunday newspaper travel sections.

Another option is to join a travel club that offers special discounts to its members. Several such organizations are **Discount Travel International** (114 Forrest Ave., Narbeth, PA 19072, tel. 215/668–2182), **Moment's Notice** (40 E. 49th St., New York, NY 10017, tel. 212/486–0503), **Traveler's Advantage** (CUC Travel

Service, 40 Oakview Dr., Trumbull, CT 06611, tel. 800/648–
4037), and **Worldwide Discount Travel Club** (1674 Meridien
Ave., Miami Beach, FL 33139, tel. 305/534–2082).

Smoking   As of 1990, smoking is banned on all routes within the 48 contig-
uous states, within the states of Hawaii and Alaska, to and
from the U.S. Virgin Islands and Puerto Rico, and on flights of
less than six hours to and from Hawaii and Alaska. The rule ap-
plies to both domestic and foreign carriers.

Canadian regulations are similar and ban smoking on all flights
of less than six hours.

On a flight where smoking is permitted, you can request a nonsmoking seat during check-in or when booking your ticket. If
the airline tells you there are no seats available in the nonsmoking section, insist on one. Department of Transportation regulations require carriers to find seats for all nonsmokers,
provided they meet check-in time restrictions. These regulations apply to all international flights on U.S. domestic carriers; however, the Department of Transportation does not have
jurisdiction over foreign carriers traveling out of, or into, the
United States.

From the U.S. by Car

The U.S. interstate highway network provides quick and easy
access to the Pacific North Coast in spite of imposing mountain
barriers. From the south, I–5 runs from the U.S.–Mexico border through California, into Oregon and Washington, and ends
at the U.S.–Canada border. Most of the population and economic development of Oregon and Washington is clustered
along this corridor. From the east, I–90 stretches from Boston
to Seattle. I–84 runs from the Midwest states to Portland.

The main entry point by car into Canada is on I–5 at Blaine,
Washington, just 30 miles south of Vancouver. Two major high-
ways enter British Columbia from the east—the Trans-Canada
Highway (the longest highway in the world, running more than
5,000 miles from St. John's, Newfoundland, to Victoria, British
Columbia) and the Yellowhead Highway, which runs through
northern British Columbia from the Rocky Mountains to
Prince Rupert.

Border-crossing procedures are usually quick and simple (*see*
Passports and Visas and Customs, above). The I–5 border
crossing at Blaine, WA, is one of the busiest anywhere between
the United States and Canada. Peak traffic times at the border
northbound into Canada are daily at 4 PM. Southbound, delays
can be expected evenings and weekend mornings. Try to plan
on reaching the border at off-peak times.

From the U.S. by Train

Amtrak (tel. 800/USA–RAIL), the U.S. passenger rail system,
has daily service to the Pacific North Coast from the midwest-
ern United States and California. The *Empire Builder* takes a
northern route from Chicago to Seattle. The *Pioneer* travels
from Chicago to Portland via Denver and Salt Lake City. The
Coast Starlight begins in Los Angeles, makes stops throughout
western Oregon and Washington, and terminates its route in

Seattle. There are no trains that cross the border from Seattle into Canada.

Canada's passenger service, **VIA Rail Canada** (tel. 800/665-0200), operates transcontinental routes on the *Canadian* three times weekly between eastern Canada and Vancouver. During the summer months, this service expands to six weekly trips on the western leg of the trip between Jasper, Alberta, and Vancouver. A second train, the *Skeena*, runs three times weekly between Jasper, Alberta, to the British Columbia port city of Prince Rupert.

From the U.S. by Bus

Greyhound/Trailways (local listings only) operates bus service to Washington, Oregon, and British Columbia from various points in the United States and Canada. Bus service in North America—though fairly economical—has not been a first-class means of travel in recent years. But Greyhound and other bus companies are putting a major effort into improving service. New amenities may include an on-board host/hostess, meals, and VCRs.

From the U.K. by Plane

Airlines and Airfares British travelers entering the Pacific North Coast can enter the main international gateways of Seattle and Vancouver. Southeast Alaska is served by regular, connecting flights to Anchorage from the United Kingdom.

At press time **British Airways** (tel. 081/897-4000) services Seattle from Heathrow. **KLM** (081/751-9000 in U.K., 800/777-5553 in U.S.) flies to Vancouver from 25 U.K. and Irish airports via Amsterdam. Also to Vancouver, **Air Canada** (tel. 081/759-2636) and **British Airways** departed from Heathrow; **Canadian Airlines International CAIL** (tel. 081/667-0666 in London, 0345/616-767 (outside London) serviced Gatwick. To Anchorage from Heathrow, **Japan Air Lines** (tel. 071/408-1000) and **British Airways** provided service.

Fares on scheduled flights vary considerably. January to March are the cheapest months to fly, and mid-week flights nearly always offer some reductions. Round-trip, peak-season fares to Seattle begin at £530 and climb to £3,690 for a first-class ticket.

Charters **Globespan Ltd.** (tel. 0293/562690), **ASAT** (tel. 0737/778560), and **Unijet** (tel. 0444/459100) with weekly flights to Vancouver, offer sizable reductions on fares. At press time, prices began at £425 round-trip. You can also find good deals through specialized ticket agencies such as **Travel Cuts** (tel. 071/637-3161). Round-trip fares to Seattle start at about £300 in the off-season.

Staying in the Pacific North Coast

Getting Around

By Plane   In the past few years, regional air travel has changed considerably in North America. Large national carriers have given up many of their shorter routes to secondary cities. But smaller, regional companies, which are often owned by, or have joint marketing and reservation systems with, larger airlines, have taken up the slack. Instead of operating jets, they often fly turboprop planes that hold 10–50 passengers.

Leading regional carriers in the U.S. Pacific North Coast are **Horizon Air** (tel. 800/547–9308) and **United Express** (tel. 800/241–6522). The two airlines provide frequent service between cities in Washington and Oregon. Horizon Air also flies internationally from Seattle to Vancouver and Victoria.

The two major regional carriers in Canada are **Air BC** (tel. 800/663–0522) and **Time Air** (tel. 800/426–7000). They serve communities throughout western Canada and have daily flights from Vancouver and Victoria into Seattle. **Air BC** also has several daily flights between Vancouver and Portland.

There is frequent jet service from Seattle to Juneau on **Alaska Airlines** (tel. 800/426–0333) and **Delta Air Lines** (tel. 800/221–1212). Alaska Airlines also serves the smaller cities of Ketchikan, Wrangell, Sitka, Petersburg, and Yakutat from Juneau. Another regional air carrier, **Markair** (tel. 800/426–6784) serves 130 points in Alaska.

With all the water surrounding the Pacific North Coast, float planes are a common and convenient means of transportation. Accommodating 5–15 passengers, the planes fly at fairly low elevations and provide a great way to see the scenery.

Air BC has float-plane service between Vancouver and Victoria harbors in addition to its regular airport service. **Lake Union Air** (tel. 800/826–1890) operates scheduled flights and charters from Seattle to Vancouver, Victoria, and other points on Vancouver Island, and the San Juan Islands. **Kenmore Air Harbor** (tel. 800/543–9595) flies charters from Seattle to many points within the region. Along with several other float-plane companies, Kenmore provides fly-in service to remote fishing resorts along the coast of British Columbia.

In Alaska, float planes (or air taxis) are an essential means of air transportation, connecting many small communities and fishing lodges.

By Train   The Pacific North Coast has a number of scenic train routes in addition to the ones operated by Amtrak and VIA Rail Canada. The **Rocky Mountaineer** (Great Canadian Railtour Co., Ltd., 340 Brooksbank Ave., Suite 104, North Vancouver, B.C. V7J 2C1, tel. 800/665–7245), is a two-day rail cruise between Vancouver and the Canadian Rockies, May–October. There are two routes—one to Banff/Calgary and one to Jasper—through landscapes considered the most spectacular in the world. An overnight hotel stop is made in Kamloops.

On Vancouver Island, VIA Rail (tel. 604/383–4324) runs the *E&N Railway* from Victoria north to Nanaimo. **BC Rail** (Box 8770, Vancouver, B.C. V6B 4X6, tel. 604/631–3500) operates daily service from its North Vancouver terminal to the town of Prince George. At Prince George, it is possible to connect with VIA Rail's *Skeena* service. BC Rail also operates a summer-time excursion steam train, the *Royal Hudson*, between North Vancouver and Squamish, at the head of Howe Sound.

A most dramatic and scenic excursion in southeastern Alaska is **The White Pass and Yukon Route** (Box 435, Skagway, AK 99840, tel. 800/343–7373). The narrow-gauge railroad carried passengers and ore from the Klondike gold mines of the Yukon to Skagway until it was closed down in the early 1980s. In 1988, the line was reopened as far as Fraser, British Columbia. Bus service is now available from Fraser to Whitehorse in the Yukon Territory.

The cruise and tour company **Holland America Line/Westours** (tel. 206/281–3535) is planning to operate a new luxury tour train between Vancouver and the Canadian Rockies beginning in 1992.

Both **Princess Cruises/Tours** (tel. 206/728–4202) and **Holland America Line/Westours** offer rail tours on the Alaska Railroad into the interior of Alaska as a post-cruise option.

By Bus **Greyhound/Trailways** (local listings only) operates regular intercity bus routes to points throughout the region. Smaller bus companies provide service within local areas. One such service, **Pacific Coach Lines** (tel. 604/662–8074), runs from downtown Vancouver to Victoria (via the British Columbia ferry system). Bus service to Alaska from the lower 48 states is possible via **Greyhound** with connections to other bus companies via White-Horse in the Yukon Territory.

Several companies operate charter bus service and scheduled sightseeing tours that last from a few hours to several days in length. Most tours can be booked locally and provide a good way for visitors to see the sights comfortably in a short period of time. **Gray Line** companies in Portland (tel. 503/226–6755), Seattle (tel. 206/624–5077), Vancouver (tel. 604/681–8687), and Victoria (tel. 604/388–5248) run such sightseeing trips.

By Car Highway travel in the Pacific North Coast is largely determined by the geography of the region. In Oregon, Washington, and British Columbia, roads that run east to west are limited to a few mountain passes. Except for a short distance north of Vancouver, there are no roads along the rugged mainland coast of British Columbia and southeast Alaska.

Alaskan cities, such as Juneau, have no direct access by road; cars must be brought in by ferry. Skagway and Haines are the only towns in southeast Alaska that can be driven to directly. The trip—a grueling 1,650 miles from Seattle—passes through British Columbia and the Yukon Territory.

The speed limit on U.S. interstate highways is 65 miles per hour in rural areas and 55 miles per hour in urban zones and on secondary highways. In Canada (where the metric system is used), the speed limit is usually 100 kilometers per hour on expressways and 80 kilometers per hour on secondary roads.

Vehicle insurance is compulsory in the United States and Canada. Motorists are required to produce evidence of insurance should they be involved in an accident. Visitors from other countries who plan to bring their own cars to the United States or Canada may find it difficult to get the proper insurance before leaving home. Upon arrival, they should contact an insurance agent or broker to obtain the necessary insurance for North America. Drivers who can prove (in writing) that they have had no claims in recent years will be eligible to purchase insurance at the lowest price.

Winter driving in the Pacific North Coast can sometimes present some real challenges. In coastal areas, the mild, damp climate contributes to roadways that are frequently wet. Winter snowfalls are not common (maybe only once or twice a year), but when snow does fall, traffic grinds to a halt. Road departments and municipalities simply do not have the equipment to handle snow, so the roadways quickly become treacherous and stay that way until the snow melts.

Tire chains, studs, or snow tires are essential equipment for winter travel in mountain areas. If you're planning to drive into high elevations, be sure to check the weather forecast beforehand. Even the main highway mountain passes can close because of snow conditions. The state or provincial highway departments operate snow advisory telephone lines during the winter months giving pass conditions.

Driving a car across the U.S.–Canada border is a simple process. Personal vehicles are allowed entry into the neighboring country, provided they are not to be left behind. Drivers of rental cars should bring along a copy of the rental contract, bearing an endorsement that states that the vehicle is permitted to cross the border.

The **American Automobile Association** (AAA) and the **Canadian Automobile Association** (CAA) provide full services to members of any of the Commonwealth Motoring Conference (CMC) clubs, including the Automobile Association, the Royal Automobile Club, and the Royal Scottish Automobile Club. Services are also available to members of the Alliance Internationale de l'Automobile (AIT), the Federation Internationale de l'Automobile (FIA), and the Federation of Interamerican Touring and Automobile Clubs (FITAC). By presenting membership cards, motorists are entitled to travel information, itineraries, maps, tour books, information about road and weather conditions, emergency road services, and travel-agency services.

By Ferry Ferries play an important part in the transportation network of the Pacific North Coast. In some areas, ferries provide the only form of access into and out of communities. In other places, ferries transport thousands of commuters a day to and from work in the cities. For visitors, ferries are one of the best ways to get a feel for the region and its ties to the sea.

The **British Columbia Ferry Corporation** (1112 Fort St., Victoria, B.C. V8V 4V2, tel. 604/386–3431 in Victoria; for 24-hour recorded schedule information, 604/656–0757 in Victoria or 604/685–1021 in Vancouver) operates one of the largest and most modern ferry fleets in the world, with 38 ships serving 42 ports of call along the British Columbia coast. More than 15 million passengers ride this fleet each year.

The busiest ferries operate between the mainland and Vancouver Island, carrying passengers, cars, campers, RVs, trucks, and buses. The company also provides scheduled service on the *Queen of the North* between Port Hardy at the northern end of Vancouver Island and the port city of Prince Rupert. From there, connections can be made to Alaskan ferries that travel still farther north, or to a VIA Rail train heading east through the Canadian Rockies. Connections also can be made with another B.C. Ferry to the Queen Charlotte Islands (reservations strongly recommended).

The *Queen of the North* sails every two days in summer and once a week in winter. Summer cruises (June–Sept.) take 15 hours (all in daylight), so passengers can enjoy every bit of the spectacular coastal scenery. Reservations are strongly recommended. For reservations, call B.C. Ferries (tel. 604/386–3431 in Victoria or 604/669–1211 in Vancouver).

The **Washington State Ferry System** (Colman Dock, Seattle, WA 98104, tel. 800/542–7052 in WA, 206/464–6400 out of state) has 23 ferries in its fleet, which carries more than 18 million passengers a year between points on Puget Sound and the San Juan Islands. Reservations are not available on any domestic routes.

If you are planning to take a ferry, try to avoid peak commuter hours. The heaviest traffic flows are eastbound in the mornings and on Sunday evenings, and westbound Saturday mornings and on weekday afternoons. The best times for travel are 9 AM–3 PM and after 7 PM on weekdays. In July and August, you may have to wait up to two hours to take a car aboard one of the popular San Juan Islands ferries. Walk-on space is always available; if you can, leave your car behind.

The transportation lifeblood of southeastern Alaska is the **Alaska Marine Highway System** (Box R, Juneau, AK 99811, tel. 907/465–3941, 907/465–3942, or 800/642–0066 from the lower 48). From their southern terminus in Bellingham, Washington, the Alaska ferries carry passengers and vehicles through the Inside Passage year-round, with stops at Prince Rupert, Skagway, Haines, Ketchikan, Sitka, Wrangell, Petersburg, Stewart, and Juneau. Smaller car ferries serve several other towns and villages in southeast Alaska. The boats take the same route as the luxury cruise ships, but at a fraction of the cost.

Staterooms are available, but cabin space is always booked months in advance. Passengers without staterooms are welcome to sleep in public lounges or on deck.

In the summer, U.S. forest rangers ride the larger ferries, offering interpretive programs along the route. Short local land tours, coinciding with ferry stopovers, are available in many communities. In the fall, winter, and spring, ferry rates are lower and senior citizens are entitled to free passage between ports in Alaska.

Clipper Navigation (2701 Alaskan Way, Pier 69, Seattle, WA 98121, tel. 800/888–2535) operates three passenger-only jet catamarans between Seattle and Victoria; each facilitates 300 people. The *Victoria Clipper* makes the scenic crossing in just 2 ½ hours; the *Victoria Clipper 2* does it in less than 3 hours; and the *Victoria Clipper 3*, which stops in Friday Harbor and Port Townsend, does the trip in 5 hours.

Black Ball Transport's (430 Belleville St., Victoria, B.C. V8V 1W9; tel. 604/386–2202 in Victoria or 206/457–4491 in Port Angeles) M.V. *Coho* makes daily crossings year-round, from Port Angeles to Victoria. The *Coho* can carry 800 passengers and 100 cars across the Strait of Juan de Fuca in 1½ hours. Advance reservations are not accepted.

Passenger-only *Victoria Express* (Box 1928, Port Angeles, WA 98362, tel. 206/452–8088; 800/633–1589 for reservations in Washington) offers a one-hour crossing of the Strait of Juan de Fuca between Port Angeles and Victoria from the end of May through the end of October.

By Cruise Ship Cruise ships travel British Columbia's Inside Passage to Alaska from mid-May through early October. Most ships start or end their seven-day journeys in Vancouver, making stops at several Alaskan ports along the way. A few companies provide land tours in conjunction with their week-long cruises into the Yukon Territory and other parts of Alaska.

More than 18 ships offer cruises to Alaska, including those operated by **Holland America Line, Princess Cruises, Cunard Line, Costa Cruises, Regency Cruise Line, Admiral Cruises, Crystal Cruises, Kloster Cruise Line,** and **World Explorer Cruises.** For more information, contact your travel agent or the Cruise Lines International Association (CLIA, 17 Battery Pl., Suite 631, New York, NY 10004, tel. 212/425–7400).

Telephones

The telephone area codes in the Pacific North Coast are 503 for Oregon; 206 for western Washington, including Seattle; 509 for eastern Washington, including Spokane; 604 for British Columbia; and 907 for Alaska, except for the town of Hyder in southeast Alaska which uses the 604 area code.

Pay telephones cost 25¢ for local calls. Charge phones are also found in many locations. These phones can be used to charge a call to a telephone company credit card, your home phone, or the party whom you are calling: You do not need to deposit 25¢.

To reach an operator for a telephone number, dial the area code for the community you wish to call, followed by 555–1212. To obtain a local number, dial 1 followed by 555–1212. You can dial most international calls direct, but if you need assistance, dial "0" to reach an operator.

Many hotels place a surcharge on local calls made from your room and include a service charge on long-distance calls. It may be cheaper for you to make your calls from a pay phone in the hotel lobby, rather than from your room.

Mail

Postal Rates Because postage rates will vary for different classes of mail and destinations, it is advisable to check with local postal authorities before mailing a letter or parcel. At press time, it costs 29¢ to mail a standard letter anywhere within the United States. Mail to Canada costs 40¢ per first ounce, and 23¢ for each additional ounce; mail to Great Britain and other foreign countries costs 50¢ per half-ounce.

First-class rates in Canada are 40¢ + 3¢ GST tax for up to 1.6 ounces of mail delivered within Canada, 46¢ + 3¢ GST tax for mail to the United States, and 80¢ + 6¢ GST tax for mail to other foreign destinations.

Receiving Mail   Visitors can have letters or parcels sent to them while they are traveling by using the following address: Name of addressee, c/o General Delivery, Main Post Office, City and State/Province, U.S./Canada, Zip Code (U.S.) or Postal Code (Canada). Contact the nearest post office for further details. Any item mailed to "General Delivery" must be picked up by the addressee, in person, within 15 days or it will be returned to the sender.

Tipping

Tips and service charges are usually not automatically added to a bill in the United States or Canada. If service is satisfactory, customers generally give waiters, waitresses, taxi drivers, barbers, hairdressers, and so forth, a tip of 15%–20% of the total bill. Bellhops, doormen, and porters at airports and railway stations are generally tipped $1 for each item of luggage.

Opening and Closing Times

Most retail stores in Washington and Oregon are open 9:30–6 seven days a week in downtown locations and later at suburban shopping malls. Downtown stores sometimes stay open late Thursday and Friday nights. Normal banking hours are weekdays 9–6; some branches are also open on Saturday morning.

In Alaska, most city retail outlets open Monday–Saturday 10–6 or 10–7. Shopping malls stay open until 8 or 9. Most banks operate 10–3.

In British Columbia, many stores close on Sunday. Outlets that cater to tourists are the notable exception. Normal banking hours in Canada are 10–3 on weekdays, with extended hours in many locations. Some banks in major cities are now open on Saturday morning.

Shopping

The Pacific North Coast offers shoppers quite a cache of locally made crafts and souvenirs. Some of the most distinctive items are produced by Northwest Native American artists, who manufacture prints, wood carvings, boxes, masks, and so forth. Shops in Seattle, Portland, and Vancouver carry a wide variety of these objects, but art collectors can find the best selection and prices in the small communities located on Vancouver Island.

Another popular "souvenir" for visitors is freshly caught salmon. Fish vendors can pack a recent catch in a special airlines-approved box that will keep the fish fresh for a couple of days. A package of smoked salmon—which will keep even longer—is another alternative.

Public markets are among the best places to purchase salmon and other gifts. Seattle's historic Pike Place Market and Vancouver's Granville Island Market offer a wonderful array of fish stalls, fresh fruit and vegetable stands, arts and crafts vendors, and small shops that sell practically everything.

Shoppers in Alaska will find good buys on gold-nugget jewelry, woven baskets, items made from jade, and specialty foods, including salmon and wild-berry products. Also available and unique to Alaska are carvings made from fossilized walrus ivory that are produced only by indigenous native carvers. Look for the "Made in Alaska" logo which indicates an item genuinely manufactured in Alaska.

Because residents of the Pacific North Coast have such an active lifestyle, many leading manufacturers and retailers of outdoor equipment and apparel have their headquarters there. Recreation Equipment Inc. (REI) has several stores in the Seattle area that sell everything from high-quality sleeping bags and backpacks to freeze-dried food and mountain-climbing equipment. Eddie Bauer, the famous recreational clothing and equipment catalog distributor and retailer, was founded in Seattle and still has outlets there. One of the world's leading athletic shoe manufacturers, Nike, is based in Oregon and has retail shops in Portland.

Sales taxes vary depending on state or province. Oregon and Alaska charge no sales tax on items purchased; Washington's tax varies between 7% and 8.2%, depending on municipality; provincial sales tax in British Columbia is 6%. Canada's Goods and Services Tax (better known as GST) is a value-added tax of 7%, applicable on virtually every purchase except basic groceries and a small number of other items. Visitors to Canada, however, may claim a full rebate of the GST on any goods taken out of the country as well as on short-term accommodations. At press time, rebates could be claimed either immediately on departure from Canada at participating Duty Free Shops or by mail. Rebate forms can be picked up at most stores and hotels in Canada or can be obtained by writing to **Revenue Canada** (Visitor's Rebate Program, Ottawa, Ontario, Canada K1A 1J5). Claims must be for a minimum of $7 and can be submitted up to a year from the date of purchase. Purchases made during multiple visits to Canada can be grouped together for rebate purposes.

Participant Sports and Outdoor Activities

Bicycling   Bicycling, a popular sport in the Pacific North Coast, appeals to both families out for a leisurely ride and avid cyclists seeking a challenge on rugged mountain trails.

Several cycling organizations sponsor trips of various lengths and degrees of difficulty. For further information, contact: **Portland Wheelmen Touring Club** (Box 40753, Portland, OR 97240, tel. 503/282–7982), **Washington State Bicycle Association** (tel. 206/329–BIKE), **Cascade Bicycle Club** (tel. 206/522–BIKE), and **Bicycling Association of British Columbia** (1200 Hornby St., Vancouver, B.C. V6Z 2E2, tel. 604/669–BIKE).

Rentals are available from bicycle shops in most cities.

Boating   The sheltered waters of Puget Sound and the Inside Passage, plus the area's many freshwater lakes, make boating one of the most popular outdoor activities in the Pacific North Coast. On sunny days, a virtual fleet of boats dot the waterways; in fact, some claimants say that there are more boats per capita in the Puget Sound area than anywhere else in the world.

Because of the region's mild climate, it is possible to enjoy boating throughout the year. Charters, which are available with or without a skipper and crew, can be rented for a period of a few hours up to several days. The calm waterways are also rated as among the best in the world for sea kayaking, an appealing way to explore the intertidal regions.

The area's swift rivers also provide challenges to avid canoers and kayakers. A word of warning, however: Many of these rivers should be attempted only by experienced boaters. Check with local residents about what dangers may lie downstream before taking to the waterways.

Climbing/ Mountaineering The mountains of the Pacific North Coast have given many an adventurer quite a challenge. It is no coincidence that many members of the U.S. expedition teams to Mt. Everest have come from this region.

With expert training and advanced equipment, mountaineering can be a safe sport, but you should never go climbing without an experienced guide. Classes are available from qualified instructors. For more information, contact: **Mazama Club** (909 N.W. 19th Ave., Portland, OR 97209, tel. 503/227–2345), **The Mountaineers** (300 3rd Ave. W, Seattle, WA 98119, tel. 206/ 284–8484), and **Rainier Mountaineering Inc.** (Paradise, WA 98397, tel. 206/569–2227).

Fishing The coastal regions and inland lakes and rivers of the Pacific North Coast are known for their excellent fishing opportunities. Fishing lodges, many of which are accessible only by float plane, cater to anglers looking for the ultimate fishing experience.

Visiting sportsmen must possess a nonresident license for the state or province in which they plan to fish. Licenses are available at sporting goods stores, bait shops, and other outlets in popular fishing areas.

For information on fishing regulations, contact: **Washington Department of Fisheries** (Administration Bldg., Room 115, Olympia, WA 98505, tel. 206/753–6600 for salmon-fishing or marine licenses, tel. 206/753–5700 for freshwater licenses), **Oregon Department of Fish and Wildlife** (506 S.W. Mill St., Portland, OR 97208, tel. 503/229–5403), or **Alaska Department of Fish and Game** (Box 3-2000, Juneau, AK 99802, tel. 907/465– 4112). In British Columbia, separate licences are required for saltwater and freshwater fishing. Information and licences for saltwater fishing can be obtained from the **Department of Fisheries and Oceans** (555 W. Hastings St., Vancouver, B.C. V6B 5G2 tel. 604/666–3545). For freshwater fishing, contact the **Ministry of Environment, Fish and Wildlife Information** (Parliament Buildings, Victoria, B.C. V8V 1X5 tel. 604/387–9737).

Most coastal towns have charter boats and crews that are available for deep-sea fishing. State and provincial tourism departments can provide further information on charters.

Golf The Pacific North Coast has many excellent golf courses, but not all of them are available to the public. Consequently, visitors may find it difficult to arrange a tee time at a popular course. If you are a member of a golf club at home, check to see if your club has a reciprocal playing arrangement with any of the private clubs in the areas that you will be visiting.

Hiking There are many trails in the Pacific North Coast that are geared to both beginning and experienced hikers. The **National Parks and Forests Outdoor Recreation Information Center** (915 2nd Ave., Room 442, Seattle, WA 98174, tel. 206/553–0170) can provide maps of trails that are well marked and well maintained. Guidebooks that describe the best trails in the area are readily available in local bookstores. The *Footsore* series of books, published by The Mountaineers (306 2nd Ave. W, Seattle, WA 98119, tel. 206/285–2665), are among the best.

Hunting Autumn visitors to the Pacific North Coast will find opportunities for deer hunting and waterfowl hunting in the coastal areas and around inland lakes. Big-game hunters, who are on the trail for elk, moose, and bear, should go to British Columbia or Alaska where outfitters are available to act as guides.

For more information on hunting facilities and licenses contact: **Washington State Game Department** (600 N. Capitol Way, Olympia, WA 98504, tel. 206/753–5700), **Oregon Department of Fish and Wildlife** (506 S.W. Mill St., Portland, OR 97208, tel. 503/229–5403), **British Columbia Ministry of Environment, Wildlife Branch** (780 Blanshard St., Victoria, B.C. V8W 2H1, tel. 604/387–9737), or **Alaska Department of Fish and Game** (Box 3-200, Juneau, AK 99802, tel. 907/465–4112).

Sailboarding The Columbia River, particularly at Hood River, Oregon, is known as the best spot in the world for windsurfing. Puget Sound and some of the inland lakes are also popular venues for the sport. Sailboard rentals and lessons are available from local specialty shops. In British Columbia, the town of Squamish is quickly becoming another major windsurfing destination.

Scuba Diving The crystal-clear waters of Puget Sound and the Inside Passage—with their diversity of marine life—present excellent opportunities for scuba diving and underwater photography. For information on dive shops, equipment rentals, and charter boats in British Columbia, contact **Dive B.C.** (707 Westminster Ave., Powell River, B.C. V8A 1C5, tel. 604/485–6267).

Skiing Skiing is by far the most popular winter activity in the area. Moist air off the Pacific Ocean dumps snow on the coastal mountains, providing excellent skiing from November through the end of March and sometimes into April. Local newspapers regularly carry snow conditions for ski areas throughout the region during the winter season.

The Whistler and Blackcomp mountains, north of Vancouver, comprise the biggest ski area in the region. Whistler Village resort boasts the longest and second-longest vertical drops (more than a mile each) of any ski area in North America. Aside from Whistler/Blackcomb, British Columbia has many other excellent ski resorts scattered throughout the province, including several only minutes from downtown Vancouver.

Washington has 16 ski areas, several of which are located just 45 miles east of Seattle in the Cascade Mountains. Other major ski resorts include Mt. Baker, Crystal Mountain, Stevens Pass, and Mission Ridge.

Oregon's primary ski facility, Mt. Bachelor, is rated one of the best ski areas in North America. Located 50 miles east of Portland, Mt. Hood offers skiing (on glaciers!) well into the summer months.

Cross-country skiing is a popular and less-expensive way to enjoy the winter wilderness. Many downhill ski resorts also feature well-marked and well-groomed cross-country trails. Washington operates a system of **SnoParks** (Office of Winter Recreation, Parks and Recreation Commission, 7150 Cleanwater La., KY-11, Olympia, WA 98504), which provides access to trails in 70 locations statewide.

Swimming Despite all the water surrounding the region, there is not as much swimming as one might expect in the Pacific North Coast. While the sandy ocean beaches attract throngs of people during the summer, most sun-worshipers spend little time in the water—it's simply too chilly!

Similarly, the waters of Puget Sound are generally too cold for swimming, and the beaches are mostly rocky. The best swimming beaches can be found around the Parksville area of Vancouver Island, where the combination of low tide, sandy beaches, and shallow water create fairly warm swimming conditions.

Many communities throughout the region have public swimming pools. Locations and hours are posted locally.

Wildlife Viewing The Pacific North Coast offers ample opportunities for viewing wildlife, both on land and on water. The best way to identify the wide range of native creatures is with a pair of binoculars and a good nature guide in hand. Books featuring regional wildlife can be found in local bookstores. Bald eagles, sea lions, dolphins, and whales are just a few of the animals that can be observed in the region.

Spectator Sports

Baseball The **Seattle Mariners** (tel. 206/628–0888 for tickets) of the American League play in the 60,000-seat indoor Kingdome. Tickets are almost always available. Baseball season runs from April to early October.

You can see the baseball stars of the future play in smaller outdoor stadiums in several cities. Teams include the **Vancouver Canadians** (tel. 604/872–5232), the **Tacoma Tigers** (tel. 206/752–7707), the **Portland Beavers** (tel. 503/223–2837), and the **Everett Giants** (tel. 206/258–3673).

Basketball The region fields two big-league basketball teams: the **Seattle SuperSonics** (tel. 206/281–5850) at the Seattle Coliseum and the **Portland Trail Blazers** (tel. 503/234–9291) at the Memorial Coliseum. Most universities and colleges in the area also have basketball programs.

Dog Racing Greyhounds race at the **Multnomah Kennel Club Dog Race Track** in Portland (tel. 503/243–2706) from May to September.

Football The **Seattle Seahawks** (tel. 206/628–0888 for tickets) of the National Football League play in the Kingdome during the fall, but games are almost always sold out. Tickets are usually available for the **British Columbia Lions** (tel. 604/280–4400) of the Canadian Football League, who play in the indoor B.C. Place Stadium in Vancouver. One of the most consistently successful university football teams in the United States is the **University**

of **Washington Huskies** (tel. 206/543–2200). They take to the gridiron at 73,000-seat Husky Stadium, which overlooks Lake Washington.

Hockey The **Vancouver Canucks** (tel. 604/254–5141) of the National Hockey League hit the ice at the Pacific Coliseum. Minorleague "junior" hockey has a strong following in both Seattle and Portland.

Horse Racing Thoroughbred horse racing takes place at **Longacres** (tel. 206/226–3131) in Seattle from April to September and at both **Portland Meadows** (tel. 503/285–9144) in Portland and **Exhibition Park** (tel. 604/254–1631) in Vancouver from April to October. Harness racing occurs from April to October at the **Cloverdale Raceway** (tel. 604/576–9141), located south of Vancouver near the U.S. border.

Powerboating Each year, thousands of spectators watch unlimited hydroplanes, or "thunder boats," race on Seattle's Lake Washington in early August as the grand finale of **Seafair** (*see* Festivals and Seasonal events in Before You Go, above).

Soccer Professional indoor soccer is played at Tacoma Dome by the **Tacoma Stars** (tel. 206/628–0888 for tickets) of the Major Indoor Soccer League. At press time, the team's future was in question.

Beaches

The Pacific coasts of Oregon, Washington, and British Columbia have long, sandy beaches that run for miles at a stretch. But the waters are often too cold or treacherous for swimming. Even in summertime, beach goers must be prepared to dress warmly.

The most accessible—and warmest—ocean beaches in the region are in Oregon, where a number of resort communities are established. Fortunately, most of the Oregon coastline has been protected as public land, so it can be enjoyed by everyone.

The beaches of Washington are more remote from the major centers of population. Seattle, for example, is located on the salt-water Puget Sound but is a two- to three-hour drive from the nearest ocean beaches. Even in summer, the beaches are never crowded.

Most of the west coast of Vancouver Island is totally isolated. Pacific Rim National Park is one of the few places where ocean beaches are accessible. On the eastern coast of Vancouver Island, there are some good swimming beaches around the town of Parksville.

The gravel beaches of Washington's Puget Sound and British Columbia's Inside Passage attract few swimmers or sunbathers, but the beaches are popular for beachcombing and viewing marine life.

Dining

Many Pacific North Coast restaurants serve local specialties such as salmon, crab, oysters, and other seafood delicacies. Seattle's Pike Place Market and Vancouver's Granville Island Market display bountiful supplies of local seafood and produce, and these are good places to scan what you might find on restaurant menus. Ethnic foods are also becoming increasingly popular, especially Asian cuisines such as Japanese, Korean, and Thai.

Portions of the Pacific North Coast are major wine-producing regions. Local wines are often featured in the best restaurants.

Restaurants are divided into the following price categories: Very Expensive, Expensive, Moderate, and Inexpensive. As a general rule, restaurants in metropolitan areas are more expensive than those outside the city. But many city establishments, especially those that feature foreign cuisine, are surprisingly inexpensive. Because of space limitations, it is impossible to include every dining establishment in the following chapters. Therefore, we have listed only those recommended as the best within each price range.

Lodging

Hotels and motels in this guidebook are divided into standard categories based on price: Very Expensive, Expensive, Moderate, and Inexpensive. Although the names of the various hotel and motel categories are standard, the prices listed under each may vary from area to area. This variation is meant to reflect local price standards: For example, a Moderate price in a large urban area might be considered Expensive in a rural region. In all cases, however, price ranges for each category are clearly stated before each listing.

Hotels Most big-city hotels cater primarily to business travelers, with such facilities as restaurants, cocktail lounges, swimming pools, exercise equipment, and meeting rooms. Room rates often reflect the range of amenities offered. Most cities also have cheaper hotels, which are clean and comfortable but have fewer upscale facilities. A new accommodations trend is all-suite hotels, which offer more intimate facilities and are gaining popularity with the business traveler. Examples are **Courtyard By Marriott** (tel. 800/321–2211) and **Embassy Suites Hotels** (tel. 800/362–2779).

Many properties offer special weekend rates, sometimes up to 50% off regular prices. However, these deals are usually not extended during peak summer months, when hotels are normally full.

Vancouver, Seattle, and Portland all have experienced major hotel building booms in the past 10 years. Most of the major chains have properties in one or all of these cities. For more information, contact: **Canadian Pacific** (tel. 800/828–7447), **Doubletree** (tel. 800/528–0444), **Four Seasons** (tel. 800/332–3442), **Hilton** (tel. 800/445–8667), **Holiday Inn** (tel. 800/465–4329), **Hyatt** (tel. 800/233–1234), **Marriott** (tel. 800/228–9290), **Ramada** (tel. 800/228–2828), **Sheraton** (tel. 800/325–3535), **Stouffer** (tel. 800/468–3751), **Westin** (tel. 800/228–3000).

Motels/Motor Inns The familiar roadside motel of the past is fast disappearing from the landscape. In its place are economical chain-run motor inns, which are strategically located at highway intersections. Some of these establishments offer very basic facilities; others provide restaurants, swimming pools, and other comforts.

Nationally recognized chains include **Best Western** (tel. 800/528–1234), **Days Inn** (tel. 800/325–2525), **La Quinta Inns** (tel.

800/531–5900), **Motel 6** (tel. 505/891–6161), **Quality Inns** (tel. 800/228–5151), **Super 8 Motels** (tel. 800/848–8888), and **Travelodge** (tel. 800/255–3050). **Nendel's** (tel. 800/547–0106), **Red Lion Inns** (tel. 800/547–8010), **Shilo Inns** (tel. 800/222–2244), and **West Coast Hotels** (tel. 800/426–0670) are regional chains.

Inns   These establishments generally are located outside cities and have anywhere from 8 to 20 rooms. Lodging is often in an old restored building with some historical or architectural significance. Inns are sometimes confused with bed-and-breakfasts in that they may include breakfast in their basic rate.

Bed-and-Breakfasts   Bed-and-breakfasts are private homes that reflect the personalities and tastes of their owners. Generally, B&Bs have 2–10 rooms, some with private baths and others with shared facilities. Breakfast is always included in the price of the room.

B&Bs in North America have flourished in recent years. Some homes advertise to the public, while others maintain a low profile. Most belong to a reservation system through which you can book a room.

Reservation services in the Pacific North Coast include **Best Canadian Bed & Breakfast Network** (1090 W. King Edward Ave., Vancouver, B.C. V6H 1Z4, tel. 604/738–7207), **Northwest Bed & Breakfast Travel Unlimited** (610 S.W. Broadway, Portland, OR 97205, tel. 503/243–7616), and **Traveller's Bed & Breakfast** (Box 492, Mercer Island, WA 98040, tel. 206/232–2345). You can book a B&B before leaving the United Kingdom through **American Bed & Breakfast, Inter-Bed Network** (31 Ernest Rd., Colchester, Essex CO7 9LQ, tel. 0206/223162).

Resorts   The Pacific North Coast has quite a variety of resorts—from rural fishing lodges to luxury destination showpieces.

Dozens of small fishing resorts nestle along the coast and within the interior of British Columbia and southeast Alaska. Most are rustic lodges, providing basic accommodations for the sports enthusiasts, but others offer such deluxe comforts as gourmet meals and hot tubs in a wilderness setting.

The Whistler Village resort in British Columbia is best known for its world-class skiing. But Whistler is equally impressive as a year-round destination with golf, tennis, swimming, mountain biking, and horseback riding.

Locals and visitors alike favor the grand settings at the Inn at Semi-Ah-Moo in Blaine, Washington, and the Rosario Resort in the San Juan Islands for getaway trips. Most of the Oregon coast is resort country; one of the state's most famous resorts, Salishan Lodge at Gleneden Beach, is located there.

Camping   Camping is a popular and inexpensive way to tour the Pacific North Coast. Oregon, Washington, Alaska, and British Columbia all have networks of excellent government-run parks that offer camping and organized activities. A few state and provincial parks will accept advance camping reservations, but most do not. Privately operated campgrounds sometimes have extra amenities such as laundry rooms and swimming pools. For more information, contact the local state or provincial tourism department.

YMCAs/YWCAs   YMCAs or YWCAs are usually a good bet for clean, no frills, reliable lodging in larger towns and cities. These buildings are often centrally located, and their rates are significantly lower than those at city hotels. Nonmembers are welcome, but they may pay slightly more than members. A few very large Ys have accommodations for couples, but usually sleeping arrangements are segregated.

Home Exchange Exchanging your home or apartment with a counterpart overseas is a surprisingly low-cost way to enjoy a vacation abroad—especially a long one. Several organizations publish lists of available homes: **International Home Exchange Service** (Box 3975, San Francisco, CA 94119, tel. 415/435–3497), **Vacation Exchange Club Inc.** (12006 111th Ave., Unit 12, Youngstown, AZ 85363, tel. 602/972–2186), **Loan-a-Home** (2 Park La., Mount Vernon, NY 10552), **Home Base Holidays** (7 Park Ave., London N13 5PG, tel. 071/886–8752), **Home Exchange Ltd.** (8 Hillside High St., Farningham, Kent DA4 0DD, tel. 0322/864527).

Credit Cards

The following credit card abbreviations have been used in this book: AE, American Express; D, Discover; DC, Diners Club; MC, MasterCard, and V, Visa.

Great Itineraries

Native Culture of the Pacific North Coast

Hundreds of years before the first white explorers reached the region, scores of Native American nations were comfortably settled in the Pacific North Coast. These "First People" profoundly influenced the development of the region, and many art forms and artifacts are displayed in museums up and down the coast.

It should be noted that this is an ambitious agenda, requiring extensive use of both the British Columbia and the Alaska Marine Highway ferry systems. Distances between points of interest in this part of North America can be great, and it is necessary to spend considerable time in transit. Because of the time involved, you may want to travel only as far as the B.C. Ferries go, instead of continuing your journey into Alaska. If you do continue on, and for any of the longer legs, it is advisable to book a stateroom when reserving passage. Nevertheless, seeing this heritage in combination with breathtaking displays of nature more than offsets any inconveniences that may be encountered.

Length of Trip 17–19 days

Getting Around From Vancouver, take the B.C. Ferry from Tsawwassen to Victoria, on Vancouver Island; Route 14 West from Victoria will take you to Sooke. All stops between Victoria and Port Hardy can be reached from Route 19, traveling northwest. The B.C. Ferry takes you from Port Hardy to Prince Rupert, on the mainland, where you can pick up Route 16 East to Hazelton. The Alaska Ferry System supplies transportation to all destinations north of Prince Rupert.

The Main Route 2 Nights: Vancouver

A great starting point, Vancouver offers much background on what you will see and experience in the tour to follow. Visit the

Vancouver Museum and the **Museum of Anthropology** to acquaint yourself with the various tribes that have inhabited the regions you'll be exploring. You can see the first of many totem poles in **Stanley Park,** and stop by the **Cartwright Gallery** on Granville Island, where temporary exhibits of Native American crafts can be seen. A meal at **Quilicum** and a shopping stop at **Images for a Canadian Heritage** should be part of your downtown Vancouver agenda.

1 Night: Victoria

Take the ferry from Tsawwassen to Victoria, capital of British Columbia, and spend some time at the **Royal British Columbia Museum** where you'll find—among many other fascinating exhibits—the Kwakiutl Indian Bighouse. In nearby Sooke, visit the **Sooke Regional Museum,** which offers extensive historical background on the Salish tribe that once flourished in this region. Call ahead for the schedule of weaving demonstrations held periodically at the museum.

1 Night: Duncan

The main draw here is the **Native Heritage Centre,** a sprawling complex devoted entirely to the culture of the tribes that have populated Vancouver Island. You can spend at least a day studying the many facets of Indian life addressed here, from interpretive dance and story telling, to carving, weaving, and native cuisine. Authentic Native American items may be purchased at **Big Foot, Modeste Mill,** and **Hills Indian Crafts.**

1 Night: Nanaimo

Petroglyph Provincial Park is named for the many distinctive rock carvings found in this area. A visit to the **Nanaimo Centennial Museum** will explain the significance of these curiosities. While you're there, you can take a look at the dioramas representing various aspects of Native American life.

1 Night: Campbell River

A 15-minute ferry ride from Campbell River takes you to the **Kwagiulth Museum and Cultural Centre** in the Cape Mudge Reserve on Quadra Island. Here you will find masks and costumes used in the Potlatch ceremonies (an event in which gifts are exchanged), spiritual gatherings convened to honor rites of passage such as birth, marriage, and death. In addition to the Potlatch regalia, the center offers tours (phone ahead), videos, dancing, and crafts demonstrations.

1 Night: Port McNeill

The B.C. Ferry takes you from Port McNeill to Alert Bay in about 40 minutes. There you'll find the **U'mista Cultural Center** (tel. 604/974–5403), which features its own collection of Potlatch masks and tribal dress, as well as jewelry, artifacts, a burial box, and videos on the prohibition of the Potlatch (which documents what happened to the native peoples) and on Spirit Lodge (a tape combining video presentations and live performers), which was previously seen at Expo '86 in Vancouver. The center focuses on the Kwakwaka'wakw, a group of 16 tribes in the area who shared the same language, Kwak'wala.

1 Night: Port Hardy–Prince Rupert (16 ½-hour ferry)

1 Night: Prince Rupert

While in Prince Rupert plan to visit the **Museum of Northern British Columbia,** which has an excellent collection of coastal Indian art as well as demonstrations of wood carving and other crafts. A boat tour of the Metlakatla Indian Village is also available through the museum.

1 Night: Hazelton

'Ksan Village, about 120 miles east of Prince Rupert on Route 16, is a side trip well worth taking. The village offers just about everything you could ask for in one location: Guided tours, native dancing, pre-European artifacts, and Potlatch entertainment can be experienced in a truly authentic setting framed by the majestic Skeena Mountains.

1–2 Nights: Prince Rupert–Ketchikan (6-hour ferry)

Your first port in Alaska, **Ketchikan,** is the fourth largest city in the state, with the added distinction of having more totem poles than any other city in the world. Recommended stops here include the **Tongass Historical Museum, Totem Bight State Historical Park,** and **Saxman Indian Village.** Also try to get a look at the mural on the campus of the University of Alaska, Southeast, titled *Return of the Eagle.*

1 Night: Ketchikan–Wrangell (5-hour ferry)

Some of the most interesting totem poles in Alaska can be found in this timber and fishing community. Visit **KikSadi Indian Park, Shakes Island,** and **Chief Shakes gravesite** for some prime examples. **Wrangell City Museum** houses an eclectic collection that includes Indian artifacts and petroglyphs. For more of the latter, walk along **Petroglyph Beach** at low tide.

1 Night: Wrangell–Sitka (17-hour ferry)

Evidence of native culture abounds in Sitka, and two attractions in particular should not be missed: The **Sheldon Jackson Museum,** which has a variety of pieces representing the full spectrum of Alaska's Native American life, and **Sitka National Historical Park,** which offers audiovisual presentations that provide interesting and informative background on native cultures.

1–2 Nights: Sitka–Juneau (8 ½-hour ferry)

The Alaska State Museum, located in Juneau—the state's capital and third largest city—has one of the finest Native American exhibits in the Pacific Northwest, and you should plan to spend as much time here as your schedule will allow. **Wickersham House** offers a more personal collection of photos, carvings, basketry, and other artifacts.

For those whose appetites are *still* not sated, the Alaska ferry continues from Juneau to Haines, where the **Sheldon Museum and Cultural Center** and the **Chilkat Center for the Arts** offer extensive exhibits as well as native dancing and demonstrations of various crafts, such as carving and weaving. For more information, *see* Off the Beaten Track for excursions to Kake, Angoon, and/or Hoonah.

Further Information Although schedules, fares, and hours of operation are listed in appropriate chapters, it is always advisable to call ahead to confirm these; they often change seasonally, sometimes for reasons that seem almost arbitrary. For ferry information, *see* Getting Around by Ferry in Staying in the Pacific North Coast,

Great Itineraries 40

above. If you wish to book staterooms, and it is advised for some of the longer legs, do so well in advance because they go quickly, especially during peak season. For details on specific attractions, consult Chapter 7, Vancouver; Chapter 8, Coastal British Columbia; and Chapter 9, Southeast Alaska.

Sampling the Wines of the Northwest

Whether you're an experienced oenophile or making the leap from simply ordering a glass of house red, you will find much to delight and instruct you among the vineyards and wineries of the Pacific Northwest. Only California produces more domestic wine than Washington State, and Oregon boasts many gold-medal winners among its varietals. This itinerary takes you through the Yakima and Willamette valleys, two major wine-producing regions of the United States. In addition to enhancing your appreciation of the grape, your route will take you through some of the most magnificent countryside in an area known for its scenery.

Length of Trip 12 days

Getting Around By car from Seattle, take I–90 east to Ellensburg and I–82 south to Yakima; 97 south takes you into Oregon. Go west on I–84 toward Hood River and pick up 35 south to 26 west; from there head west on 212 to I–205 south and 213 south into Salem. From Salem, take 22 west to 99 west, where you can go south to Corvallis or north into Portland. From Portland, take 8 west to Forest Grove.

The Main Route 2 Nights: Seattle

Take the Winslow ferry from the Seattle terminal to the **Bainbridge Island Vineyard and Winery,** or visit the **Ste. Michelle Winery** in Woodinville, 15 miles northeast of Seattle. Be sure to stop by some of the city's wine merchants who carry a wide selection of local products.

1 Night: Ellensburg

On the way to this former trading post make a stop at the **Snoqualmie Winery,** about 30 minutes from downtown Seattle. While in Ellensburg, spend an hour or two exploring the town's historical district, or visit Olmstead Park, before heading on to Yakima.

2 Nights: Yakima

You're in the heart of Washington's wine country now, with literally dozens of operations to visit. Pick up the brochure offered by the Yakima Valley Wine Growers Association; it will help you choose three or four good stops.

1 Night: Hood River

Route 97 south takes you through the **Yakima Indian Reservation** to this lovely town at the junction of the Hood and Columbia rivers. If your interests include sailboarding, you'll want to spend more time here, because Hood River is rapidly becoming this sport's most popular destination. The surrounding area is covered with orchards, and several wineries await your inspection.

2 Nights: Salem

Route 35 south from Hood River loops through some magnificent orchard country and around Mt. Hood before becoming Route 26 west. Pick up Route 212 west to Route 205 south; a few miles farther brings you to Route 213 south, which you follow right into Salem. Along this stretch you might want to stop at the **Mt. Angel Abbey,** a century-old Benedectine Seminary whose architecture alone warrants attention.

You could spend weeks exploring the **Willamette Valley Wineries** that border Route 99W (driving south) from Salem, but the concentration of establishments is so great that you can get a representative survey in a couple of days. Before leaving Salem, climb to the top of the **capitol dome** for a panoramic view of the city, valley, and mountains.

1 Night: McMinnville

Take Route 99W north to the home of **Oregon's International Pinot Noir Celebration,** which is held in August. What was true of the southern leg of this highway is even more so as you head north; use the brochure published by the Oregon Wine Center to discern between wineries.

2 Nights: Portland

Continuing north on 99W takes you through the wine towns of **Lafayette, Dundee, Newberg** and **Tualatin,** each of which has at least one site you'll want to explore. **Beaverton, Hillsboro,** and **Forest Grove**—west of Portland on Route 8—have several noteworthy establishments.

Further Information Phone ahead to the places you plan to visit; changes in season, weather, or management that might affect your itinerary can occur at any time. *See* the Exploring sections in Chapter 3, Portland; Chapter 4, Western Oregon; Chapter 5, Seattle; and Chapter 6, Washington State, for phone numbers and addresses.

Formal and Informal Florals: The Gardens of Coastal British Columbia and Washington State

British Columbia and Washington State share many things; among these are a moist climate, relatively moderate temperatures, and fertile soil. As a result, the Pacific North Coast is an area rich in varied vegetation, and residents have capitalized on this desirable condition by fashioning numerous formal gardens, shrubbery mazes, parks, and commercial flower farms throughout the area.

This excursion through Vancouver, Victoria, and Seattle and its vicinity offers you an opportunity to experience the pastoral charms of many diverse arrangements and species of vegetation, as well as a close look at many types of birds and animals, both native and exotic.

Length of Trip 7 days

Getting Around From Vancouver, take the B.C. Ferry from Tsawwassen to Victoria. From Victoria, take one of the Victoria Clippers to Seattle. From Seattle, take Route 90 east to Route 405 north to Route 522 east to Route 202 into Woodinville. From Seattle, take Route 5 north to Mt. Vernon, or south to Tacoma.

The Main Route 2 Nights: Vancouver

The **Dr. Sun Yat-Sen Gardens,** which re-create design elements found in several authentic Chinese arrangements, were constructed by native artisans using traditional methods and tools. You can appreciate the difference between the Chinese and the Japanese styles with a visit to the **Nitobe Garden,** considered to be the most authentic of its kind outside of Japan. **Queen Elizabeth Park** is the site of the Bloedel Conservatory, in which you can see free-flying tropical birds among the botanical displays. Plan to spend some time at the **Van Dusen Botanical Garden,** which contains one of the largest collections of ornamental plants in the country. Two hours east of Vancouver, just off the Trans-Canada Highway near the resort town of Harrison Hot Springs, is **Minter Gardens,** a beautifully designed oasis of color.

1 Night: Victoria

Crystal Gardens offers a dazzling array of flowers, tropical birds, and monkeys in a glass-roofed structure that was once a swimming pool. **Butchart Gardens** boasts Italian, Japanese, and English rose gardens on its 25-acre site. Also worth a look is the **Fable Cottage Estate,** 3½ acres of brightly colored blooms.

3 Nights: Seattle

Stop by the visitor center at the north end of Washington Park for information on the **Washington Park Arboretum,** where the walkways are named after flowers. In nearby Woodinville is the **Ste. Michelle Winery,** where you can stroll through formal gardens, picnic on the grounds (designed by the Olmsted family, architects of New York City's Central Park), and enjoy complimentary tastings at the winery.

About one hour north of Seattle on Route 5 is the town of Mt. Vernon, home to the commercial farms of **La Conner Flats** and **Roozengaarde,** which are open to the public. The heady fragrance, dazzling flowers, and sheer expanse of color are well worth the trip. In April, the Skagit Valley is carpeted by thousands of tulips and daffodils in an extraordinary display of color.

Tacoma, less than an hour south of Seattle on Route 5, has two noteworthy attractions. The **Seymour Botanical Conservatory,** located in Wright Park, features an extensive selection of exotic plant life inside an imposing Victorian-style greenhouse. After admiring the flower gardens and waterfront views in **Point Defiance Park,** check out the zoo and aquarium exhibits.

Further Information Obviously, the time of year you choose to visit the gardens will have much to do with the kinds of flowers you'll see; hours of operation and admission charges may change throughout the year as well. Telephone ahead for information for the season. Address and telephone listings can be found in Chapter 5, Seattle; Chapter 6, Washington State; Chapter 7, Vancouver; and Chapter 8, Coastal British Columbia.

2 Portraits of the Pacific North Coast

Pacific Northwest Microbrews: Good for What Ales You

By Jeff Kuechle

A Portland-based travel writer, Jeff Kuechle does his best to support the Northwest burgeoning microbrewery industry. His contributions have appeared in Pacific Northwest, Ford Times, Emmy, *and* L.A. Times.

Freshly poured ale sparkles a rich amber in the light of a sun-dappled May afternoon on the loading-dock beer garden of the Bridgeport Brewpub in Portland, Oregon. To the south rise the office towers of downtown Portland, which supply not a few of Bridgeport's customers. To the north is the graceful span of the Fremont Bridge, from which the tiny brewery takes its name.

The customer tips back his glass and takes a long, thirsty swallow. The ale cascades along his tongue, tweaking taste buds that for years have known only pale, flavorless industrial lagers. A blast of sweet malt explodes at the back of his mouth, counterpointing the citrusy sting of the hops. *This* is flavor, something missing from American beer for far too long.

Sip by sip, beer connoisseurs from all over the world are learning that the Pacific Northwest—particularly Portland and Seattle—has become the best place in the world outside the European continent to imbibe their favorite brew. Microbreweries (companies producing fewer than 20,000 kegs per year) can now be found in Manhattan, Minneapolis, and Maui, from Boulder, Colorado, to the Outer Banks of Cape Hatteras, but it all started in the Pacific Northwest. On any given evening, there are at least 40 locally brewed beers and ales available for tasting in pubs in Portland and Seattle, and no fewer than 30 of North America's 150-odd "cottage breweries" are located within 400 miles of Portland, the dynamic center of this brewing storm. There are more brew pubs per capita in Portland and Seattle than in any other U.S. city.

And while most East Coast entries in the microbrewing sweepstakes produce German-style lagers—the most familiar brewing style to American palates—the microbrewers of the Pacific Northwest go for wildly adventuresome bitters, stouts, and porters. "We're used to gutsy beers," says Fred Eckhardt, publisher of the Portland-based newsletter "Listen to Your Beer." "When you get grabbed by a new beer in Portland, you know you've been grabbed."

Perhaps the best place to sample hand-crafted ale is a well-run brew pub, which stimulates the human spirit with conviviality, pleasant warmth, intelligent conversation, the scent of malt, and hearty food. Combatting the chilly, damp, British-style climate of the Northwest, brew pubs become places of refuge where you can shake the tears of a hostile world from your umbrella, order a pint of cask-conditioned bitter, and savor a complex substance that caresses the senses.

These are beers, it should be noted, that would make a megabrewery marketing consultant blanch. Take Grant's Imperial Stout. So dark that even a blazing summer sun, viewed through a pint glass of the pitch-black stuff, yields not a glimmer, Imperial Stout is heavy with choice whole barley malt, citrusy Cascade hops, and honey; it contains twice the alcohol, four times the calories, and a hundred times the flavor of a Bud Light. At a time when everyone supposedly wants to stay skinny and sober, who in his right mind would brew such a beer?

Back in 1982, when Paul Shipman of the Red Hook Brewery in Seattle and Bert Grant of Grant's Ales in Yakima trundled out the first kegs of microbrewery ale tapped in America since Prohibition, they little dreamed that they were ushering in an era of modest revolutionary ferment. Not that these tiny breweries exactly have the Clydesdales quaking in their traces: Anheuser-Busch annually *spills* a thousand times more beer than Bridgeport—one of the most successful microbreweries in America—produces in a year. Still, as America's megabrewers respond to a growing demand for variety by dressing up their beers with labels like "extra gold" and "dry," then actually make their lack of flavor a selling point ("No aftertaste!"), the Northwest's thriving microbrewery industry provides a real alternative for those of us who like beer to taste like *beer*.

There's something inherently noble about a well-crafted pint, something ancient and universal. Anthropologists now theorize that agriculture and brewing may have provided the stimulus for the very foundation of human civilization. Certainly there is nothing new in the idea of a city or region being served by a number of small, distinctive breweries. More than 5,000 years ago, in Egypt, the many breweries of ancient Pelusium were as famous as the city's university. (Even then, books, beer, and scholarly contemplation went hand in hand.) Even the ancient Greeks and Romans, though more partial to wine than grain beverages, drank beer; evidence shows that there were more than 900 public houses in Herculaneum before Mt. Vesuvius sounded its fateful "last call" in AD 79.

Brewing wasn't perfected, however, until it was introduced to northern climes. Teutonic ancestors could imagine no greater paradise than Valhalla, a banquet-hall with 540 doors and an unquenchable supply of ale. For the Tudor English, ale was far more than an amusement—it was a staple of life, "liquid bread," a source of national strength, and brewers who cut corners and overcharged for an inferior product were fined heavily, imprisoned, or both. It may be a coincidence that during the 1970s Britain's Campaign for

Real Ale move ment—credited with single-handedly re-
storing fine ale to United Kingdom pubs—paralleled the
resurgence in the British economy and national pride. It
may also be a coincidence that the return of the
microbrewery ale to the Northwest signaled the end of a
bitter recession here, and the beginning of a rapid climb
into prosperity. Then again, it may not. Who knows how often the Boeing engineer or the Nike designer has, while
trading pleasantries with a new acquaintance over a glass
of hell-black stout, gotten just the idea he needed for that
important project?

"We don't want to take over the beer market," says the
most exuberant practitioner of the trade, Oregon brewpub
owner Mike McMenamin. "We just want to have our own
identity. It adds a lot of fun, and there's so little fun in the
business world today." McMenamin stands in what he calls
his "Captain Neon Fermentation Chamber." Tucked away
in Portland's West Hills, in the kitchen of a former fast-food
restaurant, McMenamin watches the yeast clouds billow
across his open fermentation tanks. A weird twisting of
neon light—blue, purple, ale-amber—casts a surrealistic
pallor over the nascent ale.

"We just love beer—we're experimenting all the time,"
says the tall, bearded McMenamin. "We want to keep on the
cutting edge of what's happening in American brewing.
When someone says 'You can't do that,' we know that's a
good place to start." Though brewing purists insist that
"real beer" should contain only four ingredients—water,
malted barley, hops, and yeast—the McMenamins reject
such notions out of hand, producing a variety of wildly distinctive brews such as raspberry stout; Java Ale, made
with fresh-ground coffee in the mash; and Wisdom Ale,
which included a collection of carefully researched ingredients designed, Mike McMenamin says, "to make you smart-
er." And whether or not the purists approve, the public
seems to, for McMenamin's seven tiny breweries—three in
Portland, one in suburban Hillsboro, one in Lincoln City at
the coast, one in Salem, and one in Eugene—can't keep up
with the demand for his products, which are sold only at his
network of 21 pubs.

Five years ago, the typical McMenamin pub was an
amalgam of fresh local microbrewery beers, cheerfully psychedelic art, wild neon sculptures, classic rock
on the jukebox, and sandwiches with names like the
Engroovenator and the Captain Neon Burger. At the most
recent additions to the McMenamin empire, you can still
find the Grateful Dead on the stereo, and fresh
microbrewery beer still flows in copious draughts—only
now most of it is produced in-house. At outlets such as the
brand-new McMenamin's on Broadway and the Thompson
Brewery in Salem, a subtle shift in focus is apparent. For
one thing, they occupy a brand-new office/retail building

and a meticulously restored Victorian house, respectively, rather than the more modest addresses of the earlier pubs. The artwork has also been reined in a bit, at least in the public areas. The McMenamins employ two house artists, Joe Cotter and Lyle Hehn, who roam from pub to pub late at night adding hand-painted scenes and details as the spirit moves them. Though much of their finest work has now been relegated to back-of-the-house areas (for example, the brewery mural at the Salem location that turns the Capitol Building into a turbo-powered spaceship, with Uncle Sam tipping his hat astride the dome), there is still ample evidence of their work: the grinning imp-face, for example, that's visible only in one of the mirrors at McMenamin's Broadway.

Each of Portland's microbreweries has its own distinctive style, its own array of products and its own army of followers, ready on the instant to debate the relative merits of Portland Ale versus Widmer Weizen. "The variety does make us work harder," says Art Larrance, one of the founders of Portland Brewing, located in an old creamery just off the railroad tracks. In this ornate pub, the brew kettle shines behind a two-story-high window beneath a skylight, and a music loft provides a view of the after-work crowd bellying up to a brass-railed bar for a pint of Grant's or the popular Portland and Timberline ales. Hot jazz swings out of the music loft every Thursday night for a live radio show sponsored by the brewery.

Inside a historic gray building just across the river from the Portland Brewing Company, Widmer Brewing co-owner and brewmaster Kurt Widmer dons a well-worn pair of Wellington boots and scampers around the wet concrete floor of his brewery preparing to pump the burbling "wort," or raw beer, in his brew-kettle to the stainless-steel fermenting tank a few feet away. The air is thick with steam and the rich fragrance of malt. Widmer tests a bit of the liquid for specific gravity—a measurement of eventual alcohol content—then, satisfied, throws a lever to begin the pumping process.

The redwood-sheathed brew kettle was custom-made to Widmer's specifications at a local metal fabrication company. Until a recent move to ritzier digs, other pieces of his equipment had more checkered pasts. The whirlpool tank, used to clarify the wort before it is fermented, began its days as a shrimp cooker in a coastal processing plant. Other vats were scavenged from area creameries. And his fermenting tanks? "Those came from the [never-completed] Pebble Springs nuclear power plant," Widmer smiles. "I picked them up for a real good price—and they're built to the highest standards in the land."

Widmer, a former Internal Revenue Service employee and homebrewer, is the Portland area's only German-style brewer. While he, like most Northwest brewers, loves the fine local hops, his products tend to emphasize malt flavors and a pleasant yeasty spiciness over the refreshing bitterness of the Northwest's English-style ales. Though one of the most recent micros to come on-line, Widmer has had no difficulty developing a following. After just four years in the marketplace, Widmer is the best-selling microbrew in the state, thanks to an extremely active marketing and distribution team. Production has climbed an average of 30%–40% every year; now that Widmer's dream brewery, located in a historic warehouse just across the Willamette River from his present location, is on-line, the company will soon exceed the legal production for a microbrewery of 20,000 kegs per annum.

"We've already vastly exceeded our projections," Widmer says. "We threw our business plan away a year ago, because it was hopelessly outdated."

From a standpoint of both business and brewing, no Portland micro is more respected than Bridgeport, the oldest. Founded in 1984 by local winemakers Dick and Nancy Ponzi, Bridgeport now combines expertly brewed English-style ales with one of the city's most popular pub operations. As originally conceived by the Ponzis and brewmaster Karl Ockert, the pub was little more than a tasting room, located in the same 1880s-vintage former rope factory as the brewery, with only a single tap, a few tables, and a dart board.

As anyone who has attempted to fight through the crush at the pub's bar on a recent Friday night can tell you, a slightly different attitude prevails at Bridgeport today. Though the atmosphere is still casual, the pub's highly regarded selection of light and dark ales, handmade pizza with a sourdough beer wort crust, and the opportunity to watch the brewers at work through steamy windows behind the bar, pack the place every night of the week.

One of the things that sets Bridgeport apart from other Portland-area breweries is the pub's skill with true cask-conditioned ales, available nowhere else in the city. Made in the traditional English style, these ales are pumped unfiltered directly into the keg at the end of fermentation, to lie undisturbed in a cool cellar for several weeks. There is no added carbon dioxide; cask-conditioned ales contain only the natural carbonation produced during the fermentation process. The result, drawn from one of the antique "beer-engine" hand-pumps at the end of the bar, is a smoother, noticeably less fizzy pint, with all the rich flavors of malt and hops allowed to shine through.

In Seattle, gems such as the Trolleyman Pub keep the Emerald City in the running with other Northwest Coast brewpubs. Tucked away in a corner of Red Hook's state-of-the-art facility in Fremont—just north of downtown Seattle—The Trolleyman poured its inaugural pint in 1988. The popular, low-key pub's five taps dispense brewery-fresh Red Hook ESB, golden Ballard Bitter, coffee-hued Black Hook porter, spicy Wheat Hook, and seasonal brews such as Winter Hook strong ale. There is one cask-conditioned tap, pouring a rotating selection of real ales.

The firelit pub, filled with long trestle tables, comfortable overstuffed furniture, and the sweet, malty aromas of new-brewed ale, is warm and inviting. From the competent kitchen flows a steady stream of hearty pub fare: black bean chili, puff pies crammed with chicken and beef, and a mean lasagne. Of particular interest to those visiting the pub will be the story of the former brewer who invited a young lady for a midnight hot-tub in the mash ton, with results worthy of the TV show *Cheers* segment. It's a Northwest legend!

So with all these beers to choose from, where do you begin? What should you look for in a microbrewery ale? First and foremost, variety. At any given time in Portland and Seattle, there are 30–40 fresh, locally made brews on tap. They range in color from pale straw to ebony-black, in strength from a standard 3½% alcohol to an ominous 8½%.

And the flavor? Well, you'll just have to taste for yourself. There is the rich sweetness of malt, counterbalanced by good bitter hops. There are the mocha java overtones of roasted barley, used in stouts and porters, and the spiciness of malted wheat. There are sweet ales and tart ales, mild inconsequential ales, and ales so charged with flavor they linger on the palate like a fine Bordeaux.

Above all else, you should look for an ale you can savor, an ale you can taste without wanting to swallow too quickly. The dearest emotion to a brewer's heart is the beer drinker's feeling of regret that the last swig is gone.

In the Footsteps of the First Settlers

By Glenn W. Sheehan

A principal investigator at SJS Archaeological Services, Inc., in Bridgeport, PA, Glenn W. Sheehan has worked extensively in the Pacific Northwest and Arctic regions.

There's a sort of primeval mystery about the majestic landscapes of the Pacific Northwest Coast, something elemental and ancient that can give you a strange sense of being dislocated in time. Drive along the coastal roads of Washington's Olympic Peninsula, for example, and you'll pass magnificent rain forest, pounding surf, and partially submerged chunks of headland stranded at sea. Every bridge you cross takes you over an ancient fishing stream where prehistoric Indians harvested salmon. The oldest trees along the road bear scars where these Indians pulled off bark strips dozens of feet long, which they used for clothing, construction work, and rope making. Stop to look out over the water, and you feel the presence of ancient whale hunters scanning the horizon for spouts among the waves.

It isn't just a question of landscape, either. Elders in the Eskimo (Inuit is the preferred term in Canada) and Indian communities along the coast still pass on stories told to them by their ancestors, stories that can sometimes be traced as far back as 1,000 years, and their tribal art is a living expression of cultures whose origins are lost in the mists of prehistory.

Despite a lack of hard evidence, many archaeologists believe the first people to inhabit the New World arrived by way of the Pacific North Coast. Unlike Columbus and the seafaring Vikings, Polynesians, Chinese, and Japanese, all of whom crossed oceans to arrive at different points in North and South America, it is believed that the first Americans came on foot. If these pioneers had boats at all, they were small ones, not designed for long-distance travel across oceans. They came via Alaska and traveled through Canada into the western United States.

Although these assertions sound feasible, there aren't any known archaeological sites to support them. The oldest documented sites in the New World are believed to be 20,000–13,000 years old; the oldest known sites in the Pacific Northwest are Indian settlements that fall at the younger end of this range, at about 13,000 years old. Why then is the Pacific Northwest Coast believed to be the point of entry for the earliest settlers? Because it's the only place where people could have walked into the New World or used their small boats to travel along the coast without excessive danger. The last Ice Age tied up so much water that ocean levels probably dropped by hundreds of feet around the world. On certain winter days today, a person can walk between Alaska and the Soviet Union on ice when the oceans

freeze over. But during the Ice Age the oceans were so reduced that the seabed was temporarily exposed as dry land,
supporting vegetation and game, with fish in the rivers and
sea mammals on the coast. So much ground was exposed, in
fact, that the Old World and the New were connected by dry
land. And though their languages and blood types differ,
evidence strongly suggests that both the Eskimos and Indians have their roots somewhere in Asia. As one Eskimo
friend of mine once said, "You know, those Chinese look an
awful lot like us. They must be descended from Eskimos."

Why then aren't there any sites to prove this migration theory? All human activity may have been confined to lower
ground levels now hidden under the ocean, reason the archaeologists. Or people may have traveled in small numbers, so their remains aren't easily detected. Or we may
have already found these sites without recognizing them as
such. Even though the two American continents were not
inhabited with people at the outset, they did have abundant
herds of large game, animals that had no fear of humans.
Hunters with such easy prey wouldn't stay in one place for
long; as they killed off their local supply of meat, or as the
animals learned how to avoid people, the hunters moved on.
So it is possible that the settlers arrived in the Pacific
Northwest, lived a nomadic life there for a while, and then
roamed on to other parts of North America and into South
America.

The first Americans came to a land we wouldn't recognize today. Most of Canada, Alaska, and the northern
United States were still under ice. Arctic weather and
the forests, animals, and plants that are found in today's far
north were prevalent halfway down the lower 48 states.
Then the weather changed: The ice sheets melted and the
ice receded north. The animal and plant distributions we
see today started to become established about 10,000 years
ago. Rivers and streams that were previously frozen
started to run fast and clear at low temperatures. Conditions for pioneering salmon became so ideal that by 5,000 or
so years ago, there were huge runs extending hundreds of
miles inland.

For hunters it was a revolutionary time. Herds of large animals started to diminish or disappear, and the big-game
hunters were increasingly confronted with more work and
less to show for their efforts. Many hunters in the Pacific
Northwest Coast, particularly those in Washington, British Columbia, and southeastern Alaska, turned to fishing
instead. Their nomadic life following the herds became a
more settled one as they switched to fishing. And as they
started to settle down, they were able to accumulate more
material things.

The first Americans moved north to south, from Alaska to
Canada and then to the lower 48 states and finally into Central America and South America. The more recent inhabi-

tants who made their living from salmon fishing, however, headed in the opposite direction, from the lower Pacific Northwest up into Canada and Alaska. The art and culture of these people spread and flourished in the Pacific Northwest and continued to do so in the centuries preceding their contact with European explorers. Archaeological sites of these fishing peoples date back 2,500 years and more.

Native Americans often moved when they felt their villages had grown too big. According to stories told by Indian elders, entire clans would depart and make new settlements along the Pacific Coast. Battles between Indian tribes, and warfare between the Eskimos and Indians, also prompted the relocation of some villages. And eventually, as the native and Euro-American economies became entwined, some Indians and Eskimos abandoned their villages. Many of these villages can still be seen today: Houses may have fallen, totem poles may have been reduced by museum acquisitions, and the forest is once again dense, but the villages are there. Not only can archaeologists find and excavate the abandoned sites of these people, they also can talk to their descendants. When an archaeologist is puzzled by an object he digs out of the ground, he can consult the elders of various Indian and Eskimo groups, who can often identify it and describe its use. And when the elders can't identify an object, they can often point researchers in the right direction.

During this prehistoric fishing era, the most prosperous natives were those of Washington, British Columbia, and southern Alaska. They had the good life, and they flaunted it. Their art was larger than life, while their potlatches (celebratory feasts) gave new meaning to the words conspicuous consumption. The success of the fishing peoples led to imitation. The natives of Kodiak Island were Eskimo, for example, and their ancestors came to the New World to fish and hunt sea mammals along the coast, rather than hunt the big land-bound game as the Indians' ancestors did. Surprising enough, however, the Kodiak people achieved a society in many ways remarkably similar to that of Indian tribes living to the east and south. Their art, archaeology, and legends demonstrate the connections.

Indian groups were open to the ways of others too. In the far north of Alaska, where trees don't grow and fish runs can be counted in dozens instead of millions, Eskimo hunters had great success in capturing large whales. Indian groups of the lower Pacific Northwest did the same, using many of the whale-hunting techniques and rituals employed by people as far away as Point Barrow on the Arctic Coast.

Although the native groups along the Pacific Northwest Coast were lucky enough to avoid outright war with the European and American settlers, they did suffer some adversity. The natives of Kodiak, for example, were viciously attacked by Russians, and many natives eventually lost land in Canada and the United States. All the natives suffered when commercial fishing and river dams reduced salmon runs, and again when Yankee whalers destroyed whales in huge numbers. Despite these setbacks, however, both the Indians and Eskimos have retained much of their culture and way of life into the present.

One of the best-known archaeological sites of these settlers is Ozette, located on the Makah Reservation in Washington's Olympic Peninsula. The finds of the site can be viewed by the public, and visitors can request permission to visit the site itself. Call the Makah Reservation (tel. 206/645–2711) for information. The village of Ozette was partially covered by a mud slide several hundred years ago. This apparent catastrophe ironically turned out to preserve the village, however, for the wet mud provided an anaerobic environment hostile to most decay-causing organisms. As a result, the mud-covered section of Ozette was preserved in its entirety, a kind of New World Pompeii.

Archaeologists usually excavate with masons' trowels because they generally dig up stone and ceramics, objects that a skillfully handled trowel won't harm. But at Ozette in the 1970s, there was a delightful obstacle to overcome. Basketry, cordage, clothing, and all kinds of soft materials had been preserved, but since they were preserved wet, they were particularly soft, and the trowels cut through them like mud. Even experienced excavators couldn't feel the damage they were doing to the objects.

A whole new excavation approach was undertaken, called "wet site" archaeology. Using water hoses to excavate the village, the archaeologists discovered that mud and debris could be washed away, leaving artifacts intact. During the handlers' first clumsy attempts at hosing down the mud, artifacts could be seen tumbling downhill with the water, but after some trial and error, the workers were able to keep even small finds in place.

One of the most exciting aspects of the Ozette excavation was the support archaeologists received from Indians living in the region. The Makah tribe encouraged archaeologists to excavate Ozette and assisted in the fieldwork; tribal members provided logistical support and helped interpret finds. And the tribe even built a museum based on the artifacts on its grounds at Neah Bay.

The Indians also helped prepare artifacts for public display, which turned out to be quite a challenge. Generally, archaeological finds of stone and ceramic pieces are preserved simply by being cleaned first in water and then glued together. But Ozette produced all kinds of perishable artifacts, objects that quickly started to deteriorate once they were removed from their muddy entombment. So the

Makah Tribe provided laboratory space and helped the archaeologists preserve and stabilize the finds.

These descendants of the ancient Indians went one step further and created a living experiment on the site. The Makah people worked outside to build a plank house, like those in Ozette, and then attempted to use the interior in the same ways their ancestors did. Life in the house was set up based upon the directions of tribal elders, historic accounts, and archaeological interpretations. In the end, the house looked as if one good mud slide would turn it into another ruined Ozette home. After this experimental period, the tribe dismantled the house and rebuilt it inside the Makah museum.

A large dugout canoe was also built for the museum. The art of making canoes had almost died out, but it was revived to capture an important part of life in Ozette. Young and old worked together to build the boat and to pass on these ancient skills.

Other archaeological sites in the area require a bit more effort to explore. From southern Alaska to Oregon, you can find hundreds of petroglyphs (rock carvings) and pictographs (rock paintings). Only a handful of them can be dated, however, so they can't be attributed to any particular group of people. Some are easily accessible, and seen by the public every day. Others are so hidden you can only find them if you happen to stumble upon them. Still other carvings are positioned at the tidal zone and consequently are under water at high tide. One worthwhile guide to the many accessible rock carvings is Beth and Ray Hill's *Indian Petroglyphs of the Pacific Northwest*.

Prehistoric Indians also carved petroglyphs on land, although mostly facing the ocean, or else overlooking a river or waterway. Pictographs, on the other hand, can be seen throughout the Northwest Coast. Some of these detailed rocks have been jackhammered from their embedded frames and carted away; others have eroded, and still others lie beneath reservoirs. But the vast majority are right where they were created, and with permission from native or nonnative landowners, or government agencies, visitors can examine them. More than 500 sites are known. One protected site open to the public is Petroglyph Park in the town of Nanaimo, on Vancouver Island. Petroglyphs at Wrangell, Alaska, are also open to the public.

The ancient craft of carving giant totem poles out of trees has survived as a living art form, with plenty of demand for new poles. Carvers today often work in public throughout the Pacific Northwest, at museums or on the grounds of institutions that have commissioned their artwork. Young workers aspire to apprentice with master carvers, and gift shops all over the region offer miniature reproductions.

The totem pole is the best-known example of current Northwest Coast tribal art, but masks, tools, and a variety of paintings and prints also continue the artistic tradition of the area. Artwork can be purchased at local galleries, many of which are located on Indian lands and are run by Indians. The choices are broader and the prices lower here than they are in the native art galleries of New York and California. The Dukuah Gallery (1971 Peninsula Rd., Ocluelet, B.C., V0R 3A0, tel. 604/726–7223) is run by native Lillian Mac and her husband, Bert Mac, the hereditary Chief of the Toquant tribe. Native artists visit and work in the gallery year-round.

The British Columbia Provincial Museum in Victoria, with its unique collection of prehistoric fish bones, is an outstanding research center, with representation from all five species of salmon and almost every other fish that might have been harvested by prehistoric natives. Each fish skeleton has been mounted on wires, with all the bones together in proper anatomical order. While this is a scientific collection, it verges on being a work of art in itself, with skeletal fish elongating and compressing into fantastic shapes.

In Vancouver, at the University of British Columbia's Museum of Anthropology, there's an excellent archaeological collection that's very accessible to the public. Visitors can open any of the Plexiglass-covered drawers to examine even the most delicate artifacts. Other artifacts can be seen at the Thomas Burke Memorial Washington State Museum at the University of Washington in Seattle, and at the Alaska State Museum in Juneau, where they also have a first-rate collection of historic baleen (fibrous plates that hang from the roof of the whale's mouth) baskets. Only native hunters and artisans are legally permitted to own unprocessed baleen.

Any overview of Northwest Coast archaeology inevitably leaves out more than it includes. Paleo-Indian sites, Russian fur-hunting activities, cave sites in Washington's channeled scablands, mastodons and mammoths, and cairns dug up 100 years ago can all be found along the Pacific Northwest Coast. And if you visit the area searching for a glimpse of the past, native people will share their stories, researchers may invite you to observe their work, artisans will explain their ancient crafts, and the museums will let you view even the most fragile artifacts. For here, one thing remains constant: the people's eagerness to document and understand the past.

3 Portland

Introduction

By Tom Barr

Tom Barr is a freelance writer and photographer whose works on the Pacific Northwest have appeared in Reader's Digest Books, USA Today, and Rotarian Magazine.

Since the 1970s, the arts, environmental issues, and history have been as important to Portlanders as the city's economic development. Evidence of this focus is in Portland's neighborhood revitalization and preservation projects as well as in the city's ambitious culture programs, which saw the establishment of a resident professional Shakespeare company and innovative neighborhood theaters. Portland's efforts have proved fruitful, as more and more visitors discover this as an attractive destination where there's a lot to do day or night, rain or shine.

Beginning in 1852, with the establishment of The Boulevard, Portland began preserving land as parks for enjoyment by future generations. As with the South Park Blocks, it is still an urban setting where one can enjoy nature. Meanwhile, the recreational system has grown to 250 parks, public gardens, and greenways. The world's smallest park, one of the nation's largest urban wildernesses, and the only extinct volcano within city limits in the continental United States are all part of the Portland parks system.

As for the arts, you'll find creations in jail hallways, office towers, banks, playgrounds, and on sides of buildings. Downtown, the brick-paved transit mall is an outdoor gallery of fountains and sculptures and, like most artistic endeavors, it elicits ambivalent feelings; since the mall is limited to buses and pedestrians, many a motorist would gladly trade a stone cat or a frothy fountain for a few extra parking spaces.

Portland, the City of Roses, also recognizes its fortuitous climate. Since 1907 it has celebrated its award-winning flowers, and today, the Portland Rose Festival is a multiweek extravaganza with auto and boat races, visiting navy ships, and a grand floral parade second in size only to Pasadena's. Other annual events are a citywide Neighborhood Fair and an Art Quake featuring everything from painting and sculpture to mime, rock and blues, symphony orchestras, and dance.

Through all these developments, the city, which began as a 1-square-mile Indian clearing, has become a metropolis of 430,000 people; the 132 square miles now include 90 neighborhoods. A center for sportswear, as well, Portland and its surroundings are home to headquarters and factories for Jantzen, Nike, and Pendleton. A variety of high-tech, shipbuilding, furniture, fabricated-metals, and other manufacturers have helped to give it a broad economic base. Geographically, the city is in a prime location. The Columbia and Willamette rivers meet at Portland and, because of them, the city ranks third as a West Coast port. Five main terminals export automobiles, steel, livestock, grain, and timber. Shipyards repair tankers and tugboats, cruise ships, and navy vessels.

Preserving the city's architecture is of major importance; in such areas as the Skidmore–Old Town, Yamhill, and Glazed Terra-Cotta National Historic Districts, 1860s brick buildings with cast-iron columns and 1890s ornate terra-cotta designs uphold the legacy of Portland's origins. Along with these historic structures, today's visitor can enjoy new art, innovative theater, fine dining, and a healthy, clean environment in which roses sometimes bloom in December and daffodils start in early February.

Essential Information

Arriving and Departing by Plane

Airports   **Portland International Airport** (tel. 503/335–1234) is located in Northeast Portland, approximately 12 miles from the city center. It is served by Alaska (tel. 503/224–2547 or 800/426–0333), Air British Columbia (800/663–8868), American (tel. 800/433–7300), American West (tel. 503/228–0737, 503/249–4363 or 800/247–5692), Continental (tel. 503/224–4560 or 800/525–0280), Delta (tel. 503/225–0830), Horizon (tel. 800/547–9308), Northwest (tel. 503/249–4804 or 800/225–2525), TWA (tel. 800/221–2000), United (tel. 503/226–7211).

Between the Airport and City Center
 By Car   From the airport, take I–84 (Banfield Freeway) west to the Burnside Street exit. Going to the airport, take I–84 east to 82nd Avenue and follow it north to the appropriate terminal from which you can check in and board your flight.

By Bus   **Raz Tranz** (tel. 503/246–3301) operates buses to downtown Portland and Lloyd Center hotels and to Amtrak and Greyhound depots. Departures are about every 30 minutes between 5:30 AM and 12:05 AM. Fare is $6 adults one way, $1 children 6–12, children under 6 free. **Tri-Met** (tel. 503/233–3511) runs about every 15 minutes to and from the airport, making regular stops every two blocks. Service begins weekdays during the hour of 5 AM and ends about 11:50 PM; weekend service starts during the hour of 5 AM and runs to about 8 PM. Exact times vary depending on which direction you're headed. Call for specific schedules: 90¢ for one- and two-zone trips; $1.20 for three zones.

By Taxi   The trip to or from the airport by taxi takes about 20 minutes. The fare is approximately $20.

Arriving and Departing

By Car   Interstate 5 enters from north and south; I–84 is the major east-side corridor, while U.S. 26 and U.S. 30 are primary east-west thoroughfares. Bypass routes are I–205, which loops through east Portland, and I–405, which arcs around western downtown.

By Train   **Amtrak** service departs from Union Station (800 N.W. 6th Ave., tel. 800/872–7245) with destinations throughout the country.

By Bus   **Greyhound/Trailways** (550 N.W. 6th Ave., tel. 503/243–2340) travels to points across the country.

Getting Around

By Car   Most city-center streets are one-way. Limited to bus traffic between Burnside Street and S.W. Madison are S.W. 5th and 6th avenues. Unless posted, it is legal to turn right on a red light. Left turns from a one-way street onto another one-way street on a red light are also legal. While most parking meters run 8 AM–6 PM, many streets have special, posted rush-hour regulations.

By Light Rail   **Metropolitan Area Express** (tel. 503/22–TRAIN), or MAX, transports passengers from S.W. 11th Avenue and Morrison

Street in the city center to Lloyd Center and to the eastern suburban community of Gresham. Twenty-seven stations, five
park-and-rides, and five transit centers are situated along the
15-mile route. Transportation operates daily, 5:30 AM–1 AM,
with a fare of 90¢ for one- and two-zone trips; $1.20 for three
zones; $3 day tickets and monthly passes are available. Senior
citizens and disabled persons pay 40¢.

By Bus **Tri-Met** (tel. 503/233–3511) operates bus service throughout
the greater Portland area. Fares are the same for both Tri-Met
and MAX, and tickets can be used on either system.

By Taxi Taxi fare is $2.00 at flag drop plus $1.50 per mile. The first person pays by meter; each additional passenger pays 50¢. Major
companies are **Broadway Deluxe Cab** (tel. 503/227–1234), **New
Rose City Cab** (tel. 503/282–7707), **Portland Taxi Company** (tel.
503/256–5400), and **Radio Cab** (tel. 503/227–1212).

Important Addresses and Numbers

Tourist The **Portland/Oregon Visitors Association** (25 S.W. Salmon St.,
Information at World Trade Center 3, tel. 503/222–2223) is open weekdays
8:30–5, Saturday 10–3.

Emergencies Dial 911 for **fire, police,** or **medical assistance.**

Hospitals **Eastmoreland Hospital** (2900 S.E. Steele St., tel. 503/231–
3490); **Emanuel Hospital and Health Center** (2801 N. Gan-
tenbein Ave., tel. 503/280–3500); **Providence Medical Center**
(4805 N.E. Glisan St., tel. 503/230–6000); **St. Vincent Hospital**
(9205 S.W. Barnes Rd., tel. 503/297–4411).

Dentists **Willamette Dental Group PC** (1933 S.W. Jefferson St., tel. 503/
292–1111); **Lombard Dental Associates PC** (3506 N. Lombard
St., tel. 503/289–0230); **Family Dental Center** (18750 S.E. Stark
St., tel. 503/666–1133 or 503/665–1133).

Late-night **Lloyd Center Pharmacy** (1302 Lloyd Ctr., tel. 503/281–4161);
Pharmacies **St. Vincent Hospital and Medical Center Pharmacy** (9155 S.W.
Barnes Rd., tel. 503/291–2630); **Woodstock Pharmacy** (4515
S.E. Woodstock Blvd., tel. 503/777–3911).

Guided Tours

Orientation **Gray Line Sightseeing** (tel. 503/226–6755) operates city tours
April 13–October 31, daily 8–5. **Rose City Riverboat Cruises**
(tel. 503/289–6665) has scheduled dinner cruises, Sunday
brunches, Portland harbor excursions, and Oregon City Falls
tours.

Walking Tours The **Portland/Oregon Visitors Association** (tel. 503/222–2223)
has self-guiding tour brochures plus maps and guides to art
galleries and select neighborhoods. Walking tours range from a
6-block jaunt in the Yamhill Historic District to a 7-mile marathon through several historic areas.

Highlights for First-time Visitors

The Grotto (*see* Tour 2)
Pioneer Courthouse Square (*see* Tour 1)
Portland Saturday Market (*see* Tour 1)
Washington Park (*see* Tour 2)
Yamhill National Historic District (*see* Tour 1)

Exploring Portland

Tour 1: Downtown Portland

Numbers in the margin correspond to points of interest on the Downtown Portland map.

The Willamette River is the east–west dividing line and Burnside Street separates north from south. While Portland's 200-foot-long blocks make them easy walking for most visitors, others may wish to explore the core by either MAX light rail or Tri-Met bus (*see* Getting Around, above).

❶ Start at **Pioneer Courthouse Square** (S.W. Broadway and S.W. Morrison St., tel. 503/223–1613), the site of the first school, the Portland Hotel, and the gathering center for the city's elite. Today it attracts everyone from street musicians and political candidates to a varied cross section of Portland's populace. Rallies and other events are held here, and it's a great place to watch people. As you make your way through the square, look down at the 64,000 bricks—each engraved with the name of a person who bought it to help pay for the square. The best time to be here is noon, when a goofy weather machine blasts a fanfare, and a shining sun, stormy dragon, or blue heron rises out of a misty cloud to confirm the day's weather.

Walk south on Broadway past first-run movie theaters and the Hilton Hotel. Cross Broadway to **The Heathman Hotel** (S.W. Broadway at S.W. Salmon St., tel. 503/241–4100), where in the lobby and restaurant a collection of 10 *Endangered Species* paintings created by Andy Warhol is featured. Among the animals portrayed on the 4½ × 4½ foot canvases are an eagle, a lion, a panda, and a rhinoceros. The hotel welcomes visitors who come in to admire the art.

❷ You are now in front of the **Portland Center for the Performing Arts** (corner of S.W. Broadway and S.W. Main St., tel. 503/248–4496), considered the "new building" and the hub of activity. Situated within the complex is the **Arlene Schnitzer Concert Hall** (also known as the Old Paramount Theater), host to the Oregon Symphony, plays, and road shows by entertainers such as Baryshnikov, Tom Jones, and Crosby, Stills and Nash. Across Main Street, but still part of the center, is the 292-seat **Delores Winningstad Theater**, used for plays and lectures. Its stage design is based on that of a Shakespearean courtyard stage. The 916-seat **Intermediate Theater**, the residence of Shakespeare Festival Portland, is also part of the complex. The section of the street connecting the old and new buildings is often blocked off for food fairs, art shows, and other events.

At the tree-lined **South Park Blocks** you may wish to photograph a fountain or the Abraham Lincoln and Teddy Roosevelt Roughrider statues en route to the **Portland Art Museum.** The
❸ museum, which includes a film center, is the region's oldest visual and media arts facility. Its treasures span 35 centuries of Asian, European, and American art with collections of Native American, regional, and contemporary art. The film center features the annual Portland International Film Festival and Northwest Film Festival. *1219 S.W. Park Ave., tel. 503/226–2811; 503/221–1156 for film schedule. Admission: $4*

Downtown Portland

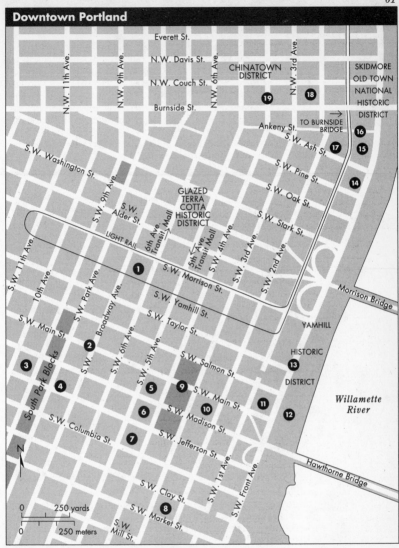

American Advertising
Museum, **18**
Central Fire
Station, **15**
Chapman and
Lownsdale Squares, **9**
Chinatown Gate, **19**
City Hall, **6**

First Interstate Bank
Tower, **7**
Governor Tom McCall
Waterfront Park and
Salmon Street
Plaza, **12**
Justice Center, **10**
Mill Ends Park, **13**
New Market Theater
Village, **17**
Oregon Historical
Center, **4**

Oregon Maritime
Museum, **14**
Pioneer Courthouse
Square, **1**
Portland Art
Museum, **3**
Portland Building, **5**

Portland Center for
the Performing Arts, **2**
Portland Civic
Auditorium, **8**
Portland/Oregon
Visitors
Association, **11**
Skidmore Fountain, **16**

nonmembers; senior citizens free Thurs.; children 4–9 free first Thurs. of the month. Open Tues.–Sat. 11–5, Sun. 1–5.

Across the South Park Blocks are the murals of Lewis and Clark and the Oregon Trail (the route the pioneers took from St. Joseph and Independence, Missouri, to the Oregon Territory). The paintings signal the entrance to **The Oregon Historical Center,** where the state's history from prehistoric times to the present is documented. Exhibits include archaeological and anthropological artifacts, ship models, and memorabilia from the Oregon Trail. A research library is open to the public. A bookstore (corner of Broadway and Madison St.) is the best source for maps and publications on Northwest history. *1230 S.W. Park Ave., tel. 503/222–1741. Admission free. Open daily 10–4:45.*

Follow Madison Avenue south to 5th Avenue, where **Portlandia,** the world's second largest hammered-copper statue (the Statue of Liberty is first) kneels on the second-story balcony of the **Portland Building.** She stands 36 feet high and was created in 1983. The building itself, one of the United States' first postmodern designs, generates strong feelings; chances are you'll either love it or hate it. The controversial structure, designed by architect Michael Graves, is buff colored with brown trim and has what seems to be a wrinkled blue ribbon wrapped around its top. The **Metropolitan Center For Public Art,** on the second floor, is a starting point for the city's public-art walking tour. Original molds of Portlandia's face and renderings of the Portland Building are displayed, in addition to ex-hibits on Portland's public art. *1120 S.W. 5th Ave., tel. 503/ 796–5111. Admission to museum free. Museum open weekdays 8–6.*

For more traditional architecture, look across Madison Avenue to the classically styled **City Hall,** a structure built in 1895 and easily recognized by the columns on the east and west sides. Though this building, which houses the mayor's and commissioners' offices, is relatively small, it's worth a walk into the lobby, where you'll find turn-of-the-century classic architecture, characterized by high ceilings, marble hallways, and pillars.

On the other side of City Hall, across Jefferson Street, is the **First Interstate Bank Tower** (1300 S.W. 5th Ave.), which is 536 feet high. The second-tallest building in Portland, it was erected in 1972 and offers panoramic views of the city to the north, south, east, and west.

Time Out While in the tower, take the elevator to **Rene's Fifth Avenue** (tel. 503/241–0710) restaurant and lounge, on the 21st floor, where moderately priced lunches are served from 11:30 to 2:30 daily. The lounge is open until 7:30.

A couple of blocks south of the tower is the **Ira Keller Fountain,** a series of man-made waterfalls built in 1971 and situated in front of the **Portland Civic Auditorium** (*see* The Arts, below). The fountain is a popular cooling-off spot in summer and a favorite Portland people-watching place. View the falls from Third Avenue for the most spectacular angle. The 3,000-seat auditorium, which is one of four theaters in the Portland Center for the Performing Arts, hosts everything from grand opera to bodybuilding contests. *222 S.W. Clay St., tel. 503/274–6560. Call for performance schedules.*

❾ If you go north on 3rd Avenue, you'll come to **Chapman** and **Lownsdale squares,** situated between Madison and Salmon streets. During the 1920s these squares were segregated: Chapman was reserved for women, and Lownsdale for men. You'll find public rest rooms at each, plus a Spanish-American War memorial at Lownsdale. The elk statue on Main Street, which separates the parks, was given to the city by former mayor David Thompson; supposedly, it honors an elk that grazed here in the 1850s.

Walking east on Main Street to Third Avenue will take you to **❿** the **Justice Center,** a beautiful building with glass bricks built into portions of the east and west sides. Because of a city ordinance requiring 1% of the development costs of new buildings to be allotted to the arts, the center's hallways are lined with travertine sculptures, ceiling mosaics, stained-glass windows, and photographic murals. Within the center is housed the county court, support offices, and the **Police Museum,** on the 16th floor, which has uniforms, guns, and badges worn by the Portland Police Department. Visitors are invited to view the artwork. *1111 S.W. 2nd Ave., tel. 503/796–3019. Admission free. Open weekdays 10–3.*

The **World Trade Center,** northeast of the Justice Center, is a trio of buildings connected by sky bridges and designed by prominent Portland architect Robert Frasca. On the ground floors of the buildings are retail stores, a restaurant, coffee shops, banks, and travel agencies. In World Trade Center **⓫** Three is the **Portland/Oregon Visitors Association,** where you can pick up maps and literature about the state. *26 S.W. Salmon St., tel. 503/222–2223. Open weekdays 8:30–5, Sat. 10–3.*

⓬ Cross Front Avenue and enter **Governor Tom McCall Waterfront Park** and **Salmon Street Plaza.** The park stretches north for approximately a mile to Burnside Street. Designed to reflect the day-to-day pace of the city, the water in Salmon Street Plaza's fountain changes formation four times during the day: during the morning commute, lunch-hour rush, evening commute, and at midnight. The plaza extends in a graceful curve out over the water, with unobstructed views of the Willamette River, several bridges, and the Riverplace Alexis Hotel and Marina (*see* Lodging, below).

⓭ Follow the park one block north to where **Mill Ends Park** sits in the middle of a traffic island on Front Avenue. At 24 inches in diameter, it has been recognized by *Guinness Book of World Records* as the world's smallest official city park.

You are now in the heart of the **Yamhill National Historic District,** a compact, 6-square-block district preserving many examples of 19th-century cast-iron architecture. Since the cast-iron facade helped support the main structure, these buildings traditionally did not need big heavy walls to bear the weight; therefore, the interior spaces could be larger and more open.

North and west of this district, along Second Avenue, you'll find several galleries featuring fine art, ceramics, photography, and posters. On the first Thursday of each month, new shows and exhibits are unveiled and most galleries stay open until 9 PM. For details call the Portland Art Museum (tel. 503/226–2811).

Oak Street marks the southern boundary and Everett Street the northern boundary of the **Skidmore Old Town National Historic District.** Portland, the region settled in 1845 (chartered as a city in 1851) by New Englanders and named for Portland, Maine, began here, and the 20-square-block district includes a variety of buildings of varying ages and architectural designs. Before its renovation, this was the city's skid row, and vestiges of that condition remain. Even in daylight you may feel more comfortable sightseeing with a companion. Don't walk here at night.

The main mast of the battleship *Oregon,* which served in three wars, stands at the foot of Oak Street. Across Front Street is 🕙 the **Oregon Maritime Museum,** whose exterior features prime street-level examples of cast-iron architecture. Inside, you'll find models of ships that plied the Columbia River, most of which were made from scratch by local model makers, some of whom work at the museum. Photo displays cover World War II, when Portland was a major military shipbuilding center. *113 S.W. Front St., tel. 503/224–7724. Admission: $2 adults, $1.25 students and senior citizens, $4.50 families. Open Fri.–Sun. 11–4; Memorial Day through Labor Day, Thurs.–Sat. 11–4.*

🕙 Next door, at the **Central Fire Station** (111 S.W. Front St.) is the **Jeff Morris Memorial Fire Museum,** where you can see antique pumps and other equipment through large plate-glass windows. Plaques explain the history of Portland fire fighting. Cast-iron medallions, capitals, and grillwork taken from other 🕙 buildings are displayed on the north wall, which faces **Skidmore Fountain,** built in 1888. Aside from being the centerpiece of the square around which many community activities take place, the fountain is renowned for its granite troughs and spouting lions' heads from which water was collected for quenching the thirsts of both men and horses.

From March through Christmas, the fountain's square is home to the **Portland Saturday Market** (also open on Sunday). Some 300 merchants sell an assortment of foods, produce, arts, and crafts. Most items are one-of-a-kind creations by the artisans. If you're looking for crystals, yard goods, beaded hats, stained glass, jewelry, flags, wood and rubber stamps, or custom footwear and decorative boots, you stand a good chance of finding it here. An assortment of street entertainers and food booths adds to the festive atmosphere. *100 S.W. Ankeny St., tel. 503/222–6072. Open Sat. 10–5, Sun. 11–4:30.*

The **Skidmore Fountain Building** (28 S.W. 1st Ave., tel. 503/227–5305), also part of the square, has three floors of baskets, jewelry, pottery, women's wear, leather crafts, imports, and other specialty shops.

🕙 If you don't find what you are looking for, try the **New Market Theater Village,** across 1st Avenue. When it opened in 1875 it was considered the grandest theater in the west. During its heyday it staged everything from Shakespeare to a prize fight with John L. Sullivan. Today, three floors of shops, several fast-food stands, a restaurant, and a bar are situated among tall brick archways and a balcony that overlooks the main floor. *50 S.W. 2nd Ave., tel. 503/228–2392. Open daily 10–6.*

⑱ Northwest of the village is the **American Advertising Museum,**
which bills itself as the only museum devoted exclusively to advertising. You may feel a bit oversold, because the museum is
small and the exhibits are limited, but you will find examples of
memorable campaigns, print advertisements, radio and TV
commercials, and a variety of novelty and specialty promotion
products, along with changing exhibits. A gift counter stocks
books and reproductions of specialty items such as pens, cups,
and pins. *9 N.W. 2nd Ave., tel. 503/226–0000. Admission: $3
adults, $1.50 children 6–12 and senior citizens. Members and
children under 6, free. Open Wed.–Fri. 11–5, Sat. noon–5.*

Time Out   If you need a break from sightseeing and shopping, stop in at
either the **Jazz de Opus** or **Opus Too Bar and Restaurant** (33
N.W. 2nd Ave., tel. 503/222–6077). Settle in the deep cushions
of the club's easy chairs and divans, lift a tall glass of beer, or
enjoy one of the moderately priced sandwiches offered here.
The recorded jazz is set on a Muzak-level volume.

During the 1890s Portland had the second-largest Chinese
community in the United States. Today the community is com-
pressed into several blocks of northwest Portland and is known
for its fine Chinese restaurants, shops, and grocery stores.
⑲ **Chinatown Gate** (N.W. 4th Ave. and Burnside St.) can be recognized by its five roofs, 64 dragons, and two huge lions, and is
the official entrance to **Chinatown.**

If you are interested in art and architecture, you may wish to
zigzag back and forth between S.W. 5th and S.W. 6th avenues
and the intersecting streets of Oak and Yamhill. This is the
heart of the **Glazed Terra Cotta National Historic District.**
Buildings from the late 1890s to mid-1910s still stand here, as
commercial and public properties. At the turn of the century
terra-cotta was an often-used material because of its availability and inexpensive cost; it could also be easily molded into decorative details that were popular at the time. Take time to look
up at the elaborate lions' heads, griffins, floral displays, and
other classical motifs that adorn many of these buildings.

Fifth and 6th avenues are lined with public art. On **5th Avenue**
you'll find a sculpture that reflects light and changing colors, a
nude woman made of bronze, a copper and redwood sculpture
inspired by the Norse god Thor, and a large limestone cat in re-
pose. **Sixth Avenue** has a steel and concrete matrix, a granite
and brick fountain, and a modern depiction of a Greek defend-
ing Crete.

A short walk west will bring you back to the beginning of the
tour.

Tour 2: Outside City Center

*Numbers in the margin correspond to points of interest on the
Outside City Center map.*

Several of Portland's prime attractions are outside its city center and require transportation to reach them. For 85¢ you can
take **Tri-Met Line 63** to the following attractions. For schedule
and route information, check with Tri-Met's Customer Assistance Office (Pioneer Courthouse Sq., tel. 503/233–3511). During summer a 4-mile round-trip narrow-gauge **train ride**
operates from the zoo to the International Rose Test Garden

and the Japanese Gardens. The fare is $2 adults, $1.50 children 3–11 and senior citizens. (*See* Getting Around, above.)

㉔ Washington Park covers 322 acres of Portland's western hills.

㉑ The **Washington Park Zoo,** established in 1887, has been a prolific breeding ground for Asian elephants. Major exhibits include an African section with rhinos, hippos, zebras, and pythons, plus an aviary with 15 species of birds. Other popular attractions include an Alaska Tundra exhibit, penguinarium, bears, and animals such as beavers, otters, and reptiles that are native to the west side of the Cascade Mountains. *4001 S.W. Canyon Rd., tel. 503/226–ROAR. Admission: $4.50 adults; $3 senior citizens; $2.50 children 3–11; free second Tues. after 3 PM. Open Memorial Day–Labor Day, daily 9:30–6; Oct.–Apr., daily 9–4.*

㉒ The **International Rose Test Garden** is the nation's oldest continuously operating site of its kind. Its three terraces include more than 10,000 bushes and 400 varieties of roses. *400 S.W. Kingston Ave., tel. 503/796–5193. Admission free. Open dawn–dusk.*

㉓ The **Japanese Gardens,** situated above the test garden, meander through 5½ acres of Washington Park. A ceremonial teahouse, Oriental pavilion, strolling pond, sand-and-stone garden, and three other gardens are among the highlights. *611 S.W. Kingston Ave., tel. 503/223–4070. Admission: $3.50 adults, $2 senior citizens and students. Open Apr.–Sept., daily 10–6; Oct.–Mar., daily 10–4.*

㉔ The **Oregon Museum of Science and Industry** (OMSI), across the zoo parking lot, is a great place for children. It includes the Northwest's largest astronomy education facility, a hands-on computer center, a space wing with a mission control center, and the Up-and-Atom stage, which explains the stranger aspects of science. *4015 S.W. Canyon Rd., tel. 503/222–2828. Admission: $5.25 adults, $4.25 senior citizens, $3.50 children 3–17. Open June 20–Sept. 4, Mon.–Thurs. and weekends 9–7, Fri. 9–7; Sept. 3–May 24, Mon.–Thurs. and weekends 9–5, Fri. 9–7.*

㉕ Next to OMSI is the **World Forestry Center,** where the spokesman is a 70-foot-tall talking tree. Outside, a 1909 locomotive and antique logging equipment are displayed, and inside are two floors of exhibits, a multi-image "Forests of the World," a collection of 100-year-old wood, and a gift shop. *4033 S.W. Canyon Rd., tel. 503/228–1367. Admission: $3 adults, $2 children 2–18 and senior citizens. Open summer, daily 9–5; after Labor Day, daily 10–5.*

㉖ Hoyt Arboretum, adjacent to Washington Park, has more than 700 species of plants, plus the nation's largest collection of coniferous trees. Ten miles of trails wind through the park to the Winter Garden and a Vietnam memorial. *4000 S.W. Fairview Blvd., tel. 503/823–3655. Admission free. Open daily dawn–dusk.*

㉗ Pittock Mansion, 1,000 feet above the city, offers superb views of the skyline, rivers, and Cascade Mountains. The 1909 mansion, which combines French Renaissance- and Victorian-style decor, was built by Henry Pittock, former editor of *The Oregonian.* Set in its own park, the opulent manor has been restored and is filled with art and antiques of the 1880s. *3229 N.W.*

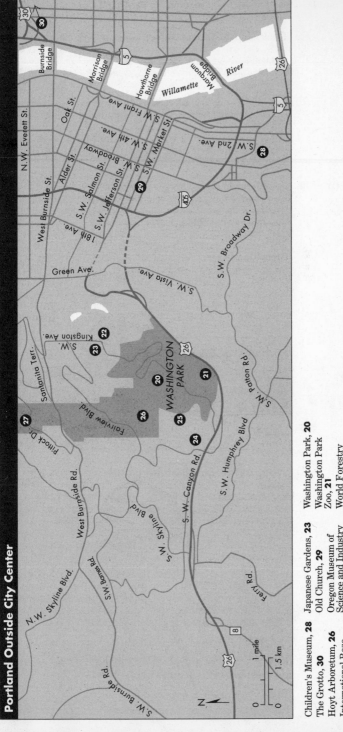

Portland Outside City Center

Children's Museum, **28**

The Grotto, **30**

Hoyt Arboretum, **26**

International Rose
Test Gardens, **22**

Japanese Gardens, **23**

Old Church, **29**

Oregon Museum of
Science and Industry
(OMSI), **24**

Pittock Mansion, **27**

Washington Park, **20**

Washington Park
Zoo, **21**

World Forestry
Center, **25**

Pittock Dr., tel. 503/248–4469. Admission: $3.50 adults, $3 senior citizens, $1.50 children 6–18. Open daily 1–5.

㉘ The **Children's Museum** offers hands-on play for children (infant–10) through changing art and craft exhibits, a clay shop, and child-size grocery store. *3037 S.W. 2nd Ave., tel. 503/823–2227. Admission: $3 adults, $2.50 children. Open Mon.–Sat. 9–5, Sun. 11–5.*

㉙ The **Old Church,** built in 1882, is a prime example of Carpenter Gothic architecture, demonstrated by rough-cut lumber, tall spires, and original stained-glass windows. Free concerts on one of the few operating Hook and Hastings pipe organs are presented each Wednesday at noon. *1422 S.W. 11th Ave., tel. 503/222–2031. Open Tues.–Sat. 11–3.*

Time Out Five blocks from the church is the **Broadway Revue** (1239 S.W. Broadway, tel. 503/227–3883) lounge, featuring nostalgic Hollywood ambience. Relax with a cold soda or beer and admire the old B-movie posters adorning the walls.

㉚ The Sanctuary of Our Sorrowful Mother, also known as **The Grotto,** is a 64-acre tract staffed by the Order of the Servants of Mary. More than 100,000 visitors per year come here to walk the Stations of the Cross trail that leads through a thick forest, and to visit a cave set in a 110-foot cliff that enshrines a marble replica of Michelangelo's *Pieta. Corner of N.E. 85th Ave. and Sandy Blvd., tel. 503/254–7371. Admission free; elevator fee: 50¢. Open May–Sept. 9–8; Oct.–Apr. 9:30–5:30.*

Portland for Free

State of Oregon Sports Hall of Fame includes 3,300 square feet of sports memorabilia associated with prominent Oregonian athletes and teams. Among those commemorated are Terry Baker, Heisman Trophy winner, and Mickey Lolich, who played for Detroit in three World Series. *900 S.W. 4th Ave. (basement of the Standard Insurance Ctr.), tel. 503/227–7466. Admission free. Open weekdays 10–3.*

What to See and Do with Children

Carousel Courtyard (N.E. 7th and 9th Aves., at Holladay St., tel. 503/230–0400) includes a working carousel, a carousel museum, and a children's theater.

Children's Museum (*see* Tour 2).

Japanese Gardens (*see* Tour 2).

Ladybug Theater (on Willamette River at the foot of S.E. Spokane St., tel. 503/232–2346 for showtimes), Portland's only theater exclusively for children, is located in **Oaks Amusement Park,** which has summer thrill rides, year-round roller skating, bingo, and miniature golf.

Oregon Maritime Museum (*see* Tour 1).

Oregon Museum of Science and Industry (*see* Tour 2).

Washington Park Zoo (*see* Tour 2).

World Forestry Center (*see* Tour 2).

Off the Beaten Track

Officers' Row Historic District and **Ft. Vancouver National Historic Site.** Depart Portland northbound on I-5 (across the Columbia River toward Vancouver, WA); take Exit 1-C and follow signs to Officers' Row. The 21 Victorian-style homes—some still private residences, others restaurants and commercial businesses—were built between 1850 and 1906. General Ulysses S. Grant and General George C. Marshall are among the notables who served here.

Ft. Vancouver is a reconstruction of the 1825 site that was the fur-trading headquarters of the Hudson's Bay Company. Tours, conducted by National Park Service staff and volunteers in period dress, take you into officers' and enlisted men's quarters and the smithy, the bakery, and other shops. Some furnishings are from the original fort. A visitor center has a museum, audiovisual program, and gift shop. *612 E. Reserve St., Vancouver, tel. 206/696-7655. Admission: $1 adults. Open daily 10-4.*

Forest Park is one of the nation's largest (4,700 acres) urban wildernesses. It is home to more than 100 species of birds and 50 species of mammals, and it includes more than 50 miles of trails. *Take Lovejoy St. west to where it becomes Cornell Rd. and follow to the park, tel. 503/248-4492. Admission free. Open dawn-dusk.*

Shopping

Shopping Districts/Streets/Malls

The main shopping area in the city center is concentrated between **S.W. 3rd** and **10th avenues** and between **S.W. Stark** and **Morrison streets.**

Clackamas Town Center (off I-205 at Sunnyside Rd., tel. 503/653-6913), with more than 180 shops and five major department stores, has one of the largest selections of merchandise in the Northwest.

The Galleria (921 Morrison St., in Fareless Sq., tel. 503/228-2748) covers a full block with three floors of 50 specialty stores, gift shops, and restaurants. MAX light-rail fare and parking are free with $10 purchase.

Pioneer Place (700 S.W. 5th Ave., in Fareless Sq., tel. 503/228-5800) has 66 specialty shops anchored by Saks Fifth Avenue, which offers two floors of high quality men's and women's clothing and jewelry, among other merchandise.

Other downtown shopping areas where you'll find an assortment of merchandise include the **Portland Saturday Market** (100 S.W. Ankeny St., tel. 503/222-6072) and the **Skidmore Fountain Building** (28 S.W. 1st Ave., tel. 503/227-5305), both part of the square surrounding the fountain. Also, the **New Market Theater Village** (50 S.W. 2nd Ave., tel. 503/228-2392) is a good place for browsing. *See* Tour 1, above, for details about the products sold.

Jantzen Beach Center (1405 Jantzen Beach Center, off I–5, tel. 503/289–5555) has 100 shops, three major department stores, a bowling alley, a triplex cinema, and an old, operating carousel.

In 1960, when it opened, **Lloyd Center** (adjacent to MAX light rail; bounded by E. Multnomah, Broadway, and 16th and 19th Aves., tel. 503/282–2511) was the largest shopping mall in the United States. With a renovation scheduled for completion in August of 1991, the center will contain more than 150 stores, three department stores, and an open-air ice-skating pavilion.

Washington Square (S.W. Hall Blvd. and Hwy. 217, tel. 503/639–8860) has six major department stores, 130 specialty shops, parking accommodations for more than 6,000 cars, vaulted skylights, and indoor landscaping. **Washington Square Too** has 20 additional stores.

Shopping in **Sellwood** (S.E. 13th St., tel. 503/233–7334) is a combination historical walking tour and venture into unusual antiques and collectibles. More than 50 antiques shops line S.E. 13th Street, along with shops specializing in specific products as well as outlet stores for sporting goods. Building dates and original occupants are identified by plaques at each store.

Department Stores **Meier and Frank** (621 S.W. 5th Ave., in Fareless Sq., tel. 503/223–0512) dates to 1857 and offers 10 floors of general merchandise at the main store downtown.

Nordstrom (701 S.W. Broadway, tel. 503/224–6666) features fine-quality apparel, accessories, and a large footwear department.

Specialty Stores

Antiques **Portland Antique Company** (1211 N.W. Glisan St., tel. 503/223–0999) spreads over 35,000 square feet and houses the Northwest's largest selection of European and English antiques.

Jack Heath Antiques (1606–1700 N.W. 23rd Ave., tel. 503/222–4663) has three buildings of china, silver, furniture, glass, jewelry, and Victorian antiques.

Sellwood Antique Row (*see* Shopping Districts, above).

Art Dealers/ For art lovers, 2nd Avenue, north and west of Yamhill Market-
Galleries place has many fine art galleries. Recommended downtown shops are **Jamison/Thomas Gallery** (1313 N.W. Glisan St., tel. 503/222–0063), representing contemporary West Coast artists and specializing in art for the advanced collector, and **Quintana Galleries of Native American Art** (139 S.W. 2nd Ave., tel. 503/223–1729), which focuses on Native American, Southwest, Navajo, and Hopi jewelry. **Quintana Galleries** (818 S.W. 1st Ave., tel. 503/228–6855) specializes in Edward Curtis photography, plus Northwest textiles, beadwork, carvings, sculptures, and paintings.

Gifts Shoppers who wish to take home local products will want to seek out the several **Made In Oregon** shops, at Portland International Airport, Lloyd Center, The Galleria, Old Town, Washington Square, or Clackamas Town Center. Merchandise ranges from books to distinctive myrtlewood, local wines, and woolen products.

Jewelry	**Pierre's Jeweler** (539 S.W. 3rd Ave., tel. 503/225–0696) sells wholesale diamonds and offers custom design, repairs, and settings.
Men's/Women's Apparel	**Norm Thompson** (1805 N.W. Thurman St., tel. 503/221–0764) offers classic fashions for men and women, innovative footwear, and one-of-a-kind gifts.

The **Portland Pendleton Shop** (900 S.W. 5th Ave., tel. 503/242–0037) carries full lines of men's and women's wear, plus Pendleton blankets.

Perfume	**Perfume House** (3328 Hawthorne Blvd., tel. 503/234–5375) has more than 600 fragrances for women and 200 for men.
Records	**Django Records** (1111 S.W. Stark St., tel. 503/227–4381) is a must for collectors of tapes, compact discs, 45s, and albums.
Toys	**Finnegan's Toys and Gifts** (922 Yamhill St., tel. 503/221–0306) is downtown Portland's largest toy store. It stocks creative, learning, art, and other toys.

Sports and Fitness

Bicycling On-street cyclists are common in Portland, and there are numerous bike paths that meander through parks and along the shoreline of the Willamette River. Designated routes include a 30-mile path along U.S. 30, through Forest Park into northwest and southwest Portland and on to the suburb of Lake Oswego. Other options are the 2 miles of promenade along the Willamette River between the Broadway and Marquam bridges, and an eastside route between the Hawthorne and Burnside bridges. Bikes can be rented at **Cascaddens Outdoor Shop** (1533 N.W. 24th Ave., tel. 503/224–4746) and **Lightning Speed Cyclery** (90 N.W. 2nd Ave., tel. 503/224–2453).

Fishing The **Columbia** and **Willamette rivers** are both major sportfishing streams with opportunities for angling virtually year-round (*see* Excursions from Portland, below).

The Willamette River offers prime fishing for rainbow trout and for cutthroat, bass, channel cats, and sturgeon. It is also a good winter steelhead stream, and salmon action lasts into June. June is also the top shad month, with some of the best fishing occurring below Willamette Falls at Oregon City. The Columbia River is known for the abundance of trout, salmon, and sturgeon that thrive in its waters.

Detailed fishing regulations are published each year, and current editions should be read before going fishing. Local sport shops are the best source of information on fishing hot spots, which change from year to year. Regulations can be obtained at local tackle shops or from the **Oregon Department of Fish and Wildlife** (506 S.W. Mill St., Portland 97201, tel. 503/229–5403).

There are numerous outfitters throughout Portland who offer guide services and rentals, including **Larry's Sport Center** (2205 E. Burnside St., tel. 503/665–6102), **Hook, Line and Sinker** (7130 S.E. Harold St., tel. 503/777–2066), and **Stewart Fly Shop** (23830 Halsey St., tel. 503/666–2471).

Golf Golfers have a choice of 18 public courses in the greater Portland area. Among the best are **Broadmoor** (3509 Columbia Blvd., tel. 503/281–1337), 18 holes; **Colwood National** (7313

N.E. Columbia Blvd., tel. 503/254–5515), 18 holes; **Glendoveer** (14015 N.E. Glisan St., tel. 503/253–7507), two 18-hole courses; and **Heron Lakes** (3500 N. Victory Blvd., tel. 503/289–1818), 27 holes.

Skiing For detailed information on cross-country and downhill ski trails, *see* Excursions from Portland, below. Two places for ski rentals are **Cascadden's Outdoor Shop** (1533 N.W. 24th Ave., tel. 503/224–4746) and **The Mountain Shop** (628 N.E. Broadway, tel. 503/288–6768).

Tennis Public indoor tennis is available at **Glendoveer Golf Course** (14015 N.E. Glisan St., tel. 503/253–7507) and the **Lake Oswego Indoor Tennis Center** (2900 S.W. Diane Dr., tel. 503/635–5550). **Portland Parks and Recreation** (tel. 503/796–5193) operates 117 outdoor courts (many with night lighting) on a first-come-first-served basis. From May 1 to September 30, outdoor courts may be reserved at Grant Park, Portland Tennis Center, and Washington Park. The **Portland Tennis Center** (324 N. 12th Ave., tel. 503/823–3189) operates four indoor courts; the **St. John's Racquet Center** (7519 N. Burlington Ave., tel. 503/823–3629) has three indoor courts.

Spectator Sports

Auto Racing Sports cars, motocross, and dragsters are featured weekends from April through September at **Portland International Raceway** (N. Victory Blvd. at West Delta Park, tel. 503/285–6635). **Portland Speedway's** (9727 N. Union Ave., tel. 503/285–2883) season runs April–September, with demolition derbies and stock-car races.

Baseball The **Portland Beavers,** a farm club of the Minnesota Twins, play at Portland Civic Stadium (1844 S.W. Morrison St., tel. 503/248–4496).

Basketball Memorial Coliseum (1401 N. Wheeler Ave., tel. 503/248–4496) is home court for the NBA's **Portland Trail Blazers.**

Greyhound Racing The season at **Multnomah Kennel Club** (223rd and Glisan Sts., tel. 503/243–2706) starts in May and continues through September.

Hockey The **Portland Winter Hawks** of the Western Hockey League play home games at Memorial Coliseum (1401 N. Wheeler Ave., tel. 503/238–4636).

Horse Racing Thoroughbred and quarter horses race, rain or shine, at **Portland Meadows** (1001 N. Schmeer Rd., tel. 503/285–9144) from October through April.

Dining

First-time visitors to Portland are likely to be surprised by both the diversity of restaurants and the low prices, when compared with other metropolitan areas. Although this city has never been known as a melting pot, lovers of ethnic foods can choose from Chinese, Cajun, French, German, Greek, Italian, Lebanese, and other cuisines. Of course, there's also Northwest cuisine, an emerging style that features local fish and domestic game, such as venison, duck, and pheasant, plus locally grown wild mushrooms and other produce. Northwest chefs try to avoid fats, oils, and high cholesterol by the means of searing and broiling.

Highly recommended restaurants are indicated by a star ★.

Category	Cost*
Very Expensive	over $25
Expensive	$20–$25
Moderate	$12–$20
Inexpensive	under $12

*per person, excluding drinks and service charge

Very Expensive
★ **Atwater's.** Perched on the 30th floor of the U.S. Bancorp Tower, Atwater's has an outstanding view of the Willamette River, the Cascade Mountains, and the city's skyline. The decor is a mix of classical pillars, Oriental art, and tile. Northwest cuisine features a variety of mushrooms, huckleberries, venison, Pacific salmon, lamb, and pheasant. A 300-label wine list of Northwest, California, and Italian vintages ranges in price from $15 to $800 per bottle. Sunday brunch is served. *111 S.W. 5th Ave., tel. 503/275–3600. Reservations advised. Dress: casual but neat. AE, D, DC, MC, V. Closed lunch.*

L'Auberge. In this French restaurant, you can dine beside the lounge fireplace with a simple supper à la carte or order a three- or six-course meal in the formal dining room. The menu, which changes weekly, emphasizes seasonal specialties, but you can count on main entrées of steak, rack of lamb or veal, and a poultry or fish dish that might include duckling, pheasant, squab, quail, sturgeon, or swordfish. *2601 N.W. Vaughn St., tel. 503/223–3302. Reservations recommended for dining room. Dress: casual. AE, D, DC, MC, V. Closed lunch.*

The Esplanade at Riverplace. The Willamette River and the marina provide a romantic setting for dining in a formal atmosphere. Borrowing traditional French cooking techniques, the chefs have produced an innovative Northwest cuisine featuring warm duck with wild greens and Stilton cheese, and lobster medallions with mahimahi. An award winning wine list and cellar boasts Northwest vintages. *Riverplace Alexis Hotel, 1510 S.W. Harbor Way, tel. 503/295–6166. Reservations advised. Dress: casual but neat. AE, D, DC, MC, V. Closed Sat. lunch.*

Genoa Restaurant. This small, crowded, but intimate Italian restaurant seats about 35 people and serves a four-course meal from 5:30, 6, and 9:30, and there's a seven-course dinner from 6 to 9:30. Since there are no windows in this somewhat dark dining room, the consistant and delicious meals have become the attraction. Emphasizing fresh meat and seafoods, the menu changes frequently but promises creative picks. Fillet of swordfish and veal loin chops are featured specials along with fish soups and seafood ravioli. *2832 S.E. Belmont St., tel. 503/238–1464. Reservations required. Dress: casual. AE, D, DC, MC, V. Closed lunch and Sun.*

Expensive
Benjamin's. Views of Portlandia and City Hall, tiles and stainless steel, huge windows, and rich brown woods and fabrics are the setting for dining that usually includes several seafood dishes. Japanese salads are a specialty along with charbroiled steaks and barbeque ribs. *112 S.W. 5th Ave., tel. 503/223–8103.*

Abou Karim, **11**

Alexis, **8**

Atwater's, **12**

l'Auberge, **1**

Benjamin's, **16**

Brasserie
Montmartre, **14**

Cajun Café and
Bistro, **2**

Couch Street Fish
House, **7**

Crepe Fare
Restaurant and
Bistro, **10**

Dan and Louis
Oyster Bar, **9**

Digger O'Dell's, **23**

The Esplanade, **17**

Fong Chong
Restaurant, **6**

Genoa Restaurant, **22**

Harrington's Bar and
Grill, **15**

Jake's Famous
Crawfish, **13**

Newport Bay
Restaurant, **18**

Papa Haydn, **3**

Rheinlander, **21**

Ringside, **5**

Roses, **4**

Salty's On The
Columbia, **19**

Salty's On the
Willamette, **24**

Sylvia's Italian
Restaurant, **20**

Portland Dining

74

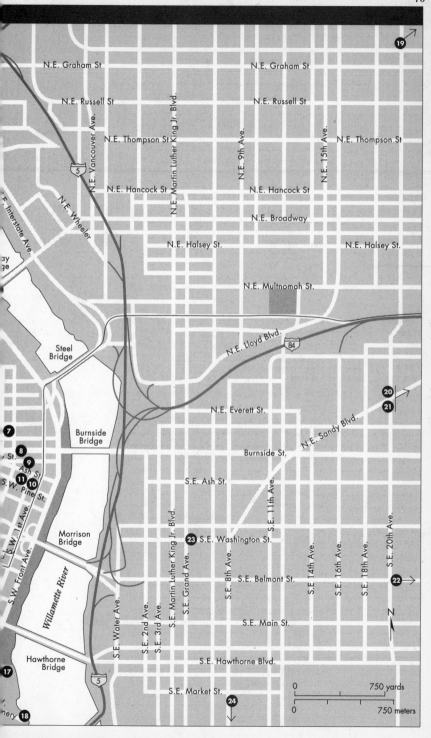

Reservations advised. Dress: casual. AE, D, MC, V. Closed weekend lunch.

★ **Couch Street Fish House.** Long recognized as one of Portland's finest restaurants, the Fish House offers an elegant atmosphere in a building dating to 1883. The decor features watercolors of oceans, antiques, and greenery interspersed with tables with high-back chairs. Chef Horst Megler's Continental cooking includes mesquite-broiled salmon, rack of lamb with port sauce and mint, prawns on chanterelles and apricots, and Maine lobster poached in court bouillon. *105 N.W. 3rd Ave., tel. 503/223–6173. Reservations advised. Dress: casual but neat. AE, MC, V. Closed lunch and Sun.*

Salty's on the Columbia and **Salty's on the Willamette.** Both have floor-to-ceiling windows overlooking the rivers, entertainment in the lounges, and a menu that is heavy on seafood, sumptuous desserts, and imaginative appetizers and salads. Featured in season are Maine lobsters with drawn butter and fresh lemon, and black tiger prawns from Taiwan baked in whiskey barbecue sauce. *On the Columbia: 3839 N.E. Marine Dr., tel. 503/288–4444; on the Willamette: foot of S.E. Marian St., tel. 503/239–8900. Reservations advised. Dress: casual. AE, DC, MC, V.*

Moderate **Brasserie Montmartre.** Although the name, the beaded lamp shades over the bar, and the murals of Paris street scenes tell you this is French, the cuisine is Continental. Rack of lamb, almond scampi, a fish or seafood catch of the day, and baked breast of chicken stuffed with Roquefort and cream cheese rolled in walnuts—all bring the locals back for more. Also, try the Saturday or Sunday brunch. *626 S.W. Park Ave., tel. 503/224–5552. Reservations advised. Dress: casual but neat. AE, DC, MC, V.*

Crepe Faire Restaurant and Bistro. Exposed brick walls, huge arched windows, and a pianist at a baby grand create the atmosphere in this casually elegant French restaurant. Crêpes are made on an exposed grill, just like in the streets of Paris. Other specialties include stuffed chicken breast, a classic chatelaine sauce, and green peppercorn chicken. *133 S.W. 2nd Ave., tel. 503/227–3365. Reservations advised. Dress: casual but neat. AE, DC, MC, V. Closed dinner Sat. and Sun.*

★ **Digger O'Dell's Oyster Bar and Restaurant.** Built in 1890 and once a theater, Digger O'Dell's offers a choice of dining in a large lounge, in an elegant open room with burgundy chairs, or an intimate balcony reached by climbing a hand-carved teak staircase. Along with seafood, the extensive Cajun menu includes blackened prime rib, sliced to order and seared to your specifications. *532 S.E. Grand Ave., tel. 503/238–6996. Reservations advised. Dress: casual. AE, D, DC, MC, V.*

Jake's Famous Crawfish. When Jake's added crawfish to its menu in 1920, it gained a national reputation. You can have your crawfish étouffé (beef-broth used for dipping), Creole, or as a pie. Sturgeon, Australian lobster tail, and a variety of oysters are also featured. Take time to enjoy the sophisticated, yet familiar feeling conveyed by the dark wood paneling, plate-glass windows, and large paintings of Mt. Hood. The back bar came around Cape Horn in the 1880s, and the chandeliers hanging from high ceilings date to 1881. *401 S.W. 12th Ave., tel. 503/226–1419. Reservations advised. Dress: casual. AE, D, DC, MC, V. Closed weekends lunch.*

Newport Bay at Riverplace. When it comes to a view, there's not a bad seat in the house; the restaurant seems to literally float on the water of the Willamette River. The circular glass dining room affords virtually a 360-degree view of the marina, bridges, river, and city skyline. Newport Bay seeks out whatever is in season worldwide, which might include Oregon spring salmon, sturgeon, Maine lobster, Australian lobster tail, Alaskan halibut, or New Zealand roughy, plus swordfish, marlin, and shark. *0425 S.W. Montgomery St., at Riverplace, tel. 503/227–FISH. Reservations advised. Dress: casual but neat. AE, D, DC, MC, V.*

Papa Haydn. This corner restaurant situated near the center of N.W. 23rd Avenue's boutiques, makes a convenient lunch or dinner stop. Sandwiches include Gruyère cheese and Black Forest ham grilled on French bread, and mesquite-grilled chicken breast on a baked roll with bacon, avocado, basil, and tomato. A favorite dinner entrée is the combination mesquite-grilled top sirloin, Italian sausage and breast of chicken, or fresh veal chop sautéed in thyme and raspberry vinegar. A large dessert list includes an award-winning meringue. *701 N.W. 23rd Ave., tel. 503/228–7317. Reservations for Sunday Brunch only. Dress: casual. AE, MC, V.*

★ **Rheinlander.** The Bavarian chalet-style building has gables and stenciled flowers painted on the outside, and the dining areas are crammed with steins, wood carvings, china, clocks, and figurines on the inside. Singing waiters and strolling musicians serenade at tables, helping make it *the* place to celebrate anniversaries and birthdays. All dinners start with Swiss-cheese fondue and Russian rye. If you're a first-timer, you may wish to sample the German cooking with a combination platter of roast pork, sauerbraten, and Cordon Bleu. A beer garden is stocked with German beer and wines. *5035 N.E. Sandy Blvd., tel. 503/288–5503. Reservations advised. Dress: casual but neat. AE, MC, V. Closed lunch.*

Ringside. Waiters in tuxedos, a fireplace, and a very dark intimate room make this the perfect setting for romantic dining. The Ringside is known for its fine wine list, onion rings, rib-eye steaks, seafood, and chicken. *2156 W. Burnside St., tel. 503/223–1513. Reservations advised. Jacket and tie suggested. AE, MC, V. Closed lunch.*

Roses. Fast a day before you go, but you may still take part of your meal home in a doggie bag. The deli sandwiches and sumptuous desserts are overwhelming. Established favorites are Reuben sandwiches on homemade Russian rye, fillet of salmon topped with lemon butter, and a seven-inch-high pecan cake with inch-thick layers of fudge icing. Roses is open for breakfast, lunch, and dinner. *315 N.W. 23rd Ave., tel. 503/227–5181. Reservations advised. Dress: casual. DC, MC, V.*

Sylvia's Italian Restaurant. This is really two restaurants. In the dining room you'll find traditional red-and-white-check tablecloths and Chianti bottles hanging from the ceiling. A separate dinner theater, seating 80–90 people and costing $22.95 per person, stages five musicals, comedies, and dramas a year—each with an eight-week or longer run; the price includes the meal and show. Traditional entrées range from spaghetti and Italian sausage to shrimp Milano with fresh mushrooms and green peppers simmered in a red sauce and white wine. *5115 N.E. Sandy Blvd., tel. 503/288–6828. Reservations advised. Dress: casual. AE, DC, MC, V. Closed lunch.*

Inexpensive **Abou Karim.** Although more than half the Lebanese menu is vegetarian, leg of lamb served on a bed of rice with lentil soup, including a full salad and pita bread, is a favorite. A special menu of meals low in saturated fats is also featured, and there is an outside area for dining in summer. A Lebanese sword, waterpipe, hanging fans, and plants create the atmosphere. *221 S.W. Pine St., tel. 503/223–5058. Reservations advised on weekends. Dress: casual. AE, MC, V.*

Alexis. The interior is as simple as the white walls and basic furnishings, but the authentic Greek flavor keeps the crowds coming. You'll find traditional Greek food such as *kalamarakia* (deep-fried squid served with *tzatziki,* a yogurt dip) and *horiatiki* (a green salad combination with feta cheese and Kalamata olives, tossed in olive oil, vinegar, and oregano). Greek beer and wine are served at the bar. *215 W. Burnside St., tel. 503/224–8577. Reservations advised. Dress: casual. AE, D, DC, MC, V. Closed weekend lunch.*

Cajun Café and Bistro. The Cajun and Creole cuisine found here includes gumbos, jambalayas, bronzed fresh fish, blackened prime rib, and chicken, all served with a basket of home-baked jalapeño cheese rolls. Microbrews, a wine list, and a full bar featuring Cajun martinis, hurricanes, and Creole Mary's help wash it all down. The dessert menu includes sweet potato pie and other Cajun/Creole delights. In 1991 a sunroom was added and when weather permits a patio is available for outside dining. *2074 N.W. Lovejoy St., tel. 503/227–0227. Reservations advised. Dress: casual. AE, D, DC, MC, V. Closed Sat. and Sun. lunch.*

★ **Dan & Louis's Oyster Bar.** You can have your oysters fried, stewed, or on the half-shell. Crab stew—virtually impossible to find elsewhere—is also a specialty. You'll also find local wines and microbrews. Founder Louis Wachsmuth, who started his restaurant in 1907, was an avid collector of steins, plates, and marine art. The trove has grown over the years to fill nearly every inch of wall, beams, nooks, and crannies. Allow time to seek out ship models, paintings on glass, and the many photographs. *208 S.W. Ankeny St., tel. 503/227–5906. Reservations required for parties of 5 or more. Dress: casual. AE, DC, MC, V.*

Fong Chong Restaurant. Although this plain, very simple spot lacks the usual vibrant Chinese-restaurant decor, there's atmosphere aplenty thanks to the Chinese grocery that shares the space. Fong Chong draws a local crowd for its specialty, salt dim sum, or the sautéed squid, fried clams with black bean sauce, and beef tripe with green onions and ginger. *301 N.W. 4th Ave., tel. 503/220–0235. No reservations. Dress: casual. No credit cards.*

Harrington's Bar and Grill. The long dark wood bar is reminiscent of a turn-of-the-century lounge, and the mirrored walls and gaudy neon lights look like leftovers from a disco, which they are. Yes, the interior styles clash, but the tasty selections help to bring attention away from the oddly decorated dining room. Broiled salmon, chicken marinated in orange juice and Southwest spices, ginger scallops sautéed, and angel hair pasta with fresh herb pesto are featured. *1001 S.W. 6th Ave., in the basement of the Security Pacific Bldg., tel. 503/243–2932. Reservations advised. Dress: casual. AE, DC, MC, V.*

Lodging

Travelers to Portland will find a variety of accommodations to suit their personal needs. Lodgings range from high-rise all-suite complexes near the airport, especially convenient for the business traveler, to elegant hotels near the city center and waterfront, which are attractive to all visitors because of their proximity to the city's two biggest attractions. For families, all-suite hotels in the southwest suburbs provide a lot of space without giving up the extras. Budget travelers will need to sacrifice convenience to the airport and downtown. Many places allow small pets, and some offer senior-citizen discounts and family plans.

Highly recommended lodgings are indicated by a star ★.

Category	Cost*
Very Expensive	over $100
Expensive	$75–$100
Moderate	$50–$75
Inexpensive	under $50

All prices are for a standard double room for two, excluding tax of 6%–9%, depending on location of the property; unless noted, all places include room/valet service and color TVs.

Airport Area   **Sheraton Airport.** Although this is the only hotel on airport property, noise is not a problem, thanks to sound-absorbing construction. All rooms have original lithographs by Northwest artists. For business travelers, the Sheraton offers everything from secretarial services to copying and mailing. *8235 N.E. Airport Way, 97220, tel. 503/281–2500 or 800/325–3535. 215 rooms; handicapped and nonsmoking rooms available. Facilities: restaurant, lounge entertainment, minibars, airport shuttle, free parking, gift shop, indoor pool, athletic facilities. AE, D, DC, MC, V. Very Expensive.*

Shilo Inn Suites Hotel. This all-suites hotel provides amenities that border on the excessive. Each room has three television sets, a personal VCR, a microwave, four telephones, refrigerators, and wet bar, and two oversize beds. The contemporary decor runs to soothing pale blues, light pinks, and light grays in both public and private areas. *11707 N.E. Airport Way, 97220, tel. 503/252–7500 or 800/222–2244. 144 rooms; handicapped and nonsmoking rooms available. Facilities: restaurant, lounge, airport shuttle, complimentary Continental breakfast, indoor pool, spa, exercise room, steam room, business service center, free local telephone calls. AE, D, DC, MC, V. Expensive–Very Expensive.*

Doubletree Club Hotel. The facility, built in 1989, is conveniently situated ¾ mile from I-205. Standard rooms are of average size and are brightly decorated in teals, maroons, and yellows. A central "club" with a large screen TV and work stations for business travelers is on the premises. *11550 N.E. Airport Way, 97220, tel. 503/252–3200 or 800/325–2525. 150 rooms; handicapped and nonsmoking rooms available. Facilities: restaurant, lounge, complimentary airport shuttle, complimentary cocktails and full breakfast, free parking, gift shop, Jacuzzi, outdoor pool. AE, D, DC, MC, V. Expensive.*

The Benson Hotel, **5**

Best Western/
Fortniter Motel, **25**

Best Western Inn at
the Convention
Center, **15**

Doubletree Club
Hotel, **22**

Embassy Suites, **3**

Greenwood Inn, **2**

Heathman, **7**

Hilton Hotel, **8**

Holiday Inn/Portland
Airport, **24**

Hotel Vintage
Plaza, **6**

Lamplighter Inn, **1**

Mallory Motor Hotel, **4**

Marriott Hotel, **10**

Portland Super 8
Motel, **19**

Ramada Inn
Airport, **23**

Red Lion/Coliseum, **12**

Red Lion/Columbia
River, **18**

Red Lion/Jantzen
Beach, **17**

Red Lion/Lloyd
Center, **16**

Riverplace Alexis
Hotel, **11**

Riverside Inn, **9**

Sheraton Airport, **20**

Shilo Inn/Lloyd
Center, **14**

Shilo Inn Suites
Hotel, **21**

Travelodge Hotel, **13**

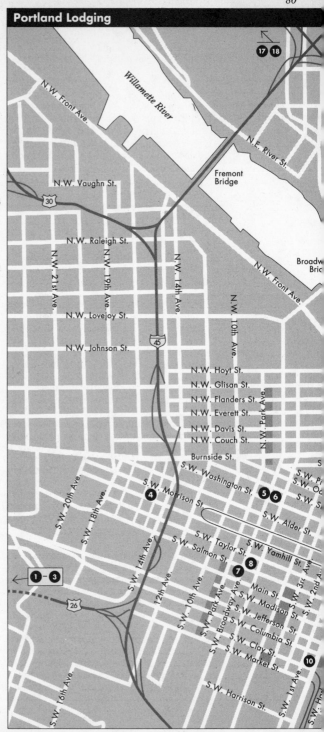

Portland Lodging

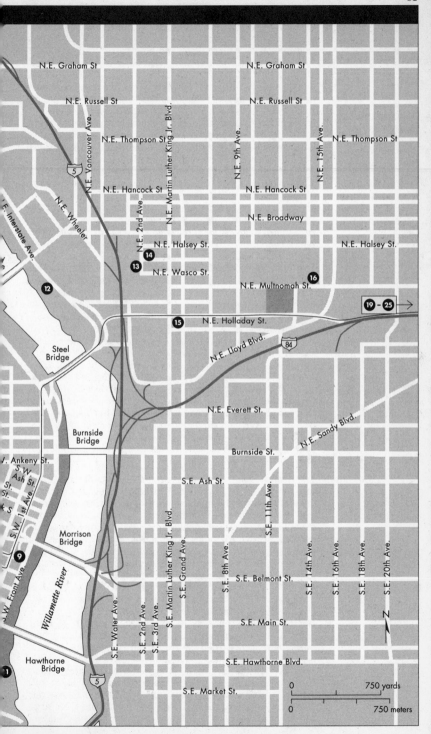

N.E. Graham St

N.E. Graham St

N.E. Russell St

N.E. Russell St

N.E. Vancouver Ave.

N.E. Thompson St

N.E. Thompson St

N.E. 9th Ave.

N.E. 15th Ave.

5

N.E. Hancock St

N.E. Hancock St

N.E. Wheeler

N.E. Broadway

N.E. Interstate Ave.

N.E. 2nd Ave.

N.E. Martin Luther King Jr. Blvd.

N.E. Halsey St.

N.E. Halsey St.

14

13

N.E. Wasco St.

16

12

N.E. Multnomah St.

19 – 25 →

15

N.E. Holladay St.

Steel
Bridge

N.E. Lloyd Blvd.

84

N.E. Everett St.

Burnside
Bridge

N.E. Sandy Blvd.

Ankeny St.

S.W.
Ash St.

St.

S

Burnside St.

S.W. 1st Ave.

S.E. Ash St.

S.E. 11th Ave.

S.W. Front Ave.

9

Morrison
Bridge

S.E. Martin Luther King Jr. Blvd.

S.E. Grand Ave.

S.E. 8th Ave.

S.E. 14th Ave.

S.E. 16th Ave.

S.E. 18th Ave.

S.E. 20th Ave.

S.E. Belmont St.

Willamette River

S.E. Water Ave.

S.E. 2nd Ave.

S.E. 3rd Ave.

S.E. Main St.

N

Hawthorne
Bridge

1

S.E. Hawthorne Blvd.

5

0   750 yards

S.E. Market St.

0   750 meters

Holiday Inn/Portland Airport. A huge multitiered Spanish fountain forms the centerpiece for fine dining and public areas in this convention-center facility. In rooms, the Spanish decor continues with green, pink, and blue pastel wall tiles. *8439 N.E. Columbia Blvd., 97220, tel. 503/256–5000 or 800/HOLI-DAY, fax 503/256–5000, ext. 149. 286 rooms; handicapped and nonsmoking rooms available. Facilities: lounge, airport shuttle, free parking, gift shop, lounge entertainment, weight room, pool, sauna. AE, D, DC, MC, V. Expensive.*

★ **Ramada Inn Airport.** This facility caters to business travelers; it includes board and conference rooms and a business center with computers, fax machines, and individual work stations. The 108 execu-suites are furnished with microwaves, wet bars, refrigerators, and living areas. Spacious one- and two-bedroom suites come equipped with a Jacuzzi, and standard rooms, with king-size beds, are tastefully decorated in quiet grays, browns, and pinks. *6221 N.E. 82nd Ave., 97220, tel. 503/255–6511 or 800/423–3047, fax 503/255–8417. 202 rooms. Facilities: restaurant, lounge, complimentary limo service to airport and car-rental companies, free parking, Jacuzzi, pool, sauna, weight room. AE, D, DC, MC, V. Expensive.*

Portland Super 8 Motel. Rooms are decorated in the chain's colors of whites, pinks, grays, and maroons, and are furnished with either one or two twin-size beds. Pets are permitted. *11011 N.E. Holman, 97220, tel. 503/257–8988. 79 rooms; including nonsmoking rooms. Facilities: suites, meeting rooms, guest laundry, copy machine, free local telephone calls, airport shuttle, free parking. AE, DC, MC, V. Moderate.*

★ **Best Western/Fortniter Motel.** Each room has a living area with queen-size bed or queen-size hide-a-bed, divan or day bed, coffee table, full kitchenette, full-size refrigerator, and a separate bedroom. Rooms have a lived-in, put-your-feet-up feel. Although there is no room service, there is a nearby restaurant that can be reached by free shuttle provided by the motel. *4911 N.E. 82nd Ave., 97220, tel. 503/255–9771 or 800/528–1234. 52 rooms. Facilities: complimentary 24-hr shuttle to airport, shuttle transfers to restaurant, 1-wk free parking, athletic-club arrangement, laundry room. AE, D, DC, MC, V. Inexpensive.*

Downtown **The Benson Hotel.** Portland's premier hotel, built in 1912, has just completed a $20 million restoration. Elegance has been maintained with the hand-carved Russian Circassian walnut and Italian white marble staircase. In the guest rooms expect to find small crystal chandeliers, inlaid mahogany doors, and original ceilings. All rooms have been enhanced with additional space, state-of-the-art movie systems, and minibars. The London Grill and Trader Vic's are among the city's finest restaurants. *309 S.W. Broadway, 97205, tel. 503/228–2000 or 800/426–0670. 290 rooms. Facilities: coffee shop, lounge, gift shop, airport-shuttle service, valet/laundry, concierge service. AE, D, DC, MC, V. Very Expensive.*

★ **Heathman.** Superior service, an award-winning restaurant, and a library of signed first editions by authors who have been guests here have earned the Heathman a reputation for quality. Elegance surrounds you in the teak lobby, in the rosewood elevators, on the mezzanine lounge overlooking a chandelier from the State House, and in the adjoining art gallery with original oil and watercolor paintings, which are changed every 90 days. Earth-tone rooms are adequate, but not overly large, and have bathrooms with lots of marble and mirrors. Many ad-join each other and can be rented as suites. *1009 S.W. Broadway, 97205, tel. 503/241–4100 or 800/551–0011. 152 rooms; handicapped and nonsmoking rooms available. Facilities: rowing machines, exercise bikes, athletic-club arrangement. AE, D, DC, MC, V. Very Expensive.*

Hilton Hotel. Situated in the heart of the financial district, the 23-story Hilton offers easy access to theaters and major department stores. But a bigger plus than the perfect location is that children stay for free. The 21st-floor executive rooms come with complimentary newspaper and bath robes. Although the property is in a constant state of renovation, some rooms, which have not recently been renovated are a bit shopworn. Recently refurbished rooms seem fresher and have new carpeting and gray-blue walls. *921 S.W. 6th Ave., 97204, tel. 503/226–1611 or 800/HILTONS. 455 rooms; handicapped and nonsmoking rooms available. Facilities: restaurant, lounge entertainment, fitness room, business center and full secretarial service, outdoor pool, barbershop, and beauty salon. AE, D, DC, MC, V. Very Expensive.*

Hotel Vintage Plaza. This new hotel, built in 1991, took its theme from the area's vineyards and features rooms with four distinct styles. A concierge club level includes two-story townhouse suites, each named after a local winery. Guests can fall to sleep while counting stars in top-floor rooms where skylights, and wall-to-wall conservatory-style windows rate highly among the special details you'll find here. Hospitality suites feature extra-large rooms with a full living area, and there are also deluxe rooms. All rooms are appointed in hunter green, deep plum, cerise, taupe, and gold; and more than 20 rooms have hot tubs. In keeping with the theme, there's plenty of shrubbery in public areas, in addition to the 10-story atrium. An extensive collection of Oregon wines is displayed in the tasting room. *422 S.W. Broadway, 97205, tel. 503/228–1212 or 800/243–0555. 107 rooms/suites. Facilities: restaurant, piano lounge, complimentary coffee and newspaper in mornings and wine in evenings, minibars, valet parking, executive gym, business center, secretarial services. AE, D, DC, MC, V. Very Expensive.*

Marriott Hotel. Emphasis on service starts with uniformed doormen and continues to the 12th floor, a concierge level. Large rooms decorated in off-whites inspire comfort and relaxation; best rooms face east to the Willamette and the Cascades. Champions Lounge, filled with sports memorabilia, is a singles hot spot on weekends. *1401 S.W. Front Ave., 97201, tel. 503/226–7600 or 800/228–9290. 500 rooms; handicapped and nonsmoking rooms available. Facilities: 3 restaurants, coffee shop, lounge entertainment, 24-hr fitness center, gift shop, indoor pool. AE, D, MC, V. Very Expensive.*

Riverplace Alexis Hotel. The Alexis maintains the feeling of a residence, with large airy rooms, wing-back chairs, teak tables, and feather pillows. It has one of the best views in Portland, with rooms overlooking the river and the marina, the city skyline, and a courtyard. *1510 S.W. Harbor Way, 97201, tel. 503/228–3233 or 800/227–1333. 84 rooms; handicapped and nonsmoking rooms available. Facilities: restaurant, lounge entertainment, athletic-club arrangement, complimentary Continental breakfast, parking in locked garage. AE, D, DC, MC, V. Very Expensive.*

Riverside Inn. The Riverside, located in the Yamhill National Historic District, presents compact rooms with a unique combination of furnishings such as brass headboards and green-checkered bedspreads, artificial flower and plants, exotic street scenes, Robert Forester prints, old books, and black-and-white photos of wild animals. Eastside rooms offer a good view of the Willamette River and its greenway. The airy café and bar features a seafood-and-steak menu. *50 S.W. Morrison St., 97204, tel. 503/221–0711 or 800/648–6640. 138 rooms; nonsmoking rooms available. Facilities: restaurant, lounge, free parking, athletic-club agreement. AE, D, DC, MC, V. Expensive.*

Mallory Motor Hotel. This older, refurbished hotel is eight blocks from the city center. A lobby with white-marble columns, mirrored walls, and moss-green carpeting lends a touch of class. The rooms are on the small side, although tastefully decorated in white and natural wood. Most of the staff has been here for years, and everyone is friendly and knowledgeable. *729 S.W. 15th Ave., 97205, tel. 503/223–6311 or 800/228–8657. 144 rooms. Facilities: restaurant, lounge, free parking. AE, DC, MC, V. Inexpensive.*

West Side **Embassy Suites.** Every room is a suite, and each has a separate living room, bedroom, wet bar with refrigerator, two color TVs, and two telephones. This nine-story structure, which sits within a block of Washington Square shopping center, surrounds an atrium of tropical plants and waterfalls. Cooked-to-order breakfast, a two-hour manager's reception with live entertainment, and free lodging for children under 12 come with rentals. *9000 Washington Sq. Rd., Tigard 97223, tel. 503/644–4654 or 800/EMBASSY, fax 503/641–4654. 253 rooms; handicapped and nonsmoking rooms available. Facilities: restaurant, lounge entertainment, courtesy limo to surrounding shops and restaurants, indoor pool, Jacuzzi, sauna, health-club arrangement, gift shop. AE, D, DC, MC, V. Very Expensive.*

Greenwood Inn. Located 10 miles west of Portland, the inn looks out onto Pacific Northwest greenery, and some rooms have a courtyard view. Though the furnishings are typical motel-issue, freshly painted walls and crisp brown-and-white color schemes give Greenwood a clean, comfortable feel. You can listen to harp music with your dinner and dance to live bands in the lounge six nights a week. *10700 S.W. Allen Blvd., Beaverton 97005, tel. 503/643–7444 or 800/289–1300 in western states. 253 rooms; handicapped and nonsmoking rooms available. Facilities: free parking, athletic-club arrangement, weight room, outdoor pool, Jacuzzi, gift shop, kitchens. AE, D, DC, MC, V. Expensive.*

Lamplighter Inn. The inn's new paint, carpeting, bedspreads, and lamps run to blues and mauves. While close to the freeway, noise coming into the hotel is muffled by highway embankments. The small shopping mall across the street has a supermarket, lounge, and sporting goods and equipment stores, and there is the Mongolian restaurant nearby. *10207 S.W. Parkway, Beaverton 97225, tel. 503/297–2211. 56 rooms. Facilities: six kitchen units. AE, MC, V. Inexpensive.*

East Side **Red Lion/Lloyd Center.** Oregon's largest hotel is the prime example of this chain in all of its flamboyance. There's plenty of brass, glass, and glitter mixed with mauves, sea-foam greens, and oak paneling. Three glass elevators and an array of contemporary chandeliers in the public areas set the tone for this highfalutin lodging. Regardless of the hour or number of people, you can expect service that runs like a well-oiled machine. Many large rooms with views of mountains to the east or city center to the west have balconies; units are decorated with wood furnishings and painted in soft muted colors. Lloyd Center and MAX light rail are across the street. *1000 N.E. Multnomah St., 97232, tel. 503/281–6111 or 800/547–8010. 476 rooms; handicapped and no-smoking rooms available. Facilities: 3 restaurants, 3 lounges, evening entertainment, airport shuttle, free parking, outdoor pool, weight room. AE, D, DC, MC, V. Expensive.*

Travelodge Hotel. Light and airy rooms come with king- or queen-size bed, sofa, and coffee table, plus full-length mirrors and cable TV. The Coliseum and Convention Center are within walking distance. *1441 N.E. 2nd Ave., 97232, tel. 503/233–2401 or 800/255–3050. 237 rooms; handicapped and no-smoking rooms available. Facilities: restaurant, airport shuttle. AE, D, DC, MC, V. Moderate–Expensive.*

Best Western Inn at the Convention Center. Rooms were redecorated in 1989 in pleasing creams and rusts. Rooms with king-size beds come with wet bars, while rooms with queen-size beds have standard furnishings. Conveniently located, the inn is four blocks west of Lloyd Center, directly across the street from the Portland Convention Center, and on the MAX line. *420 N.E. Holladay St., 97232, tel. 503/233–6331 or 800/528–1234. 95 rooms. Facilities: restaurant (serving breakfast and lunch), free parking, Jacuzzi, free local telephone calls. AE, D, DC, MC, V. Moderate.*

Red Lion/Coliseum. Many rooms and the restaurant overlook the Willamette River. Unfortunately, trains run outside the river rooms; therefore, courtside is the best choice for peace and quiet. Decorated in pinks, whites, mauve, and seafoam green, standard rooms with modern oak furnishings are pleasing. *1225 N. Thunderbird Way, 97227, tel. 503/235–8311. 213 rooms. Facilities: lounge entertainment, airport shuttle, free parking, outdoor pool. AE, D, DC, MC, V. Moderate.*

Shilo Inn/Lloyd Center. The Coliseum and Convention Center are three blocks away, and a Chinese restaurant/lounge and other dining establishments are within walking distance. Rooms have a comfortable, lived-in feeling, though they're equipped with very basic amenities. *1506 N.E. 2nd Ave., 97232, tel. 503/231–7665 or 800/222–2244. 44 rooms; non-smoking rooms available. Facilities: airport shuttle, free parking, complimentary Continental breakfast. AE, D, DC, MC, V. Moderate.*

North **Red Lion/Columbia River.** The oversize rooms have been completely refurbished since 1988, and public areas—with lots of brass, dark wood, green, and mauve colors—were redecorated in 1991. Freshly painted rooms with new carpeting overlook the mighty Columbia River. The hotel is on Hayden Island, a 100-yard stroll away from Jantzen Beach Shopping Center and the tennis courts at neighboring Red Lion Jantzen Beach. *1401 Hayden Island Dr., 97217, tel. 503/283–2111 or 800/547–8010. 351 rooms; handicapped and no-smoking rooms available. Facilities: restaurant, lounge entertainment, airport shuttle, free parking, outdoor pool, putting green, gift shop, health-club arrangement. AE, D, DC, MC, V. Very Expensive.*

Red Lion/Jantzen Beach. Built and designed by the west-coast chain as opposed to having been purchased, this property has been given special attention, resulting in larger guest rooms

with good views, particularly those on the north side that face
the Columbia River and Vancouver, Washington. Public areas
glitter with brass and bright lights that accentuate the greenery and burgundy, green, and rose color scheme. Maxi's fine
dining room features medallions of veal with gorgonzola cheese
and mushrooms; scampi flambé sautéed tableside in white
wine; or Australian rock lobster tail with drawn butter. *909 N.
Hayden Island Dr., 97217, tel. 503/283–4466. 320 rooms; handicapped and nonsmoking rooms available. Facilities: restaurant, lounge entertainment, airport shuttle, free parking,
outdoor pool, tennis courts, gift shop. AE, D, DC, MC, V. Very
Expensive.*

The Arts

"The Arts and Entertainment Guide," published each Friday
in *The Oregonian,* contains current listings of performers, productions, events, and club entertainment. The monthly *Portland Live Music Guide* gives a comprehensive listing of all clubs
and the type of entertainment featured. For current information on theater productions, call **Portland Area Theatre Alliance
Hot Line** (tel. 503/241–4903).

Theater **Artists Repertory Theatre** (1111 S.W. 10th Ave., tel. 503/242–
2400) stages six productions a year, featuring classic American
plays and new works by Northwest playwrights.
Oregon Puppet Theater stages five children's productions per
year at the CTC facilities.
Oregon Shakespeare Festival Portland (1111 S.W. Broadway,
tel. 503/248–6309) produces five contemporary and classical
productions between November and April in the 916-seat Intermediate Theater.
Portland Center for the Performing Arts (1111 S.W. Broadway,
tel. 503/248–4496) includes four theaters and schedules rock
stars, symphonies, lectures, and Broadway musicals.
Portland Repertory Theater (World Trade Center, 25 S.W.
Salmon St., tel. 503/224–4491) presents a varied season with
six productions a year by the region's oldest professional theatrical company.
Storefront Theatre (6 S.W. 3rd Ave., tel. 503/224–4001) specializes in contemporary and original productions.

Concerts **Arlene Schnitzer Concert Hall** (in Portland Center for the Performing Arts, S.W. Broadway and Main St., tel. 503/248–4496)
hosts rock stars, Broadway shows, symphonies, and classical
concerts.
Memorial Coliseum (1401 N. Wheeler Ave., tel. 503/248–4496)
has 12,000 seats and books popular rock groups and touring
shows.
Pine Street Theatre (221 S.E. 9th Ave., tel. 503/231–8382) hosts
rock, world beat, blues, and ethnic concerts in a nightclub setting.
Portland Civic Auditorium (222 S.W. Clay St., tel. 503/248–
4496), with 3,000 seats and outstanding acoustics, attracts
name country and rock performers and touring shows.
Roseland Theater (8 N.W. 6th St., tel. 503/227–0071) specializes in rock and blues in a club that accommodates up to 1,400
people.

Ballet **Oregon Ballet Theatre** (Portland Civic Auditorium, tel. 503/
227–6867) performs classical and contemporary works.

Opera   Portland Opera (1516 S.W. Alder St., tel. 503/228–1353) and its orchestra and chorus stage five productions annually at the Portland Civic Auditorium.

Symphony   Oregon Symphony (711 S.W. Alder St., tel. 503/228–1353) presents more than 40 classical, pops, children's, and family concerts per season at the Arlene Schnitzer Concert Hall.

Nightlife

Bars and   Dakota Café (239 S.W. Broadway, tel. 503/241–4151). Ameri-
Nightclubs   can cuisine and rock music have made this one of Portland's hot spots.
Key Largo Restaurant and Night Club (31 N.W. 1st Ave., tel. 503/223–9919) is a romantic night spot in an historic building with brick walls, outdoor courtyard, dance floor, Cajun food, and enough Bacall, Bogart, and Hemingway photos to justify the name.

Acoustic/Ethnic   Dublin Pub (6821 Beaverton/Hillsdale Hwy., tel. 503/297–2889) features more than 100 beers on tap, plus wine, Irish bands, and acoustic groups.
East Avenue Tavern (727 E. Burnside St., tel. 503/236–6900) features a potpourri of styles from Cajun to Irish and from bluegrass to French acoustic-guitar music.

Blues   Dandelion Pub (31 N.W. 23rd Pl., tel. 503/223–0099) offers blues six nights a week in a dark, *L*-shape room with dance floor.
Ragabones (N.W. 10th and Everett Sts., tel. 503/223–4774) features local and national blues musicians.

Country and   Jubitz Truck Stop (10310 N. Vancouver Way, tel. 503/283–1111)
Western   features country music nightly in a room that resembles a small warehouse.
The Drum (146 S.E. Division St., tel. 503/760–1400) is Portland's top country club, with traditional country and contemporary country-rock played nightly.

Jazz   Brasserie Montmarte (626 S.W. Park Ave., tel. 503/224–5552) presents solo pianists and duos on weeknights; quartets and larger groups on weekends.
The Hobbit (4420 S.E. 39th Ave., tel. 503/771–0742) has nationally prominent jazz musicians who perform on a regular basis.
Sea Food Mama's (721 N.W. 21st Ave., tel. 503/222–4121) features trios and quartets Tuesday through Saturday.

Rock   Eli's (424 S.W. 4th Ave., tel. 503/223–4241) features hard rock.

Comedy   The Last Laugh (426 N.W. 6th Ave., tel. 503/295–2844) presents headliners with national reputations.

Excursions from Portland

The Columbia River Gorge and the Oregon Cascades

There's only one reason to drive to the Columbia River Gorge and Oregon Cascades: pleasure. Sightseers, sailboarders, hikers, skiers, waterfall lovers, and fans of the Old West will all find contentment in this rugged region. The following tour will take you through the highlights of the Columbia River Gorge, where America's second-largest river (the Mississippi River ranks first) slashes through the Cascade Range. Along the way you'll pass Multnomah Falls and Bonneville Dam, the world-class windsurfing hub and rich orchardland of Hood River, and skiing and other alpine attractions of the 11,245-foot-high Mt. Hood. Finally you'll arrive in Bend, a stronghold of outdoor pleasures steeped in the traditions of the Old West.

An important note: The Columbia Gorge, the Mt. Hood area, and Bend all receive much heavier winter weather than Portland. At times, even I–84—Oregon's main east–west highway—is closed because of snow and ice. If you're planning a winter visit, be sure your car has traction devices, and carry plenty of warm clothes with you.

Getting Around
By Plane **Bend-Redmond Airport** (tel. 503/923–5012) is serviced by Horizon Airlines (tel. 800/547–9308), United Express (tel. 800/241–6522), and USAir (tel. 503/382–2228).

By Car Mt. Hood is about 50 miles from Portland; Bend is about 102 miles away. Virtually all travel in eastern and central Oregon is by car. I–84 follows the Columbia River all the way to Idaho, terminating at Salt Lake City. U.S. 197 (later U.S. 97) leaves I–84 at The Dalles and heads south to California, passing Bend along the way.

By Train **Amtrak** (tel. 800/USA–RAIL) follows I–84 through the Columbia Gorge, to Boise and beyond. From Portland, stops include Hood River and The Dalles. Once you've reached Hood River, consider taking the **Mt. Hood Railroad** (tel. 503/386–3556 or 800/TRAIN61), built in 1906, on a 44-mile round-trip scenic tour to Parkdale; or a 17-mile round-trip tour to Odell. Call for schedule information.

By Bus **Greyhound** (tel. 503/243–2323) provides service the length of the gorge and to Bend.

Scenic Drives The **Scenic Gorge Highway** (Rte. 30) leaves I–84 at Troutdale and climbs past the lush, fern-covered greenery, awesome cliff-top vistas, and thundering waterfalls. The old highway, built in the 1910s by lumber magnate Simon Benson, is a narrow and serpentine 22-mile road made expressly for sightseeing. The route is especially lovely in the fall but often impassable in winter.

The **Highway 97–Highway 218 Loop** is a 25-mile tour through some of the state's most forbiddingly beautiful high desert country. From Shaniko, take Highway 218 south to Antelope, near the now-abandoned commune of Rajneeshpuram. Follow the signs back to Highway 97 and Bend.

Important Addresses and Numbers
Tourist Information **Bend Chamber of Commerce** (63085 N. Hwy. 97, Bend 97701, tel. 503/382–3221).
Hood River County Chamber of Commerce (Port Marina Park, Hood River 97031, tel. 503/386–2000).
Mt. Hood National Forest Ranger Stations are located in Gresham (tel. 503/666–0771), Troutdale (tel. 503/695–2276), Zigzag (tel. 503/666–0704), Mt. Hood Information Center (tel. 503/622–3190), and Parkdale (tel. 503/666–0701).
Mt. Hood Recreation Association (65000 E. Hwy. 26, Welches 97067, tel. 503/622–3162 or 503/622–4822 for recreation information).

Emergencies   In most parts of the state, dialing 911 will connect you with **police, fire,** and **medical assistance.** In some rural areas, it may be necessary to call 800/452–7888, the **Oregon State Police** central dispatch line. Dial "0" to bring an **operator** to the line.

Exploring   *Numbers in the margin correspond to points of interest on the Eastern Oregon map.*

31   The tour begins at **Troutdale,** the gateway to the gorge, where the 22-mile-long **Columbia River Scenic Highway** leaves the interstate. Traveling on the well-signed route for a few miles will take you to **Crown Point,** a 730-foot-high bluff with an unparalleled 30-mile view down the gorge. Then the highway heads downhill, over graceful stone bridges built by Italian immigrant masons, past quiet forest glades and belichened cliffs, over which a dozen waterfalls pour in a single 10-mile stretch. Among the most spectacular are **Latourell, Bridal Veil, Wah-**
32   **keena, Horsetail,** and—finest of all—**Multnomah Falls,** at 620 feet. All the falls have parking areas and hiking trails, so visitors can take a close look. Multnomah Falls is by far the most popular and accessible; there's a paved (but steep) hiking trail to the bridge over the lower falls, as well as the Lakecliff Estate (*see* Dining and Lodging, below), a pleasant old stone lodge with a bar and restaurant.

33   A few miles farther along the old highway is **Oneonta Gorge.** Here you can walk up the bed of a shallow stream and through a cool green canyon that's hundreds of feet high. The walls of the narrow rift drip moisture year-round; hundreds of plant species—some found nowhere else—flourish under these conditions. About a half mile up the stream, the trail ends at lovely **Oneonta Falls.** You'll need boots or submersible sneakers—plus a strong pair of ankles—because the rocks are slippery.

Just past Oneonta Gorge, the old Scenic Highway rejoins I–84.
34   Head east to **Bonneville Dam,** Oregon's most impressive manmade attraction. The first dam ever to span the Columbia, Bonneville was dedicated in 1937 by President Franklin D. Roosevelt. Its great turbines (visible from special walkways during self-guided powerhouse tours) can produce nearly a million kilowatts, which is enough to supply 40,000 single-family homes. There is a modern visitor's center on Bradford Island complete with underwater windows for viewing migrating salmon and steelhead as they struggle up the fish ladders (April–October are the best viewing times). Nearby, **Bonneville Fish Hatchery** has ponds teeming with fingerling salmon, as well as fat rainbow trout and 6 foot-long sturgeon. A gift shop is on the premises. *Visitor's center on Bradford Island, Bonneville Lock and Dam, Cascade Locks, OR 97014, (drive over powerhouse), tel. 503/374–8820. Admission free. Open summer, daily 9–8; rest of year, daily 9–5. Fish hatchery, Star Rte. B, Box 12, Cascade Locks, OR 97014, (on Oregon shore), tel. 503/374–8393. Admission free. Open daily dawn–dusk.*

35   The town of **Cascade Locks** is inundated by the 48-mile-long **Lake Bonneville.** In pioneer days, boats needing to pass the rapids had to portage around them. In 1896, the locks that gave the town its name were completed, allowing waterborne passage for the first time. Today the locks are used by Native Americans for their traditional dip-net fishing, and Cascade Locks is notable mainly as the home port of the 600-passenger sternwheeler *Columbia Gorge.* From June through Septem-

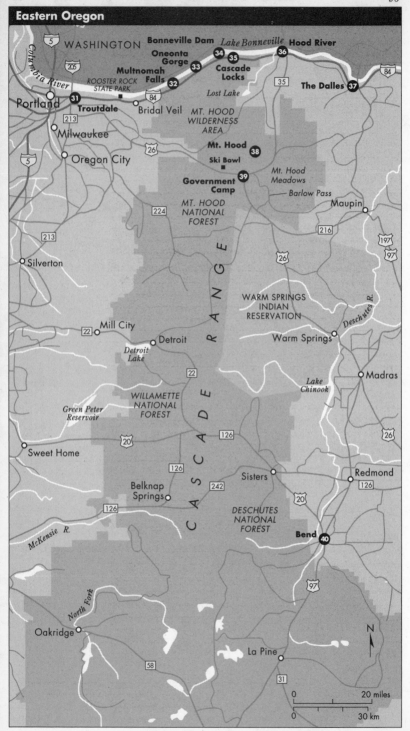

Eastern Oregon

ber, the comfortable, pleasantly appointed ship churns its way upriver, then back again, on daily two-hour excursions through some of the gorge's most awesome scenery. The company also offers lunches and brunches, and dinner-and-dancing cruises in the evenings. *Cruises leave from Marine Park in Cascade Locks, tel. 503/223-3928 or 503/374-8427. Three departures daily for excursions June–Sept. at 10, 12:30, and 3. Admission: $9.95 adults, $5.95 children 4–12. Dinner cruises embark Wed.–Fri. 7 PM; Sat.–Sun. 6:00 PM. Cruises vary in length from 90 min to 3 hours. Meal and cruise prices range from $17.95 to $31.95 for adults.*

36 For years the incessant easterly winds at **Hood River,** where the gorge widens and the scenery changes to tawny, wheat-covered hills, were nothing but a nuisance. Then somebody bolted a sail to a surfboard, and a new recreational craze was born. A fortuitous combination of factors—mainly the reliable gale-force winds blowing against the current—have made Hood River the self-proclaimed sailboarding capital of the world. Now, especially in the summer, this once-somnolent fruit-growing town swarms with colorful "boardheads," many journeying from as far away as Europe and Australia. A collection of restaurants, equipment shops, and inns has sprung up to service this trade, and Hood River is rapidly becoming one of the state's busiest tourist destinations.

Columbia Gorge Sailpark (Port Marina, tel. 503/386-2000), located on the river downtown, was one of the amenities added to encourage the boardsailing craze. It offers a boat basin, swimming beach, jogging trails, picnic tables, and rest rooms.

Situated 28 miles southwest of Hood River via signed Forest Service roads, is **Lost Lake** (tel. 503/666-0771 or 503/386-6366 for cabin reservations), one of the most photographed sites in the Pacific Northwest. Lake waters reflect the mountain and thick forests that line the shore.

37 **The Dalles,** 20 miles east, presents a placid alternative to frenetic, Californian Hood River. With its plethora of 19th-century brick storefronts and historic homes, The Dalles has a small-town, Old West feel to it, possibly because it's the traditional end of the Oregon Trail, where the wagons were loaded onto barges for the final leg of their 2,000-mile journey. The 130-year-old **Wasco County Courthouse** and the 1857-vintage **Ft. Dalles Surgeon's Quarters** have been converted to museums; both contain outstanding displays and collections illustrating the incredible pioneer ordeal. *The Courthouse Museum, 404 W. 2nd St., tel. 503/296-2231. Admission free; donations accepted. Open Oct.–May, Tues.–Sat. 11–3; June–Sept. Tues.–Sat. 11–5. Ft. Dalles Museum, 15th and Garrison Sts., tel. 503/296-4547. Admission: $2 adults, children free. Open Nov.–Feb., weekdays noon–4, weekends 10–4; Mar.–Oct. weekdays 10:30–5, weekends 10–5.*

From Hood River, Highway 35 climbs south toward the regal **38** snow-covered bulk of **Mt. Hood,** believed to be an active volcano, quiet now but capable of the same violence that decapitated nearby Mt. St. Helens in 1980. The mountain is just one feature of the 1,079,169-acre **Mt. Hood National Forest.** The all-season playground attracts more than 4 million visitors annually. You'll find 95 campgrounds and 150 lakes stocked with brown, rainbow, cutthroat, kohanee, brook, and steelhead trout. The

Sandy, Salmon, and other rivers are known for their fishing, rafting, canoeing, and swimming. Both forest and mountain are crossed by an extensive trail system for hikers, cyclists, and horseback riders. Some are half-milers, while others are day-or-longer treks. The **Pacific Crest Trail,** which begins in British Columbia and ends in Mexico, crosses here at the 4,157-foot-high Barlow Pass, the highest point on the highway.

Two miles off Highway 26, near the pass, sits **Trillium Lake** (tel. 503/666–0771), a beautiful spot for picnicking, overnight camping, and fishing for brown and rainbow trout.

Farther on, Highway 35 joins Highway 26 at 4,670-foot-high **Bennett Pass.** Turning west, you'll encounter signs to historic **Timberline Lodge** an exquisite 1930s stone and timber structure, graced with hand-forged wrought iron, intricately carved woodwork, and great stone fireplaces. The lodge has been used as a setting in many films, including *The Shining* with Jack Nicholson. At the front desk of the lodge you can pick up maps that will direct you along the network of trails, leading through alpine meadow and old growth forest. Today Timberline offers comfortable lodging and gourmet dining high (6,000 feet) on the mountain's flank and is a favorite destination of skiers, romantics and sightseers alike (*see* Dining and Lodging, below).

③⑨ **Government Camp,** just off Highway 26 west of the Timberline exit, is an alpine-flavored resort village with an abundance of lodging, restaurant, and nightlife options. It's a convenient drive to each of Mt. Hood's five ski resorts: **Timberline, Mt. Hood Meadows, Summit Ski Area, Ski Bowl** and **Cooper Spur Ski Area** (*see* Sports and Outdoor Activities, below).

During the summer months, the **Alpine Slide** at Ski Bowl, just across Highway 26 from Government Camp, gives the intrepid a chance to whiz down the slopes in a European-style toboggan run. This is heady stuff, with a marvelous view. *Hwy. 26 at milepost 53, tel. 503/272–3206. Admission: $18 adults, $12 children 11 or younger. Open June–Sept., daily 9–dusk.*

④⓪ **Bend,** a city of 20,000 sits very nearly in the center of Oregon, about two hours southeast of Mt. Hood. It occupies a countryside many visitors wouldn't even recognize as Oregon: a tawny high desert plateau, perfumed with juniper and surrounded by 10,000-foot Cascade peaks. Called Bend because it was built on Farewell Bend in the Deschutes River—here an easy-flowing river compared to the roaring cataract it will become a few miles downstream—the city is a good fueling-up spot and a nightlife mecca. It's filled with decent restaurants, dance bars, pro shops and rental places, and a surprising number of good reasonable hostelries.

While in Bend, visit the **High Desert Museum,** where you can walk through a stone-age Indian campsite; a pioneer wagon camp; a groaning, echoing old mine; an Old West boardwalk; and other lovingly detailed dioramas, complete with authentic relics, sounds, and even odors. There are outstanding exhibits on local Native American cultures, as well. The high point of the complex is the 150-acre outdoor section, which features fat porcupines, baleful birds of prey, and crowd-pleasing river otters at play aboveground and underwater. *59800 S. Hwy. 97, 6 mi south of Bend, tel. 503/382–4754. Admission: $5 adults,*

$4.50 senior citizens, $2.50 children 5–12. Open daily 9–5; closed major holidays.

Sports and Outdoor Activities

Beaches The Columbia River is lined with sandy beaches, the most famous at **Rooster Rock State Park** (tel. 503/695–2261), where both nudists and conventional bathers soak up the sun. There is a $2-per-vehicle fee on weekends and holidays from Memorial Day through Labor Day.

Bicycling With its wide bicycle path paralleling I–84, the entire length of the gorge is suitable for bicycling. The terrain is generally flat, but expect stiff and constant winds from the east. The Bend area offers many memorable venues for cyclists, including the entire **Sunriver complex** (tel. 503/593–1221), with 26 miles of paved bike paths and rentals available. Also, Highway 97 north to the **Crooked River Gorge** and the spectacular **Smith Rocks** promise breathtaking scenery and a good workout.

Canoeing and Rafting The **Deschutes River** flows north from the Mt. Thielsen Wilderness near Crater Lake, gaining volume and momentum as it nears its rendezvous with the Columbia River at The Dalles. Its upper stretches, particularly those near Sunriver and Bend, are placid and suitable for leisurely canoeing. The stretch between Madras and Maupin offers some of Oregon's most famous white-water rafting. Because of heavy use, this portion of the Deschutes is accessible by permit only; for details, call the **Central Oregon Recreation Association** (tel. 503/389–8799).

Skiing
Cross-country There are nearly 120 miles of cross-country ski trails in the **Mt. Hood National Forest;** try the trailheads at Government Camp, Trillium Lake, or the Cooper Spur Ski Area, on the mountain's northeast flank. The **Deschutes National Forest,** surrounding Bend, is even richer in Nordic trails, with more than 165 miles of them at last count. The **Mt. Bachelor Nordic Center** (tel. 503/382–2442), surrounded by 36 miles of trails, is an excellent place to begin. **Summit Ski Area** (tel. 503/382–2442) and **Ski Bowl/Multipor** (tel. 503/272–3206), among other resorts, can supply cross-country rentals, accessories, maps, and guidebooks. For ski conditions call 503/222–2211, 503/222–BOWL, 503/227–SNOW, or 503/272–3351.

Downhill **Cooper Spur Ski Area,** on the eastern slope of Mt. Hood, caters to families and has two rope tows and a T-bar. The longest run is ⅝ mile, with a 500-foot vertical drop. *Follow signs from Hwy. 135 for 1 mi to ski area, tel. 503/386–4358. Facilities: rentals, instruction, repairs, ski shop, day lodge, snack bar, restaurant.*

Mt. Bachelor, which is generally regarded as one of the 10 best ski areas in the United States, is the Northwest's largest and most complete facility. The U.S. Ski Team trains here in the spring. There are 10 lifts, including one that takes skiers all the way to the mountain's 9,065-foot summit. Vertical drop is 3,100 feet; the longest of the dozens of runs is 2½ miles. *22 mi southwest of Bend off Hwy. 97 (follow signs), tel. 503/382–7888. Open weekdays 9–4, weekends 8–4. Facilities: 6 lodges (including the new mid-mountain Pine Marten Lodge at 7,700 feet), restaurants, bars, equipment rental and repair, ski school, day care, Nordic skiing, weekly races.*

Mt. Hood Meadows is Mt. Hood's largest ski resort, with more than 2,000 skiable acres, dozens of runs, seven double chairs, one triple chair, one quad chair, a top elevation of 7,300 feet, a vertical drop of 2,777 feet, and a longest run of 3 miles. *10 mi east of Government Camp on Hwy. 35, tel. 503/337-2222. Open Mon. and Tues. 9–4:30, Wed.–Sat. 9 AM–10 PM, Sun. 9–7. Facilities: day lodge, 3 restaurants, 2 lounges, ski school, equipment rental and repair.*

Ski Bowl, the closest ski area to Portland (only 50 miles away), boasts "the most extensive night skiing in America." The complex has 60 trails serviced by four double chairs and five rope tows, a top elevation of 5,050 feet, a vertical drop of 1,500 feet, and a longest run of 3 miles. *53 mi east of Portland, across Hwy. 26 from Government Camp, tel. 503/272-3206. Open Mon.–Thurs. 9 AM–10 PM, Fri. 9 AM–11 PM, Sat. 8:30 AM–11 PM, Sun. 8:30 AM–10 PM. Facilities: 2 day lodges, mid-mountain Warming Hut, 2 restaurants, 2 lounges, sleigh rides; summer: horseback rides, go-carts, mountain and alpine bike rentals.*

Summit Ski Area has one T-bar and two rope tows. Its longest run is a half-mile, with a 400-foot vertical drop. *Box 385, Government Camp, tel. 503/272-3351. Facilities: rentals, instruction, ski shop, day lodge, cafeteria, Nordic rentals and trails.*

Timberline, a full-service family-oriented ski area, is also a favorite of snowboard skiers. The U.S. Ski team conducts summer training at Timberline, a resort famous for its Palmer Chairlift, which takes skiers to a high glacier for summer skiing. There are five double chairs and one triple chair; top elevation is 8,500 feet, with 3,600 feet of vertical drop. *60 mi east of Portland on Hwy. 26, tel. 503/231-5400. Open Sun.–Tues. 9–5, Wed.–Sat. 9 AM–10 PM. Facilities: Timberline Lodge (see Dining and Lodging, below), day lodge with fast food, cross-country skiing, lessons, equipment rental and repair.*

Dining and Lodging

Dining and Lodging ratings correspond to price charts quoted for Portland restaurants and hotels.

Bend
Dining

Le Bistro. The best restaurant in Bend has prices to match the quality. The menu features traditional French cuisine with an emphasis on fresh Oregon meat and seafood. Try the critics' choices, the highly regarded seafood Wellington and grilled duck breast with wild plum sauce. *1203 N.E. 3rd St. (Hwy. 97S), tel. 503/389-7274. Reservations suggested. Dress: casual. DC, MC, V. Closed and lunch. Expensive.*

Stuft Pizza. This new restaurant, located in a pleasant Old West Victorian storefront, specializes in hand-tossed pizza with fresh ingredients. There's also a good salad bar and regional microbrews and wines. Entertainment, including comedy, is performed on weekends. Delivery service is also available. *125 Oregon Ave., tel. 503/382-4022. No reservations. Dress: casual. MC, V. Closed major holidays. Inexpensive–Moderate.*

Deschutes Brewery & Public House. This cheery, popular brew pub features upscale Northwest cuisine and local ales and wines. Give close attention to the extensive list of lunch and dinner specials on the blackboard over the open kitchen, and try the admirable Black Butte Porter. Portions are large. *1044*

N.W. Bond St., tel. 503/382–9242. No reservations. Dress: casual. MC, V. Inexpensive.

Lodging **Lara House Bed & Breakfast Inn.** This nicely restored former boardinghouse is in a residential district overlooking Drake Park and Mirror Pond, a five-minute walk from downtown. The three spacious rooms—decorated in rose and cream—are furnished with regular mattresses or water beds. Public areas are sunny and inviting. *640 N.W. Congress St. (west on Franklin from Hwy. 97), 97701, tel. 503/388–4064. 3 rooms. Facilities: sauna, hot tub, private baths, fireplace. MC, V. Moderate.*

The Riverhouse. This 1970s hotel is a cut or two above what you'd expect to find for the very reasonable price. The surprisingly large, well-appointed guest rooms are furnished in contemporary oak, and many have river views (well worth the extra $4 charge). Perhaps the best feature is the sound of the rushing Deschutes River that you can hear from your room. *3075 N. Hwy. 97, 97701, tel. 503/389–3111 or 800/547–3928. Facilities: 3 restaurants, lounge, entertainment, indoor pool, weight room, sauna, Jacuzzi, riverside jogging trail. AE, D, DC, MC, V. Moderate.*

Cascade Locks **Cascade Inn.** This fast-food–style restaurant serves up break-
Dining fast, lunch, and dinner, which can be eaten at the counter or in the booths. Highlighting the list of home-cooked specials is the Captain's Platter, which includes prawns, fresh fish, oysters, and clams. *Columbia Gorge Ctr., tel. 503/374–8340. No reservations. Dress: casual. AE, D, MC, V. Inexpensive.*

Char Burger Restaurant. In the 225-seat dining room overlooking the Columbia River you can enjoy a variety of hamburgers plus salmon, seafood, and steak dinners and a full breakfast menu. Indian arrowhead collections, rifles, and wagon wheel chandeliers provide a western motif. Also on the premises is a gift shop and bakery. *714 S.W. Wanapa St., tel. 503/374–8477. Dress: casual. Reservations required for Sam Hills Den, which serves Sunday brunch. MC, V. Closed Thanksgiving and Christmas.*

Lodging **Scandian Motor Lodge.** Oregon pine furniture and wood paneling, colorful bedspreads, and Scandinavian wall hangings brighten otherwise standard but inexpensive rooms. *Box 398, Columbia Gorge Ctr. 97014, tel. 503/374–8417. 30 rooms with showers, no bath. Facilities: adjacent to restaurant, lounge, beauty shop, and general store. AE, DC, MC, V. Inexpensive.*

The Dalles **Ole's Supper Club.** Local folk like this establishment for its ex-
Dining cellent food, friendly and competent service, and its straightforward, no-nonsense approach. The menu, which includes Western-style food with a Continental twist, features specialties from thick slabs of prime rib to veal Oscar. It's hard to go wrong when choosing an entrée, especially when it's accompanied with a selection from the excellent wine list. *2620 W. 2nd St., tel. 503/296–6708. Reservations advised. Dress: casual. MC, V. Closed Sun., Mon., and lunch. Moderate.*

Lodging **Williams House Inn.** This Victorian home, furnished with antiques, is on the Register of National Historic Places. Sitting on 3 acres of landscaped grounds, its accommodations include a three-room suite and two rooms, each with a private balcony. *608 W. 6th St., 97058, tel. 503/296–2889. 3 rooms. AE, D, MC, V. Moderate.*

Hood River
Dining

Chianti's Ristorante. This cheerful, slightly New Wave Italian place offers both traditional pastas and more intriguing items such as its linguini Singapore (angel-hair pasta tossed with shrimp, chicken, vegetables, curry, and cream). There's a deck and outdoor barbecue so patrons can enjoy Hood River's long, warm summers. *Corner of 6th and Cascade Sts., tel. 503/386–5737. No reservations. Dress: casual. AE, MC, V. Closed lunch. Moderate.*

The Mesquitery. You'll get lean, healthy beef, chicken, and pork—grilled over aromatic mesquite—without the usual rich, cloying sauces. Instead, the owners emphasize fresh herbs and tangy marinades, with satisfying results. There's also a modest wine and beer list at this sunny, Western-flavored restaurant. *1219 12th St. (atop the hill south of the downtown core), tel. 503/386–2002. No reservations. Dress: casual. MC, V. Inexpensive–Moderate.*

White Cap Brew Pub. This modest brewery, with its glass-walled brew pub and windswept deck overlooking the Columbia, won major awards in Denver (in 1989) at the Great American Beer Festival. The food tends to hearty pub fare, but the sandwiches are substantial and the beers are outstanding. *506 Columbia St. (in the old Diamond cannery overlooking downtown Hood River), tel. 503/386–2247. No reservations. Dress: casual. No credit cards. Inexpensive.*

Lodging

Best Western-Hood River Inn. This modern hotel, built on the river within paddling distance of Hood River's Columbia Gorge Sailpark, is the address of choice for visiting windsurfers. Be sure to ask for a room with a river view. *1108 E. Marina Way, 97031, tel. 503/386–2200 or 800/828–7873. 150 rooms. Facilities: restaurant, bar, live entertainment, outdoor pool, river access. AE, D, DC, MC, V. Moderate.*

Hood River Hotel. This local landmark, built in 1913 and abandoned for more than 20 years, reopened in December 1989 after undergoing a floor-to-ceiling renovation. The results are spectacular. Public areas are rich in beveled glass, warm wood, and tasteful jade-and-cream-color fabrics. Each room is unique, but all have bare fir floors softened by Oriental carpets, four-poster beds, and skylights. There's a lively lobby bar and a Mediterranean-flavored kitchen, plus—a thoughtful touch—plenty of locked storage for sailboarders. *102 Oak St., 97031, tel. 503/386–1900. 41 rooms with private bath, plus 8 suites with kitchens and room for 5. Facilities: restaurant, outdoor café, entertainment, bar. AE, D, DC, MC, V. Moderate.*

★ **Lakecliff Estate.** This four-room bed-and-breakfast inn, just up the road from the Columbia Gorge Hotel, was the summer home of architect A. E. Doyle, who designed Portland's Classic Revival public library, U.S. Bank Building, and the Multnomah Falls Lodge. The 1908 house, built on a cliff overlooking the river, is beautifully maintained and exceptionally comfortable. A pleasant deck at the back of the house and wood-burning fireplaces in three of the rooms ensure a relaxing stay. *3820 Westcliff Dr. (exit 62), 97031, tel. 503/386–7000. 4 rooms. Facilities: restaurant, bar. MC, V. Moderate.*

Dining and Lodging

Columbia Gorge Hotel. The grande dame of gorge hotels, built by lumber baron Simon Benson as the final destination of his Scenic Highway, was restored to its original magnificence in 1979. The ambience is a bit florid, but the major attraction—the 208-foot-high waterfall—is magnificent. Public areas are decorated in coral, green, and rose, and guest rooms reveal lots of brass, wood, and antiques. Rooms with two beds overlook the formal gardens. A huge seven-course breakfast—the World Famous Farm Breakfast—is included in the price of a room (nonguests pay $22.95 for the meal). While watching the sun set on the Columbia River, you can dine on breast of pheasant with pear wine, hazelnuts, and cream; grilled venison; breast of duck; Columbia River salmon; and sturgeon. *4000 Westcliff Dr. (take exit 62), 97031, tel. 503/386–5586 or 800/345–1921. 46 rooms with private bath. Facilities: restaurant, lounge, gardens, waterfall. AE, DC, MC, V. Very Expensive.*

Mt. Hood Lodging

Valu-Inn/Mt. Hood. The inn opened in 1990, and although everything looks and smells new, it also has a comfortable, relaxed feel. The Mt. Hood National Forest is outside the east windows; rooms facing the southwest are great for watching the spectacle of night skiing at Ski-Bowl, which is literally across the street. Accommodations come in a variety of sizes, from roomy standards to king-size suites with refrigerators and Jacuzzis to double queens with kitchenettes. *87450 Government Camp Loop, 97028, tel. 503/272–3205. 55 rooms; handicapped and nonsmoking rooms available. Facilities: covered parking, laundry facilities, spa, free ski lockers, ski tuning room, Continental breakfast. AE, D, DC, MC, V. Expensive.*

Dining and Lodging
★

Timberline Lodge. This National Historic Landmark, which has withstood howling winter storms on an exposed flank of the mountain for more than 50 years, still manages to warm guests with its hospitality, hearty food, and guest rooms with fireplaces. Built as a WPA project during the Depression, everything about the lodge has a hand-crafted, rustic feel, from the wrought-iron chairs with rawhide seats to the massive hand-hewn beams. The elegant Cascade Dining Room features expertly prepared cuisine made from the freshest Oregon products. *Follow the signs from Hwy. 26 a few mi east of Zig Zag; Timberline 97028, tel. 503/272–3311 or 800/547–1406. 59 rooms, some with fireplaces. Facilities: restaurant, bar, downhill and cross-country skiing, heated outdoor pool, sauna, spa. AE, MC, V. Expensive.*

Troutdale Dining

Multnomah Falls Lodge. The lodge, with high vaulted ceilings and classic stone fireplaces, was built in 1925. Freshwater trout, salmon, and a platter of prawns, halibut, and sturgeon are specialties. In the lounge you can sample Columbia Gorge wines and a huckleberry daiquiri. A gift shop and nature center are part of the complex. *Hwy. I–84 and Columbia River Scenic Hwy., tel. 503/695–2376. Reservations accepted. Dress: casual but neat. AE, MC, V. Inexpensive–Moderate.*

Welches Dining

The Chalet Swiss. The atmosphere is authentically alpine in this country-Swiss restaurant, but it's the food that will make you want to yodel. From the creamy fondue to the nutty *buendnerfleisch*—tissue-thin slices of dry-cured beef—to the rich sautées and fresh seafood, the kitchen displays a sure and artful hand. *Hwy. 26 at Welches Rd., tel. 503/622–3600. Reservations suggested. Dress: casual. AE, DC, MC, V. Closed Mon., Tues., and lunch. Moderate.*

Dining and Lodging

The Resort at The Mountain. This sprawling resort complex, nestled among the burly Cascade foothills, has changed hands more often than a track baton. Still, it offers the mountain's most complete resort facilities, with attractive modern public areas and reasonably well-appointed rooms. With the last renovation—in 1990—came the Scottish motif, including tartans on lounge tables and light pink-and-teal floral patterns in guest rooms. Accommodations include standard rooms, huge deluxe rooms, and limited numbers of two-bedroom condos. The Highland Dining Room features Northwest cuisine, including fillet of salmon with fresh herbs and Pinot Noir wine, venison with black currant sauce, and quail sautéed with mustard. *68010 E. Fairway Ave. (follow the signs from Hwy. 26), 97067, tel. 503/ 622–3101 or 800/669–7666. 158 rooms. Facilities: 2 restaurants, 2 lounges, live entertainment, 27 holes of golf, 6 tennis courts (2 with lights), indoor and outdoor pools, outdoor spas, sauna, health club, meeting facilities, bike paths and rentals. AE, DC, MC, V. Very Expensive.*

4 Western Oregon

Introduction

By Jeff Kuechle

Visitors to Oregon will discover that the state begins in a high, sage-scented desert plateau that covers nearly two-thirds of Oregon's 96,000 square miles (roughly the same size as the United Kingdom). Moving west, the landscape rises to 10,000-foot-high alpine peaks, meadows, and lakes; plunges to fertile farmland and forest; and ends, at last, at the cold, green Pacific.

Thus, within 90 minutes' drive from Portland or Eugene you can lose yourself in the recreational landscape of your choice: a thriving wine country; scenic and uncrowded ocean beaches; lofty, snow-silvered mountain wilderness; or a monolith-studded desert used as a backdrop for many a Hollywood western. Oregonians, who have been called both the hardest-working and the hardest-playing Americans, take full advantage of this bounty. They are uncomplicated people, with down-to-earth ideals. There is a story, never confirmed, that early pioneers arriving at a crossroads of the Oregon Trail found a pile of gold quartz or pyrite pointing the way south to California. The way north, on the other hand, was marked by a hand-lettered sign: TO OREGON. Thus, Oregonians like to think that the more literate of the pioneers found their way here, while the fortune hunters continued south.

It was, however, the promise—and achievement—of wealth that quite naturally fueled Oregon's early exploration. In 1792, Robert Gray, an American trading captain, followed a trail of debris and muddy water inland and discovered the Columbia River. Shortly thereafter, British Army Lieutenant William Broughton was dispatched to investigate Gray's find, and he sailed as far upriver as the rapids-choked mouth of the Columbia River Gorge.

Within a few years, a thriving seaborne fur trade sprang up, with both American and British entrepreneurs exchanging baubles, cloth, tools, weapons, and liquor with the natives for high-quality beaver and sea-otter pelts. By 1804, American explorers Meriwether Lewis and William Clark had arrived at the site of present-day Astoria after their epic overland journey, spurring an influx of white pioneers—clerks, trappers, and traders—sent by John Jacob Astor's Pacific Fur Company in 1810. They came to claim the land from the unfortunate natives for the United States and to trade for furs. The trading part was accomplished readily enough, but the massive fir trees—some so huge that the clasped arms of 10 men couldn't encircle their bases—proved formidable, and after two months Astor's men had managed to clear just an acre.

But the "soft gold" of the fur trade proved an irresistible attraction. The English disputed American claims to the territory, on the basis of Broughton's exploration, and soon after the War of 1812 began, they negotiated the purchase of Astoria from Astor's company. It wasn't until 1846 that they formally renounced their claims in the region with the signing of the Oregon Treaty.

"Oregon Country" grew tremendously between 1841 and 1860, as more than 50,000 settlers from the eastern United States made the journey over the plains in their 10- by 4-foot covered wagons. Most settled in the Willamette Valley, where the vast majority of Oregon's 2.7 million residents still live.

As settlers capitalized on gold rush San Francisco's need for provisions and other supplies, Oregon reaped its own riches and the lawless frontier gradually acquired a semblance of civilization. The territory's 50,000 residents voted down the idea of statehood three separate times, but in 1859, Oregon became the 33rd U.S. state.

Today the state's economy is still heavily dominated by timber (Oregon is America's largest producer of softwood), agriculture (hazelnuts, fruit, berries, wine, seed crops, livestock, and dairy products), and fishing. A major high-tech center known as the Silicon Forest, producing high-speed computer hardware and sophisticated instruments has taken root west of Portland in the Tualatin Valley, side by side with the wine industry. Its proximity to Pacific Rim nations such as Japan and Korea has made Portland one of the busiest port cities on the West Coast. Tourism grows in importance here every year—Oregonians have discovered that the scenic and recreational treasures that thrill them also thrill visitors from all over the world. To cater to visitors' needs, a sophisticated hospitality network has appeared, making Oregon more accessible than ever before.

Essential Information

Important Addresses and Numbers

Tourist Information
All Oregon tourist information centers are marked with blue *I* signs from main roads. Opening and closing times vary, depending on season and individual office; call ahead for hours.

Willamette Valley/Wine Country
Ashland Chamber of Commerce and Visitors Information Center (110 E. Main St., 97520, tel. 503/482–3486).
Corvallis Convention and Visitors Bureau (420 N.W. 2nd St., 97330, tel. 503/757–1544).
Eugene-Springfield Convention & Visitors Bureau (305 W. 7th Ave., Eugene 97440, tel. 800/452–3670; 503/484–5307 or 800/547–5445 outside OR.).
Grant's Pass Visitor & Convention Bureau (1501 N.E. 6th St., 97526, tel. 503/476–5510 or 800/547–5927).
McMinnville Chamber of Commerce (417 N. Adams St., 97128, tel. 503/472–6196).
Roseburg Visitors Information Center (410 S.E. Spruce St., 97470, tel. 503/672–2648).
Salem Convention & Visitors Center (Mission Mill Village, 1313 Mill St. SE, 97301, tel. 503/581–4325).

The Oregon Coast
Astoria Area Chamber of Commerce (111 W. Marine Dr., 97103, tel. 503/325–6311).
Brookings Harbor Chamber of Commerce (97949 Shopping Center Ave., 97415, tel. 503/469–3181).
Cannon Beach Chamber of Commerce (2nd and Spruce Sts., 97110, tel. 503/436–2623).
Florence Area Chamber of Commerce (270 Hwy. 101, 97439, tel. 503/997–3128).
Lincoln City Visitors Center (3939 N.W. Hwy. 101, 97367, tel. 503/994–8378 or 800/452–2151).
Greater Newport Chamber of Commerce (555 S.W. Coast Hwy., 97365, tel. 503/265–8801 or 800/262–7844).
North Bend Tourist Information Center (1380 Sherman St., 97459, tel. 503/756–4613).

Oregon

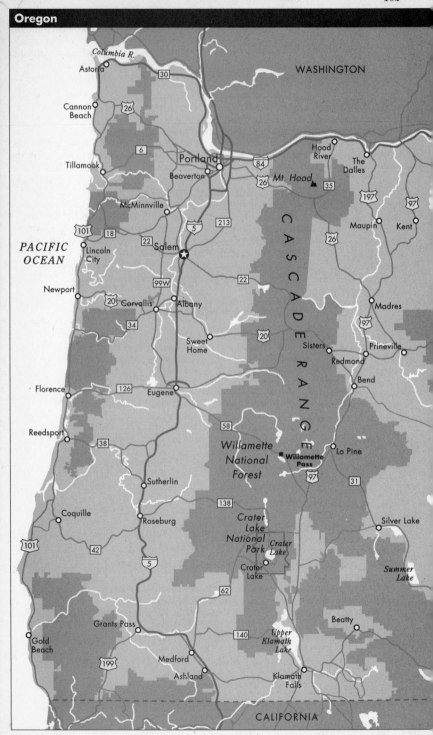

WASHINGTON

Columbia R.

Astoria

Cannon
Beach

30

26

6

Tillamook

Portland

Beaverton

Hood
River

The
Dalles

84

26 Mt. Hood

35

197

97

McMinnville

5

213

Maupin

Kent

C
A
S
C
A
D
E

26

PACIFIC
OCEAN

101

18

22 Salem

Lincoln
City

Newport

20

Corvallis

99W

Albany

22

Madras

97

Prineville

34

Sweet
Home

20

Sisters

Redmond

Florence

126

Eugene

R
A
N
G
E

Bend

Reedsport

38

58

Willamette
National
Forest

Willamette
Pass

La Pine

97

31

Sutherlin

Coquille

Roseburg

138

Crater
Lake
National
Park

Crater
Lake

Silver Lake

42

101

5

Crater
Lake

Summer
Lake

Grants Pass

62

Beatty

Gold
Beach

199

140

Upper
Klamath
Lake

Medford

Ashland

Klamath
Falls

CALIFORNIA

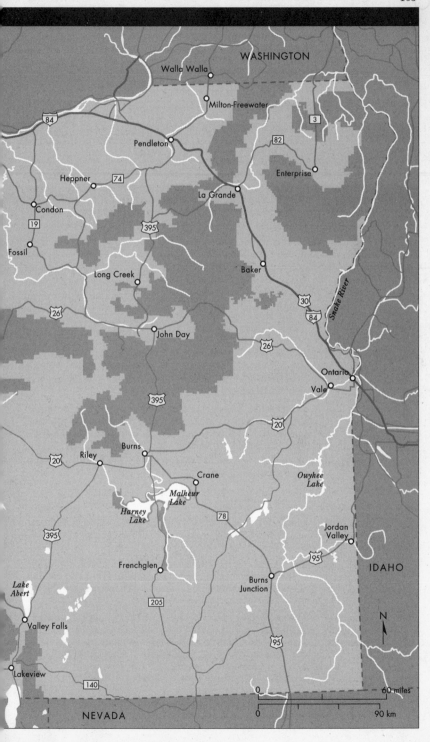

Seaside Visitors Bureau (7 N. Roosevelt Ave., 97138, tel. 503/738–6391).
Tillamook Chamber of Commerce (3705 Hwy. 101 N, 97141, tel. 503/842–7525).
Yachats Chamber of Commerce (441 Hwy. 101, 97498, tel. 503/547–3530).

Emergencies In most parts of the state, calling 911 will summon **police, fire,** or **ambulance** services; dialing "0" will bring the operator. In some rural areas, it may be necessary to dial the **Oregon State Police** at 800/452–7888.

Arriving and Departing by Plane

Airports and Airlines **Eugene Airport** (tel. 503/687–5430), the best mid-valley air destination, is serviced by American (tel. 503/342–5300), Horizon (tel. 800/547–9308), United (tel. 800/241–6522), United Express (tel. 800/241–6522), and USAir (tel. 503/345–5300).

Farther south, **Jackson County Airport** (tel. 503/772–8068), in Medford, is serviced by Horizon (tel. 800/547–9308), United (tel. 800/241–6522), United Express (tel. 800/241–6522), and USAir (tel. 503/773–9400).

Most communities along the Oregon Coast have municipal airports, but there is no major commercial service anywhere on the coast.

Arriving and Departing by Car, Train, and Bus

By Car If you are entering Oregon from the north or south, take I–5, which runs 300 miles through the Willamette Valley and the heart of Oregon. Entering from the east, take I–84, which runs from the Idaho border to Portland.

By Bus **Greyhound/Trailways** (call local listing) services the larger towns throughout the state, including Eugene (987 Pearl St., tel. 503/344–6265), La Grande (2108 Cove Ave., tel. 503/963–5165), and Medford (212 Bartlet St., tel. 503/779–2103).

By Train **Amtrak** (tel. 800/USA–RAIL) services larger towns along the I–5 and I–85 corridors.

Getting Around

By Car
Oregon Coast **Highway 101** runs the length of the coast, through vistas of shore pine and churning waves, sometimes turning inland for a few miles, then rewarding you with an awesome coastal vista.

Three Capes Loop leaves Highway 101 at Tillamook and winds past the dense forests and windswept cliffs of three protruding peninsulas: Capes Meares, Lookout, and Kiwanda (*see* The Oregon Coast in Exploring, below).

Willamette Valley/Wine Country **Highway 34** leaves I–5 just south of Albany and heads west, past Corvallis and into the Coast Range, where it follows the fish-filled Alsea River. Watch for a sign marked Alsea Falls/South Fork Road/Monroe, a mile south of Alsea. It will take you to the lovely Alsea Falls, where salmon in the spring and steelhead in the fall make prodigious leaps to clear the falls.

Highway 138 leads you through the spectacular waterfall country of the Umpqua River, east of Roseburg (watch for signs along the road), to the back door of Crater Lake National Park (*see* National and State Parks, below); in the winter, however, the road to Crater Lake is closed.

By Bus **Greyhound** (check local listing) bus routes criss-cross the state from the I–5 and I–84 corridors to the Highway 101 coastal route and Highways 20 and 97 in central and eastern Oregon. Be warned, however, that buses—particularly those running on the less-populated routes—leave sporadically and at inconvenient hours.

By Train **Amtrak's** (tel. 800/USA–RAIL) *Coast Starlight* follows I–5 south to Eugene, then enters the rugged Cascades at Oakridge; from there it follows Highwys 58 and 97 south past Diamond Peak and Crater Lake, on its way to California. The *Pioneer* runs daily from Portland to the Columbia Gorge, and parallels I–84 to the Idaho border and beyond.

Guided Tours

Orientation **Gray Line Sightseeing Tours** (Box 17306, Portland 97217, 503/285–9845) offers guided tours of scenic Oregon for both individuals and groups. Regular destinations include the Mt. Hood Loop, Oregon Coast, and Crater Lake.

Special-Interest A copy of "Discover Oregon Wineries," the free map and guide published by the **Oregon Wine Center** (1200 N.W. Front Ave., Suite 400, Portland 97209, tel. 503/228–8336), is an indispensable tool for touring wineries. It provides profiles and service information about each winery and is available at no charge where Oregon wine is sold.

Exploring

Tour 1: The Oregon Coast

Numbers in the margin correspond to points of interest on the Oregon Coast and Willamette Valley/Wine Country map.

Oregon has 300 miles of white-sand beach, not a grain of which is privately owned. Highway 101 parallels the coast from Astoria south to California, past stunning monoliths of sea-tortured rock, brooding headlands, hidden beaches, haunted lighthouses, tiny ports, and, of course, the Pacific, a gleaming gunmetal gray stretching to the horizon. With its charming hamlets (Coos Bay–North Bend–Charleston, the largest metropolis on the coast, has only 25,000 inhabitants) and endless small hotels and resorts, the Oregon Coast seems to have been created with pleasure in mind. That's even more true today, as the awesome forests and salmon runs that once produced immense fortunes dwindle and disappear. Now the locals pursue tourists who come for the endless miles of empty beaches, deep-sea charter fishing, golf, cycling, hiking, shopping, and eating.

Astoria to Newport Our journey begins in **Astoria,** where the mighty Columbia River meets the Pacific. Astoria, founded in 1811, was named for John Jacob Astor, then America's wealthiest man, who financed the original fur-trading colony here.

❶

More than 2,000 ships have been lost at the mouth of the Columbia, where the river's powerful current meets the ocean surge over shallow sandbanks. Settlers built sprawling Victori-

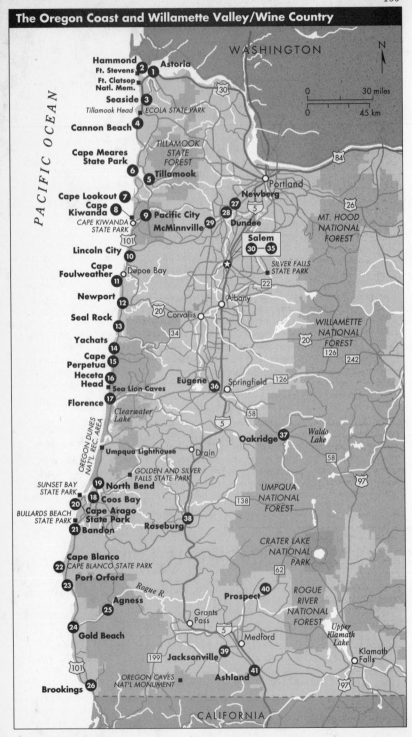

The Oregon Coast and Willamette Valley/Wine Country

WASHINGTON

PACIFIC OCEAN

0 — 30 miles
0 — 45 km

Hammond
Ft. Stevens
Ft. Clatsop
Natl. Mem.
Astoria

Seaside
Tillamook Head
ECOLA STATE PARK

Cannon Beach

TILLAMOOK
STATE
FOREST

**Cape Meares
State Park**
Tillamook

Cape Lookout
**Cape
Kiwanda**
CAPE KIWANDA
STATE PARK
Pacific City

Portland
Newberg

McMinnville
Dundee

Lincoln City
Depoe Bay

**Cape
Foulweather**

Salem
30 — 35

SILVER FALLS
STATE PARK

Newport

Albany

Seal Rock

Corvallis

Yachats

WILLAMETTE
NATIONAL
FOREST

**Cape
Perpetua**

**Heceta
Head**
Sea Lion Caves

Florence

Eugene
Springfield

MT. HOOD
NATIONAL
FOREST

Clearwater
Lake

OREGON DUNES NATL. REC. AREA

Umpqua Lighthouse
Drain

Oakridge
Waldo
Lake

GOLDEN AND SILVER
FALLS STATE PARK

SUNSET BAY
STATE PARK
North Bend
Coos Bay
**Cape Arago
State Park**
BULLARDS BEACH
STATE PARK
Bandon

UMPQUA
NATIONAL
FOREST

Roseburg

Cape Blanco
CAPE BLANCO STATE PARK
Port Orford

CRATER LAKE
NATIONAL
PARK

Agness

Rogue R.

Prospect

ROGUE
RIVER
NATIONAL
FOREST

Grants
Pass

Gold Beach

Medford

Upper
Klamath
Lake

Klamath
Falls

Brookings
OREGON CAVES
NAT'L MONUMENT
Jacksonville
Ashland

CALIFORNIA

an houses on the flanks of Coxcomb Hill, many of which have
since been restored and are no less splendid as bed-and-breakfast inns. Modern Astoria is a placid amalgamation of turn-of-
the-century small town and hard-working port city. With its
museums, inns, and fine recreational offerings, it should be one
of the Northwest's prime tourist destinations. Yet Astoria remains relatively undiscovered, even by Portlanders.

The **Columbia River Maritime Museum,** located on the downtown waterfront, is the single most interesting man-made tourist attraction on the Oregon Coast. It beguiles visitors—
particularly young ones—with exhibits ranging from the
bridge of the World War II submarine U.S.S. *Rasher* (complete
with working periscopes) and the fully operational U.S. Coast
Guard lightship *Columbia* to the personal belongings of some of
the ill-fated passengers of some of the ships that have been
wrecked here since 1811. *17th St., tel. 503/325–2323. Admission: $3 adults, $2 senior citizens, $1.50 children 6–18. Open
daily 9:30–5; closed Christmas, Thanksgiving.*

A mile up 16th Street from downtown, the **Astoria Column**—a
125-foot-high monolith atop Coxcomb Hill that was patterned
after Trajan's Column in Rome—rewards the 164-step spiral
stair climb with breathtaking views over Astoria, the Columbia River, the Coast Range, and the Pacific. *Follow signs from
downtown. Admission free. Open daily 9–dusk.*

Follow 16th Street downhill to Duane Street, then walk west
about 7 blocks to the **Flavel House,** a prim and proper Victorian
built between 1883 and 1885. The house's period furnishings,
many selected by Captain George Flavel, give insight into the
lifestyle of a wealthy 19th-century shipping tycoon. *441 8th St.,
tel. 503/325–2203. Admission: $4.50 adults, $3.50 senior citizens, $1 children 6–12. Open May–Sept., daily 10–5; Oct.–
Apr., daily 11–4.*

"Ocean in view! O! The joy!" recorded William Clark, standing
near this spot in the fall of 1805. After building a fort and
wintering over here, however, the explorers wrote "O! How
horriable is the day waves brakeing with great violence
against the shore . . . all wet and confined to our shelters." **Ft.
Clatsop National Memorial** is a faithful replica of the log stock-
ade depicted in Clark's journal. Park rangers dressed in period
garb, who perform such early 19th-century tasks as making
fire with flint and steel, lend an air of authenticity, as does the
damp and lonely ambience of the fort itself; self-guided tours
are permitted. *Follow the signs 6 mi south of Astoria on Hwy.
101, tel. 503/861–2471. Admission free. Open mid-June–Labor
Day, daily 8–6; rest of year, daily 8–5.*

To round out your historical view of the West Coast's largest
river, journey west on Highway 101, then follow signs to
Warrenton Drive toward Oregon's northwestern tip and **Ft.
➋ Stevens,** in **Hammond.** The earthworks of this 37-acre fortress
were mounded up during the Civil War, to guard the Columbia
against a rather improbable Confederate attack. During World
War II, Ft. Stevens became the only mainland U.S. military installation to come under enemy (Japanese submarine) fire since
the War of 1812. Today, the fort's abandoned gun mounts and
eerie subterranean bunkers are a memorable destination, especially for children. The corroded skeleton of the *Peter
Iredale,* a turn-of-the-century English four-master ship, pro-

trudes from the sand just west of the campground, stark evidence of the malevolence of the Pacific. The nearby state park offers 605 campsites. *Ft. Stevens State Park, Hwy. 101 (follow signs toward Hammond), tel. 503/861–2000. Admission free; summer guided truck tours of fort, $2, and underground Battery Mishler, $1.50. Open mid-May–Sept., daily 10–6; Oct.– mid-May, Wed.–Sun. 10–4.*

❸ For years, **Seaside,** 10 miles farther south on Highway 101, had a reputation as the sort of garish, arcade-filled town you would expect to find near Atlantic City, New Jersey. In the past decade it has cleaned up its act, and it now supports a bustling tourist trade with a cluster of hotels, condominiums, and restaurants surrounding the long beach. A 2-mile boardwalk parallels the shore and the stately old beachfront homes. Because it's only 90 miles from Portland, Seaside is often crowded, so it is not the place to go if you crave solitude. Be especially wary in July, when the annual Miss Oregon Pageant is in full swing, and in February, during the Trail's End Marathon.

❹ For more contemplative surroundings, go 10 miles south to Seaside's refined, artistic alter ego—**Cannon Beach**—a more mellow but trendier place for Portlanders to take in the sea air. With its tasteful weathered cedar downtown shopping district and beautiful beachfront homes, this tiny hamlet (population 1,200) is undoubtedly one of the most charming on the coast. However, the Carmel of the Oregon Coast is expensive, crowded, and afflicted with a subtle, moneyed hauteur that may grate on less-aristocratic nerves.

The town got its name when a cannon from the wrecked schooner U.S.S. *Shark* washed ashore in 1846 (the piece is now on display a mile east of town on Highway 101). Towering over the broad sandy beach is **Haystack Rock,** a vast 235-foot-high monolith that is supposedly the most-photographed feature of the Oregon Coast. The rock is temptingly accessible during some low tides, but don't be beguiled: The Coast Guard regularly airlifts stranded climbers from its precipitous sides, and falls have claimed numerous lives over the years. Every May the town hosts the **Cannon Beach Sandcastle Contest,** when thousands throng the beach to view imaginative and often startling works in this most transient of art forms. While in the town, take a walk down the main thoroughfare, **Hemlock Street** (*see* Shopping, below), a fine shopping district of art galleries, clothiers, and gift shops.

About a mile north of Cannon Beach is **Tillamook Head** and **Ecola State Park,** a popular playground of sea-sculpted rock, sandy beach, tide pools, green headlands, and panoramic views. Less-crowded **Indian Beach,** in the same park complex, is one of Oregon's rare rocky beaches. With its small, often deserted cove, mussel-encrusted rocks, and tide pools, this beach is a welcome departure from crowded Ecola.

A brisk 2-mile hike leads to the 1,100-foot-high viewpoint atop Tillamook Head. From there you'll see the old **Tillamook Rock Light Station,** which stands a mile or so out to sea. The lonely beacon, built in 1881 on a straight-sided rock, towers 41 feet above the surrounding ocean. In 1957, the lighthouse was abandoned; it is now a columbarium, or repository for the cremated remains of those who yearn for the sea.

Heading south again on Highway 101, follow signs for 10 miles to the trailhead at **Neahkahnie Mountain.** Cryptic carvings on beach rocks near here, and centuries-old Native American legends of shipwrecked Europeans, gave rise to a tale that the survivors of a wrecked Spanish mystery galleon buried a fortune in doubloons somewhere on the side of this 1,661-foot-high mountain. The treasure has never been found, but the trail to the summit provides the intrepid with a different sort of reward: unobstructed views over surf, sand, forest, and mountain. Those who visit in December and April often see pods of gray whales on their annual 14,000-mile migration.

Adventurous travelers will enjoy a sojourn at **Oswald West State Park** at the mountain's base, one of the best-kept secrets on the Pacific coast. Park your car in the lot on Highway 101 and use a park-provided wheelbarrow to trundle your camping gear down a half-mile trail. There you'll find 36 campsites, surrounded by Cape Falcon's lush old-growth forest. The beach, with its caves and little-visited tide pools, is spectacular. There are no reservations for the campsites, but a call to the park office (tel. 503/238–7488) will yield information on vacancies.

More than 600,000 visitors annually press their noses against the spotlessly clean windows at the **Tillamook County Creamery,** the largest cheese-making plant on the West Coast. Here the rich milk from the area's thousands of holstein and brown Swiss cows becomes fine Cheddar and Monterey Jack cheese, butter, and ice cream. There are wide display windows and exhibits on the cheese-making process at the visitors' center, free samples, and, of course, a gift shop. *Hwy. 101, about 2 mi north of Tillamook, tel. 503/842–4481. Admission free. Visitors' center open mid-Sept.–May, daily 8–6; June–early Sept., daily 8–8.*

Not to be outdone, **Blue Heron French Cheese Company,** a mile closer to Tillamook specializes in French-style cheeses like Camembert and Brie, as well as their own variation, a mild, creamy-veined cheese called Camemblue. The factory gift shop also sells a selection of Oregon wine and other Oregon products, such as jams and mustards. *2001 Blue Heron Dr., watch for signs from Hwy. 101., tel. 503/842–8281. Tasting room open Memorial Day–Labor Day, daily 8–8; rest of year, daily 9–5.*

❺ **Tillamook,** south of Cannon Beach, is a sort of wet Wisconsin-on-the-Pacific. The town, situated about 2 miles inland, surrounded by rich dairyland, and blessed with abundant fresh and saltwater fishing, has some of the finest scenery on the Oregon Coast, which contributes to the placid atmosphere. It lacks the aristocratic charm of Cannon Beach but has much to offer the traveler in quest of a quiet, natural retreat. In Tillamook's 1905 county courthouse, the **Pioneer Museum** has marvelous exhibits on local natural history, Native Americans, pioneers, and logging, as well as a collection of military artifacts dating back two centuries. *2106 2nd St., tel. 503/842–4553. Admission: $1 adults, 50¢ children 12–17, $5 family. Open Tues.–Sat. 8–5, Sun. and Mon. noon–5; closed Mon. Oct. 1–Mar. 15.*

Tillamook Bay, where the Miami, Kilchis, Wilson, Trask, and Tillamook rivers enter the Pacific, is a sportfishing mecca. The quarry includes silver and Chinook salmon, steelhead, sea-run cutthroat trout, bottom fish, the delectable Dungeness crab, mussels, oysters, and a variety of clams. There are abundant charter-fishing services available at **Garibaldi,** a mast-filled fishing harbor just north of Tillamook. For some of the best rock fishing in the state, try Tillamook Bay's **North Jetty.**

Leaving downtown Tillamook, going west via 3rd Street, you'll find the start of scenic **Three Capes Loop,** one of the coast's most rewarding driving experiences. Turning west on Bay Ocean Drive will take you past what was once the thriving resort town of **Bay Ocean.** More than 30 years ago, Bay Ocean washed into the sea, taking with it lots, houses, a bowling alley—almost everything. Still on the loop, at **Cape Meares State Park,** you'll have a chance to climb 100-year-old **Cape Meares Lighthouse,** open to the public from May through September. From the tower, there's a spectacular view over the cliff of the caves and the sea-lion rookery on the rocks below. A titanic, many-trunked Sitka spruce known as the Octopus Tree grows near the lighthouse parking lot.

Cape Lookout, next on the loop, has equally fine views, as well as a year-round campground. **Cape Kiwanda,** 15 miles farther south, is a favorite spot for hang gliders and surf watchers. Some of the world's best nature photographers have fallen in love with **Cape Kiwanda State Park,** where huge waves pound jagged sandstone cliffs and caves. The beach at **Pacific City,** a mile or two farther south, is one of the only places in the state where fishing dories (flat-bottom boats with high flaring sides) are launched directly into the surf, instead of from harbors or docks. During commercial salmon season in late summer, it's possible to buy salmon directly from fishermen.

If you continue south on Highway 101, you'll encounter **Lincoln City,** perhaps the single tackiest tourist trap on the coast. Here, unchecked commercial sprawl has cemented what was once a quaint collection of five smaller towns into a frenetic 7-mile strip of "factory outlet" malls, fast-food restaurants, tacky gift shops, convenience stores, and more than 50 motels. Lincoln City's only other real claim to fame is the 445-foot-long **D River,** stretching from its source in **Devil's Lake** to its mouth in the Pacific; *The Guinness Book of World's Records* lists this as the world's shortest river.

High above placid Siletz Bay, just south of Lincoln City, is **Salishan,** the most famous resort on the Oregon coast. This elegant and expensive collection of guest rooms, vacation homes, condominiums, restaurants, golf fairways, tennis courts, and covered walkways blends into a 750-acre forest preserve; if it weren't for the signs, you would hardly be able to find it.

The tiny (6-acre) harbor at **Depoe Bay** may look vaguely familiar; it was used as a setting for the Academy Award–winning film *One Flew Over the Cuckoo's Nest.* With its narrow channel and deep water, the bay is one of the most protected on the coast, and it supports a thriving fleet of commercial- and charter-fishing boats. The **Spouting Horn,** a natural cleft in the basalt cliffs on the waterfront, blasts seawater skyward during heavy weather.

If you take the **Otter Crest Loop** a mile or two south of Depoe Bay, you'll shortly arrive at **Cape Foulweather,** with its lighthouse gift shop and backward-leaning shore pines lending mute witness to the 100-mile-an-hour winds that strafe this exposed spot in winter. British explorer Captain James Cook named this 500-foot-high headland on a blustery March day in 1778.

Rejoining the highway near **Yaquina Head,** you'll find the northern city limits of **Newport,** a busy harbor and fishing town with 8,400 residents. Newport exists on two levels: the highway above, threading its way through the community's main business district; and the charming old bayfront below, which you'll find by heading east on Herbert Street. With its high-masted fishing fleet, well-worn buildings, art galleries and shops, fragrantly steaming crab kettles, and the finest collection of fresh seafood markets on the coast, Newport's bay front is an ideal place for an afternoon stroll. One of Oregon's most famous tourist attractions, the **Undersea Gardens,** gives visitors a glimpse of the world beneath the waves from its glass-walled, nautiluslike viewing chambers. Giant octopus, salmon, red snapper, crab, and ferociously ugly wolf eels are among the creatures on display. *250 S.W. Bay Blvd., tel. 503/265–2206. Admission: $5 adults, $4 senior citizens, $3 children 12–17, $2 children 5–11. Open mid-June–Labor Day, daily 9–8; Labor Day–mid-June, daily 10–5.*

Just across the Yaquina Bay is a different kind of underwater experience: Oregon State University's **Hatfield Marine Science Center.** Interpretive exhibits in the center's public aquarium explain the cycle of life in the North Pacific, as well as the natural history of the Yaquina estuary. The star of the show is the large octopus in a round low tank near the entrance—he seems as interested in human visitors as they are in him, and he has been known to reach up and gently stroke children's hands with his suction-tipped tentacles. *2030 Marine Science Dr. (head south across Yaquina Bay Bridge—Hwy. 101—and follow signs), tel. 503/867–0100. Admission free. Open Memorial Day–Labor Day, daily 10–6; Labor Day–Memorial Day, daily 10–4.*

Newport to Coos Bay South of Newport, following the highway, you'll enter a slower-paced, less-crowded section of the Oregon coast. The scenery, fishing, and other outdoor activities are just as rich as in the other towns along the way, but the commercialism and the crowds seem curiously absent.

At **Seal Rock,** chain-saw carving—a peculiar Oregon art form—reaches its pinnacle in one of the state's most unusual tourist attractions: **Sea Gulch,** a full-size ghost town inhabited by more than 300 fancifully carved wood figures. Carver Ray Kowalski wields his Stihl chain saw with virtuosity to create unique cowboys, Indians, hillbillies, trolls, gnomes, and other humorous figures. Visitors can watch him work in his adjoining studio. *East side of Hwy. 101 in Seal Rock, tel. 503/563–2727. Admission: $3.50 adults, $2.50 senior citizens, $2 children. Open daily 8–5.*

A few miles south of Seal Rock is **Yachats** (pronounced "Ya-hots"), an Indian word meaning "foot of the mountain." Among Oregon beach lovers, this tiny burg of 600 inhabitants has acquired a reputation disproportionate to its size. Yachats offers a microcosm of all the coastal pleasures: bed-and-breakfasts, excellent restaurants, deserted beaches, surf-pounded crags, fishing and crabbing. It is also one of the few places in the world where the silver smelt come inland. Every year, from May to September, hundreds of thousands of these delectable sardinelike fish swarm up the Yachats River, where dip-net fishermen eagerly await them. A community smelt-fry celebrates this bounty each July.

⑮ Three miles south of Yachats is **Cape Perpetua,** another lovely headland that towers hundreds of feet over the waves. Watch for the U.S. Forest Service Visitors Center on the east side of the highway, where you can obtain handy free maps of Cape Perpetua's miles of hiking trails, as well as of such geological features as the Devil's Churn, where the furious sea rushes into a volcanic fissure in the cliff.

⑯ Ten miles farther south, in **Heceta Head,** the lighthouse—visible for more than 21 miles—is the most powerful beacon on the Oregon coast. The structure is said to be haunted by the wife of a lighthouse keeper, who fell to her death from the cliffs shortly after the beacon was built in 1874. The building is currently being renovated by the forest service and is not open to the public at this time. Excellent views and photographic perspectives can be found at **Devil's Elbow State Park,** a few hundred yards to the south.

In 1880, a sea captain named Cox rowed a small skiff into a fissure in a 300-foot-high sea cliff. Inside, he was startled to discover a vaulted chamber in the rock, 125 feet high and 2 acres in area. Hundreds of massive sea lions—the largest bulls weighing 2,000 pounds or more—covered every available horizontal surface. Cox had no way of knowing it, but his discovery would eventually become one of the Oregon coast's most venerable and popular tourist attractions, known today as **Sea Lion Caves,** located about a mile south of Heceta Head. Visitors ride an elevator from the cliff-top ticket office down to the floor of the cavern, near sea level, to watch from above the antics of the fuzzy pups and their parents. An ancient sea-lion skeleton is on display, proof that these animals have lived here for many centuries. *91560 Hwy. 101N, tel. 503/547–3111. Admission: $5 adults, $3 children. Open Oct.–June, daily 9–6:30; July–Sept., daily 8–dusk.*

Six miles south of the caves is **Darlingtona Botanical Wayside,** another surefire child pleaser. Here, a half-mile nature walk leads through clumps of carnivorous, insect-catching cobra lilies, so named because they look like spotted cobras ready to strike. This park is most interesting in May, when the lilies are blooming. *Mercer Lake Rd., on the east side of Hwy. 101, no phone. Admission free.*

Just past Heceta Head, Highway 101 jogs inland, and the frowning headlands and cliffs of the north coast give way to the endless beaches and rolling dunes of the south. Here you'll en-
⑰ ter **Florence,** a popular destination for both tourists and retirees. The picturesque waterfront Old Town has restaurants, antiques stores, fish markets, and other wet-weather diversions.

Time Out While in Old Town, stop into **Mo's** (1436 "A" St., tel. 503/997–2185) for a rich creamy bowl of clam chowder and clear bayfront views. This coastal institution has been around for more than 40 years, and consistently provides the freshest seafood and friendly, down-home service.

Florence is the gateway to the **Oregon Dunes National Recreation Area,** a 41-mile swath of undulating camel-color sand. **Honeyman State Park,** 522 acres within the recreation area, is a popular base camp for the thousands of dune-buggy enthusiasts, mountain bikers, boaters, horseback riders, and dog-sledders (the dunes are an excellent training ground) who converge here. The dunes, some more than 500 feet high, are a vast and exuberant playground for children, particularly the sandy slopes surrounding cool **Cleawox Lake.** Facilities in the park include 381 campsites, 66 with full hookups, showers, electric stoves, and a boat ramp; there are more than 30 miles of hiking trails in the National Recreation Area. Reservations, particularly on weekends and holidays, are a must. Send request and $14 deposit by mail. *Park office, 84505 Hwy. 101, Florence 97439, tel. 503/997–3641.*

For coastal sportsmen, Winchester Bay's **Salmon Harbor** is always spoken of with reverence. A public pier, built especially for crabbers and fishermen, juts out over the bay and yields excellent results. The rockfishing from the **Winchester Bay** jetty is also popular. Salmon Harbor's excellent full-service marina was designed to provide everything an avid fisherman could possibly need, including a fish market in case the day's quest was unsuccessful. For further information, the Lower Umpqua Chamber of Commerce (tel. 503/271–3495) can assist you.

The first **Umpqua River Lighthouse,** built on the dunes at the mouth of the Umpqua River in 1857, lasted only four years before it toppled over in a storm. It took chagrined local residents 33 years to build another one. The "new" lighthouse, built on a bluff overlooking the south side of Winchester Bay, is still going strong, flashing a warning beacon out to sea every five seconds. The adjacent **Douglas County Coastal Visitors Center** has a museum featuring local history exhibits. The 50-acre **Umpqua Lighthouse Park** contains 500-foot sand dunes, the highest in the United States. *On Umpqua Hwy., west side of Hwy. 101, tel. 503/271–4631. Admission free. Hours vary, so phone ahead.*

18 **Coos Bay,** synonymous with the tall timbers that thrive here, is located 20 miles farther on Highway 101. The largest metropolitan area on the Oregon coast, it stands next to the largest natural harbor between the San Francisco Bay Area and Seattle's Puget Sound. Log trucks freighted with some of the biggest old-growth logs being cut anywhere in the world support Coos Bay's claim that it's still the world's largest lumber shipping port. But the glory days of the timber industry are over, and Coos Bay has begun to look in other directions, such as tourism, for economic prosperity.

19 Fortunately, the Coos Bay and **North Bend** metro area is also the gateway to some of the coast's most rewarding recreational experiences. For one, the Golden and Silver Falls State Park is where Glenn Creek pours over a high rock ledge deep in the old-growth forest. The 210-foot-high **Golden Falls** is the more forceful, but 200-foot-high **Silver Falls,** plunging over the same abyss a quarter-mile to the northwest, is perhaps more beautiful. *Take the Eastside-Allegany exit from Hwy. 101 at the south end of Coos Bay; follow signs to Golden and Silver Falls State Park, about 24 mi northeast.*

Coos Bay to Brookings Backtrack to Coos Bay and head west, following signs from Highway 101 to **Charleston,** a fishing village at the mouth of Coos Bay that has an almost Mediterranean quaintness about it. Four miles farther south, on Seven Devils Road, is the **South Slough National Estuarine Reserve,** where the rich and productive mud flats and tidal estuaries of Coos Bay support life ranging from algae to bald eagles to black bear. More than 300 species of birds have been sighted here; an interpretive center, guided walks, and nature trails give visitors a chance to see things up close. *Seven Devils Rd., tel. 503/888–5558. Admission free. Trails open daily dawn–dusk; interpretive center open Labor Day–Memorial Day, daily 8:30–4:30; Memorial Day–Labor Day, weekdays 8:30–4:30.*

Returning to Charleston, follow the Cape Arago Highway south toward **Sunset Bay State Park.** This placid semicircular lagoon, protected from the sea by overlapping fingers of rock, is the safest swimming beach on the Oregon coast. Leaving the park, you'll continue southbound to **Shore Acres State Park,** situated on the estate of lumber baron Louis J. Simpson. Today all that remains are the gardens, a beautifully landscaped swath of formal English and Japanese horticulture. *13030 Cape Arago Hwy., tel. 503/888–4902. Admission: $1 on weekends and holidays; otherwise free. Open daily 8–dusk.*

⓴ Just down the road from Shore Acres is **Cape Arago State Park** (end of Cape Arago Hwy., tel. 503/888–4902), surrounded by a trio of tide pool–pocked coves connected by short but steep trails. Here you'll find some of the richest and least-visited tidal rockery in the state.

㉑ Still traveling south on Highway 101, you'll reach **Bandon,** a small coastal village that bills itself as the Cranberry Capital of Oregon. Bandon, built above a walking beach with weathered monoliths, might be the most beautiful section along the coast. Follow the signs from Bandon south along Beach Loop Road, to **Face Rock Wayside** and descend a stairway to the sand, where you can watch the sunset through a veritable gallery of natural sculptures including Elephant Rock, Table Rock, and Face Rock. If the weather turns inclement, you might consider a stop at **Bullards Beach State Park,** which houses the photogenic **Bandon Lighthouse** as well as the **Bandon Historical Museum.** At the latter, a historic white clapboard coast guard station, you'll see exhibits on the three fires that have leveled Bandon. *1st St., tel. 503/347–2164. Admission: 50¢ adults, 25¢ children. Open Tues.–Sat. 10–4.*

㉒ About 20 miles south of Bandon you'll come to **Cape Blanco,** the westernmost point in the continental United States. **Cape Blanco Lighthouse,** accessible after a pleasant 6-mile drive from Highway 101 (follow signs), has been in continuous use since 1870. The 1,880-acre **Cape Blanco State Park** (tel. 503/332–6774) has campsites, hiking, and spectacular views of offshore rocks and reefs.

Many knowledgeable coastal travelers consider the stretch of
㉓ Highway 101 between **Port Orford** and Brookings (*see* below) to be the most beautiful in all of Oregon, perhaps on the entire Pacific coast. The ocean here is bluer and clearer—though not appreciably warmer—than it is farther north. The highway soars up green headlands, some hundreds of feet high, and past awesome sea-sculpted scenery: caves, towering arches, and

bridges including the man-made **Thomas Creek Bridge,** the highest span in Oregon. A word of caution: Take plenty of time to admire the scenery, but make use of the many turnouts and viewpoints along the way. This close to California, some stretches of Highway 101 are heavily trafficked, and rubber-necking can be dangerous. Ten-mile-long **Boardman State Park** offers particularly outstanding hiking trails and cliff-top views.

㉔ **Gold Beach,** about 20 miles north of the California border, is fa-mous mainly as the place the much-renowned Rogue River meets the ocean. Daily jet-boat excursions roar upstream from **Wedderburn,** Gold Beach's sister city across the bay, from late **㉕** spring to late fall. Some go to **Agness,** 32 miles upstream, where the riverside road ends and the wild and scenic portion of the Rogue begins. Other boats penetrate farther, to the wet-knuckle rapids at **Blossom Bar,** 52 miles upstream.

Gold Beach also marks the entrance to Oregon's banana belt, where mild, California-like temperatures take the sting out of winter and encourage a blossoming trade in lilies and daffodils. It's said that 90% of the pot lilies grown in the United States **㉖** come from a 500-acre area just inland from **Brookings.** You'll even see a few palm trees here, a rare sight in Oregon.

Brookings is equally famous as a commercial and sportfishing port at the mouth of the incredibly clear, startlingly turquoise-blue Chetco River. If anything, the Chetco is more highly es-teemed among fishermen and wilderness lovers alike than is the Rogue. A short jetty, popular with local crabbers and fish-ermen, offers easy and productive access to the river's mouth; salmon and steelhead running 20 pounds or larger are caught here. At **Loeb State Park**—located on the north bank of the Chetco, 10 miles east of Brookings (follow signs from Highway 101)—with its impressive grove of myrtlewood trees (they grow nowhere else in the world), you'll find 53 riverside campsites and some fine hiking trails, including one that leads to a hidden, little-known redwood grove.

Tour 2: Willamette Valley/Oregon Wine Country

During the 1940s and 1950s, researchers at Oregon State Uni-versity concluded that the Willamette Valley had the wrong cli-mate for the propagation of fine varietal wine grapes. Fortunately for wine lovers everywhere, the researchers' tech-niques were faulty, which has been proven by the success of Or-egon's burgeoning wine industry. More than 40 wineries dot the hills between Portland and Salem, and a dozen more are scattered from Newport along the I–5 corridor as far south as Ashland, on the California border. Their products—mainly cool-climate varietals like Pinot Noir, chardonnay, and Ries-ling—have won numerous gold medals in blind tastings against the best wines that California or Europe has to offer. Oregon's wine country occupies the wet, temperate trough between the Coast Range to the west and the Cascades to the east. The main concentration lies in the north, among the Willamette and Yamhill Valleys, near Portland. The warmer, drier Umpqua and Rogue Valleys, near Roseburg and Ashland—respective-ly—also produce their share of fine bottlings.

The best way to see the wine country here is to rent a car and map out your own itinerary. Strangely enough, there are no regularly scheduled bus tours at this time, though the Oregon

Wine Center (*see* Special Interest Tours in Guided Tours, above) may be able to arrange one for larger groups. Some of the state's most accomplished and hospitable wineries include (from the northern valley to the south) **Tualatin Vineyards** (Forest Grove, tel. 503/357–5005), **Shafer Vineyard Cellars** (Forest Grove, tel. 503/357–6604), **Montinore Vineyards** (Forest Grove, tel. 503/359–5012), **Ponzi Vineyards** (Beaverton, tel. 503/628–1227), **Rex Hill Vineyards** (Newberg, tel. 503/538–0666), **Veritas Vineyard** (Newberg, tel. 503/538–1470), **Autumn Wind Vineyard** (Gaston, tel. 503/538–6931), **Knudsen Erath** (Dundee, tel. 503/538–3318), **Yamhill Valley Vineyards** (McMinnville, tel. 503/843–3100), **Bethel Heights Vineyard** (Salem, tel. 503/581–2262), **Eola Hills Wine Cellars** (Rickreall, tel. 503/623–2405), **Tyee Wine Cellars** (Corvalis, tel. 503/753–8754), **Alpine Vineyards** (Alpine, tel. 503/424–5851), **Henry Estate Winery** (Umpaua, tel. 503/459–5120), **Hillcrest Vineyard** (Roseburg, tel. 503/673–3709), **Girardet Wine Cellars** (Roseburg, tel. 503/679–7252), and **Siskyou Vineyards** (Cave Junction, tel. 503/592–3727). For opening times and tour schedules, call in advance.

The following tour suggests sightseeing stops, but does not incorporate wineries. Those interested can fit one or two wineries from the above list into this itinerary. The tour begins in
㉗ **Newberg,** a graceful old pioneer town, located at a broad bend in the Willamette River about a half hour southwest of Portland. The oldest and most significant of its original structures is the **Hoover-Minthorne House,** boyhood home of President Herbert Hoover. Built in 1881, the beautifully preserved and well-landscaped frame house includes many of the original furnishings, as well as the woodshed that no doubt played a formative role in young "Bertie" Hoover's character. *115 S. River St., tel. 503/538–6629. Admission: $1.50 adults, $1 senior citizens. Open Mar.–Nov., Wed.–Sun. 1–4; Dec.–Feb., weekends 1–4.*

Driving south along Highway 99W, you'll pass through the
㉘ idyllic orchardland around **Dundee:** A haven of produce stands and tasting rooms—home to 90% of America's hazelnut crop.

㉙ Twelve miles farther southwest is **McMinnville**—the largest (population 16,000) and most sophisticated of wine-country towns—which hosts a fine collection of bed-and-breakfasts, small hotels, and restaurants. **Linfield College,** a perennial football powerhouse, is an oasis of brick and ivy in the midst of McMinnville's farmers'-market bustle, and annually hosts Oregon's **International Pinot Noir Celebration.** The college, founded in 1849, is the second oldest in Oregon, next to Willamette University. *Admissions office, 900 S. Baker St., Melrose Hall, tel. 503/472–4121, ext. 213. Open weekdays 8–5. Free guided walking tours of the campus arranged by appointment.*

Continuing south on Highway 99W, take Highway 22 west
㉚ toward **Salem**—the state capital—located precisely halfway between the North Pole and the equator on the 45th parallel, about 45 miles south of Portland, along I–5. The brightly gilded 23-foot-high bronze statue of the Oregon Pioneer atop the 140-foot capitol dome is the centerpiece of Salem's **Capitol Mall,** where Oregon's legislators convene every two years.

Numbers in the margin correspond to points of interest on the Salem map.

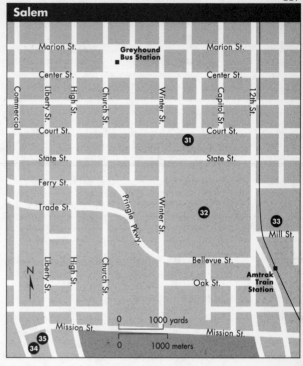

(31) Climb up 121 spiral steps to the viewing area atop the **capitol dome,** where you'll be rewarded with a panoramic view of Oregon's third-largest city, the Willamette Valley, and the mountains. (The dome is scheduled to be closed for renovation until the summer of 1993.) The **capitol complex** itself—graceless blocks of gray Vermont marble—looks as if it had been designed by a committee of career bureaucrats to frighten away the commoners. But don't be deterred—the interior is softened by some fine relief sculptures and the surprisingly deft historical murals. Tours of the rotunda, the house and senate chambers, and the governor's office leave from the information counter under the dome. *900 Court St., tel. 503/378–4423. Admission free. Open weekdays 8–5, Sat. 9–4, Sun. noon–4. Guided capitol tours available June–Aug., 9–4, on the hour; year-round by appointment.*

(32) Just across State Street but half a world away are the tradition-steeped brick buildings and immaculate greens of **Willamette University,** the oldest college in the West. Founded in 1842, Willamette has long been a mecca for aspiring politicians. Stunning **Hatfield Library,** built in 1986 of gracefully curved brick and glass, is an oasis of silent scholarship on the banks of the merry Mill Stream; tall, prim **Waller Hall,** built in 1841, is one of the five oldest buildings in the Pacific Northwest. The university hosts theatrical and musical performances, athletic events, guest lecturers, and art exhibits year-round. For information and tours, contact the university admissions office (tel. 503/370–6303).

❸❸ From 12th Street cross over to the **Mission Mill Village** and **Thomas Kay Woolen Mill Museum,** where teasel gigging, napper flock bins, and the patented Furber double-acting napper are but a few of the venerable machines and processes on display. The museum complex (circa 1889), complete with working waterwheels and mill stream, looks as if the workers have just stepped away for a lunch break, giving visitors a vivid glimpse of 19th-century manufacturing. In the same complex, the **Marion Museum of History** (tel. 503/364–2128) displays a fine collection of pioneer and Calipooya Indian artifacts. The spare simplicity of the **Jason Lee House, John D. Boon Home,** and **Methodist Parsonage,** also part of the village, invites the visitor to steal a glimpse of domestic life in the wilds of Oregon in the 1840s. In the warehouse a few steps away, specialty shops offer antiques, clothing, quilts, toys, and other handmade goods from local craftsmen. *Museum complex, 1313 Mill St. SE, tel. 503/585–7012. Admission: $4 adults, $3 senior citizens and students. Open Tues.–Sat. 10–4:30. Guided tours of historic houses and woolen mill museum leave every hour on the hour from the mill's admission desk.*

❸❹ ❸❺ **Bush's Pasture Park** and **Deepwood Estate,** situated just south of Salem's downtown district, include 105 acres of rolling lawn and formal English gardens. Also on the grounds, the 1878 **Bush House** is a creaky, gaslit Italianate monstrosity with 10 marble fireplaces. The fanciful 1894 Deepwood Estate, built in the Queen Anne style, is well worth a visit for its splendid interior woodwork and original stained glass. The houses and gardens are all on the National Historic Register. *Bush House and Bush's Pasture Park, 600 Mission St. SE, tel. 503/363–4174. Admission: $1.50 adults, $1 senior citizens, 75¢ students, 50¢ children. Open Sept.–May, Tues.–Sun. 2–5; June–Aug., Tues.–Sun. noon–5. The Deepwood Estate, 1116 Mission St. SE, tel. 503/363–1825. Admission: $2 adults, $1.50 senior citizens and students. Open Oct.–Apr., Mon., Wed., Fri. noon–2:30, Sun. 1–4:30; May–Sept., Sun.–Fri. noon–4:30.*

Numbers in the margin correspond to points of interest on the Oregon Coast and Willamette Vally/Wine Country map.

❸❻ Continuing south on I–5, you'll come to **Eugene,** 63 miles farther. The second-largest city in the state and the mid-valley's cultural hub, Eugene has more than 300 restaurants, a world-class performing arts center, and outdoor recreation "from sea level to ski level." The centerpiece of the city is the **University of Oregon,** where Nike shoes founder Phil Knight attended school. The self-proclaimed sobriquet for Eugene—Tracktown USA—and the many joggers thronging the streets and parks of the city are part of his legacy. Also, visitors may recognize the campus as the location for the filming of *National Lampoon's Animal House.* However, Oregon's liberal arts university thrives on more than the reputation of one alumnus and recognition from Hollywood. The grounds are lush and green, with more than 400 varieties of trees shading the 250-acre brick-and-ivy campus. In addition to the athletic events at **Autzen Stadium, MacArthur Court,** and **Hayward Field,** where the U of O's perennially powerful track and field team holds its meets, there are visiting arts exhibits and lecturers at the **Maude I. Kerns Art Center,** as well as a highly regarded permanent collection of Oriental art at the **University of Oregon Museum of Art.** *Admissions office: 1585 E. 13th Ave., tel. 503/346–*

3111. Open weekdays 8–noon and 1–5. Museum: 1430 Johnson La., tel. 503/346–3027. Maps and guided tours of the campus available.

If you're in the mood for a stroll or jog along the river, the **Willamette Science and Technology Center,** next to Autzen Stadium, is a good place to end your journeys. The city's well-equipped and imaginative hands-on scientific museum and planetarium features rotating exhibits designed with kids in mind; one recent offering, "Pets and People," brought forth lectures, demonstrations, and a petting zoo equipped with everything from puppies and kittens to pythons and cockroaches. The adjacent planetarium offers a rotating slate of stars and shows. *2300 Leo Harris Pkwy. Museum tel. 503/687–3619. Admission: $3 adults, $2.50 students and senior citizens, $2 children 3–17. Open Wed.–Sun. noon–6. Planetarium tel. 503/ 689–6500. Admission and hours vary.*

Time Out If you have hungry kids, or have a tough time deciding what sounds good for lunch, the food options at the **5th Street Public Market Food Pavilion** (5th and High Sts., tel. 503/484–0383), a downtown landmark, will give you plenty to choose from. They range from sit-down restaurants (Mekala's Thai Cuisine, Casablanca Mediterranean Cuisine) to decadent bakeries (the Metropol Bakery on the building's lower level is especially fine) to the bewildering international diversity of the clean, airy second-floor food esplanade, offering Greek, Mexican, English, Chinese, Italian, and nouvelle American foods.

The wineries and memorable scenic drives continue both east and west of Eugene. Highway 58 climbs into the Cascades and the Deschutes Forest, toward Willamette Pass east of the city. There, in addition to a popular ski area, you'll find the 286-foot-high Salt Creek Falls, not far from the town of **Oakridge.**

37 Westward, toward the coast, Highway 126 gives access to several wineries and trout-filled rivers before coming to Florence (*see* Tour 1, above), on the central Oregon shore.

38 Following I–5, take note of **Roseburg,** where the highway crosses the Umpqua River, a name sacred to steelhead fishermen the world over. Eight wineries (Bjelland, Callahan Ridge, Girardet, Henry Estate, Hillcrest, Jonicole, Looking Glass, and Umpqua River) can be found within an easy drive west of this sleepy farming community.

In town, the **Douglas County Museum,** one of the best county museums in the state, gives visitors a window on 8,000 years of human activity in the region. Its fossil collection, which includes a million-year-old saber-toothed tiger, is worth a stop. *At the Douglas County Fairgrounds (take exit 123 from I–5 and follow the signs), tel. 503/440–4507. Admission free; donations accepted. Open Tues.–Sat. 10–4, Sun. noon–4.*

39 If for no other reason, downtown **Jacksonville,** about 70 miles farther south and 5 miles west of I–5 on Route 238, deserves a visit for the simple reason that the entire hamlet is on the National Register of Historic Places. Clumping along the boardwalks, it's easy to imagine yourself in Jacksonville during its gold rush heyday in 1853, because several of the 80 privately owned historic structures date from this era. The **Jacksonville Museum,** located in the old Jackson County Courthouse, houses an intriguing collection of gold rush–era artifacts and a permanent exhibit called "Jacksonville! Boomtown to Home Town," outlining the rich local history. *206 N. 5th St., tel. 503/ 773–6536. Admission: $2. Open Memorial Day–Labor Day, daily 10–5; Labor Day–Memorial Day, Tues.–Sun. 10–5.*

For free maps and guides to Jacksonville's many historic structures, stop by the **Jacksonville Chamber of Commerce** (185 N. Oregon St., tel. 503/899–8118).

In many ways the town has become more important to the cultural life of Oregon than Portland or Eugene has. Jacksonville hosts the **Peter Britt Festival** (*see* The Arts, below), which attracts some of the world's best-known classical, jazz, and popular musicians every summer.

Nature lovers who want a glimpse of Rogue River's loveliest angle should plan a side trip to the **Avenue of the Boulders, Mill Creek Falls,** and **Barr Creek Falls,** just off Highway 62, near **40 Prospect** (45 miles northeast of Jacksonville). Here the wild waters of the upper Rogue water foam through volcanic boulders and the dense greenery of the **Rogue River National Forest.**

In spite of its small size and relative isolation from other towns **41** in the state, **Ashland** is also a major cultural center for Oregon. Home to the Tony Award–winning **Oregon Shakespeare Festival,** Ashland draws nearly 400,000 theater lovers to the Rogue Valley every year. Its permanent population of 16,000 swells to 50,000 or more during the peak festival months of June–September. A critical mass of excellent restaurants, bed-and-breakfasts (97 at last count), shops, and galleries combines with a salubrious climate to make Ashland one of Oregon's most popular tourist destinations.

At Ashland's **Shakespeare Festival Exhibit Center** in the festival complex, theater fans can try on costumes and view exhibits about the history of the festival. A visit to the center is included with a guided backstage tour, which takes you on a fascinating trip from the indoor Angus Bowmer Theatre, through backstage production shops, and all the way to the very heavens above the Elizabethan stage. *Festival box office, 15 S. Pioneer St., tel. 503/482–4331. Admission: $6 adults, $3 children 5–11. Tours run Feb.–Oct., Tues.–Sun. at 10 AM; reservations necessary during summer months.*

The Elizabethan Theatre overlooks lovely **Lithia Park,** a 99-acre swath of green in the center of the town. An old-fashioned bandshell, duck pond, children's playground, nature trails, and **Ashland Creek** make this a perfect spot for a pretheater picnic. Each June, to mark the opening of the outdoor season, the festival hosts a Renaissance dinner (the Feast of Will) in the park, complete with period music, dancing, and foods. Tickets ($12.50 per person) are available through the festival box office (*see* above).

What to See and Do with Children

Columbia River Maritime Museum (*see* Tour 1, above).

Ft. Stevens (*see* Tour 1, above).

The Hatfield Marine Science Center (*see* Tour 1, above).

Highway 101 between **Seal Rock** and **Honeyman State Park** (*see* Tour 1, above).

House of Mystery. This may be just a tourist trap, but then again, who knows? Peculiar kinks in the laws of physics seem to occur in this weathered old house, blithely explained by the management as the result of "a spherical field of force, half above ground and half below." The 45-minute guided tours depart whenever enough visitors accumulate. *Sardine Creek Rd., near Gold Hill (take Exit 234 from I–5), tel. 503/855–1543. Admission: $5 adults, $3.75 children 5–11. Open June–Oct., daily 8–6; Nov.–June, daily 9–5.*

Mission Mill Village (*see* Tour 2, above).

Oregon Caves National Monument (*see* National and State Parks, below).

Prehistoric Gardens. Children come face-to-face with life-size brontosaurus, tyrannosaurus rex, and other dinosaurs. *13 mi south of Port Orford on Hwy. 101, tel. 503/332–4463. Admission: $4.50 adults, $3.50 senior citizens and youths 12–18, $2.50 children 5–11. Open daily 8–dusk.*

Silver Falls State Park (*see* National and State Parks, below).

Wildlife Safari. In this 600-acre drive-through wildlife park, you'll see lions, tigers, the largest collection of cheetahs in North America, elephants, and hundreds of other exotic creatures roaming the plains of Oregon's central valley. Children are especially enthralled with the park's petting zoo. *Follow the signs from I–5 Exit 119, about 6 mi south of Roseburg, tel. 503/679–6761. Admission: $8.95 adults, $7.50 senior citizens, $5.75 children 4–12, plus $1 per vehicle. Open daily 8:30–dusk.*

National and State Parks

Crater Lake National Park. A cascade peak called Mt. Mazama decapitated itself 6,800 years ago in a volcanic explosion that spewed hot ash and pumice for hundreds of miles. Rain and snowmelt eventually filled the resulting caldera, creating a sapphire-blue lake so clear that sunlight penetrates to a depth of 400 feet. This geological curiosity, the crown jewel of the Cascades and Oregon's most famous tourist attraction, is now Crater Lake National Park. Oregon's only national park is accessible both from Roseburg (via Highway 138, about 85 miles) and from Medford (via Highway 62, about 71 miles). Visitors can drive, bicycle, or hike **Crater Lake's** 25-mile rim; feed the chipmunks along either Godfrey Glen Nature Trail or the 4-mile Castle Crest Wildflower Trail; or take a boat ride out to famous Wizard Island, a perfect miniature cinder cone protruding 760 feet above the surface of the lake. Private boats are not allowed on Crater Lake, so these tours, which leave every two hours (in the summer) from Cleetwood Cove on the lake's north side, offer a unique surface-level view of the caldera. Overnight accommodations are available at the 40-room Forest Service rental cabin complex at **Annie Creek Canyon,** south of the lake. These accommodations are far from luxurious, however; you might prefer one of the 198 campsites at nearby **Mazama Campground.** The surrounding National Forest campgrounds offer 900 additional sites. Due to conditions caused by the 6,000-foot elevation, access to the park in winter is restricted to the south and west entry roads. *Crater Lake Lodge,*

*Box 128, Crater Lake 97604, tel. 503/594–2511. Boat tour cost:
$10 adults, $5.50 children. Tours run late June–early Sept. 40
two-bedrooms, all with private bath, available June–early
Sept. Campsites are not reserved; first-come, first-served
camping information available through lodge. MC, V. Moderate.*

Oregon Caves National Monument. The "Marble Halls of Oregon," high in the verdant Siskiyou Mountains, have been en-
trancing visitors since local hunter Elijah Davidson chased a
bear into them in 1874. Huge stalagmites and stalactites, the
Ghost Room, Paradise Lost, and the River Styx are all part of a
half-mile subterranean tour that lasts about 75 minutes. The
tour includes more than 200 stairs, and is not recommended for
anyone with difficulty in walking or with respiratory or coro-
nary problems. The historic **Oregon Caves Chateau** (tel. 503/
592–3400) offers food and lodging at the monument from June 9
to September 9. *20 mi southeast of Cave Jct. (between Ashland
and Brookings) on Hwy. 46, tel. 503/592–3400. Admission:
$6.75 adults, $3.75 children 6–11. Children under 6 not
allowed in cave; child care is available. Open daily 8–7.*

Silver Falls State Park. In the lush Cascades, 26 miles east of
Salem, shallow Silver Creek roars over the lip of a mossy basalt
bowl and into a deep pool far below. The 177-foot South Silver
Falls is the main attraction in the 8,300-acre park, the largest
state park in Oregon. Thirteen other waterfalls—half of which
are more than 100 feet high—are accessible to hikers within
the park. There are picnic facilities and a WPA-era day lodge;
during the winter, the cross-country skiing is excellent. Follow
Highway 22 east to its junction with Highway 214 and follow
the signs to Silver Falls. *Headquarters, 20024 Silver Falls
Hwy. SE, Sublimity, tel. 503/873–8681. Admission free.*

Waldo Lake. This incredibly pure shield-shape lake situated
deep in the old-growth forest, 50 miles east of Eugene, is
thought by some to be the cleanest landlocked body of water in
the world. The lake is accessible after a short hike, so bring
comfortable walking attire. *Take Hwy. 58 to Oakridge, then
follow signs northwest to Waldo Lake, no phone.*

Shopping

Shopping Districts/Streets

The Oregon Coast   Hemlock Street, the main thoroughfare in **Cannon Beach,** is
lined with shops and galleries selling everything from kites to
upscale clothing, local artwork, gourmet food, wine, and coffee.

On **Newport's** Bay Boulevard, you'll find the finest group of
fresh seafood markets on the coast, as well as wood crafts from
The Wood Gallery (818 S.W. Bay Blvd., tel. 503/265–6843) and
nautical supplies including fishing equipment, hardware, and
gear from **Englund Marine Supply** (424 S.W. Bay Blvd., tel.
503/265–9275).

Willamette Valley/   You'll find a cornucopia of handmade local toys, books, doll-
Wine Country   houses, quilts, sweaters, and other items at Salem's **Mission
Mill Village Warehouse** (1313 Mill St. SE, tel. 503/585–7012).

Eugene's **5th Street Public Market** (5th and High Sts., tel. 503/
484–0383) crams nearly 100 shops—specializing in everything
from clothing to local art—into a 60-year-old warehouse surrounding a brick-paved courtyard. Every Saturday between
April and Christmas (10–5), local craftsmen, farmers, and
chefs come together to create the weekly **Eugene Saturday
Market** (8th and Oak Sts., tel. 503/686–8885), where you can
buy local artwork, dine cheaply and well, or simply watch the
people go by.

Specialty Stores

Anglers When you need to replenish your supply of mottled turkey-
wing quills, primed popper bodies, or bleached beaver, the
place to go is the **Caddis Fly Angling Shop** (168 W. 6th St., Eugene, tel. 503/342–7005 or 800/825–7005).

Antiques Oregon's largest permanent antiques show is housed in a lovingly restored 1910 schoolhouse at the **Lafayette Schoolhouse
Antique Mall** (Hwy. 99, 5 mi north of McMinnville, tel. 503/864–
2720). A vast assortment of antiquities, from china and toys to
Native American artifacts, are on sale in a three-story showroom.

Food **Josephson's** (106 Marine Dr., Astoria, tel. 503/325–2190 or outside OR, 800/772–3474) is one of the Oregon coast's oldest commercial smokehouses (tours offered), preparing Columbia
River Chinook salmon in the traditional alder-smoked and lox
styles. Smoked shark, tuna, oysters, mussels, sturgeon, scallops, and prawns are also available by the pound or in sealed
gift packs.

Mail-order **Harry and David's** and **Jackson & Perkins** (2518 S. Pacific Hwy.,
Medford, tel. 503/776–2121 or 503/776–2000) are two of the
largest mail-order companies in the world: Harry and David for
fruit and gift packs; Jackson & Perkins for roses. **Harry and
David's Country Store,** located in the same complex, is the only
retail outlet for their products, most of which are grown in the
famous Bear Creek Orchards. Free tours leave the store hourly
on the half hour on weekdays.

Sports and Outdoor Activities

Bicycling

For the past 20 years Oregon has set aside 1% of its highway
funds for the development and maintenance of bikeways
throughout the state, resulting in one of the most extensive
networks of bicycle trails in the country. Write or call for the
free "Oregon Bicycling Guide" (Bicycle Program Manager, Oregon Dept. of Transportation, Room 200, Transportation
Bldg., Salem 97310, tel. 503/378–3432). A second excellent
publication, "Mountain Bike Guide to Oregon" (Oregon Dept.
of Transportation, Parks and Recreation Division, 525 Trade
St. SE, Salem 97310) costs $5.50, plus postage.

The Oregon Coast The **Oregon Coast Bike Route** parallels Highway 101 and the
coastline from Astoria to Brookings. There are numerous de-

tours for scenic loops, hikes, and waysides; though the terrain is far from mountainous, it does have its share of hills and headlands. For mountain bikers, the **Oregon Dunes National Recreation Area** near Florence offers a unique challenge.

Willamette Valley/Wine Country *Eugene*

Eugene is particularly esteemed as a cyclists' town. **Pedal Power** (535 High St., downtown Eugene, tel. 503/687–1775, and 877 E. 13th St., near Univ. of Oregon, tel. 503/343–2488), local cycle stores, rents bikes by the hour, day, or week. The **River Bank Bike Path,** originating in Alton Baker Park on the Willamette's north bank, is a level and leisurely introduction to this exercise-oriented city's two-wheel topography. Also in the park, try the **Prefontaine Trail,** which travels through level fields and forests for 1½ miles.

Yamhill Valley The 25 miles of Highway 18 between Dundee and Grand Ronde, in the Coast Range, roll through the heart of the Yamhill Valley wine country; wide shoulders and relatively light traffic earned the route a "most suitable" rating from the "Oregon Bicycling Guide."

Canoeing and Rafting

There is excellent canoeing on most coastal bays and tidal estuaries and lakes. Virtually all rivers flowing from the Willamette Valley and the I–5 corridor offer memorable rafting and canoeing experiences, ranging from a placid float through lush forests to an adrenaline-pumping plunge through roaring maelstroms of rock and frigid water.

For wet-knuckle enthusiasts (rafters), two rivers stand out: the exuberant **McKenzie,** west of Eugene, and the especially challenging **Rogue,** near the California border. Many parts of the Rogue are still true wilderness, with no road access. Deer, bear, eagles, and other wild creatures are abundant here. Many guide services offer overnighters and longer trips, aboard either rafts or powerful jet boats, which roar upstream from Gold Beach on the coast. **Oregon Guides and Packers** (Box 10841, Eugene 97440, tel. 503/683–9552) will help you find a professional guide service—an absolute necessity on both the McKenzie and the Rogue rivers.

Fishing

The mountains and bountiful rainfall in western Oregon have given birth to some of the finest fishing lakes and rivers in North America. Though overfishing and logging-caused siltation have vastly depleted the runs, many types of fish are still abundant: Native rainbow and sea-run cutthroat trout; wily steelhead reaching 20 pounds and larger; sturgeon; and, greatest prize of all, the fat chinook salmon (weighing up to 50 pounds) that return every spring. Silver and Chinook salmon and the delectable Dungeness crab are the prime quarry the entire length of Oregon's shoreline. Steelhead, flounder, sea-run cutthroat trout, red snapper, lingcod, perch, greenling (whose flesh is a startling electric blue), and dozens of other species are accessible from jetties, docks, and riverbanks from Astoria to Brookings. There are a bewildering number of options available to visiting fishermen, from self-guided boat and shore trips to guided adventures to seagoing charters. Major charter fleets are available from most towns along the coast;

the amenities and fruitful waters of Astoria, Reedsport, and Brookings are particularly esteemed. Ocean salmon season begins in earnest in late June and usually runs through mid-September. For information about fishing options in the specific area you'll be visiting, it's best to contact the local chamber of commerce or visitors' center (*see* Important Addresses and Numbers in Essential Information, above). Although it's hard to go wrong on any of the Coast Range streams or high-mountain lakes, fly-and-bait fishing is internationally famous on the **McKenzie, Umpqua, Rogue,** and **Chetco** rivers. In **Crater Lake,** massive rainbow trout, some three feet in length, cruise the depths in profusion. The fish thrive because there is no boat fishing allowed. You'll need to bring your own tackle, and no license is necessary, but you're not allowed to use organic baits that might cloud the lake—it's lure fishing only.

To fish in most areas of Oregon, out-of-state visitors need a yearly ($35.50), 10-day ($21), or one-day ($5) nonresident angler's license; those fishing for salmon and steelhead need an additional salmon/steelhead tag ($5.50), available from any local sporting goods store.

Golf

Oregon's 136 golf courses run the gamut from layouts designed by top pros such as Robert Trent Jones, to easy pitch-and-putt par 3s, in settings ranging from the blue Pacific to high mountain meadows to the sagebrush and lodgepole pine of central Oregon.

The Oregon Coast
Florence **Ocean Dunes Golf Links** (3345 Munsel Lake Dr., tel. 503/997–3232), 18 holes.

Gold Beach **Cedar Bend Golf Course** (Hwy. 101 N, tel. 503/247–6911), nine holes.

Lincoln City **Devils Lake Golf & Racquet Club** (3245 Clubhouse Dr., tel. 503/994–8442), nine holes.

Neskowin **Neskowin Beach Golf Course** (48405 Hawk St., tel. 503/392–3377), nine holes.

Newport **Agate Beach Golf Club** (4100 N. Coast Hwy., tel. 503/265–7331), nine holes.

North Bend/Coos Bay **Kentuck Golf Course** (Kentuck Inlet, North Bend, tel. 503/756–4464), 18 holes; **Sunset Bay Golf Course** (6905 Cottrell La., Coos Bay, tel. 503/888–9301), nine holes.

Reedsport **Forest Hills Golf Club** (1 Country Club Dr., tel. 503/271–2626), nine holes.

Seaside **Seaside Golf Club** (451 Ave. U, tel. 503/738–5261), nine holes.

Tillamook **Alderbrook Golf Club** (7300 Alderbrook Rd., tel. 503/842–6413), 18 holes.

Willamette Valley/Wine Country
Corvallis **Trysting Trees Golf Club** (34028 Electric Rd., tel. 503/752–3332), 18 holes; **Golf Club of Oregon** (905 Spring Hill Dr. N, Albany, tel. 503/928–8338), 18 holes; **Pineway Golf Club** (30949 Pineway Rd., Lebanon, tel. 503/258–8919), 9 holes.

Eugene/Springfield **Fiddler's Green Golf Course** (91292 Hwy. 99 N, tel. 503/689–8464), 18 holes; **Laurelwood Golf Course** (2700 Columbia St., tel. 503/687–5321), nine holes; **Oakway Golf Course** (2000 Cal Young Rd., tel. 503/484–1927), 18 holes; **Riveridge Golf Course**

(3800 N. Delta Hwy., tel. 503/345–9160), 18 holes; **McKenzie River Golf Course** (41723 Madrone St., Springfield, tel. 503/896–3454), nine holes; **Emerald Valley Golf Course** (83293 Dale Kuni Rd., Creswell, tel. 503/484–6354), 18 holes.

Medford/Ashland **Bear Creek Golf Course** (2355 S. Pacific Hwy., Medford, tel. 503/773–1822), nine holes; **Cedar Links Golf Course** (3155 Cedar Links Dr., tel. 503/773–4373), 18 holes; **Oak Knoll Golf Course** (3070 Hwy. 66, Ashland, tel. 503/482–4311), nine holes.

Newberg/ **Bayou Golf & Country Club** (9301 S.W. Bayou Dr., McMinn-
McMinnville ville, tel. 503/472–4651), 18 holes; **Riverwood Golf Club** (21050 S.E. Riverwood Rd., Dundee, tel. 503/864–2667), nine holes.

Roseburg **Sutherlin Knolls** (1919 Recreation La., Sutherlin, tel. 503/459–4422), 18 holes.

Salem **Salem Golf Club** (2025 Golf Course Rd., tel. 503/363–6652), 18 holes; **McNary Golf Club** (6255 River Rd. N, Keizer, tel. 503/393–4653), 18 holes; **Battle Creek Golf Club** (6161 Commercial St. SE, tel. 503/585–1402), 18 holes.

Skiing

Cross-country The Willamette Valley itself is temperate and generally receives only a few inches of snow a year, but the **Coast Range,** the **Cascades,** and, farther south, the **Siskiyous** are all Nordic skiers' paradises, crisscrossed by hundreds of miles of trails. Every major ski resort in the state offers Nordic skiing; you can also set off down your choice of Forest Service trails and logging roads. If you're unsure where to begin, the **City of Eugene Parks and Recreation Department** (tel. 503/687–5329) takes cross-country snow campers on overnight loops around both **Crater Lake** and **Waldo Lake.**

See also **Willamette Pass** and **Mt. Bailey,** below.

Downhill **Willamette Pass.** Though most Oregon downhillers congregate around Mt. Hood and Mt. Bachelor (*see* Chapter 3, Portland) there is some excellent skiing to the south as well. Willamette Pass, 6,666 feet high in the Cascades Mountains, packs an annual average snowfall of 300 inches atop 18 runs. With a vertical drop of 1,525 feet, there are three triple chairs, one double chair, and one rope tow; lift lines are refreshingly short. Other facilities include 13 miles of Nordic trails, Nordic and downhill rentals, repairs, instruction, ski shop, day care, bar, and restaurant. *Hwy. 58, 69 mi SE of Eugene, tel. 503/484–5030. Open Nov.–Dec. 31, Wed.–Sun. 9–4; Jan. 1–Apr., Wed.–Sat. 9–9, Sun. 9–4.*

Mt. Ashland. This cone-shape Siskiyou peak has some of the steepest runs in the state. There are two triple and two double chair lifts, accommodating a vertical drop of 1,150 feet; the longest of the 22 runs is 1 mile. Facilities include rentals, repair, instruction, ski shop, restaurant, and bar. *18 mi SW of downtown Ashland; follow the signs from I–5, tel. 503/482–2897 or 800/547–8052. Open winter daily 9–4; night skiing Thurs.–Sat. 4–10.*

Snowcat Skiing **Mt. Bailey.** If you *really* crave solitude (and detest lift lines), this is the guide service for you. First you ride in heated snowcats to the summit of Mt. Bailey, an 8,300-foot peak not far from Crater Lake. Then you attack the virgin powder on 4 miles of runs, with a vertical drop of 3,000 feet. The excursions are limited to 12 skiers a day, but be warned—this is downhill for advanced intermediates and experts only. Tours leave Diamond Lake Resort daily at 7 AM. Facilities at resort include three restaurants, bar, lodging, downhill and Nordic ski rentals, and Nordic trails. *Diamond Lake Resort, 76 mi east of Roseburg on Hwy. 138, tel. 503/793–3333. Reservations required. Season runs Nov.–May.*

Spectator Sports

Baseball   The **Eugene Emeralds,** the Kansas City Royals' Northwest League (Class A) affiliate, play 38 home games at **Civic Stadium** (2077 Willamette St., Eugene, tel. 503/342–5367) from June to September.

Basketball   The **Oregon State Beavers** play their home games at **Gill Coliseum** (26th and Washington Sts., on the OSU campus, Corvallis, tel. 503/737–4455). The **University of Oregon's Ducks** seldom fare as well as the Beavers, but seeing a home game at **MacArthur Court** (1601 University St., on the U of O campus, Eugene, tel. 800/932–3668) is a real experience.

Football   The **University of Oregon Ducks** play their home games at **Autzen Stadium** (2700 Centennial Blvd., tel. 800/932–3668). The **Oregon State Beavers** play theirs at **Parker Stadium** (26th and Western Sts., on the OSU campus, tel. 503/737–4455).

Beaches

Virtually the entire 300-mile coastline of Oregon is a clean, quiet white-sand beach, publicly owned and accessible to all. A word of caution: The Pacific off the Oregon Coast is not the mild-mannered playmate it becomes in southern California. It is 45°–55°F year-round, a temperature that can be described as brisk at best and numbing at worst. Tides and undertows are strong, and swimming is not advised. When fishing from the rocks, always watch for sneaker or rogue waves, and never play on logs near the water—they roll without warning in the surf, and have cost numerous lives over the years. Above all, watch children closely while they play in or near the ocean.

Everyone has a favorite beach, but Bandon's **Face Rock Beach** is justly renowned as perhaps the state's loveliest beach for walking, while the beach at **Sunset Bay State Park** on Cape Arago, with its protective reefs and encircling cliffs, is probably the safest for swimming. Nearby, **Oregon Dunes National Recreation area** adds extra cachet to Florence's beaches. Fossils, clams, mussels, and other eons-old marine creatures, easily dug from soft sandstone cliffs, make **Beverly Beach State Park** (5 miles north of Newport) a favorite with young beachcombers.

Dining and Lodging

In wine districts everywhere, eating and living well is high on the list of priorities. The Oregon wine country, which includes the Willamette and Rogue valleys from Newberg to Ashland, is no exception. The regional gastronomy is enlivened by an extensive collection of excellent ethnic restaurants, from Italian to Vietnamese to Eastern European, as well as some expert practitioners of nouvelle cuisine. Eugene, with its longtime emphasis on good living, and Ashland, with its world-famous Oregon Shakespeare Festival, are particularly noted for the excellence and diversity of their restaurants.

Lodging choices are equally varied. In addition to the ever-popular and flourishing numbers of bed-and-breakfasts, Wild West resorts (complete with buffalo and stagecoach), rustic fisherman's lodges, and plenty of chain facilities are available in all price ranges.

The Oregon Shakespeare Festival has stimulated one of the most extensive networks of B&Bs in the country—nearly 100 in all. High season for Ashland-area B&Bs is June–October. Expect to pay $75–$100 per night, which includes breakfast for two; during the off-season, $50–$80. Deciding which one to patronize can be a bewildering task. The **Ashland B&B Clearinghouse** (tel. 503/488–0338) and **Ashland B&B Reservation Network** (tel. 503/482–2337) offer free, unbiased advice to connect travelers with more than 450 options available in the area.

Highly recommended restaurants and lodgings are indicated by a star ★.

Dining	Category	Cost*
	Expensive	over $17
	Moderate	$9–$16
	Inexpensive	$5–$9

per person, not including tip and beverages

Lodging	Category	Cost*
	Expensive	over $90
	Moderate	$40–$90
	Inexpensive	$25–$40

All prices are for a standard double room, excluding tax of 6%–9%, depending on location of the property.

The Oregon Coast

Astoria
Dining

Pier 11 Feed Store Restaurant & Lounge. This spacious restaurant, decorated with linen and crystal, overlooks the Columbia River from the windows of this renovated pier/warehouse. The friendly staff serves hearty and abundant fish, steaks, and prime rib. The cioppino is a massive helping packed with clams, crab, oysters, shrimp, and fish, and it is large enough to feed three people. *Foot of 11th St., tel. 503/325–0279. Reservations accepted. Dress: casual. MC, V. Moderate.*

Columbian Café. The locals love this small, unpretentious diner with its south-of-the-border decor that's heavy on the chili pepper Christmas lights and religious icons. Fresh, simple food—crepes with broccoli, cheese, and homemade salsa for lunch; grilled salmon and pasta with lemon-cream sauce for dinner—is served by a modest staff that usually includes the owner. Come early, though, since this place draws crowds. *1114 Marine Dr., tel. 503/325–2233. No reservations. Dress: casual. No credit cards. Closed Sun.; Mon.–Tues. lunch. Inexpensive.*

Lodging **Red Lion Inn.** The only north-coast outlet of this reliable north-western chain sits right on the Columbia River, beneath the Astoria Bridge; there's a decent view of the river from the guest-room balconies. The small rooms and public areas, formerly decorated in an unfortunate combination of blue and purple, have been renovated in soothing earth tones. *400 Industry St., 97103, tel. 503/325–7373 or 800/547–8010. 124 rooms. Facilities: restaurant, lounge, cable TV. AE, D, DC, MC, V. Moderate–Expensive.*

★ **Franklin Street Station Bed & Breakfast.** The ticking of clocks and the mellow marine light filtered through leaded-glass windows set the tone at this velvet-upholstered Victorian, built in 1900 on the slopes above downtown Astoria. Each of the five immaculate guest rooms has a private bath. Breakfasts are huge, hot, and satisfying; there's always a plate of brownies and a pot of coffee in the kitchen. *1140 Franklin St., 97103, tel. 503/325–4314. 5 rooms. MC, V. Moderate.*

Grandview Bed & Breakfast. This huge, turreted mansion lives up to its name, and then some—decks and telescopes look out over Astoria, with the Columbia River and Washington beyond. The interior is bright and airy, with scrubbed hardwood floors and comfortable, lace-filled rooms. The breakfast specialty is bagels with cream cheese and smoked salmon from Josephson's (*see* Shopping, above). *1574 Grand Ave., 97103, tel. 503/325–5555 or 800/488–3250. 8 units (3 1-bedroom units, 3 2-bedroom units) with private bath. D, MC, V. Moderate.*

Bandon **Bandon Boatworks.** A local favorite, this romantic jetty-side
Dining eatery serves up its seafood, steaks, prime rib, and rack of lamb with a view of the Coquille River Harbor and the historic Bandon Lighthouse. Try the panfried oysters flamed with brandy and anisette, or the quick-sautéed seafood combination that's heavy on scampi and scallops. *S. Jetty Rd., tel. 503/347–2111. Reservations suggested. Dress: casual. AE, MC, V. Closed Jan.; Mon. Moderate.*

Lord Bennett's. Some come to this modern cliff-top restaurant for the excellent food; the prawns sautéed with butter, brandy, cream, and mustard are especially fine. Even better is the house lobster, sautéed with shallots, mushrooms, brandy, and cream then broiled with hollandaise. Most guests, however, come for the sunsets seen through picture windows that overlook Face Rock Beach. The lounge features live music on weekends, and Sunday breakfasts are particularly good. *1695 Beach Loop Dr., tel. 503/347–3663. Reservations suggested. Dress: casual. AE, MC, V. Moderate.*

Lodging **Inn at Face Rock.** This modern, cheerful resort sits just across Beach Loop Drive from Bandon's fabulous walking beach. The rooms are spacious, soothing, and well-furnished; nearly half have ocean views. The interior is clean and contemporary, decorated in a cream-and-sand color scheme, and some rooms have kitchenettes and fireplaces. *3225 Beach Loop Rd., 97411, tel. 503/347–9441. Facilities: restaurant, bar, spa, 9-hole golf course, some fireplace and kitchen units available, cable TV. AE, MC, V. Moderate.*

Brookings **Mama's Authentic Italian Food.** The decor is down-home
Dining trattoria, typically styled to accompany the homestyle Italian food served here. Meals are still cooked (and often served) by the owner, an 85-year-old task mistress who keeps the efficient staff on their toes. The tender pasta, crusty pizza, and slow-

simmered sauces keep this small and simply furnished restaurant always busy. *703 Chetco Ave., tel. 503/469–7611. Reservations accepted. Dress: casual. MC, V. Inexpensive.*

Lodging **The Chetco Inn.** Not to be confused with the Chetco River Inn (*see* below), this once-grand 44-room hotel was the destination of choice for a Who's Who of Hollywood stars in the 1930s. It's a bit rough around the edges, currently, but is in the middle of a lengthy and detailed renovation. It's not the Ritz, but it's a good choice for fishermen because of its central location and reasonable rates. *417 Fern St., 97415, tel. 503/469–5347. 44 rooms. D, MC, V. Inexpensive.*

Dining and Lodging **Chetco River Inn.** Thirty-five acres of private forest surround
★ this splendidly remote fishing lodge, located 17 miles up the pale-blue Chetco River from Brookings. There are three guest rooms (all share a bath), plus a library, a comfortable common room, and a crackling fireplace. Fishing-guide service is available upon request, as are gourmet dinners cooked by the hosts. The rooms feature thick comforters and panoramic views of river and forest; hearty dinners might star a nickel-bright salmon fresh from the stream. *21202 High Prairie Rd. (follow North Bank Rd; the road follows the north bank of the Chetco River), 97415, tel. 503/469–2114, ext. 4628 (radio phone) or 800/327–2688. MC, V. Moderate.*

Cannon Beach **The Bistro.** Cannon Beach's most romantic restaurant is small
Dining and intimate, filled with flowers, candlelight, and classical mu-
★ sic. The menu features imaginative, Continental-influenced renditions of fresh local seafood dishes in a four-course fixed-price menu; expect monstrous scampi and tender razor clams to appear as specials. This intimate, 12-table nonsmoking establishment is not inexpensive, but it is arguably the best meal in town. *263 N. Hemlock St., tel. 503/436–2661. Reservations suggested. Dress: casual. MC, V. Closed lunch weekends. Expensive.*

Dooley's West Texas Barbecue. You'll get tangy barbecued and mesquite-grilled chicken, ribs, and beef at this new addition to Cannon Beach's well-developed restaurant scene. (It moved from Astoria last year.) What makes this restaurant different from other barbecue joints is that the meat is meticulously fat-free and the chicken is skinless and lean. Locals pack this small (15 tables), down-home place for the evening buffet and live music. *123 S. Hemlock St., tel. 503/436–1827. No reservations. Dress: casual. MC, V. Moderate.*

Dooger's. This is the original Dooger's, not to be confused with the newer branch a few miles south in Cannon Beach, though both are much beloved by local families. The seafood is fresh and expertly prepared, and the decor—warm floral tones and wood paneling—makes this a comfortable, contemporary restaurant. The creamy clam chowder may also be the best on the coast. *505 Broadway, tel. 503/738–3773; other location: 1371 S. Hemlock St., tel. 503/436–2225. No reservations. Dress: casual. MC, V. Inexpensive–Moderate.*

Charleston **The Portside Restaurant.** This unpretentious restaurant over-
Dining looking the busy Charleston boat basin is a gem, with utterly fresh fish brought to the kitchen by the restaurant's own fishing boat, the *Portside I*. The nautically furnished restaurant overlooks the harbor through picture windows. Preparation is simple, usually with a touch of garlic butter, tomato, white wine, or cream. Try the steamed Dungeness crab with drawn

butter or, better, come Friday night for the scrumptious all-you-can-eat seafood buffet ($13.95). *8001 Kingfisher Rd. (follow Cape Arago Hwy. from Coos Bay), tel. 503/888–5544. Reservations accepted. Dress: casual. AE, DC, MC, V. Moderate.*

Coos Bay **The Blue Heron Bistro.** You'll get subtle preparations of local
Dining seafood, chicken, and homemade pasta with an international flair at this busy bistro. There are no flat spots on the far-ranging menu; the innovative soups and desserts are also excellent. The skylighted, tile-floored dining room seats about 70 amid natural wood and blue linen. Outside seating area is fine in good weather, blue awnings and colorful Bavarian window boxes add a festive touch. For breakfast, the omelets are as filling as they are innovative. *100 Commercial St., tel. 503/267–3933. Reservations suggested for large groups. Dress: casual. MC, V. Moderate.*

★ **Kum-Yon's.** If you have a hankering for something Oriental but can't decide on a cuisine, this small multiethnic restaurant on Coos Bay's main drag will fit the bill. You'll find everything from sushi to *kung pao* shrimp to Korean short ribs on the voluminous menu. The preparations are average, and the ambience resembles nothing so much as a Seoul Burger King, but the portions are satisfying and the prices are ridiculously low. *835 S. Broadway, tel. 503/269–2662. Reservations accepted. Dress: casual. MC, V. Inexpensive.*

Lodging **This Olde House B & B.** The charm and care that have gone into
★ the creation of this sprawling Victorian, four blocks up the hill from downtown Coos Bay, are matched only by the charm and warmth of its owners. Each room is a treasure trove of antiques and oddities collected over the past 40 years. You'll never sleep better, or eat better when you awake; the breakfast, including heavenly french toast with fresh berries, home-made caramel syrup, and great coffee, is included in room rate. *202 Alder Ave., 97420, tel. 503/267–5224. 4 rooms, 1 with private bath. No credit cards; personal checks accepted. Moderate.*

Florence **Bridgewater Seafood Restaurant.** The venerably salty ambi-
Dining ence of Florence's photogenic bay-front Old Town permeates this spacious fish house. Steaks, salads, and, of course, plenty of fresh-caught seafood are the mainstays at this creaky-floored Victorian-era restaurant. *1297 Bay St., tel. 503/997–9405. Reservations accepted. Dress: casual. AE, MC, V. Moderate.*

The Windward Inn. One of the south coast's most elegant eateries, this tightly run ship prides itself on its vast menu, master wine list, home-baked breads and desserts, and array of fresh seafood. The interior reflects the refined atmosphere, with the elegant decor and furnishings. *3757 Hwy. 101 N, tel. 503/997–8243. Reservations suggested. Dress: casual but neat. AE, D, DC, MC, V. Closed Mon. Labor Day–Memorial Day. Moderate.*

Lodging **Driftwood Shores Surfside Resort Inn.** The chief amenity at this resort is the location, just north of Florence and directly above one of the longest, emptiest walking beaches on the coast. The rooms and public areas fall a bit short of elegant, but they're comfortable, equipped with kitchens. Some rooms have fireplaces and balconies (on the rooms on the ocean side). *88416 1st Ave. (take Heceta Beach Rd. from Hwy. 101, about 3 mi north of Florence), 97439, tel. 503/997–8263 or outside OR, 800/824–8774. 122 rooms. Facilities: restaurant, bar, indoor pool, spa,* *sauna, in-room kitchens in most units, cable TV. AE, D, DC, MC, V. Moderate.*

Gleneden Beach
Dining

Chez Jeanette. This whitewashed, French country cottage nestles in the shore pine between Highway 101 and the ocean, and it seems a continent or so away from the frenetic tourism of downtown Lincoln City. The atmosphere is quiet, with fireplace, antiques, linen, and crystal. The food is wonderful: Try the carpetbagger steak, a thick fillet stuffed with tiny local oysters, wrapped in bacon and sauced with crème fraîche, scallions, spinach, and bacon. The rest of the menu puts a Parisian spin on the local bounty from the sea, sky, and pasture. *7150 Old Hwy. 101 (turn west from Hwy. 101 at the Salishan entrance; take the first left and go ¼ mi south), tel. 503/764–3434. Reservations necessary. Dress: casual but neat. AE, D, MC, V. Closed lunch; Sun.–Mon. Oct.–June. Expensive.*

★ **Gourmet Dining Room at Salishan.** The resort's main dining room, a roomy multilevel expanse of hushed waiters, hillside ocean views, and snow-white linen, has built an enviable reputation on its showy Continental cuisine. House specialties include fresh local fish, game, beef, and lamb; the fettuccine with fat scallops and salmon caviar is heavenly. By all means make a selection from the wine cellar, the largest in the state. *Hwy. 101 at Gleneden Beach, tel. 503/764–2371. Reservations advised. Jacket and tie suggested. AE, D, DC, MC, V. Closed lunch. Expensive.*

Lodging

Salishan Lodge. For most visitors, this is *the* resort on the Oregon coast. From the soothing, silvered-cedar ambience of its guest rooms, divided into eight complex units nestled into a 750-acre hillside forest preserve, Salishan embodies a uniquely Oregonian elegance. The quiet, spacious rooms each have wood burning fireplaces, balconies, and walls decorated by Northwest artists. Add to its setting collections of wine (there are 20,000 bottles in the cellar here), and original art, and you'll understand why the timeless atmosphere also carries perhaps the steepest price tag on the coast. *Hwy. 101 at Gleneden Beach, 97388, tel. 503/764–2371; outside OR, 800/547–6500. 200 rooms. Facilities: 3 restaurants, bar, private beach access, indoor pool, spas and saunas, indoor and outdoor tennis courts, 18-hole golf course, men's and women's weight rooms, children's playground, conference facilities. AE, D, DC, MC, V. Expensive.*

Gold Beach
Dining

The Captain's Table. You can trust this popular local eatery for ultratender Midwest corn-fed beef, a solid touch with fresh seafood, and a nice view out over the ocean. The antique-filled dining room is on the smallish side, providing a cozy atmosphere; the service is excellent. *1295 S. Ellensburg Ave., tel. 503/247–6308. No reservations. Dress: casual. MC, V. Closed lunch. Moderate.*

Lodging

Ireland's Rustic Lodges. Eight original one- and two-bedroom cabins filled with rough-hewn charm, plus 27 newer motel rooms, are available in this spectacularly landscaped setting. Each unit has a fireplace and a deck overlooking the sea, with venerable furnishings in a black, brown, rust, and beige color scheme. For the price, you can't beat this accommodation. *1120 S. Ellensburg Ave., 97444, tel. 503/247–7718. 40 units; nonsmoking rooms available. Facilities: decks, fireplaces, ocean views. No credit cards; personal checks accepted. Inexpensive–Moderate.*

Dining and Lodging **Tu Tu Tun Lodge.** This famous, richly appointed fishing resort
★ sits right on the clear blue Rogue River, 7 miles upriver from
Gold Beach. This is a small place, and all units are furnished
with rough-and-tumble, rustic charm. Private decks overlook
the river and the surrounding old-growth forest. The lodge dining room serves rib-sticking breakfast, lunch, and dinner; the
latter are open to nonguests with reservations and consist of a
five-course fixed-price meal that changes nightly. Portions are
dauntingly huge. *96550 N. Bank Rogue, 97444, tel. 503/247–
6664. 16 rooms, 2 suites, one 3-bedroom house. Facilities: restaurant, bar, heated outdoor pool, 4-hole golf course, horseshoes, hiking, boat dock and ramp, salmon and steelhead
fishing, jet-boat excursions. D, MC, V. Expensive. Closed
Nov. 2–Apr.*

Lincoln City **The Bay House.** Rapacious development has robbed Lincoln
Dining City proper of much of its former wistful charm, but if you head
★ slightly south of town, you can at least eat well. Particularly
satisfying cuisine can be found here, in a charming bay-side
house transformed into one of the Oregon coast's most extraordinary restaurants. These are meals to linger over while gazing
out over sunset-gilded Siletz Bay: crab cannelloni, rack of lamb,
pasta with escargots and garlic, roast duck with cherries. The
wine list is extensive; the service, impeccable. The interior,
crammed with antiques and flowers is especially conducive to a
romantic evening. *5911 S.W. Hwy. 101, tel. 503/996–3222. Reservations necessary. Dress: neat but casual. MC, V. Closed
lunch. Expensive.*

Lighthouse Brew Pub. This westernmost outpost of the Portland-based McMenamin brothers' microbrewery empire has
the same virtues as their other establishments: fresh local ales,
including several brewed on the premises; good unpretentious
sandwiches, burgers, and pasta; cheerfully eccentric decor—
of particular note is the psychedelic artwork by Northwest
painters. At this two-level shopping center pub, there's an unexpected plus in the ocean views. Families are welcome. *4157
N. Hwy. 101, tel. 503/994–7238. No reservations. Dress: casual. MC, V. Inexpensive.*

Lodging **Ester Lee Motel.** Perched on a bluff overlooking the cold green
Pacific through panoramic windows, this small whitewashed
motel has attracted a devoted repeat business through a simple, elegant approach to the innkeeping business. For the
price, there are some nice amenities, including wood-burning
fireplaces and full kitchens. Make sure to request a unit in the
older section of the hotel; the rooms are larger, furnished in
rustic knotty pine, with brick fireplaces and picture windows.
*3803 S.W. Hwy. 101, 97367, tel. 503/996–3606. 54 units. Facili-
ties: kitchens, cable TV. D, MC, V. Moderate.*

Manzanita **Blue Sky Café.** There is a quirky, cheerful atmosphere here,
Dining conveyed through the eclectic table furnishings, the jungle of
plants, stained glass and butcher paper-covered tables. Menu
specialties such as pesto prawns and creamy homemade soups
such as ham, apple, and blue cheese bisque make this tiny hole-
in-the-wall restaurant worth a special trip from Cannon Beach
or Tillamook. *154 Laneda St., tel. 503/368–5712. Reservations
accepted. Dress: casual. MC, V. Closed breakfast and lunch.
Moderate.*

Newport **Tables of Content.** The restaurant at the outstanding Sylvia
Dining Beach Hotel offers a well-plotted eight-course, fixed-price ($15

per person) menu that changes nightly. Chances are the main character will be fresh local seafood, perhaps a moist grilled salmon fillet in sauce Dijonnaise, with a supporting cast of sautéed vegetables, fresh-baked breads, rice pilaf, and a decadent dessert. The interior is functional, especially the family-size tables. *267 N.W. Cliff St. (follow signs west from Hwy. 101 to Nye Beach), tel. 503/265–5428. Reservations necessary. Dress: casual. MC, V. Closed lunch. Moderate.*

Don Petrie's Italian Food Co. A little hole-in-the-sand place with a strong local following, this tidy, Spartan restaurant serves some of the best seafood lasagna you'll ever eat. Get there early, especially on weekends, as the place fills up with locals. *613 N.W. 3rd St., tel. 503/265–3663. No reservations. Dress: casual. MC, V. Closed lunch. Inexpensive.*

Mo's. There are several Mo's restaurants, scattered from Lincoln City to Coos Bay. All are always busy, attesting to the quality of the food and the friendly, hardworking staff. Mo's chowder, a creamy, velvet-textured potion flavored with bacon and onion and studded with tender potatoes and clams, is famous; her grilled oysters and cioppino are merely delicious. The decor is hoary and nautical, but never mind—just consider yourself lucky to get a table. Kids love this place for its great chowder and picnic-table informality. *622 S.W. Bay Blvd., tel. 503/265–2979; other locations in Lincoln City (860 S.W. 51st St., tel. 503/996–2535), Florence (1436 Bay St., tel. 503/997–2185), and Coos Bay (700 S. Broadway, tel. 503/269–1323). No reservations. Dress: casual. No credit cards. Inexpensive.*

Lodging **The Embarcadero.** This luxurious bay-front resort has everything you're looking for in coastal accommodations. The location—at the east end of Bay Boulevard—is outstanding, offering great views over Yaquina Bay and its graceful bridge. The rooms and public areas are modern and posh, decorated heavily with rough-hewn native woods and ceramic tiles. Spacious suites have one or two bedrooms, with bayside deck, fireplace, and kitchen. *1000 S.E. Bay Blvd., 97365, tel. 503/265–8521. 129 rooms. Facilities: restaurant, bar, indoor pool, sauna, spa, private marina, boats, fishing rentals, decks, harbor views, kitchen and fireplace units available. AE, D, DC, MC, V. Moderate–Expensive.*

★ **The Sylvia Beach Hotel.** Book a reservation far in advance for this unique beachfront hotel; some weekends are fully booked as much as a year in advance. The owners have restored this 1912-vintage hostelry along a literary theme; each of the 20 antique-filled guest rooms is named for a famous writer, and no two are decorated alike. The Poe Room, for instance, sports a pendulum swinging over the bed. The Christie, Twain, and Colette rooms are the most luxurious; all have fireplaces, decks, and great ocean views. Upstairs is a well-stocked, split-level library, with decks, a fireplace, slumbering cats, and too-comfortable chairs. Complimentary mulled wine is served there nightly at 10. And in the morning, a hearty breakfast buffet (included in room rate) with homemade pastries, cereals, hot quiche, or frittata is offered. *267 N.W. Cliff St., 97365, tel. 503/265–5428. Facilities: restaurant, library. No smoking allowed inside; no TVs or phones. AE, MC, V. Moderate.*

Port Orford **The Whale Cove.** The food at this unprepossessing restaurant is
Dining legendary—rich, subtle, and worth the drive from Portland,
★ let alone any of the surrounding coastal communities. Take the

broiled salmon with wasabe butter: it's moist, flaky, and perfectly enhanced by the sauce. Surroundings are romantic, with an artist's flair for the dramatic: flowers everywhere, Handel on the stereo, great views over the sun-bronzed Pacific, and paintings by the chef. The Sunday brunch is concocted from the finest, freshest available fruits, meats, and seafood. *190 6th St., tel. 503/332–7575. Reservations suggested. Dress: casual. MC, V. Closed lunch and Tues. dinner. Moderate.*

Seaside
Dining

Lazy Susan Café. This nonsmoking establishment is the place to come for breakfast in Cannon Beach, with its cheerful, wood-and-oilcloth decor. Excellent entrées include a substantial order of waffles topped with fruit and orange syrup, oatmeal, quiche, and omelets. Whatever your choice, don't leave without tasting the fresh-baked muffins and home fries. *126 N. Hemlock St., in Coaster Sq., tel. 503/436–2816. No reservations. Dress: casual. No credit cards. Closed dinner; Tues.–Wed.; Sun. lunch, but open for breakfast. Inexpensive.*

Lodging

Hallmark Resort at Cannon Beach. Cozy rooms with fireplaces, spas, and the best views in Cannon Beach make this triple-decker oceanfront resort the destination of choice for the north coast. Rooms, adorned with oak-tiled baths and spacious balconies, favor a soothing color scheme. Their large size makes them ideal for families or couples looking for a romantic splurge. *1400 S. Hemlock St., 97110, tel. 503/436–1566 or 800/345–5676. 123 rooms, 5 oceanfront rental homes. Facilities: restaurant, lounge, indoor pool, sauna, spa, weight room, children's pool, cable TV, in-room refrigerators, covered parking, free newspaper delivered daily. AE, D, DC, MC, V. Expensive.*

Webb's Scenic Surf. This quiet, small family-operated hotel is a throwback to simpler times in Cannon Beach, before trendiness translated into big resorts and $500 weekends. Located on the beach, Webb's provides panoramic views of the ocean. The austerely furnished rooms, many with kitchens and fireplaces, are functional, clean, and have comfortable beds. For the budget traveler, this is the best deal in town. *255 N. Larch St., 97110, tel. 503/436–2706. 14 rooms. Facilities: kitchens, cable TV. MC, V. Inexpensive.*

Waldport
Lodging
★

The Cliff House Bed-and-Breakfast. The view from Yaquina John Point (once an Indian chief's headquarters), on which this inn sits, is exquisite, and the ambience is enhanced considerably by the presence of this extraordinary B&B. The huge, romantic, old house, once a bordello, is filled with an Aladdin's trove of antiques, including a 500-year-old sleigh bed that once adorned a French manor house. Lacquered screens, Chinese porcelains, deep, comfortable furnishings, and a garden filled with fairy lights complete the ambience. The breakfasts are as sumptuous as the surroundings. *1 block west on Adahi Rd. off Hwy. 101, 97394, tel. 503/563–2506. 5 rooms with private bath. MC, V. Moderate.*

Yachats
Dining
★

La Serre. Don't be dismayed by the vaguely steak-and-salad-bar ambience at this skylit, plant-filled restaurant—the chef's deft touch with impeccably fresh seafood attracts knowledgeable diners from as far away as Florence and Newport. Try the tender geoduck clam, breaded with parmesan cheeese and flash-fried in lemon garlic butter. A reasonably priced wine list and mouth-watering desserts complete the package. La Serre also serves Sunday brunch. *2nd and Beach Sts., tel. 503/547–3420. Reservations accepted. Dress: casual. AE, MC, V. Closed lunch; Jan.; Mon.–Tues. Oct.–June. Moderate.*

New Morning Coffeehouse. Exquisite fresh-baked breads and desserts, salads, sandwiches, and fine coffee make this airy sunlit café worth a stop. *4th St. and Hwy. 101, tel. 503/547–3848. No reservations. Dress: casual. No credit cards. Closed dinner. Closed Mon.–Tues. Oct.–June. Inexpensive.*

Lodging **Ziggurat.** You'll have to see this four-story cedar-and-glass pyramid, rising from the tidal grasslands, to believe it; and you'll need to spend a night or two here, serenaded by the wind and the sea, to fully appreciate it. Odd angles, Scandinavian furnishings, and artworks gathered from the owner's world travels lend an eccentric but welcoming air. Ask for the fourth-floor master bedroom if it's available, because the best views in the house make it the most romantic. *95330 Hwy. 101, 97498, tel. 503/547–3925. 3 rooms, 1 with private bath. Facilities: sauna. No credit cards. No smoking inside. Closed mid-Dec.–Jan. 1. Moderate.*

Dining and Lodging **The Adobe.** Yachats is a beautiful and relaxed alternative to some of the more intensely touristy communities to the north, and this quiet and unassuming resort motel is right at home here. Many of the rooms have wood-burning fireplaces, and all have the low-key, knotty-pine, high-ceiling ambience you look for in a coastal getaway. Rooms are on the smallish side, but warm and inviting, with high-beamed ceilings and picture windows framing noble views. The Adobe restaurant offers sweeping views and quality Continental cuisine. The loft above the bar offers a panoramic vantage for storm- and whale-watching. *1555 Hwy. 101, 97498, tel. 503/547–3141. 60 units. Facilities: restaurant, bar, spa, sauna, cable TV, refrigerators, coffee makers. Reservations accepted. Dress: casual. AE, D, DC, MC, V. Moderate.*

Willamette Valley/Wine Country

Ashland Dining ★ **Chateaulin.** One of southern Oregon's most romantic restaurants occupies a little ivy-covered storefront a block from the Shakespeare Festival center. It dispenses elegant French food, local wine, and impeccable service with equal facility. Try fresh loin of lamb with a sauce of balsamic vinegar, shallots, veal stock and cream, washed down with a bottle of Ponzi Pinot noir. *52 E. Main St., tel. 503/482–2264. Reservations necessary, especially during Shakespeare season (June–Oct.). Dress: casual but neat; tie is acceptable. AE, DC, MC, V. Closed lunch. Moderate–Expensive.*

The Back Porch Barbecue. This down-home outdoor restaurant (the cavernous outdoor seating area of Señor Gator's, a popular Mexican restaurant) serves up Texas-style barbecued steaks, ribs, and chicken, with ice-cold beer to wash it all down. Located mostly on a deck beside the creek, the Back Porch offers a refreshing, lush view, suitable scenery for such a simple place. *92 ½ N Main St., tel. 503/482–4131. No reservations. Dress: casual. MC, V. Closed Nov.–Apr. Moderate.*

Thai Pepper. Spicy Thai-style curries and stir-fries are the specialties at this elegantly-appointed restaurant perched above musical Ashland Creek. With an interior filled with local art, rattan, linen, and crystal, the restaurant feels like a French café in downtown Bangkok. The house special is spicy curry, but try the coconut prawns as well as the Thai beef salad appetizer for starters. *84 N. Main St., tel. 503/482–8058. Reservations suggested. Dress: casual. MC, V. Closed lunch Sun.–Mon. Moderate.*

Rogue Brewery & Public House. Ashland's first brew-pub (a nonsmoking establishment indoors) serves pizza and other hearty pub food, as well as a rotating selection of 4–6 ales brewed on the premises, including Rogue Golden, Ashland Amber, and Shakespeare Stout. A deck overlooks the creek. *31 B Water St., tel. 503/488–5061. No reservations. Dress: casual. MC, V. Inexpensive.*

Lodging **The Mt. Ashland Inn.** Deserving special mention, this is one of
★ the most unusual B&Bs in the area. The 5,000-square-foot lodge was hand built from cedar logs cut from the owners' 160-acre property, located just a mile or two from the summit ski area on Mt. Ashland. The views are as magnificent as the forested setting; Pacific Crest Trail runs through the parking lot, and views of Mt. Shasta and the rest of the Siskiyou Mountains. On the inside, a huge stone fireplace, hand-stitched quilts, and natural wood provide welcoming warmth. *550 Mt. Ashland Rd. (take exit 5 from I–5 and follow the signs toward the ski area), Box 944, 97520, tel. 503/482–8707. 5 rooms with private bath, plus separate guest house with hot tub, small meeting room. MC, V. Moderate–Expensive.*

Best Western Bard's Inn. If you're looking for a nicely appointed commercial hotel, close to the theaters but not too expensive, this 38-unit property fits the bill. A rose garden surrounds the pool, and Rogue Valley views can be seen from every window. Inside, original artwork, created by contemporary local artists, hangs on the walls. The rooms, though on the small side, are freshly furnished in knotty pine and neutral tones. *132 N. Main St., 97520, tel. 503/482–0049 or 800/528–1234. Facilities: restaurant, bar, outdoor pool, hot tub. AE, D, DC, MC, V. Moderate.*

Dining and Lodging **Winchester Country Inn.** Another favorite with locals and knowledgeable visitors, this 1886-vintage restaurant/inn, with guest rooms upstairs, serves superb food from a small but imaginative menu. The duck à la Bigarde (roast duck in a sauce of duck stock, caramel, brandy, and fresh fruit) is ambrosial; the homemade scones, crab Benedict, and duck hash with orange hollandaise, served for Sunday brunch, are equally memorable. Set among manicured gardens, the airy, high-windowed dining rooms lend a feeling of casual elegance. *35 S. 2nd St., 97520, tel. 503/488–1113. Reservations recommended. Dress: casual but neat. MC, V. Closed lunch; Mon. Oct.–May. Moderate–Expensive.*

Bellevue **Augustine's.** First explore the Lawrence Gallery, with its fine
Dining collection of local art. Then enter the adjoining Oregon Wine Tasting Room to sample the wares of more than 20 Yamhill Valley wineries. Finally, go upstairs to the tastefully-decorated dining room, with its modern furnishings and rustic views, where you'll enjoy fresh local seafood, lamb, and beef, all simply prepared and lightly sauced. The wine list is as extensive as it is reasonably priced; many local vintages are available by the glass, a nice concession to those with moderation in mind. Give the Sunday brunch a try, too. *19706 Hwy. 18 (7 mi west of McMinnville), tel. 503/843–3225. Reservations suggested.*

Dress: casual. MC, V. Closed Tues.; Mon. Labor Day–Memorial Day. Moderate.

Corvallis
Dining

Papagayo. For years this was the best Mexican restaurant in Oregon, with true aficionados making the three-hour round-trip journey from Portland with the regularity of religious pilgrims. It wasn't, however, for the decor, which favors earths, reds, ochres, and Mexican pottery knick-knacks, but for the food. Although there is more competition now, the meals are still simple and delicious. The menu favors mesquite-grilled beef and chicken and handmade renditions of traditional Mexican favorites. *550 N.W. Harrison St. (downtown, 5 min from the university), tel. 503/757–8188. Reservations suggested. Dress: casual. AE, D, MC, V. Closed Mon.; weekend lunch. Moderate.*

The Gables. This quiet, elegant eatery, with all dark wood has earned a reputation over the years as Corvallis's most romantic restaurant. The menu is about what you would expect: steaks, straightforward seafood, local lamb, and prime rib. The portions are huge and satisfying. The well-stocked wine cellar can be reserved as a dining room for small groups and special occasions. *1121 N.W. 9th St., tel. 503/752–3364. Reservations suggested. Dress: casual. AE, DC, MC, V. Closed lunch. Moderate.*

Novak's Hungarian Paprikas. Locals can't say enough about this unpretentious family-run restaurant, located a few miles east of Corvallis in Albany. Its Hungarian owners turn out native specialties such as *kolbasz* (homemade sausages with sweet-and-sour cabbage) and beef *szelet* (crispy batter-fried cutlets) with virtuosity. The restaurant's only drawback is its lack of a liquor license, so no alcohol is permitted. *2835 Santiam Hwy., Albany, tel. 503/967–9488. Reservations suggested. Dress: casual. MC, V. Closed Sat. lunch. Inexpensive–Moderate.*

Lodging

Madison Inn. One of the Willamette Valley's most venerable B&Bs—opened more than a decade ago by the current owner's mother—is this sprawling five-story Tudor that overlooks Central Park in downtown Corvallis. Eight guest rooms are available; all but one, the Matt & Mike Room, share a bath. *660 Madison Ave., 97330, tel. 503/757–1274. 8 rooms. MC, V. Moderate.*

Eugene
Dining

Chanterelle. In a city quietly renowned for its restaurants, this is where the smart money comes when it wants a superb meal in a memorably romantic setting. Seasonal, regional European-inspired cuisine is on the menu here; the chef's touch is equally deft with game and local beef or lamb as it is with seafood. The 12-table restaurant, in an old warehouse across from the 5th Street Public Market, is warm and intimate, and is filled with crystal and fresh flowers. *207 E. 5th Ave., tel. 503/484–4065. Reservations suggested. Jacket and tie suggested. AE, MC, V. Closed lunch; Sun.–Mon.; last 2 wks of Mar.; last week of Aug.; 1st week of Sept.; major holidays. Expensive.*

The Excelsior Café. This elegant Victorian restaurant, with its hardwood floors, closet-size bar and accomplished chefs, is a university tradition. The sparely decorated dining room, shaded by blossoming cherry trees in the spring, has a quiet, scholarly ambience. Despite the simple setting, there is nothing spare about the food here: Glorious fresh-baked breads and desserts and imaginative, well-executed sandwiches, pastas, sautées, and grills form the backbone of the menu. Also try the excellent Sunday brunch. *754 E. 13th Ave., tel. 503/342–6963. Reservations accepted for parties of 6 or more. Dress: casual but neat; tie acceptable. AE, DC, MC, V. Closed weekend lunch. Moderate.*

Zenon Café. You never know what you'll find on the menu here—Thai, Italian, down-home barbecue, South American—but chances are you'll find it memorable and expertly prepared. The decor is clean, modern, simple, so as not to detract from the real stars: The entrees, desserts like Black Velvet cake, a Willamette Valley wine list that changes as often as the menu. There's a fine local wine list, as well. *898 Pearl St., tel. 503/343–3005. No reservations. Dress: casual. MC, V. Moderate.*

Poppi's Anatolia. For years a joyful, slightly seedy taverna called Poppi's near the University of Oregon campus distributed home-style Greek food, retsina (very dry Greek white wine), Aegean beer, and music with equal liberality. Now Poppi's has moved downtown, changed names slightly, and generally spruced up. The food—particularly a lovely moussaka and *kalamarakia* (fried squid)—is still great, and the atmosphere is still as exuberant as a slightly more upscale clientele will allow. *992 Willamette St., tel. 503/343–9661. Reservations accepted for parties of 6 or more. Dress: casual. MC, V. Closed Sun. lunch. Inexpensive.*

Lodging **The Mapletree Inn.** This sprawling five-bedroom Queen Anne–
★ style home has graced this corner near the university since 1903, but it wasn't until quite recently that anyone thought about turning it into a B&B. An extensive renovation, finished in 1990, has done just that—and it's a stunner. From its quiet antique-filled rooms to the well-stocked CD player in the living room and the wraparound sitting porch out front, this place feels like home. A glorified Continental breakfast, consisting of coffee, juice, fresh-baked breads, and pastries, is served in the dining room each morning. *412 E. 13th Ave., 97401, tel. 503/344–8807. 5 rooms, 3 with full bath, 2 with their own showers and shared toilet. MC, V. Moderate.*

Motel 6. Those who've stayed at a Motel 6 before know what to expect from this ultra-unassuming chain: a clean, well-maintained room, a swimming pool, and not much else. This 59-room specimen on the southern outskirts of Eugene provides exactly that—plus a quiet, surprisingly panoramic view over the Coburg Hills. The rather garish rooms are fine for sleeping, with functional, but not very plush furnishings. *3690 Glenwood Dr. (take the Glenwood exit from I–5), 97403, tel. 503/687–2395. Facilities: outdoor pool, 24-hr room service. AE, D, DC, MC, V. Inexpensive.*

Jacksonville **The Jacksonville Inn.** The eight guest rooms and basement din-
Dining and Lodging ing room of this 1863-vintage inn remind you of what the Wild
★ West might have been, had Leona Helmsley been in charge of the arrangements. Four-poster beds, scrubbed floors, and spotless old antiques are maintained with scrupulous attention to detail. The Continental fare and 600-label wine cellar in the dining room are among the best in southern Oregon. Fresh razor clams and veal dishes are house specialties here. You'll need to book well in advance, particularly from late June to August, when the Peter Britt Festival draws thousands of visitors here. *175 E. California St., 97530, tel. 503/899–1900. Reservations suggested. Dress: casual but neat. AE, D, DC, MC, V. Closed Mon. lunch.*

McKenzie Bridge
Lodging

The Log Cabin Inn. This romantic log cabin inn, on the banks of the wild, fish-filled McKenzie River, is an appropriate romantic weekend getaway. The inn is furnished with antique furniture, new beds and baths, and each room has a river view. The restaurant, featuring a decadent homemade beer-cheese soup, buffalo, venison, quail, salmon, and a famous marionberry cobbler, is delightful. *McKenzie Hwy., 97413, tel. 503/822–3432. 8 rooms. Facilities: excellent fishing, river views, restaurant, lounge. MC, V. Moderate.*

McMinnville
Dining
★

Nick's Italian Café. Ask any wine maker in the valley to name his favorite wine-country restaurant, and chances are that Nick's would head the list. It's not the decor—Nick's occupies a modestly furnished former dinette—but it might be Nick's voluminous wine cellar, a veritable New York Public Library of local vintages. The food is spirited and simple, reflecting the owner's northern Italian heritage. The five-course fixed-price menu changes nightly, but you should look for the steak with capers and the tender asparagus, simply grilled with olive oil. *521 E. 3rd St., tel. 503/434–4471. Reservations recommended. Dress: casual but neat. No credit cards; personal checks accepted. Closed lunch; Mon. Moderate.*

Roger's. With its emphasis on fresh fish, and its jaunty maritime decor and pleasant stream-side location (there's patio dining in the summer), this restaurant is a local family favorite. Great french fries and large, simply prepared seafood, coupled with reasonable prices, are the reason. *2121 E. 27th St., tel. 503/472–0917. Reservations accepted. Dress: casual but neat. AE, DC, MC, V. Closed lunch. Moderate.*

Lodging
★

Mattey House Bed & Breakfast. This 100-year-old Historic Register, Victorian-style home was built by English immigrant Joseph Mattey, a prosperous local butcher. Its current owners, the Irvins, rescued it in 1986, filling the vast old place with family antiques and hand-screened wallpapers. Now, with its cheerful marble fireplace and gourmet breakfasts (poached pears with raspberry sauce and scrambled eggs with smoked salmon are typical fare), this B&B is an area favorite. *10221 N.E. Mattey La., off Hwy. 99 W, ¼ mi south of Lafayette, 97128, tel. 503/434–5058. 4 rooms, 1 with private bath. MC, V. No smoking allowed inside. Moderate.*

Safari Motor Inn. This motel on McMinnville's main drag is more functional than fancy. The clean, comfortable accommodation in a wonderfully central wine-country location has modest rates and modern, up-to-date furnishings. *345 N. Hwy. 99 W (corner of 19th St.), 97128, tel. 503/472–5187. 90 rooms. Facilities: coffee shop, bar, modest weight room, Jacuzzi. AE, D, DC, MC, V. Inexpensive.*

Medford
Lodging
★

Under the Greenwood Tree. Regular guests at this B&B are hard-pressed to decide which they like most: the luxurious and romantic rooms, the stunning 10-acre gardens, or the breakfasts cooked by the owner, a Cordon Bleu chef. The interior is decorated with Renaissance splendor. Four hundred-year-old oaks hung with hammocks shade the inn itself, a 125-year-old farmhouse exuding French Country charm. There's a manicured 1-acre croquet lawn and a creaky three-story barn for exploring; an outbuilding holds the covered wagon that brought the property's original homesteaders westward on the Oregon Trail. *3045 Bellinger La. (midway between Medford and Ash-*

land; take Exit 27 from I–5 and follow Steward to Bellinger, about 3 mi), 97501, tel. 503/776–0000. MC, V. Expensive.

Motel 6. It's not the Savoy, but it's clean and cheap. Color schemes are primary; a typical room might contain a durable green bed with quarter-operated "music fingers," a color TV, table and chairs, and spartan bath. Perhaps one of the best attributes of this chain hotel is its close proximity to not only the Shakespeare Festival but also the Mt. Ashland ski area and Crater Lake. *950 Alba Dr. (off I–5 exit 27), 97504, tel. 503/773–4290. 167 units. Facilities: outdoor pool, nearby skiing. AE, D, DC, MC, V. Inexpensive.*

Oakland
Dining

Tolly's. Stroll past the Victorian ice-cream parlor downstairs and up to the second-floor opulent oak- and antique-filled upstairs dining room, where steaks, chicken, veal, shellfish, and salmon receive tender and multiethnic treatment. On any given night six or seven different countries, from Indonesia to Italy, might be represented on the menu, which features favorites such as lamb loin in a pan juice demiglaze and filet royale, topped with scampi, artichoke hearts, and lobster sauce. *115 Locust St. (take Exit 138 from I–5 to Oakland), tel. 503/459–3796. Reservations recommended. Dress: casual. AE, MC, V. Closed Mon. dinner. Moderate.*

Salem
Dining
★

The Inn at Orchard Heights. This handsome hilltop restaurant is filled with the sound of trickling water and soft classical music, and panoramic views overlooking the lights of the capital city. The deftly handled Continental menu, relying heavily on fresh local seafood, beef, and pasta, is enlivened by the European chef/owner's rich sauces. Standbys include fresh prawns stuffed with crabmeat, and pan-fried New York steak with pepper-cream sauce. *695 Orchard Heights Rd. NW (across the Willamette River from downtown Salem off Hwy. 221), tel. 503/378–1780. Reservations advised. Dress: casual but neat. AE, DC, MC, V. Closed weekend lunch; Sun. Moderate.*

Pilar's Restaurant. This small, romantic restaurant, with its skylit brick dining room, occupies the restored Reed Opera House in downtown Salem. Fresh pasta and seafood are the most prominent pillars of the Italian-inspired menu, but watch for the nightly specials featuring dishes such as salmon-stuffed black pasta ravioli in creamy salmon sauce. There's a nice salad bar, as well, which accompanies the entrées. *189 Liberty St. NE, tel. 503/371–1812. Reservations suggested. Dress: casual. AE, MC, V. Inexpensive–Moderate.*

Thompson Brewery & Public House. The atmosphere of this funky southern outpost of a Portland-based brew-pub empire is 60s-vintage rock-and-roll memorabilia and hand-painted woodwork in a series in the small intimate rooms. The food—mostly hearty sandwiches, salads, and pasta dishes—is good and remarkably cheap; families are welcome. There are 21 beer taps behind the bar, most pouring fresh local microbrews. Several, including Java Ale and Terminator Stout, are made on the premises in a tiny brewery enlivened by colorful original artwork. The surreal rendering of the state capitol as a spaceship, with Uncle Sam waving his hat astride the dome, is especially noteworthy. Tours are gladly welcomed. *3575 Liberty Rd. S (a 10-min drive south of the Capitol Mall), tel. 503/363–7286. No reservations. Dress: casual. MC, V. Inexpensive.*

Lodging

Chumaree Hotel. This is a clean, functional, 11-year-old hotel about five minutes from the capitol; its chief virtue is its location, in addition to a few unexpected luxuries, such as the spacious Jacuzzis in the presidential suites. Views of the freeway are not particularly desirable, but the remodeling, completed in 1991, enhanced the baths and public rooms. *3301 Market St. NE, 97301, tel. 503/370–7888 or 800/248–6273. 150 rooms. Facilities: indoor pool, sauna. AE, D, DC, MC, V. Moderate.*

State House Bed & Breakfast. Though the capital's only B&B tends to get a bit of the State Street noise, it makes up for the inconvenience in location and luxury; it's a five-minute walk from the Capitol Mall and Willamette University, and it has a large hot tub overlooking Mill Creek. The decor, in lacy, floral fabrics of sky blue and salmon, is a little fussy but warm. Ask for the Grand Suite—Hank Aaron once slept there, and besides, it's the nicest room in Salem. Cabins, perfect for the family, are available in addition to rooms in the main building. *2146 State St., 97301, tel. 503/588–1340. 4 rooms, plus 2 cottages overlooking Mill Creek; 2 rooms with private bath. D, MC, V. Moderate.*

Steamboat
Dining and Lodging
★

The Steamboat Inn. Oregon's most famous fishing lodge, first brought to the world's attention in travel articles by Western writer Zane Grey in the 1930s, sits high above the emerald North Umpqua River. A veritable Who's Who of the world's top fly fishermen still converge on this very special nook in the Cascades every fall to try their luck against the 20-pound steelhead that haunt these waters. Others come simply to relax in the reading nooks or on the broad decks of the riverside guest cabins. Another renowned activity here is to partake in the nightly Fisherman's Dinner, a multicourse feast served around a massive 50-year-old sugar-pine dinner table. There are 12 sleep cabins in all, four with kitchens. Especially during July–October, the prime fishing months, you'll need to make reservations well in advance. *Steamboat, 97447 (about 40 mi east of Roseburg on Hwy. 138), tel. 503/498–2411. Facilities: restaurant, world-class fishing, riverside location, nearby hiking, wildlife viewing, fishing equipment rentals and sales. Guide services available. MC, V. Moderate–Expensive.*

Talent
Dining

Chata. Locals rave about the food, the service, and the warm atmosphere at this Eastern European restaurant, run by a Polish immigrant couple and their children. Try the piroshki (meat or vegetable-filled dumplings in a delicate sour-cream sauce) or the *co za bimba* ("What a party!" in Polish)—a thick T-bone steak sautéed with fresh mushrooms, so named because that's what someone in meat-scarce Poland might say if presented with such a feast. *1212 S. Pacific Hwy. (Hwy. 99), tel. 503/535–2575. Reservations suggested. Dress: casual. MC, V. Closed lunch. Moderate.*

Yamhill
Lodging
★

Flying M Ranch. The mysterious red "M" signs begin in downtown Yamhill and continue west for 10 miles into the Chehalem Valley, in the foothills of the Coast Range. Following them will bring you to the 625-acre Flying M Ranch, perched above the steelhead-filled Yamhill River. The centerpiece of this charming complex is the great log lodge, decorated in a style best described as Daniel Boone eclectic and featuring a bar carved from a single six-ton tree trunk. Guests have their choice of cabins (the cozy, hot tub–equipped Honeymoon Cabin is the nicest) or 28 riverside hotel units. Parents should take note, however: There are no TVs or telephones. Be sure to book ahead for a Flying M specialty: the Steak Fry Ride, where guests, aboard their choice of horse or a 120-year-old stage-coach, ride into the mountains to the ranch's elk camp for a feast of barbecued steak with all the trimmings. *From Newberg, take Hwy. 240 west to Yamhill, then follow the small red Flying M signs west to 23029 N.W. Flying M Rd., 97148, tel. 503/662–3222. 28 units, 7 cabins, more than 100 campsites. Facilities: restaurant, bar, live entertainment, swimming hole, tennis court, basketball court, horseshoe pits, horseback riding, fishing, hiking. AE, D, DC, MC, V. Moderate–Expensive. Closed Dec. 24–25.*

The Arts and Nightlife

The Arts

Ashland Every year, nearly 400,000 *Hamlet*-quoting fanatics descend on Ashland for the **Oregon Shakespeare Festival** (Box 158, Ashland 97520, tel. 503/482–4331). In three different theaters from February through October, this accomplished repertory company stages some of the finest Shakespearean productions you're likely to see on this side of Stratford—plus works by Ibsen, Williams, and other more modern writers. There are backstage tours, noon lectures, and Renaissance music and dancing before each outdoor performance. The best time to go is from June through October, when the 1,200-seat Elizabethan Theatre, an atmospheric re-creation of Shakespeare's Globe, is operating. Be forewarned that tickets are difficult to come by—the festival generally operates at 98% of capacity, and you'll need to book ahead.

Eugene The **Hult Center For the Performing Arts** (1 Eugene Ctr., Eugene 97401, tel. 503/342–5746) is an airy, spacious confection of glass and native wood, containing two of the most acoustically perfect theaters on the West Coast. In the course of a typical year, the complex hosts everything from Broadway shows to ballet, from heavy-metal music to Haydn.

Jacksonville Every summer some of the finest musicians in the world gather in this historic Wild West town for the **Peter Britt Festival** (Box 1124, Medford 97501, tel. 503/773–6077 or 800/882–7488), a weekly series of outdoor concerts and theater presentations lasting from late June to early September. Contemporary and classical performances are held in a natural amphitheater on the estate of early photographer Peter Britt.

Nightlife

Lounges, restaurants, and bars throughout Western Oregon provide the outlet for the region's nightly entertainment. In Salem, visit the **Union Street Oyster Bar** (445 State St., tel. 503/362–7219). In Ashland, the after-theater crowd (including many of the actors) congregates in the bar at **Chateaulin** (52 E. Main St., tel. 503/482–2264) for a nightcap. The **Rogue Brewery and Public House** (318 Water St., tel. 503/488–5061) caters to a younger crowd.

5 Seattle

Introduction

By Adam Woog and Loralee Wenger

Adam Woog is a Seattle-based freelance writer whose works have appeared in the Village Voice, Seattle Times, *and* Japan Times. *Loralee Wenger is the former travel editor for* Pacific Northwest *magazine and a freelance writer whose articles have appeared in the* San Francisco Examiner, Washington Post, Parade *magazine, and* Glamour *magazine.*

Seattle is defined by water. There's no use denying the city's damp weather, or the fact that its skies are cloudy for much of the year. People in Seattle don't tan—goes the joke—they rust. Vendors at the city's waterfront Public Market sell T-shirts that read "Seattle Rain Festival: January through December."

But Seattle is also defined by a different sort of water. A variety of rivers, lakes, and canals bisect steep hills, creating a series of distinctive areas along the water's edge that provide for a variety of activities. Funky fishing boats and floating homes, swank yacht clubs and waterfront restaurants, exist side by side.

But a city is defined by people as well as by its layout, and the people of Seattle—some half million within the city proper, another 2 million in the surrounding Puget Sound region—are a diversified bunch. Seattle has long had an active Asian and Asian-American population, as well as being home to well-established communities of Scandinavians, Afro-Americans, Jews, Native Americans, Hispanics, and other ethnic groups.

True, it's impossible to accurately generalize about such a varied group. Still, the prototypical Seattleite was pithily summed up by a *New Yorker* cartoon several years ago in which one arch-eyebrowed East Coast matron says to another, "They're backpacky, but nice." And it's true, nearly everyone in Seattle shares a love for the outdoors.

Aided by the proximity of high mountains (the Cascades to the east, the Olympics to the west) and water (both salt water and fresh water are everywhere), Seattle's vigorous outdoor sports are perennial favorites. The city's extensive park system (designed by Frederick Law Olmsted, creator of New York City's Central Park) and miles of secluded walking and bicycling paths add to one's appreciation of Seattle's surroundings.

On the other hand, the climate tends to foster an easygoing, indoor lifestyle, too. Overcast days and long winter nights help make Seattle a haven for moviegoers and book readers—the city is often used by Hollywood as a testing ground for new films and, according to independent bookstore sales and per-capita book purchases, the city ranks in the highest category.

Shedding its sleepy-town image, Seattle is one of the fastest-growing cities in the United States. For years, giant aerospace manufacturer Boeing was the only major factor in the area's economy besides lumber and fishing—the staples of the Northwest Coast. But as the 1962 World's Fair (and its enduring symbol, the Space Needle) signaled a change from small town to medium-size city, so the 1990s Goodwill Games announced the city's new role as a respected international hub. Seattle is now a major seaport and a vital link in Pacific Rim trade, and the evidence of internationalism is everywhere, from the discreet Japanese script identifying downtown department stores (i.e., "Nordstrom" written as "Katakana") to the multilingual recorded messages at Seattle-Tacoma International Airport.

The town that Sir Thomas Beacham once described as a "cultural wasteland" now has all the trappings of a full-blown big city, with ad agencies and artists' co-ops, symphonies and ballet companies. A variety of magazines compete with the two daily newspapers. There's an innovative new convention center, a covered dome for professional sports, a world-renowned theater scene, an excellent opera company, and a strong music world.

As the city grows, though, it is also beginning to display big-city problems. Increases in crime, drug abuse, homelessness, and poverty are coupled with a decline in the quality of the public schools. Construction of new skyscrapers has disrupted downtown life for years. Suburban growth, meanwhile, is rampant; nearby Bellevue, the largest suburb, has swollen in just a few years from a quiet farming community to the second-largest city in the state. Further, the area is plagued with one of the worst traffic problems in the country. But Seattleites are a strong political group with a great love for their city and a commitment to maintaining its reputation as one of the most livable in the country.

Essential Information

Arriving and Departing by Plane

Seattle-Tacoma International Airport is 20 miles from downtown Seattle, and is served by Air BC (tel. 206/467–7928), Air Canada (tel. 206/467–7928), Alaska (tel. 206/433–3100), American (tel. 800/433–7300), America West (tel. 206/763–0737), British Airways (tel. 800/247–9297), Canadian (tel. 800/426–7000), Coastal (tel. 206/433–6343), Continental (tel. 206/624–1740), Delta (tel. 206/433–4711), Harbor (tel. 800/521–3450), Hawaiian (tel. 800/367–5320), Horizon (tel. 800/547–9308), Japan (tel. 800/525–3663), Northwest (tel. 206/433–3500), Pan American (tel. 800/221–1111), TWA (tel. 206/447–9400), Thai (tel. 206/467–0600), United (tel. 206/441–3700), United Express (tel. 206/441–3700), and USAir (tel. 206/587–6229).

Between the Airport and Center City
By Bus
Gray Line Airport Express (tel. 206/626–6088) operates buses from major downtown hotels from 6:10 AM to 11:45, with departures every 20–30 minutes, depending on hotel. Fare: $7 one-way, and $12 round-trip.

Shuttle Express (tel. 206/622–1424) offers service to and from the airport. Fares are $14 for singles one-way or $21 for two one-way tickets.

By Taxi Taxis to the airport take 30–45 minutes; the fare is about $25.

Arriving and Departing by Car, Bus, and Train

By Car I–5 enters Seattle from the north and south, I–90 from the east.

Washington law requires all passengers to be buckled into seat belts. Children under age 5 should use car seats. Cars are allowed to turn right at a red light after stopping to check for oncoming traffic.

By Bus Seattle is served by **Greyhound** (8th Ave. and Stewart St., tel. 206/624–3456), a nationwide bus line.

By Train **Amtrak** (303 S. Jackson St., tel. 800/USA–RAIL) provides rail transportation from Seattle.

Getting Around Seattle

By Car Many downtown streets are one-way, so a map with arrows is especially helpful. Main thoroughfares into downtown are Aurora Avenue (the part through downtown is called the Alaskan Way Viaduct) and I–5.

By Bus **Metropolitan Transit** (821 2nd Ave., tel. 206/553–3000) provides a free-ride service in the downtown-waterfront area. Fares to other destinations range from 55¢ to $1.25, depending on the zone and time of day.

By Ferry The **Washington State Ferry System** (tel. 206/464–6400 or 206/464–2000, ext. 5500) is the largest in the world. Ferries leave from downtown Seattle for Winslow (Bainbridge Island) and Bremerton (Kitsap Peninsula) several times daily. Foot-passenger ferries travel to Vashon Island and Southworth (Kitsap Peninsula). Car and passenger ferries leave from Fauntleroy, in West Seattle, to Vashon Island and Southworth; from Edmonds, north of Seattle, to Kingston; and from Mukilteo, further north, to Clinton (Whidbey Island). In Anacortes, about 90 minutes north of Seattle, ferries depart for the San Juan Islands and for Vancouver Island, British Columbia. Fares range from as low as $1.10 for children 5–11 and senior citizens traveling the Mukilteo to Clinton route, to $31.25 for a car and driver going one way from Anacortes to Sydney.

Victoria Clipper I and **II** (tel. 206/448–5000), passenger catamarans, leave from Pier 69. They make the trip to Victoria in 2½ hours and depart four times daily in the summer; two times daily in spring and fall, and once daily in winter. Fares are $79 round-trip. Reservations are necessary.

By Monorail The **Monorail** (tel. 206/684–7200), built for the 1962 World's Fair, runs direct from Westlake Center to the Seattle Center every 15 minutes. Hours are Sunday–Thursday 9–9 and Friday and Saturday 9 AM–midnight. Fare is 60¢ each way; free for children under 6.

By Trolley **Waterfront trolleys** (tel. 206/553–3000) run from Pier 70 into Pioneer Square. Fares (55¢ nonpeak and 75¢ for travel during peak hours) are the same as bus fares.

By Taxi The taxi fare is $1.20 at the flag drop and $1.40 per mile. Major companies are **Farwest** (tel. 206/622–1717) and **Yellow Cab** (tel. 206/622–6500).

Important Addresses and Numbers

Tourist Information The **Seattle/King County Convention and Visitors Bureau** (800 Convention Pl., tel. 206/461–5840), at the I–5 end of Pike Street, can provide you with maps and information about lodging, restaurants, and attractions throughout the city.

Emergencies For **police, ambulance,** or **other emergencies,** dial 911.

Hospitals Area hospitals with emergency rooms include **Harborview Medical Center** (325 9th Ave., tel. 206/223–3074) and **Virginia Mason Hospital** (925 Seneca St., tel. 206/583–6433).

Pharmacies **Fred Meyer** (417 Broadway Ave. E, tel. 206/323–6586) is open until 10 PM.

Guided Tours

Orientation   Several guided tours of Seattle's waterfront and nearby areas
are available, primarily during summer months. From Pier 55,
Seattle Harbor Tours offers one-hour tours exploring Elliott
Bay and the Port of Seattle. The vessel is the *Goodtime III*,
part of the biggest charter fleet in Seattle. Sailings vary according to season, with up to six daily during peak months.
*Pier 55, Suite 201, 98101, tel. 206/623–1445. Cost: $8.50 adults,
$7.50 senior citizens, $6 youths 12–17, $4 children 5–12.*

Major Northwest Tours offers a 2¼-hour tour from Pier 56 of the
harbor and the Hiram Chittendan Locks, with a return by bus.
*1415 Western Ave., Suite 503, Seattle 98101, tel. 206/292–0595.
Tours depart noon and 3. Cost: $17 adults, $9 children.*

Gray Line offers guided bus tours of the city and environs,
ranging in scope from a daily 2½-hour spin to a six-hour "Grand
City Tour." The company also offers various specialized tours,
including the Boeing 747-767 plants, Mt. Rainier, dinner
cruises, and Seattle's waterways by boat. *All departures from
the downtown Sheraton, 1400 6th Ave., tel. 206/626–5208. Free
transfer service from major downtown hotels. Reservations required.*

Special-Interest   From Pier 56, **Tillicum Village Tours** sails across Puget Sound
to Blake Island, south of Bainbridge Island, for a four-hour ex-
amination of traditional Native American life. A dinner including steamed clams and salmon is served, and presentations are
given of dances, wood carving, and other aspects of West Coast
Indian culture. *Pier 56, tel. 206/443–1244. Tour schedule varies
during the year, with up to 3 tours leaving daily during peak
months. Cost: $35 adults, $32 senior citizens, $24 youths 13–
19, $14 children 6–12, $7 children 3–5; children under 3 free.*

The **Spirit of Puget Sound** runs dinner cruises in Elliot Bay evenings from 7–10 on a sleek, 175-foot yacht. The cruise includes
beef, salmon, and chicken buffet dinner; a 30-minute Broadway
revue; and 1 hour of dancing to a five-piece band. Moonlight
cocktail cruises set sail at 11:30 and return at 2 AM, and feature
a nightclub atmosphere. *2819 Elliot Ave., Suite 204, Seattle
98121, tel. 206/443–1439. Cost for dinner cruise ranges from
$36.70–$40.80, depending on weekends or weeknight travel; for
moonlight cruises, $14 per person. Call for schedules.*

Gray Line (*see* above).

Seattle's Chinatown, now known as the International District,
reflecting its multicultural flavor, is one of the largest Asian-
American enclaves in North America. **Chinatown Discovery
Tours** offers groups (and individuals on a space-available basis)
a three-hour tour of the area that includes such sights as a fortune cookie factory, a Chinese market, and an herb dispensary.
Tours end with a traditional dim sum or dinner banquet. *Box
3406, 98114, tel. 206/236–0657. Cost varies depending on tour.
Tours offered Tues.–Sat., several times during the day and
evening.*

One of the most beloved of Seattle's tours is the **Underground
Tour,** begun in 1965 by feisty entrepreneur/historian Bill
Speidel as an effort to help preserve the then-derelict Pioneer
Square area. This 90-minute walking tour explores (with
tongue-in-cheek narration) the rough-and-tumble history of

early Seattle; the Great Fire of 1889, which destroyed most of downtown; and the fascinating below-ground sections of Pioneer Square that have been abandoned (and built on top of) since 1907. This tour, however, is not wheelchair- or stroller-accessible, as six flights of stairs are involved. *Departure from Doc Maynard's Public House, 610 1st Ave., tel. for reservations, 206/682–4646; tel. for schedules, 206/682–1511. Cost: $4.75 adults, $3.50 senior citizens and youths 13–17 or with valid student ID, $2.25 children 6–12, children under 6 free. Reservations recommended. Tours run daily except Easter, Thanksgiving, Christmas Eve, Christmas Day, and New Year's Day. Tour schedule varies with season, with up to 7 tours daily in summer.*

Self-Guided   Also worth exploring are the unusual self-guided tours found in "Steps to Enjoying Seattle's Public Art," an illustrated brochure published by the Seattle Arts Commission. It describes walks and drives to see more than 1,000 innovative works of **art in public places**. Among these treasures are brass dance-steps inlaid on the sidewalks of Broadway, whirligigs festooning a neighborhood power substation, an "ark" of animals at Woodland Park Zoo, murals on downtown high rises, and a "sound garden" of acoustical sculptures in a lakeside park. "Steps to Enjoying Seattle's Public Art" is free from the Seattle Arts Commission (305 Harrison St., 98109, tel. 206/684–7171).

Ballooning   **Balloon Depot** (16138 N.E. 87th St., Redmond 98052, tel. 206/881–9699) offers 90-minute balloon flights for $99–$125 per person, with a half-price discount for children under age 11 who are accompanied by an adult. **Lighter Than Air Adventures** (21808 N.E. 175th St., Woodinville 98072, tel. 206/788–2454) has evening flights lasting 30 minutes–one hour for $125 per person, as well as morning flights lasting one–two hours and featuring a champagne brunch for $145 per person. The **Great Northwest Aerial Navigation Company** (7616 79th Ave. SE, Mercer Island 98040, tel. 206/232–2023) specializes in longer flights and gourmet picnics, lasting about four hours, surveying the Snohomish Valley north and east of Seattle. Morning and evening picnic flights, $145 on weekends, $130 weekdays; flights only, $105.

Highlights for First-time Visitors

Kingdome (*see* Exploring Seattle, below).
Pioneer Square (*see* Exploring Seattle, below).
Seattle Center (*see* Exploring Seattle, below).
Space Needle (*see* Exploring Seattle, below).

Exploring Seattle

Numbers in the margin correspond to points of interest on the Downtown Seattle map.

Downtown   Downtown Seattle is bounded by the Kingdome to the south, the Seattle Center to the north, I–5 to the east, and the waterfront to the west. You can reach most points of interest by foot, bus, or the monorail. Bear in mind that Seattle is a city of hills, so comfortable walking shoes are a must.

❶ Start at the **Seattle Visitor Information Center** to pick up maps, brochures, and listings of events. *666 Stewart St., tel. 206/461–*

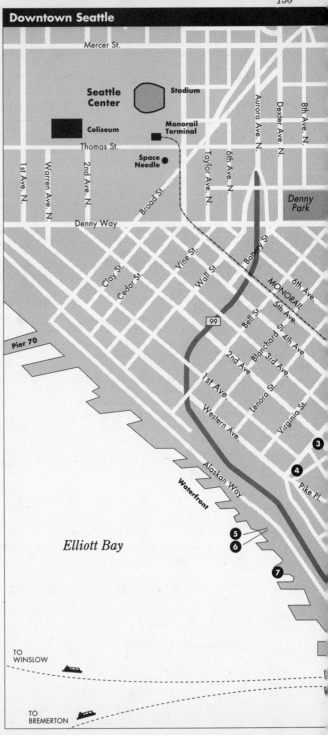

Downtown Seattle

Mercer St.

Seattle Center

Stadium

Coliseum

Monorail Terminal

Thomas St.

Space Needle

Aurora Ave. N.

Dexter Ave. N.

8th Ave. N.

Taylor Ave. N.

6th Ave. N.

1st Ave. N.

Warren Ave. N.

2nd Ave. N.

Denny Park

Broad St.

Denny Way

Clay St.

Cedar St.

Vine St.

Wall St.

Battery St.

6th Ave.

MONORAIL

5th Ave.

99

Bell St.

St. 4th Ave.

Blanchard 3rd Ave.

2nd Ave.

1st Ave.

Lenora St.

Virginia St.

Western Ave.

Pier 70

Alaskan Way

Waterfront

Pike Pl.

3

4

5

6

7

Elliott Bay

TO WINSLOW

TO BREMERTON

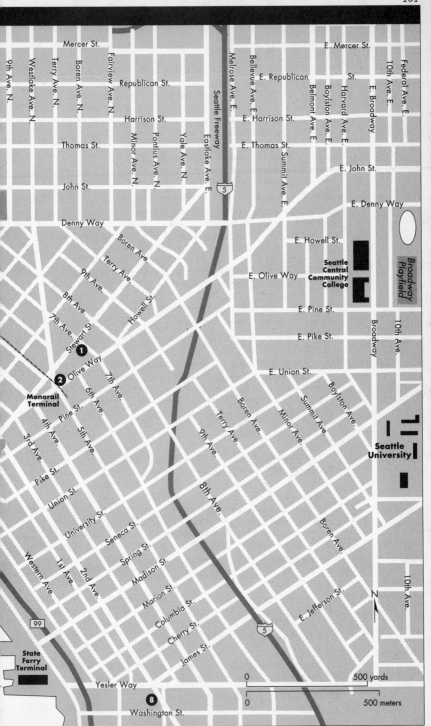

5840. Open weekdays 8:30–5. Other location at the Seattle Center, adjacent to the Space Needle, tel. 206/000–0000. Open Memorial Day–Labor Day.

From the Information Center, you can proceed either north or south. If you choose the latter, take Westlake Avenue to **2 Westlake Center** (*see* Shopping, below), a complex completed in 1989, in spite of the controversy surrounding its construction. The conflict occurred between city residents—some of whom objected to the 27-story office tower and three-story shopping structure with enclosed walkways—and favored, instead, the large grassy park without commercial buildings. In any case, the center is a major terminus for buses and the monorail, which goes north to Seattle center. *1601 5th Ave., tel. 206/467–1600. Open weekdays 9:30–9.*

Make your way from 5th Avenue west to 2nd Avenue. The **3** doors to the new **Seattle Art Museum** will open in the winter of 1991, and the five-story building, designed by post-modern theorist Robert Venturi, is a work of art in itself. The building features a limestone exterior with large-scale vertical fluting, accented by terra-cotta, cut granite, and marble. The museum displays an extensive collection of Asian, Native American, African, Oceanic, and pre-Columbian art, a café, and gift shop. *1320 2nd Ave., tel. 206/625–8900. Admission: $2 adults, $1 senior citizens and students, children under 6 free; free admission on Thurs. and Sun.; free tours Tues.–Sun. at 2, Thurs. at 7. Open Tues.–Sat. 10–5, Thurs. 10–9, Sun. noon–5. Closed Mon., Thanksgiving, Christmas, and New Year's Day.*

4 Go west one block to 1st Avenue and one block north to the **Pike Place Market**, a Seattle institution. It began in 1907 when the city issued permits to farmers allowing them to sell produce from their wagons parked at Pike Place. Later, the city built stalls that were allotted to the farmers on a daily basis. At one time the market was a madhouse of vendors hawking their produce, haggling over prices; some of the fishmongers still carry on this kind of frenzied banter, but chances are you won't get them to waver on their prices. Urban renewal almost killed the market, but just as planners were about to do away with it, city voters led by the late architect Victor Steinbreuck (for whom the park near the market was named) rallied and voted it to be a historical asset. Many of the buildings have been restored, and the project is now connected by stairs and elevator to the waterfront. You can still find fresh seafood (which can be packed in dry ice for your flight home), produce, cheese, Northwest wines, bulk spices, tea, coffee, and arts and crafts sold here. *1st Ave. at Pike St., tel. 206/682–7453. Open Mon.–Sat. 9–6, Sun. 11–5.*

From the market, take the stairs or elevator down to the waterfront. In the early days, the waterfront was the center of activity in Seattle; today it stretches some 19 blocks, from Pier 70 and Myrtle Edwards Park in the north, where there is a bicycle and jogging trail, down to Pier 51 in Pioneer Square.

Pier 70, to the south of the park, is a large warehouse converted to shops, galleries, restaurants, and bars.

5 At the base of the Pike Street Hillclimb at Pier 59 is the **Seattle Aquarium**, showcasing Northwest marine life. Sea otters and seals swim and dive in their pools, and the "State of the Sound" exhibit shows aquatic life and the ecology of Puget Sound. *Pier 59, tel. 206/386–4320. Admission: $5.75 adults, $3.50 youths and senior citizens, $2.50 children 6–12, children under 6 free. Open daily 10–7.*

6 Next to the aquarium is the **Omnidome Film Experience,** which includes subjects such as the eruption of Mt. St. Helens and a study of sharks and whales. *Pier 59, tel. 206/622–1868. Admission: $5.95 adults, $4.95 youths 13–18 and senior citizens, $3.95 children 6–12, children under 6 free; combination tickets for the Omnidome and aquarium: $9.95 adults, $6.75 youths 13–18 and senior citizens, $5.10 children 6–12. Open daily 10–5.*

7 The **historical marker** indicating the landing of the ship *Portland,* on July 17, 1897, is at Pier 58. The ship brought gold and news of the Klondike gold rush; shops at this pier continue to commemorate the event with gold-rush theme merchandise.

From Pier 51 at the foot of Yesler Way, walk a couple of blocks east to **Pioneer Park,** where an ornate iron and glass pergola stands. This was the site of Henry Yesler's (one of Seattle's first businesspeople) pier and sawmill and Seattle's original business district. In 1889, a fire destroyed many of the wood-frame **8** buildings in the area now known as **Pioneer Square,** but the industrious residents and businesspeople rebuilt them with brick and mortar.

The term Skid Row originated here, when timber was logged off the hill and sent to the sawmill. The skid road was made of small logs laid crossways and greased so the freshly cut timber could slide down to the mill. With the Klondike gold rush, this area became populated with saloons and brothels; businesses gradually moved north, and the old pioneering area deteriorated. Eventually, drunks and bums hung out on Skid Road, and the term changed to Skid Row. Today, Pioneer Square encompasses about 18 blocks and includes restaurants, bars, shops, and the city's largest concentration of art galleries. In Pioneer Square is the **Klondike Gold Rush National Historical Park** and interpretive center. The center provides insight on the story of Seattle's role in the 1897–98 gold rush through film presentations, permanent exhibits, and gold-panning demonstrations. *117 S. Main St., tel. 206/442–7220. Admission free. Open daily 9–5, except major holidays.*

Numbers in the margin correspond to points of interest on the Metropolitan Seattle map.

9 Walk a half block east on Main Street, and two blocks south on Occidental Avenue to the **Kingdome,** Seattle's covered stadium where the Seattle Seahawks NFL team and the Seattle Mariners baseball team play. The 650-feet-diameter stadium was built in 1976 and has the world's largest self-supporting roof, which sits 250 feet high. If you're interested in the inner workings, take the one-hour guided tour. *201 S. King St., tel. 206/296–3111 for information. Admission: $3 adults, $1.50 children and senior citizens.*

10 To the east is a 40-square-block area known as the **International District** (the ID). Inhabited by about one-third Chinese and one-third Filipino, other residents come from all over Asia. The ID began as a haven for Chinese workers after they finished the

Boeing Field, **21**
Henry Art Gallery, **18**
International
District, **10**
Kingdome, **9**
Museum of History
and Industry, **19**
Nippon Kan
Theater, **11**
Seattle Center, **13**
Space Needle, **14**
Thomas Burke
Memorial Washington
State Museum, **17**
University of
Washington, **16**
Washington Park
Arboretum, **20**
Wing Luke
Museum, **12**
Woodland Park
Zoo, **15**

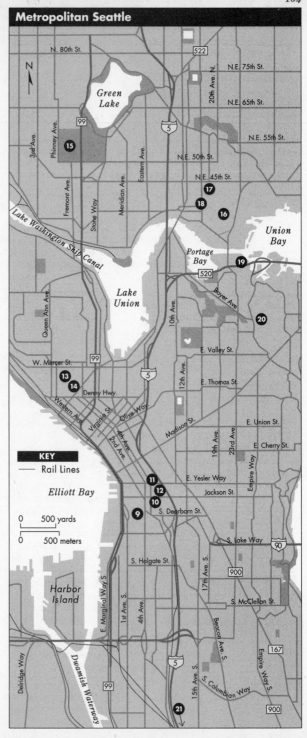

Metropolitan Seattle

N. 80th St.

522

N.E. 75th St.

N

20th Ave. N.

N.E. 65th St.

*Green
Lake*

99

N.E. 55th St.

5

3rd Ave.

Phinney Ave.

15

N.E. 50th St.

Eastern Ave.

N.E. 45th St.

17

Meridian Ave.

18

16

Stone Way

Fremont Ave.

*Union
Bay*

Lake Washington Ship Canal

*Portage
Bay*

19

520

*Lake
Union*

Boyer Ave.

10th Ave.

20

Queen Ann Ave.

E. Valley St.

W. Mercer St.

99

12th Ave.

E. Thomas St.

13

14

Denny Hwy.

5

Western Ave.

Virginia St.

Olive Way

Madison St.

19th Ave.

E. Union St.

4th Ave.

23rd Ave

E. Cherry St.

2nd Ave.

Empire Way

KEY

Rail Lines

E. Yesler Way

11

Elliott Bay

12

Jackson St.

10

0   500 yards

9

S. Dearborn St.

0   500 meters

S. Lake Way

90

S. Holgate St.

17th Ave. S.

900

*Harbor
Island*

S. McClellan St.

E. Marginal Way S.

1st Ave. S.

4th Ave.

Beacon Ave. S.

167

Delridge Way

15th Ave. S.

S. Columbian Way

Empire Way S.

99

Duwamish Waterway

5

21

900

Transcontinental Railroad. The community has remained intact, despite the anti-Chinese riots in Seattle during the 1880s and the World War II Japanese-American internment. The district, which includes many Chinese, Japanese, and Korean restaurants, also houses herbalists, massage parlors, acupuncturists, and about 30 private clubs for gambling and socializing. The most notorious club is the **Wah Mee Club,** on Canton Avenue, where a multiple murder linked to gangs and gambling occurred in 1983. **Uwajimaya** (519 6th Ave. S, tel. 206/624–6248), one of the—if not *the*—largest Japanese stores on the West Coast, is in this district as well. Here you will find china, gifts, fabrics, housewares, and a complete supermarket with an array of Asian foods.

Time Out If you're feeling a need to rest your feet a bit by now, stop in at **Okazuya,** the Asian snack bar (tel. 206/624–6248) in Uwajimaya. You can get noodle dishes, sushi, tempura, humbow, and other Asian dishes for carryout or to eat in.

From Uwajimaya, continue north on 6th Street to Washington Street. In summer, as you walk up the hill, you can see the many gardens tended by residents of the ID.

⓫ Historically, the **Nippon Kan Theater** (628 S. Washington St., tel. 206/467–6807) was the focal point for Japanese-American activities, including kabuki theater. Renovated and reopened in 1981 as a national historic site, it presents many Asian-interest productions, including the Japanese Performing Arts series, which runs from October through May.

⓬ The final stop on the southbound Downtown Seattle tour will be at the **Wing Luke Museum,** named for the first Asian person to be elected to a Seattle city office, where exhibits emphasize Oriental history and culture. An acupuncture exhibit demonstrates how needles are inserted into parts of the body to release blocked energy and promote healing. Other elements of the permanent collection includes costumes, fabrics, crafts, basketry, and Chinese traditional medicines. *407 7th Ave. S, tel. 206/623–5124. Admission: $2.50 adults, $1 senior citizens and students, 50¢ children. Open Tues.–Fri. 11–4:30, weekends noon–4; closed Mon.*

North of To explore outside the downtown area, take the 4th Avenue bus
Downtown to Westlake Center, where you can pick up the Monorail to
⓭ **Seattle Center,** a 74-acre complex built for the 1962 Seattle World's Fair. It includes an amusement park, the very popular Space Needle with restaurant and observation deck, theaters,
⓮ the Coliseum, exhibition halls, museums, and shops. The **Space Needle,** a Seattle landmark easily recognized from almost anywhere in the downtown area, looks much like something from the "Jetsons" cartoon show. The glass elevator to the observation deck offers an impressive view of the city.

Time Out The **Space Needle Lounge** (tel. 206/443–2100), on the observation deck (one floor above the Space Needle Restaurant), offers fabulous views of Elliot Bay and Queen Anne Hill. The black-and-grey exterior decor emphasizes the 1960s style of the Needle. Ask the bartender for the special "Spirit of the Needle" cocktail or choose from the full bar.

From downtown or from the Seattle Center, take Highway 99
(Aurora Ave. N) north across the Aurora Bridge to the 50th
⑮ Street exit; follow signs to the **Woodland Park Zoo,** where many
of the animals are free to roam their section of the total of 92
acres. The African savannah and the new elephant house are
popular features. Wheelchairs and strollers can be rented. *N.
59th St. and Fremont Ave., tel. 206/684–4800. Admission:
$4.50 adults, $2.25 children 6–17 and senior citizens, children
under 5 free. Open summer, daily 9:30–6; winter, daily 10–4.*

From the Woodland Park Zoo, take the 50th Street exit to 15th
Avenue NE, the head south to 45th Street. Turn east for a few
⑯ blocks to the entrance of the 33,500-student **University of Washington.** The U-Dub, as locals call it, was founded in 1861. On the
northwestern corner of the beautifully landscaped campus is
⑰ the **Thomas Burke Memorial Washington State Museum,** Washington's natural history and anthropological museum. The museum has been renovated recently and features exhibits on
cultures of the Pacific region and the state's 35 Native American tribes. *17th Ave. NE and N.E. 45th St., tel. 206/543–5590.
Admission free; special exhibit fees vary. Open Mon.–Wed.
and Fri.–Sun. 10–5, Thurs. 10–8.*

⑱ Going south, on the west side of the campus is the **Henry Art
Gallery,** which displays paintings from the 19th and 20th centuries, textiles, and traveling exhibits. *15th Ave. NE and N.E.
41st St., tel. 206/543–2280. Admission: $3 adults, $1.50 students and senior citizens; free Thurs. Open Tues.–Fri. 10–5,
Thurs. 10–9, weekends 11–5; closed Mon.*

Close to the university's Husky Stadium, off Montlake and
⑲ Lake Washington boulevards, is the **Museum of History and Industry.** An 1880s-era room and a Seattle time-line depict the
city's earlier days. Other rotating exhibits from the permanent
collection and traveling exhibits are displayed. *2700 24th Ave.
E, tel. 206/324–1125. Admission: $3 adults, $1.50 children 6–
12, children under 6 free. Open daily 10–5.*

At the museum pick up a brochure of self-guided walking tours
⑳ of the nearby **Washington Park Arboretum.** The arboretum's
Rhododendron Glen and Azalea Way are in full bloom from
March through June. During the rest of the year, other plants
and wildlife flourish. A new visitor center at the north end of
the park is open to instruct you on the species of flora and fauna
you'll see here. *2300 Arboretum Dr. E, tel. 206/325–4510. Admission free. Park open daily 7 AM–sunset; visitor center open
daily 10–4.*

㉑ If you have your own plane, land at **Boeing Field** to see the **Museum of Flight.** (You can also get there by metro bus #174 that
follows Second Avenue from downtown Seattle.) The **Red Barn,**
the original Boeing airplane factory, houses an exhibit on the
history of aviation. The **Great Gallery,** a dramatic structure designed by Seattle architect Ibsen Nelson, contains more than
20 airplanes—suspended from the ceiling and on the ground—
dating back to the Wright brothers. For a complete lesson, take
the free hour-long Boeing tour. *9404 E. Marginal Way S, tel.
206/764–5720. Admission: $5 adults, $3 children 6–16, children under 6 free. Open Mon.–Wed. and Fri.–Sun. 10–5,
Thurs. 10–9; closed Christmas.*

Seattle for Free

Rainier Brewery, located 2 miles south of the Kingdome on I–5, offers 30-minute tours of the premises that conclude with free samples for adults of the locally made beer. Daily tours are followed by a tasting. If you don't want to drive, take the #130 bus from downtown. *3100 Airport Way S, tel. 206/622–2600. Tours weekdays 1–6. No children under 3.*

Gallery Walk (begin at any gallery in Pioneer Square, tel. 206/587–0260), an open house hosted by Seattle's art galleries, explores new local exhibits the first Thursday of every month, starting at 5.

Thomas Burke Memorial Washington State Museum (*see* Exploring Seattle, above).

The **Charles and Emma Frye Art Museum** features a large collection of Munich School and American School paintings. *704 Terry Ave., tel. 206/622–9250. Open Mon.–Sat. 10–5, Sun. noon–5.*

The **Elliott Bay Book Company** (101 S. Main St., tel. 206/624–6600) hosts lectures and readings by authors of local and international acclaim. Most are free, but phone ahead to be sure.

Recreational Equipment, Inc. (REI, tel. 206/323–8333), the largest consumer co-op in the United States, hosts free programs on travel, adventure, and outdoor activities at Seattle (1525 11th Ave.), Bellevue (15400 N.E. 20th St.), and Federal Way (2565 Gateway Center Blvd. S) locations, starting at 7 PM every Thursday, and at Lynnwood (4200 194th St. SW) at 7 PM on Tuesdays.

Seattle's summer concerts, the **Out To Lunch Series** (tel. 206/623–0340), runs from mid-June to early September every weekday at noon in various parks, plazas, and atriums in downtown. Concerts feature local and national musicians and dancers. Call ahead for schedule and location.

What to See and Do with Children

Burke-Gilman Trail (*see* Sports and Fitness, below) offers good bike trails for children.

Burke Thomas Memorial Washington State Museum (*see* Exploring Seattle, above).

Elliott Bay Book Company (*see* Seattle for Free, above) hosts a children's story hour at 11 AM the first Saturday of the month.

Green Lake (*see* Sports and Fitness, below).

Museum of Flight (*see* Exploring Seattle, above).

Myrtle Edwards Park (*see* Exploring Seattle, above).

Seattle Aquarium (*see* Exploring Seattle, above).

Seattle Children's Museum is a colorful, spacious facility at the Seattle Center's Center House. An infant-toddler area features a giant, soft ferryboat for climbing and sliding. A bubble area helps children learn about shapes and gravity. The pretend neighborhood lets children play in a post office, café, fire station, grocery store, and more. Intergenerational programs, special exhibits, and workshops are offered. *Fountain level of Seattle Center House, 305 Harrison St., tel. 206/441–1768. Admission: $3, children under 1 free. Open Tues.–Sun. 10–5.*

Seattle Children's Theater is nationally recognized for its artistic excellence. Five plays per year, performed at the PONCHO Theatre, are presented by professional actors and are appropriate for children ages five and older and their families. *N. 50th St. and Freemont Ave. N, at south entrance to the Woodland Park Zoo, tel. 206/633–4567. Admission: $14 adults, $8.25 senior citizens, students, and children. Call for the performance schedule.*

Off the Beaten Track

Touring **brew pubs**—drinking establishments attached to actual breweries—is a congenial and educational alternative to usual city attractions. Seattle, as well as a good portion of the Pacific Northwest, has become a hotbed for microbrews (high-quality beers made for local distribution). Note that all brew pubs below serve a variety of food and nonalcoholic beverages. If live music is performed, a cover charge may be required; otherwise admission is free.

The **Pacific Northwest Brewing Co.,** located in the heart of Pioneer Square, offers six mild beers that reflect the taste of its British owner. The elegantly decorated interior—smooth high-tech design, blended with antiques and brewing equipment in full view—fits not only the personality of Richard Wrigley, the proprietor, but also the downtown location. *322 Occidental Ave. S, tel. 206/621–7002. Open Tues.–Sat. 11:30 AM–midnight.*

Near the north end of the Fremont Bridge, just 8 miles from downtown, is the **Trolleyman,** birthplace of the much-loved Ballard Bitter and Red Hook Ale. The premises mixes Northwest style—whitewashed walls and a nonsmoking policy—with a cozy British pub atmosphere that includes a fireplace and ample armchairs. *3400 Phinney Ave. N, tel. 206/548–8000. Open weekdays 8:30 AM–11 PM, Sat. 11–11, Sun. noon–6. Tours given weekdays at 3, weekends at 1:30, 2:30, 3:30, and 4:30.*

Catering to the nearby university crowd, the **Big Time Brewery** resembles a typical college pub, with a moose head on the walls and co-ed decor. Pale ale, amber, and porter are always on tap; specialty brews change monthly. *4133 University Way NE, tel. 206/545–4509. Open daily 11:30 AM–1 AM.*

Noggins, in the downtown Westlake Mall, offers at least five distinctive beers at a given time. *Westlake Mall, 400 Pine St., tel. 206/682–BREW. Open Mon.–Thurs. 9 AM–11 PM, Fri. and Sat. 9 AM–midnight, Sun. 11–9.*

Technically not a brew pub, **Cooper's Northwest Alehouse,** located north of the University District, nonetheless deserves mention as the mecca of Northwest microbreweries. Twenty-one of its 22 brews are specialties from all over the West Coast, and the staff is awesomely knowledgeable about their subtle distinctions between the brews. If you don't come for the drink, come for the dart tournaments that are played on a regular ba-

sis. *8065 Lake City Way NE, tel. 206/522–2923. Open weekdays
3 PM–2 AM, Sat. 1 PM–2 AM, Sun. 1 PM–midnight.*

Perhaps the best way to tour the pubs without worrying about
who's driving is to take a four-hour tour offered by **Northwest
Brewery & Pub Tours** (4224 1st Ave. NE, tel. 206/547–1186).
The $26 fee includes free tastings and van transportation on
weekend afternoons and Monday evenings. Reservations are
required.

If your preference is grapes, visit **Ste. Michelle Winery,** one of
the oldest wineries in the state. It's located 15 miles northeast
of Seattle, nestled on 87 wooded acres that were once part of
the estate of lumberman Fred Stimson. Some of the original
1912 buildings are still on the property, including the family
home—the manor house—which is on the National Register of
Historic Places. Trout ponds, a carriage house, a caretaker's
cottage, and formal gardens are part of the original estate. The
landscaping, created by New York's Olmsted family (designers
of New York City's Central Park), has been restored, and the
gardens feature hundreds of trees, shrubs, and plants. Visitors
are invited to picnic and explore the grounds. Delicatessen
items, wines, and wine-related gifts are available at the winery shop. In the summer, the company hosts a series of nationally recognized performers and arts events in the
amphitheater. *14111 N.E. 145th St., Woodinville, tel. 206/488–
1133. From downtown Seattle take I–90 east, then go north on
I–405. Take Exit 23 east (S.R. 522) to the Woodinville exit.
Complimentary wine tastings and cellar tours are available
daily 10–4:30, except for holidays.*

Another option if you're looking to go off the beaten track is to
visit the Hiram M. Chittenden Locks, more commonly called
the **Ballard Locks,** part of the 8-mile Lake Washington Ship Canal linking Lakes Washington and Union with the salt water of
Shilshole Bay and Puget Sound. Completed in 1917, the locks
currently service some 100,000 boats yearly by raising and low-
ering water levels anywhere from 6 to 26 feet.

The locks themselves are fascinating to watch as a variety of
commercial fishing boats and pleasure craft go through them,
but there are several other sights nearby that are well worth
seeing. The **Fish Ladder** has 21 levels that allow fish to swim
upstream on a gradual incline. A series of lighted windows lets
visitors watch several varieties of salmon and trout—an estimated half-million fish yearly—as they migrate upstream.
(This, by the way, is where various attempts are being carried
out to prevent sea lions, including the world-famous Herschel,
from depleting the salmon population.)

On the north side of the locks is a fine 7-acre **ornamental garden**
of native and exotic plants, shrubs, and trees. Also on the north
side is a staffed visitor center with displays on the history and
operation of the locks, and several fanciful sculptures by local
artists. Along the south side is a lovely 1,200-foot promenade
with a footbridge, fishing pier, and observation deck. *North
entrance, 3015 N.W. 54th St., west of the Ballard Bridge. Locks
tel. 206/783–7001; visitor center tel. 206/783–7059. Visitor center open daily 10–7; closed in winter, Tues., Wed.; locks open
year-round, except for maintenance.*

Two legendary performers—rock guitarist Jimi Hendrix and
kung-fu movie star Bruce Lee—are buried in the Seattle area;

their graves are popular sites for fans wishing to pay respects. In addition, there is a memorial to Hendrix, a Seattle native, overlooking the African Savannah exhibit at Woodland Park Zoo; appropriately enough, it's a very big rock.

Jimi Hendrix's grave site is at the Greenwood Cemetery, in Renton. *From Seattle, take I–5 south to the Renton exit, then I–405 past Southcenter to Exit 4B. Bear right under the freeway, take a right along Sunset Blvd. 1 block and right again up 3rd St. Continue 1 mi and go right at the 3rd light; the cemetery is on the corner of 3rd and Monroe Sts., tel. 206/255–1511. Open daily until dusk. Inquire at the office; a counselor will direct you to the site.*

Bruce Lee's grave site is at the Lakeview Cemetery on the north slope of Capitol Hill. *1554 15th Ave. E, directly north of Volunteer Park, tel. 206/322–1582. Open weekdays 9–4:30. Inquire at the office for a map.*

Shopping

Shopping Districts

Westlake Center (1601 5th Ave., tel. 206/467–1600) lies in the middle of downtown Seattle. The new three-story steel-and-glass building contains 80 upscale shops, as well as covered walkways to Seattle's three major department stores, **Nordstrom's, Frederick & Nelson,** and **The Bon.**

Pike Place Market (*see* Exploring Seattle, above).

The **University District** (University Ave., north and south of 45th St., tel. 206/527–2567) has an eclectic mixture of such student-oriented imports as ethnic jewelry and South American sweaters; a few upscale shops; and the city's largest concentration of bookstores.

Seattle's **Fremont area** (N. 35th St. and Fremont Ave. N, north of the ship canal and the Fremont Bridge), a remnant from hippie days, offers products of a different variety—namely funky and used. There's the **Daily Planet** (3416 Fremont Ave. N, tel. 206/633–0895), and **Guess Where** (615 N. 35th St., tel. 206/547–3793) for vintage clothing. At **Armadillo & Co.** (3510 Fremont Pl. N, tel. 206/633–4241) you'll find jewelry, T-shirts, and other armadillo-theme accessories and gifts. The **Frank & Dunya Gallery** (3418 Fremont Ave. N, tel. 206/547–6760) features unique art pieces, from furniture to jewelry. You'll also find **Dusty Strings** (3406 Fremont Ave. N, tel. 206/634–1656) a hammered dulcimer shop.

Capitol Hill's **Broadway Avenue** features clothing stores, high-design housewares shops, espresso bars, and restaurants. An unusual boutique is the **Bead Works** (233 Broadway Ave. E, tel. 206/323–4998).

Northgate Mall, located 10 miles north of downtown, encompasses 118 shops including **Nordstrom's, The Bon, Lamonts,** and **J.C. Penney.** *I–5 and Northgate Way, tel. 206/362–4777. Open Mon.–Sat. 9:30–9:30, Sun. 11–6.*

Southcenter Mall contains 140 shops, which are anchored by major department stores. *I–5 and I–405 in Tukwila, tel. 206/246–7400. Open Mon.–Sat. 9:30–9:30, Sun. 11–6.*

Bellevue Square, an upscale shopping center about 8 miles east of Seattle, houses more than 200 shops and includes a children's play area, the Bellevue Art Museum, and covered parking. *N.E. 8th St. and Bellevue Way, tel. 206/454–8096. Open Mon.–Sat. 9:30–9:30, Sun. 11–6.*

Specialty Stores

Antiques | **Antique Importers** (640 Alaskan Way, tel. 206/628–8905) carries mostly English oak antiques.

Art Dealers | **Michael Pierce Gallery** (600 Pine St., tel. 206/447–9166) specializes in limited-edition prints and paintings on paper.

Art Glass | The **Glass House** (311 Occidental Ave. S, tel. 206/682–9939), Seattle's only working glass studio, features one of the largest displays of glass in the city.

Chocolates | **Cafe Dilettante** (416 Broadway Ave. E, tel. 206/329–6463) is well-known for its mouth-watering dark chocolates. Recipes come via Julius Rudolf Franzen, who obtained them from the kitchen of the imperial court of Russia when he was commissioned by Czar Nicholas II as master pastry chef. Later, he was master chocolatier to Franz Joseph I, emperor of Austria.

Crafts | **Pike Place Market** (*see* Exploring Seattle, above).
Flying Shuttle Ltd. (607 1st Ave., tel. 206/343–9762) displays handcrafted jewelry, whimsical folk art, handknits, and handwoven garments.

Jewelry | **Fireworks Gallery** (210 1st Ave. S, tel. 206/682–8707; 400 Pine St., tel. 206/682–6462) features whimsical earrings and pins.
Fourth & Pike Building houses many retail/wholesale jewelers, including **Turgeon-Raine Jewelers** (9th floor, tel. 206/447–9488), an exceptional store with a sophisticated but friendly staff.

Leather and Luggage | **Bergman Luggage Co.** (1930 3rd Ave., tel. 206/448–3000) features luggage in a variety of prices and materials.

Men's Apparel | **Jeffrey-Michael** (1318 4th Ave., tel. 206/625–9891) provides a fine line of traditional, business, and casual men's clothing.
Mario's (1513 6th Ave., tel. 206/223–1461) offers a wide selection of contemporary men's wear.

Outdoor Wear and Equipment | **REI** (1525 11th Ave., tel. 206/323–8333) sells clothing as well as outdoor equipment including water bottles, tents, bikes, and freeze-dried food in a creaky, funky building on Capitol Hill.
Eddie Bauer (5th Ave. and Union St., tel. 206/622–2766) features sports and outdoor apparel.

Toys | **Magic Mouse Toys** (603 1st Ave., tel. 206/682–8097) carries two floors of toys, from small windups to giant stuffed animals.
Great Windup (Pike Place Market, tel. 206/621–9370) carries all sorts of windup action toys.

Wine | **Delaurenti Wine Shop** (1435 1st Ave., tel. 206/340–1498) has a knowledgeable staff and a large selection of Northwest Italian wines.
Pike & Western Wine Merchants (Pike Pl. and Virginia St., tel. 206/441–1307 or 206/441–1308) carries a wide selection of Northwest wines from small wineries.

Women's Apparel | **Boutique Europa** (1015 1st Ave., tel. 206/624–5582) features sophisticated clothing from Europe.

Littler's (Rainier Sq., tel. 206/223–1331) offers classic fashions
for women.
Local Brilliance (1535 1st Ave., tel. 206/343–5864) showcases
fashions from local designers.

Sports and Fitness

Participant Sports

"The best things in life are free" is a homily that holds true, at
least in part, when it comes to keeping fit in this most health-
oriented of cities. Walking, bicycling, hiking, and jogging require little money; pay-as-you-go alternatives such as golf, kayak, sailboat, or sailboard rentals require only marginally more.

Bicycling   Although much of Seattle is so hilly that recreational bicycling
is strenuous, many residents nonetheless commute by bike.
The trail circling **Green Lake** and the **Burke-Gilman Trail** are
popular among recreational bicyclists, although at Green Lake
the crowds of joggers and walkers tend to impede fast travel.
The Burke-Gilman Trail is a city-maintained trail extending for
12.1 miles along Seattle's waterfront from Lake Washington
nearly to Salmon Bay along an abandoned railroad line; it is a
much less congested path. **Myrtle Edwards Park,** north of Pier
70, has a two-lane path for jogging and bicycling. For general
information about Seattle's parks and trails, call the Seattle
Parks Department (tel. 206/684–4075).

A number of shops around Seattle rent mountain bikes as well
as standard touring or racing bikes and equipment. Among
them are **Greg's Greenlake Cycle** (7007 Woodlawn Ave. NE, tel.
206/523–1822) and **Mountain Bike Specialists** (5625 University
Way NE, tel. 206/527–4310).

Fishing   There are plenty of good spots for fishing on **Lake Washington,**
Green Lake, and **Lake Union,** and there are several fishing piers
along the **Elliott Bay** waterfront. A number of companies operating from **Shilshole Bay** also offer charter trips for catching
salmon, rock cod, flounder, and sea bass. A couple of the many
Seattle-based charter companies are **Ballard Salmon Charter**
(tel. 206/789–6202) and **Seattle Salmon and Bottom Fishing**
(tel. 206/292–0595).

Golf   There are almost 50 public golf courses in the Seattle area.
Among the most popular municipally run courses are **Jackson**
Park (1000 N.E. 135th St., tel. 206/363–4747) and **Jefferson**
Park (4101 Beacon Ave. S, tel. 206/762–4513). For more infor-
mation, contact the Seattle Parks and Recreation Department
(tel. 206/684–4075).

Jogging, Skating,   **Green Lake** is far and away Seattle's most popular spot for jog-
Walking   ging and the 3-mile circumference of this picturesque lake is
custom-made for it. Walking, bicycling, roller skating, fishing,
and lounging on the grass and feeding the plentiful waterfowl
are also popular pastimes here. In summer, a large children's
wading pool on the northeast side of the lake is a popular gathering spot. Several outlets clustered along the east side of the
lake offer skate and cycle rentals.

Other good jogging locales are along the **Burke-Gilman Trail,**
around the reservoir at **Volunteer Park,** and at **Myrtle Edwards**
Park, north of the waterfront.

Sports and Fitness 163

Skiing Snoqualmie Pass in the Cascade Mountains, about an hour's drive east of Seattle on I-90, has a number of fine resorts offering both day and night downhill skiing. Among them: **Alpental, Ski Acres, Snoqualmie Summit** (for all areas: 3010 77th St. SE, Mercer Island 98040, tel. 206/232-8182). All of these areas rent equipment and have full restaurant/lodge facilities.

For ski reports for these areas and the more distant White Pass, Crystal Mountain, and Stevens Pass, call 206/634-0200 or 206/634-2754. For recorded messages about road conditions in the passes, call 206/455-7900.

Tennis There are public tennis courts in many parks around the Seattle area. For information, contact the King County Parks and Recreation Department (tel. 206/296-4258).

Water Sports It stands to reason that sailboating and powerboating are popu-
Boating lar in Seattle. **Sailboat Rentals & Yachts** (2046 Westlake Ave. N, tel. 206/281-9176), on the west side of Lake Union, rents sailboats, with or without skippers, 14-38 feet in length, by the hour or the day. **Wind Works Rentals** (7001 Seaview Ave. NW, tel. 206/784-9386), on Shilshole Bay, rents sailboats ranging from 25 to 40 feet on the more challenging waters of Puget Sound, with or without skippers and by the half-day, day, or week. **Seacrest Boat House** (1660 Harbor Ave. SW, tel. 206/932-1050), in West Seattle, rents 18-foot aluminum fishing boats, with or without motors, by the hour or the day.

Kayaking Kayaking—around both the inner waterways (Lake Union, Lake Washington, the Ship Canal) and open water (Elliott Bay)—is a terrific and easy way to get an unusual view of Seattle's busy waterfront. **The Northwest Outdoor Center** (2100 Westlake Ave. N, tel. 206/281-9694), on the west side of Lake Union, rents one- or two-person kayaks and equipment by the hour or week and provides both basic and advanced instruction. Canoes and rowing shells are also available.

Sailboarding Lake Union and Green Lake are Seattle's prime sailboarding spots. Sailboards can be rented year-round at the **Bavarian Surf Shop** (711 N. Northlake Way, tel. 206/545-9463), on Lake Union. Lessons are available.

Spectator Sports

Baseball The **Seattle Mariners,** an American-league team, play April through early October at the Kingdome (201 S. King St., tel. 206/628-3555).

Basketball The **Seattle SuperSonics,** an NBA team, play October through April at the Seattle Center Coliseum (1st Ave. N, tel. 206/281-5850).

Boat Racing The **unlimited hydroplane** (tel. 206/628-0888) races cap Seattle's Seafair festivities, from mid-July through the first Sunday in August. The races are held on Lake Washington near Seward Park, and tickets cost $10-$20. Weekly **sailing regattas** are held in the summer on Lakes Union and Washington. Call the Seattle Yacht Club (tel. 206/325-1000) for schedules.

Football Seattle's NFL team, the **Seahawks,** play August through December in the Kingdome (201 S. King St., tel. 206/827-9777).

Dining

By John Doerper

Food editor of
Washington
*magazine, John
Doerper is a local
food critic and
travel writer whose
pieces have
appeared in* Travel
& Leisure *and*
Pacific Northwest
Magazine.

Highly recommended restaurants are indicated by a star ★.

Category	Cost*
Very Expensive	over $35
Expensive	$25–$35
Moderate	$15–$25
Inexpensive	under $15

**per person, excluding drinks, service, and sales tax (about
7.9%, varies slightly by community)*

**American/
Continental**
★

Canlis. This sumptuous restaurant is almost more of a Seattle
institution than a place of fine dining, dating from a time when
steak served by kimono-clad waitresses was the pinnacle of
high living in the city by the sound. Little has changed here
since the '50s. The restaurant is still very expensive, very good
at what it does, and very popular, and the view across Lake Union is as good as ever (though curtained off by a forest of recently built high rises on the far shore). Besides the famous steaks
there are equally famous oysters from Quilcene Bay and fresh
fish in season, cooked to a turn. *2576 Aurora Ave. N, tel. 206/
283–3313. Reservations advised. Jacket required. AE, DC,
MC, V. Closed lunch and Sun. Very Expensive.*

Landau's. Conceived by Hong Kong transplants David and
Mary Jane Landau, this elegant dining spot has established itself as the East Side's top restaurant. The interior is a harmony
of pastel-color walls, polished granite, Oriental artworks, huge
flower arrangements, and plush carpeting. The menu, like the
Hong Kong original, consists mostly of Continental dishes,
with a creative sprinkling of Chinese, Indian, and East/West
dishes. Vegetables, seafood, veal, pork, and even steaks are
prepared with uncommon flair. Try the cream of mushroom
soup (made from scratch), the homemade pâté, or the crab
cannelloni. *500 108th Ave. NE, tel. 206/646–6644. Reservations
accepted. Jacket required. AE, DC, MC, V. Closed Sat. lunch
and Sun. Expensive.*

Place Pigalle. Despite its French name, this is a very American
restaurant and a popular place with locals. Large windows look
out over Elliott Bay and, in nice weather, are open to admit the
salt breeze. Bright flower bouquets lighten up the café tables,
and the friendly staff makes you feel right at home in this small,
intimate restaurant located behind a meat market in the Pike
Place Market's main arcade. Seasonal meals feature seafood
and local ingredients. Go for the rich oyster stew, the fresh
Dungeness crab (available only when it is truly fresh), or the
fresh fish of the day baked in hazelnuts. *Pike Place Market, tel.
206/624–1756. Reservations advised. Dress: casual but neat.
MC, V. Closed Sun. Moderate.*

★ **Vic & Mick's Nine-10 Cafe.** Victor Rosellini has done more for
the Seattle dining scene than anyone else in town in his 40-odd
years behind his famous reservation podium. Trained in San
Francisco, he was the first to introduce such amenities as white
tablecloths and wine lists to Seattle. The Nine-10 is his latest
venture (in partnership with fellow restaurateur Mick Mc-
Hugh). In the 1970s McHugh set a new tone for Seattle restau-

rants by introducing clubby atmosphere with lots of dark wood, polished brass, genteel prints, and a saloonlike atmosphere. The Nine-10 fits this mold snugly. The menu is basically Continental with an Italian flair, and a number of well-cooked local foods are thrown in for variety. The recipes have been carried over from two of Victor Rosellini's previous establishments, and Seattleites are lining up to once again taste the famous Four-10 sandwich; the Italian-style sautéed tenderloin tips; the veal scaloppine saltimbocca; the spaghettini with Italian meatballs; and the cappelletti with fresh chopped tomatoes, cream, and pesto. *910 2nd Ave., tel. 206/292–0910. Reservations advised. Dress: casual but neat. AE, DC, MC, V. Closed Sat. lunch and Sun. Moderate.*

Beeliner Diner. A long, narrow storefront, Formica tables, and vinyl settees make for a surprisingly comfortable diner. The food is classic diner fare—a throwback to the 1950s—with thick burgers, french fries, meat loaf, macaroni and cheese, and huge chili dogs. Even though a sign says EAT IT AND BEAT IT, you're encouraged to linger over coffee and pie. *2114 N. 45th St., tel. 206/547–6313. No reservations. Dress: casual. No credit cards. Closed Mon. lunch, Sun. Inexpensive.*

Caveman Kitchen. Despite its out-of-the-way location in suburban Kent, this low-key establishment is Seattle's favorite barbecue joint. It's almost southern in concept, except that the late Dick Donley, who started the place, perfected the cooking of meat over smokey alder or apple wood instead of hickory. His children now run the place and old-timers insist nothing has changed; the ribs, chicken, turkey, salmon, and sausage are as good and moist as ever. Also try the beans, coleslaw, and bread pudding. There's no inside seating, but in nice weather you can sit outside at picnic tables and, if you choose, pick up beer at the store across the street. *807 West Valley Hwy., Kent, tel. 206/854–1210. No reservations. Dress: casual. MC, V. BYOB. Inexpensive.*

Asian
★
Wild Ginger. This restaurant's specialty is Pacific Rim cookery—primarily tasty and eclectic Asian fare—including southern Chinese, Vietnamese, Thai, and Korean dishes served in a warm, clubby dining room. The *satay* (chunks of beef, chicken, or vegetables skewered and grilled, and usually served with a spicy peanut sauce) bar, where you can sit to sip local brews and eat tangy, elegantly seasoned skewered seafood or meat until 2 AM, has quickly become a favorite local hangout. In the dining room, daily specials, based on seasonally available products, make meals exciting. No wonder the locals come back again and again. Be sure to start your meal with satay and wandering sage soup, and don't neglect the sweetly flavored duck, a house specialty. *1400 Western Ave., tel. 206/623–4450. Reservations advised. Dress: casual but neat. AE, CB, DC, MC, V. Closed Sun. lunch. Moderate.*

Chinese
Linyen. This comfortable restaurant comes into its own late at night, when Seattle celebrities mingle here with chefs from Chinatown restaurants. The standard fare is Cantonese, in the new light style, but you're best off to stick to the blackboard specials: clams in black bean sauce, geoduck, spicy chicken, and fish dishes. The dart games in the bar are a popular—and heated—diversion. *424 7th Ave. S, tel. 206/622–8181. Reservations advised. Dress: casual but neat. AE, DC, MC, V. Closed lunch. Moderate.*

Chau's Chinese Restaurant. This small, very plain place on the

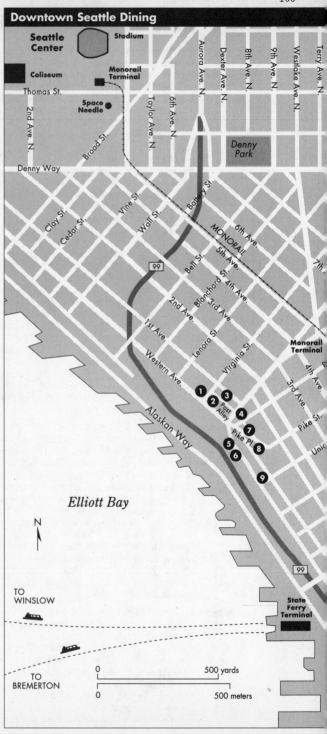

Downtown Seattle Dining

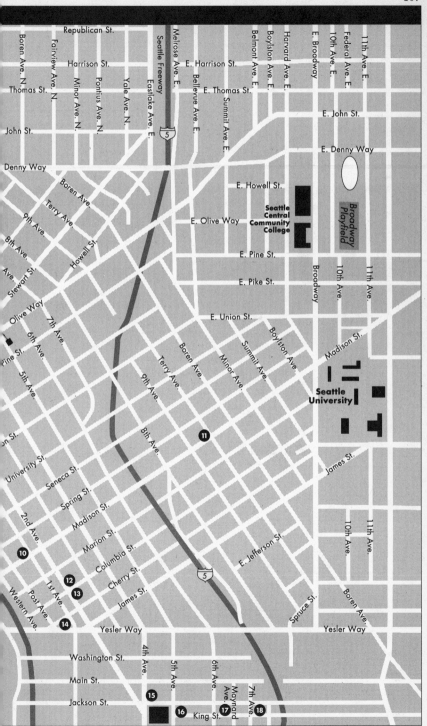

A. Jay's, **32**
Bahn Thai, **30**
Beeliner Diner, **25**
Cafe Juanita, **27**
Canlis, **26**
Caveman Kitchen, **34**
Cucina! Cucina!, **29**
Landau's, **28**
Le Tastevin, **31**
Pacifica, **19**
Ray's Boathouse, **24**
Rover's, **33**
Saleh Al Lago, **20**
Salvatore Ristorante
Italiano, **22**
Santa Fe Cafe, **21, 23**

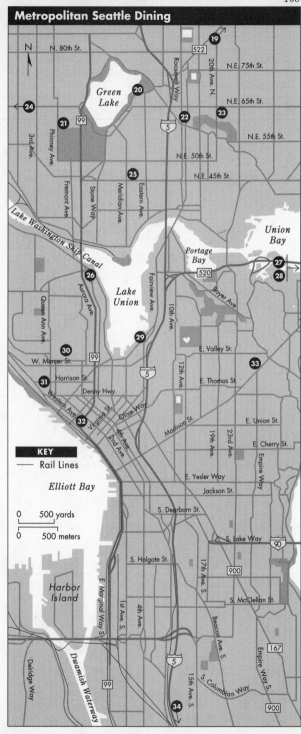

Metropolitan Seattle Dining

outer limits of Seattle's Chinatown serves great seafood, such as steamed oysters in garlic sauce, Dungeness crab with ginger and onion, and geoduck. Avoid the standard dishes of the Cantonese repertoire that dominate much of the menu, and stick to the seafood and specials. *310 4th Ave. S, tel. 206/621–0006. Reservations advised. Dress: casual. MC, V. Closed weekend lunch. Inexpensive.*

Deli **A. Jay's.** This small, simple place proves that homey deli fare can be very good. For breakfast, try one of the half-dozen fluffy, overstuffed omelets or a thick, well-seasoned frittata. Bagels come with plenty of cream cheese and good lox. Coffee flows freely, and the service is friendly. You can sit and talk without being rushed. At lunch you'll discover large sandwiches (good pastrami), burgers, and soup. *2619 1st Ave., tel. 206/441–1511. Reservations advised. Dress: casual. AE, MC, V. Closed nights and weekends. Inexpensive.*

Three Girls Bakery. It's a 13-seat glassed-in lunch counter behind a bakery outlet, serving sandwiches and soups to hungry folks in a hurry. Go for the chili and a hunk of Sicilian sourdough. Another idea is to buy a loaf at the takeout counter, get smoked salmon at the fish place next door, and head for a picnic table in Waterfront Park. *Pike Place Market, 1514 Pike Pl., tel. 206/622–1045. No reservations. Dress: casual. No credit cards. No alcohol. Closed nights and Sun. Inexpensive.*

French **Campagne.** Overlooking Pike Place Market and Elliott Bay, Campagne is intimate and urbane. White walls, picture windows, and colorful modern prints set the up tone; wood floors with Oriental rugs add a touch of class. The lusty flavors of Provence pervade the menu in such dishes as chicken stuffed with goat cheese and fresh herbs, salmon in a cognac and champagne butter sauce, garlic sausage and duck leg served on red cabbage, and *pan bagna* (ratatouille with goat cheese sandwich). The chef's interpretation of salade Niçoise comes with local Blue Lake beans, Niçoise olives, and fresh seared (and thus very tender) tuna. A lamb salad (thinly sliced lamb served on a bed of greens with goat cheese) is perfectly seasoned. Occasionally the service can be brusque, but the food more than makes up for grumpy waiters. *Inn at the Market, 86 Pine St., tel. 206/728–2800. Reservations advised. Jacket required. AE, MC, V. Expensive.*

Le Tastevin. This restaurant may have set a new tone for Seattle's French restaurants when it opened several years ago. Instead of dark wood and subdued lighting, you'll find a sunny, trellised dining room, bright with light wood and green plants, and racks of wine bottles along the far walls. The windows face west, toward the Olympic Mountains and colorful sunsets. Since Le Tastevin can't make up its mind whether it serves classical French or Northwest nouvelle cuisine, you're likely to find such dishes as salmon, bouillabaisse, or sweetbreads with port sauce paired with berry soups, fresh halibut with tart fruit puree, or steamed pink scallops served whole in the shell, like clams. Cream, the staple of traditional French cookery, is almost absent. For dessert, you should not miss the fresh fruit ices—made daily from scratch—or the wine sorbets. As an alternative to the expensive regular lunch menu, try the bar lunch, that's just as good. In the late afternoon, during happy hour, inexpensive dishes and great snack food are served. The wine list is vast, spanning many countries and vintages, and quite reasonably priced. *19 W. Harrison St., tel. 206/283–0991.*

Reservations advised. Jacket required. AE, DC, MC, V. Closed Sat. lunch and Sun. Expensive.

Rover's. This is French cooking at its best, with a daily menu based on what is locally available. Specialties include salmon, pheasant, quail, venison, and rabbit in elegant yet surprisingly light sauces. The enormous pasta dishes are among Seattle's best. Recently, chef/owner Thierry Rautureau has experimented with sea urchin roe and truffles, and walnuts and wild mushrooms. The setting is highly romantic, in a small house with a garden. Herbs and flowers grow in flower beds just outside the windows. Service is excellent—friendly but not obtrusive. *2808 E. Madison St., tel. 206/325-7442. Reservations advised. Dress: casual but neat. AE, MC, V. Closed lunch and Mon. Moderate.*

Irish **Kells.** Tucked into an old brick building along the Pike Place Market's most romantic thoroughfare, you'll forget you're in America when you step through the door of this pub. The accoutrements, too, look like they've been brought over from the old country: bar, taps, wood paneling, sporting prints are all very Irish, down to the accents and politics. The food is simple but tasty: Irish stew, leg of lamb, meat pies. Guinness and Harp on tap are very fresh, or try one of the hearty Northwest brews. The place rings with live Irish music Wednesday through Saturday nights. Kells is very friendly and feels an instant home away from home. In summer there's limited outdoor seating in the alley. *Pike Place Market, 1916 Post Alley, tel. 206/728-1916. Reservations advised. Dress: casual but neat. MC, V. Closed Sun. Moderate.*

Italian **Saleh Al Lago.** This very fashionable spot with a view of Green
★ Lake and the park serves up some of the best Italian fare in the city. The well-lit dining room with light pinks and pastels invites simple, well-paced evening dining and choices such as the antipasti, fresh pasta, and veal dishes are always excellent. Be sure to try the ravioli *al mondo mio*, the chef's special ravioli (filling and sauce vary), or the *tagliatelle* (flat, ribboned egg pasta) with champagne and caviar. Even deceptively plain fare, like grilled breast of chicken with olive oil and fresh herbs, is superb here, with just the right—very light—touch. *6804 E. Greenlake Way N, tel. 206/522-7943. Reservations advised. Jacket required. AE, MC, V. Closed Sat. lunch and Sun. Expensive.*

Cafe Juanita. This comfortable, casual place—decorated with beige linens and offering wonderful views from the windows—is more than just a restaurant. There's a winery in the basement, and the vintages made there—bottled under owner/chef/winemaker Peter Dow's Cavatappi label—are available upstairs. The veal scaloppine and chicken dishes can be a bit on the rich and buttery side, but there's plenty of inexpensive Italian wine on the lengthy wine list to dilute the cream. *9702 N.E. 120th Pl., Kirkland, tel. 206/823-1505. Reservations advised. Dress: casual but neat. MC, V. Closed lunch. Moderate.*

Cucina! Cucina! This is where Seattle goes for fun and good food. The restaurant and its large deck overlook Lake Union, Seattle's downtown lake, which is large enough to accommodate oceangoing ships. Of the many lakefront restaurants, Cucina has the best view, the most sheltered deck (to guard against cold winds that can spring up even on warm summer afternoons), and the friendliest service. Some of the waiters and waitresses double as fashion models at local studios (which adds glitz and chic to the place). The restaurant itself is simple in design, with concrete tabletops in the bar and colorful surroundings. The food is basic Italian, with a good selection of lightly sauced pasta and seafood dishes and a tempting assortment of one-person pizzas topped with wild mushrooms, smoked chicken, and even salmon. If you're out on the deck, expect seaplanes buzzing above the restaurant as they prepare to land on the lake. *901 Fairview Ave. N, tel. 206/447–2782. Reservations advised. Dress: casual but neat. AE, MC, V. Closed Sun. lunch. Moderate.*

Trattoria Mitchelli. This archetypal Seattle storefront café is usually noisy and crowded, especially in the wee hours of the morning (the place stays open till 4 AM), and has a Bohemian-like atmosphere that's fast-paced and friendly, though you're never rushed. The food is a bargain and comes in plentiful portions: heaping servings of Italian pasta, sandwiches, and antipasti. *84 Yesler Way, tel. 206/623–3885. No reservations. Dress: casual. AE, CB, DC, MC, V. Moderate.*

Salvatore Ristorante Italiano. You have to wait for a table in this small storefront restaurant, but most customers don't consider that an obstacle. Go for one of the four or five specials, which always include individual pizzas, pasta dishes, and meat and fish courses, chalked onto the blackboard above the kitchen window. Chef/owner Salvatore Anania learned the fine art of pizza making in Paris, but his pasta dishes hark straight back to his native Calabria. Be sure to try the *pesce misto*, a delightful seafood stew whose contents are very mutable—and very Italian. The wine list has some locally rare Italian bottlings. *6100 Roosevelt Way NE, tel. 206/527–9301. No reservations. Dress: casual. MC, V. Closed Sat. lunch and Sun. Inexpensive.*

Japanese   **Takara.** Kuma-san in full action can look like a character from a Japanese wood-block print: the famed swordsman Miyamoto Musashi getting ready to fight heaven and earth. But there's nothing bellicose about this ever-smiling sushi chef—except for his determination to serve only the freshest seafood for sushi and sashimi. It's the freshness of the raw materials and the quality of the knife handling (one is almost tempted to say swordsmanship) that's making Kuma-san the hottest sushi chef in town. He's been known to create a perfect rose from translucent slices of raw tuna, and he can form a phoenix in full flight from a lump of rice (for the body), golden salmon caviar (to simulate the iridescent back feathers), and sparkling *nori* seaweed (for the head, beak, and wings). No wonder Japanese businessmen flock here for lunch. The dining room serves classic Japanese dishes using Northwest ingredients. The salmon teriyaki is superb, and so is the steamed black cod. *Pike Place Market Hillclimb, 1501 Western Ave., tel. 206/682–8609. Reservations advised for dining room, no reservations for sushi bar. Dress: casual but neat. AE, MC, V. Beer and sake. Closed Sun., except May–Labor Day. Moderate.*

Japanese/Korean   **Han Il.** This upstairs, upscale Korean restaurant overlooks an urban square in Seattle's Asian shopping district. Classic Korean barbecue, prepared on gas burners at your table, comes with a plethora of side dishes and dipping sauces. But the much less expensive luncheon specials are just as good. Barbecued chicken, pork, or beef come to the table with kimchi (the Han Il's version of this Korean cabbage pickle has just the right degree of pungency and is piquant but not overspiced), plus *daikon* radish pickles, a tangy sea vegetable salad, rice, a couple of tempura prawns, and a bottomless pot of tea. *409 Maynard Ave. S, tel. 206/587–0464. Reservations advised. Dress: casual. MC, V. Inexpensive.*

Mexican **El Puerco Lloron.** Don't be put off by the cafeteria line and the studied "sleazy-south-of-the-border" bar look. The fresh, handmade tortillas have great texture, and the fillings are endowed with all the right flavors. The chili relleno is tops. But it almost doesn't matter what you order—tacos, *taquitos,* tamales—they're all good. The salsas are zesty and the beer is cold. *Pike Place Market Hillclimb, 1501 Western Ave., tel. 206/624–0541. No reservations. Dress: casual. AE, MC, V. Inexpensive.*

Northwest **Cafe Alexis.** This is a small intimate, but elegant place that's
★ highlighted by the tapestry wall coverings, teal-colored walls, and wood-burning fireplace. In addition, it offers one of the more imaginative menus in town, with a fare that changes according to the seasons. Expect artistically arranged salads with uncommon ingredients like grilled trout and dressings like avocado-mint crème fraîche with smoked salmon or curried walnuts; steamed clams and mussels in spicy peanut–black bean sauce; king salmon steamed over aromatic herbs and served with a lemon-thyme-ginger butter; and other seasonal fish grilled and seasoned to perfection. The braised veal shank with sun-dried tomatoes, herb *pistou,* and grilled polenta is very tender and flavorful; the roast duck breast with cardamom hazelnut sauce and apple catsup is a fowl delight. *Alexis Hotel, 1007 1st Ave., tel. 206/624–3646. Reservations advised. Jacket required. AE, D, DC, MC, V. Expensive.*

Hunt Club. Owner Barbara Figueroa may be the most accomplished chef in Seattle, a suitable match for this very traditional, almost clubby restaurant with dark wood and plush seats and innovative and exciting food. Besides perfectly prepared lamb with shiitake mushrooms in Madeira sauce, or seasonal king salmon with Pinot noir butter, you may happen upon such surprising fare as green cattail spikes (the texture of asparagus, the flavor of artichokes), *salicornia* (a fleshy herb grown in salt marshes), or just plain corn fritters. There are occasionally odd desserts—jalapeño sorbet, anyone? Ask for local goat cheeses on your cheese platter. *Sorrento Hotel, 900 Madison St., tel. 206/622–6400. Reservations advised. Jacket required. AE, DC, MC, V. Expensive.*

Cafe Sport. This trendy Pike Place Market restaurant—affiliated with the athletic club next door—prepares some of the city's most original and delicious cookery in a modern dining room decorated with muted tones, fresh flowers, and white linens. A few of the best seafood choices include *sake kasu* cod and lingcod in a spicy peanut and coconut sauce. But the fare can be quite eclectic, since the ever-changing menu varies wildly depending on the availability of seasonal products and the whim of the cooks. You might walk in one day and find dishes that would do the finest Italian restaurant proud, from a well-designed antipasto platter to a succulent osso buco with wild mushrooms. Another time, you might think you have accidentally stepped into a Thai café, an American diner (replete with cheeseburger and fries), or perhaps a New England fish house. That sort of eclectic approach is fraught with danger, but at Cafe Sport it works. *2020 Western Ave., tel. 206/443–6000. Reservations advised. Dress: casual but neat. AE, DC, MC, V. Moderate.*

Pacifica. Located in the heart of the Woodinville wine country—25 miles east of Seattle—this airy country place is Washington's first "wine country" restaurant. The lushly green valley grows few grapes, but much wine is made here from grapes brought in from eastern Washington. Seafood dishes and meats are handled with a light touch; the homemade sausages—including pesto chicken sausage and Milwaukee-style beer sausage—alone are worth the trip. Taste wines nearby at the Château Ste. Michelle, French Creek, and Salmon Bay wineries. *14450 Woodinville–Redmond Rd., Woodinville, tel. 206/487–1530. Reservations advised. Dress: casual but neat. AE, MC, V. Closed Mon. Moderate.*

Seafood **Ray's Boathouse.** The view of Puget Sound may be the drawing card here, but the seafood is impeccably fresh and well prepared. Perennial favorites include broiled salmon, sake kasu cod, prawns baked in their shells, and superb (lingcod) fish 'n chips. Ray's has a split personality: a fancy dining room downstairs, a café and bar upstairs. Go for the café, where prices are lower and the food is just as good as in the more formal setting downstairs. In warm weather, sit outside and watch boats float past almost below your table. The gap in the rocky shore is the mouth of Seattle's ship canal, which runs to Lakes Union and Washington. You can't get bored: Pilot boats, tugs, fishing boats, pleasure yachts—a continuous stream of marine vessels flows past. *6049 Seaview Ave. NE, tel. 206/789–3770. Reservations advised for window seats in dining room; no reservations for café. Dress: casual but neat. AE, DC, MC, V. Moderate.*

★ **Emmet Watson's Oyster Bar.** This small oyster bar may be a bit hard to find: It's in the back of the Pike Place Market's Soames-Dunn Building and fronts a small flower-bedecked (from spring through fall) courtyard. The decor is unpretentious, the inside booths are cramped, and a seat at the bar (in rainy weather) or in the courtyard (when the sun shines) is hard to find. But Seattleites know their oysters, and this is the locals' favorite hangout. The place is worth the special effort, for the oysters are very fresh (and come in a great number of varieties) and the beer list is ample (50 or more selections, from local microbrews to fancy imports). Both oysters and beer are very inexpensive. If you don't like oysters, try the salmon soup or the fish-and-chips (large flaky pieces of fish with very little grease). *Pike Place Market, 1916 Pike Pl., tel. 206/448–7721. No reservations. Dress: casual. No credit cards. Closed dinner and Sun. Inexpensive.*

Southwest **Santa Fe Cafe.** In this casual dining room you can enjoy such spicy New Mexican dishes as green-chili burritos made with blue-corn tortillas. Interesting brews on tap help mitigate the heat of such fiery fare as the red-chili burrito (it's so hot, the waiter warns you as you order). Other choices are less *picante*, but still flavorful: the green-chili stew, the blue-corn crepes, the red or green enchiladas. Chili relleno may come in the form of a quiche. The thick, hand-patted flour tortillas are uncommonly flavorful; sauces are made from red and green chilis brought in from New Mexico. The 65th Street location offers a cozier, homey appeal, with its woven rugs and dried flowers, and is popular with graduate students and professors. The Phinney Avenue restaurant is slicker and more chic; skylights fill the place with light that brightens the soft pink-and-mauve color scheme. Visitors from Santa Fe admit that this is about as authentic as it gets. *Two locations: 2255 N.E. 65th St., tel. 206/*

524–7736; 5910 Phinney Ave. N, tel. 206/783–9755. Reservations advised. Dress: casual but neat. MC, V. Closed weekend lunch and Mon. Moderate.

Steaks **Metropolitan Grill.** This favorite lunch spot of the executive crowd serves custom-aged, mesquite-broiled steaks in a classic steakhouse atmosphere. The steaks—the best in Seattle—are huge and come with baked potatoes or pasta. This is not food for timid eaters: Even the veal chop is extra thick, and the hamburger ("Western Ground Sirloin Steak") is so big that one person may have problems finishing it. Among the accompaniments, the onion rings and sautéed mushrooms are tops. Don't be surprised if you hear more Japanese than English as you eat here: The place is so popular with visiting businessmen that there's a menu in Japanese, too. *818 2nd Ave., tel. 206/624–3287. Reservations advised. Dress: casual but neat. AE, CB, DC, MC, V. Closed Sun. lunch. Moderate.*

Thai **Bahn Thai.** Thai cooking is ubiquitous in Seattle—it almost can be considered a mainstream cuisine. Because of the variety of dishes and the quality of the preparations, the Bahn Thai, one of the pioneers of local Thai food, is still one of the best and most popular. Start your meal with a skewer of tangy chicken or pork satay or with the *tod mun goong* (spicy fish cake), and continue with hot-and-sour soup and one of the many prawn or fish dishes. The deep-fried fish with garlic sauce is particularly good—and you can order it very hot. This restaurant promises a relaxed—particularly romantic—atmosphere in the evenings. *409 Roy St., tel. 206/283–0444. Reservations advised. Dress: casual but neat. AE, DC, MC, V. Closed weekend lunch. Inexpensive.*

Vietnamese **Hien Vuong.** Talk about unpretentious: This small café, set in
★ the International District, is about as plain as such places get in Seattle, but the food is superb. Aficionados make special trips for the Cambodian soup and the shrimp rolls. The peanut dipping sauce is more flavorful than usual. Do try the papaya with beef jerky—it's unusual but very enjoyable. The prices are incredibly low, just one reason why this is one of the best lunch places in town. Parking can be a problem here. *502 S. King St., tel. 206/624–2611. No reservations. Dress: casual. No credit cards. No alcohol. Closed Tues. Inexpensive.*

Lodging

There is no shortage of lodging in Seattle. The variety ranges from the elegant deluxe hotels of downtown to the smaller, less expensive hotels in the University District; from the string of budget motels along Aurora Avenue North (Hwy. 99), many of which are legacies of the 1962 World's Fair, to the big new hotels strung along Pacific Highway South (Hwy. 99) that accommodate travelers near Seattle-Tacoma International Airport. Also available are a number of bed-and-breakfast accommodations: For more information, contact the **Washington State Bed-and-Breakfast Guild** (2442 N.W. Market St., Seattle, WA 98107, tel. 509/548–7171) or the **Pacific Bed & Breakfast Agency** (701 N.W. 60th St., Seattle, WA 98107, tel. 206/784–0539).

Highly recommended hotels are indicated by a star ★.

Category	Cost*
Very Expensive	over $150
Expensive	$100–$150
Moderate	$50–$100
Inexpensive	under $50

per room, double occupancy, not including 14.1% combined hotel and state sales tax

Downtown Seattle
Very Expensive

★ **Alexis.** The Alexis is an intimate hotel in an artfully restored historic 1901 building on 1st Avenue near the waterfront, the Public Market, and the new Seattle Art Museum. Guests are greeted with complimentary sherry at this small, quietly understated elegant hotel. The 54 rooms are decorated in subdued colors, with mauve as a primary color, and some suites feature Jacuzzis, wood-burning fireplaces, and some marble fixtures. Unfortunately, there are no views in this simple hotel; rooms facing the avenue can be noisy. Cafe Alexis, an elegant dining room in wine and green colors with a marble fireplace, located on the ground floor of the hotel, features fine Northwest cuisine. Amenities include complimentary Continental breakfast, shoe shines, morning newspaper, and guest membership at the Seattle Club, the place to be seen working out. *1007 1st Ave., 98104, tel. 206/624–4844 or 800/426–7033; fax 206/621–9009. 54 rooms. Facilities: restaurant, café/bar, access to health club, steam room. AE, CB, MC, V.*

★ **Four Seasons Olympic Hotel.** The Olympic is Seattle's most elegant hotel. In 1982, Four Seasons restored it to its 1920s grandeur, with the public rooms furnished with marble, thick rugs, wood paneling, armchairs, and potted plants. Palms and skylights in the Garden Court provide a relaxing background for lunch, afternoon tea, or dancing to the Fred Radke swing band on the weekends. The Georgian Room, the hotel's premier dining room, exudes Italian Renaissance elegance, while Shuckers, oyster bar is more casual. The 450 rooms, less luxurious than the public rooms, feature period reproductions. Amenities include valet parking, 24-hour room service, stocked bar, chocolates on your pillow, complimentary shoe shines, and a bathrobe in the room for each guest. Locals drop in occasionally to pamper themselves with a massage and swim at the health club. *411 University St., 98101, tel. 206/621–1700 or 800/223–8772; fax 206/682–9633. 450 rooms. Facilities: 3 restaurants, health club, indoor pool. AE, DC, MC, V.*

Stouffer Madison Hotel. This new high-rise hotel, located between downtown and I–5, was built in 1983. Peach and green are the identifying colors of the Stouffer Madison, and the rooms are equipped with wood cabinets and marble countertops and have good views of downtown, Elliott Bay, and the Cascade Mountains. Club Level floors (25 and 26) feature their own concierge, complimentary Continental breakfast, and a library. The health club includes a 40-foot rooftop pool and a Jacuzzi. *515 Madison St., 98104, tel. 206/583–0300 or 800/468–3571; fax 206/622–8635. 554 rooms. Facilities: 2 restaurants, lounge, indoor pool, Jacuzzi, health club, indoor parking. AE, D, DC, MC, V.*

Expensive **Edgewater.** The only hotel situated on Elliott Bay, the Edgewater is an institution, known for the now-defunct tradition of guests' fishing from their waterside windows. In 1988 the new

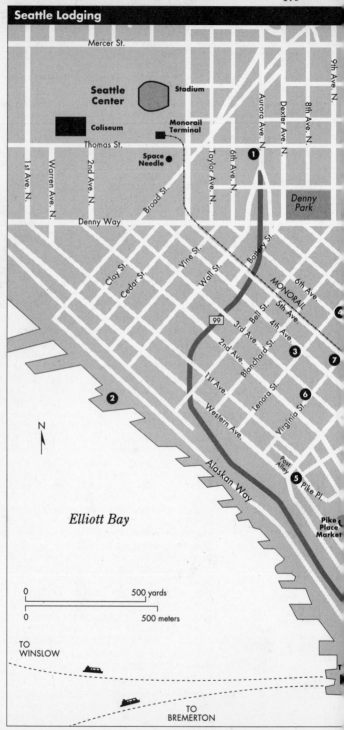

Seattle Lodging

Mercer St.

9th Ave. N.

Westlake Ave. N.

Terry Ave. N.

Boren Ave. N.

Fairview Ave. N.

Republican St.

Harrison St.

Thomas St.

Minor Ave. N.

Pontius Ave. N.

Yale Ave. N.

Eastlake Ave. E.

Seattle Freeway

John St.

Denny Way

18 19

Melrose Ave. E.

Bellevue Ave. E.

E. Republican

E. Mercer St.

10th Ave. E.

Federal Ave. E.

St.

Harvard Ave. E.

Boylston Ave. E.

E. Broadway

E. Harrison St.

Belmont Ave. E.

Summit Ave. E.

E. Thomas St.

E. John St.

E. Denny Way

Broadway Playfield

Boren Ave.

Terry Ave.

9th Ave.

8th Ave.

7th Ave.

Howell St.

Stewart St.

4

7

Olive Way

7th Ave.

6th Ave.

Monorail Terminal

Pine St.

5th Ave.

4th Ave.

3rd Ave.

9

Pike St.

Union St.

Pike Place Market

10

2nd Ave.

1st Ave.

University St.

11

12

Seneca St.

14

Post Ave.

13

Madison St.

15

Spring St.

16

8

E. Howell St.

Seattle Central Community College

E. Olive Way

E. Pine St.

E. Pike St.

Broadway

10th Ave.

E. Union St.

Boren Ave.

Terry Ave.

Minor Ave.

Summit Ave.

Boylston Avenue

Seattle University

9th Ave.

8th Ave.

17

Boren Ave.

99

State Ferry Terminal

Western Ave.

Marion St.

Columbia St.

Cherry St.

James St.

E. Jefferson St.

10th Ave.

5

25 26 27 28

Yesler Way

20 24

Washington St.

owners banned hotel fishing and remodeled the 250 rooms, and the results are magnificent. The lobby features oak furnishings and comfortable chairs and sofas, with a fireplace and a panoramic bay window from which you can sometimes see sea lions frolicking by. Spacious rooms on the water provide views of ferries, barges, and the Olympic Mountains and are decorated in green-and-blue rustic Northwest plaids and unfinished wood furnishings. *Pier 67, 2411 Alaskan Way, 98121, tel. 206/728–7000 or 800/624–0670; fax 206/441–4119. 250 rooms. Facilities: restaurant, bar, free parking. AE, DC, MC, V.*

Seattle Sheraton Hotel and Towers. The Sheraton is a modern, 840-room hotel catering largely to conventioneers, as it is conveniently located near the Washington State Convention & Trade Center. The lobby features an art-glass collection by Dale Chihuly, a Northwest artist of international repute. The Towers (top five floors) feature larger, more elegant rooms with concierge. Within the complex is a diverse selection of restaurant entertainment options, including Banners, which offers an authentic Japanese breakfast, buffet luncheon, and Continental menu; Gooey's (named after the geoduck, a large, sausagelike northwestern clam that is the subject of many jokes), the bar/disco nighttime hot spot; and Fullers, one of the best restaurants in Seattle, serving nouvelle cuisine using local ingredients. *1400 6th Ave., 98101, tel. 206/621–9000 or 800/325–3535; fax 206/621–8441. 840 rooms. Facilities: 2 restaurants, 2 bars, health club, indoor pool. AE, D, DC, MC, V.*

★ **Sorrento.** This deluxe European-style hotel, originally built in 1909 for the Alaska-Yukon Exposition and since restored to its original elegance, is relatively small and has an intimate, cordial atmosphere. Sitting high on First Hill, it has wonderful views overlooking downtown and the waterfront. The rooms are smaller than in modern hotels, but are quiet and very comfortable; they're decorated in understated, elegant earth tones. The stylish Hunt Club restaurant features exquisite Continental and Northwest dishes by chef Barbara Figueroa, while the dark-paneled Fireside Lounge in the lobby is a warm and inviting locale for sipping coffee, tea, or a cocktail. Other amenities include a complimentary limousine service within the downtown area, concierge, and guest privileges at a nearby athletic club. *900 Madison St., 98104, tel. 206/622–6400; fax 206/625–1059. 76 rooms, 42 suites. Facilities: restaurant, lounge, access to health club. AE, DC, MC.*

Moderate–Expensive **Inn at the Market.** This is a sophisticated but unpretentious hotel adjacent to the Pike Place Public Market. It combines the
★ best aspects of a small, deluxe hotel with the informality of the Pacific Northwest, offering a lively setting that's perfect for travelers who prefer originality and personality over big-hotel amenities. The rooms are spacious and tastefully decorated with comfortable modern furniture and small touches such as fresh flowers and ceramic sculptures. Ask for a room with views of the Market and Elliott Bay. An added plus is a 2,000-square-foot deck, furnished with Adirondack chairs and overlooking the water and the market. There are three restaurants that are not part of the hotel but share the building: Campagne (*see* Dining, above); the Gravity Bar, an ultratrendy hangout with a variety of juices and coffees; and Cafe Dilettante for light meals, fine chocolates and coffees. *86 Pine St., 98109, tel. 206/443–3600; fax 206/448–0631. 65 rooms; nonsmoking rooms*

available. Facilities: 3 restaurants, access to health club and spa, room service, TV. AE, D, DC, MC, V.

Mayflower Park Hotel. This pleasant older hotel, built in 1927, is conveniently connected with Westlake Center and the Monorail terminal to Seattle Center. Brass fixtures and antiques give both the public and private spaces a muted Oriental feel, and the service is similarly unobtrusive and smooth. The rooms are somewhat smaller than in modern hotels, but the Mayflower Park is so sturdily constructed that it is much quieter than many modern downtown hotels. *405 Olive Way, 98101, tel. 206/ 623–8700; fax 206/382–6997. 182 units, including 14 suites; nonsmoking rooms available. Facilities: restaurant, lounge, access to health club. AE, DC, MC, V.*

Seattle Hilton. This Hilton is a favorite for conventions and meetings, particularly because of its central location. Rooms are furnished in the same nondescript, but tasteful style as Hiltons worldwide, with soothing color schemes. One of its two restaurants, the Top of the Hilton, has excellent views of the city and well-prepared variations of salmon steak and other local specialties. An underground passage connects the Hilton with a shopping concourse, Rainier Square, as well as the 5th Avenue Theater and the Washington State Convention Center. *1301 University St., 98101, tel. 206/624–0500, 800/542–7700, or 800/426–0535; fax 206/682–9029. 237 rooms, including 6 suites; nonsmoking rooms available. Facilities: 2 restaurants, lobby, top-floor lounges, gift shop. AE, D, DC, MC, V.*

Warwick Hotel. The Warwick manages to combine its somewhat large size with an intimate European-style charm. Service is friendly and leisurely (but not slow), and the rooms are understated without being bland. All rooms have small balconies and good views of downtown. There is live entertainment nightly in the Liaison restaurant and lounge. *401 Lenora St., 98121, tel. 206/443–4300; fax 206/448–1662. 230 units, including 4 suites; nonsmoking rooms and handicapped rooms available. Facilities: 24-hr courtesy transportation within downtown, pool, Jacuzzi, exercise room, sauna. AE, D, DC, MC, V.*

Westin Hotel. The large high-rise hotel, located just north and east of the Public Market, is easily recognized by its twin-tower cylindrical shape. With this design, all rooms, equipped with balconies, can maximize the terrific views of the waterfront and Lake Union. Inside, the rooms are airy and bright, though furnished in a plain but high-quality style. The informal Market Cafe, the more formal Palm Court, and the famous Trader Vic's, as well as three lounges, are located in-house. *1900 5th Ave., 98101, tel. 206/728–1000 or 800/228–3000; fax 206/728– 2259. 865 rooms, including 47 suites; nonsmoking and handicapped rooms available. Facilities: 3 restaurants, 3 lounges, indoor pool, Jacuzzi, sauna, exercise and weight rooms, voice mail for guests, concierge service. AE, CB, D, DC, MC, V. 50% discounts Fri. and Sat. nights.*

Moderate **Pacific Plaza.** Built in 1929 and refurbished in 1989, this hotel now reflects its original character. The rooms and furnishings, reminiscent of the 1920s and 1930s, are appropriate for singles or couples but are too small to comfortably accommodate a family. Because of its downtown location and modest rates, the Plaza is a fairly good bargain for anyone who is not seeking contemporary luxury. *400 Spring St., 98104, tel. 206/623–3900 or 800/426–1165; fax 206/623–2059. 160 rooms. Facilities: 2* *restaurants, complimentary Continental breakfast. AE, DC, MC, V.*

WestCoast Camlin Hotel. This 1926 Seattle hotel/motor inn was recently remodeled, and the renovation turned out a gracious lobby featuring Oriental carpets, large mirrors, and lots of marble. Located on the edge of the downtown office area, but close to the convention center, the reasonably priced hotel is popular with business travelers. Rooms ending with 10 are best because they feature windows on three sides, and all have working spaces with a chair and table, along with gray-and-maroon cushioned chairs for relaxing. One drawback to staying here, though, is that the heating, air-conditioning, and ventilation system can be noisy. *1619 9th Ave., 98101, tel. 206/682–0100 or 800/426–0670; fax 206/682–7415. Facilities: restaurant, lounge, outdoor pool. AE, D, DC, MC, V.*

Inexpensive **Seattle YMCA.** This accommodation has 198 units and is a member of the American Youth Hostels Association. Rooms are clean and plainly furnished with a bed, phone, desk, and lamp. Rooms cost $25–$50; dorm units, designed to accommodate four people each, cost $14. *909 4th Ave., 98104, tel. 206/382–5000. 198 units. Facilities: pool, health club. No credit cards.*

Youth Hostel: Seattle International. Situated near the Pike Place Market is a bright, clean youth hostel with 126 dormitory-style beds, kitchen, dining room, lounge, and small library for about $10 a night. It's closed between 11 and 4 daily and has a midnight curfew on weeknights. *84 Union St., 98101, tel. 206/622–5443. 126 units. No credit cards.*

Seattle Center **Park Inn Club & Breakfast.** This 1960s-vintage motel, set off
Moderate Aurora Avenue (Hwy. 99), is relatively close to Seattle Center. The decor is typical of its vintage, not fancy but comfortable, and service is friendly and brisk. Continental breakfast, cafeteria, weight room, and play area for children make this lodging a good value. *225 Aurora Ave. N, 98107, tel. 206/728–7666. 160 rooms, nonsmoking rooms available. Facilities: indoor pool, Jacuzzi, parking. AE, MC, V.*

Sixth Avenue Inn. This small but comfortable motor hotel a few blocks north of downtown is a suitable location for families and business travelers. Rooms are pleasant, with standard-issue but well-maintained decor and color schemes; the service is cheerful. This is the hotel of choice for musicians playing at Dimitriou's Jazz Alley, the highly regarded club across the street where jazz buffs may spot a hero or two. *2000 6th Ave., 98121, tel. 206/441–8300; fax 206/441–9903. 166 rooms; nonsmoking rooms available. Facilities: restaurant, lounge. AE, DC, MC, V.*

Inexpensive **Meany Tower Hotel.** Built in 1931 and completely remodeled
★ several times, this is a pleasant hotel just a few blocks from the University of Washington campus. It has managed to retain much of its old-fashioned charm, with a muted-peach color scheme throughout, brass fixtures, and careful, attentive service. The rooms, especially those on the higher floors, have good views of the college grounds and surrounding areas, such as Green Lake and Lake Union. Other amenities include room service and a complimentary morning paper. The Meany Grill on the ground floor serves breakfast, lunch, and dinner; there is a large street-level lounge, as well. *4507 Brooklyn Ave. NE, 98105, tel. 206/634–2000; fax 206/634–2000. 55 rooms;*

nonsmoking rooms available. Facilities: restaurant, lounge. AE, DC, MC, V.

University Plaza Hotel. This is a full-service motor hotel, just on the other side of I–5 from the University of Washington campus, thus it is popular with families and others having business in the area. The mock-Tudor decor gives its lobby and other public areas a slightly outdated feel, but the service is cheerful and the rooms are spacious and pleasantly decorated in teak furniture, with pale pinks and grays being the predominant colors. The rooms on the freeway side can be noisy. *400 N.E. 45th St., 98105, tel. 206/634–0100; fax 206/633–2743. 135 rooms; nonsmoking rooms available. Facilities: restaurant, lounge, outside heated pool, beauty parlor, fitness room. AE, D, DC, MC, V.*

Seattle-Tacoma Airport
Expensive

Red Lion/Sea-Tac. The Red Lion is a popular, hospitable 850-room, full-service convention hotel. Built about 1970, it was recently remodeled in mauve, teal, and gray. Rooms are spacious and bright, with large panoramic balconies; the corner "King Rooms" feature wrap-around balconies and have the best views. Furnishings include chests of drawers, comfortable chairs, a dining table, and desk; this is the perfect accommodation for the business traveler who plans on doing some work between meetings. *18740 Pacific Hwy. S, 98168, tel. 206/246–8600; fax 206/242–9727. 850 rooms. Facilities: restaurant, coffee shop, 2 lounges, 24-hr workout facility with outdoor pool. AE, D, DC, MC, V.*

Moderate–
Expensive

Doubletree Inn and **Doubletree Suites.** These two hotels, situated across the street from each other, are adjacent to Southcenter Shopping Mall and convenient to the myriad of business-park offices there. Rooms at the Inn are smaller and less lavish, but perfectly fine and are at least $25 less than rooms at the Suites. Suites, decorated in neutrals, mauves, and pinks, feature a queen-size sofa, table and chairs, and a wet bar in the living room. Vanity area includes a full-size closet with mirrored doors. The room rate includes complimentary buffet breakfast for up to four people per room and two drinks in the bar nightly. *Doubletree Inn, 205 Strander Blvd., Tukwila 98188, tel. 206/246–8220. 200 rooms. Facilities: dining room, coffee shop, lounge, outdoor pool. Doubletree Suites, 16500 Southcenter Pkwy., Tukwila 98188, tel. 206/575–8220; fax 206/575–4743. 221 suites. Facilities: restaurant, lounge, health club, indoor pool, Jacuzzi, sauna, 2 racquetball courts. Doubletree Inn: Moderate; Doubletree Suites: Moderate–Expensive. AE, D, DC, MC, V (for both).*

Seattle Airport Hilton. This relatively small hotel (for the Hilton chain) has an intimate, original feel accentuated by its oak furnishings and cozy fireplace in the lobby, and paintings with Northwest scenery decorating the lobby. The large rooms are presently undergoing a renovation that will make them brighter and livelier with shades of peach and blue. This is also conveniently located: only a half-hour drive from downtown, and a 10-minute drive from Southcenter shopping mall. *17620 Pacific Hwy. S, 98188, tel. 206/244–4800; fax 206/439–7439. 173 rooms. Facilities: restaurant, sports bar, health facilities, outdoor pool, complimentary shuttle to airport. AE, D, DC, MC, V.*

★ **Seattle Marriott.** A surprisingly luxurious and substantial hotel for being in a non-downtown location, this Marriott, built in 1981, features a five-story-high, 20,000-square-foot tropical atrium that's complete with waterfall, dining area, indoor pool, and lounge. The newly renovated rooms are decorated in greens and mauve with dark wood and brass furnishings. Gambits, an in-house jazz club, books nationally known acts that play. *3201 S. 176th St., 98188, tel. 206/241–2000, international reservations tel. 800/228–9290; fax 206/248–0789. 459 rooms; nonsmoking rooms available. Facilities: restaurant, jazz club, 2 whirlpools, health club, games room, airport shuttle, concierge service. AE, D, DC, MC, V. Special rates available to AAA and AARP members; package rates available for weekends.*

Moderate **Holiday Inn Sea-Tac.** This 260-room hotel, built in 1970, has recently been remodeled with an atrium lobby, and a more private garden room, convenient for meeting people. The Top of the Inn revolving-view restaurant features singing waiters. *17338 Pacific Hwy. S, 98188, tel. 206/248–1000 or 800/HOLIDAY; fax 206/242–7089. 260 rooms. Facilities: restaurant, coffee shop, lounge, health club, indoor pool, Jacuzzi. AE, DC, MC, V.*

Bellevue/Kirkland **Red Lion Bellevue.** This 10-story hotel was built in 1982 with a
Expensive large airy atrium full of trees, shrubs, and flowering plants. The property also has a formal dining room, a lounge with two dance floors and 350 oversize rooms, many decorated in mauve and sea-foam green. Rooms have either king- or queen-size beds and two-room suites feature wet bars and spas or Jacuzzis. *300 112th Ave. SE, Bellevue 98004, tel. 206/455–1300 or 800/274–1415; fax 206/454–0466. 350 rooms. Facilities: 2 restaurants, lounge, health club, outdoor pool. AE, D, DC, MC, V.*

★ **Woodmark Hotel.** This new hotel, built in 1989, is the only one situated on the shores of Lake Washington; downtown Kirkland is only a few steps away from the hotel. Its 100 contemporary-style rooms face the water, courtyard, or street and are tastefully furnished in European-style luxury, with earth tones, heavy comforters, and numerous amenities such as terry-cloth bathrobes and fragrant soaps. Comfortable chairs surround the fireplace in the large, open lobby, and a circular staircase descends past a huge bay window and vast view of Lake Washington to the lounge. *1200 Carillon Point, Kirkland 98033, tel. 206/822–3700 or 800/822–3700; fax 206/822–3699. 100 rooms. Facilities: restaurant, access to health club. AE, MC, V.*

Moderate–Expensive **Hyatt Bellevue.** This is a deluxe new high-rise complex in the heart of downtown Bellevue, within a few blocks of Bellevue Square and other fine shopping. The exterior looks like any other sleek high rise, but the interior has such oriental touches as antique Japanese *tansu* (wood chests of drawers) and huge displays of fresh flowers. The rooms are decorated in similarly understated ways, with dark wood and earth tones predominating, and the service is impeccable. Some rooms have been specially designed for Japanese travelers, and come complete with slippers and Japanese meals; others are deluxe suites with two bedrooms, bar facilities, and meeting rooms with desks and full-length tables. The Eques restaurant serves excellent and reasonably priced breakfast, lunch, and dinner; an English-style pub serves a variety of drinks as well as lunch and dinner. *900 Bellevue Way NE, 98004, tel. 206/462–2626; fax 206/646–7567. 382 units, including 30 suites and deluxe suites; nonsmoking rooms available. Facilities: restaurant, pub, 24-*

hr room service, access to health club and pool. AE, D, DC, MC, V.

Moderate **Best Western Greenwood Hotel.** This hotel/motor inn features 176 rooms, 16 of which are town-house suites, suitable for two–four people, with sleeping lofts and wood-burning fireplaces. Rooms are clean; those in the corporate wing face the courtyard and are larger and more quiet than the others. These rooms provide thick terry robes for guest use. The hotel is about eight blocks or a 20-minute walk from Bellevue Square. A complimentary appetizer buffet, offered in the lounge weekdays between 5 PM and 7 PM, is substantial and includes seafood and roast beef, and sometimes is built around a theme, such as Mexican or Scandinavian cuisine. *625 116th Ave. NE, Bellevue 98004, tel. 206/455–9444 or 800/445–9444; fax 206/455–2154. 176 rooms. Facilities: restaurant, coffee shop, lounge, outdoor pool. AE, D, DC, MC, V.*

The Arts and Nightlife

The Arts

In recent years Seattle has gained a world-class reputation as a theater town, and it also has a strong music and dance scene for local, national, and international artists. A good handle on what's happening in town can be found in any of several periodicals. Both the *Seattle Times* and *Post-Intelligencer* have pull-out sections on Friday detailing most of the coming week's events. *Seattle Weekly*, which hits most newsstands on Wednesday, has even more detailed coverage and arts reviews. *The Rocket*, a lively free monthly, covers music news, reviews, and concert information, with an emphasis on rock and roll.

Ticketmaster (tel. 206/628–0888) provides (for an added fee) tickets to most productions in the Seattle area through charge-by-phone. **Ticket/Ticket** (401 Broadway E, tel. 206/324–2744) or **Pike Place Market Information Booth** (1st Ave. and Pike St., tel. 206/682–7453 ext. 26) sell half-price tickets for most events on the day of the performance.

Part of the legacy left by the 1962 World's Fair is a series of performance halls at **Seattle Center** (305 Harrison St., tel. 206/684–8582). Seattle also boasts two fine examples of the classic (and beautifully renovated) early 20th-century music hall—the **Fifth Avenue** (1308 5th Ave., tel. 206/625–1900) and the **Paramount** (907 Pine St., tel. 206/682–1414). Other prominent venues are the **Moore Theater** (1932 2nd Ave., tel. 206/443–1744), the small but acoustically outstanding **Broadway Performance Hall** (1625 Broadway, tel. 206/323–2623) at Seattle Central Community College, and **Kane** and **Meany halls** on the University of Washington campus (tel. 206/543–4880).

The **Cornish College of the Arts** (710 E. Roy St., tel. 206/323–1400) is an internationally recognized school that also serves as home to a number of distinguished professional performing groups. These groups stage productions September–May, ranging from dance and jazz to art lectures and multimedia performances. Of particular note are the Professional Acting Conservatory and the renowned Cornish New Performance Group, which often premieres important new pieces of music.

Theater The **Seattle Repertory Theater** (Bagley Wright Theater at Seattle Center, 155 Mercer St., tel. 206/443–2222) presents a variety of high-quality programming, from classics to new plays. During its October–May season, six mainstage productions and three smaller shows (in the adjoining PONCHO Forum) are presented.

The **New City Arts Center** (1634 11th Ave., tel. 206/323–6800) is home to a wide range of experimental performances, produced by a resident company as well as in conjunction with major national and international artists. Its annual output includes six plays, a director's festival and a playwright's festival, three dance concerts, a monthly film showing, and a lively, late-night monthly cabaret.

The **Empty Space Theater** (107 Occidental Ave. S, tel. 206/467–6000) has a strong reputation for introducing Seattle to new playwrights. The season generally runs October–July, with five or six mainstage productions plus several smaller shows throughout the season.

The **Fifth Avenue Musical Theater Company** (Fifth Avenue Theater, 1308 5th Ave., tel. 206/625–1468) is a resident professional troupe that mounts four lavish musicals between October and May each year, with each run lasting about two weeks. (During the rest of the year, this chinoiserie-style historical landmark, carefully restored to its original 1926 condition, hosts a variety of other traveling musical as well as theatrical performances.)

The **Intiman Theater** (Playhouse at Seattle Center, 2nd and Mercer Sts., tel. 206/624–4541) presents the great plays with enduring themes of world drama in an intimate, high-quality setting. The season generally runs May–November.

The **Evergreen Theater Company** (305 Harrison St., tel. 206/443–1490) offers non-Equity but professional musical theater in an intimate setting. (None of its 158 seats is more than 25 feet from the stage.) It stages five productions a season, September–May.

The **Group Theater** (3940 Brooklyn Ave. NE, tel. 206/543–4327) is a multicultural troupe that prides itself on presenting socially provocative works—old and new—by artists of varied cultures and colors. The season runs September–June, and the Group also mounts a special summertime playwrights' festival. Of the regular season's six productions, one is always the popular *Voices of Christmas*, a study of the holidays with consideration to cultural differences and ethnic and emotional barriers.

A Contemporary Theater (100 W. Roy St., tel. 206/285–5110) specializes in developing works by emerging playwrights, including at least one world premiere every year. The season runs May–November, and every December ACT mounts a popular production of Dickens's *A Christmas Carol*.

The **Bathhouse Theater** (7312 W. Greenlake Dr. N, tel. 206/524–9108) produces six productions on a year-round schedule, specializing in innovative updates on classics. In addition, it mounts numerous free public shows in various Seattle parks.

The **Village Theater** (120 Front St. N, Issaquah, tel. 206/392–2202) produces high-quality family musicals, comedies, and dramas September–May in Issaquah, a town east of Seattle.

Dance **Pacific Northwest Ballet** (Opera House at Seattle Center, tel. 206/547–5920) is a resident company and school that presents 60–70 performances annually. Its Christmastime production of *The Nutcracker*, with choreography by Kent Stowell and sets by Maurice Sendak, has become a beloved Seattle tradition.

Allegro Dance Company (Broadway Performance Hall, 1625 Broadway, tel. 206/32–DANCE) presents the best in local and regional choreography, with some productions that include other elements of the performing arts. It schedules about 10 concerts a year between September and June.

Meany Hall for the Performing Arts (University of Washington campus, tel. 206/543–4880) presents important national and international companies, September–May, with an emphasis on modern and jazz dance.

On the Boards (Washington Performance Hall, 153 14th Ave., tel. 206/325–7901) presents and produces a wide variety of contemporary performances, including not only dance but also theater music, and multimedia events by local, national, and international artists. Although the main subscription series runs October–May, OTB events happen nearly every weekend year-round.

Music **Civic Light Opera** (11051 34th Ave. NE, tel. 206/363–2809) is a non-Equity, semipro company that offers three or four high-quality productions per season of large-scale American musical theater. The season runs roughly October–May.

Seattle Symphony (Opera House at Seattle Center and other locations, tel. 206/443–4747) presents some 120 concerts September–June in Seattle and around the world and—under the musical direction of Gerard Schwartz—continues to uphold its long tradition of excellence.

Northwest Chamber Orchestra (tel. 206/343–0445) is the Northwest's only professional chamber music orchestra. At the Moore Theater, the Nippon Kan, and other venues, it presents a full spectrum of music, from Baroque to modern. The season, generally September–May, includes a Bach festival every fall, a spring subscription series, and special holiday performances in December.

A number of other organizations sponsor classical series throughout the year. An integral part of Seattle's strong early music scene is the **Early Music Guild** (tel. 206/325–7066), which presents regional, national, and international artists in various intimate settings during a season running roughly September–May. The 100-year-old **Ladies Musical Club** (tel. 206/328–7153), composed of professional or retired musicians, sponsors four or five important recitals each year by internationally-known artists.

For live rock concerts, the **Moore Theater** (1932 2nd Ave., tel. 206/443–1744) and the **Paramount** (907 Pine St.; for tickets and information, Ticketmaster, tel. 206/628–0888) are elegant former movie/music halls that now host visiting and national rock acts.

Opera **Seattle Opera** (Opera House at Seattle Center, Mercer St. at 3rd Ave., tel. 206/443–4711) is a world-class opera company, generally considered to be one of the top organizations in

America. During the August-May season, it presents six performances of six productions.

Nightlife

For a city of relatively small size, Seattle has a remarkably strong and diverse music scene. On any given night, you can hear high-quality live sounds at a variety of venues. There's a particularly strong blues circuit, a lively folk/bluegrass/Celtic scene, and a steady diet of good local jazz provided by the many internationally known teachers and students at the Cornish School. The two areas with the highest concentration of clubs are Pioneer Square and Ballard; the clubs and taverns in both areas often place an emphasis on high-quality blues and R&B.

Bars and Nightclubs
Bars with waterfront views are plentiful in Seattle. Among the best: on the Ship Canal, **Hiram's at the Locks** (5300 34th Ave. NW, tel. 206/784–1733); on Lake Union, the **Lakeside** (2501 N. Northlake Way, tel. 206/634–0823) and **Arnie's** (1900 N. Northlake Way, tel. 206/547–3242); and on Shilshole Bay, **Ray's Boathouse** (6049 Seaview Ave. NW, tel. 206/789–3770) and **Anthony's Home Port** (6135 Seaview Ave. NW, tel. 206/783–0780).

Panoramic views of the city can be found at the **Mirabeau** (1001 4th St., tel. 206/624–4550), on the 46th floor of the Seafirst Building, and at the **Space Needle** (Seattle Center, tel. 206/443–2100), where the revolving restaurant provides a 360-degree view over the course of an hour.

Other fine places for a drink downtown are the **Garden Court** (411 University St., tel. 206/621–1700) at the Four Seasons Olympic, a rather formal and elegant locale; the **J&M Cafe** (201 1st Ave. S, tel. 206/624–1670), a lively and casual Pioneer Square joint; and, near the Kingdome, **F.X. McRory's** (419 Occidental Ave. S, tel. 206/623–4800), famous for its huge selection of single-malt whiskies and equally huge singing bartender.

Folk Clubs
Backstage (2208 N.W. Market St., tel. 206/781–2805) is an often-packed basement venue in Ballard that has a lively mix of national and local acts with the emphasis on world music, offbeat rock, and new folk.
Kells (1916 Post Alley, tel. 206/728–1916), a snug Irish-style pub, is located near the Public Market and plays live Celtic music Wednesday–Saturday starting at 9 PM.
Murphy's Pub (2110 45th St. NE, tel. 206/634–2110) features open-mike Wednesdays, with Irish and other folk music on Friday and Saturday in this cozy neighborhood bar.
New Melody Tavern (5213 Ballard Ave. NW, tel. 206/782–3480), a lively and casual Ballard bar, is the mecca of serious Seattle folkies. Irish, bluegrass, and other music is played nightly.

Blues/R&B Clubs
The **Ballard Firehouse** (5429 Russell St. NW, tel. 206/784–3516) is the music mecca in the heart of Ballard, with an emphasis on local and national blues acts.
Chicago's (315 1st Ave. N, tel. 206/282–7791) features Chicago-style pizza and other kinds of good, reasonably priced Italian food in this restaurant just west of the Seattle Center. Live blues is played on weekends.
Doc Maynard's (610 1st Ave., tel. 206/682–4649) is another

R&B-oriented tavern with a small and always jam-packed dance floor.

Larry's (209 1st Ave. S, tel. 206/624–7665) features live R&B and blues nightly in an unpretentious, friendly, and usually jam-packed tavern/restaurant in Pioneer Square.

Old Timer's Cafe (620 1st Ave., tel. 206/623–9800) is a popular Pioneer Square restaurant and bar with live music—mostly R&B—nightly.

Owl Cafe & Tavern (5140 Ballard Ave. NW, tel. 206/784–3640) is a casual and popular tavern near the Ballard waterfront, with good food, live R&B nearly every night, and a spacious dance floor.

The **Scarlet Tree** (6521 Roosevelt Way NE, tel. 206/523–7153), a neighborhood institution, is a restaurant and bar just north of the University District. Great burgers and live R&B are offered nightly.

Jazz Clubs   **Dimitriou's Jazz Alley** (2037 6th Ave., tel. 206/441–9729) is a downtown club with nationally known, consistently high-quality performers every night but Sunday. Excellent dinners are served before the first shows.

Gambits (3201 S. 176th St., tel. 206/241–2000), in the Marriott Hotel near Seattle-Tacoma airport, is an attractive lounge that features nationally known jazz acts on a regular basis.

Latona Tavern (6423 Latona Ave. NE, tel. 206/525–2238) is a funky, friendly, often jazz-oriented, neighborhood bar at the south end of Green Lake with a variety of local musicians nightly.

Lofurno's (2060 15th Ave., tel. 206/283–7980), located south of the Ballard Bridge, offers reasonably priced Italian food and jazz nightly.

New Orleans Creole Restaurant (114 1st Ave. S, tel. 206/622–2563) is a popular Pioneer Square restaurant with good food and live jazz nightly—mostly top local performers but occasionally national acts as well.

Rock Clubs   **Central Tavern** (207 1st Ave. S, tel. 206/622–0209) is a crowded Pioneer Square tavern with an ever-changing roster of local and national rock acts.

OK Hotel (212 Alaskan Way, tel. 206/621–7903), a small venue near Pioneer Square, is dedicated to national and local rock and experimental music.

Parker's (17001 Aurora Ave. N, tel. 206/542–9491) was a venerable North Seattle teen palace of the '50s and '60s but has since become a more sophisticated dinner-and-show venue for a variety of rock artists, often nationally known acts.

Squid Row Tavern (518 E. Pine St., tel. 206/322–2031), an avant-garde and very casual tavern on Capitol Hill, features ultranew rock and occasional poetry readings.

The **Square on Yesler** (111 Yesler St., tel. 206/447–1514) has high-quality live rock and R&B Thursday through Saturday.

Vogue (2018 1st Ave., tel. 206/443–0673), a club in Belltown, the artist's community just north of the Public Market, presents a variety of au courant local and national rock.

Comedy Clubs   **Comedy Underground** (2225 Main St., tel. 206/628–0303), a Pioneer Square club (literally underground, beneath Swannie's), presents stand-up comedy nightly, with Monday and Tuesday reserved as open-mike nights; the other nights are mixtures of nationally known and local comics.

Giggles (5220 Roosevelt Way NE, tel. 206/526–JOKE), in the

University District, presents the best of local and nationally known comedians six nights a week, with late shows on weekend nights.

Dance Clubs   In Pioneer Square, there are several popular, chic clubs featuring recorded dance music, including the **Celebrity** (313 2nd Ave. S, tel. 206/467–1111), the **Hollywood Underground** (323 2nd Ave. S, tel. 206/628–8964), and the **Borderline** (608 1st Ave., tel. 206/624–3316).

In the downtown area, **Fitzgerald's on Fifth** (1900 5th Ave., tel. 206/728–1000) and **Pier 70** (2815 Alaskan Way at Broad St., tel. 206/624–8090) are dance clubs that feature Top-40 music nightly.

Ballroom Dancing   The U.S. Amateur Ballroom Dancing Association's local chapter (tel. 206/822–6686) sponsors regular classes and dances throughout the year. These are either at the **Avalon Ballroom** (1017 Stewart St.) or **Carpenter's Hall** (2512 2nd Ave.). The **Washington Dance Club** (1017 Stewart St., tel. 206/628–8939) sponsors Friday-night workshops on various styles, and the **All-City Dance Club** (2245 N.W. 57th St., tel. 206/747–2707) hosts regular Saturday-night get-togethers.

Excursions from Seattle

The heavily developed I–5 corridor runs through Seattle, north to Vancouver, British Columbia, or south to Portland, Oregon. But venturing off this ribbon of highway—either toward the mountains in the east or the water to the west—will quickly bring the traveler to some relatively isolated areas. Five of the many excellent trips that can be taken from Seattle are to Winslow on Bainbridge Island, a short but delightful ferry ride from downtown across Puget Sound; the scenic Snoqualmie Falls, where snowcapped mountains meet lush farmland; Whidbey Island and the San Juan Islands, with scenic beaches, rolling countryside, and good fishing; or Leavenworth, a mock Bavarian village high in the Cascade Mountains.

Winslow

On a nice day, there's no better way to escape Seattle than on board a Washington State Ferry for a trip across Puget Sound. It's a great way to watch seagulls, sailboats, and massive container vessels in the sound—not to mention the surrounding scenery, which takes in the San Juan Islands, the Kitsap Peninsula and Olympic Mountains, Mt. Rainier, the Cascade Mountains, and the Seattle skyline. Even when the weather isn't all that terrific, travelers can stay snug inside the ferry, have a snack, and listen to the folk musicians who entertain the cross-sound commuters. Winslow combines a small-town atmosphere with scenic country surroundings.

Tourist Information   **Bainbridge Island Chamber of Commerce** (166 Winslow Way, tel. 206/842–3700) has free maps that detail shops, restaurants, and sights.

Getting There   Although there are several ferries that leave from the Seattle
By Ferry   area (*see* Getting Around Seattle, above), probably the best one for a single-day excursion is the ferry to **Winslow,** on Bainbridge Island. The advantages of walking on board are obvious; it's cheap (only $3.30 for a round-trip ticket) and hassle-

free (no long waits in lines of frustrated drivers during peak commute hours or on weekends).

The Winslow ferry leaves from Seattle's busy downtown terminal at Colman Dock (Pier 52, south of the Public Market and just north of Pioneer Square), and the trip takes about a half-hour each way.

A word on ferries in general: The Washington State Ferry System, the biggest in the United States, includes vessels ranging from the 40-car *Hiyu* to jumbo ferries capable of carrying more than 200 cars and 2,000 passengers each. They connect points all around Puget Sound and the San Juan Islands. There is no smoking allowed in public areas.

If you do take your car, there are several points to note: Passengers and bicycles always load first unless otherwise instructed. Prior to boarding, lower antennas. Only parking lights should be used at night, and it is considered bad form to start your engine before the ferry docks.

Sunny weekends are heavy traffic times all around the San Juans, and weekdays at commuting times for ferries headed into or out of Seattle are also crowded. Peak times on the Seattle runs are sunny weekends, eastbound in the morning and Sunday nights, as well as westbound Saturday morning and weekday afternoons. Since no reservations are accepted on Washington State Ferries (except for the Sidney–Anacortes run during summer), arriving at least a half-hour before a scheduled departure is always advised. *Colman Dock, Pier 52, tel. 206/464–6400, 206/464–2000 (press #5500 for schedules), or 800/543–3779, in WA. 800/542–7052; for information concerning Winslow, 206/464–6990. Cost: Winslow ferry auto and driver: $6.65; passenger (in car or as walk-on) $3.30; senior citizens and disabled persons half-fare; children under 5 free; no extra charge for bicycles. Special rates for mobile homes and other oversize vehicles. Schedules vary according to season and time of day, but generally ferries leave daily every 30–40 min, early morning–2 AM.*

Once you reach the Winslow terminal, walk north up a short hill on Olympic Drive to Winslow Way; about ¼ mile farther north on Olympic is the **Bainbridge Island Vineyard and Winery** (682 S.R. 305, tel. 206/842–9463), which is open for tastings and tours Wednesday–Sunday noon–5.

If you turn west on Winslow Way, you'll find yourself in town, with several square blocks of interesting antiques shops, clothing stores, Scandinavian gift shops, galleries, restaurants, and other services. Shopping in Winslow is a refreshing change from the bustle of most big towns: There are usually only a few customers, and shopkeepers tend to carry on protracted, friendly conversations with natives and visitors alike.

Snoqualmie Falls

Driving east out of Seattle, you'll travel through bucolic farmland with snowcapped mountains in the background. Spring and summer snowmelt turns the Snoqualmie River into a thundering torrent as it cascades through a 268-foot rock gorge (100 feet higher than Niagara Falls) to a 65-foot-deep pool below.

Tourist Information For information on Snoqualmie call the **Seattle/King County Visitors Bureau** (800 Convention Pl., tel. 206/461–5840).

Getting There Snoqualmie, Exit 27 off I-90, is about 30 miles east of Seat-
By Car tle.

Snoqualmie is the site of the first major electric plant in the Northwest to use falling water as a power source, and the world's first completely underground electric generating facility. The power plant, started in 1889, is a National Historic Civil Engineering Landmark; plant No. 2 was added just downstream from the falls in 1910 and expanded in 1957. Electricity from the two power plants provides enough power to serve 16,000 homes.

A 2-acre park, including an observation platform 300 feet above the Snoqualmie River, offers a view of the falls and surrounding area. Hike the **River Trail,** a 3-mile round-trip route through trees and open slopes, ending with a view from the base of the falls. (Note: Be prepared for an uphill workout on the return to the trailhead.)

Steam locomotives power vintage trains on **Puget Sound** and **Snoqualmie Valley Railway.** The 75-minute trip travels through woods and farmland, stopping briefly at Snoqualmie Falls. Railroad artifacts and memorabilia are displayed at both the Snoqualmie Depot (Hwy. 202, in downtown Snoqualmie) and Railroad Park Depot in downtown Northbend. For children, a special Santa train runs the first two weekends in December and a spook train runs the last two weekends in Oct.; tickets for all special trips must be prepurchased. *Box 459, Snoqualmie, tel. 206/888–3030. Admission: $6 adults, $5 senior citizens, $4 children. Trains operate Sept., May, and June, weekends; Oct. and Apr., Sun.; July–Aug., Fri.–Sun. Call for departure times.*

Snoqualmie Falls Forest Theater produces three plays a summer (the Passion Play, a melodrama, and a well-known classic performed by acting students and community theater performers) in the 250-seat outdoor amphitheater near Fall City, usually on Friday and Saturday nights and Sunday afternoons. *From I–90 take Exit 22 and go 4 mi; take a right on David Powell Rd., follow signs, continue through gate to parking area. 36800 S.E. David Powell Rd., tel. 206/222–7044. Admission: $8.50; for another $9 per person, you can enjoy a salmon or steak barbecue after the matinee and before the evening performances. Reservations required for dinner.*

Snoqualmie Pass is the site of three ski areas—Alpental, Ski Acres, and Snoqualmie Summit for downhill and cross-country skiing in winter and spring, and for hiking in the summer (*see* Sports and Fitness, above).

The **Snoqualmie Winery** (1000 Winery Rd., tel. 206/888–4000) offers daily tours, tastings, and great views.

Dining **The Herbfarm.** If there is such a thing as Northwest Cuisine,
★ then The Herbfarm must rank as its temple. But the attraction here surpasses the fine, fresh food: This restaurant offers intimate, elegant dining among wildflower bouquets, Victorian-style prints, and a friendly staff. Try such delicacies as goat's milk cheese and parsley biscuits, green pickled walnuts in the husk, fresh salmon with a sauce of fresh garden herbs, and sorbet of rose geranium and lemon verbena. There's only one

drawback: The Herbfarm is commonly booked up months ahead of time, which means you should plan a meal long before you're getting to Seattle. Is all that effort worth it? Yes. Only wine is served. *From I–90, Exit 22, go 3 mi. 32804 Issaquah-Fall City Rd., Fall City, tel. 206/784–2222. Some 75% of the 24 seats for each lunch or special dinner are reserved on Apr. 10 starting at 9 AM. The other 6 seats can be reserved by phoning at 1 PM the Fri. before you wish to go. Allow 2 hours for lunch ($39.50 per person) and the garden tour. 8 twilight dinners, including five fine wines, are scheduled in the summer ($82–$89 per person). Dress: casual but neat. Restaurant closed Mon.–Thurs.; closed dinner; closed Jan.–early Apr. MC, V. Expensive.*

Dining and Lodging **Salish.** This lodge at the top of the falls has been rebuilt and is operated by the Oregon-based Salishan Lodge. Eight of the 91 rooms look out over the falls, and others have a view upriver. Rooms have an airy feeling with wood furniture and window seats or balconies. You can sit in the whirlpool bath and open a window to view the fire in the flagstone fireplace. The Salish restaurant, which serves three meals daily, also has a widespread reputation for its Sunday brunch that includes course upon course of eggs, bacon, fish, fresh fruit, pancakes, and its renowned oatmeal. *37807 Snoqualmie-Fall City Rd., Fall City 37807, tel. 206/888–2556. 91 rooms. Facilities: 2 restaurants, lounge, health club, country store. Reservation for restaurant necessary. Dress for restaurant: casual; jacket and tie recommended for dinner. AE, DC, MC, V. Expensive.*

Puget Sound and the San Juan Islands

Whidbey Island and the San Juan Islands are the jewels of Puget Sound. Because the islands are reachable only by ferry or airplane, with the exception of Whidbey, which can be reached via a bridge from the north end of the island (90 minutes from Seattle), the islands beckon to souls longing for a quiet change of pace, whether it be kayaking in a cove, walking a deserted beach, or nestling by the fire in an old farmhouse.

Unfortunately, solitude can be a precious commodity in summer when the islands, particularly the San Juans, are overrun with tourists. On weekends and even some weekdays, expect to wait at least three hours in line once you arrive at the ferry terminal. You will face the same challenge or worse if you return Sunday afternoon or evening.

Island residents enjoy their peace and quiet; while some of them rely on tourism, many do not, and they would just as soon not have their country roads and villages jammed with "summer people." So it should come as no surprise that tourism and development are hotly contested issues on the islands.

One way to avoid crowds and the possibility of a cantankerous island resident is to plan a trip in the spring, fall, or winter. Reservations are a must any time in the summer and are advised for weekends in the off-season, too. Because Whidbey Island is more accessible to the mainland, its sandy beaches, villages, and viewpoints make it a perfect day-trip destination.

Tourist Information For information concerning Puget Sound and its islands, contact the **San Juan Tourism Cooperative** (Box 65, Lopez 98261, tel. 206/468–3663).

Getting There **Coastal Airways** (tel. 800/547–5022) and **Chart Air** (tel. 800/237–
By Plane 1101) fly to the San Juan Islands from Seattle-Tacoma International; **Harbor Airlines** (tel. 800/521–3450) flies to Whidbey Island from the airport, as well.

Lake Union Air (tel. 206/284–0300 or 800/826–1890) and **Kenmore Air** (tel. 206/486–8400, 800/832–9696 in WA, or 800/423–
5526 outside WA) fly float planes from Lake Union in Seattle to
the San Juan Islands and can arrange charter flights to
Whidbey Island.

By Car To reach the **San Juan Islands,** drive north on I–5 to La Conner;
go west on 536 to 20W and follow signs to Anacortes; pick up
the Washington State Ferry (*see* below).

Whidbey Island can be reached via the Mukilteo-to-Clinton
ferry, or you can drive from Seattle along I–5, heading west on
Hwy. 20; cross the dramatic Deception Pass via the bridge at
the north end of the island.

By Ferry The **Washington State Ferry System** (tel. 206/464–6400 or 800/
542–9052) provides car and passenger service from Mukilteo to
Clinton (Whidbey Island). From Anacortes, about 90 miles
north of Seattle, ferries depart for the San Juan Islands.

A.I.T. Waterways (tel. 206/671–1137) takes passengers from
Bellingham, Orcas, and Friday Harbor.

Calm Sea Charters (tel. 206/385–5288) runs a passenger service
from Port Townsend and Friday Harbor.

Guided Tours **Discovery Washington** (Box 14493, Seattle 98114, tel. 206/838–
6043) runs tours of Puget Sound, and customizes itineraries.

Grey Line Water Sightseeing (500 Wall St., Suite 31, Seattle
98121, tel. 206/441–1887) operates three-and-a-half-hour nature cruises through the San Juan Islands.

The **Mosquito Fleet** (Box 196, Langley, WA 98260, tel. 206/
321–0506 or 800/235–0506; fax 206/321–4122) offers several
cruises of Whidbey Island and Deception Pass from mid-May–
October.

The **Rosario Princess** (#5 Harbor Esplanade, Bellingham
98225, tel. 206/734–8866) conducts whale-watching, nature,
and island cruises on an 83-foot tour boat.

Western Prince Cruises (tel. 206/378–5315) charters boats for
half days during the summer; in the spring and fall bird-watching and scuba diving tours are offered. Cruises depart from
Friday Harbor.

Bear in mind that Whidbey, a 50-mile island, is mostly rural
with undulating hills, gentle beaches, and little coves.

*Numbers in the margin correspond to points of interest on the
Puget Sound map.*

This tour begins at the southern tip of Whidbey, before pro-
gressing to Lopez, Orcas, and San Juan Islands. Naturally, on
an island such as Whidbey, wildlife is plentiful, and it's not unusual to see eagles, great blue herons, and oyster catchers, as
well as Orcas, gray whales, dolphins, and otters. Perhaps the
❶ best view of the sea creatures can be had from **Langley,** the
quaint town that sits atop a 50-foot-high bluff overlooking the
southeastern shore. In the heart of town, particularly along

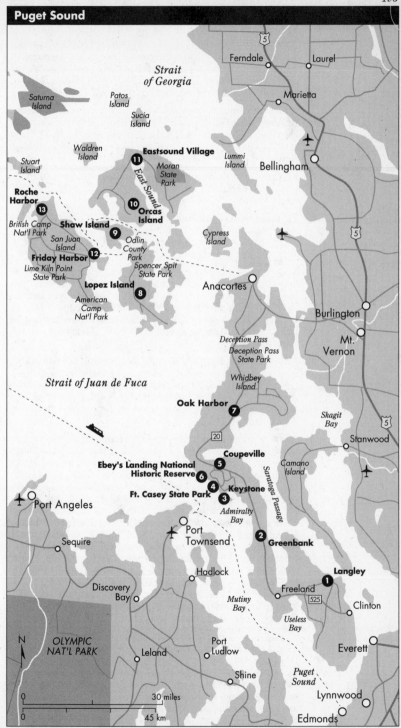

Puget Sound

Strait of Georgia

Ferndale

Laurel

Marietta

Saturna Island

Patos Island

Sucia Island

Waldren Island

Stuart Island

Eastsound Village

⑪

Moran State Park

Lummi Island

Bellingham

East Sound

Roche Harbor

⑬

British Camp Nat'l Park

⑩ **Orcas Island**

Shaw Island

⑨

San Juan Island

⑫

Odlin County Park

Friday Harbor

Lime Kiln Point State Park

Spencer Spit State Park

Cypress Island

Anacortes

Lopez Island

⑧

American Camp Nat'l Park

Burlington

Mt. Vernon

Deception Pass

Deception Pass State Park

Strait of Juan de Fuca

Whidbey Island

Oak Harbor ⑦

Skagit Bay

Stanwood

20

Coupeville

⑤

Ebey's Landing National Historic Reserve ⑥

④

Camano Island

Saratoga Passage

Keystone ③

Ft. Casey State Park

Admiralty Bay

Port Angeles

Sequire

② **Greenbank**

Port Townsend

Hadlock

Langley ①

Freeland

525

Clinton

Discovery Bay

Mutiny Bay

Useless Bay

Everett

N

OLYMPIC NAT'L PARK

Leland

Port Ludlow

Shine

Puget Sound

Lynnwood

Edmonds

0   30 miles
0   45 km

First Street, there are boutiques that sell art, glass, antiques, jewelry, and clothing.

About halfway up this long, skinny island is Whidbey's town of ❷ **Greenbank,** home to the historically recognized **Loganberry Farm.** The 125-acre site is now the place of production for the state's newest spirit, Whidbey's Liqueur. *657 Wonn Rd., tel. 206/678-7700. Admission free. Tours offered daily 10-4.*

While in Greenbank, you may want to see the 53-acre **Meerkerk Rhododendron Gardens,** with 1,500 native and hybrid species of rhododendrons, numerous walking trails, and ponds. The best time for viewing the flowers in full bloom is in April and May. *Resort Rd., Greenbank, tel. 206/321-6682. Admission free.*

❸ Farther north you'll come to **Keystone,** an important town because it is the port of call for the ferry bound for Port Townsend on the Olympic Peninsula.

❹ **Ft. Casey State Park** (tel. 206/678-4519), just north of Keystone, is one of three forts built in 1890 to protect Puget Sound. Today it offers a small interpretive center, camping, picnic sites, fishing, and a boat launch.

❺ About two-thirds of the way up this long island is **Coupeville,** home of many restored Victorian houses and one of the largest National Historic Districts in the state. The town was founded in 1852 by Captain Thomas Coupe; his house, built in 1853, is one of the state's oldest. The town is also the site of the new **Island County Historical Museum** (908 N.W. Alexander St., tel. 206/678-3310).

❻ **Ebey's Landing National Historic Reserve** (tel. 206/678-4636), west of Coupeville, is a 22-acre area including Keystone, Coupeville, and Penn Cove. Established by Congress in 1980, the reserve is the first and largest of its kind. It is dotted with some 91 nationally registered historical structures, farmland, parks, and trails.

❼ About 11 miles farther north is **Oak Harbor,** which derived its name from the Garry oaks in the area. It was settled by Dutch and Irish immigrants in the mid-1800s, and several Dutch windmills are still in existence. Unfortunately, the island's largest city has not maintained the sleepy fishing-village pace that much of the rest of the island follows. Instead, Oak Harbor has the look of suburban sprawl, with strips of fast-food restaurants and service stations. Just north of Oak Harbor is **Whidbey Island Naval Air Station** (tel. 206/257-2286), at which group tours can be arranged. At **Deception Pass State Park,** 3 miles from the naval base, take some time to notice the spectacular view and stroll among the madrona trees with their reddish-brown peeling bark. While walking across the bridge, you won't be able to miss seeing the dramatic gorge below, well-known for its tidal currents. The Deception Pass bridge links Whidbey to Fidalgo Island and the mainland. From here it's just a short distance to Anacortes and ferries to the San Juans.

There are 172 named islands in the San Juan archipelago, although at low tide the islands total 743 and at high tide, 428. Sixty are populated, and 10 are state marine parks. Ferries stop at Lopez, Shaw, Orcas, and San Juan; other islands, many privately owned, must be reached by private plane or boat. In any case, the San Juans are a gold mine for naturalists, because they are home to more than 80 orcas, a few minke whales, seals, dolphins, otters, and more than 60 active pairs of breeding bald eagles.

⑧ The first ferry stop is **Lopez Island,** with old orchards, weathered barns, and pastures of sheep and cows. Because of the relatively flat terrain, this island is a favorite for bicyclists. Two popular parks to note are **Odlin County Park** and **Spencer Spit State Park.**

⑨ At the next stop, **Shaw Island,** Franciscan nuns wear their traditional habits while running the ferry dock. You may notice that few people get off here; the island is mostly residential, and tourists rarely stop.

⑩ **Orcas,** the next in line, is a large, mountainous, horseshoe-shape island. Roads sweep down through wide valleys and rise to marvelous hilltop views. A number of little shops featuring the island's cottage industries—jewelry, weaving, pottery—
⑪ are in **Eastsound Village,** the island's business and social center situated in the middle of the horseshoe. Walk along Prune Alley, where you'll find a handful of small shops and restaurants.

On the other side of the horseshoe from the ferry landing, following aptly named Horseshoe Highway, is **Moran State Park** (Star Rte., Box 22, Eastsound 98245, tel. 206/376–2326). The ranger station will supply information, but applications for camping permits within the park for Memorial Day through Labor Day must be received by mail, at least two weeks prior to requested date. From the summit you of the 2,400-foot **Mt. Constitution** can have panoramic views of the San Juans, the Cascades, the Olympics, and Vancouver Island.

⑫ The last ferry stop in the San Juans is at **Friday Harbor** on San Juan Island, with a colorful, active waterfront that always conveys a holiday feeling. Although Friday Harbor—the island's county seat—is the largest town, it is also the most convenient destination for visitors traveling on foot. The shops here cater to tourists, offering clever crafts, gifts, and whimsical toys. A short walk from the ferry dock, the **San Juan Historical Museum** displays a number of farm implements used by early settlers. *405 Price St., tel. 206/378–3949. Admission free. Open June–Aug., Wed.–Sat. 1–4:30.*

Standing at the ferry dock, you'll recognize the **Whale Museum** by the mural of the whale painted on the wall. To reach the entrance, walk up Spring Street and turn right on First Street. This modest museum doesn't attempt to woo you with expensive exhibits; models of whales, whale skeletons, baleen, recordings of whale sounds, and videos of whales are the attractions. The museum also offers workshops on marine mammals and San Juan ecology. *62 1st St. N, tel. 206/378–4710. Admission: $2.50 adults, $2 senior citizens, $1 children 3–12. Open June–Sept., daily 10–5; Oct.–May, daily 11–4.*

For an opportunity to see whales cavorting in the water, go to **Lime Kiln Point State Park,** just 6 miles from Friday Harbor. This viewpoint is America's first official whale-watching park, situated on San Juan's west side. The best seasons to visit are late spring, summer, and fall. *6158 Lighthouse Rd., tel. 206/ 378–2044. Admission free. Open daily 6:30 AM–10 PM. Day-use only; no camping facilities.*

The **San Juan Island National Historic Park** is a unique attraction, with two camps that attest to the island's benign history.

For a number of years both the Americans and British occupied San Juan Island. In 1859, a Yank killed a Brit's pig, thus setting off tempers (on both sides) that had been ready to explode. Both nations sent armed forces to the island, but no gunfire was exchanged in the Pig War, which lasted from 1859 to 1872. The proof of this scuffle is the existence of the **British Camp,** with a blockhouse, commissary, and barracks, and of the armaments that remain from the American Camp. The Visitor Center headquarters is at **San Juan Island Chamber of Commerce Office** (125 Spring St., tel. 206/378–2240). Phone ahead to check when the center is open and in June through August to find out about guided hikes and historical re-enactments of life in an 1860s-era military camp.

⓭ Roche Harbor, at the northern end of San Juan, is an elegant site with well-manicured lawns, rose gardens, cobblestone waterfront, hanging flower baskets on the docks, the Hotel de Haro, and its restaurant and lounge.

Shopping
Lopez Island
The **Chimera Gallery** (Lopez Village, tel. 206/468–3265) is a local artists' cooperative.

Grayling Gallery (Hummel Lake Rd., tel. 206/468–2779) features the work of a sculptor and a painter who live and work on the premises.

Orcas Island **Darvill's Rare Print Shop** (Eastsound, tel. 206/376–2351) specializes in antique and contemporary prints.

San Juan Island **Ravenhouse Art** (1 Spring St. W, Friday Harbor, tel. 206/378–2777) features watercolors, oil paintings, jewelry, and pottery.

Cabezon Gallery (60 1st St. W, tel. 206/378–3116) features works of local artists.

Waterworks Gallery (315 Argyle St., Friday Harbor, tel. 206/378–3060) emphasizes marine art.

Whidbey Island On Whidbey Island, **Langley's First Street** offers a number of unique items. You can meet the artist and shop owner, Gwenn Knight, at **The Glass Knight** (214 1st St., Langley, tel. 206/321–6283), where her glass art and jewelry is for sale.

Annie Steffen's (101 1st St., tel. 206/321–6535) specializes in hand-painted, handwoven, and hand-knit apparel and jewelry.

The **Childers/Proctor Gallery** (302 1st St., Langley, tel. 206/321–2978) exhibits and sells paintings, jewelry, pottery, and sculpture.

Sports and Outdoor Activities
Bicycling
Orcas Island: **Key Moped Rental** (Box 279, Eastsound, tel. 206/376–2474) rents mopeds during the summer.

Wildlife Cycles (Box 1048, Eastsound, tel. 206/376–4708) has bikes for rent at various roadside stands during the summer.

San Juan Island: **San Juan Island Bicycles** (380 Argyle St., Friday Harbor, tel. 206/378–4941) has a reputation for good service as well as equipment.

Susie's Mopeds (Box 1972, Friday Harbor, tel. 206/378–5244) offers mopeds for rent.

Whidbey Island: **The Pedaler** (5603½ S. Bayview Rd., tel. 206/321–5040) has bikes to rent.

Fishing *San Juan Islands:* You can fish year-round for bass and trout at **Hummel Lake** on Lopez Island, and at **Egg** and **Sportsman lakes** on San Juan Island. On Orcas, there are three lakes at **Moran State Park** that are open to fishing from late April through October.

You can go saltwater fishing through **Buffalo Works** (tel. 206/378–4612), **Captain Clyde's Charters** (tel. 206/378–5661), **Custom Designed Charters** (tel. 206/376–5105), and **King Salmon Charters** (tel. 206/468–2314).

Whidbey Island: You can catch salmon, perch, cod, and bottomfish from the Langley dock. Supplies are available from the **Langley Marina** (202 Wharf St., tel. 206/321–1771).

Water Sports On the **San Juan Islands:**

Lopez Island: **Islander Lopez Resort** (tel. 206/468–6121) and **Islands Marine Center** (tel. 206/468–3377) have most standard marina amenities.

Orcas Island: **Deer Harbor Resort & Marina** (tel. 206/376–4420), **Lieber Haven Marina Resort** (tel. 206/376–4420), and **West Sound Marina** (tel. 206/376–2314) offer standard marina facilities and more. **Russell's Landing/Orcas Store** (tel. 206/376–4389) has gas, diesel, tackle, and groceries at the ferry landing. For small boat and motor rentals, sales, and service, try **Eastsound Marine** (tel. 206/376–4420).

San Juan Island: **Port of Friday Harbor** (tel. 206/378–2688), **San Juan Marina** (tel. 206/378–2841), and **Roche Harbor Resort** (tel. 206/378–2155) have standard marina facilities; Port of Friday Harbor and Roche Harbor are also U.S. Customs Ports of Entry.

On **Whidbey Island:**

Langley's small boat harbor (tel. 206/321–6765) offers moorage for 35 boats, utilities, and a 160-foot fishing pier, all protected by a 400-foot timber-pile breakwater.

Marine State Parks (tel. 206/753–2027) are accessible by private boat only. No moorage or camping reservations are available, and fees are charged at some parks from May through Labor Day. Fresh water, where available, is limited. Island parks are **Blind, Clark, Doe, James, Matia, Patos, Posey, Stuart, Sucia,** and **Turn.** All have a few campsites; there are no docks at Blind, Clark, Patos, Posey, or Turn islands.

Skippered sailing charters are available through **Amante Sail Tours** (tel. 206/376–4231), **Custom Designed Charters** (tel. 206/376–2927), **Harmony Sailing Charters** (tel. 206/468–3310), **Kismet Sailing Charters** (tel. 206/468–2435), **Nor'wester Sailing Charters** (tel. 206/378–5478), and **Wind N' Sails** (tel. 206/378–5343).

Bare-boat sailing charters are available through **McKinney Marine Inc.** (tel. 206/468–2130), **Snug Harbor Marina** (tel. 206/378–4762), and **Wind N' Sails** (tel. 206/378–5343).

If you are kayaking on your own, beware of ever-changing conditions, ferry and shipping landings, and strong tides and currents. Go ashore only on known public property. Day trips and longer expeditions are available from **Shearwater Sea Kayak Tours** (tel. 206/376–4699), **Doe Bay Resort** (tel. 206/376–2291), **Black Fish Paddlers** (tel. 206/376–4041), **San Juan Kayak Expeditions** (tel. 206/378–4436), and **Seaquest** (tel. 206/378–5767).

Beaches *Orcas Island:* The best beaches on this island include the low bank beach at **Odlin County Park** (Rte. 2, Box 3216, tel. 206/468–2496) and a mile of waterfront at **Spencer Spit State Park** (Rte. 2, Box 3600, tel. 206/468–2251).

San Juan Island: You'll find 10 acres of beachfront at the **San Juan County Park** (380 Westside Rd. N, Friday Harbor, tel. 206/378–2992).

Whidbey Island: Beaches are best on Whidbey Island's west side, where the sand stretches out to the sea and you have a view of the shipping lanes and the Olympic Mountains. **Maxwelton Beach** (Maxwelton Beach Rd.), popular with the locals, is on the west side of the island. **Possession Point** (west on Coltas Bay Rd.) includes a park, a beach, and a boat launch. **Forts Casey** and **Ebey** offer more hiking trails and bluff outlooks than wide, sandy beaches. **West Beach,** north of the forts, is a stormy beach with lots of driftwood.

Dining *Rates correspond to Seattle Dining chart.*

Orcas Island **Christina's.** Here you will find an elegant atmosphere whether you dine inside, on the enclosed porch, or on the rooftop terrace with views of East Sound. The emphasis is on fresh, local seafood, with some of the best salmon entrées in the Northwest. Other specialties include grilled breast of chicken with an eggplant and pepper stuffing and mouthwatering desserts. *North Beach Rd. and Horseshoe Hwy., tel. 206/376–4904. Reservations suggested. Dress: neat but casual. AE, DC, MC, V. Moderate–Expensive.*
Bilbo's Festivo. This house with a courtyard features stucco walls, Mexican tiles, wood benches, and weavings from New Mexico. The menu features Bilbo's renditions of burritos, enchiladas, and other Mexican favorites. With a typical entrée being orange-sauce marinated chicken grilled over mesquite and served with fresh asparagus, potatoes, and salad. Sunday brunch, featuring pan dulce—a Mexican sweet bread and omelets with tortillas—is also served. *Northbeach Rd. and A St., Eastsound, tel. 206/376–4728. No reservations. Dress: casual. AE, MC, V. Closed Mon.; lunch Tues.–Wed. Inexpensive–Moderate.*

San Juan Island **Duck Soup Inn.** This Mediterranean-inspired kitchen emphasizes fresh local fish such as squid sautéed in butter and olive oil and served in a fresh tomato sauce, Wescott Bay oysters from across the island, and mussels in a tomato-wine sauce. There is a good list of Northwest, California, and European wines. *3090 Roche Harbor Rd., tel. 206/378–4878. Reservations suggested. Dress: casual. No credit cards; checks accepted. Closed winter; rest of year, closed dinner Mon.–Tues. Expensive.*
Springtree Eating Establishment and Farm. Meals are prepared from organically grown produce on the farm, and entrées include such items as cod with a fresh citrus and garden mint sauce, seafood chowder, and meal-size salads. Lots of plants and chintz fabrics decorate the interior, and patio dining is available, too, but the service is mediocre at best. *Spring St., tel. 206/378–4848. Reservations suggested. Dress: casual. MC, V. Moderate.*

Whidbey Island **Garibyan Brothers Café Langley.** Terra-cotta tile floors, antique oak tables, Italian music, and the aromas of garlic, basil, and oregano are the backdrop to your lunch or dinner. Greek salads, vegetarian eggplant, fresh mussels, lamb loin chops, moussaka, and lamb shish kebabs are just some of the menu selections. *113 1st St., Langley, tel. 206/221–3090. Reservations suggested. Dress: neat but casual. MC, V. Moderate.*

Star Bistro. This black, white, and red bistro, atop the Star Store, serves up Caesar salads, shrimp-and-scallop linguine, and gourmet burgers. *201½ 1st St., Langley, tel. 206/221–2627. No reservations. Dress: casual. AE, MC, V. Moderate.*

Dog House Backdoor Restaurant. This somewhat run-down waterfront grub house serves large, juicy burgers, offers a great view of Saratoga Passage, and provides a pool table. *230 1st St., Langley, tel. 206/321–9996. No reservations. Dress: casual. No credit cards. Inexpensive.*

Lodging *Rates correspond to Seattle Lodging chart.*

Lopez Island **Edenwild.** The imposing gray Victorian-style farmhouse, surrounded by rose gardens, looks as if it's a restored island building, but actually it was newly opened in 1990. Rooms feature whitewashed oak floors, a muted gray interior, and white painted woodwork, along with botanical prints, lace curtains from Scotland, leaded glass windows, and some antiques. A three-course breakfast is served in the dining room. *Box 271, Lopez Island, WA 98261, tel. 206/468–3238. 7 double rooms with baths. Facilities: bicycle rentals, kennel in garage. MC, V. Expensive.*

Mackaye Harbor Inn. At the south end of Lopez Island, across the road from MacKaye Harbor, is this inn, a two-story frame Victorian-style home. The 1920s sea captain's house with ½ mile of beach features rooms with golden oak and brass details and wicker furniture; three guestrooms have views of the harbor. Owners Robin, who is Swedish, and Mike Bergstrom take turns cooking breakfast, which often includes Scandinavian specialties. Mike also provides guided kayak tours. *Box 1940, Lopez Island, WA 98261, tel. 206/468–2253. 5 rooms. Facilities: kayak tours, bikes, rowboat. MC, V. Moderate.*

Orcas Island **Rosario Spa & Resort.** Originally built by shipbuilding magnate Robert Moran (who was told he had six months to live), this Mediterranean-style mansion cost $1.5 million in 1905, and includes six tons of copper for the roof. The interior of the mansion, now the dining room and spa, is of fine teak and mahogany. Moran lived another 30 years, and now the mansion is on the National Register of Historic Places. Fire codes prohibit rental of guest rooms in the old structure, so villas and hotel units were added after Rosario was converted to a resort in 1960. These guest rooms are not spectacular like the mansion, but they do have decent views and most have decks or patios. *Horseshoe Hwy., Eastsound 98245, tel. 206/376–2222. 179 rooms. Facilities: dining room, indoor pool, 2 outdoor pools, health spa, sauna, whirlpool, games room, tennis courts, marina with boat rentals, fishing, hiking. AE, DC, MC, V. Expensive.*

Orcas Hotel. Sitting on the hill overlooking the Orcas Island ferry landing is this three-story, red-roofed Victorian hotel with a wrap-around porch and white picket fence. Dating to 1900, when construction first began, the lodging is on the National Register of Historic Places. The dining room, open to the public, overlooks the ferry landing and gardens, and the parlor is decorated in Victorian antiques. Guest rooms feature wicker, brass, antique furnishings, and feather beds, and some units have small sun decks. Breakfast is in the dining room and guests order off the menu, which includes French toast, omelets, and other egg dishes. *Box 155, Orcas, WA 98280, tel. 206/376-4300; fax 206/376-4399. 12 rooms. Facilities: restaurant, lounge. AE, DC, MC, V. Moderate-Expensive.*

Turtleback Farm. Just 15 minutes from the Orcas Island ferry landing is this forest-green with white trim inn, set on 80 acres of meadow, forest, and farmland in the shadow of Turtleback Mountain. The inside is spacious and airy with an absence of frills. Guest rooms have easy chairs, good beds with woolen comforters made from the fleece of resident sheep, some antiques, cream colored muslin curtains, and views of meadows and forest. Breakfast, cooked by Susan Fletcher and served by her husband, Bill, can be taken in the dining room or on the deck overlooking the valley. *R.R. 1, Box 650, Eastsound, WA 98245, tel. 206/376-3914. 7 rooms. No facilities. MC, V. Moderate-Expensive.*

Doe Bay Village Resort. This is a rustic place that is actually an International Youth Hostel, personal-growth center, and retreat. The resort feels faintly countercultural: leftover from its earlier days as an artists colony. Units vary from dormitory rooms to cottages, some with sleeping quarters only and access to shower house and community kitchen; other units feature kitchens and baths. The peaceful, scenic grounds are great for walks or sitting and reading. *S.R. 86, Olga 98279, tel. 206/376-2291. 100 units. Facilities: natural-food café, general store, guided kayak trips, hot tub, massage therapist. AE, MC, V. Inexpensive-Moderate.*

San Juan Islands   **Roche Harbor Resort.** Choice of cottage, condominium, or rooms in the 1886 restored Hotel de Haro are the options here. It's better to look at the old hotel than to actually stay in that part of the resort, since guest rooms are fairly shabby or, at best, rustic. *Box 1, Friday Harbor 98250, tel. 206/378-2155. 60 rooms. Facilities: restaurant, swimming pool, tennis court, boat moorage for 200 yachts, complete boating facilities, 4,000-ft airstrip. MC, V. Moderate-Expensive.*

Blair House. Just 4 blocks uphill from the ferry landing in Friday Harbor on more than an acre of landscaped grounds is Blair House. The two-story gray Victorian house with dormer windows and a wide wraparound porch, now furnished with wicker chairs and table, was built in 1909 and has been enlarged several times. Rooms are decorated around farm animal themes with country-print wallpapers, color-coordinated linens and ivory comforters on the beds. Guests can eat breakfast in the large dining room, on the front porch, or alongside the outdoor pool. *345 Blair Ave., Friday Harbor, WA 98250, tel. 206/378-5907. 7 rooms, 1 cottage. Facilities: cable TV, outdoor pool, hot tub. AE, MC, V. Moderate.*

Hillside House. Less than a mile outside of Friday Harbor, this contemporary house sits on a hill, providing stunning views of the harbor and Mt. Baker. The home features a large living room, kitchen, and deck with views of the harbor and Mt. Baker. All of the comfortable guest rooms have sophisticated decor. Queen-size beds, oak chests, and one- or two-person window seats are in all rooms. The Robinsons, who own the inn, encourage guests to use the recycled books in the hallway—take one or leave one—and provide badminton, horseshoes, and a cable swing (a present from guests with fond memories of their stay) in the yard. Breakfast includes entrées made from resident hens' eggs, island jams, and fresh berries. *365 Carter*

Ave., Friday Harbor, WA, tel. 206/378–4730. 6 rooms. Facilities: access to health club in town. MC, V. Moderate.

San Juan Inn. This restored 1873 inn is comfortable but modestly furnished and within walking distance of the ferry terminal. Rooms, which are all on the second floor, are small but include brass, iron, or wicker beds, and some antiques. Breakfast of muffins, coffee, and juice is served each morning in a parlor overlooking the harbor. *50 Spring St., Box 776, Friday Harbor 98250, tel. 206/378–2070. 10 rooms. No facilities. MC, V. Moderate.*

Whidbey Island **Cliff House.** This luxury house, situated in near Freeland, sleeps one-two couples in a secluded setting overlooking Admiralty inlet. The three-story house, one side nearly all glass, affords romantic views to the couple enjoying the elegant bedroom loft. Rain and occasionally snow whisk through the open-air atrium in the middle of the house. Guests are pampered with fresh flowers, a huge stone fireplace, and miles of driftwood beach. *5440 Windmill Rd., Freeland 98249, tel. 206/321–1566. 1 room. Facilities: fireplace, spa, art collection. No credit cards. Expensive.*

Guest House Cottages. This B&B, just outside Greenbank, includes a luxurious log lodge for one couple, four private cottages, and a three-room suite in a farmhouse located on 25 acres of forest and pastureland. The accommodations are cozy, with fireplaces, stained-glass pieces, and country antique furnishings. *835 E. Christianson Rd., Greenbank 98253, tel. 206/678–3115. 6 units. Facilities: fireplaces, microwaves, some kitchens, swimming pool, exercise room, spa. Expensive.*

Dining and **Deer Harbor Inn.** The original log lodge—situated on a knoll
Lodging overlooking Deer Harbor—was the first resort built on the is-
Orcas Island land (1915) and is now the dining room of the inn. A newer log cabin features eight spacious, airy rooms with peeled log furniture; views; balconies; and breakfast delivered to your door in a picnic baskets. Although large, the dining room, which specializes in fresh seafood, feels cozy, with its natural wood and floral prints, and has an adjoining deck for outdoor dining. *Box 142, Eastsound 98243, tel. 206/376–4110. 8 units. No facilities. Reservations in restaurant suggested. Dress: casual. AE, MC, V. Moderate.*

Whidbey Island **Inn at Langley.** This concrete and wood Frank Lloyd Wright-
★ inspired structure perches on the side of a bluff descending to the beach. Guest rooms feature Asian-style decor using neutrals, wood and glass, and spectacular views of Saratoga Passage and the Cascade Mountains. Entering the inn's Country Kitchen restaurant is like walking into someone's living room—no maître d' or coatroom. A huge fireplace rises before you, and then you notice tables for two unobtrusively lining the walls. On the other side of the fireplace is the "great table," which seats 10. Dinner may include locally gathered mussels in a black bean sauce, breast of duck in a loganberry sauce, or rich Columbia River salmon. Appetizers, side dishes, salad greens so fresh they have never touched a refrigerator, and desserts such as a bowl of island-grown strawberries with cream round out the satisfying entrées. Continental breakfast is served Monday–Wednesday, 8–10, for guests of the inn. Dinner starts promptly at 7, with a glass of sherry and a tour of the wine cellar. *400 1st St., Langley, tel. 206/221–3033. 24 rooms. Facili-*

ties: restaurant. Reservations in restaurant necessary. Jacket
and tie suggested. MC, V. Expensive.

Captain Whidbey Inn. There are a wide variety of accommodations offered by this inn, including the original madrona log inn
(listed on the National Register of Historic Places), cottages, a
duplex, and houses with views of Penn Cove. Inn rooms are rustic, though they feature a few antiques, but do have feather
beds and shared baths. Lagoon rooms are large and have private baths. Cottages and the duplex have one or two bedrooms,
sitting rooms, some kitchens, fireplaces, and private baths.
The dining room, serving breakfast, lunch, and dinner, is cozy
with dark paneling, soft lighting, and several tables overlooking Penn Cove. *2072 W. Captain Whidbey Inn Rd., Coupeville
98239, tel. 206/678–4097. 33 units. Facilities: bicycles and row-
boats available. Reservations for restaurant suggested. Dress:
neat but casual. MC, V. Moderate.*

The Arts   On the San Juan Islands, check performance schedules at the
Orcas Performing Arts Center (Box 567, Eastsound 98245, tel.
206/376–ARTS) and the **San Juan Community Theatre** (100 2nd
Ave., Friday Harbor 98250, tel. 206/378–3210.)

Leavenworth

On the way to Leavenworth, traveling northeast from Seattle
along I–5 and U.S. 2, visitors will pass through the densely
forested mountain country along the Skykomish River. At the
summit, in the Stevens Pass/Leavenworth area, the main attractions are the towering Cascades. (Leavenworth itself has
an elevation of 1,170 feet; the surrounding mountains rise to
8,000 feet.) Some of the best skiing, hiking, rock climbing, rafting, canoeing, and snowshoeing in the Northwest starts at
Leavenworth, and the town itself is well worth exploring.

In the early '60s, Leavenworth was a moribund village that had
once been a center for mining and railroading. Civic leaders
seeking ways to revitalize the area decided to capitalize on the
town's spectacular alpine setting; the result is a charming (and
only sometimes overly cute) center for both winter and summer
sports. Shopkeepers and hostelers, maintaining the town's
buildings in gingerbread Tyrolean style and sponsoring events
modeled after those found in a typical Bavarian village, keep a
European spirit of simple elegance alive in a setting that is never short of spectacular.

The many specialty shops, restaurants, and hotels almost all
subscribe to the Bavarian theme. There are restaurants specializing in Bavarian food; candy shops with gourmet Swiss-
style chocolate; shops featuring music boxes, nutcrackers, and
other Bavarian specialties; and charming European-style pension hotels. (There's even a laundromat called Die Washerie.)
Throughout the year the village engages in festivities that reflect the alpine theme.

Tourist   **Leavenworth Chamber of Commerce** (703 U.S. 2, 98826, tel.
Information   509/548–5807).

Getting There   Small airports in Wenatchee, Cashmere, and Lake Wenatchee
By Plane   serve the Leavenworth area.

By Car   Leavenworth is about 120 miles from Seattle, north on I–5 to
Everett and east on U.S. 2. To return, take the long scenic loop
by continuing on U.S. 2 past Leavenworth, then south on High-

way 97 to Cle Elum, and back to Seattle on I-90 across Snoqualmie Pass.

By Bus   Greyhound (tel. 509/548-7414) serves Leavenworth with two
westbound and two eastbound buses daily, year-round. The
bus stop is at the Kountry Kitchen restaurant on U.S. 2 at the
east end of town.

Sports and   Leavenworth's setting in the mountains can be appreciated
Outdoor Activities   from a car, of course, but the main attraction here is a variety of
vigorous outdoor sports in the backcountry.

Cross-Country and   The beginning and advanced skier will find more than 20 miles
Downhill Skiing   of maintained cross-country ski trails in the Leavenworth area.
Meanwhile, Stevens Pass has downhill slopes and lifts for every
level of skier. Several shops in Leavenworth rent and sell ski
equipment. For more information, contact the **Leavenworth
Winter Sports Club** (Box 573, 98826, tel. 509/548-5115).

Golf   Those hankering for more placid sports can try the **Leavenworth Golf Club** (Box 247, 98826, tel. 509/548-7267), an 18-hole,
par-71 course with a pro shop and clubhouse.

Hiking and Rock   Leavenworth also offers hiking trails that take in some of the
Climbing   most breathtaking vistas in the entire Cascades. There are
more than 320 miles of scenic trails in the Leavenworth Ranger
District alone, including **Hatchery Creek, Icicle Ridge,** the **En-
chantments, Tumwater Canyon, Fourth of July Creek, Snow
Lake, Stuart Lake,** and **Chatter Creek.** Contact the **Leavenworth Ranger District** (600 Sherburne St., 98826, tel. 509/782-
1513) for more details, or consult one of the many fine books detailing backcountry hikes in the Northwest. Rock climbing is
also popular because of the solid granite cliffs in the area.

Horseback Riding   The hourly and daily horseback rides and pack trips at **Eagle
Creek Ranch** (7951 Eagle Creek Rd., Leavenworth 98826, tel.
509/548-7798) may also be appealing to the less rugged.

White-Water Rafting   Rafting is a popular sport during March-July, with the prime
high-country runoff in May and June. The **Wenatchee River,**
which runs through Leavenworth, is generally considered the
best white-water river in the state—a Class 3 (out of six on a
scale of difficulty) on the International Canoeing Association
scale. Depending on the season and location, anything from a
relatively calm scenic float to an invigorating white-water
shoot is possible on the Wenatchee or on one of several other
nearby rivers. Some rafting outfitters and guides in the Leavenworth area are **Northern Wilderness River Riders** (10645
Hwy. 209, Leavenworth 98826, tel. 509/548-4583), **Wenatchee
Whitewater and Scenic Float Trips** (Box 12, Cashmere 98815,
tel. 509/782-2254), and **Leavenworth Outfitters** (21588 S.R.
207, Leavenworth 98826, tel. 509/763-3733).

Dining   *Rates correspond to Seattle Dining chart.*

Cougar Inn. This stylish family restaurant is about 25 miles
outside Leavenworth on the shores of Lake Wenatchee. Locals
often come by boat and tie up at the restaurant's dock. The atmosphere is very pleasant, with lots of natural wood, airy
rooms, great views of the lake and, in summer, a big outside
deck. The hearty American-style Sunday brunch is especially
popular, but breakfast, lunch, and dinner are also served daily.
The menu, featuring burgers, steaks, and prime rib, is rather
unadventurous, but the food is well-prepared and the service

friendly. *23379 S.R. 207, Lake Wenatchee, tel. 509/763–3354. Reservations advised, especially for Sun. brunch. Dress: casual. AE, MC, V. Moderate.*

Reiner's Gasthaus. Authentic central European cuisine with a Hungarian/Austrian accent is presented in this small, cheerful restaurant. The decor is heavy on the pine furnishings and thick drapes, with lots of vintage photos and other knickknacks on the walls to look at, and the service is bustling and friendly. Music is performed on weekend evenings: Usually a jolly accordion player is featured. Specialties include pork schnitzel and Hungarian goulash; these and all the reasonably priced and well-prepared dinners include hearty soups and salads. *829 Front St. (upstairs), tel. 509/548–5111. No reservations. Dress: casual. MC, V. Moderate.*

Baren Haus. Good, unpretentious food is served in a big, high-ceiling beer-hall-style room. It can get crowded and noisy in this spacious place that's decorated with blue tablecloths and large booths. House specialties include German-style sandwiches (such as bratwurst on grilled whole-wheat bread, with sauerkraut and hearty mustards) and pizzas. *208 9th St., tel. 509/548–4535. Reservations accepted, except during festival time. Dress: casual. MC, V. Inexpensive.*

Danish Bakery. Tasty homemade pastries, good strong espresso drinks, and a self-serve coffee bar are the attractions in this small, pleasant shop. The decor is tastefully done with dark woods and mural paintings, and the service is fast and friendly. This is a perfect place to escape the crowds on the sidewalks. *731 Front St., tel. 509/548–7514. No reservations. Dress: casual. No credit cards. Inexpensive.*

Lodging   The number of hotels, motels, B&Bs, and long-term-rental cabins in Leavenworth has increased in recent years as the area has become more popular among hikers and skiers. **Bavarian Bedfinders** (905 Commercial St., Suite 1, tel. 800/323–2920) matches travelers with more than 100 facilities such as condominiums, private cabins, and small lodges, in Leavenworth and around the state, and it also books dinner reservations, snowmobile tours, sleigh rides, and more. Their services are free to guests.

Rates correspond to the Seattle Lodging chart.

Der Ritterhof. This is a relatively new and large hotel on the highway to Leavenworth from Seattle. Its 51 units, decorated in fairly standard-issue motel style, include suites that sleep six comfortably; some units have small kitchenettes. Amenities include a recreation area, barbecue pit, and volleyball and badminton courts on the lawn. The service is friendly and efficient. *190 Hwy. 2, 98826, tel. 509/548–5845 or 800/255–5845. 51 rooms. Facilities: outdoor heated pool, hot tubs. AE, MC, V. Moderate–Expensive.*

Pension Anna. This small, family-run Austrian-style pension in the middle of the village has a farmhouse atmosphere. Although it's newly built, it has a distinctly old-fashioned feel; rooms and suites are decorated with sturdy, pine antique furniture, with such added touches as fresh flowers and comforters on the beds. Two of the suites have whirlpool baths, and all except the ground-level rooms have small balconies. The two largest suites have fireplaces and handsome four-poster beds. A hearty European-style breakfast (cold cuts, meats, cheeses, soft-boiled eggs), inclusive in the room price, is served in a breakfast room decorated in traditional European style with crisp linens, pine decor, dark green curtains, and (of course) a cuckoo clock. The staircases to the upper floors are quite steep. *926 Commercial St., 98826, tel. 509/548–6273. 11 units. Facilities: TV. Moderate–Expensive.*

Evergreen Motel. Popular with hikers and skiers, the pleasant Evergreen was built in the 1930s and still has a lot of the charm of the old-fashioned roadside inn it once was. Some of its two-bedroom suites have fireplaces and/or kitchens (though no utensils), while some have multiple beds and can sleep up to six comfortably. Thus, although there are only 26 units, the motel's capacity is about 80 guests. Complimentary Continental breakfast is offered by a very friendly staff and the motel is one block from downtown. *1117 Front St., 98826, tel. 509/548–5515 or 800/327–7212. 26 rooms. AE, D, DC, MC, V. Moderate.*

Edelweiss Hotel. This is an unpretentious hotel above the restaurant of the same name. Small rooms, plainly furnished and with either shared or private baths, are available. This is not the place to spend a romantic weekend, but if you're on a budget and simply need a place to lay your head, the Edelweiss's price ($15 for a single room, no view or TV) is hard to beat in this hotel-hungry town. The service is genial but sometimes harried, and the staircase is steep. *843 Front St., 98826, tel. 509/548–7015. 14 units. MC, V. Inexpensive.*

6 Washington State

Introduction

By Loralee Wenger and Adam Woog

Twenty years ago, Washington State and Seattle were virtual backwaters in the country's landscape. The nation had first awakened to this corner of the world via the press given the 1962 Seattle World's Fair, but even so, Seattle was still nowheresville, stuck on the corner of the continental map.

For the most part, Washingtonians didn't care what the rest of the country thought of them; they were too busy hiking, backpacking, mountain climbing, and sailing. Before outdoor adventures were popular in the rest of the country, they were commonplace for Washington residents. For northwesterners, adventuring isn't so much the in thing to do as it is the expression of a yearning to join with the mighty and majestic forces of nature. Now, the Northwest is one of the country's foremost locations for outdoor activities.

Washington boasts a host of scenic attractions that beckon the sightseer as well as the adventurer. To the west, the Olympic Peninsula's rain forest drips with moss, waterfalls, and sprawling greenery. The 5,200-foot-high Hurricane Ridge offers spectacular views of the Olympic Mountains and the Straits of Juan de Fuca. The state's coastline along the western shores of the Olympic Peninsula and the Long Beach Peninsula is punctured with inlets, coves, and secluded harbors, many of which are accessible to visitors via the Washington State Ferry System, the world's largest ferry operation.

Across Puget Sound, Mt. Rainier reigns over the Cascade Mountains. The mild climate and regular rainfall of western Washington make for lush stands of Douglas fir, western red cedar, and the Renoiresque washes of color in the springtime blossoms of rhododendrons and azaleas. Crossing the Cascades into central and eastern Washington, patchwork quilts of irrigated fruit orchards; miles of rolling, treeless prairie; and stands of golden grain prevail—and so does eastern Washington's extreme weather.

The state's contrasts in landscape have spilled over to its residents. Battles have been hard-fought between Native American and non–Native American fishermen, between land developers and environmentalists, and now, between residents and an influx of prospective residents, purportedly Californians hellbent on Los Angelesizing Puget Sound. These conflicts underscore the vigor with which Washingtonians defend their turf. With a strong economy, the outlook for the state is a healthy one, and visitors can expect to feel welcome here as long as they continue to respect the state's bounty and leave it intact for others to enjoy.

Essential Information

Important Addresses and Numbers

Tourist Information State Offices

Northwest Tourism Region (c/o Anacortes Chamber of Commerce, 1319 Commercial Ave., Anacortes 98221, tel. 206/293–3832).
Washington State Department of Tourism (Dept. of Trade and Economic Development, General Administration Bldg., Olympia, WA 98504, tel. 206/753–5600).

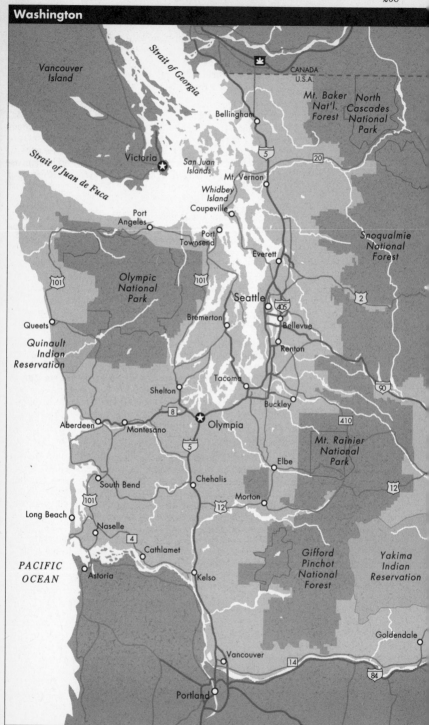

Washington

Vancouver
Island

Strait of Georgia

CANADA
U.S.A.

Mt. Baker
Nat'l.
Forest

North
Cascades
National
Park

Bellingham

Strait of Juan de Fuca

Victoria

San Juan
Islands

Mt. Vernon

20

Whidbey
Island
Coupeville

Snoqualmie
National
Forest

Port
Angeles

Port
Townsend

Everett

2

Olympic
National
Park

101

Seattle

405

Queets

Bremerton

Bellevue

Quinault
Indian
Reservation

Renton

90

Tacoma

Shelton

Buckley

8

410

Aberdeen

Montesano

Olympia

5

Mt. Rainier
National
Park

Elbe

12

South Bend

Chehalis

101

Morton

12

Long Beach

Naselle

4

Cathlamet

Gifford
Pinchot
National
Forest

Yakima
Indian
Reservation

PACIFIC
OCEAN

Astoria

Kelso

Goldendale

Vancouver

14

84

Portland

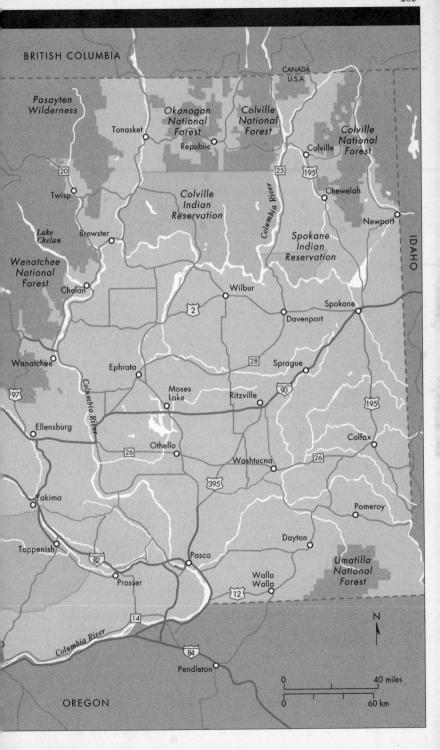

Bellingham/ Whatcom/Skagit Counties	**Bellingham/Whatcom County Visitors and Convention Bureau** (904 Potter St., Bellingham 98226, tel. 206/671–3990). **Ferndale Chamber of Commerce** (5640 Riverside Dr., Ferndale, WA 98248, tel. 206/384–3042). **North Cascades National Park** (2105 Hwy. 20, Sedro Woolley 98264, tel. 206/856–5700).
Long Beach Peninsula	**Long Beach Visitors Bureau** (Intersection of Hwys. 101 and 103, Seaview 98644, tel. 206/642–2400, 800/451–2542 in WA, 800/451–2540 in OR, ID, or northern CA).
Olympic Peninsula	**Superintendent, Olympic National Park** (600 E. Park Ave., Port Angeles 98362, tel. 206/452–4501). **Supervisor, Olympic National Forest** (801 S. Capitol Way, Box 2288, Olympia 98507, tel. 206/753–9535).
Tacoma	**Tacoma-Pierce County Visitors and Convention Bureau** (950 Pacific Ave., Suite 450, 98401, tel. 206/627–2836).
Emergencies	Throughout Washington State, except on Orcas Island and Long Beach Peninsula, dial 911 for **police, ambulance,** or other emergencies. On Orcas dial "0" or 206/468–3663; on Long Beach dial 206/642–2911 for police and 206/642–2316 for fire.

Arriving and Departing by Plane

Airports and Airlines *Bellingham/ Whatcom/Skagit Counties*	**Seattle-Tacoma International Airport** (*see* Essential Information in Chapter 7), about a two-hour drive south from Bellingham, is served by most major airlines. **Vancouver International Airport** (*see* Essential Information in Chapter 7), in British Columbia, is 1½ hours away by car. Major airlines use this facility, which includes a main terminal building with three levels. Smaller airports are in **Bellingham, Lynden,** and **Blaine.**
Between the Airport and City Center	**Bellingham Airporter** (tel. 206/733–3600 or 800/235–5147) and **Greyhound Bus Lines** (tel. 206/624–3456) offer ground transportation from Sea-Tac to Bellingham.
Long Beach Peninsula	Although there is no regular air service to the Long Beach peninsula, charters from **Astoria Flight Center** (1140 S.E. Flightline Dr., Warrenton, OR 97146, tel. 503/861–1222) fly among the cities of Portland, Astoria, and Seaside in Oregon, and Seattle, and Ilwaco in Washington.
Olympic Peninsula	To reach destinations in the Olympic Peninsula, pick up a commuter flight from Seattle-Tacoma airport to fly to small airports in **Port Angeles, Forks,** or **Hoquiam.**
Tacoma	Tacoma is about a half-hour's drive south of **Seattle-Tacoma International Airport. Capitol Airporter** (tel. 206/572–9544), **Greyhound Bus Lines** (tel. 206/624–3456), and **Affordable Limousine** (tel. 206/827–8940) provide service to Tacoma. Two smaller fields, the **Tacoma Narrows Airport** (tel. 206/591–5759) and the **Pierce County Airport** (tel. 206/593–4698), offer services to and from smaller destinations in the Northwest.

Arriving and Departing by Car, Train, Bus, and Ferry

By Car	**Interstate 5** is the main north–south route, passing through Tacoma and Bellingham.

From Tacoma, **Highway 16** goes west across the Tacoma Narrows Bridge to Gig Harbor and the Kitsap Peninsula; **Highway 410** heads east toward Mt. Rainier.

Looping around the Olympic Peninsula is **Highway 101,** branching off via Route 8 from I–5.

To reach Long Beach Peninsula, take **Route 8** (Ocean Beaches exit from I–5) to **Highway 107** at Montesano to Highway 101S to Seaview. From Portland, take **Highway 30** to Astoria, crossing the Columbia River Bridge and go west onto Highway 101N to Ilwaco.

To reach the Yakima Valley, take **I–90** east from Seattle to Ellensburg and **I–82** south to Yakima.

By Train   **Amtrak** (tel. 800/USA–RAIL) serves major cities and towns throughout the state.

By Bus   **Greyhound/Trailways** (tel. 206/733–5251 in Bellingham, 206/627–0687 in Tacoma, 206/357–5541 outside WA) provides access to most major cities. In Tacoma, **Pierce Transit** (tel. 206/581–8000) is the public bus system that covers most of the county. Public transportation in Bellingham is frequent and dependable.

By Ferry   The **Washington State Ferry System** (tel. 206/464–6400 or 800/542–9052) is the largest in the world. Ferries leave from downtown Seattle for Winslow (Bainbridge Island) and Bremerton (Kitsap Peninsula) several times daily. At press time, passenger ferries to Vashon Island and Southworth (Kitsap Peninsula) are due to start soon. Car and passenger ferries leave from Fauntleroy, in West Seattle, to Vashon Island and Southworth; from Edmonds, north of Seattle, to Kingston; and from Mukilteo, farther north, to Clinton (Whidbey Island). In Anacortes, about 90 minutes north of Seattle, ferries depart for the San Juan Islands and for Vancouver Island, British Columbia.

Guided Tours

Orientation   **Northwest Adventures, Inc.** (7616 79th Ave. S.E., Mercer Island 98040, tel. 206/232–1490) represents tour operators throughout the state.

Discovery Washington (Box 14493, Seattle 98114, tel. 206/838–6043) runs tours of Seattle and Puget Sound, as well as custom itineraries.

Gray Line Water Sightseeing (500 Wall St., Suite 310, Seattle 98121, tel. 206/441–1887) offers two-hour cruises of the Seattle waterfront and five-hour combination land/water tours. From Blaine, Gray Line operates three-and-a-half-hour nature cruises through the San Juans.

Christy's Escorted Tours (4655 Guide Meridian, Bellingham 98226, tel. 206/734–9361) organizes two–five-day trips and extended United States-Canada tours of 10–38 days.

Puget Sound & See (3608 70th Ave. Court West, Tacoma 98466, tel. 206/564–1711) runs daily tours of Tacoma, Mt. Rainier, and Mt. St. Helens.

Special-Interest   **Evergreen Travel Service** (19505 44th Ave. W, Lynnwood 98036, tel. 206/766–1184) specializes in tours for the disabled.

Rosario Princess (#5 Harbor Esplanade, Bellingham 98225, tel. 206/734–8866) conducts whale-watching, nature, and island cruises on an 83-foot tour boat.

Wineries **Blue Mountain Express** (1037 Winslow Ave., Richland 99352, tel. 509/946–7375) visits wineries throughout eastern Washington.

Transcascade (609 E. Yakima Ave., Yakima 98907, tel. 509/452–9402) tours Yakima Valley wineries.

Exploring Washington State

Bellingham/Whatcom and Skagit Counties

Numbers in the margin correspond to points of interest on the Bellingham/Whatcom and Skagit Counties map.

North of Seattle on the way to Vancouver, British Columbia, I–5 passes through the beautiful Skagit River Valley and Skagit and Whatcom counties. The gentle farmlands and low foothills along this route are often wrapped in mist, resembling a delicate Japanese pen-and-ink drawing of a nature scene. Off to the east, however, rising sharply from the foothills, are the anything-but-delicate Cascade Mountains.

Aside from the beauty, there are many interesting sights in the area, and a good place to start—and a perfect launching point for exploration—is the town of **Bellingham,** where you'll witness the best of several worlds, including an intellectual college atmosphere and a bustling fishing and lumber industry in a lush and beautiful setting.

There are a variety of places to go in and around Bellingham, but a convenient start is downtown, at the **Whatcom County Museum of History and Art.** The beautiful, huge redbrick Victorian building houses permanent exhibits of the early coal and lumbering industries, Native American artifacts, and local waterfowl; other traveling exhibits, on a variety of subjects, are shown on a regular basis. *121 Prospect St., tel. 206/676–6981. Admission free. Open Tues.–Sun. noon–5.*

Traveling by car or on foot, go northwest from downtown to Holly Street, across the mouth of Whatcom Creek. Turning right on C Street will bring you to the **Maritime Heritage Center,** an urban park that pays tribute to Bellingham and its fishing industry. Self-guided tours allow visitors to learn about hatcheries and salmon life cycles, see salmon-rearing tanks and fish ladders, go angling for salmon and trout, and watch salmon spawning. *1600 C St., tel. 206/676–6806. Admission free. Open weekdays 9–5.*

Go about ¼ mile down Holly Street or Roeder Avenue to F Street and Bellingham's northern **waterfront.** The harbor here, including the **Squalicum Harbor Marina** (Roeder Ave. and Coho Way, I–5 Exits 253 and 256), the second-largest marina on Puget Sound and the home to more than 1,700 commercial and pleasure boats, makes for good dock-walking, fishing, lounging, and picnicking. There are several other points on Bellingham's shoreline from which to engage in any of these ac-

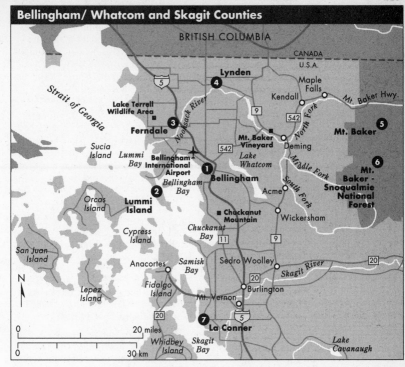

tivities, including **Boulevard Park** (S. State St. and Bayview Dr., tel. 206/676–6985), an excellent waterfront park, with 14 acres and a ½ mile of shoreline located midway between downtown and Old Fairhaven; and **Marine Park** (foot of Harris St., in Old Fairhaven), a small but popular spot for sunset-watching and crabbing, which is close to the Alaska Marine Highway terminal.

On a hill, overlooking downtown and Bellingham Bay, is the picturesque campus of **Western Washington University** (516 High St., tel. 206/676–3000). To get there take Garden Street from the north or College Drive from the south. There is a fine collection of outdoor sculptures scattered around the campus, including works by Mark DiSuvero, Isamu Noguchi, Richard Serra, and George Rickey.

Before leaving downtown Bellingham, pick up Alabama Street going east. Just before reaching Lake Whatcom, turn left onto Sylvan Street, which will take you to the **Big Rock Garden,** an extensive, unusual nursery and the Garden of Art, an outdoor retail sculpture gallery with hundreds of beautiful azaleas, rhododendrons, Japanese maples, and other plants and trees, and trails interspersed with multi-media fountains, bells, and sculpture. The best time to visit is May–June, peak season for the shrubs. *2900 Sylvan St., Bellingham, tel. 206/734–4167. Admission free. Open Mar.–Nov., Mon.–Sat. 9–5:30, Sun. 11–5.*

An option out of the city is to take Highway 11 (Chuckanut Dr.) south for a 23-mile drive into Skagit County, alongside beautiful **Chuckanut Bay.** On one side is the steep and heavily wooded Chuckanut Mountain; on the other are stunning views westward over Puget Sound and the San Juan Islands. Many university professors and others have attractive houses built along this stretch of road. Beginning by **Fairhaven Park** in the Old Fairhaven neighborhood and joining up with I–5 in the flat farmlands near Bow, in Skagit County, the full loop can be made in a few hours. Several good restaurants are located toward the southern end of the drive, so planning your excursion to include a lunch stop is a good idea.

While in the area, stop at the **Rose Garden** at Fairhaven Park. It was developed in the early 1900s and is used as a testing site by the American Rose Society. Fairhaven Park also has numerous hiking trails and picnic grounds, a playground, tennis courts, playing fields and a wading pool. *107 Chuckanut Dr., tel. 206/ 676–6985. Admission free. Open year-round; roses are best seen in summer months.*

At the southern end of Chuckanut Drive is the **Rock Point Oyster Company,** a wonderfully funky and friendly operation where visitors can watch oysters being harvested, sorted, shucked, and sent on their way. Fresh Pacific oysters and a variety of other shellfish are sold by a very helpful staff. Ask to see the incredible pink scallops; they swim in their tanks by "biting" the water. *188 Chuckanut Dr., Bow, tel. 206/766– 6002. Admission free. Open weekdays 8–5, weekends 1–5.*

Another alternative route from Bellingham is to take Exit 250 west off I–5 to the ferry terminal at Fisherman's Cove dock. The passenger/car ferry will take you on a 10-minute ride across to **Lummi Island.** The 10-mile-long mountainous and largely uninhabited spot in Bellingham Bay makes a great day trip, especially if you're going to bike or hike. At the **Lummi Indian Reservation,** visitors can observe a fascinating aqua cultural station where salmon and oyster are raised commercially. *From Exit 250, go west on Slater Rd. and Haxton Rd. Aquacultural station, 2612 Haxton Way, Bellingham, tel. 206/ 734–8180. Admission free. Open weekdays 8–4:30; tours by appointment.*

Farther north off I–5 is **Ferndale** (Exit 262), a charming town and longtime dairy-farming community in the Nooksack Valley, 18 miles north of Bellingham. Among its chief attractions is **Pioneer Park,** which features a number of 1870s log buildings, including a granary, Whatcom County's first church, a hotel, and several historic houses. The buildings have been restored and converted into period museums through which the public can wander and learn about the town's history. *1st and Cherry Sts. (2 blocks south of Main St.), tel. 206/384–3042. Admission free. Open May–Oct., Tues.–Sun. noon–5; tours run daily on the hour.*

Also in Ferndale is the **Hovander Homestead Park,** a National Historic Site with a model farm complete with Victorian-era farmhouse, barnyard animals, water tower, vegetable gardens, and antique farm equipment. Surrounding it are 60 acres of walking trails, picnic grounds, and access to fishing in the Nooksack. *5299 Nielsen Rd., Ferndale, tel. 206/384–3444. Admission free. Office open Mon., Wed., Fri. 8 AM–9 PM; park Thurs.–Sun. noon–6. Tours of farmhouse May–Sept., daily on the hour.*

About a mile away is **Tennant Lake Natural History Interpretive Center,** situated in the Nielsen House, an early homestead. There are exhibits, nature walks around the lake, and an observation tower from which the 200 acres of marshy habitat, eagles, and other wildlife can be seen. The unusual **Fragrance Garden**—with herbs and flowers—is designed for the sight-impaired and can be explored by following Braille signs. *5236 Nielsen Rd., Ferndale, tel. 206/384–3444. Admission free. Open Thurs.–Sun. noon–6.*

At **Lake Terrell Wildlife Preserve,** visitors can observe a wide variety of waterfowl that live throughout this 11,000-acre spread. In the fall you can hunt pheasants and western Washington species of waterfowl; catfish, perch, bass, and cutthroat can be fished year-round. *5975 Lake Terrell Rd., Ferndale, tel. 206/384–4723. Admission free. Open weekdays 8–5.*

From Ferndale, take Highway 539 north and east to **❹ Lynden**—a small dairying town that has preserved its conservative Dutch heritage. Only recently have Sunday retail store closures become voluntary instead of mandatory, and drinking alcoholic beverages is prohibited in establishments where dancing occurs. **Lynden Farm Tours** (7026 Noon Rd., tel. 206/354–3549) offers tours of working farms in the area. Residents and shopkeepers make a conscious effort to keep alive their Dutch heritage; though much of the result is kitschy-cute, some good examples of traditional Dutch architecture are evident. **Downtown Lynden** features a four-story windmill (which doubles as an inn), a minimall called Delft Square, the Dutch Village Shopping Mall, and a miniature indoor canal. On special occasions, shopkeepers can be seen wearing traditional Dutch clothing, right down to the wood clogs.

Probably the single biggest tourist attraction near Bellingham **❺** is **Mt. Baker,** part of the Cascade range. At 10,778 feet high, this sharp peak is visible from several points, as is the adjacent and photogenic **Mt. Shuksan,** which stands at an elevation of **❻** 9,038 feet. **Mt. Baker–Snoqualmie National Forest,** as well as the foothills, forests, streams, and country villages you will pass through on the road from Bellingham, provides endless opportunity for exploration. Along the 60-mile route east from Bellingham (on the Mt. Baker Highway, also called Highway 542) are several excellent stopping points. Among the pleasant mountain towns are **Deming, Kendall, Maple Falls,** and **Glacier,** all of which have a variety of good, old-fashioned cafés and shops. Near Deming, the small **Mt. Baker Vineyards** (4298 Mt. Baker Hwy., Everson, tel. 206/592–2300) is open to the public, with daily tours and a tasting room. Be sure to taste the very special plum wine.

Just past the town of Glacier is the turnoff to **Coleman Glacier;** the thundering, 170-foot-high **Nooksack Falls,** only a short walk from the road; and the **Mt. Baker ski area** (*see* Sports and Outdoor Activities, below).

Time Out If you're about ready for a mountain picnic, at Deming go south on Highway 9 to the town of **Van Zandt.** Be sure to stop at **Everybody's Store** (the only public building in town), a longtime local favorite place to stock up on exotic foods and goodies. Everything from "nickel pickle" dill pickles to homemade sausage, cheeses, bialys—not to mention toys, imported clothes, and regular foodstuffs—can be found here.

Continue south along the **Nooksack River Valley,** through the small towns of **Clipper** and **Acme,** then cut over at **Wickersham** and back to Bellingham along **Lake Whatcom,** for a splendid afternoon's drive.

❼ Driving south for about 30 miles on I–5 and Route 1 from Bellingham will bring you to **La Conner,** a small fishing village and arts community west of Mount Vernon, at the mouth of the Skagit River. Such painters as Morris Graves, Kenneth Callahan, Guy Anderson, and Mark Tobey set up shop here in the 1940s, and it has been an artist's haven ever since. A concerted effort has been made in recent years to make La Conner a tourist destination; the number of good shops and restaurants have consequently shot up, but the increased traffic also means that in summer this usually sleepy town becomes clogged and congested.

Many of the shopkeepers and gallery owners in La Conner carry free copies of a helpful visitor's guide, published by the **Chamber of Commerce** (Lime Dock, 109 N. 1st St., tel. 206/466–4778). Interesting attractions that you won't want to miss are the **Volunteer Fireman's Museum** (1st St., no phone), with turn-of-the-century equipment on display; the **Gaches Mansion** (2nd and Calhoun Sts., tel. 206/466–4288), a Victorian house that is now an exhibition space and museum for area artists, called the Northwest School of La Conner; and the **Skagit County Historical Museum** (501 4th St., tel. 206/466–3365).

Outside the village of La Conner is the fertile flatland of the Skagit River Valley. Many farms grow huge batches of commercial flowers—especially daffodils and tulips—and depending on the season, it is possible to view these huge fields of bright colors as you drive the back roads. One of the commercial gardens open to the public is **La Conner Flats** (1588 Best Rd., tel. 206/424–8531). At various times throughout the year, tulips (the main crop), rhododendrons, roses, and flowering cherry trees may be seen. Another garden is **Roozengaarde** (1587 Beaver Marsh Rd., tel. 206/424–8531), one of the largest growers of tulips, daffodils, and irises in the United States.

Tacoma

Numbers in the margin correspond to points of interest on the Tacoma map.

Like many towns in the Northwest, Tacoma's history is tied inextricably with lumber and fishing, and with the two-fisted men and women who did the labor. Today, Tacoma is still a hardworking, largely blue-collar town, and it is struggling hard to overcome the bum rap it has acquired over the years. Although the reputation—based on the city's high crime rate and the pollution from the many nearby pulp mills and smelters—is partly deserved, Tacoma is doing much to clean up its act; it appears that the "City of Destiny" is finally getting a little respect.

Tacoma deserves the respect, too. Looking beyond the surface of this city of 174,500, the visitor will find lovely residential neighborhoods, handsome brick buildings, fine views of Com-

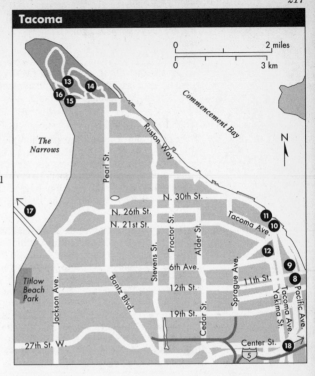

mencement Bay, a world-class zoo, a tremendously active port (so busy, in fact, that it's stealing the thunder of its larger neighbor to the north), and the dominating presence of nearby Mt. Rainier. The city is also a convenient jumping-off point for exploring some wonderful locations in south-central Washington: the Cascade Mountains, the state capital of Olympia, and—across the Tacoma Narrows Bridge—the sleepy fishing villages of the Kitsap Peninsula.

8 While downtown visit the **Tacoma Art Museum,** where you'll find a rich collection of American and French paintings, as well as Chinese jades and imperial robes. There is a permanent children's gallery and an ongoing series of high-quality changing exhibitions. Native Tacoman Dale Chihuly, generally recognized as the greatest living glass sculptor, recently donated a number of important pieces to the museum. *12th St. and Pacific Ave., tel. 206/272–4258. Admission free; donations accepted. Open Mon.–Sat. 10–5, Sun. noon–5.*

9 The **Pantages Theater,** designed by the famous theater architect B. Marcus Pritica, is a beautifully restored example of early 20th-century Greco-Roman music-hall style, which features classical figures, ornate columns, arches, and reliefs. Once the locale of performances by such varied entertainers as W.C. Fields, Mae West, Charlie Chaplin, Bob Hope, and Stan Laurel, it is now the home of the Tacoma Symphony and BalleTacoma, as well as visiting musical and theatrical productions. The Pantages is part of the Broadway Center for the Performing Arts, which also includes the home of the Tacoma

Youth Symphony, which opened in the fall of 1991. *901 Broadway, tel. 206/591–5890. Tours Thurs. between 1–4, free with reservations.*

In the Pantages Building, around the corner from the main entrance, are the offices of the **Bing Crosby Historical Society,** which house a fascinating collection of memorabilia about Der Bingle, perhaps Tacoma's most famous favorite son. *Tel. 206/627–2947 or 206/627–4722. Admission free; donations accepted. Open weekdays 11–3.*

⑩ At the north end of downtown is **Stadium High School,** an elaborate building designed in 1891 as a luxury hotel for the Northern Pacific Railroad (Tacoma was once the railroad's terminus); it was converted to a high school in 1906 after a fire left only the outer shell. The château-style building, with classic European details, is still used as such by the Tacoma School District. *111 N. E St., tel. 206/596–1325.*

⑪ The nearby **Washington State Historical Society,** housed in a newly remodeled building, features exhibitions on the natural, Native American, pioneer, maritime, and industrial history of the state. Its pioneer, Alaskan, and Native American displays are the largest on the Pacific Coast. *315 N. Stadium Way, tel. 206/593–2830. Admission: $2. Open Mon.–Sat. 10–4, Sun. noon–5.*

Time Out If the weather's cooperative, pick up a sandwich to go at the **Judicial Annex** (311 S. 11th St., tel. 206/272–3501) or at the **Ark Delicatessan** (1140 Court C, tel. 206/383–3354) and take it to Wright Park (*see* below) for a picnic.

⑫ **Wright Park** is a pleasant 30-acre park in the middle of town, just north of the downtown area. Lawn-bowling, a children's playground, and picnicking are the favorite activities here. The park's chief feature is the **W. W. Seymour Botanical Conservatory,** a lovely Victorian-style greenhouse with an extensive collection of exotic flora. *Park, between 6th and Division Sts., Yakima and Tacoma Aves. Conservatory, nearest corner on 4th and G Sts., tel. 206/591–5331. Admission free; donations accepted. Open daily 8:30–4:20.*

⑬ Leave the heart of the city by driving northeast along Commencement Bay or Ruston Way and turn right on Pearl Street, bringing you to the entrance of one of Tacoma's most interesting attractions: 700-acre **Point Defiance Park,** one of the largest urban parks in the country. In addition to its various museums, this huge tract of land that juts into the western part of Commencement Bay offers extensive footpaths and hiking trails, a variety of flower gardens, the densely wooded Five Mile Drive, and some spectacular views of the waterfront. *5400 N. Pearl St., tel. 206/591–5335. Admission free. Open June–Aug., daily 10–7; Sept.–May, weekdays 10–4, weekends 10–7.*

⑭ On the grounds of the park is the **Point Defiance Zoo and Aquarium,** founded in 1890 and generally considered one of the top zoos in the country. Using the Pacific Rim as its theme, it has blossomed (since an extensive renovation in 1986) into an impressive example of humane and innovative trends in zoo administration. Natural habitats and super-close vantage points let visitors observe a wide variety of whales, walruses, sharks, polar bears, octopuses, apes, reptiles, and birds. Both the zoo and aquarium have gained international reputations for the expert caretakers who treat injured wildlife. *Tel. 206/591–5335. Admission: $5.75 adults, $5.25 senior citizens and disabled persons, $4 children 5–17, $1.75 children 3–4. Open Sept.–May, daily 10–4; July and Aug., daily 10–7; closed Thanksgiving and Christmas.*

⑮ Part of Point Defiance is **Ft. Nisqually**—a painstakingly restored Hudson Bay Trading Post, originally built as a British outpost on the Nisqually Delta in the 1830s and relocated as a WPA project to Point Defiance in 1935. Tours of the fort are offered, where guides point out kitchens, stables, bunkhouses, and other parts of the fur-trading post. Near the site is the **⑯ Camp Six Logging Museum,** a 20-acre museum featuring restored original bunkhouses, hand tools, and historic logging equipment. A 15-mile-long steam donkey train ride takes you around old bunk cars and a 240-ton skidder. *Ft. Nisqually, tel. 206/591–5339. Admission free. Open Jan.–Oct., daily 10–6. Logging museum, tel. 206/752–0047. Admission free; train ride $2 adults, $11 children 3–12 and senior citizens. Open Memorial Day–Sept., Wed.–Sun. 10–6. Special Santa trains run in Dec.*

⑰ From Point Defiance, take Highway 16 for 8 miles to **Gig Harbor,** a tiny village retreat inhabited by musicians, artists, sailing enthusiasts, and general layabouts. The beautiful and well-protected harbor is home to a number of unusual bed-and-breakfasts, a string of boutiques and antiques shops, and a lively marina full of both working fishing boats and pleasure crafts. Continuing north along the highway you'll pass many small farms, rolling hills, and fine beaches that are good for beachcombing and clamming.

Although the 35-mile drive southeast along Route 161 will take **⑱** you away from the city, the trip to the **Northwest Trek Wildlife Park** will be time well spent. The land, administered by the Metropolitan Park District of Tacoma, is 435 acres of forest and meadow within which bison, beavers, bobcats, bighorn goats, moose, elk, bald eagles, and more can be observed from a guided tram tour. The **Cheney Discovery Center,** in the park, features a live butterfly atrium and a 150-gallon fish tank with many varieties of native fish, such as salmon and trout. *11610 Trek Dr. E, Eatonville, tel. 206/832–6116. Admission: $6.25 adults, $5.25 senior citizens, $4 children 5–17, $2 children 3–4. Open year-round at 9:30 AM; closing times vary so call ahead. Tram tours run hourly from 10 AM.*

The Olympic Peninsula

Numbers in the margin correspond to points of interest on the Olympic Peninsula map.

The rugged Olympic Peninsula is the most northwestern corner of the continental United States. Much of it is wilderness, with the magnificent Olympic National Park and National Forest at its heart. The peninsula has tremendous variety: the wild Pacific shore, the sheltered waters along the Hood Canal and the Strait of Juan de Fuca, the rivers of the Olympic Rain Forest, and the towering Olympic Mountains.

Although the region's economy—primarily revolving around lumber and fishing—assures some ties to the outside world,

Olympic Peninsula

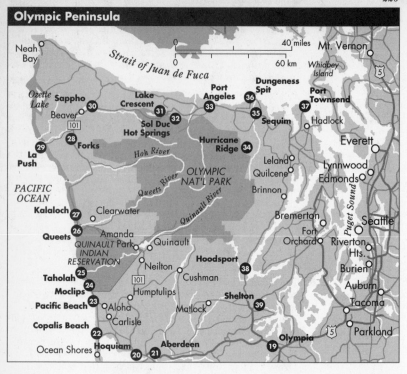

the peninsula is, in many ways, isolated and largely self-sufficient. Its inaccessible terrain and the unique climates caused
by the Olympic Mountains add to this feeling of separateness:
The mountains trap incoming clouds, creating both a rain forest
to the west and a dry "rain shadow" area on the east. As a result, the peninsula has both the wettest and the driest climates
in the entire coastal Pacific Northwest.

A benefit of this somewhat ambiguous environment is that
wildlife takes to it—and flourishes. Visitors in search of the
great outdoors, however, should be aware that much of the
Olympic Peninsula is stringently protected. Within the National Park, all hunting, firearms, and off-road vehicles are prohibited, as is any disturbance to plants or wildlife. Although
hunting and fishing are permitted in portions of the National
Forest, many areas are maintained as complete wilderness.
Furthermore, Native American tribal regulations restrict access to, and activity within, certain parts of reservations;
check with local authorities for details.

Because of the rugged terrain and some difficult roads, much of
the peninsula is accessible only to backpackers, but the 300-
mile loop made by Highway 101 provides glimpses of some of its
most interesting features. The various side roads off 101,
meanwhile, offer excellent (if sometimes unpaved) opportunities for further exploration of more remote towns, beaches, and
mountains. This section describes a journey clockwise, primarily around Highway 101 (although jaunts from the main drag
are suggested), beginning and ending in Olympia.

⑲ Olympia, Washington State's capital, is often overrun with government activity; the legislative season determines whether this town at the southern end of Puget Sound is bustling or somnolent. But even in full swing, the city still retains an air of laid-back relaxation. Spend time in the capitol area, where many of the political activities of Washington State take place. Consider taking a tour of the stately **Legislative Building.** This handsome Romanesque structure boasts a 287-foot dome that closely resembles the Capitol Building in "the other Washington." State Senate and Representative sessions can be viewed from visitors' galleries. The surrounding grounds feature carefully maintained rose gardens (best in summer) and Japanese cherry trees that are in glorious bloom around the end of April. Also worth a visit is the modern **State Library,** located directly behind the Legislative Building. It is open to the public during regular business hours, and boasts a variety of artwork, including wonderful murals by two renowned Washington artists, Mark Tobey and Kenneth Callahan, and exhibits devoted to early state history. *Legislative Bldg., Capitol Way between 10th and 14th Aves., tel. 206/586–TOUR. Admission free. Tours offered daily, on the hour from 10–3.*

Traveling south along Capitol Way to 21st Street—a pleasant walk or a short drive—will bring you to the **State Capitol Museum,** housed in a handsome building that dates from the 1920s and was once the mansion of a local banker. Permanent and temporary exhibits of local art, history, and natural history are displayed, including the permanent collections of rare local Native American baskets. *211 W. 21st St., tel. 206/753–2580. Admission free; donations accepted. Open Tues.–Thurs. 10–4, weekends noon–4; closed Mon.*

A few blocks east of the Capitol campus on Union Avenue, at its intersection with Plum Street and adjacent to City Hall, the sister cities of Olympia and Yashiro, Japan, have recently collaborated on a beautiful **Japanese garden** complete with a waterfall, bamboo grove, carp pond, and stone lanterns. *Cnr of Union and Plum Sts., tel. 206/357–3370. Admission free. Open daily 10–10.*

Wolfhaven, just 15 miles south of the city on Old Highway 99, is a unique facility offering hour-long walk-through guided tours of a 60-acre refuge and sanctuary for wolves and other canines. On Friday and Saturday evenings in the summer the facility reopens at 7 PM for the public howl-in. *3111 Offut Lake Rd., tel. 206/264–HOWL. Admission for daily tours: $5 adults, $2.50 children 6–15, children under 6 free; for Howl-in: $6 adults, $3 children 6–15. Open May–Sept., daily 10–5; Oct.–Apr., Wed.–Sun. 10–4.*

Leaving Olympia, travel west along Highway 101 and State Routes 8 and 12 to Gray's Harbor and the twin seaports of **⑳ ㉑ Hoquiam** and **Aberdeen.** In spring, thousands of migratory shorebirds and peregrine falcons come to Bowerman Basin, west of Hoquiam on State Route 109.

An option from Hoquiam would be to drive north on Route 109, ㉒ passing through resorts and ample beach areas such as **Copalis** ㉓ ㉔ **Beach, Pacific Beach,** and **Moclips** on your way to the Quinault ㉕ Indian Reservation and the tribal center of **Taholah.** You should know, however, that access to the coastline at some points here is restricted to tribal members. Taholah is a rustic town, and the main attraction for tourists here, as elsewhere on the peninsula, is the vast amounts of pristine scenery, rather than a commercialized town center.

Another route to follow from Hoquiam is Highway 101 north, along the west fork of the Hoquiam River (through the wonderfully named town of Humptulips) to picturesque Quinault Lake **26 27** and west to the ocean at **Queets** and **Kalaloch.** The stretch of coastal highway north of Kalaloch has many well-marked trails, each a ¼ mile or less in length, that lead to spectacular Pacific beaches.

Continue north on 101 for about 20 miles before taking the Hoh Road east to the spectacular Hoh Rain Forest, a complex and rich ecosystem of conifers, hardwoods, grasses, mosses, and other flora that shelters such wildlife as elk, otter, beaver, salmon, and even flying squirrels. The average rainfall here is 145 inches a year. The **Hoh Visitor Center,** located at the campground and ranger center at road's end, has information, nature trails, and a museum. There are several interpretive facilities to help visitors prepare for the nature trails, and naturalist-led campfire programs and walks are conducted daily July and August. *Hoh Rd., 1.5 mi north of the Hoh River Bridge; the Visitor Center is 20 mi further. Tel. 206/374–6925. Park admission: $3. Visitor Center open June–Aug., daily 9–7; Sept.–May, daily 9–5 (staff often not available in winter, but center remains open).*

28 North on Highway 101 is the little town of **Forks,** famous throughout the Northwest for its lavish and enjoyable Fourth of July celebrations (which actually lasts three days). This is classic Americana with a Northwest twist: parades featuring giant logging trucks along with the Shriners and royalty, demolition derbies, marathon runs and dances, arts and crafts, fireworks, and lots of food. Every year one lucky tourist family is showered with free food, lodging, and gifts, for being selected "Tourist of the Day." For details about festivities write to Forks Old Fashioned Fourth of July (Box 881, 98331) or Forks Chamber of Commerce (Box 1249, 98331, tel. 206/374–2531).

From Forks take La Push Road west for about 15 miles to the **29** town of the same name. **La Push** is a beautiful coastal village and the tribal center of the Quileute Indians. (One theory about the town's name is that it is a variation on the French *la bouche,* the mouth; this makes sense, since it's located at the mouth of the Quilayute River.) Several points along this road have short trails with access to the ocean, fabulous views of offshore islands, and stark rock formations. The north branch of the La Push detour is the road to **Rialto Beach,** a picnic area and campsite.

North and east, Highway 101 enters the **Soleduck River Valley,** **30** famous for its abundant salmon fishing. At **Sappho,** Burnt Mountain Road branches northward off to Route 112 (paved but slow) and eventually leads to **Neah Bay, Capes Flattery** and **Alava, Shi-Shi Beach,** and **Ozette Lake** (the largest body of fresh water in the state). Eight miles east of Sappho is the **Soleduck Hatchery** (tel. 206/327–3246), operated by the Washington State Department of Fisheries and offering a variety of interpretive displays about the many aspects of fish breeding.

31 The deep azure of **Lake Crescent,** about 12 miles farther along, is outstandingly beautiful, and the area has abundant campsites, resorts, trails, canoeing, and fishing. Among Lake Crescent's famous guests was Franklin D. Roosevelt, whose negotiations with U.S. senators and Park Department officials at the Lake Crescent Lodge in 1937 led directly to the creation of the Olympic National Forest. The original lodge buildings of 1915 are still in use, well-worn but comfortable.

32 Twelve miles south on Soleduck Road (which meets Highway 101 a mile west of the western tip of Lake Crescent) is **Sol Duc Hot Springs.** Native Americans have known about the soothing waters of these springs for generations, and since the first resort opened there tourists have known about it as well. There are three hot sulfur pools ranging in temperature from 98° to 104°. The Sol Duc Hot Springs Resort, a venerable institution dating from 1910, has a series of cabins, a restaurant, and hamburger stand. It is not necessary to stay at the resort to use the hot springs. *Soleduck Rd. and Hwy. 101, tel. 206/327–3583. Admission: $3.95. Open mid-May–Sept., daily 9–9.*

33 Back on Highway 101 east, you will soon come to **Port Angeles,** a bustling commercial fishing port and an access route to Canada. Directly across the Strait of Juan de Fuca is Victoria, British Columbia, which can be reached via the private Black Ball Ferry Line (tel. 206/457–4491). Among the points of interest in P.A., as its residents fondly refer to it, is the **Clallam County Historical Museum.** This handsome Georgian building, constructed in 1914 as a courthouse, has exhibitions of artifacts and photo displays detailing the lifestyles of the people, both Native American and white, who lived in this timber-rich and seagoing community. *4th and Lincoln Sts., tel. 206/452–7831, ext. 364. Admission free; donations accepted. Open June–Aug., Mon.–Sat. 10–4; Sept.–May, weekdays 10–4.*

Also interesting is the casual but well-appointed **aquarium** of the Arthur D. Feiro Marine Laboratory, operated as a joint venture by the City of Port Angeles and Peninsula College. Many kinds of local sea life, including octopuses, scallops, rockfish, and anemones, are on display, with new varieties and specimens arriving often. The tour is self-guided, but friendly volunteers are always on hand to answer questions. *Port Angeles City Pier, tel. 206/452–9277. Admission: $1 adults, 50¢ children 6–12, children 5 and under free. Open June–Aug., daily 10–8; Sept.–May, weekends noon–4.*

34 **Hurricane Ridge,** 17 miles south of Port Angeles, rises nearly a mile above sea level and offers spectacular views of the Olympics, the Strait of Juan de Fuca, and Vancouver Island. Despite the point's height, the road grade leading to it is easily negotiated by automobile. In the summer, rangers lead hikes and give interpretive talks on local geology, and flora and fauna. The numerous nature trails range in difficulty from disabled-accessible paths to advanced climbs, and provide an opportunity to see wildflowers such as glacier lilies and lupine, as well as animals such as mountain goats and marmots. In winter, when accessible, the area has miles of cross-country ski routes and a modest downhill ski operation. *3002 Mt. Angeles Rd., tel. 206/452–4501, ext. 230. Visitor center open daily 9–4.*

35 A wide variety of animal life, present and past, can be found in the charming town of **Sequim,** 17 miles east of Port Angeles on Highway 101, and in the fertile plain at the mouth of the **36** Dungeness River to the north of the town. **Dungeness Spit,** part of the Dungeness National Wildlife Refuge and one of the longest natural spits in the world, is home to thousands of migratory waterfowl as well as clams, oysters, and seals. This picturesque locale features a lighthouse on the end of the spit in addition to its abundant natural beauty; there is no formal interpretive center, but large displays provide information about what can be seen. A 65-site campground nearby is operated by Clallam County. *About 3 mi north on Kitchen Rd. (4 mi west of Sequim). Campground tel. 206/683–5847. Wildlife Refuge tel. 206/683–5037. Admission: $2 per family per day.*

In 1977, 12,000-year-old mastodon remains were discovered near Sequim and today are displayed at the **Sequim-Dungeness Museum,** where you can look at these Ice Age creatures as well as at exhibits on Captain Vancouver, the early Klallam Indians, and the area's pioneer towns. *175 W. Cedar St., tel. 206/683–8110. Admission free; donations accepted. Open May–Sept., Wed.–Sun., noon–4; Oct.–Nov. and mid-Feb.–Apr., weekends noon–4; closed Dec.–mid-Feb.*

The nearby **Sequim Natural History Museum,** part of the Peninsula Cultural Arts Center, features exhibits and collections detailing the abundant birds and wildlife of the Olympic Peninsula's salt-water beaches, marshlands, and forests. More than 80 birds and mammals enliven the scenes. *503 N. Sequim Ave. Admission free; donations accepted. Open Wed., Sat., Sun. noon–4; closed Dec.–mid-Feb.*

About 10 miles east of Sequim, State Route 20 turns northward ㊲ another 12 miles to **Port Townsend,** a charming town with a fine waterfront along which runs a series of handsome brick buildings that date from the 1870s. These have been carefully restored and now house a variety of attractive shops, restaurants, and services. High up on the bluff are several large gingerbread-trimmed Victorian homes, many of which have been turned into elegant B&Bs. While Port Townsend is a flourishing arts community, with a high proportion of writers, musicians, and artists in residence, the restored buildings of **Fort Worden,** a former Navy base, are the center for a variety of popular annual arts festivals.

Backtracking from Sequim, Highway 101 travels south along the west side of Hood Canal, past abundant oyster-picking and clam-digging areas. The **Hama Hama Oyster Company** is a retail store south of the town of Eldon, where you can buy fresh salmon, mussels, crab, shrimp, and other seafoods, as well as a variety of pickled and smoked items. Picnic tables outside provide a fine place in which to have a meal al fresco. Especially worth a look and maybe a sample are the store's live examples of geoducks (pronounced gooey-ducks), giant cousins to the clam. *N. 35959 Hwy. 101, tel. 206/877–5811. Admission free. Open daily 8:30–5:30.*

About 10 miles farther, near the southern bend of the canal and ㊳ the town of **Hoodsport,** is the **Hoodsport Winery,** which produces a number of fine wines—from chardonnays and Reislings to gooseberry and rhubarb. The winery is open to the public; the friendly staff gives tours and tastings on an informal basis as requested. *N. 23501 Hwy. 101, tel. 206/877–9894. Admission free. Open daily 9–7.*

Branching off to the west from the middle of town is the Staircase Road, which leads to **Lake Cushman.** This is not only an important source of water for Tacoma's powerhouse on Hood Canal, but it is also the trailhead to numerous hiking trails, including one to the spectacular **Staircase Rapids** on the Skokomish River. The steep country gives rise here to rushing cataracts and boulder-strewn rapids, broken up by deep pools where Dolly Varden trout rest.

Driving south on Highway 101 through the sawmill town of **㊴ Shelton** will bring you back to Olympia.

Long Beach Peninsula

Numbers in the margin correspond to points of interest on the Long Beach Peninsula map.

If the waters of the Pacific and the mighty Columbia River had met in a less turbulent manner, a huge seaport might sit at the river's mouth. Instead, the entrance to the Columbia is quite unpopulated. Dotted with fishing villages and cranberry bogs, it is worlds apart from Seattle—3½ hours southwest—and Portland, 2 hours away. The Long Beach Peninsula, just north of the river's mouth, is rich for the naturalist who enjoys bird-watching, hiking, or beachcombing; the history buff; or the gourmet. It is the perfect place to hole up in front of a crackling fire and indulge in a good book or venture out to witness a winter storm (and there are plenty of them). Locals warn that it is *not* a place to swim. Shifting sands underfoot and tremendous undertows account for several drownings each year.

The Long Beach Peninsula's natural bounty is borne of the water and coastline. The peninsula boasts the longest uninterrupted stretch (28 miles) of sandy beach in North America. Unfortunately, the locals act as if it were private property, greedily claiming their right to drive cars, trucks, recreational vehicles, and motorcycles up and down this pristine belt of sand. Despite what the practice may do to clamming beds or the psyche of solitary beachcombers, it continues. At least in 1990 the state legislature decided to close about 40% of the beach to motor vehicles from April through Labor Day.

In 1990, a ½-mile-long wood boardwalk (stretching from Balstad Street South to South 10th Street) was installed, along with stairs to the beach access, disabled-accessible ramps, plenty of benches, and telescopes. Since no vendors are permitted, the addition offers unobstructed views of the beach and bird life.

Inland a mile or two, the peninsula-area marshes are a haven to migrating birds, particularly the graceful, white trumpeter swans. The old-growth red-cedar grove on Long Island is believed to have sprouted some 4,000 years ago and is home to the endangered spotted owl, the marbled murelet, and other birds and small mammals. Following this tour will allow you to take in some of the unique features of Long Beach Peninsula.

㊵ **Fort Columbia State Park and Interpretive Center,** one of 27 coastal defense units of the U.S. Army, was built in 1903 to house as many as 200 men at one time. Many of the fort's 30 structures have been restored to their original state. Illustrating barracks life at the fort is an interpretive center in one of the old accommodations, and a museum in the fort commander's quarters depicts military family life. A hike up Scarborough Hill behind the fort gives a breathtaking view of the

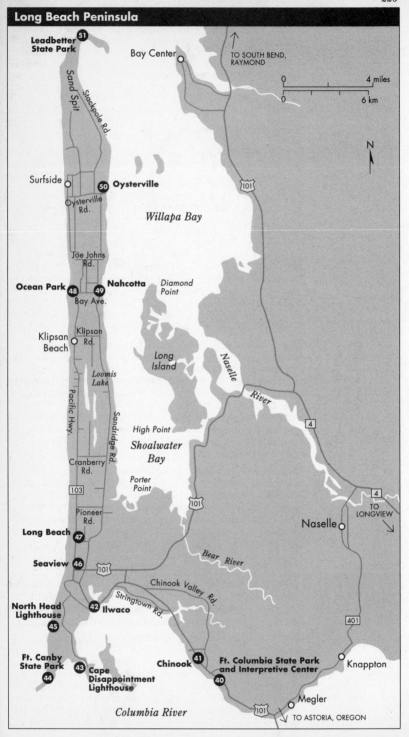

Long Beach Peninsula

Leadbetter
State Park 51

Bay Center

TO SOUTH BEND,
RAYMOND

4 miles

6 km

Sand Spit

Stackpole Rd.

N

Surfside

50 Oysterville

Oysterville
Rd.

Willapa Bay

Joe Johns
Rd.

Ocean Park 48 49 Nahcotta

Bay Ave.

*Diamond
Point*

Klipsan
Beach

Klipsan
Rd.

*Loomis
Lake*

*Long
Island*

Naselle

Pacific Hwy.

Sandridge Rd.

High Point

*Shoalwater
Bay*

Cranberry
Rd.

Porter
Point

4

River

103

Pioneer
Rd.

101

4

TO
LONGVIEW

Long Beach 47

Naselle

Seaview 46

101

Bear   River

Chinook Valley Rd.

North Head
Lighthouse

42 Ilwaco

Stringtown
Rd.

45

401

Ft. Canby
State Park

43 Cape
Disappointment
Lighthouse

Chinook 41

Ft. Columbia State Park
and Interpretive Center

Knappton

44

40

Megler

101

Columbia River

TO ASTORIA, OREGON

peninsula and the Columbia River. *Hwy. 101, 2 mi east of Chinook, tel. 206/777–8221. Admission free. Open May–Sept., daily 6:30 AM–dusk; Oct. 16–Apr. 1, Wed.–Sun. 8 AM–dusk.*

41 Two miles farther is **Chinook,** named for a Native American tribe that helped William Clark and Meriwether Lewis during their stay on the Pacific Coast. The **Sea Resources Hatchery Complex** offers tours of the hatchery and fish-rearing ponds that are used to teach high-school students the basics of salmon culturing and marine industrial arts. *Houchen St., tel. 206/ 777– 8229. Admission free. Phone ahead to arrange a tour.*

42 The next town along the coast is **Ilwaco,** a small fishing community of about 600. From 1884 to 1910, gill-net and trap fishermen fought each other with knives, rifles, and threats of lynchings over ownership and access to their fishing grounds. Today, the port is home to salmon, crab, tuna, charter fishing, and other commercial boats. The **Ilwaco Heritage Museum** uses excellent dioramas to present the history of southwestern Washington, beginning with the Native Americans; moving on to the influx of traders, missionaries, and pioneers; and concluding with the contemporary industries of fisheries, agriculture, and forests. The museum also houses a model of the peninsula's "clamshell railroad," a narrow-gauge train that transported passengers and mail along the beach. The railbed on which the train ran was made of ground-up clam and oyster shells. *115 S.E. Lake St., tel. 206/642–3446. Admission: $1.25 adults, $1 senior citizens, 50¢ children under 12. Open May– Aug., Mon.–Sat. 9–5, Sun. noon–4; Sept.–Apr., Mon.–Sat. 9–5, Sun. noon–5.*

43 **Cape Disappointment Lighthouse,** first used in 1856, is one of the oldest lighthouses on the West Coast. The cape was named by English fur trader Captain John Meares in 1788 because of his unsuccessful attempt to find the Northwest Passage. Construction of the lighthouse suffered when the boat *Oriole,* carrying materials for the project, sank 2 miles offshore.

44 **Ft. Canby State Park** was an active military installation until 1957, when it was turned over to the Washington State Parks and Recreation Commission. Many of the bunkers that guarded the mouth of the Columbia remain today. The park attracts beachcombers, ornithologists, and fishermen, and it offers viewing spots for watching huge waves crash against the Columbia River Bar during winter storms. *Robert Gray Dr. (Box 488), 2½ mi southwest of Ilwaco, off Hwy. 101; tel. 206/642– 3078 or 800/562–0990. Admission free. Open Apr.–Oct. 15, daily 6:30 AM–dusk; Oct. 16–Mar., daily 8 AM–dusk.*

In the park is the **Lewis & Clark Interpretive Center,** which was built in 1976 and covers the 8,000-mile round-trip journey of the Corps of Volunteers for Northwest Discovery from Wood River, Illinois, to the mouth of the Columbia River. Artwork, photographs, and original journal entries are arranged along a series of ramps, which take visitors from the planning of the expedition to a view of the Pacific from Cape Disappointment. *Tel. 206/642–3029 or 604/642–3078. Open Memorial Day–Labor Day, daily 9–5; Labor Day–Memorial Day, weekends 10–3.*

The U.S. Coast Guard Station Cape Disappointment is the largest search-and-rescue station on the Northwest coast, and its operations saved or assisted some 3,000 people in 1989. The **National Motor Life Boat School** is a graduate course in conquering fear. The only school of its kind, it teaches elite rescue crews from around the world advanced skills in navigation, mechanics, firefighting, lifesaving, the capabilities and limitations of the motor lifeboats, and safe rescues. The rough conditions of the Columbia River Bar provide a practical training for the regular surf drills. The observation platform on the North Jetty at Ft. Canby State Park is a good viewing spot for watching the motor lifeboats. *Tel. 206/642–2384. Informal tours available daily 9–5.*

45 **North Head Lighthouse,** also one of the oldest in the area, was built in 1899 to help skippers sailing from the north who could not see the Cape Disappointment Lighthouse. Before the lighthouses were built, a variety of less-sophisticated signals, such as notched trees, white rags, or bonfires, was used. Volunteers residing in Astoria had to paddle across the river and hike 12 miles up the cape to place the signals.

46 **Seaview** is an unincorporated community including several homes dating back to the 1800s. The **Shelburne Inn** (*see* Dining and Lodging, below), built in 1896, is the last turn-of-the-century hotel that still accommodates visitors. Another historic building is the **Sou'wester Lodge,** built by U.S. Senator Henry Winslow Corbett in 1892.

47 **Long Beach,** a community of 1,200, caters to tourists with its go-carts, bumper cars, amusement park, and beach activities.

48 **Ocean Park** is the commercial center of the peninsula's north end. It was founded as a camp for the Methodist Episcopal Church of Portland in 1883, but the law that once prohibited the establishment of saloons and gambling houses no longer exists. The **Taylor Hotel,** built in 1892 on Bay Avenue and N Place, houses retail businesses including a coffee shop and is the only structure from the early days that is open to the public.

49 Across the way, on the bay side, is **Nahcotta,** the site of an active oyster industry. Oysters are shucked and canned on the docks on Willapa Bay, and you can sample them at the **Ark** (273 Sandridge Rd., tel. 206/665–4133), a restaurant on the old Nahcotta Dock. Nahcotta, named for a Native American chief, was once the northernmost point on the peninsula's narrow-gauge railway, and the schedule is still posted in the Nahcotta Post Office. The town's port is a good place from which to view Long Island, home of an old-growth cedar forest that can only be reached by private boat.

50 **Oysterville,** established in 1854, did not survive the oyster industry's decline. The native shellfish were fished to extinction and were replaced with a Japanese oyster, but Oysterville never made a comeback. Tides have washed away homes, businesses, and a Methodist church, but the village still exists, and free maps inside the vestibule of the restored **Oysterville Church** direct you through this town, which is now on the National Register of Historic Places. For more information on the town, write to the **Oysterville Restoration Foundation** (Box 1, Oysterville 98641).

51 **Leadbetter State Park,** at the northernmost tip of the peninsula, is a wildlife refuge and good spot for bird-watching. The dune area at the very tip of the point is closed from April to Au-

gust to protect the nesting snowy plover. Black brants, sandpi-
pers, turnstones, yellowlegs, sanderlings, knots, and plovers
are among the 100 species biologists have recorded at the point.
*Robert Gray Dr., 2 mi south of Ilwaco, tel. 206/642–3078. Open
Apr. 1–Oct. 15, daily 6:30 AM–dusk; Oct. 16–Mar. 31, daily 8
AM–dusk.*

Yakima Valley Wine Country

*Numbers in the margin correspond to points of interest on the
Yakima Valley map.*

America's second-largest producer of wines, Washington state
has been blessed with just the right soil, latitude, growing season, and climate that work together for premium grape and
wine production. Its vineyards share the same latitude (46 degrees) and growth cycle of the great French wine-producing
regions of Bordeaux and Burgundy. The Columbia and Yakima
valleys have a low average rainfall, and irrigation allows for
careful moisture control during critical growth phases. Warm
sunny days build heavy sugars and cool nights help to retain
high acids in the grapes. The results are balanced wines of superior flavor and quality.

Eastern Washington has some 11,000 acres planted in vineyards of cabernet sauvignon, Johannesburg Riesling, chardonnay, sauvignon blanc, chenin blanc, grenache, merlot,
semillon, muscat, and Gewürztraminer grapes. Yakima Valley,
the viticultural center of the state, is home to the largest group
of wineries. Wine operations vary from small wineries on the
back of residential property to large, commercial operations.
Barrels are tapped and wine tasting begins about the last week
of April. The **Yakima Valley Wine Grower Association** (Box 39,
Grandview, WA 98930) publishes a brochure that lists local wineries with tasting-room tours and maps of the region.

52 The first stop is 10 minutes south of Yakima at **Staton Hills Winery** (2290 Gangl Rd., Wapato, tel. 509/877–2112), just east of I–
82. The building, with a huge stone fireplace and commanding
view of the valley, is surrounded by three vineyard trellis systems, showing an efficient method of grape growing.

Zillah, a town named after the 17-year-old daughter of a rail-
53 road manager, features six wineries. Small **Bonair Winery** (500
S. Bonair Rd., Zillah, tel. 509/829–6027), which specializes in
chardonnay, is run by the Puryear family who, after 10 years of
amateur wine making in California, took up commercial pro-
54 duction in the Yakima Valley. **Hyatt Vineyards Winery** (2020
Gilbert Rd., Zillah, tel. 509/829–6333) specializes in estate-
bottled table wines, and premium dessert wines are produced
55 under the Thurston Wolfe label. **Zillah Oakes Winery** (Box
1729, Zillah, tel. 509/829–6990) produces wine from vineyards
56 on the southern slopes of the Rattlesnake Mountains. **Quail
Run Vintners** (1500 Vintage Rd., Zillah, tel. 509/829–6235),
producers of Covey Run wines, is one of the valley's largest
wineries, with expansive decks and grounds offering commanding views of the surrounding vineyards and orchards. Inside you can watch the wine-making through windows off the
tasting room.

57 **Portteus Vineyards** (5201 Highland Dr., Zillah, tel. 509/829–
6970) limits its production to cabernet sauvignon and

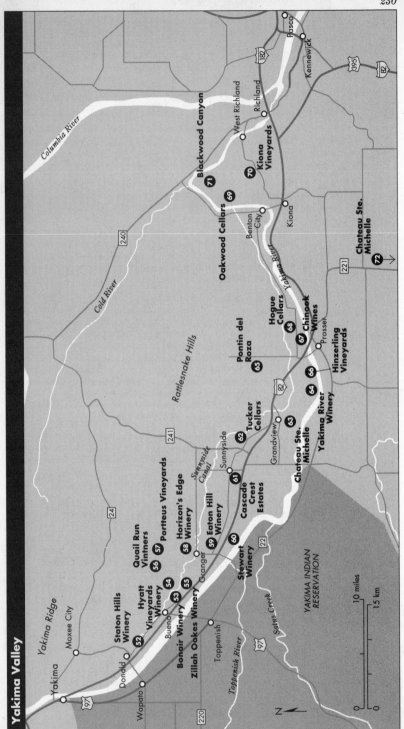

Yakima Valley

chardonnay from grapes grown at a 1,440-foot elevation in the
58 hills above Zillah. **Horizon's Edge Winery** (4530 E. Zillah Dr.,
Zillah, tel. 509/829–6401) takes its name from its tasting room
view of the Yakima Valley, Mt. Adams, and Mt. Rainier. The
winery produces champagne, barrel-fermented chardonnays,
Pinot noir, cabernet sauvignon, and muscat canelli.

59 Granger's **Eaton Hill Winery** (530 Gurley Rd., Granger, tel.
509/854–2508), located in the restored Rinehold Cannery building, produces white Riesling and semillon. You may see fruit
60 pickers working outside the **Stewart Winery** (1711 Cherry Hill
Rd., Granger, tel. 509/854–1882), located atop Cherry Hill. In
sunny weather, tastings are held on the large deck overlooking
the cherry orchard.

61 Sunnyside's **Cascade Crest Estates** (111 E. Lincoln Ave.,
Sunnyside, tel. 509/839–9463) is the state's fourth-largest producer of award-winning wines. The winery produces some 12
varietals, from light semillon to cabernet sauvignon and
62 merlot. The **Tucker Cellars** (Rte. 1, Box 1696, Sunnyside, tel.
509/837–8707) family produces some 20,000 gallons of wine annually. Their market, just east of Sunnyside on Highway 12,
sells the family's homegrown fruit and vegetables, in addition
to wine.

63 The state's oldest winery is **Chateau Ste. Michelle** (W. 5th and
Ave. B, Grandview, tel. 509/882–3928), in Grandview, where
many of the company's red wines are made in a building dating
back to the 1930s. The European-style open-top fermenters
and a collection of wood aging tanks are featured.

64 Several wineries are found in the Prosser area. The **Yakima
River Winery** (Rte. 1, Box 1657, Prosser, tel. 509/786–2805),
specializing in barrel-aged red wines and dessert wines, is
65 southwest of town. The name **Pontin del Roza** (Rte. 4, Box 4735,
Prosser, tel. 509/786–4449) comes from the owners, the Pontin
family, and the Roza, the irrigated, south-facing slopes of the
Yakima Valley where the grapes are grown.

66 **Hinzerling Vineyards** (1520 Sheridan Rd., Prosser, tel. 509/
786–2163), operated by the Wallace family, is the valley's oldest family-owned winery, specializing in estate-grown cab-
67 ernets and late harvest wines. East of Prosser is **Chinook
Wines** (Wine Country Rd., Box 387, Prosser, tel. 509/786–
2725), operated by Kay Siman and Clay Mackey, vintners
known for their dry wines.

68 **Hogue Cellars** is housed at the Prosser Industrial Park, east of
Chinook Wines. Three generations of the Hogue family have
farmed in the Yakima Valley, and in 1982 they produced their
first wine in the family's mint shed. Hogue Cellars includes a
tasting room, reception room, and gift shop featuring Hogue
Farm's foods and wines and other locally made products. *Box
31, Prosser, tel. 509/786–4557. Gift shop open daily 10–5.*

69 Farther east are three small wineries including **Oakwood Cellars** (Rte. 2, Box 2321, Benton City, tel. 509/588–5332), where
70 almost all the work is done by hand; **Kiona Vineyards** (Rte. 2,
Box 2169E, Benton City, tel. 509/588–6716), producers of the
first commercial Lemberger released in this country; and
71 **Blackwood Canyon** (Rte. 2, Box 2169H, Benton City, tel. 509/
588–6249), known for its Old World wine-making techniques.

72 The largest winery in the area is **Chateau Ste. Michelle** (Box 231, Hwy. 221, Columbia Crest Dr., tel. 509/875–2061) at Patterson. The imposing 16-acre estate is situated in the hills above the Columbia River near the Washington–Oregon border, and the winery itself is in a building that covers more than 9 acres.

What to See and Do with Children

Children's Museum Northwest is a hands-on exploratory museum for children. Exhibits include a fire station, TV station, puppet-making workshop, and science center. *106 Prospect St., Bellingham, tel. 206/733–8769. Admission: $2 adults, $1 children. Open Tues.–Fri. noon–5, Sat. 10–5, Sun. noon–5.*
Ilwaco Heritage Museum (*see* Long Beach Peninsula, above).
Lewis & Clark Interpretive Center (*see* Long Beach Peninsula, above).
Northwest Trek Wildlife Park (*see* Tacoma, above).
Point Defiance Zoo and Aquarium (*see* Tacoma, above).
Sequim-Dungeness Museum (*see* The Olympic Peninsula, above).

Shopping

Bellingham

Shopping Districts and Malls The **Old Fairhaven District** (12th and Harris Sts.) consists of a number of square blocks of beautifully restored 1890s brick buildings housing a variety of restaurants, taverns, galleries, and specialty boutiques. To get there, take Exit 250 from I–5, then take Old Fairhaven Parkway west.

In **Old Town** (Lower Holly St.), in downtown Bellingham, there are a number of good antiques shops, second-hand stores, fish markets, hobby shops, and outdoor recreation equipment suppliers. The surrounding area also has small shops and a pleasant small-town atmosphere. Public parking is available on the street or at the Parkade (corner of Commercial and Holly Sts.).

Bellis Fair (I–5 Exits 256 and 256B, jct. I–5 and Guide Meridian, tel. 206/734–5022) is a glossy new regional shopping mall a few miles north of downtown. It has five department stores, several restaurants, and more than 120 other shops, including a multiplex movie theater.

Long Beach Peninsula

Specialty Shops The **Bookvendor** (101 Pacific Ave., Long Beach, tel. 206/642–2702) stocks an extensive supply of children's books, classics, and travel books as well as art supplies.
Gray Whale Gallery & Gifts (105 Pacific Ave., Long Beach, tel. 206/642–2889) features Northwest art, cards, jewelry, and cranberry products from the peninsula.
Long Beach Kites (104 Pacific Ave. N, Long Beach, tel. 206/642–2202) offers myriad kites, from box kites, dragons, and fighters to 19 varieties of stunt kites, *and* free repairs are made.
North Head Gallery (600 S. Pacific Ave., Long Beach, tel. 206/642–8884) has the largest selection of Elton Bennett originals,

plus Bennett's reproductions and works from other Northwest artists.

The Olympic Peninsula

Shopping Districts The single best locale for the confirmed shopaholic is the water-front array of boutiques and stores in **Port Townsend,** all of which feature a good selection of Northwest arts and crafts.

Tacoma

Shopping Districts and Malls **Freighthouse Square Public Market,** on the corner of 25th and D streets, is a former railroad warehouse, now converted into several small, unpretentious shops. The emphasis is on local arts and crafts, and there's also a weekend farmer's market, several informal snack bars, and restaurants. The biggest shopping mall in the Pacific Northwest is the **Tacoma Mall** (tel. 206/475–4565), 1½ miles south of Tacoma Dome. The mall has more than 150 department stores, specialty shops, services, and restaurants for the devoted shopper.

Specialty Shops **Antique Row** (Broadway and St. Helens St., between 7th and
Antiques 9th Sts.) is comprised of some 30 high-quality antiques stores: perfect for browsing on a rainy afternoon. A surprisingly wide variety of items is available—from high quality to decidedly funky, Native American crafts to antique fishing gear, circus memorabilia to fine furniture. Proprietors are generally friendly and knowledgeable.

Sports and Outdoor Activities

Bicycling

Bellingham/Whatcom/ Skagit Counties **Chuckanut Drive** and **Lummi Island** are favorite bicycling routes. Also good is the flat land around **La Conner,** to the south of Bellingham. To the north, **Lynden** is beautiful country, where tulip farms enliven the scenery in the spring. For rentals, try **Fairhaven Bicycle and Ski** (1103 11th St., tel. 206/733–4433) and **Franz Gabl's** (1515 Cornwall St., tel. 206/733–5888).

Long Beach Good areas for bicycling include Ft. Canby and North Head roads, Sandridge Road to Ocean Park and Oysterville, and Highway 101 from Nasselle to Seaview along Willapa Bay.

Tacoma Bicycling is especially popular in the **Puyallup Valley** to the east and the **Kitsap Peninsula.** A number of shops in Tacoma, Puyallup, Gig Harbor, and Port Orchard rent bicycles and equipment.

Climbing

Tacoma **Rainier Mountaineering** (tel. 206/627–6242) offers one-day snow and ice courses during the summer. This group also sponsors guided summit climbs and five-day climbing seminars. The summit climb is not necessarily restricted to experienced climbers, but it is not for people who are out of shape.

Fishing

Long Beach Salmon, rock cod, lingcod, flounder, perch, sea bass, and sturgeon are popular and plentiful for fishing. A free fishing guide is available from the **Port of Ilwaco** (Box 307, 98624, tel. 206/642–3143).

The clamming season varies depending on the supply, but is a popular pastime here. For details call the **Washington Department of Fisheries** (tel. 206/753–6552) or the **fisheries shellfish lab** (tel. 206/665–4166) in Nahcotta.

The Olympic Peninsula Trout and salmon fishing is particularly abundant in rivers throughout the peninsula. In **Neah Bay,** halibut and salmon are the target of charter fishing operations such as **Olson's Resort** (Box 216, Sekiv 98381, tel. 206/963–2311). In **Aberdeen** and **Hoquiam,** bottomfish and salmon are the primary catches. For information concerning fishing in the Olympic Peninsula, contact **Olympic Peninsula Tourism Council** (Box 303, Port Angeles 98362, tel. 206/457–4491 or 206/457–3599).

Tacoma The snow-fed lakes and streams of **Mt. Rainier** are a fisherman's dream. Among the varieties available are cutthroat, rainbow, steelhead, and eastern brook trout; bass, bluegill, crappie, and perch; and Chinook salmon. Licenses are available at most sporting goods stores, or through the **Washington Department of Fisheries** (115 General Adm. Bldg., Olympia 98504, tel. 206/753–6552).

Golf

Bellingham A public course designed by Arnold Palmer is at the **Inn at Semiahmoo Golf Club** (tel. 206/371–7005), a luxury resort near Blaine and the Canadian border on Semiahmoo Spit. There are also public 18-hole courses at **Birch Bay** (tel. 206/371–2026), **Sudden Valley** (tel. 206/734– 6435), and **Lake Padden Park** (tel. 206/676–6989).

Long Beach The peninsula has two nine-hole golf courses, the **Peninsula Golf Course** (tel. 206/642–2828), on the northern edge of Long Beach, and the **Surfside Golf and Country Club** (tel. 206/665–4148), located 2 miles north of Ocean Park.

Tacoma Tacoma has several fine golf courses, including **North Shore** (tel. 206/927–1375), with 18 holes and several small unpretentious shops; **Allenmore** (tel. 206/627–7211), with 18 holes; **Highlands** (tel. 206/759–3622), a nine-hole course; and **Meadowpark** (tel. 206/473–3033), with 18 holes plus a nine-hole course as well.

Hiking

Long Beach Hiking trails are available at **Ft. Canby** (tel. 206/642–3078 or 800/562–0990) and **Leadbetter** (tel. 206/642–3078) state parks.

The Olympic Peninsula Both the ocean and mountain areas offer numerous hiking trails for all levels. For details, contact the **National Park Service** (Box 2208, Olympia, tel. 206/753–9534).

Tacoma **Mt. Rainier National Park** (tel. 206/569–2211) has more than 300 miles of hiking trails, from easy to advanced.

Horseback Riding

Long Beach Horseback riding is popular on the beach, and rentals are available at **Skippers** (S. 9th St. and Beach Access Rd., tel. 206/642–3676). For beach access, riders are asked to use South 10th Street rather than Bolstad Street.

Skiing, Cross-Country

The Olympic Peninsula **Hurricane Ridge,** south of Port Angeles, offers miles of cross-country ski trails. Contact **Port Angeles Visitor Center** (121 E. Railroad St., 98362, tel. 206/452–2363) for information.

Tacoma The **Ski Touring Center** (Box 108, Ashford 98304, tel. 206/569–2283) at Longmire, operated by Mt. Rainier Guest Services, rents cross-country ski equipment and provides lessons for those who want to explore the isolated meadows and forests of Rainier in winter.

Skiing, Downhill

Bellingham Mt. Baker's **Heather Meadows** (1017 Iowa St., tel. 206/734–6771) facility has the longest ski season in the state, lasting from roughly November–March.

The Olympic Peninsula **Hurricane Ridge** (tel. 206/452–4501) has a modest ski operation, with two rope tows and a poma lift.

Tacoma Sixty-four miles east of Tacoma is **Crystal Mountain** (Rtes. 410 and 123 at Crystal Mountain Rd., tel. 206/663–2265), a world-class ski resort with activities year-round. The elevation is 7,000 feet, with 34 runs and 2,300 acres of skiable terrain for all levels. Services include full resort amenities and equipment rentals. **Crystal Mountain Express** (tel. 206/455–5505) coaches leave from six locations, including Sea-Tac Airport, every morning.

Water Sports

Bellingham/Whatcom/ Skagit Counties Several lakes near Bellingham offer ample opportunity for water sports, including **Lake Padden Park** (4882 Samish Way, tel. 206/676–6989) and **Bloedel Donovan Park** (2214 Electric Ave., tel. 206/676–6888), on the northwest shore of Lake Whatcom.

Long Beach Peninsula **Whale-watching** is a popular activity on Long Beach Peninsula. Gray whales pass by here twice a year: December through February, on their migration from the Arctic to their winter breeding grounds in California and Mexican waters; and March through May, on the return trip north. At press time there are no charters offered in the Long Beach area, but lighthouses offer good viewpoints. The best conditions exist in the mornings, when seas are calm and overcast conditions reduce the glare. Look on the horizon for a whale blow—the vapor, water, or condensation that spouts into the air when the whale exhales. Once a blow is spotted, there are likely to be others. Whales often make up to six shorter, shallow dives before a longer dive that can last as long as 10 minutes.

Spectator Sports

The **Tacoma Stars** indoor soccer team play about 26 home games from October through April at the Tacoma Dome (2727

E. D St., tel. 206/572–7827). The **Tacoma Tigers,** a Pacific Coast League Triple-A baseball team, plays 72 home games a year at the 8,000-seat Cheney Stadium (Rte. 16, just west of Tyler St., tel. 206/591–5491).

National and State Parks and Forests

Birch Bay State Park (5105 Helwig Rd., Blaine 98230, tel. 206/ 371–2800), 10 miles from the Canadian border, encompasses almost 200 acres, including a large campground and plenty of room for clamming, fishing, golf, swimming, and hiking.

Dash Point State Park (5700 S.W. Dash Pt. Rd., tel. 800/562– 0990), 5 miles northeast of Tacoma, is a fine beach for picnicking, camping, or beachcombing, and it has excellent views of nearby Vashon Island.

Larrabee State Park (245 Chuckanut Dr., tel. 206/676–2093), 6 miles from Bellingham, has nearly 1,900 acres of forest and park and 3,600 feet of shoreline. The **Interurban Trail** is 6 miles of former train track along the water, paralleling part of Chuckanut Drive. It's now devoted to nonmotorized biking, walking, jogging, and horseback riding. The trailhead begins in the north near 24th Street and Old Fairhaven Parkway, and in the south near Larrabee State Park.

Mt. Baker–Snoqualmie National Forest (*see* Bellingham/ Watcom and Skagit Counties, above).

Mt. Rainier National Park located 74 miles southeast of Tacoma, features the magnificent, 14,410-foot Mt. Rainier—the fifth-highest mountain in the lower 48 states. It's so big that it creates its own weather system. But the park isn't just this incredible volcanic peak; it also encompasses nearly 400 square miles of surrounding wilderness. Within its boundaries are more than 300 miles of hiking trails, from easy to advanced, as well as good lakes and rivers for fishing, ice caves and glaciers, isolated cross-country skiing spots, and ample camping facilities. Among the wildlife in the park are bear, mountain goat, deer, elk, eagles, beavers, and mountain lions; the abundant flora includes Douglas fir, hemlock, cedar, ferns, and wildflowers. The aptly named **Paradise,** at an altitude of 5,400 feet, is the usual starting point for climbs to Rainier's summit during the summer months. The **Henry M. Jackson Visitor's Center** has exhibits, films, and a 360-degree view of the summit and surrounding peaks. A number of hiking trails to various points lead off from here. At 6,400 feet, the **Sunrise Visitor's Center** is the highest point accessible by car at Rainier. A gift and camping-supplies shop is here, as well as the trailheads of several hikes. (*See* Dining and Lodging, below, for accommodations.) *To Mt. Rainier, follow Hwy. 5 south and east, or Hwy. 410 east and south. Both roads meet up at Cayuse and Chinook passes (often closed in winter) to form a full circle around the park. Henry M. Jackson Visitor's Center, tel. 206/569–2211. Jackson and Sunrise open Memorial Day–Labor Day, weekdays 9–7, weekends and holidays 10–5.*

Olympic National Park and Olympic National Forest, two of the most outstanding pieces of natural beauty in America, were established in 1938, and feature such diversified areas as the wind-swept beaches at La Push and Cape Alava, the lush green of the Hoh Rain Forest, the 60-odd active glaciers of the Olympic Mountains, and the high Alpine beauty of Hurricane Ridge. Wildlife such as elk and eagle, as well as plant life such as wildflowers and Douglas Fir, flourish here, in large part due to the prohibition of all hunting, firearms and, offroad vehicles, as well as any disturbance of plants or wildlife. Fishing, however, is permitted without a state license within the park, though punchcards for salmon and steelhead are required and certain waters are subject to regulation. In the National Forest, hunting and fishing are permitted in areas, though some portions are maintained as complete wilderness. For more information, contact Superintendant, Olympic National Park (600 E. Park Ave., Port Angeles 98362, tel. 206/452–4501) or Forest Supervisor, Olympic National Forest (Box 2288, Olympia 98507, tel. 206/753–9535).

Dining and Lodging

Dining Highly recommended restaurants are indicated by a star ★.

Category	Cost*
Very Expensive	over $35
Expensive	$25–$35
Moderate	$15–$25
Inexpensive	under $15

cost per person, excluding drinks, service, and 8.1% sales tax

Lodging Highly recommended hotels are indicated by a star ★.

Category	Cost*
Very Expensive	over $140
Expensive	$90–$140
Moderate	$50–$90
Inexpensive	under $50

For a double room, excluding 8.1% tax and service.

Ashford
Dining and Lodging
★

Alexander's Country Inn. Built in 1912 as a luxury hotel, this B&B near the southwest entrance to the park has attracted a fiercely loyal clientele since its recent restoration to grandeur. Carefully decorated rooms have choice antiques and added touches, such as hand-sewn quilts and delicate floral wallpaper. A wheelchair-accessible suite with a separate entrance has recently been added, but it blends in well with the original building. Breakfasts (price included) are simple but well done, and might feature omelets, French toast, fruit, croissants, juice, and coffee. The excellent restaurant, open to guests and nonguests, bakes its own bread and desserts; a variety of fresh fish and pasta dishes, such as chicken fettucine, are also specialties. *37515 Star Rte. 706 E., tel. 206/569–2300. Reservations in restaurant recommended. Dress: casual. Restaurant closed weekdays in winter. MC, V. Moderate-Expensive.*

Bellingham
Dining
★

Il Fiasco. Although the food can be pricey, this restaurant, translated to "the flask," is considered one of the best restaurants in Bellingham, offering an ambitious northern Italian menu, a sophisticated decor, knowledgable staff, and a good wine list that mixes Italian and local vintages. Many of the entrées, such as the fresh crab ravioli or a luscious lasagne made with lamb, fontina cheese, spinach, and polenta, can be ordered as appetizers; an entire meal can thus be concocted entirely from the appetizer list, a practice that is not only accepted, but even encouraged by the friendly waitpersons. *1309 Commercial St., tel. 206/676-9136. Reservations advised. Dress: casual. MC, V. Closed Sat., Sun. lunch. Expensive-Very Expensive.*

La Belle Rose. A very good French country restaurant run by an expatriate Frenchwoman, Mariette Wood, who emphasizes fresh ingredients and home baking. The extremely small dining room with just six tables, is cozily and romantically decorated. Seafood is the specialty, reflecting the restaurant's waterfront location in the Harbor Center Building, though there are choice meat dishes as well. Typical menu listings may include salmon *en sauce verte* (herb mayonnaise sauce) or sausage prepared Alsatian style and accompanied by crisp sauerkraut. *1801 Roeder Ave., suite 102, tel. 206/647-0833. Reservations necessary. Dress: casual. MC, V. Closed Sun.-Mon. dinner; Sun.-Wed. lunch. Expensive.*

Douglas House. This renovated house with lots of windows that offer great views of Mt. Baker and the Cascade Mountains also serves some great meals. Highly recommended dishes are prime rib, seafood, and the fabulous cheesecake for dessert. *2254 Douglas Dr., tel. 206/384-5262. Reservations advised. Dress: casual. MC, V. Closed lunch, Mon. and Tues. Moderate.*

Oyster Creek Inn. This small eatery, best described as Northwest eclectic, is set in a sharp switchback near the southern end of Chuckanut Drive. The window tables overlook the creek and bay, to compliment the already wonderful atmosphere. Oysters, cooked a variety of imaginative ways, stand out, while an excellent wine list drawn exclusively from Washington State vineyards—is also featured. Sunday brunch, with classic dishes, such as salmon omelets and fries, is offered. *190 Chuckanut Dr., Bow, tel. 206/766-6179. Reservations suggested. Dress: casual. AE, MC, V. Moderate.*

Pacific Café. This restaurant, next door to the historic Mt. Baker Theater in downtown Bellingham, features a variety of seafood and pasta dishes with an Asian twist; typical menu listings include dishes such as Alaska spot prawns in a garlicky black bean sauce and rib steak with a plum-oyster sauce. Portions are large (but the spicing can be mild), but you'll want to save room for one of the wickedly good desserts, such as the chocolate eclairs. The café's understated decor, like the food, is Asian-influenced: white walls, rice-paper screens, wood shutters. *100 N. Commercial St., tel. 206/647-0800. Reservations advised. Dress: casual. AE, MC, V. Closed Sat. lunch, Sun. dinner. Moderate.*

Rhododendron Café. Homemade soups, seafood, and fresh salads comprise the foundations upon which the ever-changing specials menu is built in this generally excellent restaurant. Specials vary according to the market and may include marinated snapper with a toasted nut sauce or mussel-vegetable soup. The locally famous pies and other luscious desserts should be sampled. The restaurant, located at the very southern (and out of the way) end of Chuckanut Drive—near the tiny town of Bow—is pleasant and unpretentious in its decor, and has usually cheerful and fast service, though when things get crowded it can slow up. *553 Chuckanut Dr., Bow, tel. 206/766-6667. Reservations accepted. Dress: casual. MC, V. Closed Mon., Tues. Moderate–Inexpensive.*

Colophon Cafe. Incorporated into the Village Bookstore, this restaurant offers hearty soups such as Brazilian peanut butter, as well as good sandwiches and ice cream. *1208 11th St., Old Fairhaven, tel. 206/647–0092. No reservations. Dress: casual. MC, V. Inexpensive.*

Lodging **Schnauzer Crossing.** A meticulously kept garden surrounds three sides of this elegant B&B, with Lake Whatcom on the fourth. Besides a large and gracious common sitting room, each of its two guest rooms offers something different: The larger has a huge bed, garden views, a fireplace, and a small sitting room, while the smaller has a view of the lake and a choice little library. Friendly owners Donna and Vermont McAllister serve ample gourmet breakfasts. *1807 Lakeway Dr., 98226, tel. 206/733–0055 or 206/734–2808. 2 rooms. Facilities: Jacuzzi, tennis court, outdoor hot tub, boating facilities. No smoking or pets. MC, V. Expensive.*

Best Western Lakeway Inn. A large, bustling hotel in downtown Bellingham, this accommodation is popular with tourists, especially those from Vancouver. Located near the big Fred Meyers shopping complex, there are plenty of things to keep the whole family occupied. Children under 12 stay for free when sharing a room with their parents. *714 Lakeway Dr., 98225, tel. 206/671–1011 or 800/547–0106; fax 206/676–8519. 132 rooms. Facilities: café, piano lounge, indoor pool, sauna, weight room, free shuttle service to airport or ferry. AE, D, DC, MC, V. Moderate.*

Park Motel. Because of its "children under 12 free" policy, this is a popular family motel, and since it's close to the university, it's also often occupied by the visiting parents of students. The strictly standard-issue decor and furnishings are functional, but comfortable, and some are equipped with kitchens. *101 N. Samish Way, 98225, tel. 206/733–8280; fax 206/738–9186. 56 rooms; nonsmoking rooms available. Facilities: Jacuzzi, sauna. AE, DC, MC, V. Moderate.*

Chinook **The Sanctuary.** This restaurant, in a turn-of-the-century *Dining* church building, offers fine cuisine and a quiet atmosphere with soft lighting and stained-glass windows. Swedish meatballs are a specialty, but the menu also features local seafood, prime rib, veal, an extensive wine list, and delicious homemade desserts. *Hwy. 101 and Hazel St., tel. 206/777–8380. Reservations recommended. Dress: neat but casual. AE, MC, V. Closed lunch; Mon.–Tues., Oct.–Apr. Moderate–Expensive.*

Cle Elum **Mama Vallone's Steakhouse and Inn.** The Vallones use tradi-*Dining and Lodging* tional recipes from their Italian homeland to design the menu for this cozy and informal restaurant. Although it's notorious for its great pasta, the pasta and *fagioli* soup (a tomato-based soup with vegetables and beans) and the *bagna calda* (a bath of olive oil, garlic, anchovies, and butter for dredging vegetables and meat) are favorites. Also try the Sunday brunch, which may feature ravioli or tortellini along with standard eggs and ham buffet. The inn upstairs was built in 1906 as a boardinghouse for unmarried miners; today three moderately priced rooms with private baths and antique reproduction furnishings are available. *302 W. 1st St., tel. 509/674–5174. 3 rooms. No fa-*

*cilities. Reservations for restaurant suggested. Dress: casual.
AE, DC, MC, V. Closed Mon. and lunch. Moderate.*

Copalis Beach
Lodging

Iron Springs Resort. Located 3 miles north of Copalis Beach on
Route 109, this string of 25 individual cottages can accommodate anywhere from 2 to 10 people—perfect for families. Each
has its own fireplace and kitchen; older cabins are decorated in
a dimly lit but pleasantly funky style, while newer ones (Nos.
22–25) are spiffier; only No. 6 has no view, but others have superb beach, river, and forest views and access. *Box 207,
Copalis Beach 98535, tel. 206/276–4230. 25 units. Facilities:
heated and covered pool. AE, MC, V. Moderate.*

Forks
Dining and Lodging

Kalaloch Lodge. This facility, set in the lush Olympic National
Forest, is a hodgepodge mixture of old cabins, new log cabins,
old lodge, and new hotel. Lodge rooms are clean, airy, and comfortable, and most have terrific ocean views. Some of the rooms
in the modern part—Sea Crest House—have fireplaces and
decks. The old cabins can be pretty basic (drafty in winter,
with minimal kitchens and other amenities), but are fine for informal stays and for getting a sense of what the wild Washington coast was like in "the good old days." The newer log cabins
convey a similar feeling, but are a little spiffier, while the lodge
offers few resort-type amenities, but abundant opportunities
for beachcombing, hiking, and other robust activities. Good
fresh salmon and oysters highlight the menu in the restaurant,
though the rest of the fare can be disappointingly ordinary.
*Hwy. 101 (HC 80, Box 1100), Forks-Kalaloch 98331, tel. 206/
962–2271. 58 rooms and cabins. Facilities: restaurant (dress:
casual; reservations accepted). AE, MC, V. Moderate–Expensive.*

Gig Harbor
Dining
★

Neville's Shoreline. This pleasant, accommodating restaurant
in the heart of Gig Harbor's marina is rather dark inside, but
window tables offer excellent views of the water. Northwest
seafood is the specialty here—try especially the simply but
well-prepared salmon and clams. Come also for Sunday brunch.
*8827 N. Harborview Dr., tel. 206/851–9822. Reservations ad-
vised. Dress: casual. AE, D, MC, V. Moderate.*

Tides Tavern. This noisy, cheerful waterfront bar-cum-restau-
rant has been going strong since 1904. The food is standard-
category tavern grub—sandwiches, pizza, burgers—but is
much better than the usual indifferent run; shrimp salad is a
house specialty. When the sun's out, the deck serves as the popular locale. If you arrive by boat or seaplane you can tie up right
at the tavern. *2925 Harborview Dr., tel. 206/858–3982. No reservations. Dress: casual. MC, V. Inexpensive.*

Lodging
★

Olde Glencove Hotel. Situated above a secluded cove on Puget
Sound, this charming Victorian hotel was built originally as a
resort in 1896 and now ranks on the National Register of Historic Places. The setting—lush lawns, veranda, pond, antique-
laden common, and private rooms—makes the Olde Glencove a
popular locale for local weddings. Amenities include a full gourmet breakfast and afternoon hors d'oeuvres; the lodgings, all
with views of the Sound, include two suites with private bath
and separate entrances, and two rooms with shared bath. *9418
Glencove Rd., 98335, tel. 206/884–2835. From Hwy. 16, take
Purdy-Shelton exit (S.R. 302) to Key Center; turn left, then
right at bottom of hill. MC, V. Moderate.*

Ilwaco **Inn at Ilwaco.** This New England–style church, built in 1928,
Lodging has been renovated as a B&B. All but two of the nine guest
rooms are upstairs in the old Sunday-school rooms and all are
cozily furnished with some antiques, armoires, and eyelet or
printed chintz curtains and coverlets. The lobby, with upholstered sofas, chairs, and tables with loads of books, and the
breakfast area are in the former church parlor. For performances meetings, classes, and weddings, the inn makes use of
the converted sanctuary, which is now a 120-seat theater.
Breakfast may include such delicacies as apple-walnut pancakes, homemade muffins, fresh fruit, and cereal. *120 Williams
St. NE, 98624, tel. 206/642–8686. 9 rooms, 7 with private bath.
No facilities. MC, V. Moderate–Expensive.*

La Conner **Hotel Planter.** This recently renovated hotel is the oldest in La
Lodging Conner and is on the National Register of Historic Places.
Bright and airy rooms are filled with attractive antiques and
handmade furniture, and offer fine views either of La Conner's
main street or the waterfront. *715 1st St., 98257, tel. 206/466–
4422. 12 rooms, some with private baths. Facilities: hot tub.
AE, MC, V. Moderate.*

Long Beach **Dog Salmon Cafe & Lounge.** Even if you don't eat here, it's
Dining worthwhile to look inside this family restaurant, decorated
with replicas of Northwest Coast Native American carvings
and paintings of bear, beaver, and salmon on wood-paneled
walls. Fare ranges from hamburgers to spicy Cajun shrimp linguini. *113 Hwy. 103, in downtown Long Beach, tel. 206/642–
2416. No reservations. Dress: casual. MC, V. Inexpensive–
Moderate.*
My Mom's Pies. Although this place, whose residence is in a
mobile home, keeps very irregular hours, it's worth dropping
by. Specialty pies include banana whipped cream, chocolate almond, pecan, sour-cream raisin, and fresh raspberry. The
menu also includes clam chowder and quiche. *Hwy. 103 and
12th St. S, tel. 206/642–2342. No reservations. Dress: casual.
MC, V. Closed dinner and Mon. Inexpensive.*

Lodging **The Breakers Motel and Condominiums.** These contemporary
condominiums have one- and two-bedroom units and are located on the beach. Since they are individually owned, the decor varies, but all are modern, comfortable, and clean. *Box 428,
98631, tel. 206/642–4414 or 800/288–8890. 114 rooms, some
with kitchenettes. Facilities: indoor heated pool and spa, playground. MC, V. Moderate–Expensive.*
Nendels. This modern motel, set just behind the sand dunes,
presents a variety of rooms with different views, but those in
the newer building offer the best scenery. Furnishings are nice
and new, but a significant drawback is that the walls are so thin
you can often hear conversations in adjoining rooms and in the
stairwells. *Box 793, 98631, tel. 206/642–2311 or 800/547–0106.
72 rooms. Facilities: outdoor heated spa. Moderate–Expensive.*

Moclips **Ocean Crest Resort.** Set high on a bluff above a spectacular
Dining and Lodging stretch of the Pacific, this resort hotel has one- and two-bedroom units with airy decor, fireplaces, cedar paneling, and su-
perb views. Some have kitchens and/or fireplaces; access to the
beach is down a steep wooded walkway. The Ocean Crest restaurant features those panoramic ocean views and standard but
well-prepared, ample food: eggs, hash browns, good coffee and
muffins at breakfast, fresh seafood for lunch and dinner.

There's also a gift shop and a snug bar tastefully decorated with Native American artifacts. *Hwy. 109 (18 mi north of Ocean Shores), 98562, tel. 206/276–4465. 45 rooms. Facilities: recreation area with pool, Jacuzzi, weight room. AE, MC, V. Moderate.*

Mt. Baker **Mt. Baker Lodging & Travel.** These self-contained cabins and
Lodging chalets nestled in a lovely wooded setting 17 miles west of the Mt. Baker National Forest offer units of varying sizes, from snug hideaways suitable for couples to larger chalets good for families or groups. Each rustic but clean and charming unit has a woodstove or fireplace, and comes stocked with linen, firewood, and towels. For families with children, cribs and toys are available from the friendly office staff. *Box 472, Glacier 98244, tel. 206/599–2453. Facilities: some units equipped with VCRs, hot tub, sauna. MC, V. Moderate.*

Nahcotta **The Ark.** The Ark, sitting adjacent to the Nahcotta oyster dock,
Dining has excellent cuisine. The house specialty is seafood—especially oysters, but leave room for the splendid desserts—cranberry Grand Marnier mousse and blackberry bread pudding, for example. The bar presents less expensive, lighter fare, including soup and sandwiches. *273 Sandridge Rd., tel. 206/665–4133. Reservations recommended. Dress: casual. AE, MC, V. Expensive.*

Olympia **La Petite Maison.** Imaginative French food is the specialty of
Dining this converted 1890s farmhouse, generally considered Olympia's premier fine dining establishment. The ambience— one of quiet elegance—created by the classical music, unobtrusive service, and crisp linens accompanying the food support the restaurant's reputation. Entrées range from delicately prepared local seafood (look especially for the Shelton clams) to marinated lamb or duck with blackberry sauce. A good wine list and excellent desserts, such as a Grand Marnier torte, round out the menu. *2005 Ascension Way, tel. 206/943–8812. Reservations recommended. MC, V. Closed Sun.; Sat. lunch, Mon. dinner. Moderate–Expensive.*

Lodging **Westwater Inn.** This is a large but friendly hotel, close to downtown Olympia and the Capitol grounds, with striking views of Capitol Lake, the Capitol Dome, and the surrounding green hills. The rooms are spacious and comfortable; those facing the water are especially appealing. There are two good restaurants in the hotel: a modest coffee shop called Tiffin's and Ceazan's, a restaurant with a fine view that also serves very decent sandwiches and full meals, mostly imaginative American food, for modest prices. *2300 Evergreen Park Dr., 98502, tel. 206/943–4000. 191 rooms; disabled and nonsmoking rooms available. Facilities: 2 restaurants, coffee shop, lounge, outdoor pool, Jacuzzi. AE, D, MC, V. Moderate.*

Pacific Beach **Sandpiper Beach Resort.** This resort is a modern, four-story
Lodging complex of clean, attractive, and fully equipped suites; most have a sitting room, dining area, fireplace, small kitchen, porch, bedroom, and bath. Penthouse suites have an extra bedroom and cathedral ceilings. There are also five cottages and a few one-room studios. Despite an ugly playground that mars the beach view, the building is attractive, with the wood exterior blending well with the surrounding woods and water. This is definitely the place for a getaway: no in-room phones, no pool, no TV, no restaurant. *Rte. 109 (1½ mi south of Pacific Beach)*

Box A, 98571, tel. 206/276–4580. 30 rooms. No facilities. MC, V. Moderate.

Paradise
Dining and Lodging

Paradise Inn. At an elevation of 5,400 feet, this large, old-fashioned lodge offers excellent views of Mt. Rainier and Nisqually Glacier from nearly every one of its rooms. The best part about it, aside from its splendid location, is the spacious common lobby, which has exposed wood-beam construction, two huge stone fireplaces, Indian rugs, and Western decor. The full-service dining room, with a menu that leans toward heavy and rather bland meat or frozen-fish dishes, is a famous gathering place for leisurely Sunday brunches in summer; in addition, the lodge has a small snack bar and a snug, crowded lounge with plenty of rough natural wood for decor. *Hwy. 706, (c/o Mt. Rainier Guest Services, Box 108, Star Rte., Ashford 98304), tel. 206/569–2275. Reservations recommended. Dress: casual. MC, V. Closed Nov.–mid-May. Moderate–Expensive.*

Port Angeles
Dining

C'est Si Bon. This is a locally famous French restaurant run by a French expatriate couple, Norbert and Michele Juhasz. Probably the most elegant restaurant on the decidedly informal Olympic Peninsula, C'est Si Bon has bold art on the walls, fine linen on the tables, and a good view of rose gardens and the Olympic Mountains. Sophisticated and generally good service compliments the classic menu. *Escargots en Pernod, fruits de mer au gratin,* or a hearty onion soup are typical appetizers; entrées include salmon, duck, and prawns with tomato and garlic. There is an excellent wine list, and desserts are also good, especially the chocolate mousse. *2300 Hwy. 101E (4 mi east of Port Angeles), tel. 206/452–8888. Reservations advised. Dress: casual. AE, CB, DC, MC, V. Closed Mon. and lunch. Expensive.*

First Street Haven. Small and informal, this place is tucked quietly into the storefronts of downtown Port Angeles, but is a good place for high-quality breakfasts and lunch. The service is always friendly and fast, the decor cheerful but unpretentious. Fresh salads, thick sandwiches, well-prepared fajitas and chili, and homemade quiche are featured; good espresso drinks and desserts are offered, too. Sunday brunches include well-prepared, hearty standard fare. *107 E. 1st St. (at Laurel), tel. 206/457–0352. No reservations. Dress: informal. No credit cards. No alcohol. Closed dinner. Inexpensive.*

Lodging

Sol Duc Hot Springs Resort. This is a comfortable, casual resort, dating from the turn of the century, but managing to be spiffed-up just enough without becoming slick and soulless. Consisting of 32 minimally outfitted cabins, the resort presents a pleasant and cheery atmosphere. All units have separate bathrooms, and some have kitchens. There is also an outdoor hamburger stand and an attractive inside dining room serving unpretentious meals (breakfast, lunch, and dinner) drawing on the best of the Northwest: salmon, crab, fresh vegetables, and fruit. *12 mi south of Hwy. 101 on Soleduck Rd. (Box 2168), 98362, tel. 206/327–3583. 32 units and camping and RV facilities. Facilities: restaurant, hot springs, outdoor pool. Reservations for restaurant necessary. Dress: casual. MC, V. Closed mid-Oct.–mid-May. Moderate.*

Tudor Inn. This 1910 Tudor-style house, fully refurbished and turned into a pleasant B&B, is only about 12 blocks from the Victoria-bound ferry dock. Adding to the quiet style of this inn are the antique furnishings and library; from the biggest and most pleasant of the five guest rooms you get spectacular water views (and private bath). The cheerful and efficient owners—the Glasses—serve breakfast in classic English style, which includes eggs, bacon, and muffins, as well as a generous afternoon tea with plenty of fresh scones and other goodies. *1108 S. Oak St., 98362, tel. 206/452–3138. 5 units. No facilities. No smoking. MC, V. Moderate.*

Dining and Lodging **Lake Crescent Lodge.** This old but comfortable accommodation with a big main lodge and small cabins overlooks the beautiful deep-blue Lake Crescent. Units in the lodge are minimal—bathrooms down the hall, dimly lit rooms—but the setting makes up for sparse amenities. Trout fishing, hiking, evening nature programs, and boating are all on the bill. The food in the restaurant is nothing special, but the service is cheerful and efficient, appealing to young college students enjoying a summer away from the city. *6540 E. Beach Rd., 98362, tel. 206/928–3325. Facilities: restaurant, fishing, boating. AE, DC, MC, V. Closed mid-Nov.–Apr. Inexpensive.*

Port Townsend
Dining
★ **Fountain Café.** This small cafe, set off the main tourist drag, is one of the best restaurants in Port Townsend. Fine linens and fresh flowers dress up the unpretentious dining room, and a cheerful staff furthers the welcoming tone of this café. You can count on seafood and pasta specialties with imaginative and always-changing twists: smoked salmon in black porter sauce, for instance. This is a local hot spot, as evidenced by the occasional wait (usually short) for a table, and a particular favorite with Port Townsend's local heroes, including the zany globe-trotting juggling troupe known as the Flying Karamazov Brothers; if they're in town, you may be treated to an impromptu perfomance of a fine-cutlery-on-the-nose balancing act. *920 Washington St., tel. 206/385–1364. Reservations advised. Dress: casual. MC, V. Moderate.*

Salal Café. Featuring home-style cooking and daily specials, this cooperatively-run restaurant shines among early-morning breakfast joints. Try one of many variations on the potato-egg scramble for lunch, seafood and regional American style meals are good, portions ample, and prices reasonable. Try to get a table in the glassed-in back room, which faces a plant-filled courtyard. *634 Water St., tel. 206/385–6532. No reservations. Dress: casual. No credit cards. Closed dinner and Tues. Inexpensive.*

Lodging **James House.** A splendid antiques-filled Victorian-era B&B in the heart of downtown Port Townsend and located across the street from the Whidbey Island ferry dock, this inn presents a homey atmosphere in a terrific location. Each of the two parlors has fireplace and library, and a portion of the guest rooms overlook the water front views. In the formal dining room, simple but elegant Continental-style breakfasts are served. In addition to being on the National Register of Historic Places, the James lays claim to being the first B&B in the Northwest. *1238 Washington St., 98368, tel. 206/385–1238. 12 rooms. No facilities. Call for restrictions. MC, V. Moderate–Expensive.*

Palace Hotel. This friendly B&B in the historic downtown section of Port Townsend is tastefully decorated to reflect its 1889 construction date and its former history as a bordello. The narrow, steep brick building facade is pleasant to look at, but there is no elevator, a consideration if getting around is difficult for you. On the up side, the Palace is conveniently located close to the town's shopping and sightseeing district. *1004 Water St., 98368, tel. 206/385–0773. 15 units, 1 with kitchenette. No facilities. AE, D, MC, V. Moderate.*

Tides Inn. You might recognize this place from the movie *An Officer and a Gentleman*, which was filmed around Port Townsend and Fort Worden. (The hotel is the scene of those steamy love scenes between Richard Gere and Debra Winger.) There are even *Officer and a Gentleman*–theme rooms available, complete with stills from the movie and a VCR for private viewing of the film. The Tides is a comfortable, unfancy motel, about six blocks from downtown, with good views of the water. An informal but adequate Continental breakfast is served every morning, and kitchens are available in both single rooms and suites; all the rooms have TVs and phones, and some have private decks. *1807 Water St., 98368, tel. 206/385–0595. 21 units. Facilities: Jacuzzis in some rooms. AE, CB, DC, MC, V. Moderate.*

Quinault Lodging **Lake Quinault Lodge.** This lodge is set on a perfect glacial lake in the midst of the Olympic National Forest. Spectacular old-growth forests are an easy hike away, and there is abundant salmon and trout fishing. The medium-size and quite deluxe lodge, built in 1926 of cedar shingles, includes delightfully decorated public rooms with antiques and a fireplace. The restaurant food is expensive but generally bland and unadventuresome; the old-fashioned bar is lively and pleasant. Hiking and jogging trails are within easy access. Lake Quinault Lodge is especially popular with conventions and other groups. *S. Shore Rd. (Box 7), 98575, tel. 206/288–2571. 89 rooms. Facilities: restaurant, bar, Jacuzzi, indoor pool, sauna, golf course, games room. MC, V. Expensive.*

Roslyn Dining **Roslyn Café.** This funky café has a number of trappings from the past that, along with its good food, make it so popular. High ceilings, a jukebox with the original 78s, and neon in the window bring nostalgia to the place. The hamburgers with spinach and onions are mouthwatering, but entrées also include such offerings as fresh halibut in dill sauce. Desserts are decadent. *28 Pennsylvania Ave., tel. 509/649–2763. No reservations. Dress: casual. No credit cards. Closed Mon. Inexpensive–Moderate.*

Seaview Dining ★ **The Shoalwater Restaurant.** The Shoalwater Restaurant at the Shelburne Inn, has been acclaimed by *Gourmet, Bon Appétit,* and *Travel & Leisure,* so you dine in good company here. Seafood bought from the fishing boats to the restaurant's back door, is as fresh as it can be; local mushrooms and salad greens are gathered from the peninsula's woods and gardens. Exquisite desserts are the creation of Ann Kischner, a master pastry chef, and an extensive wine list and Northwest microbrews on tap in the Heron & Beaver Pub are featured. Also try the Sunday brunch. *Pacific Hwy. and N. 45th St., tel. 206/642–4142. Reservations recommended. Dress: casual but neat. AE, MC, V. Closed Fri.–Mon. lunch; Oct.–May, Wed. Moderate–Expensive.*

42nd Street Cafe. This much-needed, middle-of-the-road restaurant is nestled comfortably between deep-fried seafood and fries on one end of the peninsula's restaurant spectrum and expensive gourmet fare on the other. The café, which opened last year, emphasizes home-cooked food and features a new menu daily. "We both thought my father had retired in Mexico," said

Robert Guy. Instead, Dad—named Leonard—had moved to
the peninsula to bake the restaurant's breads and make the
tasty corn relish and conserves. Grilled Willapa Bay oysters
are tender and succulent and halibut and salmon are grilled or
poached. The raisin cream pie for dessert is heavenly. Prices
include soup, salad, vegetable, potato, entrée, and dessert.
*Hwy. 103 and 42nd St., tel. 206/642–2323. Reservations ac-
cepted for 5 or more persons. Dress: casual. V. Inexpensive–
Moderate.*

Lodging **Shelburne Inn.** This bright and cheerful, antiques-filled inn
was built in 1896 by Charles Beaver and is now listed on the National Register of Historic Places. It also is right on the highway, which can make it noisy, so the best picks are rooms on the
west side. Most of the rooms have balconies, private baths,
queen-size beds with handmade quilts. *Hwy. 103 and N. 45th
St., 98644, tel. 206/542–2442. 16 rooms. Facilities: pub, restaurant. AE, MC, V. Expensive.*

Sou'wester. A stay at the Sou'wester promises a bohemian experience that begins with your choice of accommodation: rooms
and apartments in a historic lodge, cabins, or classic mobile-
home units on the surrounding property just behind the beach.
The lodge was built in 1892 as the summer retreat for Henry
Winslow Corbett, a Portland banker, timber baron, shipping
and railroad magnate, and U.S. senator. Units in the lodge are
not "decorated"—instead they are the repository of things
carefully collected over the years, including handmade quilts
and original paintings and drawings. Stays of at least a month
are welcomed in the lodge. Proprietors Len and Miriam Atkins
came to Seaview from South Africa, by way of Israel and Chicago, where they worked with the late psychologist Bruno Bet-
telheim, and they are always up for a stimulating conversation.
Soirees and chamber-music concerts sometimes occur in the
parlor. Cabins and trailers have cooking facilities and instead of
a B&B downstairs, there is a B&MYODB—"make your own
damned breakfast" (in the Atkins' homey kitchen). *Beach Access Rd. (Box 102), 98644, tel. 206/642–2542. 3 rooms with
shared bath and kitchen; 4 cabins; 6 trailers. Facilities: adjacent to beach. MC, V. Inexpensive–Moderate.*

Sequim **Eclipse Café.** Spring rolls, *con oc* (pancake filled with bacon and
Dining green onion and dipped in a pungent mixture of fish paste, hot
peppers, and hoisin sauce), and Hong Kong fried ice cream are
just a few of the delights cooked up by Cambodian chef Lay Yin
Wells and her husband, Tom Wells, in this unexpected gem of a
place. The decor is decidedly unpretentious—like a standard-
issue roadside café—but the food is consistently interesting,
and the service is friendly and fast. *144 S. 5th St. (near the
Landmark Mall), tel. 206/683–2760. Reservations advised.
Dress: informal. No credit cards. No alcohol. Closed Wed.–
Fri.; closed dinners except weekends by reservation only. Inexpensive.*

Tacoma **Pacific Rim Restaurant.** This much-praised upscale restaurant,
Dining undoubtedly the best in Tacoma, has an inventive menu, genuinely friendly staff, and the atmosphere of an elegant Victorian
club. Fresh seafood and Italian fare are the specialties, and
chef and co-owner Lenore Nolan-Ryan prepares some favorites
with an Asian influence, culminating in such unusual dishes as
grilled salmon in a cucumber-wasabi sauce. The desserts are
also grand, especially the cremé brûlée. *100 S. 9th St., tel. 206/*

627–1009. Reservations advised. Dress: casual. AE, MC, V. Expensive.

Harbor Lights. This waterfront institution, appropriately adorned with nautical furnishings including glass floats, stuffed fish, and life preservers, hasn't changed since the 1950s. The specialties are also classics: seafood, steaks, chops, and shellfish, but the steamed clams (in season) and good, ungreasy fish and chips are particular favorites. Service is generally efficient despite the crowds usually found here. There's a good waterfront view of Commencement Bay if you're lucky enough to snag a window seat. *2761 Ruston Way, tel. 206/752–8600. Reservations advised. Dress: casual. AE, DC, MC, V. Moderate.*

The Lobster Shop. This classic seafood restaurant has two locations; the older, on Dash Point, is cozier than the newer in-town spot, although both have fine views of Commencement Bay. Dash Point's rustic feel makes for an especially good spot to while away a long winter evening. Both restaurants specialize in simply prepared seafood, with salmon the perennial favorite. There's a cocktail lounge in the newer location, and beer and wine are available in the older. *6912 Soundview Dr. NE (off Dash Point Rd.), tel. 206/927–1513; and 4013 Ruston Way, tel. 206/759–2165. Reservations advised. Dress: casual. AE, DC, MC, V. Moderate.*

The Antique Sandwich Company. Open daily for breakfast, lunch, and dinner, this pleasant deli-style café specializes in hearty soups and sandwiches, classic children's food like waffles and PB&J sandwiches, and well-prepared espresso drinks. Old posters on the walls, plastic bears for serving honey on the tables, and a toy-covered play area for children (which doubles as a music stage) help set the restaurant's cheerful, casual mood. On weekends come hear live folk and classical music; Tuesday evening is open-mike night. *5102 N. Pearl St., 2 blocks from the entrance to Point Defiance Park, tel. 206/752–4069. No reservations. Dress: casual. AE, MC, V. No alcohol. Inexpensive.*

Lodging **Sheraton Tacoma Hotel.** This attractive high rise is located in the heart of downtown, and is a popular site for conventions. The executive suites on the top floors (24th and 25th) have concierge service and Continental breakfasts. Amenities for the other rooms include great views of Commencement Bay and/or Mt. Rainier from almost every angle, and modern decor in elegant muted tones. Also on hand in the hotel are a lively European-style café, the Wintergarden, as well as a less formal restaurant and a lobby-level cocktail lounge. The Rose Room lounge at the top of the hotel has a well-stocked bar and a diverse lunch and dinner menu of seafoods, salads, and other fresh foods. *1320 Broadway Plaza, 98402, tel. 206/572–3200. 372 rooms. Facilities: restaurants, lounge, health club. AE, DC, MC, V. Expensive.*

Tacoma Dome Hotel. Situated near the Tacoma Dome, this hotel caters to people coming to see musical, sporting, and other events held there. Basic, standard-issue rooms are offered, with few amenities, but there is free airport service and pets are allowed. *2611 E. E St., 98421, tel. 206/572–7272. 164 rooms. Facilities: restaurant, lounge. AE, MC, V. Moderate–Expensive.*

Tenino
Dining
★

Alice's Restaurant. This homey restaurant, set in a rural farmhouse adjacent to the Johnson Creek Winery in the lovely Skookumchuck Valley, offers a cheerful, simple ambience reminiscent of a Norman Rockwell rendering. The food is surprisingly sophisticated and prix-fixe dinner costs vary depending on the entrée. These elegant six-course meals are innovative takes on classic American cuisine and are accompanied, naturally, by Johnson Creek wines. Vegetable appetizers, soup, a fish course, and home-baked bread are among the preludes to the robust entrées, which might be anything from wild game to oysters or steak. *19248 Johnson Creek Rd. E, tel. 206/264–2887. Reservations required. Dress: casual. MC, V. Closed Mon., Tues., and lunch. Moderate.*

The Arts and Nightlife

The Arts

In Bellingham, the **Museum of Natural History** and **Art and Allied Arts** (121 Prospect St., tel. 206/676–6981) sponsor monthly walks downtown, among the many art galleries.

On Long Beach Peninsula, call **The Playhouse Community Theater** (120 William St., NE, Ilwaco 98624, tel. 206/642–8686) for a calendar of events.

Western Washington University (*College of Fine Performing Arts, Western Washington College, 516 High St., tel. 206/676–3866*) has a high quality performing arts scene with classical music and theater presentations by local and national performers.

Nightlife

In Bellingham, **Speedy O. Tubs Rhythmic Underground** (*1305 11th St., Old Fairhaven, tel. 206/734–1539*) features rock and blues, rock and roll, and a drumming circle.

On the Olympic Peninsula, the **Fourth Avenue Tavern** (210 E. 4th Ave., Olympia, tel. 206/786–1444), a cheerful beer-and-wine joint offers live rock music on weekends. A favorite with locals, featuring live rock and roll on weekends, is **Back Alley** (923 Washington St., Port Townsend, tel. 206/385–2914).

7 Vancouver

Introduction

By Terri Wershler

Terri Wershler, publisher of Brighouse Press, a regional book publisher, is also the author of The Vancouver Guide.

Vancouver is a young city, even by North American standards. While three to four hundred years of settlement may make cities like Québec and Halifax historically interesting to travelers, Vancouver's youthful vigor attracts visitors with powerful elements not yet ground down by time. Vancouver is a mere 105 years old; it was not yet a town in 1870, when British Columbia became part of the Canadian confederation.

Vancouver's history, such as it is, remains visible to the naked eye. Eras are stacked east to west along the waterfront like some horizontal, century-old archaeological dig—from cobbled, late-Victorian Gastown to shiny postmodern glass cathedrals of commerce grazing the sunset.

The Chinese were among the first to recognize the possibilities of Vancouver's setting. They came to British Columbia during the 1850s seeking the gold that inspired them to name the province *Gum-shan*, or Gold Mountain. They built the Canadian Pacific Railway that gave Vancouver's original townsite a purpose—one beyond the natural splendor that Royal Navy Capt. George Vancouver admired during his lunchtime cruise around its harbor on June 13, 1792. The transcontinental railway, along with its Great White Fleet of clipper ships, gave Vancouver a full week's edge over the California ports in shipping tea to New York at the dawn of the 20th century.

Vancouver's natural charms are less scattered than in other cities. On clear days, the mountains appear close enough to touch. Two thousand-acre wilderness parks lie within the city limits. The saltwater of the Pacific and fresh water direct from the Rocky Mountain Trench form the city's northern and southern boundaries.

Bring a healthy sense of reverence when you visit: Vancouver is a spiritual place. For its original inhabitants, the Coast Salish peoples, it was the sacred spot where the mythical Thunderbird and Killer Whale flung wind and rain all about the heavens during their epic battles—how else to explain the coast's occasional climatic fits of temper? Devotees of a later religious tradition might worship in the sepulchre of Stanley Park or in the polished, incense-filled quiet of St. James Anglican Church, designed by English architect Sir Adrian Gilbert Scott and perhaps Vancouver's finest building.

Vancouver has a level of nightlife possible only in a place where the finer things in life have never been driven out to the suburbs and where sidewalks have never rolled up at 5 pm. There is no shortage of excellent hotels and restaurants here either. But you can find good theater, accommodations, and dining almost anywhere these days. Vancouver's *real* culture is in its tall fir trees practically downtown and its towering rock spires close by, the ocean at your doorstep and people from every corner of the earth all around you.

Essential Information

Arriving and Departing by Plane

Airport and Airlines International Airports — Vancouver International Airport is on an island about 14 kilometers (9 miles) south of downtown. The main terminal building has three levels: departures, international arrivals, and domestic arrivals; a small south terminal building services flights to secondary destinations within the province. **American Airlines** (tel. 800/433–7300), **Continental** (tel. 604/222–2442), **Delta** (tel. 604/682–5933), **Horizon Air** (800/547–9308), and **United** (tel. 604/683–7111) fly into the airport. The two major domestic airlines are **Air Canada** (tel. 604/688–5515) and **Canadian Airlines** (tel. 604/279–6611).

Other Facilities — **Air BC** (tel. 604/278–3800) offers 30-minute harbor-to-harbor service (downtown Vancouver to downtown Victoria) several times a day. Planes leave from near the Bayshore Hotel. Harbor-to-harbor service (Seattle to Vancouver) is run by **Lake Union Air** (tel. 800/826–1890). **Helijet Airways** (tel. 604/273–1414) has helicopter service from downtown Vancouver to downtown Victoria. The heliport is near Vancouver's Pan Pacific Hotel.

Between the Airport and Downtown — The drive from the airport to downtown is 20–45 minutes, depending on the time of day. Airport hotels offer free shuttle service to and from the airport.

By Bus — The **Airport Express** (tel. 604/273–9023) bus leaves the domestic arrivals level of the terminal building every 15 minutes, stopping at major downtown hotels and the bus depot. It operates from 5:30 AM until 12:30 AM. The fare is $7.25.

By Taxi — There are taxi stands in front of the terminal building on the domestic and international arrivals levels. Taxi fare to downtown is about $20. Area cab companies are **Yellow** (tel. 604/681–3311), **Black Top** (tel. 604/731–1111), and **MacLures** (tel. 604/731–9211).

By Limousine — Limousine service from **Airlimo** (tel. 604/273–1331) costs about the same as a taxi to downtown: The current rate is about $26.

Arriving and Departing

By Car — From the south, I-5 from Seattle becomes **Highway 99** at the U.S.–Canada border. Vancouver is a three-hour drive from Seattle. Avoid border crossings during peak times: holiday weekends, Friday evenings, Saturday mornings, and Sunday afternoons and evenings.

Highway 1, the **Trans-Canada Highway,** enters Vancouver from the east. If you enter the city after rush hour (8:30 AM), you should not have a problem with traffic.

By Ferry — **BC Ferries** operates two major ferry terminals outside Vancouver. From Tsawwassen to the south (an hour's drive from downtown), ferries sail 38 kilometers (24 miles) to Victoria on Vancouver Island and through the Gulf Islands (the small islands between the mainland and Vancouver Island). From Horseshoe Bay (30 minutes north from downtown), ferries sail a short distance up the coast and to Nanaimo on Vancouver Island. Call (tel. 604/685–1021) for departure and arrival times.

Vancouver Exploring *(Boxes Refer to Detail Maps)*

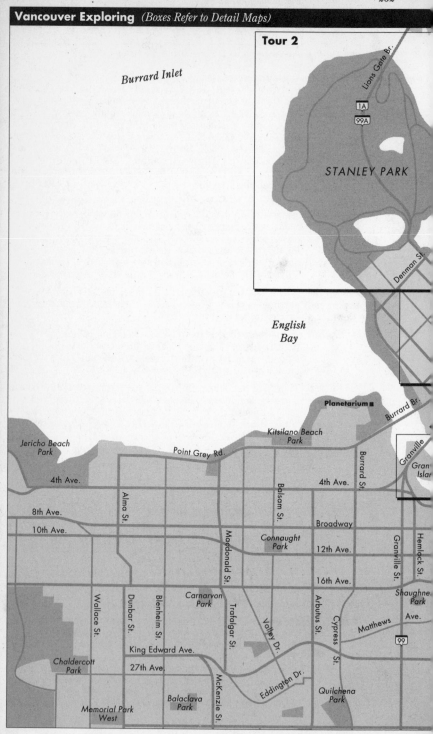

Tour 2

Burrard Inlet

Lions Gate Br.

1A
99A

STANLEY PARK

Denman St.

English
Bay

Planetarium ■

Burrard Br.

Kitsilano Beach
Park

Jericho Beach
Park

Point Grey Rd.

Granville

Gran
Islan

4th Ave.

4th Ave.

Burrard St.

Alma St.

Balsam St.

8th Ave.

Broadway

10th Ave.

Connaught
Park

12th Ave.

Granville St.

Hemlock St.

Macdonald St.

16th Ave.

Shaughne
Park

Wallace St.

Dunbar St.

Blenheim St.

Carnarvon
Park

Trafalgar St.

Arbutus St.

Cypress
St.

Ave.

Matthews

99

Valley Dr.

King Edward Ave.

27th Ave.

Chaldercott
Park

McKenzie St.

Eddington Dr.

Quilchena
Park

Memorial Park
West

Balaclava
Park

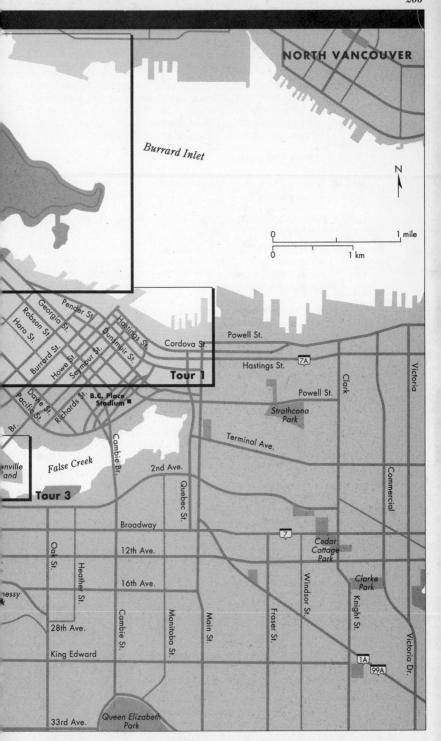

By Train The **VIA Rail** (tel. 800/561–8630) station is at Main Street and Terminal Avenue. VIA provides service through the Rockies to Banff. Passenger trains leave the **BC Rail** (tel. 604/631–3500) station in North Vancouver for Whistler and the interior of British Columbia. There is no Amtrak service from Seattle.

By Bus **Greyhound** (tel. 604/661–8747) is the biggest bus line servicing Vancouver. The **Vancouver bus depot** is at the corner of Dunsmuir and Cambie streets, a 10-minute walk from Georgia and Granville streets. **Quick Shuttle** (tel. 604/591–3571) bus service runs between Vancouver and Seattle four times a day.

Getting Around

By Car Although no freeways cross Vancouver, rush-hour traffic is not yet horrendous. The worst rush-hour bottlenecks are the North Shore bridges, the George Massey Tunnel on Highway 99 south of Vancouver, and Highway 1 through Coquitlam and Surrey.

By Subway Vancouver has a one-line, 25-kilometer (15-mile) rapid transit system called **SkyTrain** that travels underground downtown and is elevated for the rest of its route to New Westminster. Trains leave about every five minutes. Tickets must be carried with you as proof of payment. They are sold at each station from machines; correct change is not necessary. You may use transfers from Sky Train to Seabus and BC Transit buses (*see* below) and vice versa.

By Bus Exact change is needed to ride the buses: $1.25 adults, 65¢ for senior citizens and children 5–13. Books of 10 tickets are sold at convenience stores and newsstands; look for a red, white, and blue "Fare Dealer" sign. Day passes, good for unlimited travel after 9:30 AM, cost $3.50 for adults. They are available from fare dealers and any SeaBus or SkyTrain station.

By Taxi It is difficult to hail a cab in Vancouver; unless you're near a hotel, you'd have better luck calling a taxi service. Try **Yellow** (tel. 604/681–3311), **Black Top** (tel. 604/731–1111), or **MacLures** (tel. 604/731–9211).

By SeaBus The **SeaBus** is a 400-passenger commuter ferry that crosses Burrard Inlet from the foot of Lonsdale (North Vancouver) to downtown. The ride takes 13 minutes and costs the same as the transit bus. With a transfer, connection can be made with any BC Transit bus or SkyTrain.

Important Addresses and Numbers

Tourist Information **Vancouver Travel Infocentre** (1055 Dunsmuir St., tel. 604/683–2000) provides maps and information about the city, and is open in summer, daily 8–6; in winter, Monday–Saturday 9–5. A kiosk, located at Stanley Park in the Aquarium parking lot, is open mid-May–September, daily 10–6. The kiosk in Pacific Centre Mall is open daily in summer, Monday–Saturday 9:30–5, Sunday noon–5; in winter, Monday–Saturday 9–5. Eaton's department store downtown also has a tourist information counter that is open all year.

Embassies There are no embassies in Vancouver, only consulates and trade commissions: **United States** (1075 W. Georgia St., tel. 604/685–4311) and **United Kingdom** (800–1111 Melville St., tel. 604/

683–4421). For a complete listing, see the Yellow Pages under consulates.

Emergencies Call 911 for **police, fire department,** and **ambulance.**

Hospitals and **St. Paul's Hospital** (1081 Burrard St., tel. 604/682–2344), a ma-
Clinics jor downtown hospital, has an emergency ward. **Medicentre** (1055 Dunsmuir St., lower level, tel. 604/683–8138) is a drop-in clinic on the lower level of the Bentall Centre.

Dentist The counterpart to Medicentre is **Dentacentre** (1055 Dunsmuir St., lower level, tel. 604/669–6700), and is next door.

Late-night **Shopper's Drug Mart** (1125 Davie St., tel. 604/685–6445) is open
Pharmacy until midnight every night except Sunday, when it closes at 9 PM.

Road Emergencies **BCAA** (tel. 604/293–2222) has 24-hour emergency road service for members of AAA or CAA.

Travel Agencies **American Express Travel Service** (1040 W. Georgia St., tel. 604/669–2813), **Hagen's Travel** (210–850 W. Hastings St., tel. 604/684–2448), **P. Lawson Travel** (409 Granville St., tel. 604/682–4272).

Opening and Closing Times

Banks traditionally are open Monday–Thursday 10–3 and Friday 10–6, but many banks have extended hours and are open on Saturday, particularly in the suburbs.

Museums are generally open 10–5, including Saturday and Sunday. Most are open one evening a week as well.

Hours at **department stores** are Monday–Wednesday and Saturday 9:30–6, Thursday and Friday 9:30–9, and Sunday noon–5. Many smaller stores are also open Sunday. Robson Street and Chinatown are particularly good for Sunday shopping.

Guided Tours

Orientation **Gray Line** (tel. 604/681–8687), the largest tour operator, offers the 3½-hour Grand City bus tour year-round. Departing from the Hotel Vancouver, the tour includes Stanley Park, Chinatown, Gastown, English Bay, and Queen Elizabeth Park, and costs about $31. **City and Nature Sightseeing** (tel. 604/683–2112) accommodates up to 14 people in vans that run a 3½-hour City Highlights Tour for $25 (pick-up available from any downtown location). A short city tour (2½ hours) is offered by **Vance Tours** (tel. 604/222–1966) in their minibuses and costs $20.

North Shore tours usually include any or several of the following: a gondola ride up Grouse Mountain, a walk across the Capilano Suspension Bridge, a stop at a salmon hatchery, the Lonsdale Quay Market, and a ride back to town on the SeaBus. Half-day tours cost about $45 and are offered by **Landsea Tours** (tel. 604/687–5640), **Harbour Ferries** (tel. 604/687–9558), **Gray Line** (tel. 604/681–8687), **City and Nature** (tel. 604/683–2112), and **Pacific Coach Lines** (tel. 604/662–7575).

Air Tours Tour the mountains and fjords of the North Shore by helicopter for $149 per person for 45 minutes: **Vancouver Helicopters** (tel. 604/683–4354) flies from the Harbour Heliport downtown. Or see Vancouver from the air for $55 for 20 minutes: **Harbour Air's**

(tel. 604/688–1277) seaplanes leave from beside the Bayshore Hotel.

Boat Tours The Royal Hudson, Canada's only functioning steam train, heads along the mountainous coast up Howe Sound to the coastal logging town of Squamish. After a break to explore, you sail back to Vancouver via the M.V. *Britannia*. This highly recommended excursion costs $45, takes 6½ hours, and is organized by **Harbour Ferries** (tel. 604/687–9558). Reservations are necessary.

The **S.S.** *Beaver* (tel. 604/682–7284), a replica of a Hudson Bay fur-trading vessel that ran aground here in 1888, does two trips. One is the Harbour Sunset Dinner Cruise, a three-hour trip with a mesquite-grilled salmon dinner; the other is a daytime trip up Indian Arm with salmon for lunch. Each is about $35. Reservations are necessary.

Harbour Ferries (tel. 604/687–9558) takes a 1½-hour tour of the Burrard Inlet in a paddle wheeler. Including pick-up from a downtown hotel, the cost is $18.

Fraser River Tours (tel. 604/250–3458 or 604/584–5517) will take you on a 4-hour tour of a fascinating working river—past log booms, tugs, and houseboats. The cruiser, *Atria Star*, leaves from Westminster Quay Market (a handy destination from downtown via SkyTrain) and costs $25.

Personal Guides **Fridge's Early Motion Tours** (tel. 604/687–5088) covers Vancouver in a Model-A Ford convertible. Minimum charge is $45 or $18 per person for an hour-long trip around downtown, Chinatown, and Stanley Park.

AAA Horse & Carriage (tel. 604/681–5115) will pick you up at your downtown hotel and take you for a ride in Stanley Park for $100 an hour.

Walking Pick up "A Self-Guided Walking Tour of Downtown Vancouver," published by Tourism Vancouver (Vancouver Travel Infocentre, 1055 Dunsmuir St., tel. 604/683–2000).

Exploring Vancouver

Orientation

The heart of Vancouver—which includes the downtown area, Stanley Park, and the West End high-rise residential neighborhood—sits on a peninsula bordered by English Bay and the Pacific Ocean to the west; by False Creek, an inlet on which you will find Granville Island, to the south; and to the north by Burrard Inlet, the working port of the city, past which loom the North Shore mountains. The oldest part of the city—Gastown and Chinatown—lies at the edge of Burrard Inlet, around Main Street, which runs north–south and is roughly the dividing line between the east side and the west side. All the avenues, which are numbered, have east and west designations.

Highlights for First-time Visitors

Chinatown (*see* Tour 1: Downtown Vancouver)
English Bay (*see* Tour 2: Stanley Park)
Granville Island (*see* Tour 3: Granville Island)

Robson Street (*see* Shopping, below)
Stanley Park (*see* Tour 2: Stanley Park)

Tour 1: Downtown Vancouver

*Numbers in the margin correspond to points of interest on the
Tour 1: Downtown Vancouver map.*

❶ You can logically begin your downtown tour in either of two
ways. If you're in for a day of shopping, amble down **Robson
Street** (*see* Shopping, below), where you'll find any item from
souvenirs to high fashions, from espresso to muffins.

❷ If you opt otherwise, start at **Robson Square,** built in 1975 and
designed by architect Arthur Erickson to be the gathering
place of downtown Vancouver. The complex, which functions
from the outside as a park, encompasses the Vancouver Art
Gallery and government offices and courts that have been built
under landscaped walkways, a block-long glass canopy, and a
waterfall that helps mask traffic noise. An ice-skating rink and
restaurants occupy the below-street level.

❸ The **Vancouver Art Gallery** that heads the Square was a neoclas-
sical-style 1912 courthouse until Erickson converted it in 1980.
Notice some original details: The lions that guard the majestic
front steps and the use of columns and domes are features bor-
rowed from ancient Roman architecture. In the back of the old
courthouse, a more modest staircase now serves as a speakers'
corner. *750 Hornby St., tel. 604/682–5621. Admission: $3.75
adults, $2.25 students and senior citizens; free Thurs. eve.
Open Mon., Wed., Fri., and Sat. 10–5, Thurs. 10–9, Sun.
noon–5.*

❹ Adjacent to the art gallery, on Hornby Street, is the **Hotel Vancouver** (1939), one of the last of the railway-built hotels. (The
last one built was the Chateau Whistler, in 1989.) Reminiscent
of a medieval French castle, this château style has been incorporated into hotels throughout every major Canadian city.
With the onset of the Depression, construction was halted
here, and the hotel was finished only in time for the visit of
King George VI in 1939. It has been renovated twice: During
the 1960s it was unfortunately modernized, but the more recent refurbishment is more in keeping with the spirit of what is
the most recognizable roof on Vancouver's skyline. The exteri-
or of the building has carvings of malevolent gargoyles at the
corners, an ornate chimney, Indian chiefs on the Hornby Street
side, and an assortment of grotesque mythological figures.

❺ **Christ Church Cathedral** (1895), across the street from the Hotel Vancouver, is the oldest church in Vancouver. The tiny
church was built in a Gothic style with buttresses and pointed
arched windows and looks like the parish church of an English
village. By contrast, the cathedral's rough-hewn interior is
that of a frontier town, with Douglas-fir beams and carpenter
woodwork that offers excellent acoustics for the frequent ves-
pers, carol services, and Gregorian chants presented here. *690
Burrard St., tel. 604/682–3848.*

❻ The **Marine Building** (1931), at the foot of Burrard Street, is
Canada's best example of Art Deco style. Terra-cotta bas-
reliefs depict the history of transportation: Airships, biplanes,
steamships, locomotives, and submarines are figured. These
motifs were once considered radical and modernistic adorn-

258

Tour 1: Downtown Vancouver

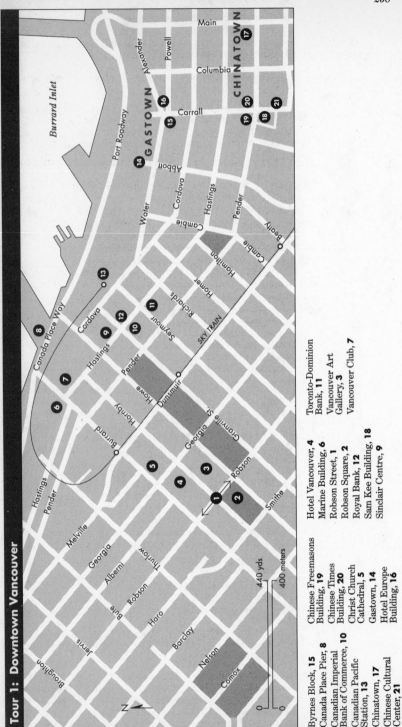

Byrnes Block, **15**
Canada Place Pier, **8**
Canadian Imperial
Bank of Commerce, **10**
Canadian Pacific
Station, **13**
Chinatown, **17**
Chinese Cultural
Center, **21**

Chinese Freemasons
Building, **19**
Chinese Times
Building, **20**
Christ Church
Cathedral, **5**
Gastown, **14**
Hotel Europe
Building, **16**

Hotel Vancouver, **4**
Marine Building, **6**
Robson Street, **1**
Robson Square, **2**
Royal Bank, **12**
Sam Kee Building, **18**
Sinclair Centre, **9**

Toronto-Dominion
Bank, **11**
Vancouver Art
Gallery, **3**
Vancouver Club, **7**

ments since most buildings were still using classical or Gothic ornamentation. From the east, the Marine Building is reflected in bronze by 999 West Hastings, and in silver from the southeast by the Canadian Imperial Bank of Commerce. Stand on the corner of Hastings and Hornby streets for the best view of the Marine Building.

A nice walk is along Hastings Street—the old financial district. Until the 1966–1972 period, when the first of the bank towers and underground malls on West Georgia Street were developed, this was Canada's westernmost business terminus. The temple-style banks, businessmen's clubs, and investment houses survive as evidence of the city's sophisticated architec-
7 tural advances prior to World War I. The **Vancouver Club,** built between 1912 and 1914, was a gathering place for the city's elite. Its architectural design is reminiscent of private clubs in England that were inspired by Italian Renaissance palaces. The Vancouver Club is still a private businessmen's club. *915 W. Hastings St., tel. 604/685–9321.*

8 The foot of Howe Street, north of Hastings, is **Canada Place Pier.** Converted into Vancouver's Trade and Convention Center after Expo 86, Canada Place was originally built on an old cargo pier to be the off-site Canadian pavilion. It is dominated at the shore end by the luxurious Pan Pacific Hotel (*see* Lodging, below), with its spectacular three-story lobby and waterfall. The convention space is covered by a fabric roof shaped like 10 sails, which has become a landmark of Vancouver's skyline. Below is a cruise-ship facility, and at the north end are an Imax theater, restaurant, and outdoor performance space. A promenade runs along the pier's west side with views of the Burrard Inlet harbor and Stanley Park. *999 Canada Pl., tel. 604/682–1070.*

9 Walk back up to Hastings and Howe streets to the **Sinclair Centre.** Vancouver's outstanding architect, Richard Henriquez, has knitted four government office buildings (built 1905–1939) into an office-retail complex. The two Hastings Street buildings—the 1905 post office with the elegant clock tower and the 1913 Winch Building—are linked with the Post Office Extension and Customs Examining Warehouse to the north. Painstaking and very costly restoration involved finding master masons—the original terrazzo suppliers in Europe—and uncovering and refurbishing the pressed-metal ceilings.

Canada has a handful of old chartered banks; the oldest and
10 most impressive of these is the former **Canadian Imperial Bank of Commerce** headquarters (1906–1908) at Hastings and Granville streets; the columns, arches, and details are of typically
11 Roman influence. The **Toronto-Dominion Bank,** one block east, is of the same style, but was built in 1920.

Backtracking, directly across from the CIBC on Hastings
12 Street, is the more Gothic **Royal Bank.** It was intended to be half of a symmetrical building that was never completed, due to the Depression. Striking, though, is the magnificent hall, ecclesiastical in style, reminiscent of a European cathedral.

13 At the foot of Seymour Street is the **Canadian Pacific Station,** the third and most pretentious of three CPR passenger terminals. Built 1912–1914, this terminal replaced the other two as the western terminus for Canada's transcontinental railway. After Canada's railways merged, the station became obsolete until a 1978 renovation turned it into an office-retail complex and SeaBus Terminal. Murals in the waiting rooms show passengers what kind of scenery to expect on their journeys across Canada.

From Seymour Street, pick up Water Street, on your way to **14 Gastown.** Named after the original townsite saloon keeper, "Gassy" Jack Deighton, Gastown is where Vancouver originated. Deighton arrived at Burrard Inlet in 1867 with his Indian wife, a barrel of whiskey, and few amenities. A statue of Gassy Jack stands on the north side of Maple Tree Square, the intersection of five streets, where he built his first saloon.

When the transcontinental train arrived in 1887, Gastown became the transfer point for trade with the Orient and was soon crowded with hotels and warehouses. The Klondike gold rush encouraged further development until 1912, when the "Golden Years" ended. The 1930s–1950s saw hotels being converted into rooming houses and the warehouse district shifting elsewhere. The area gradually became unattended and rundown. However, both Gastown and Chinatown were declared historic areas and revitalization projects are underway.

15 The **Byrnes Block** building was constructed on the corner of Water and Carrall streets (the site of Gassy Jack's second saloon) after the 1886 Great Fire. The date is just visible at the top of the building above the door where it says "Herman Block," which was its name for a short time. The extravagantly detailed Alhambra Hotel that was situated here was luxury class for the time, at a cost of a dollar a night.

Tucked behind 2 Water Street is **Blood Alley** and **Gaoler's Mews.** Once the site of the city's first civic buildings—the constable's cabin and courthouse, and a two-cell log jail—today the cobblestone street with antique streetlighting is the home to architectural offices.

16 The **Hotel Europe** (1908–1909), a flatiron building at Powell and Alexander streets, was billed as the best hotel in the city, and was Vancouver's first reinforced concrete structure. Designed as a functional commercial building, the hotel lacks ornamentation and fine detail, a style unusually utilitarian for the time.

From Maple Tree Square, walk three blocks up Carrall Street **17** to Pender Street, where **Chinatown** begins. There was already a sizable Chinese community in British Columbia because of the 1858 Cariboo gold rush in central British Columbia, but the biggest influx from China occurred in the 1880s, during construction of the Canadian Pacific Railway, when 15,000 laborers were imported. The Chinese were among the first inhabitants of Vancouver, and some of the oldest buildings in the city are in Chinatown.

Even while doing the hazardous work of blasting the railbed through the Rocky Mountains, the Chinese were discriminated against. The Anti-Asiatic Riots of 1907 stopped growth in Chinatown for 50 years and immigration from China was discouraged by more and more restrictive policies, climaxing in a $500 head tax during the 1920s.

In the 1960s the city council was planning bulldozer urban renewal for Strathcona, the residential part of Chinatown, and freeway connections through the most historic blocks of Chinatown were charted. Fortunately, plans were halted and today Chinatown is an expanding, vital district fueled by investment from Vancouver's most notable newcomers—immigrants from Hong Kong. It is best to view the buildings in Chinatown from the south side of Pender Street, where the Chinese Cultural Center stands. From here you'll get a better view of important details that adorn the upper stories. The style of architecture typical in Vancouver's Chinatown is patterned on that of Canton, and won't be seen in any other Canadian cities.

⑱ The corner of Carrall and East Pender streets, now the western boundary of Chinatown, is one of the neighborhood's most historic spots. Standing at 8 West Pender Street is the **Sam Kee Building,** recognized by *Ripley's Believe It Or Not!* as the narrowest building in the world. The 1913 structure still exists, with its bay windows overhanging the street and a basement that burrows under the sidewalk.

⑲ The **Chinese Freemasons Building** (1901) at 1 West Pender Street has two completely different styles of facades: The side facing Chinatown displays a fine example of Cantonese-imported recessed balconies; on the Carrall Street side, the standard Victorian style common throughout the British Empire is displayed. It was in this building that Dr. Sun Yat-sen hid for months from the agents of the Manchu dynasty while he raised funds for its overthrow, which he accomplished in 1911.

⑳ Directly across Carrall Street is the **Chinese Times Building,** constructed in 1902. Inside, there is a hidden mezzanine floor from which police officers could hear the clicking sounds of clandestine mah-jongg games played after sunset. Attempts by vice squads to enforce restrictive policies against the Chinese gamblers proved fruitless because police were unable to find the players who were hidden on the secret floor.

㉑ Planning for the **Chinese Cultural Center** and Dr. Sun Yat-sen Gardens (1980–87) began during the late-1960s; the first phase was designed by James Cheng, a former associate of Arthur Erickson. The cultural center has exhibition space, classrooms, and meeting rooms. The **Dr. Sun Yat-sen Gardens** located behind the cultural center, were built by 52 artisans from Suzhou, the Garden City of the People's Republic. The gardens incorporate design elements and traditional materials from several of that city's centuries-old private gardens and are the first living classical Chinese gardens built outside China. As you walk through the gardens, remember that no power tools, screws, or nails were used in the construction. *Dr. Sun Yat-sen Gardens. 578 Carrall St., tel. 604/689–7133. Admission: $3.50 adults, $2.50 senior citizens and students, $7 family. Open May–Sept., daily 10–8; Oct.–Apr., daily 10–4:30.*

Tour 2: Stanley Park

Numbers in the margin correspond to points of interest on the Tour 2: Stanley Park map.

A 1,000-acre wilderness park just blocks from the downtown section of a major city is a rarity, but is one of Vancouver's major attractions. In the 1860s, due to a threat of American invasion, the area that is now Stanley Park was set aside as a military reserve (though it was never needed). When the City of Vancouver was incorporated in 1886, the council's first act was to request that the land be set aside for a park. In 1888 permission was granted and the grounds were named Stanley Park after Lord Stanley, then Governor-General of Canada (the same person after whom hockey's Stanley Cup is named).

An afternoon in Stanley Park gives you a capsule tour of Vancouver that includes beaches, the ocean, the harbor, Douglas fir and cedar forests, and a good look at the North Shore mountains. The park sits on a peninsula and along the shore is a 9-kilometer (5½-mile) long pathway called the seawall. You can walk or bicycle all the way around, or follow the shorter route, suggested below.

Bicycles are for rent at the foot of Georgia Street near the park entrance. Cyclists must ride in a counterclockwise direction and stay on their side of the path. A good place for pedestrians (22) to start is at the foot of Alberni Street beside **Lost Lagoon.** Go through the underpass and veer right to the seawall.

(23) The old wood structure that you pass is the **Vancouver Rowing Club,** a private athletic club (established 1903), a bit farther (24) along is the **Royal Vancouver Yacht Club.**

(25) About ½ kilometer (⅓ mile) away is the causeway to **Deadman's Island,** a former burial ground for the local Salish Indians and the early settlers. It is now a small naval training base called the HMCS *Discovery* that is not open to the public. Just ahead (26) is the **Nine O'Clock Gun,** a cannonlike apparatus that sits by the water's edge. Originally used to alert fishermen of a curfew ending weekend fishing, now it automatically signals every night at 9.

(27) Farther along is **Brockton Point,** and its small but functional lighthouse and foghorn. The **totem poles,** which are situated more inland, make a popular photo spot for tourists. Totem poles were not carved in the Vancouver area; these were brought to the park from the north coast of British Columbia and were carved by the Kwakiutl and Haida peoples late in the last century. These cedar poles with carved animals, fish, birds, or mythological creatures were like a family coat-of-arms or crest.

(28) At kilometer 3 (mile 2) is **Lumberman's Arch,** a huge log archway dedicated to the workers in Vancouver's first industry. Beside the arch is an asphalt path that leads back to Lost Lagoon, for those who want a shorter walk. (This is about a third of the (29) distance.) This path also leads to the **Vancouver Public Aquarium,** with killer and beluga whale shows several times a day. Also part of this attraction is the humid Amazon rain-forest gallery, through which you can walk, with its piranhas, giant cockroaches, alligators, tropical birds, and jungle vegetation. Other displays show the underwater life of coastal British Columbia, the Canadian arctic, and other areas of the world. The Clamshell Gift Shop next to the aquarium is the best spot in town for quality souvenirs and gifts, most with an emphasis on natural history. *Aquarium, tel. 604/682–1118. Admission: $8 adults, $7 senior citizens and youths, $5 children 5–12. Open daily in summer 9:30–8; daily in winter 10–5:30. Clamshell open July–Labor Day, daily 9:30–8; rest of year, daily 10–6.*

(30) Next to the aquarium is the **Stanley Park Zoo,** a friendly place, easily seen in an hour or two. Except for the polar bears, most

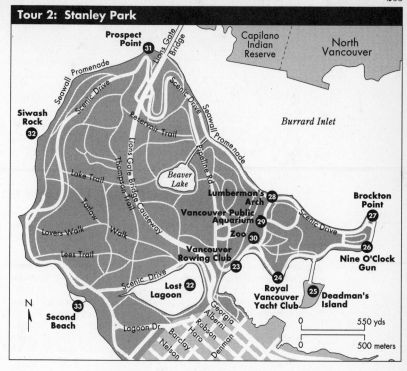

Tour 2: Stanley Park

Prospect Point · 31 · Lions Gate Bridge

Capilano Indian Reserve · North Vancouver

Siwash Rock · 32

Burrard Inlet

Seawall Promenade · Scenic Drive · Reservoir Trail · Pipeline Rd · Seawall Promenade

Lions Gate Bridge Causeway · Thompson Trail · Lake Trail

Beaver Lake

Lumberman's Arch · 28

Vancouver Public Aquarium · 29

Zoo · 30

Brockton Point · 27

Nine O'Clock Gun · 26

Tatlow Walk · Lovers Walk · Lees Trail

Vancouver Rowing Club · 23

Scenic Drive · Lost Lagoon · 22

Royal Vancouver Yacht Club · 24

Deadman's Island · 25

N

Second Beach · 33

Georgia · Alberni · Robson · Haro · Dennman · Barclay · Nelson · Lagoon Dr.

0 ___ 550 yds

0 ___ 500 meters

of the animals are small—monkeys, seals, exotic birds, penguins, and playful otters.

About 1 kilometer (¾ mile) farther is the **Lions Gate Bridge**—the halfway point of the seawall. On the other side of the bridge is **Prospect Point,** where you can see cormorants in their seaweed nests on the ledges along the cliffs. The large black diving birds are recognized by their long necks and beaks; when not nesting, they often perch atop floating logs or boulders. Another remarkable bird found along the shore in the park is the beautiful great blue heron. Reaching up to 4-feet tall with a wing span of 6 feet, the heron preys on passing fish in the waters here. The oldest heron rookery in British Columbia is in the trees around the zoo.

Continuing around the seawall you will come to the **English Bay** side and the beginning of sandy beaches. The imposing rock just off shore is **Siwash Rock.** Legend tells of a young Indian who, about to become a father, bathed persistently to wash his sins away so that his son could be born pure, and for his devotion he was blessed by the gods and immortalized in the shape of Siwash Rock. Two small rocks, said to be his wife and child, are just up on the cliff above the site.

Time Out Along the seawall is one of Vancouver's best restaurants, the **Ferguson Point Teahouse.** Set on the great lawn among Douglas fir and cedar trees, the restaurant is the perfect stopover for a summer weekend lunch or brunch. If you just want a snack, a park concession stand is also at Ferguson Point.

㉝ The next attraction along the seawall is the large saltwater pool at **Second Beach.** In the summer it is a children's pool with life-guards, but during winter the pool is drained and skate-boarders perform stunts. At the pool you can take a shortcut back to Lost Lagoon. To take the shortcut, walk along the per-pendicular road behind the pool that cuts into the park. The wood footbridge that's ahead will lead you to a path along the south side of the lagoon and to your starting point at the foot of Alberni or Georgia street.

If you continue along the seawall, it will emerge out of the park into a high-rise residential neighborhood, the **West End.** You can walk back to Alberni Street along Denman Street where there are plenty of places to stop for coffee, ice cream, or a drink.

Tour 3: Granville Island

Numbers in the margin correspond to points of interest on the Tour 3: Granville Island map.

Granville Island was just a sandbar until World War I when the nearby creek was dredged for access to the sawmills that lined the shore. Sludge heaped on the sandbar gradually created the island that was then used to house supplies for the logging in-dustry. In 1971 the federal government bought the island with an imaginative plan to refurbish it and introduce a public mar-ket, marine activities, and artisans' studios. The opposite shore of False Creek was the site of the 1986 World's Fair and is now part of the largest urban redevelopment plan in North America.

The small island is almost strictly commercial except for a small houseboat community. Most of the previously used industrial buildings and tin sheds have been retained, but are painted in upbeat reds, yellows, and blues. The government regulates the types of businesses that settle on Granville Island; only busi-nesses involving food, crafts, marine activities, and the arts are permitted here.

Access on foot to Granville Island starts with a 15-minute walk from downtown Vancouver to the south end of Thurlow Street. From a dock behind the Vancouver Aquatic Center, the Gran-ville Island ferry leaves every six minutes for the short trip across False Creek to the Granville Island Public Market. These pudgy boats are a great way to see the sights on False Creek, but for a longer ride, go to the Maritime Museum (1905 Ogden St., tel. 604/737–2211). For more information call Gran-ville Island Ferries (tel. 604/684–7781).

Another option is to take a 20-minute ride on a BC Transit (tel. 604/261–5100) bus. Take a UBC, Granville, Arbutus, Cambie, or Oak bus from downtown to Granville and Broadway and transfer to the Granville Island bus No. 51. Parking is limited, but if you must take a car, go early in the week and early in the day to avoid crowds. Parking is free for only three hours; an al-ternative is to use the pay parking buildings on the island if you can find a space.

㉞ The ferry to Granville Island will drop you off at the **Granville Island Public Market.** Although there are a few good food stores outside, most stalls are enclosed in the 50,000-square-foot building. Since the government allows no chains, each out-

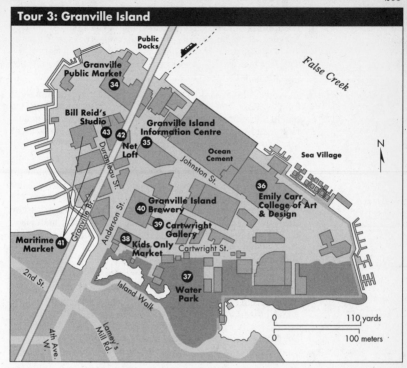

Tour 3: Granville Island

let is unique, and most are of good quality. You probably won't
be able to leave the market without a snack, espresso, or fix-
ings for a lunch out on the wharf. Don't miss the charcoal-
grilled oysters from **Sea-kist,** fish chowder or bouillabaisse
from the **Stock Market,** fresh fudge at **Olde World Fudge,** or
smoked salmon from the **Salmon Shop.** In the summer you'll see
mounds of raspberries, strawberries, blueberries, and even
more exotic fruits like persimmons and lychees. On the water
side of the market is lots of outdoor seating. *Public Market.
Tel. 604/666–5784. Open June–Aug., daily 9–6; closed Mon.
Sept.–May except holidays.*

35 The **Granville Island Information Centre,** kitty-corner to the
market, is a good place to get oriented with the island. Maps
are available and a slide show depicts the evolution of Granville
Island. Ask here about special-events days; perhaps there's a
boat show, outdoor symphony concert, dance performance, or
some other happening. *1592 Johnston St., tel. 604/666–5784.
Open daily 10–6.*

Continue walking south on Johnston Street, along a clockwise
loop of the island. Next is **Ocean Cement,** one of the last of the
island's former industries; its lease does not expire until the
year 2004.

36 Next door is the **Emily Carr College of Art and Design.** Just inside the front door, to your right, is the **Charles H. Scott Gallery.** This gallery hosts contemporary multi-media exhibits.
*1399 Johnston St., tel. 604/687–2345. Open daily 11–5, Thurs.
11–8.*

Past the art school, on the left, is one of the only **houseboat communities** in Vancouver; others have been banned by the city because of problems with sewage and property taxes. The owners of this community appealed the ban and won special status. Take the boardwalk that starts at the houseboats and continues partway around the island.

37 As you circle around to Cartwright Street, stop in **Kakali** at number 1249, where you can watch the process of making fine handmade paper from all sorts of materials like bluejeans, herbs, and sequins. Another unusual artisan on the island is the glassblower at 1440 Old Bridge Street, around the corner.

The next two attractions will make any child's visit to Granville Island a thrill. First, on Cartwright Street, is the children's **38** **water park**, with a wading pool, sprinklers, and a fire hydrant made for children to shower each other. A bit farther down, be-**39** side Isadora's restaurant, is the **Kids Only Market,** with two floors of small shops selling toys, arts-and-crafts materials, dolls, records and tapes, chemistry sets, and other sorts of kid stuff. *Water park. 1318 Cartwright St., tel. 604/665–3425. Admission free. Open June–Aug., daily 10–6. Kids Only Market. 1496 Cartwright St., tel. 604/689–8447. Open June–Aug., daily 10–6; Sept.–May, Tues.–Sun. 10–6.*

40 Across from the Kids Only Market is the **Cartwright Gallery,** which hosts such temporary exhibits as native Indian and local crafts and intriguing traveling exhibits. *1141 Cartwright St., tel. 604/687–8266. Open Tues.–Sat. 10–5, Sun. 11–3.*

41 At the **Granville Island Brewery,** next door, you can take a half-hour tour every afternoon; at the end of the tour, sample the Granville Island Lager that is produced here and sold locally in most restaurants. *Tel. 604/688–9927. Admission free. Tours run Mon.–Fri. at 2; Sat. and Sun. at 1 and 3.*

Cross Anderson Street and walk down Duranleau Street. On your left, the scuba diving pool in **Adrenalin Sports** marks the **42** start of the **Maritime Market,** a string of businesses all geared to the sea. The first walkway to the left, Maritime Mews, leads to marinas and dry docks. There are dozens of outfits in the Maritime Market that charter boats (with or without skippers) or run cruise-and-learn trips.

Another way to take to the water is by kayak. Take a lesson or rent a kayak from **Ecomarine Ocean Kayak Center** (1668 Duranleau St., tel. 604/689–7575). Owner John Dowd is considered *the* expert on Pacific Northwest ocean kayaking.

Time Out **Bridges** (1696 Duranleau St., tel. 604/687–4400), in the bright yellow building across from the market, is a good spot to have lunch, especially on a warm summer's day. Eat on the spacious deck that looks out on the sailboats, fishing boats, and other water activities.

The last place to explore on Granville Island is the blue building **43** next to Ecomarine on Duranleau Street, the **Net Loft.** The loft is a collection of small, quality stores—good places to find a gift to take home: bookstore, crafts store/gallery, kitchenware shop, postcard shop, custom-made hat shop, handmade paper store, British Columbian native Indian gallery, do-it-yourself jewelry store, and more reside here.

Behind Blackberry Books, in the Net Loft complex, is the
⑭ **studio of Bill Reid,** British Columbia's most respected Haida
Indian carver. His *The Raven and the First Men* (which took
five carvers more than three years to complete) is in the Museum of Anthropology (*see* Other Museums, below). Reid's Pacific
Northwest Coast Indian artworks are world-renowned. Although you can't visit the studio, there are large windows
through which you can look.

Since you have come full circle, you can either take the ferry
back to downtown Vancouver, or stay for dinner and catch a
play at the **Arts Club** (tel. 604/687–1644) or **Waterfront Theater**
(tel. 604/685–6217).

Other Museums

The **Maritime Museum** traces the history of marine activities on
the west coast. Permanent exhibits depict the port of Vancouver, the fishing industry, and early explorers; the model ships
on display are a delight. Traveling exhibits vary, but always
have a maritime theme. Guided tours are led through the dou-
ble-masted schooner, the *St. Roch*, the first ship to sail in both
directions through the treacherous Northwest Passage. A
changing variety of restored heritage boats, from different cultures, are moored behind the museum and a huge Kwakiutl totem pole stands out front. *North foot of Cypress St., tel. 604/
737–2211. Admission: $4 adults, $2.50 children, students, and
senior citizens, $8 families; free Wed. eve. Open daily 10–5,
Wed. 10–9. Access available by the Granville Island ferries.*

The **Museum of Anthropology,** focusing on the arts of the Pacific Northwest Indians, is Vancouver's most spectacular museum. Situated on the campus of the University of British
Columbia, the museum is housed in an award-winning glass
and concrete structure designed by Arthur Erickson. In the
Great Hall are large and dramatic totem poles, ceremonial
archways, and dugout canoes—all adorned with carvings of
frogs, eagles, ravens, bears, and salmon. Also showcased are
exquisite carvings of gold, silver, and argillite (a black stone
found in the Queen Charlotte Islands). Masks, tools, and costumes from many other cultures are also displayed. A ceramics
wing, housing 600 pieces from 15th- to 19th-century Europe
opened in 1990. *6393 N.W. Marine Dr., tel. 604/228–3825. Admission: $4 adults, $2 youths (13–18) and senior citizens, $1
children; free on Tues. Open Tues. 11–9, Wed.–Sun. 11–5.*

Science World is in a gigantic shiny dome that was built for
Expo 86 for an Omnimax Theater—the world's largest dome
screen. Science World is not a traditional museum, but is very
much hands-on. Visitors are encouraged to touch and to participate in the theme exhibits. A special gallery, the Search Gallery, is aimed at younger children, as are the fun-filled
demonstrations given in Center Stage. *1455 Québec St., tel.
604/687–7832. Admission to Science World: $7 adults, $4.50
senior citizens and children. Admission to Omnimax is the
same; for admission to both you get a discount. Open daily
10–5, Saturday 10–9.*

Vancouver Museum displays permanent exhibits that focus on
the city's early history and native art and culture. Life-size
replicas of an 1897 CPR passenger car, trading post, Victorian
parlor, and a real dugout canoe are highlights. Also on the site

are the Planetarium and Observatory (*see* Off the Beaten Track, below). *1100 Chestnut St., tel. 604/736–7736. Admission: $5 adults, $2.50 senior citizens and children. Open Tues.–Sun. 10–5 in winter, daily 10–5 in summer.*

Parks and Gardens

Nitobe Garden is a small (2.4-acre) garden that is considered the most authentic Japanese garden outside Japan. The circular path around the park symbolizes the cycle of life and provides a tranquil view from every direction. In April and May cherry blossoms are the highlight, and in June the irises are magnificent. *1903 West Mall, Univ. of B.C., tel. 604/228–4208. Admission: $1.75 adults, $1 senior citizens and students, free Wed. and every day Oct. 11–Mar. 17. Open daily 10–dusk in summer; Mon.–Fri. in winter; phone for specific closing times.*

Pacific Spirit Park (W. 16th Ave., tel. 604/224–5739) is a 1,000-acre park that is bigger and more rugged than Stanley Park. Pacific Spirit's only amenities are 30 miles of trails, a few washrooms, and a couple of signboard maps. Go for a wonderful walk in the west coast woods—it's hard to believe that you are only 15 minutes from downtown Vancouver.

Queen Elizabeth Park has lavish gardens and lots of grassy picnicking spots. Illuminated fountains; the botanical Bloedel Conservatory, with tropical and desert zones and 20 species of free-flying tropical birds; and other facilities including 20 tennis courts, lawn bowling, pitch and putt, and a restaurant are on the grounds. *Cambie St. and 25th Ave., tel. 604/872–5513. Admission to conservatory: $2.70 adults, $1.35 senior citizens and students, $5.40 family ticket. Open May–Sept., daily 10–9; Oct.–Apr., daily 10–5.*

Van Dusen Botanical Garden was a 55-acre golf course, but is now the grounds of one of the largest collections of ornamental plants in Canada. Native and exotic plant displays include the shrubbery maze and the rhododendrons in May and June. *5251 Oak St. at 37th Ave., tel. 604/266–7194. Admission: $4.25 adults, $2.15 senior citizens and youths (13–18), $8.50 family ticket. Open 10–dusk.*

Vancouver for Free

Several public galleries and museums are free on certain days: The **Vancouver Art Gallery** (750 Hornby St., tel. 604/682–5621) is free on Thursday evenings; the **Maritime Museum** (1950 Ogden St., tel. 604/737–2211) is free Wednesday evenings for shanty-singing night; the **Museum of Anthropology** (6393 N.W. Marine Dr., tel. 604/228–3825) is free Tuesday. The **Vancouver Museum** (1100 Chestnut St., tel. 604/736–7736) is free on the first Thursday evening of every month. It is also free every Tuesday for senior citizens.

Also free is the **Beatles Museum** (456 Seymour St., tel. 604/685–8841), with memorabilia from the early years of the Fab Four.

What to See and Do with Children

Stanley Park Zoo (*see* Tour 2: Stanley Park, above).

The **miniature steam train** in Stanley Park, just five minutes northwest of the aquarium, is a big hit with children as it chugs through the forest.

Splashdown Park (Hwy. 17, just before the Tsawwassen Ferry causeway, tel. 604/943–2251), 38 kilometers (24 miles) outside Vancouver, is a giant water-slide park with 11 slides (for toddlers to adults), heated water, picnic tables, and minigolf.

Richmond Nature Park (No. 5 Rd. exit from Hwy. 99, tel. 604/ 273–7015), with its displays and games in the Nature House, is geared toward children. Guides answer questions and give tours. Since the park sits on a natural bog, rubber boots are recommended if it's been wet, but a boardwalk around the duck pond makes some of the park accessible to strollers and wheelchairs.

Maplewood Farms (405 Seymour River Pl., tel. 604/929–5610), a 20-minute drive from downtown Vancouver, is set up like a small farm, with all the barnyard animals for children to see and pet. Cows are milked every day at 1:15.

Kids Only Market (*see* Tour 3: Granville Island, above).

The Planetarium (1100 Chestnut St., tel. 604/736–3656), on the same site as the Vancouver Museum in Vanier Park, has astronomy shows each afternoon and evening, and laser rock music shows later in the night.

Science World (*see* Other Museums, above)

Off the Beaten Track

On the North Shore you can get a taste of the mountains and test your mettle at the **Lynn Canyon Suspension Bridge** (Lynn Headwaters Regional Park, North Vancouver, tel. 604/987– 5922), which hangs 240 feet above Lynn Creek. Also on the North Shore is the **Capilano Fish Hatchery** (4500 Capilano Rd., tel. 604/987–1411), with exhibits about salmon.

If the sky is clear, the telescope at the **Gordon Southam Observatory** (1100 Chestnut St., in Vanier Park, tel. 604/738–2855) will be focused on whatever stars or planets are worth watching that night. While you're there, visit the planetarium on the site.

Shopping

Unlike many cities where suburban malls have taken over, Vancouver's downtown area is still lined with individual boutiques and specialty shops. Stores tend to be open every day and on Thursday and Friday nights.

Shopping Districts

The immense **Pacific Center Mall,** in the heart of downtown, connects Eaton's and The Bay department stores, which stand at opposite corners of Georgia and Granville streets. Pacific Center is on two levels and is mostly underground.

A new commercial center is developing around **Sinclair Center** (*see* Tour 1, above), which caters to sophisticated and upscale tastes.

On the opposite side of Pacific Center, stretching from Burrard to Bute streets, is **Robson Street**—the place for fashion-conscious clothing. Chockablock with small stores and cafés, it is Vancouver's liveliest street and provides many excellent corners for people-watching.

Two other shopping districts, one on **West 41st Avenue,** between West Boulevard and Larch Street, in Kerrisdale, and the other on **West 10th** from Discovery Street west, are both in upscale neighborhoods and have quality shops and restaurants.

Fourth Avenue, from Burrard to Balsam streets, offers an eclectic mix of stores (from sophisticated women's clothing to surfboards and Jams), with an emphasis on sports shops.

In addition to the Pacific Center Mall, **Oakridge Shopping Center** at Cambie Street and 41st Avenue has chic, expensive stores that are fun to browse.

Ethnic Districts **Chinatown** (*see* Tour 1, above)—centered around Pender and Main streets—is an exciting and animated place for restaurants, exotic foodstuffs, and distinctive architecture.

Commercial Drive (around East 1st Avenue) is the heart of the **Italian community,** here called Little Italy. You can sip cappuccino in coffee bars where you may be the only one speaking English, buy sun-dried tomatoes, real Parmesan, or an espresso machine.

The **East Indian shopping district** is on Main Street around 50th Avenue. Curry houses, sweet shops, grocery stores, and sari shops abound.

A small **Japantown** on Powell Street at Dunlevy Street is made up of grocery stores, fish stores, and a few restaurants.

Department Stores

The two biggest department stores in Vancouver, **Eaton's** and **The Bay,** are Canadian owned and located downtown and at most malls. The third, **Woodward's,** is a local chain and is found only in British Columbia and Alberta. The flagship store is in the Oakridge Shopping Center.

Flea Markets

A huge flea market (703 Terminal Ave., tel. 604/685–0666), with more than 300 stalls, is held Saturday, Sunday, and holidays from 8 to 4. This is easily accessible from downtown via SkyTrain.

Auctions

On Wednesday at noon and 7 PM, auctions are held at **Love's** (1635 W. Broadway, tel. 604/733–1157). **Maynard's** (415 W. 2nd Ave., tel. 604/876–6787) also has home furnishings auctions on Wednesday at 7 PM. Phone for times of art and antiques auctions.

Specialty Stores

Antiques A stretch of antiques stores runs along Main Street from 19th to 35th avenues. On 10th Avenue near Alma are a few antiques stores that specialize in Canadiana, including **Folkart Interiors** (3715 W. 10th Ave.), and **Old Country Mouse Factory** (3720 W. 10th Ave.). Also try **Canada West** (3607 W. Broadway). For very refined antiques, see **Artemis** (321 Water St.) in Gastown. For Oriental rugs, go to Granville Street between 7th and 14th avenues.

Art Galleries There are many private galleries throughout Vancouver. The best of them are: **Bau-Xi** (3045 Granville St., tel. 604/733–7011), **Buschlen-Mowatt** (1445 W. Georgia St., tel. 604/682–1234), **Diane Farris** (1565 W. 7th Ave., tel. 604/737–2629), **Equinox** (2321 Granville St., tel. 604/736–2405), and the **Heffel Gallery** (2247 Granville St., tel. 604/732–6505).

Books The best general bookstores are **Duthie's,** located downtown (919 Robson St.) and near the university (4444 W. 10th Ave.), and **Blackberry Books** (1663 Duranleau St.) on Granville Island.

Specialty bookstores include: **The Travel Bug** (2667 W. Broadway) and **World Wide Books and Maps** (736 Granville St., downstairs) for travel books, **Vancouver Kidsbooks** (3083 W. Broadway), **Sportsbooks Plus** (230 W. Broadway), and **Pink Peppercorn** (2686 W. Broadway) for cookbooks, and **William McCarley** (213 Carrall St.) for design and architecture.

Most of the secondhand and antiquarian dealers such as **William Hoffer** (60 Powell St.) and **Colophon Books** (407 W. Cordova St., upstairs), are in the Gastown area. A block or two away are **McLeod's** (455 W. Pender St.), **Ainsworth's** (321 W. Pender St.), and **Bond's** (319 W. Hastings St.). **Lawrence Books** (3591 W. 41st Ave.) is out of the way but is probably the best used bookstore in town.

Children's Stores An unusual children's store worth checking out is **The Imagination Market** (528 Powell St.), an oddball warehouse-type store selling recycled industrial goods for arts and crafts materials: barrels of metallic plastic, feathers, fluorescent-colored paper, buttons, bits of Plexiglas, and other materials by the bagful.

Clothing
Men Several quality men's clothing stores are in the business district: **Edward Chapman** (833 W. Pender St.) has conservative looks; **E.A. Lee** (466 Howe St.) is stylish; **Leone** (757 W. Hastings St.) is ultra-chic; and **Polo Country** (375 Water St.) offers a casual line of Ralph Lauren.

A few blocks away, at Pacific Center, are **Harry Rosen** and **Holt Renfrew,** both on the upper level. If your tastes are traditional, don't miss **George Straith** (900 W. Georgia St.) in the Hotel Vancouver.

On Robson Street, a more trendy shopping area, are **Ralph Lauren** (No. 1123) and **Club Monaco** (No. 1153), for casual wear.

Outside downtown Vancouver there are two men's boutiques selling Italian imports: **Mondo Uomo** (2709 Granville St.) and **Boboli** (2776 Granville St.).

In Kerrisdale, two excellent men's clothing stores are **Finn's** (2159 W. 41st Ave.) and, across the street, **S. Lampman** (2126 W. 41st Ave.).

Women For women's fashions, visit **E.A. Lee** (466 Howe St.), **Wear Else?** (789 W. Pender St.), **Leone** (757 W. Hastings St.), and the more conservative **Chapy's** (833 W. Pender St.), all in the business district. Nearby is the casual **Polo Country** (375 Water St.).

On Robson Street, look for **Margareta** (No. 948), **Ralph Lauren** (No. 1123), **Alfred Sung** (No. 1143), **Club Monaco** (No. 1153), and a lingerie shop, **La Vie en Rose** (No. 1001). For shoes, try **Aldo** (No. 1016), **Pegabo** (No. 1137), and **Stephane de Raucourt** (No. 1024). Off Robson is **Morgan** (813 Hornby St.).

Two expensive and very stylish import stores in South Granville are: **Boboli** (2776 Granville St.) and **Bacci** (2788 Granville St.). Nearby, one of the largest and best shoe stores in town is **Freedman Shoes** (2867 Granville St.).

On the west side **Enda B.** (4346 W. 10th Ave.) and **Wear Else?** (2360 W. 4th Ave.) are the largest and best stores for high-quality fashions, but there's also **Bali Bali** for the more exotic (4462 W. 10th Ave.) and **Zig Zag** (4424 W. 10th Ave.) for fashion accessories.

Gifts Want something special to take home from British Columbia? The best places for quality souvenirs are the **Vancouver Art Gallery** (750 Hornby St.) and the **Clamshell Gift Shop** at the aquarium in Stanley Park. The **Salmon Shop** in the Granville Island Public Market will wrap smoked salmon for travel. Downtown, Haida and Salish Indian art is available at **Images for a Canadian Heritage** (779 Burrard St.). Near Granville Island is **Leona Lattimer** (1590 W. 2nd Ave.), where the inside of her shop is built like an Indian longhouse and is full of Indian arts and crafts ranging from cheap to priceless.

Sports and Outdoor Activities

Participant Sports

Biking **Stanley Park** (*see* Tour 2 in Exploring Vancouver, above) is the most popular spot for family cycling. Rentals are available here from **Bayshore Bicycles** (745 Denman St., tel. 604/688–2453) or around the corner at **Stanley Park Rentals** (676 Chilco St., tel. 604/681–5581).

Another biking route is along the north or south shore of **False Creek.** Rent bikes at **Reckless Rider** (1840 Fir St., tel. 604/736–7325), near Granville Island.

Fishing You can fish for salmon all year in coastal British Columbia. **Sewell's Landing Marina** (6695 Nelson St., Horseshoe Bay, tel. 604/921–7461) organizes a daily four-hour trip on Howe Sound or has hourly rates on U-drives. **Bayshore Yacht Charters** (1601 W. Georgia St., tel. 604/682–3377) has a daily five-hour fishing trip; boats are moored five minutes from downtown Vancouver. **Island Charters** (Duranleau St., Granville Island, tel. 604/688–6625) arranges charters or boat shares and supplies all gear.

Golf Lower Mainland golf courses are open all year. **Fraserview Golf Course** (tel. 604/327–3717), a spacious course with fairways well defined by hills and mature conifers and deciduous trees, is the busiest course in the country. Fraserview is also the most central, about 20 minutes from downtown. **Seymour Golf and Country Club** (tel. 604/929–5491), on the south side of Mt. Seymour, on the North Shore, is a semiprivate club that is open to the public on Monday and Friday. One of the finest public courses in the country is **Peace Portal** (tel. 604/538–4818), near White Rock, a 45-minute drive from downtown.

Health and Fitness Clubs Both the **YMCA** (955 Burrard St., tel. 604/681–0221) and the **YWCA** (580 Burrard St., tel. 604/683–2531) downtown have drop-in rates that let you participate in all activities for the day. Both have pools, weight rooms, and fitness classes; the YMCA has racquetball, squash, and handball courts. Two other recommended clubs are: **Chancery Squash Club** (202–865 Hornby St., tel. 604/682–3752) and **Tower Courts Racquet and Fitness Club** (1055 Dunsmuir St., lower level, tel. 604/689–4424), both with racquet courts, weight rooms, and aerobics.

Hiking **Pacific Spirit Park** is a 1,000-acre wilderness park, with 30 miles of hiking trails (*see* Parks and Gardens, above).

The **Capilano Regional Park,** (*see* Off the Beaten Track, in Exploring Vancouver, above), on the North Shore, provides a scenic hike.

Jogging The seawall around **Stanley Park** (*see* Tour 2 in Exploring Vancouver, above), is 9 kilometers (5½ miles) and gives an excellent minitour of the city. A shorter run of 4 kilometers (2½ miles) in the park is around **Lost Lagoon**.

Skiing
Cross-country The best cross-country skiing is at **Hollyburn Ridge** in Cypress Park (tel. 604/925–2704).

Downhill Vancouver is two hours away from **Whistler/Blackcomb** (Whistler Resort Association, tel. 604/685–3650; snow report, tel. 604/687–7507), one of the top ski spots in North America.

There are three ski areas on the North Shore mountains, close to Vancouver, with night skiing. The snow is not as good as at Whistler and runs are generally used by novice, junior, and family skiers or those who want a quick ski after work. **Cypress Park** (tel. 604/926–5612; snow report, tel. 604/926–6007) has the most and the longest runs; **Grouse Mountain** (tel. 604/986–0661; snow report, tel. 604/980–6262) has extensive night skiing, restaurants, and bars; and **Mt. Seymour** (tel. 604/986–2261; snow report, tel. 604/986–3444) is the highest in the area, so the snow is a little better.

Water Sports
Kayaking Rent a kayak from **Ecomarine** (tel. 604/689–7575) on Granville Island (*see* Tour 3 in Exploring Vancouver, above).

Rafting The Thompson, the Chilliwack, and the Fraser are the principal rafting rivers in southwestern British Columbia. The Fraser River has whirlpools and big waves, but for frothing white water, try the Thompson and Chilliwack rivers. Trips range from three hours to several days. Some well-qualified outfitters that lead trips are: **Kumsheen** (Lytton, tel. 604/455–2296; in B.C., tel. 800/482–2269), **Hyak** (Vancouver, tel. 604/734–8622), and **Canadian River Expeditions** (Vancouver, tel. 604/736–4449).

Sailing Several charter companies offer a cruise-and-learn vacation, usually to the Gulf Islands. The five-day trip is a crash course teaching the ins and outs of sailing. The **Westcoast School of Seamanship** (Granville Island, tel. 604/689–9440), **Sea Wing**

(Granville Island, tel. 604/669–0840), **Pacific Quest** (Granville Island, tel. 604/682–2205), and **Blue Orca** (Granville Island, tel. 604/687–4110) offer this package.

Windsurfing Rental shops clustered on the west side of town include: **Surf City** (420 W. 1st Ave., tel. 604/872–8585), **The Windsurfing Shop** (1793 W. 4th Ave., tel. 604/734–7245), and at **Windsure** (Jericho Beach, tel. 604/224–0615). Boards can also be rented at **Jericho Beach** or **English Bay Beach** (Davie and Denman Sts.).

Spectator Sports

The **Vancouver Canucks** (tel. 604/254–5141) of the National Hockey League play in the Coliseum October–April. The **Canadians** (tel. 604/872–5232) play baseball in an old-time outdoor stadium in the Pacific Coast League. Their season runs April–September. The **B.C. Lions** (tel. 604/681–5466) football team scrimmage at the B.C. Place Stadium downtown June–November. Tickets are available from Ticketmaster (tel. 604/280–4444).

Beaches

An almost continuous string of beaches runs from Stanley Park to the University of British Columbia. Children and hardy swimmers can take the cool water but most others prefer to sunbathe; these beaches are sandy with grassy areas running alongside. Note that liquor is prohibited in parks and on beaches. For information on beaches, call the **Parks Department of the City of Vancouver** (tel. 604/681–1141).

Kitsilano Beach. Kits Beach, with a lifeguard, is the busiest of them all—transistor radios, volleyball games, and sleek young bodies are ever-present. The part of the beach nearest the Maritime Museum is the quietest. Facilities include a playground, tennis courts, heated saltwater pool (good for serious swimmers to toddlers), concession stands, and many nearby restaurants to cafés.

Point Grey Beaches. Jericho, Locarno, and Spanish Banks begin at the end of Point Grey Road. This string of beaches has a huge expanse of sand, especially in the summer and at low tide. The shallow water here is warmed slightly by the sun and the sand and so is best for swimming. Farther out, toward Spanish Banks, you'll find the beach becomes less crowded, but the last concession stand and washrooms are at Locarno. If you keep walking along the beach just past Point Grey, you'll hit Wreck Beach, Vancouver's nude beach. It is also accessible from Marine Drive at the university but there is a fairly steep climb from the beach to the road.

West End Beaches. Second Beach and Third Beach, along Beach Drive in Stanley Park, are large family beaches. Second Beach has a guarded saltwater pool. Both have concession stands and washrooms. Farther along Beach Drive, at the foot of Jervis Street, is Sunset Beach, a surprisingly quiet beach considering the location. A lifeguard is on duty, but there are no facilities.

Dining

Among other allures, experiencing Vancouver's diverse gas-
tronomical pleasures makes a visit to the city worthwhile. Restaurants appear throughout Vancouver—from the bustling
downtown area to trendy beach-side neighborhoods—making
the diversity of the establishment's surroundings as enticing as
the succulent cuisine they serve. A new wave of Chinese immigration and Japanese tourism has brought a proliferation of upscale Chinese and Japanese restaurants, offering dishes that
would be at home in their own leading cities. Restaurants featuring Pacific Northwest fare—including homegrown regional
favorites such as salmon and oysters, accompanied by British
Columbia and Washington State wines—have become some of
the city's leading attractions.

Highly recommended restaurants are indicated by a star ★.

Category	*Cost
Very Expensive	over $41
Expensive	$31—$40
Moderate	$21—$30
Inexpensive	under $20

*per person, including appetizer, entrée and dessert; exclud-
ing drinks, service, and sales tax

American

Isadora's. Not only does Isadora's offer good coffee, a menu
that ranges from samosas to lox and bagels, and children's specials, but there is also an inside play area packed with toys, and
restrooms with changing tables accommodate families. In the
summer, the restaurant opens onto Granville Island's water-
park, so kids can entertain themselves. Service can be slow,
but Isadora's staff is friendly. *1540 Old Bridge St., Granville
Island, tel.604/681–8816. Reservations required for 6 or more.
Dress: casual. Closed dinner Mon. Sept–May. MC, V. Inexpensive.*

Nazarre BBQ Chicken. The best barbecued chicken in several hundred miles comes from this funky storefront on Commercial Drive. Owner Gerry Moutal massages his chickens
for tenderness before he puts them on the rotisserie, then
bastes them in a mixture of rum and spices. Chicken comes
with roasted potatoes and a choice of mild, hot, extra hot,
or hot garlic sauce. You can eat in, at one of four rickety tables, or take out. *1408 Commercial Dr., tel. 604/251–1844.
No reservations. Dress: casual. No credit cards. Inexpensive.*

**Cambodian/
Vietnamese**

Phnom Penh Restaurant. A block away from the bustle of
Keefer Street, the Phnom Penh is part of a small cluster of
Southeast Asian shops on the fringes of Chinatown. Simple,
pleasant decor abounds: arborite tables, potted plants, and
framed views of Ankor Wat on the walls. Hospitable staff
serves unusually robust Vietnamese fare including crisp, peppery garlic prawns fried in the shell and slices of beef crusted
with ground salt and pepper mixed in the warm beef salad. *244
E. Georgia St., tel. 604/682–5777. No reservations for lunch;*

276

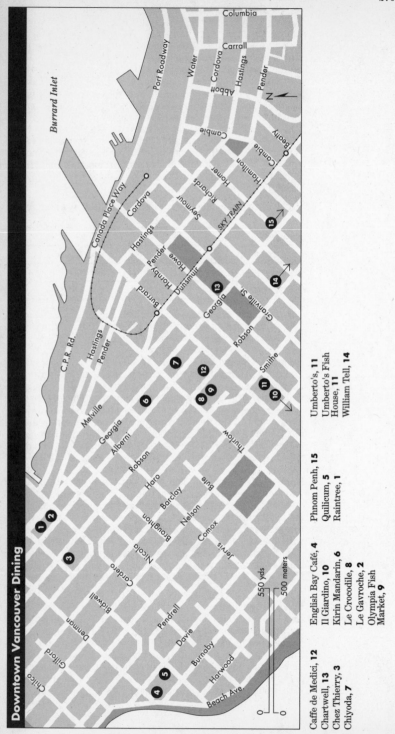

Downtown Vancouver Dining

Caffe de Medici, **12**
Chartwell, **13**
Chez Thierry, **3**
Chiyoda, **7**

English Bay Café, **4**
Il Giardino, **10**
Kirin Mandarin, **6**
Le Crocodile, **8**
Le Gavroche, **2**
Olympia Fish
Market, **9**

Phnom Penh, **15**
Quilicum, **5**
Raintree, **1**

Umberto's, **11**
Umberto's Fish
House, **11**
William Tell, **14**

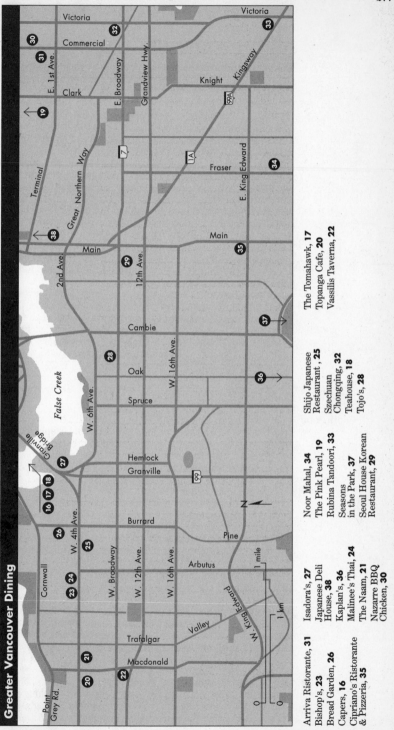

277

Greater Vancouver Dining

Arriva Ristorante, **31**
Bishop's, **23**
Bread Garden, **26**
Capers, **16**
Cipriano's Ristorante & Pizzeria, **35**

Isadora's, **27**
Japanese Deli House, **38**
Kaplan's, **36**
Malinee's Thai, **24**
The Naam, **21**
Nazarre BBQ Chicken, **30**

Noor Mahal, **34**
The Pink Pearl, **19**
Rubina Tandoori, **33**
Seasons in the Park, **37**
Seoul House Korean Restaurant, **29**

Shijo Japanese Restaurant, **25**
Szechuan Chongqing, **32**
Teahouse, **18**
Tojo's, **28**

The Tomahawk, **17**
Topanga Cafe, **20**
Vassilis Taverna, **22**

advised for dinner. Dress: casual. MC, V. Closed Tues. Inexpensive.

Chinese **Kirin Mandarin Restaurant.** Kirin, located two blocks from
★ most of the major downtown hotels, presents attentively
served Chinese food in posh, elegant surroundings. Live fish in
tanks set into the slate green walls remind one of aquariums
displayed in a lavishly decorated home. Drawn from a smattering of northern Chinese cuisines, dishes include Shanghai-style
smoked eel, Peking duck, and Szechuan hot-and-spicy scallops.
*1166 Alberni St., tel. 604/682–8833. Reservations advised.
Dress: neat but casual. AE, MC, V. Closed for 2 days, 15 days
after Chinese New Year. Moderate.*

★ **The Pink Pearl.** In the world of Cantonese restaurants, biggest
may very well be best: This 650-seat restaurant certainly wins
the prize in this city. The huge, noisy room features tanks of
live seafood—crab, shrimp, geoduck, oysters, abalone, rock
cod, lobsters, and scallops. Menu highlights include clams in
black bean sauce, crab sautéed with five spices (a spicy dish
sometimes translated as crab with peppery salt), and Pink
Pearl's version of crispy-skinned chicken. Arrive early for dim
sum on the weekend if you don't want to be caught in the lineup.
*1132 E. Hastings St., tel. 604/253–4316. Reservations advised.
Dress: casual. AE, MC, V. Inexpensive.*

★ **Szechuan Chongqing.** Although fancier Szechuan restaurants
can be found, the continued popularity of this unpretentious
white tablecloth restaurant in a revamped fried chicken franchise speaks for itself. Try the Szechuan-style fried green
beans, steamed and tossed with spiced ground pork or the
Chongqing chicken—a boneless chicken served on a bed of
spinach cooked in dry heat until crisp, giving it the texture of
dried seaweed and a salty, rich, and nutty taste. *2495 Victoria
Dr., tel. 604/254–7434. Reservations advised. Dress: casual.
AE, MC, V. Inexpensive.*

Continental **Chartwell.** Named after Sir Winston Churchill's country home
★ (a painting of which hangs over the green marble fireplace), the
flagship dining room at the Four Seasons Hotel (*see* Lodging,
below) looks like an upperclass British men's club. Floor-to-
ceiling dark wood paneling, deep leather chairs to sink back in
and sip claret, plus a quiet setting make this the city's top spot
for a power lunch. Chef Wolfgang von Weiser (formerly of the
Four Seasons in Toronto) cooks robust, inventive Continental
food. A salad of smoked loin of wild boar comes sprinkled with
hazelnuts; the seafood pot au feu is served with fennel bread
and aioli. Conclude the meal with port and Stilton. *791 W. Georgia St., tel. 604/689–9333. Reservations advised. Jacket required. AE, DC, MC, V. Expensive.*

Seasons in the Park. Seasons has a commanding view over the
park gardens to the city lights and the mountains beyond. A
comfortable room with lots of light wood, white tablecloths,
and deep-pile carpeting, this restaurant in Queen Elizabeth
Park serves a conservative Continental menu with standards
such as grilled salmon with fresh mint and roast duck with Bing
cherry sauce. *Queen Elizabeth Park, tel. 604/874–8008. Reservations advised. Dress: neat but casual. AE, MC, V. Closed
Christmas Day. Expensive.*

★ **The Teahouse Restaurant at Ferguson Point.** The best of the
Stanley Park restaurants is perfectly poised for watching sunsets over the water, especially from its newer wing, a glassed-
in room that conveys a conservatory-like ambience. Although

the teahouse has a less innovative menu than its sister restaurant, Seasons in the Park, certain features, including the cream of carrot soup, duck in cassis, and the perfectly grilled fish don't need any meddling. For dessert, there's baked Alaska—a natural for this restaurant. *Ferguson Point in Stanley Park, tel. 604/669–3281. Reservations required. Dress: neat but casual. AE, MC, V. Closed Christmas Day. Expensive.*

The William Tell. Silver underliners, embossed linen napkins, and a silver flower vase on each table set the tone of Swiss luxury. The William Tell's 27-year reputation for excellent Continental food continues at its quarters on the main floor of the Georgian Court Hotel, located 10 minutes from the central business district. Chef Pierre Dubrelle, a member of the gold medal-winning Canadian team at the 1988 Culinary Olympics, offers locally raised pheasant with glazed grapes and red wine sauce, sautéed veal sweetbreads with red onion marmalade and marsala sauce, as well as the Swiss specialty *Buendnerfleisch* (paper-thin slices of air-dried beef). Professional and discreet service contribute to the restaurant's excellence. *765 Beatty St., tel. 604/688–3504. Reservations advised. Jacket required at dinner. AE, DC, MC, V. Expensive.*

English Bay Café. Downstairs, the English Bay Café is a noisy tapas bistro serving nachos, crabcakes, and other grazing food. Upstairs, in the more serious dining room, you'll find the chef's fondness for venison and racks of lamb. Regardless of the level, however, when you look out the windows, it's all the same: With English Bay just two lanes of traffic away, you're guaranteed a glorious view of the sunset. Both bars are substantial; the bistro offers a large choice of imported beers, while the upstairs features jalapeño-pepper martinis. Valet parking is available and well worth the money. *1795 Beach Ave., tel. 604/669–2225. Reservations required. Dress: casual downstairs; neat but casual upstairs. AE, DC, MC, V. Moderate.*

Deli/Bakery **The Bread Garden Bakery, Café & Espresso Bar.** What began as a croissant bakery has taken over two neighboring stores, and is now the ultimate Kitsilano 24-hour hangout. Salads, smoked salmon pizzas, quiches, elaborate cakes and pies, giant muffins, and cappuccino bring a steady stream of the young and fashionable. The Bread Garden To Go, next door, serves over-the-counter, but you may still be subjected to an irritatingly long wait in line; things just don't happen fast here. *1880 W. 1st Ave., tel. 604/ 738–6684; 812 Bute St., tel. 604/688–3213. No reservations. Dress: casual. DC, MC, V. Inexpensive.*

★ **Kaplan's Deli, Restaurant and Bakery.** Tucked into a mini-mall on Oak Street (the road that leads to the Tsawwassen ferries and Seattle), Kaplan's is the traveler's last chance for authentic Jewish deli food before leaving town. Eat in at booths, or take your chopped liver, chopped herring, lox, and home-made corned beef with you. The bakery makes justly famous cinnamon buns. *5775 Oak St., tel. 604/263–2625. No reservations. Dress: casual. MC, V. Closed Jewish holidays. Inexpensive.*

East Indian **Rubina Tandoori.** If one must single out the best East Indian
★ food in the city, then Rubina Tandoori, 20 minutes from downtown, ranks as a top contender. The large menu spans most of the subcontinent's cuisines, and the especially popular *chevda* (East Indian salty snack,) gets shipped to fans all over North America. Maitre d' Shaffeen Jamal has a phenomenal memory for faces. Nonsmokers get the smaller, funkier back room with the paintings of coupling gods and goddesses; smokers get the

big, upholstered banquettes in the new room. *1962 Kingsway, tel. 604/874–3621. Reservations advised on weekends. Dress: casual. AE, MC, V. Closed lunch Sun. Moderate.*

Noor Mahal. The only Lower Mainland restaurant that specializes in South Indian food, the Noor Mahal provides good-sized portions at a reasonable price in authentic surroundings. The pink walls help to create the light and airy decor. Try a *dosa*—a lacy pancake made from bean, rice, and semolina flour, stuffed with curried potatoes, shrimp, or chicken—for lunch. Owners Susan and Paul Singh double as staff so service can be slow and harried during busy periods. *4354 Fraser St., tel. 604/873–9263. Reservations advised on weekends. Dress: casual. AE, MC, V. Closed lunch Mon. and Tues. Inexpensive.*

French **Le Gavroche.** Time has stood still in this charming turn-of-the-
★ century house, where a woman dining with a man will be offered a menu without prices. Featuring classic French cooking, lightened—but by no means reduced—to nouvelle cuisine, Le Gavroche's menu also includes simple listings such as smoked salmon with blinis and sour cream. Other options may be as complex as smoked pheasant breast on a puree of celeriac, shallots, and wine with a light truffle sauce. The excellent wine list stresses Bordeaux. Tables by the front window promise mountains and water views. *1616 Alberni St., tel. 604/685–3924. Reservations advised on weekends. Jacket and tie advised. AE, DC, MC, V. Closed Dec. 24–Jan. 1. Expensive.*

Chez Thierry. This cozy bistro on the Stanley Park end of Robson Street adds pizzazz to a celebration: Owner Thierry Damilano stylishly slashes open champagne bottles with a sword on request. The country-style French cooking emphasizes seafood. Try watercress and smoked salmon salad; fresh tuna grilled with artichokes, garlic, and tomatoes; and apple tarte Tatin for dessert. During the week the intimate dining room promises a relaxing meal; on the weekend, however, with every one of the 16 tables jammed, the restaurant gets noisy. *1674 Robson St., tel. 604/688–0919. Reservations required on weekends. Dress: casual. AE, DC, MC, V. Closed lunch; Dec. 24–26. Moderate.*

★ **Le Crocodile.** Why do people want to sit packed tighter than sardines in this tiny bistro? Because chef Michael Jacob serves extremely well-cooked simple food at very moderate prices. His Alsatian background shines with the caramelly, sweet onion tart. Anything that involves innards is superb, and even old standards such as duck à l'orange are worth ordering here. The one flaw? A small, overpriced wine list. *818 Thurlow St., tel. 604/669–4298. Reservations required. Jacket advised. AE, MC, V. Closed lunch; Sat., Sun. Moderate.*

Greek **Vassilis Taverna.** The menu in this family-run restaurant, located in the heart of the city's small Greek community, is almost as conventional as the decor: checked tablecloths and mandatory paintings of white fishing villages and the blue Aegean Sea. At Vassilis, though, even standards become memorable due to the flawless preparation. The house specialty is a deceptively simple *kotopoulo* (a half-chicken, pounded flat, herbed, and charbroiled); the lamb fricassee with artichoke hearts and broad beans in an egg-lemon sauce is more complicated, though not necessarily better. Save room for a *navarino*, a creamy custard square topped with whipped cream and ground nuts. *2884 W. Broadway, tel. 604/733–3231. Reserva-*

*tions advised on weekends. Dress: casual. AE, DC, MC, V.
Closed lunch Mon.; Sat. and Sun. Moderate.*

Health Food   **Capers.** Hidden in the back of the most lavishly handsome
health food store in the Lower Mainland, Capers (open for
breakfast, lunch, and dinner), drips with earth-mother chic:
wood tables, potted plants, and heady smells from the store's
bakery. Breakfast starts weekdays at 7, weekends at 8. Eggs
and bacon? Sure, but Capers serves free-range eggs, and bacon
without additives. Feather-light blueberry pancakes,
crammed with berries star here. The view of the water com-
pensates for service that can be slow and forgetful. *2496 Marine Dr., W. Vancouver, tel. 604/925-3316. No reservations.
Dress: casual. MC, V. Inexpensive.*

★   **The Naam Restaurant.** Vancouver's oldest alternative restaurant is now open 24 hours, so those needing to satisfy a late-
night tofu burger craving, rest easy. The Naam has left its caf-
feine- and alcohol-free days behind, and now serves wine, beer,
cappuccinos, and wicked chocolate desserts, along with the
vegetarian stir-fries. Wood tables and kitchen chairs make for
a homey atmosphere. On warm summer evenings, the outdoor
courtyard at the back of the restaurant welcomes diners. *2724
W. 4th Ave., tel. 604/738-7151. Reservations required for 6 or
more. Dress: casual. MC, V. Inexpensive.*

Italian   **Caffe de Medici.** It takes shifting gears as you leave the stark
★   concrete walls of the Robson Galleria behind and step into this
elegant restaurant with its ornate molded ceilings, rich green
velvet curtains and chair coverings, and portraits of the Medici
family. But after a little wine, an evening's exposure to courtly
waiters, and a superb meal, you may begin to wish the outside
world conformed more closely to this peaceful environment.
Although an enticing antipasto table sits in the center of the
room, consider the *Bresaola* (air-dried beef marinated in olive
oil, lemon, and pepper) as a worthwhile appetizer. Try the rack
of lamb in a mint, mustard, and Martini & Rossi sauce. Any of
the pastas is a safe bet. *1025 Robson St., tel. 604/669-9322.
Reservations advised. Jacket advised. AE, DC, MC, V. Closed
lunch Sat. and Sun. Expensive.*

Arriva Ristorante. Commercial Drive Italian restaurants, like
Chinese restaurants in Chinatown, are best looked at with a
skeptical eye. The best of the breed are elsewhere, what's left is
often found cranking out North Americanized travesties of the
home country's food. Arriva is one Little Italy restaurant
that's worth the drive, and a welcome find if you've spent the
day shopping in Italian groceries. There's a version of spaghet-
ti and meatballs on the menu, ziti with spicy squid sauce, and a
fusili with wild game—"Bambi and Bugs Bunny," as the waiters have affectionately coined it. The antipasto plate includes a
heaping order of octopus, shrimp, roasted red peppers, cheese,
sausage, and fat lima beans in a herby marinade. Don't miss the
orange sherbet served in a hollowed-out orange for dessert.
*1537 Commercial Dr., tel. 604/251-1177. Reservations ad-
vised. Dress: casual. AE, MC, V. Closed lunch Sat. and Sun.
Moderate.*

Il Giardino di Umberto, Umberto's. First came Umberto's, a
Florentine restaurant serving classic northern Italian food, in-
stalled in a century-old Vancouver home at the foot of Hornby
Street. Then, next door, Umberto Menghi built Il Giardino, a
sunny, light-splashed restaurant styled after a Tuscan house.
This restaurant features braided breast of pheasant with po-

lenta and reindeer filet with crushed peppercorn sauce. Where
Il Giardino attracts a regular young, moneyed crowd,
Umberto's is more quiet and sedate. Fish is treated either Ital-
ian style—rainbow trout grilled and served with sun-dried to-
matoes, black olives, and pine-nuts—or with a taste of the far
east, as in yellow-fin tuna grilled with wasabi butter. *Il
Giardino, 1382 Hornby St., tel. 604/669–2422. Umberto's, 1380
Hornby St., tel. 604/687–6316. Reservations advised. Dress:
neat but casual. AE, DC, MC, V. Umberto's closed lunch and
Sun. Moderate.*

Cipriano's Ristorante & Pizzeria. Formerly a Greek pizza parlor, Cipriano's has been transformed into an Italian restaurant,
with green-white-and-red walls representing the Italian flag,
Mama-mia!—inexpensive and hearty Italian food is the mainstay here, including good pizza, even better pasta, and the
"Pappa" lasagna. *3995 Main St., tel. 604/879–0020. Reservations accepted. Dress: casual. V. Closed lunch. Inexpensive.*

Japanese
★

Tojo's. Hidekazu Tojo is a sushi-making legend here. His handsome blond-wood tatami rooms, on the second floor of a new
green-glass tower in the hospital district on West Broadway,
provide proper ambience for intimate dining, but Tojo's 10-seat
sushi bar stands as the centerpiece. With Tojo presiding, this is
a convivial place for dinner, and a ringside seat for watching
the creation of edible art. Although tempura and teriyaki dinners will satisfy, the seasonal menu is more exciting. In October, ask for *dobbin mushi*, a soup made from pine mushrooms
that's served in teapot. In spring, try sushi made from scallops
and pink cherry blossoms. *777 W. Broadway, No. 202, tel. 604/
872–8050. Reservations advised on weekends. Dress: neat but
casual. AE, MC, V. Closed Mon.; Dec. 24–26. Expensive.*

Chiyoda. The robata bar curves like an oversize sushi bar
through Chiyoda's main room: On one side are the customers
and an array of flat baskets full of the day's offerings; on the
other side are the robata chefs and grills. There are 35 choices
of things to grill, from squid, snapper, and oysters to eggplant,
mushrooms, onions, and potatoes. The finished dishes, dressed
with sake, soy, or *ponzu* sauce, are dramatically passed over on
the end of a long wooden paddle. If Japanese food only means
sushi and tempura to you, check this out. *1050 Alberni St., tel.
604/688–5050. Reservations accepted. Dress: casual. AE, MC,
V. Closed lunch Sat. and Sun. Moderate.*

Shijo Japanese Restaurant. Shijo has an excellent and very
large sushi bar, a smaller robata bar, tatami rooms, and a row of
tables overlooking bustling Fourth Avenue. The epitome of
modern urban Japanese chic is conveyed through the jazz music, handsome lamps with a patinated bronze finish, and lots of
black wood. Count on creatively prepared sushi, eggplant
dengaku topped with light and dark miso paste and broiled,
and shiitake *foil yaki* (fresh shiitake mushrooms cooked in foil
with *ponzu* sauce). *1926 W. 4th Ave., tel. 604/732–4676. Reservations advised. Dress: casual. AE, MC, V. Closed lunch, Sat.
and Sun. Moderate.*

Japanese Deli House. The least expensive sushi in town is
served in this high-ceilinged room on the main floor of a turn-of-
the-century building on Powell Street, once the heart of
Vancouver's Japantown. Along with the standard sushi-bar
menu, Japanese Deli House makes a pungent but tender hot
ginger squid appetizer from baby squid caught off the Thai
coast, and a geoduck appetizer in mayonnaise worth wandering

off the beaten path for. Food is especially fresh and good if you can make it an early lunch: Nigiri sushi and sushi rolls are made at 11 AM for the 11:30 opening. *381 Powell St., tel. 604/681–6484. No reservations. Dress: casual. No credit cards. Closed Mon. Inexpensive.*

Korean   **Seoul House Korean Restaurant.** The shining star in a desperately ugly section of East Broadway, Seoul House is a bright restaurant, decorated in Japanese style, that serves a full menu of Japanese and Korean food. The best bet is the Korean Barbecue, which you cook at your table. A barbecue dinner of marinated beef, pork, chicken, or fish comes complete with a half dozen side dishes—*kim chee* (Korea's national pickle), salads, stir-fried rice, and pickled vegetables—as well as soup and rice. Service can be chaotic in this very popular restaurant. *36 E. Broadway, tel. 604/874–4131. Reservations advised. Dress: casual. MC, V. Closed lunch Sun. Inexpensive.*

Mexican   **Topanga Cafe.** Arrive before 6:30 or after 8 PM to avoid waiting in line for this 40-seat Kitsilano classic. The California-Mexican food hasn't changed much in the 14 years the Topanga has been dishing up fresh salsa and homemade tortilla chips. Quantities are still huge and prices are low. Kids can color blank menu covers while waiting for food; a hundred or more of the clientele's best efforts are framed and on the walls. *2904 4th Ave., tel. 604/733–3713. No reservations. Dress: casual. MC, V. Closed Sun. Inexpensive.*

Nouvelle   **Bishop's.** John Bishop established Vancouver's most influential
★   restaurant seven years ago, serving a variety of cuisines from northern Italian to nouvelle and East–West crossover. Penne with grilled eggplant, roasted peppers, and basil pasta cohabits the menu with marinated loin of lamb with ginger and sesame. The small white rooms—their only ornament some splashy, expressionist paintings—are favored by Robert de Niro when he's on location in Vancouver. *2183 W. 4th Ave., tel. 604/738–2025. Reservations required. Dress: casual. AE, DC, MC, V. Closed 1st week in Jan. Expensive.*

Pacific Northwest   **Quilicum.** Only a few blocks from English Bay, this downstairs "longhouse" serves the original Northwest Coast cuisine: bannock bread, baked sweet potato with hazelnuts, alder-grilled salmon, and soap-berries for dessert. Try the authentic, but odd dish—oolichan grease—that's prepared from candlefish. Native music is piped in, and Northwest Coast masks (for sale) peer out from the walls. *1724 Davie St., tel. 604/681–7044. Reservations advised. Dress: casual. AE, MC, V. Closed lunch Sat. and Sun. Moderate.*

★   **The Raintree.** This cool, spacious restaurant offers a local menu and wine list; the latter won a 1988 award from the *Wine Spectator* for its British Columbia, Washington, and Oregon choices. Raintree bakes its own bread, makes luxurious soups, and has pumped-up old favorites such as a slab of apple pie for dessert. With main courses, which change daily depending on market availability, the kitchen teeters between willfully eccentric and exceedingly simple. Specials could include Queen Charlotte abalone and side-stripe shrimps stir fried with scallions and spinach in chamomile essence, or grilled lamb chops with a mint and pear puree. *Leon's Bar and Grill*, on the ground floor, stocks local beers and a respectable number of single malt scotches. The pub-food menu, under the direction of chef Rebecca Dawson, includes organic-beef burgers and vegetarian chili. *1630 Alberni St., tel. 604/688–5570. Reservations advised on weekends. Dress: casual. AE, DC, MC, V. Closed Dec. 24–26. Moderate.*

The Tomahawk. North Vancouver was mostly trees 65 years ago, when the Tomahawk first opened. Over the years, the original hamburger stand grew and mutated into part Northwest Coast Indian kitsch museum, part gift shop, and part restaurant. Renowned for its Yukon breakfast—five slices of back bacon, two eggs, hash browns, and toast—the Tomahawk also serves gigantic muffins, excellent French toast, and pancakes. The menu switches to burgers named after Indian chiefs for lunch and dinner. *1550 Philip Ave., tel. 604/988–2612. No reservations. Dress: casual. AE, MC, V. Inexpensive.*

Seafood **Olympia Fish Market and Oyster Co. Ltd.** Some of the city's best fish and chips are fried in this tiny shop located behind a fish store in the middle of the Robson Street shopping district. The choice is halibut, cod, prawns, calamari, and whatever's on special in the store, served with genuine—never frozen—french fries. *1094 Robson St., tel. 604/685–0716. No reservations. Dress: casual. No credit cards. Inexpensive.*

Thai **Malinee's Thai.** The city's most consistently interesting Thai
★ food can be found in this typically Southeast Asian–style room, tapestries adorning the walls. The owners, two Canadians who lived several years in Thailand, can give you detailed descriptions of every dish on the menu. Steamed fish with ginger, pickled plums, and red chili sauce is on the regular menu; a steamed whole red snapper, marinated in oyster sauce, ginger, cilantro, red pepper, and lime juice is a special worth ordering when available. *2153 W. 4th Ave., tel. 604/737–0097. Reservations advised. Dress: casual. AE, DC, MC, V. Closed lunch Sat. and Sun.; Mon. Moderate.*

Lodging

Lodging has become a major business for Vancouver, a fairly young city that hosts a lot of Asian businesspeople who are used to an above-average level of service. Although by some standards pricey, properties here are highly competitive, and you can expect the service to reflect this trend.

Highly recommended lodgings are indicated by a star ★.

Category	Cost*
Very Expensive	over $180
Expensive	$120–$180
Moderate	$80–$119
Inexpensive	under $80

All prices are for a standard double room for two, excluding 10% provincial accommodation tax, 15% service charge, and 7% goods and services tax. Non-Canadians are eligible for a rebate on the goods and services tax paid for hotel accommodations.

Very Expensive **Four Seasons.** The 28-story hotel is adjacent to the Vancouver Stock Exchange and is attached to the Pacific Centre shopping

285

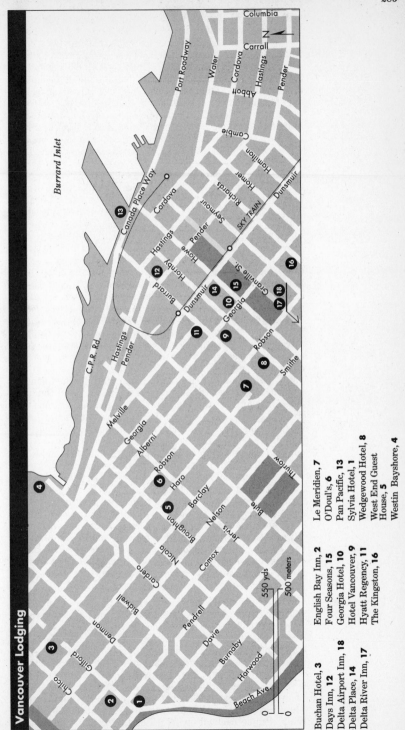

Vancouver Lodging

Buchan Hotel, **3**
Days Inn, **12**
Delta Airport Inn, **18**
Delta Place, **14**
Delta River Inn, **17**

English Bay Inn, **2**
Four Seasons, **15**
Georgia Hotel, **10**
Hotel Vancouver, **9**
Hyatt Regency, **11**
The Kingston, **16**

Le Meridien, **7**
O'Doul's, **6**
Pan Pacific, **13**
Sylvia Hotel, **1**
Wedgewood Hotel, **8**
West End Guest
House, **5**
Westin Bayshore, **4**

mall. Standard rooms are not large; corner deluxe or deluxe Four Seasons rooms are recommended. Expect tasteful and stylish decor in the rooms and hallways that provide a calm mood despite the bustling hotel. A huge sun deck and indoor-outdoor pool are part of the complete health club facilities. Service is outstanding and the Four Seasons has all the amenities. The formal dining room, Chartwell (*see* Dining, above), is one of the best in the city. *791 W. Georgia St., V6C 2T4, tel. 604/689–9333; in Canada, 800/268–6282; in the U.S., 800/332–3442; fax 604/684–4555. 317 doubles, 68 suites. Facilities: restaurant, café, bars, indoor-outdoor pool, sun deck, weight room, aerobics classes, sauna, Jacuzzi, ping-pong. AE, DC, MC, V.*

★ **Le Meridien.** The Meridien feels more like an exclusive guest house than a large hotel. The lobby has sumptuously thick carpets, enormous displays of flowers, and a newsstand situated discreetly down the hall. The rooms are even better, furnished with rich, dark wood, in a style that is reminiscent of 19th-century France. Despite the size of this hotel, the Meridien in Vancouver has achieved and maintained a level of intimacy and exclusivity. The **Café Fleuri** serves the best Sunday brunch in town (plus a chocolate buffet on Friday and Saturday evenings), and **Gerard,** a formal French restaurant, is a special-occasion place. The bar has lots of leather, dark wood, wingback chairs, and a fireplace. *845 Burrard St., V6Z 2K6, tel. 604/682–5511 or 800/543–4300, fax 604/682–5513. 350 doubles, 47 suites. Facilities: restaurant, café, bar, business center, handicapped rooms, health club with pool, Jacuzzi, sauna, steam room, tanning bed, masseur, hairdresser, weights, exercise equipment, adjoining apartment hotel. AE, DC, MC, V.*

★ **Pan Pacific.** Canada Place sits on a pier right by the financial district and houses the luxurious Pan Pacific Hotel (built in 1986 for the Expo), the Vancouver Trade and Convention Centre, and a cruise ship terminal. The lobby has a dramatic three-story atrium with a waterfall, and the lounge, restaurant, and café all have huge expanses of glass, so that you are rarely without a harbor view or mountain backdrop. Earth tones and Japanese detail give the rooms an understated elegance. Make sure you get a room that looks out on the water. The health club has a $10 fee that's well worth the price. The Pan Pacific is a grand, luxurious, busy hotel, but it is not a pick for an intimate weekend getaway. *300–999 Canada Pl., V6C 3B5, tel. 604/662–3223; in Canada, 800/663–1515; in the U.S., 800/937–1515; fax 604/685–8690. 468 doubles, 40 suites. Facilities: 3 restaurants, bar, health club with indoor track, sauna, steam room, state-of-the-art aerobics equipment, weights, massage and Shiatsu, sports lounge with wide-screen TV, squash, racquetball, and paddle-tennis courts, heated outdoor pool. AE, DC, MC, V.*

Expensive–Very Expensive **Westin Bayshore.** This hotel is the closest thing to a resort that you'll find in the downtown area. Because the Bayshore is perched right on the best part of the harbor, because it is a five-minute walk from Stanley Park, because of the truly fabulous view, and because of its huge outdoor pool, sun deck, and grassy areas, it is the perfect place to stay during the summer, especially for a family. The tower is the newer section, so rooms there are better furnished, larger, and offer the best view of the water. The café is okay but avoid the dining room, Trader Vic's; you can do much better at several neighborhood restaurants. People commuting from Seattle via Lake Union Air (downtown-to-downtown service) will find it handy that the floatplanes land at the Bayshore. *1601 W. Georgia St., V6G 2V4, tel. 604/682–3377 or 800/228–3000; fax 604/687–3102. 481 doubles, 38 suites, 2 handicapped floors. Facilities: restaurant, café, bars, free shuttle service downtown, bicycle rentals, marina with fishing and sailing charters, health club with indoor and outdoor pools, Jacuzzi, sun deck, masseur, sauna, pool table. AE, DC, MC, V.*

Expensive **Delta Airport Inn.** It's not a view or a shoreline that make this place (five minutes from the airport) a resort, it's the facilities on the 12-acre site: three swimming pools (one indoor), four all-year tennis courts with a pro (matching list for partners), an outdoor fitness circuit, squash courts, aqua-exercise classes, outdoor volleyball nets, golf practice net, a play center for children, summer camps for 5- to 12-year-olds, and a playground. In spite of its enormity, the atmosphere is casual and friendly. There are two guest-room towers and a few low-rise buildings for convention facilities. The rooms are nothing special, but all the extras, and the hotel's close proximity to the airport, make it worthwhile. The Japanese restaurant is expensive and all show. *10251 St. Edwards Dr., V6X 2M9, tel. 604/278–9611; in Canada, 800/268–1133; in the U.S., 800/877–1133; fax 604/276–1122. 460 doubles, 4 suites. Facilities: restaurant, café, bar, free shuttle to airport and shopping center, meeting rooms. AE, DC, MC, V.*

Delta Place. This 18-story hotel was built in 1985 by the luxurious Hong Kong Mandarin chain but was sold to Delta Hotels in 1987. The rates have gone down but the surroundings have not changed. The lobby is restrained and tasteful—one has to look for the registration desk. A slight Oriental theme is given to the deluxe furnishings and dark, rich mahogany is everywhere. Most rooms have small balconies and the studio suites are recommended since they are much roomier and only slightly more expensive than a standard room. The business center has secretarial services, work stations, cellular phones for rent, and small meeting rooms. The restaurant and bar are adequate and the location is perfect; the business and shopping district is a five-minute walk away. *645 Howe St., V6C 2Y9, tel. 604/687–1122; in Canada, 800/268–1133; in the U.S., 800/877–1133; fax 604/689–7044. 181 doubles, 16 suites. Facilities: restaurant, bar, squash and racquetball courts, lap pool, weight room. AE, DC, MC, V.*

Delta River Inn. This hotel, on the edge of the Fraser River, is two minutes from the airport. Rooms on the south side get the best view. Although renovations began in 1990, the River Inn still has a way to go to compete with others in the price range. The rooms do not have the style and pizzazz that some have. All the dark wood in the hotel gives it an out-of-date feel, but the hotel is convenient. The marina attached to the hotel organizes fishing charters. Food does not seem to be a priority with Delta. *3500 Cessena Dr., V7B AC7, tel. 604/278–1241; in Canada, 800/268–1133; in the U.S., 800/877–1133; fax 604/276–1975. 410 doubles, 6 suites. Facilities: jogging route, free shuttle to airport, shopping center, and extensive health club at the nearby Delta Airport Inn. AE, DC, MC, V.*

★ **Hotel Vancouver.** The Hotel Vancouver, built in 1939 by the Canadian National Railway, is a grand old lady of the château-style hotels that appear in Canadian cities. It commands a regal position in the center of things across from the fountains of the art gallery. Standard rooms are nothing special, but are decorated in a more classic style than those of the Hyatt or the Four Seasons. But the hotel has a category called Entré Gold: two floors with all the extra services and amenities. Entré Gold suites have a luxurious amount of space, French doors, graceful wingback chairs, and fine mahogany furniture. The style and elegance of the Hotel Vancouver leaves its mark here. The hotel's restaurants and bars are adequate. *900 W. Georgia St., V6C 2W6, tel. 604/684–3131; in Ontario and Quebec, 800/268–9420; rest of Canada, 800/268–9411; in the U.S., 800/828–7447; fax 604/662–1937. 466 doubles, 42 suites, handicapped rooms. Facilities: 2 restaurants, 2 bars, two-line telephones, health club with lap pool, exercise machines, tanning bed, sun deck. AE, DC, MC, V.*

Hyatt Regency. The 17-year-old Hyatt is in the midst of a badly needed $11-million renovation, but the location is still perfect. The Hyatt's standard rooms are the largest in the city, and are decorated in deep, dramatic colors and dark wood. Ask for a corner room with a balcony on the north or west side. The lobby, however, can't escape the feel of a large convention hotel. The Hyatt has two special features: Camp Hyatt and the Regency Club. The Camp Hyatt has organized evening activities for children. For a small fee, the Regency Club gives you the exclusivity of two floors accessed by keyed elevators, your own concierge, a private lounge with a stereo and large TV, complimentary breakfast, 5 PM hors d'oeuvres, and evening pastries. Robes and special toiletries are also in the Regency Club rooms. For a hotel restaurant, Fish & Co. is unusual in that the room is casual, the atmosphere fun, and the food good. The Gallery Lounge is one of the most pleasant in town. Health club facilities are available, but they leave much to be desired. *655 Burrard St., V6C 2R7, tel. 604/687–6543 or 800/233–1234, fax 604/689–3707. 612 doubles, 34 suites. Facilities: restaurant, café, 2 bars, health club. AE, DC, MC, V.*

O'Doul's. Set on a lively street with loads of shops and restaurants, this hotel is a five-minute walk from either the heart of downtown or Stanley Park. This is a great location if you're traveling with teenagers who want time on their own. It was built in 1986 in a long, low style and feels like a very deluxe motel. The rooms are what you'd expect from any mid-range hotel, with modern decor and pastel color schemes, but the place is very well maintained. The deluxe rooms (with king-size beds) face Robson Street, and are worth the price, especially off-season when rates plummet. *1300 Robson St., V6E 1C5, tel. 604/684–8461 or 800/663–5491, fax 604/684–8326. 119 doubles, 11 suites. Facilities: 3 telephones in every room, pool, Jacuzzi, steam rooms, exercise machines. AE, DC, MC, V.*

★ **Wedgewood Hotel.** This hotel upholds a reputation for being a small, elegant hotel run by an owner who fervently cares about her guests. The intimate lobby is decorated in fine detail with polished brass, a fireplace, and tasteful artwork. All the extra touches are here, too: nightly turn-down service, afternoon ice delivery, dark-out drapes, flowers growing on the balcony, terry-cloth robes, and morning newspaper. No tour groups or conventions stop here; the Wedgewood's clients are almost exclusively corporate, except on weekends when it turns into a honeymoon retreat. Health facilities are next door at the excellent Chancery Squash Club. The lounge and restaurants couldn't be better. It's a treasure. *845 Hornby St., V6Z 1V1, tel. 604/689–7777 or 800/663–0666, fax 604/688–3074. 60 dou-*

bles, 33 suites. Facilities: 2 restaurants, bar, use of the adjacent Chancery Squash Club with 7 squash courts, weight room, aerobics, sauna, and whirlpool. AE, DC, MC, V.

Moderate **Days Inn.** For the businessperson looking for a bargain, this location is tops. The six-story, 71-year-old Days Inn (formerly the Abbotsford) is the only moderately priced hotel in the business core, and the recent renovations of the guest rooms and the lobby have made this accommodation even more agreeable. This is a basic accommodation but rooms are bright, clean, and functional. Standard rooms are very large but there is no room service and few amenities. Suites 310, 410, 510, and 610 have a harbor view. The bar, the **Bombay Bicycle Club,** is a favorite with businesspeople. *921 W. Pender St., V6C 1M2, tel. 604/ 681–4335 or 800/663–1700, fax 604/681–7808. 74 doubles, 11 suites. Facilities: restaurant, 2 bars, free parking. AE, DC, MC, V.*

★ **English Bay Inn.** The English Bay Inn, in a newly renovated 1930s house, is two blocks from the ocean and Stanley Park in a quiet residential part of the West End. The five small guest rooms—each with private bath—have wonderful sleigh beds with matching armoires and brass lighting fixtures. The common areas are generous and elegantly furnished: The sophisticated but cozy parlor has wingback chairs, a fireplace, and French doors opening onto the front garden. A sunny English country garden graces the back of the inn. Breakfast is served in a rather formal dining room furnished with a Gothic dining room suite and an 18th-century grandfather clock. *1968 Comox St., V6G 1R4, tel. 604/683–8063. 5 rooms. Facilities: off-street parking. AE, MC, V.*

★ **Georgia Hotel.** Across from the Four Seasons, this hotel is a five-minute walk from the business district. This handsome 12-story hotel, built in 1927, has such Old-World features as an oak-paneled lobby, ornate brass elevators, and a subdued, genteel atmosphere. Although it's lacking in special amenities, the Georgia is a reliable and satisfactory deal. Rooms are small but well furnished, with nothing worn around the edges. Executive rooms have an almost-separate seating area. Rooms facing the art gallery have the best views. *801 W. Georgia St., V6C 1P7, tel. 604/682–5566 or 800/663–1111, fax 604/682–8192. 310 doubles, 4 suites. Facilities: restaurant, 3 bars. AE, DC, MC, V.*

★ **West End Guest House.** The bright-pink exterior of this delightful Victorian house may throw you: The gracious front parlor with its early 1900s furniture is more indicative of the charm of the place. Most of the rooms are small but are extraordinarily handsome because of the high brass beds, antiques, gorgeous linen, and dozens of old framed pictures of Vancouver. All rooms have phones, TVs, and new bathrooms. There's a veranda for people-watching, and a back deck for sunbathing. A full breakfast is included and can be served in bed. The inn's genial hosts, Charles and George, have learned that it is the little things that make the difference, including an evening glass of sherry, duvets and feather mattress-pads, and a pantry where guests can help themselves to tea or snacks. The inn is in a residential neighborhood that is a 15-minute walk from downtown and Stanley Park and two minutes from Robson Street. This is a nonsmoking establishment. *1362 Haro St., V6E 1G2, tel. 604/ 681–2889. 7 rooms. Facilities: off-street parking. MC, V.*

Inexpensive **Buchan Hotel.** This three-story 1930s building is conveniently
★ set in a tree-lined residential street a block from Stanley Park,

a block from shops and restaurants on Denman Street, and a 15-minute walk from the liveliest part of Robson Street. The hallways appear a bit institutional, but the rooms are bright and clean. Furnishings, in good condition, consist of a color TV, and a wood-grained arborite desk and chest of drawers. The rooms are small and the bathrooms tiny. None of the rooms have phones and you have to park on the street, but with this location you probably won't use your car much. Rooms on the east side are brightest and overlook a park; front corner rooms are the biggest. A popular restaurant with an eclectic menu is in the basement and is open for dinner. *1906 Haro St., V6G 1H7, tel. 604/685–5354. 60 rooms, 30 with private bath. Facilities: TV lounge, laundry room. AE, DC, MC, V.*

The Kingston. The Kingston is a small budget hotel in a location convenient for shopping. It is an old-style, four-story hotel, with no elevator—the type of establishment you'd find in Europe. The spartan rooms are small, immaculate, and share a bathroom down the hall. All rooms have phones but no TVs. Rooms on the south side are brighter. Continental breakfast is included. *757 Richards St., V6B 3A6, tel. 604/684–9024. 60 rooms, 7 with bath. Facilities: sauna, coin-op laundry, TV lounge, free nighttime parking. AE, MC, V.*

★ **Sylvia Hotel.** Perhaps the Sylvia Hotel is the best bargain in Vancouver, but don't count on staying here June–August unless you've booked six months ahead. What makes this hotel so popular are its low rates and near-perfect location: about 25 feet from the beach, 200 feet from Stanley Park, and a 20-minute walk from downtown. Vancouverites are particularly fond of the eight-story ivy-covered brick building—it was once the tallest building in the West End and the first to open a cocktail bar in the city, in 1954. It's part of the local history and was declared a protected heritage building in the 1970s. Rooms are unadorned and have basic plain furnishings that have probably been around for 20 years—not much to look at but the view and price make it worthwhile. Suites are huge and all have kitchens, making this a perfect family accommodation. There is little difference between the old and new wings. *1154 Gilford St., V6G 2P6, tel. 604/681–9321. 97 doubles, 18 suites. Facilities: restaurant, lounge, free parking. AE, DC, MC, V.*

The Arts and Nightlife

For information on events, look in the entertainment section of the *Vancouver Sun;* also, Thursday's paper has complete listings in the **"What's On"** column, and the **Arts Hotline** (tel. 604/684–ARTS). For tickets to major events, book through **Ticketmaster** (tel. 604/280–4444).

The Arts

Theater   The **Vancouver Playhouse** (Hamilton St., tel. 604/872–6722) is the most established venue in Vancouver. The **Arts Club Theatre** (tel. 604/687–1644), with two stages on Granville Island (1585 Johnston St.) and performances all year, is the most active. Both feature mainstream theatrical shows. **Carousel Theater** (tel. 604/669–3410), which performs off-off Broadway shows at the **Waterfront Theatre** (1405 Anderson St.) on Granville Island, and **Touchstone** (tel. 604/687–8737), at the Firehall Theater (280 E. Cordova St.), are smaller but lively companies.

The **Back Alley Theatre** (751 Thurlow St., tel. 604/688–7013) hosts **Theatresports,** a hilarious improv event. The **Vancouver East Cultural Centre** (1895 Venables St., tel. 604/254–9578) is a multipurpose performance space that always hosts high-caliber shows.

Music   The **Vancouver Symphony Orchestra** (tel. 604/684–9100) and the **CBC Orchestra** (tel. 604/662–6000) play at the restored **Orpheum Theatre** (601 Smithe St.). Choral groups like the **Bach Choir** (tel. 604/921–8012), the **Cantata Singers** (no tel.), and the **Vancouver Chamber Singers** (tel. 604/738–6822) play a major role in Vancouver's classical music scene. The **Early Music Society** (tel. 604/732–1610) performs medieval, renaissance, and baroque music throughout the year, and hosts the summer concerts of the most important Early Music Festival in North America. Concerts by the **Friends of Chamber Music** (no tel.) and the **Vancouver Recital Society** (tel. 604/736–6034) are always of excellent quality.

Vancouver Opera (tel. 604/682–2871) stages four productions a year, usually in October, January, March, and May at the **Queen Elizabeth Theatre** (600 Hamilton St.). Productions are high caliber with both local and imported talent.

Dance   The **Dance Hotline** (tel. 604/872–0432) has information on upcoming events. Watch for **Ballet BC's Dance Alive!** series, presenting visiting or local ballet companies (from the Kirov to Ballet BC), as well as the modern dance series, **Discover Dance.** Most performances by these companies can be seen at the Orpheum or the Queen Elizabeth Theatre (*see* above). Local modern dance companies worth seeing are **Karen Jamison, Judith Marcuse,** and **Anna Wyman.**

Film   Two theaters have distinguished themselves by avoiding the regular movie fare: **The Ridge** (3131 Arbutus St., tel. 604/738–6311), which generally plays foreign films; and **Pacific Cinémathèque** (1131 Howe St., tel. 604/688–3456), which goes for even more esoteric foreign and art films. The **Vancouver International Film Festival** (tel. 604/685–0260) is held in September and October in several theaters around town.

Nightlife

Bars and Lounges   The **Gérard Lounge** (845 Burrard St., tel. 604/682–5511) at Le Meridien Hotel is probably the nicest in the city because of the fireplaces, wingback chairs, dark wood, and leather. The **Bacchus Lounge** (845 Hornby St., tel. 604/689–7777) in the Wedgewood Hotel is stylish and sophisticated. The **Gallery Lounge** (655 Burrard St., tel. 604/687–6543) in the Hyatt is a genteel bar, with lots of windows letting in the sun and views of the action on the bustling street. The **Garden Lounge** (791 W. Georgia St., tel. 604/689–9333) in the Four Seasons is bright and airy with greenery and a waterfall, plus big soft chairs you won't want to get out of. For a more lively atmosphere, try **Joe Fortes** (777 Thurlow St., 604/669–1940), or **Night Court** (801 W. Georgia St., tel. 604/682–5566) in the Georgia Hotel.

The **English Bay Cafe** (1795 Beach Ave., tel. 604/669–2225) is the place to go to catch the sunset over English Bay. **La Bodega** (1277 Howe St., tel. 604/684–8815) beneath the Chateau Madrid is a popular Spanish tapas bar.

Two bars on Granville Island catering to the after-work crowd are **Bridges** (tel. 604/687–4400), near the Public Market, and the upscale **Pelican Bay** (tel. 604/683–7373) in the Granville Island Hotel, at the other end of the island.

Music While discos come and go, lines still form every weekend at
Discos **Richard's on Richards** (1036 Richards St., tel. 604/687–6794) for live and taped Top-40 music.

Jazz A jazz and blues hotline (tel. 604/682–0706) gives you current information on concerts and clubs. **Carnegie's** (1619 W. Broadway, tel. 604/733–4141), **Café Django** (1184 Denman St., tel. 604/689–1184), and the **Alma Street Cafe** (2505 Alma St., tel. 604/222–2244), all restaurants, are traditional venues with good mainstream jazz.

Rock The **Town Pump** (66 Water St., tel. 604/683–6695) is the main venue for local and touring rock bands. The **Soft Rock Cafe** (1925 W. 4th Ave., tel. 604/736–8480) is decidedly more upscale. There's live music, dinners, and weekend lineups. The **86th Street Music Hall** (750 Pacific Blvd., tel. 604/683–8687) serves up big-name bands.

Casinos A few casinos have been licensed recently in Vancouver and proceeds go to local charities and arts groups. Downtown there is the **Royal Diamond Casino** (535 Davie St., tel. 604/685–2340) and the **Great Canadian Casino** (2477 Heather St., tel. 604/872–5543) in the Holiday Inn.

Comedy **Yuk Yuks** (750 Pacific Blvd., tel. 604/687–5233) is good for a few laughs.

Excursion 1: Victoria

Introduction

Victoria, originally Fort Victoria, was the first European settlement on Vancouver Island and is the oldest city on Canada's west coast. It was chosen in 1842 by James Douglas to be the Hudson's Bay Company's most western outpost. Today it's a compact seaside town laced with tea shops and gardens. Though it's quite touristy during the high summer season, it's also at its prettiest, with flowers hanging from turn-of-the-century building posts and strollers feasting on the beauty of Victoria's natural harbor.

Tourist Information

Tourism Victoria (812 Wharf St., tel. 604/382–2127; mailing address, 612 View St., Victoria V8W 1J5) is open 9–9 June–Sept. 4 and 9–5 the rest of the year.

Arriving and Departing by Plane

BC Air (tel. 604/688–5515) provides both airport and harbor-to-harbor service from Vancouver to Victoria. Flights from Vancouver's international airport to Victoria's depart every hour from 8:15 AM. Harbor-to-harbor service runs every half hour from Coal Harbour in downtown Vancouver to Empress Harbour in Victoria. Both flights take about 35 minutes.

Arriving and Departing by Ferry

The **British Columbia Ferry Corporation** runs frequent ferry service from Vancouver to Victoria year-round. For information call 604/669–1211.

Getting Around

By Bus The **BC Transit System** runs a fairly extensive service throughout Victoria and the surrounding areas. Tourists may want to consider an all-day pass that allows passengers unlimited rides during the day at a cost of $3 for adults, $2 for students and senior citizens. Passes are sold at many outlets in downtown Victoria, including Eaton Centre and Harbour Square Ticket Centre.

For more information about passes and schedules, call 604/382–6161.

By Taxi Taxis are readily available throughout Victoria and can always be hailed outside hotels.

Exploring Victoria

Numbers in the margin correspond to points of interest on the Downtown Victoria map.

❶ For the most part, **Victoria** is a walker's city; most of its main attractions are located downtown or are a few blocks from the core. Attractions on the outskirts of downtown can easily be reached by bus or a short cab ride (though taxis can be alarmingly expensive). In the summer you have the added option of horse-drawn carriages, bicycle, boat, or double-decker bus tours.

❷ A logical place to begin this tour is at the **Visitors Information Centre,** located along the waterfront. Pick through numerous leaflets, maps, and tourism information concerning Victoria, Vancouver Island, ferries, entertainment, and accommodations. *812 Wharf St., tel. 604/382–2127. Open July, Aug., daily 9–9; May, June, Sept., Oct., daily 9–7; Nov.–Apr., daily 9–5.*

❸ Just across the way is the recently renovated **Empress Hotel,** a symbol both of the city and of the Canadian Pacific Railway. Originally opened in 1908, the hotel was designed by Francis Rattenbury, whose works dot Vancouver. The Empress is another of the great châteaus built by Canadian Pacific, the still-current owners who also built the Chateau Frontenac in Québec City, Chateau Laurier in Ottawa, and Chateau Lake Louise. The $55 million facelift has been a hot topic of discussion in traditional Victoria, though not all of the comments have been positive; criticism aside, the ingredients that made the 488-room hotel a tourist attraction in the past are still alive. Stop in for high tea—served at hour-and-a-half intervals during the afternoon. The experience may lend to your appreciation of the lobby's high-beamed ceiling and wood floors. In the basement of the hotel is an informative collection of historical photos and items from the hotel's early days. *721 Government St., tel. 604/384–8111. Proper dress required; no jeans, shorts, or T-shirts.*

Also, in the north wing of the Empress is **Miniature World,** where small replicas of people, trains, and historical events are displayed. The exhibit seems at times like a mix of fact and fic-

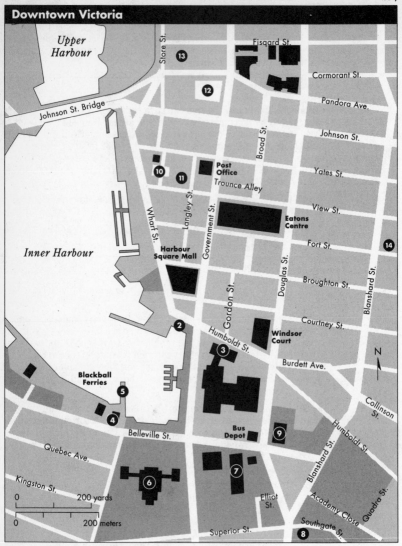

Downtown Victoria

Upper Harbour

Store St.

Fisgard St.

Cormorant St.

Pandora Ave.

Johnson St. Bridge

Broad St.

Johnson St.

Yates St.

Post Office

Trounce Alley

Langley St.

Wharf St.

Inner Harbour

Harbour Square Mall

Government St.

View St.

Eatons Centre

Fort St.

Broughton St.

Gordon St.

Douglas St.

Courtney St.

Blanshard St.

Humboldt St.

Windsor Court

Burdett Ave.

N

Collinson St.

Blackball Ferries

Belleville St.

Bus Depot

Quebec Ave.

Kingston St.

0   200 yards

0   200 meters

Humboldt St.

Blanshard St.

Academy Close

Elliot St.

Quadra St.

Superior St.

Southgate St.

Bastion Square, **10**

Beacon Hill Park, **8**

Chinatown, **13**

Craigdarroch Castle, **14**

Crystal Gardens, **9**

Empress Hotel, **3**

Legislative/Parliament Buildings, **6**

Maritime Museum, **11**

Market Square, **12**

Pacific Undersea Garden, **5**

Royal British Columbia Museum, **7**

Royal London Wax Museum, **4**

Visitors Information Centre, **2**

tion, though many of the models are delicately laid out. *649 Humbolt St., tel. 604/385–9731. Admission: $6 adults, $5 children 12–17, $4 children under 12; children under 10 and disabled persons with escort free. Open mid-June–mid-Sept., daily 8:30–10 PM; mid-Sept.–mid-June, daily 9–5:30.*

4 A short walk around the harbor leads you to the old CPR Steamship Terminal, also designed by Rattenbury and completed in 1924. Today it is the **Royal London Wax Museum,** housing more than 200 wax figures, including replicas of Queen Victoria, Elvis, and Marilyn Monroe. *470 Belleville St., tel. 604/388–4461. Admission: $6 adults, $5 students and senior citizens, $3 children 5–12. Open May–end of July, daily 8 AM–9 PM; end of July–Aug., daily 8 AM–11:30 PM; Sept.–Apr., daily 9:30–5.*

5 Next to the wax museum is the **Pacific Undersea Garden,** where more than 5,000 marine specimens are on display in their natural habitat. You also get performing scuba divers and Armstrong the giant octopus. Unfortunately, there are no washrooms, and the site is not wheelchair accessible. *490 Belleville St., tel. 604/382–5717. Admission: $6 adults, $5.50 senior citizens, $4.50 children 12–17, $2.75 children 5–11. Open Oct.–end of May, daily 10–5; summer, daily 9–9; closed Christmas. Shows run about every 45 minutes.*

6 Across Belleville Street is the **Legislative Parliament Buildings** complex. The stone exterior building, completed in 1897, dominates the inner harbor and is flanked by two statues: Sir James Douglas, who chose the location of Victoria, and Sir Matthew Baille Begbie, the man in charge of law and order during the gold-rush era. Atop the central dome is a gilded statue of Captain George Vancouver, who first sailed around Vancouver Island; a statue of Queen Victoria stands in front of the complex; and outlining the building at night are more than 3,000 lights. Another of Rattenbury's creations, the complex gives a good example of the rigid symmetry and European elegance that characterize much of the city's architecture. The public can watch the assembly, when it's in session, from the galleries overlooking the Legislative Chamber. *501 Belleville St., tel. 604/387–3046. Admission free. Tours run several times daily, and are conducted in at least 4 languages in summer and 3 in winter. Open Sept.–June, weekdays 8:30–5; summer, daily 8:30–5:30.*

7 Follow Belleville Street one block east to reach the **Royal British Columbia Museum.** Adults and children can wander for hours through the centuries, beginning with the present and going back 12,000 years. In the prehistoric exhibit, you can actually smell the pines and hear the calls of mammoths and other ancient wildlife. Other exhibits allow you to explore a turn-of-the-century town, with trains rumbling past; in the Kwakiutl Indian Bighouse, the smell of cedar envelopes you, while piped-in potlatch songs tell the origins of the genuine ceremonial house before you. Also explored in this museum are the industrial era, fur trading, pioneering, and the effects of modern history on native Indian cultures. *675 Belleville St., tel. 604/387–3014. Admission: $5 adults, $3 students and senior citizens, $2 children 6–18 and disabled persons, children under 6 free. Open Oct.–Apr., daily 10–5:30; May–Sept., daily 9:30–7; closed Christmas and New Year's Day.*

A walk east on Belleville Street to Douglas Street will lead you
8 to the **Beacon Hill Park,** a favorite place for joggers, walkers,
and cyclists. The park's southern lawns offer one of the best
views of the Olympic Mountains and the Strait of Juan de Fuca.
There are also athletic fields, lakes, walking paths, abundant
flowers, and a wading pool and petting farm for children.

From the park, go north on Douglas Street and stop off at the
9 **Crystal Gardens.** Opened in 1925 as the largest swimming pool
in the British Empire, this glass-roof building—now owned by
the provincial government—is home to flamingos, macaws, 75
varieties of other birds, hundreds of blooming flowers, walla-
bies, and monkeys. At street level there are several boutiques
and Rattenbury's Restaurant, one of Victoria's well-fre-
quented establishments. *713 Douglas St., tel. 604/381–1213.
Admission: $6 adults, $4 children 6–16 and senior citizens.
Open Oct.–Apr., daily 10–5:30; summer, daily 9–9.*

From Crystal Gardens continue on Douglas Street going north
10 to View Street, west to **Bastion Square,** with its gas lamps, restaurants, cobblestone streets, and small shops. This is the spot
James Douglas chose as the original Fort Victoria in 1843 and
the original Hudson's Bay Company trading post. Today fashion boutiques and restaurants occupy the old buildings. At the
Wharf Street end of the square are some benches where you
can rest your feet and catch a great view of the harbor. While
you're here, you may want to stop in at what was Victoria's
11 original courthouse, but is now the **Maritime Museum of British
Columbia.** Dugout canoes, model ships, Royal Navy charts,
photographs, uniforms, and ships bells chronicle Victoria's
seafaring history. A seldom-used 100-year-old cage lift, believed to be the oldest in North America, ascends to the third
floor. *28 Bastion Sq., tel. 604/385–4222. Admission: $4 adults,
$3 senior citizens, $1 children 6–18, children under 6 free.
Open Sept. 16–June 16, daily 9:30–4:30; June 17–Sept. 15, daily 9:30–6:30; closed Christmas and New Year's Day.*

West of Government Street, between Pandora Avenue and
12 Johnson Street is **Market Square,** offering a variety of specialty
shops and boutiques and considered one of the most picturesque shopping districts in the city. At the turn of the century
this area—once part of Chinatown—provided everything a visitor desired: food, lodging, entertainment. Today the square
has been restored to its original, pre-1900s character.

Just around the corner from Market Square is Fisgard Street,
13 the heart of one of the oldest **Chinatowns** in Canada. It was the
Chinese who were responsible for building much of the Canadian Pacific Railway in the 19th century; and their influences still
mark the region. If you enter Chinatown from Government
Street, you'll walk under the elaborate Gate of Harmonious Interest, made from Taiwanese ceramic tiles and decorative panels. Along the street, merchants display fragile paper lanterns,
embroidered silks, imported fruits, and vegetables. **Fan Tan
Alley,** situated just off Fisgard Street, holds claim not only to
being the narrowest street in Canada but also to having been
the gambling and opium center of Chinatown, where mah-
jongg, fantan, and dominoes games were played.

A 15-minute walk, or short drive, east on Fort Street will take
14 you to Joan Crescent, where **Craigdarroch Castle** stands. This
lavish mansion was built as the home of British Columbia's first

millionaire, Robert Dunsmuir, who oversaw coal mining for the Hudson's Bay Company (he died before the castle's completion in about 1890). Recently converted into a museum depicting turn-of-the-century lifestyle, the castle is strikingly authentic, with elaborately framed landscape paintings, stained-glass windows, carved woodwork—precut in Chicago for Dunsmuir and sent by rail—and rooms for billiards and smoking. The location offers a wonderful view of downtown Victoria from the fifth-floor tower; guided tours are given. *1050 Joan Crescent, Victoria, tel. 604/592–5323. Admission: $5 adults, $4 senior citizens and children 12 and older. Open mid-June–Aug., daily 9–7:30; Sept.–mid-June, daily 10–5.*

What to See and Do with Children

Anne Hathaway's Cottage, tucked away in a unique English-village complex, is a full-size replica of the original thatched home in Stratford-Upon-Avon, England. The building and the 16th-century antiques inside are typical of Shakespeare's era. The Olde England Inn, on the grounds, is a pleasant spot for tea or a traditional English-style meal. You can also stay in one of the 50 antiques-furnished rooms, some complete with four-poster beds. *429 Lampson St., Victoria, V9A 5Y9, tel. 604/388–4353. Admission: $4.50 adults, $2.95 senior citizens and children 8–17, children under 8 free. Open June–Sept., daily 9–9; rest of year, daily 10–4. Guided tours leave from the inn during the winter, and directly from the cottage in summer. From downtown Victoria, take the Munro bus to the door.*

Dominion Astrophysical Observatory, maintained by the National Research Council of Canada, has a 72-inch telescope that transmits pictures of planets, star clusters, and nebulae. A museum display around the inside of the domed building provides a quick lesson in astrophysics, and video monitors are set up for visitors' easy viewing. *Off W. Saanich Rd. (Hwy. 17), 16 km (10 mi) from Victoria on Little Saanich Mt., tel. 604/383–0001. Admission: free. Open Mon.–Fri. 9–4:30; Apr.–Oct., Mon.–Fri. 9–4:30, Sat. 9 PM–11 PM.*

Sealand of the Pacific. Featured at this aquarium are Orcas (killer whales), seals, and sea lions, with poolside shows every hour. The setting itself is an attraction, offering one of the finest views of the Strait of Juan de Fuca in the Victoria area. *1327 Beach Dr., Oak Bay, tel. 604/598–3373. Admission: $6.50 adults, $5 children 12–17, $2.75 children 5–11. Open June–Sept., daily 10–6; Sept.–May, daily 10–5; closed Mon. and Tues. in Nov., Jan., Feb.*

Shopping

Shopping in Victoria is easy. Virtually everything can be found in the downtown area, beginning at the Empress and walking north along Government Street. In succession you'll hit **Roger's Chocolates and English Sweet Shop** (tel. 604/384–7021), for fine chocolates; **George Straith Ltd.** (tel. 604/384–6912) for woolens; **Piccadilly Shoppe British Woolens** (tel. 604/384–1288) for women's woolens; **Gallery of the Arctic** (tel. 604/382–9012), for quality Inuit art; **Munro's Books** (tel. 604/382–2464), for the best selection of Victoriana in the city; and **Old Morris Tobacconist, Ltd.** (tel. 604/382–4811) for unusual pipe tobacco blends.

The **Eaton's Centre** at Government and Fort streets is both a department store and a series of small boutiques, with a total of 140 shops and restaurants. For upscale boutiques, visit **Bastion Square** and **Windsor Court,** at the corner of Douglas and Humboldt. Market Square, between Johnson and Pandora, has three stories of specialty shops.

At last count, Victoria had 60-plus **antiques shops** specializing in coins, stamps, estate jewelry, rare books, crystal, china, furniture, or paintings and other works of art. A short walk on Fort Street going away from the harbor will take you to **Antique Row** between Blanshard and Cook streets. **Waller Antiques** (tel. 604/388–6116) and **Newberry Antiques** (tel. 604/388–7732) offer a wide selection of furniture and collectibles. You will also find antiques on the west side of Government Street near the **Old Town.**

Chinatown is marked by the red Gate of Harmonious Interest. On Fisgard Street shops offer merchandise and meals straight from the Orient. You must visit the little shops of **Fan Tan Alley,** a walkway between two buildings so small that two people have a difficult time passing without one giving way.

Sports and Outdoor Activities

Golf Though **Victoria Golf Club** (1110 Beach Dr., Victoria, tel. 604/595–2433) is private, it's open to other private-club members. This windy course is the oldest (built in 1893) in British Columbia and offers a spectacular view of the Strait of Juan de Fuca. **Uplands Golf Club** (3300 Cadboro Bay Rd., Victoria, tel. 604/592–1818) is a flat, semi-private course (it becomes public after 2). **Cedar Hill Municipal** (1400 Derby Rd., Victoria, tel. 604/595–3103) is a public course with up-and-down terrain. **Royal Oak Inn Golf Club** (4680 Elk Lake Dr., Victoria, tel. 604/658–1433) is the newest nine-hole course in the area. **Gorge Vale Golf Club** (1005 Craigflower Rd., Victoria, tel. 604/386–3401) is a semiprivate course, but is open to the public. It has punitive traps and a deep gorge that eats up golf balls. **Glen Meadows Golf and Country Club** (1050 McTavish Rd., Sidney, tel. 604/656–3921), situated near the ferry terminal, is a semiprivate course that's open to the public at select times.

Dining and Lodging

Dining **Chez Daniel.** One of Victoria's old standbys, Chez Daniel offers dishes that are rich, though the nouvelle influence has found its way into a few of the offerings. The interior, following a burgundy color scheme, seems to match the traditional rich, caloric cuisine. The wine list is varied and the menu has a wide selection of basic dishes: rabbit, salmon, duck, steak. This is a restaurant where you linger for the evening in the romantic atmosphere. *2524 Estavan Ave., tel. 604/592–7424. Reservations advised. Jacket advised. AE, MC, V. Closed lunch and Sun.–Mon. Expensive.*

★ **La Ville d'Is.** This seafood house is one of the best bargains in Victoria in terms of quality and price. Run by Michel Duteau, a Brittany native, the restaurant is cozy and friendly, with an outside café open May–October. An extensive, imaginative wine list features bottles from the Loire Valley that go well with the seafood, rabbit, lamb, and beef tenderloin specials. Try the *perche de la nouvelle Zelande* (orange roughie in muscadet with herbs) or lobster soufflé for a unique taste. *26 Bastion Sq., tel. 604/388–9414. Reservations advised. Dress: casual but neat. AE, MC, V. Closed Sun. and Jan. Expensive.*

Chez Pierre. Established in 1973, this is the oldest French restaurant in Victoria; and the downtown location, combined with an intimate, rustic decor, creates a pleasant ambience. House specialties include canard à l'orange (duckling in orange sauce), rack of lamb, and British Columbia salmon. Although a tourist destination, this restaurant has managed to maintain its quality over the years. *512 Yates, tel. 604/388–7711. Reservations advised. Dress: casual but neat. AE, MC, V. Closed lunch and Sun.–Mon. Moderate–Expensive.*

Camilles. This restaurant is romantic, intimate, and one of the few West Coast-cuisine restaurants in Victoria. House specialties such as Zinfandel chicken, papaya brochettes (prawns wrapped around chunks of papaya in a lime and jalapeño marinade), phyllo-wrapped salmon (fresh fillet of salmon in phyllo pastry) are all served in generous portions. Camilles also has an extensive wine cellar, uncommon in Victoria. *45 Bastion Sq., tel. 604/381–3433. Reservations advised. Dress: casual but neat. AE, MC, V. Closed lunch and Sun.–Mon. Moderate.*

French Connection. Located in one of Victoria's Heritage homes, built in 1884, the restaurant has maintained the character of the time. From the outside, ornate details indicate the French tradition that you will find in the service and on the menu. The food is prepared with care, with an emphasis on the sauces. *512 Simcoe St., tel. 604/385–7014. Reservations required. Dress: casual. AE, MC, V. Closed Sat.–Mon. lunch and Sun. Moderate.*

★ **Pagliacci's.** If you want Italian food, Pagliacci's is a must. Featured are dozens of pasta dishes, quiches, veal, and chicken in marsala sauce with fettuccine. The pastas are freshly made in-house. The orange-color walls are covered with photos of Hollywood stars, so there's always something to look at here. *1011 Broad St., tel. 604/386–1662. No reservations. Dress: casual. MC, V. Moderate.*

Le Petite Saigon. This is a small, intimate café-style restaurant, offering a quiet dining experience with beautifully presented meals and a fare that is primarily Vietnamese, with a touch of French. The crab, asparagus, and egg swirl soup is a specialty of the house, and combination meals are a cheap and tasty way to learn the menu. *1010 Langley St., tel. 604/386–1412. Dress: casual. AE, MC, V. Closed Sat. lunch and Sun. Inexpensive–Moderate.*

Cafe Mexico. This is a spacious, red-brick dining establishment just off the waterfront, serving hearty portions of Mexican food, such as pollo chipolte (grilled chicken with melted cheddar and spicy sauce, on a bed of rice). Bullfight ads and cactus plants decorate the restaurant, reinforcing its character and theme. *1425 Store St., tel. 604/386–5454. Reservations accepted. Dress: casual. AE, MC, V. Inexpensive.*

Periklis. Standard Greek cuisine is offered in this warm, Taverna-style restaurant, but there are also steaks and ribs on the menu. On the weekends you can enjoy Greek and belly dancing, but be prepared for the hordes of people who come for the entertainment. *531 Yates St., tel. 604/386–3313. Reservations accepted. Dress: casual. Closed weekend lunch; during summer, open Sat. lunch. AE, MC, V. Inexpensive.*

★ **Six-Mile-House.** This 1855 carriage house is a Victoria landmark. The brass, carved oak moldings, and stained glass, set a festive mood for the evening. The menu is constantly changing, but always features seafood selections and burgers. Try the cider or one of many international beers offered. *494 Island Hwy., tel. 604/478-3121. Reservations accepted. Dress: casual. MC, V. Inexpensive.*

★ **Wah Lai Yuen.** Although Chinatown seems to be offering less-interesting restaurants than before, this one has managed to maintain its character. It's a small corner of authenticity, combining Cantonese cuisine with wonderful baked goods including pork and curry beef buns. The portions are enormous and the price is right. *560 Fisgard St., tel. 604/381-5355. Reservations accepted. Dress: casual. No credit cards. Closed Mon. Inexpensive.*

Lodging **The Bedford Hotel.** This European-style hotel, located in the heart of downtown, is reminiscent of San Francisco's small hotels, with personalized service and strict attention to details. In keeping with the theme, rooms follow an earthen color scheme, and many have goose-down comforters, fireplaces, and Jacuzzis. Meeting rooms and small conference facilities are available also, making this a good businessperson's lodging. Gourmet breakfast is included in the room rate. *1140 Government St., V8W 1Y2, tel. 604/384-6835 or 800/665-6500; fax 604/386-8930. 40 rooms. Facilities: restaurant, pub. AE, MC, V. Very Expensive.*

★ **The Empress Hotel.** This is Victoria's dowager queen with a face-lift. First opened in 1908, it recently underwent a multi-million dollar renovation that has only enhanced its Victorian charm. In the renovation process, stained glass, carved archways, and hardwood floors were rediscovered and utilized effectively. Forty-six new rooms were added and the others were brought up to modern standards, something the hotel desperately needed. A new entrance has been constructed, in addition to the new rooms and re-landscaped grounds. The Empress dominates the inner-harbor area and is the city's primary meeting place for politicians, locals, and tourists. This is one of Victoria's top tourist attractions, so don't expect quiet strolls through the lobby. *721 Government St., V8W 1W5, tel. 604/384-8111, or 800/268-9411 in Canada, and 800/828-7447 in U.S.; fax 604/381-4334. 488 rooms. Facilities: 2 restaurants, café, 2 lounges, conference center, indoor pool, sauna, health club, in-room movies, cable TV, Christmas discount, family discount. AE, DC, MC, V. Very Expensive.*

★ **Hotel Grand Pacific.** This is a new hotel and one of Victoria's finest, with modern motifs and international service standards. Overlooking the harbor, and adjacent to the legislative buildings, the hotel accommodates business and vacationing people looking for comfort, convenience, and great scenery; all rooms have terraces, with views of either the harbor or the Olympic Mountains. The health club is elaborate, equipped with Nautilus, racquetball court, and sauna. *450 Québec St., V8V 1W5, tel. 604/386-0450 or 800/663-7550; fax 604/383-7603. 149 rooms. Facilities: restaurant, lounge, sauna, whirlpool, fitness center, convention facilities, underground parking, indoor pool. AE, DC, MC, V. Very Expensive.*

★ **Holland House Inn.** Two blocks from the inner harbor, legislative buildings, and ferry terminals, this nonsmoking hotel has a sense of casual elegance. Some of the individually designed rooms have original fine art created by the owner, and some have four-poster beds and fireplaces. All rooms have private

baths and all but two have their own balconies. A gourmet
breakfast is served and included in room rates. You'll recognize
the house by the picket fence around it. *595 Michigan St., V8V
1S7, tel. and fax 604/384–6644. 10 rooms. Facilities: lounge.
AE, DC, MC, V. Expensive–Very Expensive.*

Victoria Regent Hotel. Originally built as an apartment, this is
a posh, condo-living hotel that offers views of the harbor or
city. The outside is plain, with a glass facade, but the interior is
sumptuously decorated with warm earth tones and modern
furnishings; each apartment has a living room, dining room,
deck, kitchen, and one or two bedrooms with bath. *1234 Wharf
St., V8W 3H9, tel. 604/386–2211 or 800/663–7472; fax 604/386–
2622. 47 rooms. Facilities: restaurant, free parking, laundromat. AE, DC, MC, V. Expensive–Very Expensive.*

Captain's Palace Hotel and Restaurant. This is a unique lodging, contained within three Victorian-era mansions, and located only one block from the legislative buildings. Once a one-
bedroom B&B, it has expanded to 16 guest rooms and a restaurant. Rooms, decorated in florals and pastels, offer different
extras: some have private baths with claw-foot tubs, others
have balconies. Although the restaurant provides ample breakfasts—included in the room price—don't overlook offerings in
the neighborhood for dinner. Ask about special honeymoon,
holiday, and blossom-time packages. *309 Belleville St., V8V
1X2, tel. 604/388–9191; fax 604/388–7606. 16 rooms. Facilities:
restaurant, money exchange, bicycles. AE, MC, V. Moderate–
Very Expensive.*

Oak Bay Beach Hotel. This Tudor-style hotel, located in Oak
Bay, on the southwest side of the Saanich Peninsula, is well removed from the bustle of downtown. There's a wonderful atmosphere here, though; the hotel, situated oceanside,
overlooks the Haro Strait, and catches the setting sun. The interior decor is as dreamy as the grounds, with antiques and
flower prints decorating the rooms. The restaurant, Tudor
Room by the Sea, is average, but the bar with its cozy fireplace
is truly romantic. *1175 Beach Dr., V8S 2N2, tel. and fax 604/
598–4556. 51 rooms. Facilities: restaurant, pub, yacht for
cruises, access to health club. AE, DC, MC, V. Moderate–Very
Expensive.*

★ **Abigail's.** A Tudor country inn with gardens and crystal chandeliers, Abigail's is not only posh, but also conveniently located
four blocks east of downtown. All guest rooms are lavishly detailed with a rose, peach, and mint color scheme. Down comforters, and Jacuzzis and fireplaces in some add to the
luxurious atmosphere. There's a sense of elegant formality
about the hotel, noticed especially in the guest library and sitting room, where you'll want to spend an hour or so in the evening relaxing. Breakfast, included in the room rate, is served
from 8 to 9:30 in the downstairs dining room. *906 McClure St.,
V8V 3E7, tel. 604/388–5363; fax 604/361–1905. 16 rooms. MC,
V. Expensive.*

★ **The Beaconsfield Inn.** Built in 1875 and restored in 1984, the
Beaconsfield has a feel of Old World charm. Dark mahogany
wood appears throughout the house; down comforters and
some canopy beds and claw-foot tubs adorn the rooms, reinforcing the Victorian style of this residentially situated inn. Some
of the rooms have fireplaces and Jacuzzis. An added plus is the
guest library and conservatory/sun room. One block away, a
new addition—the Humboldt House—offers three more romantic rooms. Full breakfast, with homemade muffins, and a

cocktail hour (6–7 PM), with sherry, cheese, and fruit, are included in the room rates. *998 Humboldt St., V8V 2Z8, tel. 604/ 384–4044; fax 604/384–4044. 12 rooms. Facilities: library, Jacuzzi. MC, V. Expensive.*

Chateau Victoria. This 19-story hotel, situated across from Victoria's new Conference Centre, near the inner harbor and the Royal British Columbia Museum, promises wonderful views from its upper rooms and its rooftop restaurant. Following a Victorian motif, the rooms are warm and spacious, some with balconies or sitting areas and kitchenettes. *740 Burdett Ave., V8W 1B2, tel. 604/382–4221 or 800/663–5891; fax 604/380– 1950. 178 rooms. Facilities: restaurants, lounge, indoor pool, whirlpool, meeting rooms, courtesy vans to ferry, access to health club. AE, MC, V. Expensive.*

Dashwood Manor. One of those small, intimate places for which you're always on the lookout, Dashwood Manor is on the waterfront next to Beacon Hill Park and is truly a find. Be aware, however, that this inn is a modestly furnished inn, and sloping ceilings and sometimes peculiar layout reflect its age. This Heritage Tudor mansion, built in 1912 on property once owned by Governor Sir James Douglas, offers panoramic views of the Strait of Juan de Fuca and the Olympic Mountains. Three rooms in this B&B have fireplaces. In the afternoon, join the other guests for sherry or brandy, or relax in the small library. *1 Cook St., V8V 3W6, tel. 604/385–5517. 14 rooms. MC, V. Moderate–Expensive.*

Admiral Motel. Located on the Victoria harbour and along the tourist strip, this motel is right where the action is, although it is relatively quiet in the evening. If you're looking for a basic, clean lodging, the Admiral is just that. The amicable owners take good care of the newly refurbished rooms, and small pets are permitted. *257 Belleville St., V8V 1X1, tel. 604/388–6267. 29 rooms, 23 with kitchens. Facilities: cable TV, free parking, laundry. AE, MC, V. Inexpensive–Moderate.*

★ **Craigmyle Guest House.** In the shade of Craigdarroch Castle, about 2 kilometers (1 mile) from the downtown core, this lodge, built in 1913, has a special view of the castle. The rooms are quietly elegant and simple, with decor reminiscent of Laura Ashley prints; most units have private bath. The Edwardian touches are best felt in the main lounge, where you'll find high ceilings and a huge fireplace. A hearty English-style breakfast, with homemade preserves, porridge, and eggs, is a main attraction here. *1037 Craigdarroch Rd., V8S 2A5, tel. 604/595– 5411, fax 604/370–5276. 19 rooms, 15 with private bath. MC, V. Inexpensive–Moderate.*

The Arts and Nightlife

The Arts
Galleries

The Art Gallery of Greater Victoria is considered one of Canada's finest art museums and is home to large collections of Chinese and Japanese ceramics and other art, and also to the only authentic Shinto shrine in North America. The gallery hosts about 40 different temporary exhibitions yearly. *1040 Moss St., Victoria, tel. 604/384–4101. Admission: $3 adults, $1.50 students and senior citizens, children under 12 free; free Thurs. after 5, though donations are accepted. Open Mon.–Wed., and Fri.–Sat. 10–5, Thurs. 10–9, Sun. 1–5.*

Geert Maas Sculpture Gardens, Gallery, and Studio. World-class sculptor Geert Maas exhibits his art in an indoor gallery and a one-acre garden, in the hills above Kelowna. Maas, who works in bronze, stoneware, and mixed media, creates distinctive abstract figures with a round and fluid quality. He also sells medallions, original paintings, and etchings. *R.R. #1, 250 Reynolds Rd., Kelowna, V1Y 7P9, tel. 604/860–7012. Admission free. Open year-round, call for exact hours.*

Music The **Victoria Symphony** has a winter schedule and a summer season, playing out of the weathered **Royal Theatre** (805 Broughton St., Victoria, tel. 604/383–9711) and at the **University Centre Auditorium** (Finnerty Rd., Victoria, tel. 604/721–8559). The **Pacific Opera Victoria** performs three productions a year in the 800-seat **McPherson Playhouse** (3 Centennial Sq., tel. 604/386–6121), adjoining the Victoria City Hall. The **Victoria International Music Festival** (tel. 604/736–2119) features internationally acclaimed musicians, dancers, and singers each summer from the first week in July through late August.

Theater Live theater activity includes the **Belfry Theatre** (1291 Gladstone Ave., Victoria, tel. 604/385–6815), **Phoenix Theatre** (Finnerty Rd., tel. 604/721–8000) at the University of Victoria, **Victoria Theatre Guild** (805 Langham Ct., tel. 604/384–2141), **McPherson Playhouse** (3 Centennial Sq., tel. 604/386–6121).

In Prince George visit the **Prince George Playhouse** (2833 Recreation Place, tel. 604/563–8401). In Kelowna the **Sunshine Theatre Company** (1304 Ellis, tel. 604/763–4025) stages productions.

In Kamloops call the **Sagebrush Theatre Company** (821 Munro St., tel. 604/372–0966) or the **Western Canada Theatre Company** (1025 Lorne St., tel. 604/372–3216) for schedule information.

Nightlife After 8 PM, **Tudor House Hotel Pub** (533 Admirals Rd., tel. 604/389–9943) becomes a pub attracting the younger set. There's a dance floor and large screen for disco and video entertainment nightly.

Harpo's (15 Bastion Sq., tel. 604/385–5333) features live music, with visits from internationally recognized bands.

Excursion 2: Mayne Island

Introduction

The Gulf Islands lie in the Gulf of Georgia, between Vancouver and Victoria. The southern islands Galiano, Mayne, Saturna, Pender, and Salt Spring (the most commercialized) are warmer, have half the rainfall of Vancouver, and are graced with smooth sandstone rocks and beaches. Marine birds are numerous, and unusual vegetation such as arbutus trees (a leafy evergreen with red peeling bark) and Garry oaks make the islands very different from other areas around Vancouver. Writers, artists, craftspeople, weekend cottagers, and retirees take full advantage of the undeveloped islands.

For a first visit to the Gulf Islands, make a stopover on Mayne, the most agricultural of the group. In the 1930s and 1940s the island produced vegetables for Vancouver and Victoria until the Japanese farmers who worked the land were interned during World War II. Mayne's close proximity to Vancouver and its manageable size (even if you're on a bicycle) make it accessible and feasible for a one- or two-day trip. A free map, published by the islanders, is available on the ferry or from any store on Mayne.

Arriving and Departing by Ferry

BC Ferry (tel. 604/685–1021 for recorded message; for reservations, 604/669–1211) runs frequent service from outside Vancouver and Victoria to the Gulf Islands. The trip to Mayne Island takes about 1½ hours, and a couple of sailings run each day. Call for a 24-hour recorded phone message of crossings. If you plan on taking a car, it is often necessary to make reservations a couple of weeks in advance, especially if you are traveling on the weekend. Go mid-week if possible.

Getting Around

By Bicycle Because Mayne Island is so small (20 sq km, or 8 sq mi) and scenic, it is great territory for a vigorous bike ride, though the small hills make it not-quite-a-piece-of-cake. Renting a bike in Vancouver is a good idea, unless the weather looks iffy; then it would be worth taking a car. Some B&Bs have bicycles; ask for them to be set aside for you when making your reservation. A few bicycles are for rent at the island's only gas station (604/539–5411) at Miners Bay.

By Car The roads on Mayne Island are narrow and winding.

Exploring Mayne Island

Mayne Island saw its heyday around the turn of the century when passenger ships traveling from Victoria and Vancouver stopped to enjoy Mayne's natural beauty. Late-19th-century wood houses, hotels, and a church still stand today among the newer A-frames, log cabins, and split-level homes. Although there is no real town on Mayne, except for a few commercial buildings and homes around Miners Bay, you will find eagles, herons, and rare ducks; sea lions and black-tail deer; quiet beaches, coves, and forest paths; and warm, dry weather in the summer.

Starting at the ferry dock at **Village Bay,** head toward Miners Bay via Village Bay Road. A small white sign on your left will indicate the way to **Helen Point,** previously an Indian reservation, which presently has no inhabitants. Indian middens at Village Bay show that the island had been inhabited for 5,000 years by Cowichan Indians from Vancouver Island who paddled to Mayne Island in dugout canoes. If you choose to go all the way to Helen's Point (about a two-hour, round-trip walk), you can look north across **Active Pass** (named for the turbulent waters).

If you continue on Village Bay Road, head toward **Miners Bay,** a little town about 2 kilometers (1.2 miles) away. This commercial hub has a post office, restaurant, health-food store, gas station, bakery (with espresso), a general store, and a secondhand bookstore. Look for the House of Taylor (tel. 604/539–5283), an arts-and-crafts gallery that features local works. Also, visit the **Plumbers Pass Lockup;** formerly a jail, it is now a minuscule museum with local history exhibits.

Time Out Stop at the **Springwater Lodge** (tel. 604/539–5521), built in 1892 and the oldest operating hotel in British Columbia. The deck of the Springwater overlooks the bay and is a fine place for a cold soda or beer on a sunny day.

From Miners Bay head east on Georgina Point Road. About a mile away is **St. Mary Magdalene Church,** which doubles as an Anglican and United church. If Pastor Larry Grieg is around, he'll show you the century-old building, but the cemetery next to the church is even more interesting. Generations of islanders—the Bennetts, Georgesons, Maudes, and Deacons—whose names are all over the Mayne Island map—are buried here. Across the road, a stairway leads down to the beach.

At the end of Georgina Point Road is the **Active Pass Lighthouse.** The grassy grounds, open to the public every day from 1 to 3, are great for picnicking. Bald eagles are often on the shore along with many varieties of ducks (waterfowl is most abundant in spring and fall).

Head back down Georgina Point Road a short way and turn left on Waugh Road, left on Porter Road, and right to the end of Edith Point Road. A path leads off into the woods to **Edith Point,** an hour's walk away. The path is a bit steep in parts—not recommended for small children—but the sunny smooth sloping sandstone at the point is a real enticement. Many of the beaches on Mayne are on the north or east side, but at Edith Point you can take advantage of the full southern exposure. If the tide is out, beachcomb your way back to your car.

From Edith Point Road, go back along Waugh Road a short distance to Campbell Bay Road. Take this to Fernhill Road (which becomes Bennett Bay Road), heading east to **Bennett Bay,** the island's most popular beach. Just past the junction of Bennett Bay and Wilkes roads, beyond the Marisol Cottages, a small green sign on the right indicates beach access. The beach is wide and long and the bay is shallow, so the water warms up nicely. (Don't expect washrooms or concession stands in the Gulf Islands.) The mountain looming in the distance is Washington State's Mt. Baker. The nicest part of the beach is to your left if you are facing the water.

The last stop on the tour is **Mount Parke,** which was declared a wilderness park in 1989. Access is from Village Bay Road, where you will see a timber archway naming Mt. Parke. Drive up as far as you can until you see the sign that says "No Vehicles Beyond This Point." It is then about a 15-minute walk to the highest point on the island and a stunning, almost 360-degree view of Vancouver, Active Pass, and Vancouver Island. You may be face-to-face with eagles using the updraft to maintain their cruising altitude.

Dining and Lodging

Dining **Mayne Mast.** A nautical theme in blues and grays is appropriate for the Mayne Mast, ensconsed in a 1940s house with a large sunny deck facing Miners Bay. This family restaurant is open every day for breakfast, lunch, and dinner. Fish and chips made with red snapper is the most popular item on the menu, followed closely by the steak, prawn, and scallop dinner. *Village Bay Rd., tel. 604/539–3056. MC, V. Moderate.*

Dining and Lodging
Fernhill Lodge and Herb Farm. The lodge has built its reputation on friendly service, distinctive rooms, and historical dinners. Odds are the chef and owner, Brian Crumblehume, will be serving the Cleopatra, Chaucer, or Roman dinners. If you're not staying at the lodge, you must make a dinner reservation by 1 PM. Breakfasts are more traditional and are fabulous. They feature fresh-squeezed orange juice, freshly baked buns and muffins, good coffee, and eggs and sausages. In the summer, reserve in advance. You have a choice of seven rooms: the Jacobean, Oriental, Canadiana, Moroccan, East Indian, 18th-century French, or Victorian. *Fernhill Rd., Box 140, V0N 2J0, tel. 604/539-2544. Facilities: bicycles, sauna under the trees, sun room, library, piano, herb garden. MC, V. Moderate.*

Lodging
Oceanwood Country Inn. Set in 10 wooded acres on the waterfront, The Oceanwood offers eight deluxe rooms. Seven of them have a view of Navy Channel, which separates Mayne Island from North Pender. All have private bath and some have whirlpools, French doors, fireplaces, or terraces. Each room is individually decorated but features Canadian pine, Victorian mahogany, and romantic chintzes. During the winter, theme weekends are built around wine tastings, nature outings, murder mysteries, and the like. Room rates include breakfast and afternoon tea. The inn is open to the public daily for dinner and Sunday brunch. The menu focuses on wines and seasonal foods from the Pacific Northwest such as grilled salmon or warm scallop salad. No children or pets allowed. *630 Dinner Bay Rd., V0N 2J0, tel. 604/539-5074, fax 604/539-3002. Facilities: bicycles, sauna, hot tub, conference room, library, games room with bridge tables. AE, MC, V. Expensive.*

Blue Vista Resort. The sizable '60s-style cabins, decorated with rumpus room–style family furnishings, are about 100 feet from the beach at Bennett Bay. This is the best family accommodation on the island, because units are complete with kitchens and there are no restrictions on pets. Owners Gerry and Naomi Daignault can also provide bicycles, barbecues, and a rowboat. *Arbutus Rd., V0N 2J0, tel. 604/539-2463. MC, V. Inexpensive.*

Root Seller Inn. This warm and friendly country-style bed-and-breakfast is in a 1924 clapboard house a mile from the ferry dock. The location is popular with people getting around on foot or by bicycle because it is in the heart of activity at Miners Bay—within walking distance of stores and the pub. The four large rooms in this rustic house are furnished in old Canadiana oak and share two baths. The honeymoon suite has a fireplace and the family room sleeps five people. Guest rooms on the south side overlook the huge front deck and Miners Bay. There are picnic facilities for guests in the shady backyard. The lounge has a TV and a VCR. Breakfast is served in the dining room at a long communal table. *Box 5, Village Bay Rd. V0N 2J0, tel. 604/539-2621. Inexpensive.*

8   British Columbia

Introduction

By Ray Chatelin

Travel writer Ray Chatelin is a columnist for Province, *and contributing editor to* Business Travel Management Magazine. *His articles have appeared in a wide variety of travel and music publications worldwide.*

Updated by Philip Joseph

Canada's third-largest province (only Québec and Ontario are bigger), British Columbia occupies almost 10 percent of Canada's total surface area, stretching from the Pacific Ocean to the provinces of Alberta, Saskatchewan, and Manitoba; and from the U.S. border to the Yukon and Northwest territories. It spans more than 360,000 square miles, making it larger than every American state except Alaska.

But size alone doesn't account for British Columbia's popularity as a vacation destination. Even easterners, content in the fact that Ontario and Québec form the industrial heartland of Canada, admit that British Columbia is the most spectacular part of the nation, with salmon-rich waters, abundant coastal scenery, and stretches of snow-capped peaks.

The region's natural splendor has ironically become the source of one of its more serious conflicts. For more than a century, logging companies have depended on the abundant supply of British Columbia wood, and whole towns are still centered around the industry. But environmentalists and many residents see the industry as a threat to the natural surroundings. Compromises have been achieved in recent years, but the issue is far from resolved.

The province used to be very British and predictable, reflecting its colonial heritage, but no longer. Vancouver, for example, has become an international city whose relaxed lifestyle is spiced by a rich and varied cultural scene embracing large Japanese, Chinese, Italian, and Greek communities. Even Victoria, which clings with restrained passion to British traditions and lifestyles, has undergone an international metamorphosis in recent years.

No matter how modern the province, evidence of the earliest settlers, Pacific Coast Indians (Haida, Kwakiutl, Nootka, Salish, and others), who occupied the land for more than 12,000 years before the first Europeans arrived en masse in the late 19th century, remains.

But material proof of their heritage may not be enough for today's Native Indians who often face social barriers that have kept them from the mainstream of the province's rich economy. Although some have gained university educations and have fashioned careers, many are just now beginning to make demands on the nonnative population. In dispute are thousands of square miles of land claimed as aboriginal territory, some of which is located within major cities such as Vancouver, Prince George, and Prince Rupert.

Although the issue of ownership remains inconclusive, testimony of British Columbia's roots is apparent throughout the province, from small-town boutiques to big-city dining establishments. Native arts, such as wood-carved objects and silver-etched pendants, fetch top dollar from visitors and residents alike, and Native Indian restaurants prepare authentic culinary delights from traditional recipes.

Essential Information

Important Addresses and Numbers

Tourist Information For information concerning the province contact the **Ministry of Tourism and Provincial Secretary** (Parliament Buildings, Victoria V8V 1X4, tel. 604/387–1642). More than 140 communities in the province have **Travel Infocentres.**

The principal regional tourist offices are: **Tourism Association of Southwestern B.C.** (304–828 W. 8th Ave., Vancouver V5Z 1E2, tel. 604/876–3088); **Tourism Association of Vancouver Island** (302–45 Bastion Sq., Victoria V8W 1J1, tel. 604/382–3551); **Okanagan–Similkameen Tourist Association** (104–515 Hwy. 97 S, Kelowna V1Z 3J2, tel. 604/769–5959); **High Country Tourist Association** (403–186 Victoria St., Box 962, Kamloops V2C 6H1, tel. 604/372–7770); **North By Northwest Tourism** (3840 Alfred Ave., Box 1030, Smithers V0J 2N0, tel. 604/847–5227); **Rocky Mountain Visitors Association** (495 Wallinger Ave., Box 10, Kimberley V1A 2Y5, tel. 604/427–4838); **Prince Rupert Convention and Visitors Bureau** (100 McBride St., Box 669 CMG, Prince Rupert V8J 3S1, tel. 604/624–5637); **Kootenay Country Tourist Association** (610 Railway St., Nelson V1L 1H4, tel. 604/352–6033); **Cariboo Tourist Association** (190 Yorkston St., Box 4900, Williams Lake V2G 2V8, tel. 604/392–2226); **Peace River Alaska Highway Tourist Association** (106319–100th St., Box 6850, Fort St. John V1J 4J3, tel. 604/785–2544).

For information on Whistler, contact the **Whistler Resort Association** (Box 1400, Whistler, B.C. V0N 1B0; in Whistler, tel. 604/932–3928; reservations, tel. 604/932–4222; in Vancouver, tel. 604/685–3650; in the U.S., tel. 800/634–9622). In Whistler Village an information booth at the front door of the Conference Center is open 8:30–8.

A provincial government **Travel Infocentre** (tel. 604/932–5528) is on the main highway, about a mile south of Whistler.

Emergencies Dial **911** in Vancouver and Victoria; dial **0** elsewhere in the province for **police, ambulance,** or **poison control.**

Hospitals British Columbia has hospitals in virtually every town, including: in Victoria, **Victoria General Hospital** (35 Helmcken St., tel. 604/727–4212); in Prince George, **Prince George Regional Hospital** (2000 15th Ave., tel. 604/565–2000 or for emergencies, 604/565–2444); in Kamloops, **Royal Inland Hospital** (311 Columbia St., tel. 604/374–5111); in Kelowna, **Kelowna General Hospital** (2268 Pandosy St., tel. 604/862–4000).

Late-night Pharmacies All-night pharmacies are unknown in British Columbia, even in the largest cities, although some pharmacies do offer after-hours emergency numbers. Generally, emergency prescriptions can be filled through major hospitals. The following is a list of some pharmacies that could provide assistance: in Victoria, **McGill and Orme Pharmacies** (649 Fort St., tel. 604/384–1195); in Prince George, **Hart Drugs** (3789 W. Austin Rd., tel. 604/962–9666); in Kamloops, **Kipp-Mallery I.D.A. Pharmacy** (273 Victoria St., tel. 604/372–2531); in Kelowna, **Willits-Taylor Rexall Drugs** (444 Bernard St., tel. 604/763–7525).

Arriving and Departing by Plane

Airports and Airlines British Columbia is served by **Victoria International Airport** and **Vancouver International Airport**. Domestic airports are in most cities. **Air Canada** (tel. in Vancouver, 604/688–5515; in the U.S., 800/458–5811) and **Canadian Airlines International** (tel. in Vancouver, 604/279–6611; in the U.S., 800/426–7000) are the two dominant carriers. **Air B.C.** (tel. in Vancouver, 604/688–5515; in the U.S., 800/663–0522) is the major regional line, and runs daily flights between Seattle and Victoria.

Arriving and Departing by Car, Bus, and Boat

By Car Driving time from Seattle to Vancouver is about 2½ hours. From other Canadian regions, there are three main routes leading into British Columbia: through Sparwood, in the south, take Highway 3; from Jasper and Banff, in the central region, travel on Route 1 (TransCanada) or Highway 5; and through Dawson Creek, in the north, follow Highways 2 and 97.

By Bus **Greyhound** (tel. in Vancouver, 604/662–3222; in Seattle, 206/624–3456) connects destinations throughout British Columbia with cities and towns throughout the Pacific North Coast.

By Boat There is year-round water service (closed Christmas) between Victoria and Seattle via the *Victoria Clipper* (tel. 800/888–2535).

Washington State Ferries (tel. in Victoria, 604/656–1531; in Seattle, 206/464–6400) cross daily, year-round, between Sidney, just north of Victoria, and Anacortes, WA. **Black Ball Transport** (tel. in Victoria, 604/386–2202; in Seattle, 206/622–2222) operates between Victoria and Port Angeles, WA.

Getting Around

By Air
Queen Charlotte Islands **Trans Provincial Airlines** (tel. in Prince Rupert, 604/627–1341; in Sandspit, 604/637–5355) charters floatplanes between Sandspit, Masset, Queen Charlotte City, and Prince Rupert daily except Christmas, December 26, and New Year's Day.

Vancouver Island **Helijet** (tel. 604/273–1414) helicopter service is available from downtown Vancouver to downtown Victoria.

By Car Major roads in British Columbia, and most secondary roads, are paved and well-engineered. Mountain driving is slower, but more scenic. There are no roads on the mainland coast once you leave the populated areas of the southwest corner near Vancouver.

Car Rentals Most major agencies, including **Avis, Budget,** and **Hertz,** service cities throughout the province (*see* Renting and Leasing Cars in Chapter 1).

By Bus **Greyhound** (tel. 604/662–3222) serves the area with hundreds of stops within the province.

North of Vancouver Island **Farwest Bus Lines** (tel. 604/624–6400) serves Prince Rupert, Terrace, Kitimat, Stewart, and Smithers.

Vancouver Island **Pacific Coach Lines** (tel. in Victoria, 604/385–4411 or 800/661–1725) operates service to Victoria from Vancouver via B.C. Ferries. **Island Bus Lines** (tel. 604/385–4411) serves the Vancouver Island area. **Maverick Coach Lines** (tel. 604/255–1171) services Nanaimo from Vancouver, via B.C. Ferries (*see* below).

Whistler **Maverick Coach Lines** (tel. 604/255–1171) has buses leaving every couple of hours from the bus depot in downtown Vancouver. The bus stops at Whistler Village and the fare is $13 one way. During ski season, the last bus leaves Whistler at 10 PM.

Perimiter Transportation (in B.C., tel. 800/663–4265; outside B.C., tel. 604/261–2299) has daily service, November–May, from Vancouver Airport to Whistler. Reservations are necessary; the ticket booth is on the arrivals level of the airport.

By Ferry **B.C. Ferries** (tel. in Vancouver, 604/685–1021; in Victoria, 604/656–0757; in Nanaimo, 604/753–6626) has an efficient cross-strait ferry service from Tsawwassen and Horseshoe Bay (both just outside of Vancouver) to Vancouver Island (Victoria and Nanaimo), and the Gulf Islands. Ferries usually depart on the hour 7 AM–9 PM and can carry about 360 cars and 1,500 passengers. Ferries also run from Powell River, Campbell River, Comox, and Port McNeill to the Gulf Islands; from Port Hardy to Prince Rupert; and from Prince Rupert to the Queen Charlotte Islands, although schedules vary greatly. When traveling with car during summer months, expect a long line and delays. All summer travelers should book well in advance. For schedule information call the numbers above for a 24-hour recorded message.

By Train **BC Rail** (in Vancouver, tel. 604/984–5246 or 604/631–3500; in Prince George, tel. 604/564–9080) travels from Vancouver to Prince George, a 463-mile route including daily service to Whistler. **Via Rail** (tel. 800/561–8630) offers service between Prince Rupert and Prince George.

Vancouver Island **Esquimalt & Nanaimo Rail Liner** (450 Pandora Ave., Victoria V8W 1N6, tel. 604/383–4324 or 800/561–8630), operated by Via Rail, travels from Victoria to Courtenay and returns. It leaves Victoria's Pandora Avenue Station daily at 8:15 AM, arrives in Courtenay by 12:50 PM, and departs 25 minutes later for a 5:45 PM return.

Guided Tours

Orientation The following operators offer familiarization tours throughout the province: **Classic Holidays Tour & Travel** (102–75 W. Broadway, Vancouver, B.C. V5Y 1P1, tel. 604/875–6377); **Klineburger Worldwide Travel** (3627 1st Ave. S., Seattle, WA 98134, tel. 604/343–9699). and **Sea to Sky** (1928 Nelson St., W. Vancouver, B.C., V7V 2P4, tel. 604/984–2224).

Special-interest Nature Tours A few Vancouver Island–based companies that conduct whale-watching tours are: **Subtidal Adventures** (Box 78, Ucluelet V0R 3A0, tel. 604/726–7336), **Inter-Island Excursions** (Box 393, Tofino V0R 2Z0, tel. 604/725–3163), **Ocean Pacific Whale Charters Ltd.** (Box 590, Tofino V0R 2Z0, tel. 604/725–3919), **Tofino Sea-Kayaking Company** (320 Main St., Tofino, V0R 2Z0, tel. 604/725–4222), and, near Port Hardy, **Stubbs Island Charters** (Telegraph Cove V0N 3J0, tel. 604/928–3185).

Ecosummer Expeditions (1516 Duranleau St., Vancouver V6H 3S4, tel. 604/669–7741) runs ecological tours of the Queen Charlotte Islands.

Exploring British Columbia

Orientation

When traveling by car, keep in mind that more than three quarters of British Columbia is mountainous terrain. Trips that appear relatively short may take longer, especially in the northern regions and along the coast, where roads are often narrow and winding. In certain areas—most of the uninhabited west coast of Vancouver Island, for example—roads do not exist.

Within British Columbia, there is a vast range of climates, largely a result of the province's size, its mountainous topography, and its border on the Pacific. Vancouver Island, surrounded by Pacific waters, experiences relatively mild winters and summers (usually above 32 degrees winter, below 80 degrees summer), although it rains a lot in the winter. Likewise, the northern coast around Prince Rupert and the Queen Charlotte Islands has wet winter months and few extremes in temperature. But as you move inland, and especially toward the Peace River region in the north, the climate becomes much colder. In the southern interior, the Okanagan Valley has an arid climate, with temperatures dropping below the freezing level in winter and sometimes reaching 90 degrees during the summer.

This chapter covers Vancouver Island, the west coast, the Queen Charlotte Islands, and the Okanagan Valley. Vancouver is covered in Chapter 6.

Highlights for First-time Visitors

Craigdarroch Castle (*see* Other Points of Interest)
Naikoon Provincial Park (*see* Tour 3: North of Vancouver Island)
O'Keefe Historic Ranch (*see* Tour 4: Okanagan Valley)
Pacific Rim National Park (*see* Tour 2: Vancouver Island)
Royal British Columbia Museum (*see* Tour 1: Victoria)

Tour 1: Vancouver Island

Numbers in the margin correspond to points of interest on the British Columbia and Vancouver Island maps.

①
② **Vancouver Island,** the largest island on the west coast, stretches 450 kilometers (280 miles) from **Victoria** (*see* Excursion 1: Victoria in Chapter 6) in the south to Cape Scott, although 97% of the population live between Victoria and Campbell River (halfway up the island); 50% of them live in Victoria itself. Geographically, the differences between the east and west are impressive. The western side is wild, often inhospitable, with just a handful of small settlements. Virtually all of the island's human habitation is on the eastern coast where the weather is gentler and the topography is low-lying.

The cultural heritage of the island is Native Indian from the Kwakiutl, Nootka, and Coastal Salish groups. Native Indian art and cultural centers flourish throughout the region, especially in the lower section of the island. These centers enable visitors to catch a glimpse of contemporary Indian culture.

Mining, logging, and tourism are the important island industries. But environmental issues, such as logging practices by British Columbia's lumber companies, are becoming important to islanders—both native and non-native. Residents are working to reach a happy medium between the island's wilderness and its economy that is dependent on industrial development and tourism.

❸ Beginning your driving tour from Victoria, take Highway 14 west to **Sooke,** (26 miles, or 42 kilometers, west of Victoria), a logging, fishing, and farming community. **East Sooke Park,** on the east side of the harbor, offers 3,500 acres of beaches, hiking trails, and meadows with wild flowers. You can also visit the **Sooke Region Museum and Travel Infocentre,** with Salish and Nootka crafts, artifacts from 19th-century Sooke, barbecued salmon, and strawberry shortcake on the front lawn during the summer, and plenty of information about the region. *2070 Phillips Rd., Box 774, V0S 1N0, tel. 604/642–6351. Admission free; donations accepted. Open summer, daily 9–6; winter, Tues.–Sun. and holiday Mon., 9–5; closed Christmas.*

Time Out **Seventeen Mile House** (5196 Sooke Rd., Victoria, tel. 604/642–5942) is on the road to Sooke from Victoria. Stop here for English pub fare, a beer, or fresh local seafood. Built as a hotel, the house is an education in turn-of-the-century island architecture, as well.

The adventurous can take Highway 14 west and pick up the logging road from Port Renfrew back to the east coast; however, conditions on the gravel road may be hazardous, especially on weekdays with the trucks rolling by. The more reliable route backtracks to Victoria, then up the eastern coast of Vancouver Island, toward Nanaimo, the mid-island B.C. Ferries terminal **❹** point. On your way you'll pass through the town of **Duncan** (about 60 kilometers, or 37 miles, north of Victoria), nicknamed "city of totems" for the many totem poles that dot the small community. The two carvings behind the City Hall are worth a short trip off the main road. Duncan is also home to the **Native Heritage Centre.** Covering 13 acres of land on the banks of the Cowichan River, the center features an Indian big house, interpretive dance presentations, an arts-and-crafts gallery that focuses on carvings and weaving traditions, and picnic meals of smoked salmon next to the river. *200 Cowichan Way, Duncan, tel. 604/746–8119. Admission: $5.50 adults, senior citizen and student rates, children 6 and under free. Open May–Sept., daily 10–9; Oct.–Apr., call for schedule.*

Also in Duncan is the **B.C. Forest Museum.** More a park than a museum, the attraction spans more than 40 hectares (100 acres), combining indoor and outdoor exhibits that focus on the history of forestry in British Columbia. You begin by riding an original steam locomotive over an old wood trestle bridge to the main exhibit, which features logging and milling equipment. *RR 4 Trans-Canada Hwy., tel. 604/746–1251. Admission: $4.50 adults, $3.50 senior citizens and children 13–18, $2 children 6–12. Open late-Apr.–late-Sept., daily 9:30–6; closed rest of year.*

Vancouver Exploring *(Boxes Refer to Detail Maps)*

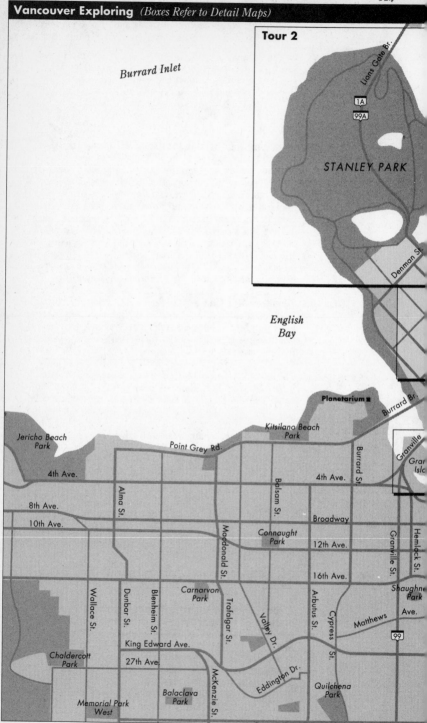

Tour 2

Burrard Inlet

Lions Gate Br.

1A
99A

STANLEY PARK

Denman St.

English
Bay

Planetarium ■

Burrard Br.

Granville

Gran
Isla

Kitsilano Beach
Park

Jericho Beach
Park

Point Grey Rd.

Burrard St.

4th Ave.

4th Ave.

Alma St.

Balsam St.

8th Ave.

10th Ave.

Broadway

Connaught
Park

Macdonald St.

12th Ave.

Granville St.

Hemlock St.

16th Ave.

Carnarvon
Park

Shaughne
Park

Wallace St.

Dunbar St.

Blenheim St.

Trafalgar St.

Valley Dr.

Arbutus St.

Cypress St.

Matthews

Ave.

99

King Edward Ave.

27th Ave.

McKenzie St.

Eddington Dr.

Quilchena
Park

Chaldercott
Park

Balaclava
Park

Memorial Park
West

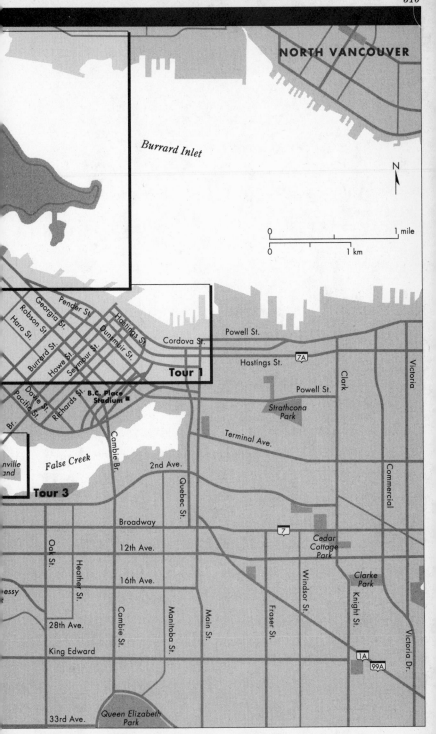

NORTH VANCOUVER

Burrard Inlet

N

| 0 | | 1 mile |
| 0 | | 1 km |

Pender St.

Georgia St.

Robson St.

Haro St.

Burrard St.

Howe St.

Hastings St.

Dunsmuir St.

Seymour St.

Cordova St.

Powell St.

Hastings St. 7A

Powell St.

Clark

Victoria

Tour 1

Dave St.

Pacific St.

Richards St.

**B.C. Place
Stadium** ■

Strathcona
Park

Br.

Cambie Br.

Terminal Ave.

False Creek

nville
nd

Tour 3

2nd Ave.

Quebec St.

Commercial

Broadway

7

Cedar
Cottage
Park

Oak St.

Heather St.

12th Ave.

16th Ave.

Clarke
Park

essy

28th Ave.

Cambie St.

Manitoba St.

Main St.

Fraser St.

Windsor St.

Knight St.

Victoria Dr.

King Edward

1A 99A

33rd Ave.

*Queen Elizabeth
Park*

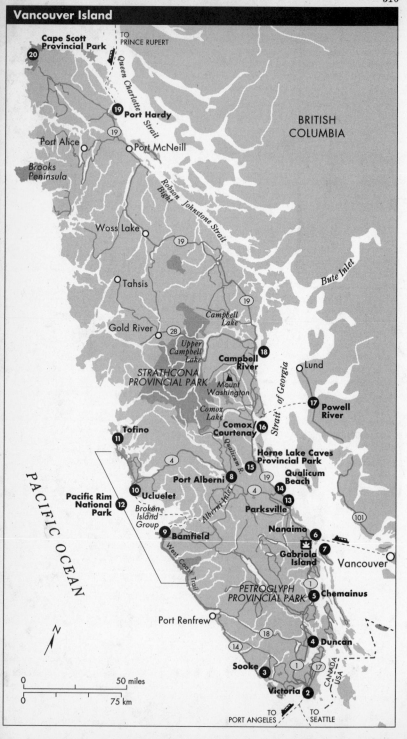

Vancouver Island

TO PRINCE RUPERT

BRITISH COLUMBIA

20 Cape Scott Provincial Park

19 Port Hardy

Port Alice

Port McNeill

Queen Charlotte Strait

Brooks Peninsula

Robson Bight

Johnstone Strait

Woss Lake

Bute Inlet

Tahsis

Campbell Lake

Gold River

Upper Campbell Lake

STRATHCONA PROVINCIAL PARK

18 Campbell River

Lund

Mount Washington

Comox Lake

Strait of Georgia

17 Powell River

16 Comox/Courtenay

11 Tofino

Horne Lake Caves Provincial Park

15

10 Ucluelet

Pacific Rim National Park

12

Broken Island Group

8 Port Alberni

Qualicum R.

Alberni Inlet

14 Qualicum Beach

13 Parksville

9 Bamfield

West Coast Trail

Nanaimo **6**

7

Gabriola Island

Vancouver

PACIFIC OCEAN

PETROGLYPH PROVINCIAL PARK

5 Chemainus

Port Renfrew

4 Duncan

18

14

3 Sooke

17

2 Victoria

CANADA USA

N

0 — 50 miles
0 — 75 km

TO PORT ANGELES TO SEATTLE

⑤ Just north of Duncan, the small town of **Chemainus** has become known recently for the bold epic murals that decorate its landscape. Once dependent on the lumber industry, the town began to revitalize in the early 1980s when its mill closed down. Since then, more than 25 murals depicting local historical events have been painted around town by international artists. Restaurants, shops, cafés, and coffee bars have added to the town's growth. Footsteps on the sidewalk lead you on a self-guided tour of the murals.

⑥ **Nanaimo,** across the strait of Georgia from Vancouver, is about an hour's drive from Victoria. Throughout the Nanaimo region, petroglyphs (Indian rock carvings) representing humans, birds, wolves, lizards, sea monsters, and supernatural creatures can be found. The **Nanaimo Centennial Museum** (100 Cameron St., tel. 604/753–1821) will give you information about local carvings. Eight kilometers (5 miles) south of town is the **Petroglyph Provincial Park,** where designs estimated to have been carved thousands of years ago can be seen along the marked trails that begin at the parking lot.

⑦ Nanaimo is a convenient departure point for other island activities. A 20-minute ferry ride leaves from town for **Gabriola Island,** a rustic, rural island equipped with lodging; and a 10-minute ferry takes you to **Newcastle Island,** where you can picnic, ride your bicycle, walk on trails leading past old mines and quarries, and wait for glimpses of deer, rabbits, and eagles.

⑧ As you continue north on Highway 19, you have the option of taking Highway 4 west to Port Alberni and the lower west-coast towns. **Port Alberni** is about an 80-kilometer (49-mile) drive from Nanaimo and is mainly a pulp-and-sawmill town and a stopover for those on the way to Ucluelet and Tofino, though fishermen will want to take advantage of the salmon-rich waters. While you're there, consider taking a breathtaking trip down the Alberni Inlet to the open sea aboard the *Lady Rose*, a Scottish ship, built in 1937. The *Lady Rose* leaves the Argyle Street dock Tuesday, Thursday, and Saturday (and Sunday in July and August) for the four-hour cruise to **Bamfield,** a remote
⑨ village of about 200. Bamfield's seaside boardwalk affords an uninterrupted view of ships heading up the inlet to Port Alberni. Oddly, for a place this small, it is well equipped to handle overnight visitors. The west coast is invaded every summer by fishermen, kayakers, scuba divers, and hikers. Bamfield is also a good base from which to take boating trips to the Broken Group Islands and hikes into the West Coast Trail (*see* below). From early June to mid-September the *Lady Rose* and *Francis Barkley* sail for Ucluelet on Monday, Wednesday, and Friday. It's a unique trip and deserves all the accolades it receives. Most of the trips, to both Bamfield and Ucluelet, stop at the Broken Group Islands, but call ahead to make sure. *Argyle St. dock, tel. 604/723–8313. Bamfield fare: $30; Broken Group Islands fare: $32; Ucluelet fare: $35. Sailings depart daily at 8AM.*

⑩ North of Bamfield are Ucluelet and Tofino—the whale-watching capitals of Canada, if not of the whole west coast of North America. The two towns are quite different in character, though both are relaxed in the winter and swell to several times their sizes in summer. **Ucluelet,** which in the Indian language means "people with a safe landing place," is totally focused on the sea. Fishing, water tours, and whale watching are the primary activities. Whale watching is big business, with a variety of charter companies that take tourist boats to greet the 20,000 gray whales that pass within a short distance of Ucluelet on their migration to the Bering Sea every March–May.

⑪ **Tofino,** on the other hand, is more commercial, with beachfront resorts, motels, and several unique bed-and-breakfast establishments. But the surrounding area remains natural. You can walk along the beach discovering caves on the way, cruise around the ancient forests of Meares Island, or take an hour-long water taxi to the hot springs north of town.

Ucluelet and Tofino bookend the Long Beach section of the ⑫ **Pacific Rim National Park** (Box 280, Ucluelet, V0R 3A0, tel. 604/726–7721), the first national marine park in Canada. The park itself comprises three separate areas—Long Beach, the Broken Group Islands, and the West Coast Trail. Each accommodates a specific interest.

The unit of **Long Beach** gets its name from an 11-kilometer (7-mile) strip of hard-packed white sand strewn with twisted driftwood, shells, and the occasional Japanese glass fishing float. Needless to say, the beach is a favorite spot during the summer and you often have to fight heavy traffic along the twisting 85 kilometers (53 miles) of Highway 4 from Port Alberni.

The 100 islands of the **Broken Group Islands** can be reached only by boat. Many boating tours are available from Ucluelet, which rests at the southern end of Long Beach, and from Bamfield. The 100 islands are alive with sea lions, seals, and whales. The sheltered lagoons of Gibralter, Jacques, and Hand islands offer protection and good boating conditions, but go with a guide.

The third element of the park is the **West Coast Trail** that stretches along the coast from Bamfield to Port Renfrew. It can be traveled only on foot and takes an average of six days to complete. The 77-kilometer (47-mile) trail is for experienced hikers and follows part of the coast called the "Graveyard of the Pacific," so called because of the large number of shipwrecks that occurred there. After the SS *Valencia* ran aground in 1906, killing all the crew and passengers, the Canadian government constructed a lifesaving trail to help future victims of shipwrecks reach safe ground. The trail remains, with demanding bogs, steep slopes and gullies, cliffs (with ladders), slippery boardwalks, and insects. Although the difficult West Coast Trail presents many obstacles for hikers, the rewards are the panoramic views of the sea, dense rain forest, sandstone cliffs with waterfalls, and wildlife that includes gray whales and seals. It's open from mid-May to late-September. The north end, from Bamfield to Nitinat, is open year-round.

Heading back to the east coast from Port Alberni, stop off at **Cathedral Grove,** located in Macmillan Provincial Park on Highway 4. Walking trails lead you past Douglas fir trees and western red cedars, some about 800 years old. Their remarkable height creates a spiritual effect, as though you were gazing at a cathedral ceiling. At the junction of highways 4 and 19 is ⑬ **Parksville**—one of the east island's primary resort areas with lodges and waterfront motels catering to families, campers, and boaters. In **Rathtrevor Provincial Park,** 1½ kilometers (about 1 mile) south of Parksville, high tide brings ashore the warmest ocean water in British Columbia. Swimmers should time their visits accordingly.

⓮ Just 12 kilometers (7 miles) north of Parksville is **Qualicum Beach,** known largely for its salmon fishing and opportunities for beachcombing along the long, sandy beaches. The nonprofit **Old School House Gallery and Art Centre** (122 Fern Rd. W., tel. 604/752–6133), with nine working studios, shows and sells the work of local artists and artisans.

Continue north, then head west off the highway and follow signs for about 15 kilometers (9 miles) to Horne Lake and the **⓯** **Horne Lake Caves Provincial Park.** Three of the six caves are open at all times. If you decide to venture in, bring along a flashlight, warm clothes, and a hard hat, and be prepared to bend and even crawl. Riverbend Cave, spanning 383 meters (1,259 feet), requires ladders and ropes in some parts, and can only be explored with a guided tour. Spelunking lessons and tours are offered for all levels, from beginner to advanced. *Tel. 604/248–3931. Fees for tours vary depending on ability level. Reservations suggested for tours.*

Between the Horne Lakes turnoff and the twin cities of Comox and Courtenay is tiny Buckley Bay, where ferries leave for **Denman Island,** with connecting service to **Hornby Island.** Denman offers old-growth forests and long sandy beaches, while Hornby's spectacular beaches have earned it the nickname of "the undiscovered Hawaii of British Columbia." Many artists have settled on the islands, establishing studios for pottery, jewelry, wood carving, and sculpture.

⓰ **Comox** and **Courtenay** are on the edge of **Strathcona Provincial Park,** and are commonly used as a base for anyone skiing Mt. Washington in the winter. Strathcona, the largest provincial park on Vancouver Island, encompasses **Mt. Golden Hinde,** at 2,200 meters (7, 218 feet) the island's highest mountain; and **Della Falls,** Canada's highest waterfall, reaching 440 meters (1,443 feet). The park's multitude of lakes and 161 campsites attract summer canoers, fishermen, and wilderness campers, and the **Strathcona Park Lodge and Outdoor Information Center,** well known for its wilderness-skills programs, provides information on the park's facilities. *Information Center, Hwy. 28, on Upper Campbell Lake, about 45 km (28 mi) west of Highway 19, Box 2160, Campbell River, V9W 5C9, tel. 604/286–3122.*

⓱ From Comox, you can take a 75-minute ferry east across the Strait of Georgia to **Powell River,** a city established around the MacMillan pulp-and-paper mill, which opened in 1912. Renowned as a year-round salmon-fishing destination, the Sunshine Coast town has 30 regional lakes that offer exceptional trout fishing, as well. For information contact **Powell River Travelinfo Center** (6807 Wharf St., tel. 604/485–4701).

⓲ **Campbell River** is ringed by shopping centers that make it look like a free-zoned mess. But people don't come here for the aesthetics, they come for the fish; some of the biggest salmon ever caught on a line have been landed just off the coast of Campbell River. At the mouth of the town's namesake, you can vie for membership in Campbell River's Tyee Club, which would allow you to fish in a specific area, and possibly land a giant chinook. Requirements for membership in the club include registering and landing a tyee (a spring salmon weighing 30 pounds or more). Coho salmon and cutthroat trout are also plentiful in the river. *Travel Information Center, 1235 Island Hwy., Box 400, Campbell River, V9W 5B6, tel. 604/286–0764. Open late-June–Labor Day, daily 8–8; rest of year, Mon.–Fri. 9–5.*

Pods of resident Orcas are nearby year-round in Johnstone Strait; and in one area, Robson Bight, they like using the beaches to rub against. Because of their presence, Robson Bight has been made into an ecological preserve: Whales must not be disturbed by human observers there. Some of the island's best whale-watching tours, however, are conducted nearby, out of Telegraph Cove, a village built on pilings over water.

⑲ Farther north is **Port Hardy,** the departure and arrival point for B.C. Ferries going through the Inside Passage to and from Prince Rupert, the coastal port serving the Queen Charlotte Islands. During the summer the town can be extremely crowded, so book your accommodations well in advance. If you choose to continue to the northernmost point on Vancouver Island, drive about 60 kilometers (about 37 miles) on logging
⑳ roads to reach **Cape Scott Provincial Park,** a wilderness camping region designed for well-equipped and experienced hikers. At Sand Neck, a strip of land that joins the cape to the mainland of the island, you can see both the eastern and western shores at once.

Tour 2: North of Vancouver Island

㉑ Cruising the 274-nautical-mile **Inside Passage,** between Port Hardy on northern Vancouver Island and Prince Rupert, is a sail through sheltered marine highway that follows a series of natural channels behind protective islands along the green-and-blue shaded British Columbia coast. The undisturbed landscape of rising mountains and humpbacked islands has a prehistoric look that leaves an indelible impression.

After a short segment in the open ocean, the 410-foot MV *Queen of the North* ducks in behind Calvert Island into Fitz Hugh Sound. From there, its route is protected from ocean swells all the way through Finlayson and Grenville channels, which are flanked by high, densely wooded mountains that rise steeply, in places, from narrow channels. The *Queen of the North* carries 750 passengers and 157 vehicles, and takes close to an entire day to make the Port Hardy to Prince Rupert trip. The ship has plenty of deck space plus lounge areas, a self-serve cafeteria, and a satisfactory restaurant that offers a plentiful buffet. Sleeping rooms are available for an additional fee. Children can play in the Captain Kids Room. *British Columbia Ferry Corporation, 1112 Fort St., Victoria V8V 4V2, tel. 604/ 386–3431. Cost varies according to room, vehicle, and time of season. Reservations required for the cruise and advised for hotel accommodations at ports of call. Oct. 1–April 30 sailings are once weekly; May 1–May 31 sailings twice-weekly; June 1– Sept. 30 sailings daily, departing on alternate days from Port Hardy and Prince Rupert; departure time 7:30 AM, arrival time 10:30 PM. Schedule and fares subject to change.*

An alternative to the ferry cruise along the Inside Passage is one of the more expensive luxury-liner cruises that sail along the B.C. coast (*see* Chapter 1) from Vancouver to Alaska.

㉒ Prince Rupert, the final stop on the B.C. Ferries route through the Inside Passage, is about 750 air kilometers (465 miles) northwest of Vancouver, though it takes more than 20 hours to drive the mountainous 1,500 kilometers (936 miles). Prince Rupert has a mild but wet climate, so take rain gear.

The town lives off fishing, fish processing, logging, saw- and pulp-mill operations, and deep-sea shipping. A gondola ride to the top of Mt. Hays, located just outside the downtown area, offers magnificent views on a clear day of the industrial harbor, the Queen Charlotte Islands, and the mountains of Alaska. You can ski Mt. Hays during the winter and picnic in the summer. Prince Rupert is also a place where British Columbia's cultural heritage is quite evident. The **Museum of Northern British Columbia** has one of the finest collections throughout the province of coastal Indian art, some artifacts dating back 10,000 years. Also featured are native artisans who carve totem poles in the carving shed and, during the summer, a 2½-hour boat tour of the harbor and Metlaktla Indian village. *1st Ave. and McBride St., Prince Rupert, tel. 604/624–3207. Admission: free; donations accepted. Open Sept–May, Mon.–Sat. 10–5; June–Aug., Mon–Sat. 9–9, Sun. 9–5.*

From Prince Rupert you can continue on to explore either the Alaskan Panhandle, interior British Columbia, or the Queen Charlotte Islands. If you wish to proceed north through the Alaskan waterways to Skagway, board the **Alaska Marine Highway System ferry** (tel. in Prince Rupert, 604/627–1745 or 800/642–0066), which docks alongside the *Queen of the North* in Prince Rupert. Alaska ferries travel this route daily in the summer; and between two and four times a week otherwise.

To see interior British Columbia, take Highway 16. En route **㉓** you'll pass through or near such communities as **Terrace,** with a hot springs complex at the Mt. Layton Resort and excellent **㉔** fishing in the Skeena River; **Kitimat** (on Highway 37, south of **㉕** Highway 16); **Hazelton,** a town rich in the culture of the Gitksan and Wet'suwet'en peoples (*see* 'Ksan in Other Points of Inter- **㉖** est, below); and the serene **Lakes District,** before coming to **㉗ Prince George** (Tourism Prince George, 1198 Victoria St., V2L 2L2, tel. 604/562–3700), British Columbia's third-largest city and the northern part of the province's hub.

The other choice from Prince Rupert is to visit the popular va- **㉘** cation destination, the **Queen Charlotte Islands,** or misty islands. Though once the remote preserve of the Haida Indians, the archipelago is now easily accessed by ferry. Today the Haidas make up only one sixth of the population, but they continue to infuse the island with a sense of the Haida past and contribute to the logging and fishing industries, and to tourism, as well. Haida elders lead tours—an essential service if you want to reach the isolated, abandoned villages. Though the region has become a popular tourist destination, limited accommodations make it necessary to reserve guest rooms well in advance.

The *Queen of Prince Rupert* (tel. in Prince Rupert, 604/624–9627) sails four to five times a week between June and September, and can easily accommodate recreational vehicles. Crossing the Hecate Strait from Prince Rupert to Skidegate, near Queen Charlotte City on Graham Island takes about six hours. Schedules vary, so call ahead, a good idea anyway because the boat fills up quickly. The **MV Kwuna,** a B.C. Ferries ship, con-

nects Skidegate Landing to Alliford Bay on Morseby Island,
with 12 twenty-minute sailings daily. Access to smaller islands
off Graham Island (the northernmost and largest of the group
of 150) and Morseby Island is by boat or air, but plans should be
made in advance through a travel agent.

In the Queen Charlottes, there are 150 kilometers (93 miles) of
paved road, most of it on Graham Island, connecting Queen
Charlotte City in the south to Massett in the north. Some of the
other islands are laced with gravel roads, most of which can be
accessed with any sturdy car or RV. The six islands that make
up the biggest portion of the group are **Langara, Graham,
Moresby, Louise, Lyell,** and **Kunghit,** with Graham the largest.
The rugged, rocky west coast of the archipelago faces the
ocean, while the east coast has many broad sandy beaches.
Throughout, the mountains and shores are often shrouded in
fog and rain-laden clouds, adding to the mysteriousness of the
islands.

Naikoon Provincial Park (tel. 604/557–4390), in the northeast
corner of Graham, preserves a large section of the unique wilderness found here, where low-lying swamps, pine and cedar,
lakes, beaches, trails, and wildlife combine to create an intriguing environment. Take the 5-kilometer (3-mile) walk from
the Tlell Picnic Site to the beach, and on to the bow section of
the old wooden shipwreck of the *Pezuta,* a 1928 log-hauling vessel. On the southern end of Graham Island, the **Queen Charlotte
Islands Museum** has a small but impressive display of Haida totem poles, masks, and carvings of both silver and argillite (a
hard black slate). There is also a natural history exhibit, which
gives interesting background on the wildlife of the islands. *Box
RR1, 2nd Beach, Skidegate V0T 1S0, tel. 604/559–4643. Admission: $2 adults, $1 senior citizens, children 12 and under
free. Open Apr.–late-Oct., weekdays 9–5, weekends 1–5; winter, Tues.–Sun. 1–5.*

If you have time on Graham Island, drive up to Old Massett on
the northern coast, site of the **Ed Jones Haida Museum.** Exhibits here include totems and artifacts. Nearby, artists sell their
work from their homes. South of Graham, in and around South
Moresby National Park Reserve, lie most of the better-known
abandoned Haida villages, accessible by water. Visiting some
of the villages requires at least several days, and lots of planning for the wilderness. You (or your tour) need to contact the
Skidegate Band Council and the Canadian Parks Services before you go.

For more information on the Queen Charlotte Islands, contact
the Queen Charlotte Islands Chamber of Commerce (Box 38,
Massett V0T 1M0, tel. 604/559–4666).

Tour 3: Okanagan Valley

The Okanagan Valley is part of a highland plateau between the
Cascade range of mountains on the west and the Monashee
mountains on the east. Dominating the valley is Okanagan
Lake, a vacation hot-spot for tourists from the west coast and
Alberta. In summer months it can be difficult to find rooms.

The valley includes Penticton to the south, Kelowna in the middle, and Vernon at the north end. Between are the recreational
and resort communities of **Summerland, Peachland, Westbank,**

and **Oyama.** These communities situated along the lake are popular tourist destinations and have camping facilities, motels, and cabins. Favorite local lore attests to the legendary Ogopogo, a snakelike creature that inhabits the lake between Peachland and Summerland. Though small in size (only 3% of the province's total land mass), the area contains the interior's largest concentration of people. Kamloops, though not officially a part of the Okanagan, is a convenient passageway from Fraser Canyon and Thompson Valley.

The valley is the fruit-growing capital of Canada, producing apricots, cherries, pears, plums, apples, and peaches. A visit to the region from mid-April through early June promises to jolt to your senses, with the brightness of spring blossoms, and a sweet smell in the air that can't be found later in the summer.

㉙ Kamloops, 50 minutes northeast of Vancouver by air and 425 kilometers (260 miles) from Vancouver, is surrounded by 500 lakes, providing an abundant source of trout, Dolly Varden, and kokanee. During late-September and October, however, attention turns to the sockeye salmon, when thousands of these fish—intent on breeding—return home to their birth waters in Adams River (only 65 kilometers, 40 miles, east of Kamloops off the Trans Canada Highway).

Once every four years—the last one was 1990—the sockeye run reaches a massive scale, as more than a million salmon pack the waters and up to 500,000 visitors come to observe. The **Roderick Haig-Brown Conservation Area,** which protects the 11-kilometer (7-mile) stretch of Adams River, is the best place to watch.

Vernon, Kelowna, and Penticton, running south along Highway 97, like to believe each has a distinct personality, but local rivalries aside, this is actually one large unit. Okanagan Lake is their glue, offering recreation, lodging, and restaurants.

㉚ Of the three, **Vernon** is the least dependent on tourism, organized instead around forestry and agriculture. The city borders on two other lakes besides Okanagan, the most enticing of which is Kalamalka Lake. The Kalamalka Lake Provincial Park has warm waters, and some of the most scenic viewpoints and hiking trails in the region. Ten kilometers (6 miles) north of Vernon, the **O'Keefe Historic Ranch** gives visitors a window on cattle-ranch life at the turn of the century. The O'Keefe mansion is a late-19th-century log house opulently furnished with original antiques. On the grounds, which now comprise 62 acres, there are a Chinese cooks' house, St. Ann's Church, a blacksmith shop, a reconstructed general store, and a display of the old Shuswap and Okanagan Railroad. Also featured are a contemporary restaurant and gift shop. *9830 Hwy. 97, 12 km (8 mi) north of Vernon, tel. 604/542–7868. Admission: $4 adults, $3 senior citizens and children 13–18, $2 children 6–12; family and group rates available. Open mid-May–mid-Oct., daily 9–5.*

㉛ Kelowna, the largest city in the Okanagan, is home to **Father Pandosy's Mission** (tel. 604/860–8369), the first non-native settlement in the region, founded in 1859. The city also offers the area's only tour of a fruit orchard; a covered wagon, pulled by a tractor, takes you on the hour-long narrated excursion. *2750 KLO Rd., East Kelowna, tel. 604/769–4719. Admission: $6.50* *adults, $5.50 senior citizens, accompanied children free. Open July 1–early Sept., weekdays 10–4, weekends 10–12.*

Kelowna is the geographic center of the valley's wine industry, with **Calona Wineries** (1125 Richter St., tel. 604/762–9144), British Columbia's oldest and biggest wine factory. Also around Kelowna are smaller, but more intimate wineries, including **Gray Monk Cellars** (1055 Camp Rd., 8 km, 5 mi west of Winfield, off Hwy. 97, tel. 604/766–3168), and **CedarCreek Estate Winery** (14 km, 8.5 mi south of Kelowna, off Hwy. 97, tel. 604/764–8866).

㉜ Penticton is the most tourist-oriented of the three. While its winter population is about 25,000, its population in summer nears 130,000. An 11-kilometer (5-mile) drive south on Highway 97 takes you to the **Okanagan Game Farm,** with more than 650 species of wild animals from around the world. Further south, off Highway 3 and along the American border, **Cathedral Provincial Park** (tel. 604/494–0321) features 81,500 acres of lakes and rolling meadows, teeming with such animals as mule deer, mountain goats, and California bighorn sheep. To reach the main part of the park, either take the six-hour hike, or arrange (and pay in advance) for the Cathedral Lake Resort (located on the premises) to escort you by four-wheel drive. There are 16 campsites in the park.

Tour 4: Whistler

㉝ If you think of skiing when you hear mention of **Whistler,** British Columbia, you're thinking on track. Whistler and Blackcomb mountains, part of the Whistler Resort Association, are the two biggest ski mountains in North America; there's summer glacier skiing, the longest vertical drop in North America, and the most advanced lifts in the world. At the base of the mountains is Whistler Village—a small community of lodgings, restaurants, pubs, gift shops, and boutiques. With more than 28 hotels arranged within a five-minute walk between the mountains, the site is buzzing with activity. Culinary options within the village range from burgers to French, Japanese to deli cuisine; and nightly entertainment runs the gamut from sophisticated piano bars to casual pubs.

Adjacent to the area is the 78,000-acre **Garibaldi Provincial Park,** with dense mountainous forests splashed with hospitable lakes and streams. But even if you don't want to roam much farther than the village, there are five lakes for canoeing, fishing, swimming, and windsurfing, and many nearby hiking and mountain-bike trails.

In the winter, the village buzzes with skiers taking to the slopes in vibrantly colored attire, but as the scenery changes from winter's snow-white to summer's lush-green landscapes, the mood of Whistler changes, too. Things seem to slow down a bit, and the resort sheds some of its competitive edge and welcomes a more relaxed, slower-paced environment. Even the local golf tournaments and the triathlon are interspersed with Mozart and bluegrass festivals.

No matter what the season, though, Whistler Village is very accessible to the pedestrian. Anywhere you want to go within the resort is at most five minutes away, and parking lots are just outside the village. The bases of Whistler and Blackcomb mountains are also just at the edge; in fact, you can ski right into the lower level of the Chateau Whistler Hotel, and all 1,220 of the village's hotel rooms are less than 1,000 feet from the lifts.

If you are interested in a tour of the area, **Alpine Adventure Tours** (tel. 604/932–2705) has a Whistler history tour of the valley and a Squamish day trip. **Caledon's Carriage Tours** (tel. 604/932–1272) will give you a tour around the village in a horse and buggy.

Other Points of Interest in British Columbia

Butchart Gardens, situated on the 130-acre Butchart estate about 21 kilometers (13 miles) north of downtown Victoria, offers more than 700 varieties of flowers and includes Italian, Japanese, and English rose gardens. During the summer, many of the floral exhibits are illuminated at night. Once a limestone quarry, the grounds were transformed in 1904 when Canadian cement pioneer Robert Butchart began building bridges and walkways and planting shrubs and flowers on the 50-acre site. Also on the premises is a gift shop, teahouse, and restaurants. *800 Benvenuto Ave., Victoria, tel. 604/652–5256. Admission: $9.50 adults, $5 children 12–17, $1 children under 12 excluding GST. Prices and schedules vary greatly depending on time of year; call ahead.*

A 15-minute drive northeast of downtown Victoria will take you to **Craigflower Farmhouse,** once the residence of Kenneth McKenzie, the overseer of one of the first farms established by the Hudson's Bay Company. The original structure—completed in 1856—and most of the furniture remain. While at the farmhouse, ask for a tour of the **Craigflower Schoolhouse,** constructed 1854-55 from lumber supplied by the sawmill at the farm. Inside, the sloping door frames and tilting fireplace support the local legend that tells of drunken workers who built this one-room schoolhouse that operated until 1911. *110 Island Hwy., tel. 604/387–4697. Schoolhouse: 2765 Admirals Rd. Admission: $3.25 adults, $2.75 students and senior citizens, $1.25 children over 6. Supplemental charge for schoolhouse. Open mid-May–June, Sept., Thurs.–Mon. 10–5; July, Aug., daily 10–5. Tours of the farmhouse are given upon request.*

Fable Cottage Estate, located 20 minutes from downtown Victoria, is 3½ acres of brightly flowered gardens with a 609-square-meter (2,000-square-foot) home, modeled on an English thatched cottage and offering spectacular ocean views. *Off Hwy. 17 on Marine Dr., Victoria, tel. 604/658–5741. Admission: $7.50 adults, $6.50 senior citizens, $4 children 13–17, $3 children 5–12. Open early Mar.–late-Oct., daily 9–dusk.*

'Ksan, set in Interior British Columbia, 291 kilometers (180 miles) from Prince Rupert, is a re-created Gitksan Indian village. The brightly painted community of six longhouses is a replica of the one that stood on the same site when the first explorers arrived in the last century. The **National Exhibition Centre and Museum** displays works and artifacts from the Upper Skeena River region. A workshop, often used by 'Ksan artists, is open to the public, and three other longhouses can be visited on a 45-minute tour: One features contemporary masks and robes, another has song-and-dance dramas in the summer. A gift shop and museum are on the grounds. *Box 326, Hazel-*

ton, tel. 604/842–5544. Admission: $4.50 adults, $3 senior citizens, $2.50 students, $1.50 children 5–12. Open May–mid-Oct., daily 9–6; mid-Oct.–Apr., Mon–Fri. 9–5. Tours given in summer, on the hour.

Scenic Drives From downtown Victoria, get on Dallas Road and follow the scenic route signs for a **marine drive around Victoria** that takes you past a residential area, along pebble beaches, and into the city's mansion area known locally as the Tweed Curtain, reflecting its house designs and residents' British lifestyles. The road continues past Beacon Hill Park (the street name changes to Beach Drive), Gonzales Point, through the township of Oak Bay, and past Uplands Park, with its stone-gate entrance leading to the huge estates of Uplands. After passing the east side of the University of Victoria, the route will eventually reach Sidney, from which you can take a ferry across to the mainland and head over to Vancouver.

The **Gold Rush Trail** is a 640-kilometer (400-mile) route along which the frontiersmen traveled in search of gold in the 19th and early 20th centuries. The interior British Columbia trail begins just below Prince George in the north, and extends to Lilooet in the south, but juts off at points in between. Following the route you can travel through Quesnel, Williams Lake, Wells, Barkerville, along the Fraser Canyon, and Cache Creek. Most towns and communities through which the trail passes have re-created villages, history museums, or historic sites that help to tell the story of the gold-rush era. For more information contact the **Cariboo Tourist Association** (Box 4900, Williams Lake V2G 2V8, tel. 604/392–2226, or in U.S. 800/663–5885).

Shopping

Okanagan Valley The **Peter Flanagan Okanagan Pottery Studio** (tel. 604/767–2010), located on Highway 97 in Peachland, sells handcrafted ceramics.

Prince Rupert Native art and other local crafts are available at **Studio 9** (516 3rd Ave. W tel. 604/624–2366).

Queen Charlotte The **Haida** Indians carve valuable figurines from the hard,
Islands black slate called argillite. The specific variety used by the Haidas is found only on the islands. Their works can be found at the **Adams Family House of Silver** (tel. 604/626–3215), in Old Masset, behind the Ed Jones Haida Museum, and at **Joy's Island Jewellers** (tel. 604/559–4742) in Queen Charlotte City. Other island specialties are silk screen prints and silver jewelry.

Vancouver Island Duncan is the home of Cowichan Indian wool sweaters, handknitted by the native Indians. A large selection is available from **Hills Indian Crafts** (tel. 604/746–6731) and **Big Foot Trading Post** (tel. 604/748–1153), both located on the main highway, about 1½ kilometers (1 mi) south of Duncan. Also check out **Modeste Wool Carding** (tel. 604/748–8983), about a half mile off the highway in nearby Koksilah.

Sports and Outdoor Activities

Canoeing and Kayaking   You'll see lots of canoes and kayaks at the many lakes and rivers near **Whistler.** If you want to get in on the fun, rentals are available at Alta Lake at both **Lakeside Park** and **Wayside Park.** Another spot that's perfect for canoeing is the **River of Golden Dreams,** either from Meadow Park to Green Lake or upstream to Twin Bridges. Kayakers looking for a thrill may want to try **Green River** from Green Lake to Pemberton. Call **Whistler Outdoor Experience** (tel. 604/932–3389) or **Whistler Kayak Adventures** (tel. 604/932–6615) for equipment or guided trips.

Fishing   Miles of coastline and thousands of lakes, rivers, and streams bring more than 750,000 fishermen to British Columbia each year. The waters of the province hold 72 species of fish (22 of them sport fish), including Chinook salmon and rainbow trout. An annual freshwater fishing license is about $20 for Canadians, $18 for B.C. residents. For a nonresident or non-Canadian, it's about $16 for six days, and $30 annually. A saltwater fishing license for one day costs $3.75 for Canadian residents and non-Canadians, and is available at virtually every fishing lodge and sporting goods outlet in the province. Annual licenses are about $11 for non-B.C. Canadians and $37 for non-Canadians.

Whistler   **Green River Fishing Guides** (tel. 604/932–3474) will take care of anything you need—equipment, guides, four-wheel-drive transportation. All five of the lakes around Whistler are stocked with trout, but the area around **Dream River Park** is one of the most popular fishing spots. Slightly farther afield, try **Cheakamus Lake, Daisy Lake,** and **Callaghan Lake.**

Golf   There are more than 200 golf courses in British Columbia and the figure is growing quickly. The province is now an Official Golf Destination of the PGA Tour in Canada and of the American PGA tour. Greens fees are about $20–$35. The topography in British Columbia tends to be mountainous, and many courses have fine views as well as some of the most treacherous approaches to greens in Canada.

Okanagan Valley   The Okanagan has a central tee-time booking service for out-of-town golfers that lists all of the Okanagan/interior British Columbia courses below. *Box 342, Westbank V0H 2A0, tel. 604/768–7500, call collect. Open May 15–Oct. 15, Mon.–Fri. 9–5; leave message if no one is there.*

Gallaghers Canyon Golf Resort (4320 McCulloch Rd., Kelowna, tel. 604/861–4000) is one of the most challenging courses in British Columbia, with long, rolling and twisting fairways. **Kelowna Golf and Country Club** (1297 Glenmore Dr., Kelowna, tel. 604/763–2736) is a private club that favors straight drivers; visitors are welcome but advised to avoid weekends. **Osoyoos Golf and Country Club** (20th Ave., Osoyoos, tel. 604/495–7003) provides a green setting in the dry, parched hills; only two of the 12 par-fours on the course are under 350 yards. Visitors are welcome. **Penticton Golf and Country Club** (799 Eckhardt Ave. W., Penticton, tel. 604/492–8727) has 10 acres of water hazards, challenging traps, and bunkers; it is a private club that welcomes visitors. **Rivershore Golf Course** (off Old Shuswap Rd., Kamloops, tel. 604/573–4622) is a Robert Trent Jones–designed course, and is one of British Columbia's longest at 7,007 yards. Visitors are welcome. **Salmon Arm Golf Club** (3400 Hwy. 97B, Salmon Arm, tel. 604/832–4727) welcomes visitors to its hilly terrain. **Shadow Ridge Golf Club** (3770 Bullman Rd., Kelowna, tel. 604/765–7777) is a relatively new course, set in a valley and surrounded by orchards. **Summerland Golf and Country Club** (Paradise Flats, 6.5 km (4 miles) west of Highway 97, Summerland, tel. 604/494–9554) is slightly off the beaten track, but has two distinctly different nines with the front nine clear and the back nine cut through a pine forest. **Twin Lakes Golf Club** (Hwy. 3A, Kaleden, tel. 604/497–5359) has an on-site RV park.

Whistler Arnold Palmer designed the par-72 championship **Whistler Golf Course** (tel. 604/932–4544), which is said to be a "good four-iron shot from the village." The course is very scenic, fairly flat, and challenging for the experienced, but pleasant for beginners.

Hunting All hunters for game—moose, bear, mountain goat and sheep, caribou, deer, birds—need licenses. Of the 112 species of mammals that dwell in British Columbia, 74 of them are peculiar only to this province. Nonresidents of Canada are required to be accompanied by a licensed guide while hunting big game in British Columbia. More than 300 outfitters provide the service. Prices vary depending on species and length of trip, but equipment, including a tent, food, and transportation is usually part of the package. For more information contact the **B.C. Wildlife Branch** (780 Blanshard St., Victoria V8V 1X5, tel. 604/387–9737).

Skiing British Columbia has hundreds of kilometers of groomed cross-
Cross-country country (Nordic) ski trails in the provincial parks and more than 40 cross-country resorts. Most downhill destinations have carved out Nordic routes along the valleys, and there are literally thousands of more trails in unmanaged areas of British Columbia.

For cross-country enthusiasts, **Manning Park Resort** (Manning Park V0X 1R0, tel. 604/840–8822) en route to the Okanagan, east of Hope, is one of the finest in the province and is located about 200 kilometers (124 miles) east of Vancouver. It also has downhill facilities, which are just as popular as the Nordic program. On Vancouver Island, **Mt. Washington** (*see* below) has Nordic facilities.

Downhill With more than half the province situated higher than 4,200 feet above sea level, new downhill courses are constantly opening. At the moment, more than 40 major resorts have downhill facilities.

On Vancouver Island, **Mt. Washington Ski Resort Ltd.** (Box 3069, Courtenay V9N 5N3, tel. 604/338–1386), with more than 30 runs and an elevation of 5,200 feet, is the largest ski area on Vancouver Island, and the third-largest in terms of visitors, in the province. Located in the Comox Valley, it's a modern, well-organized mountain with snowpack averaging 472 inches a year. It also has 30 kilometers (19 miles) of double trackset Nordic trails. Other island ski areas are **Forbidden Plateau** (2050 Cliffe Ave., Courtenay V9N 2L3, tel. 604/334–4744), located near Mt. Washington, with 15 runs and a fall of 1,150 feet; and **Mt. Cain** (Box 1225, Port McNeill V0N 2R0, tel. 604/956–

3849), on the northern part of the island near the community of Sayward off Highway 19, with 16 runs and a fall of 1,500 feet.

The Okanagan Valley region, four hours east by car from Vancouver, or one hour by air, offers some of the best ski bargains in the province. **Big White Ski Resort** (Box 2039, Station R, Kelowna V1X 4K5, tel. 604/765–3101) is the highest ski area in British Columbia, though Whistler has a longer free fall. The resort has more than 40 runs, hotels, restaurants, and, like Whistler, is in the process of rapidly expanding. **Silver Star Mountain Resorts Ltd.** (Box 2, Silver Star Mtn. V0E 1G0, tel. 604/542–0224), with 35 runs, offers well-lighted night skiing. The complete village at the base of the mountain has enough hotels to accommodate 650 people. **Apex Alpine** (275 Rosetown Ave., Penticton V2A 3J3, tel. 604/493–3200) has 36 runs and is the largest ski resort in South Okanagan. On-mountain condominiums—many for rent—can accommodate a total of 350.

Kootenay Country, a southeastern section of British Columbia that includes the Rockies, Purcells, Selkirks, and Monashees mountain ranges, features two major resorts: **Whitewater** (Box 60, Nelson V1L 5P7, tel. 604/354–4944), with more than 20 runs and a lot of powder skiing; and **Red Mountain Resorts** (Box 670, Rossland V0G 1Y0, tel. 604/362–7700), which spans two mountains and three mountain faces, and has 30 runs.

The resorts in the High Country reflect British Columbia's most diverse topographical area. At 3,100 feet of vertical drop, **Tod Mountain** (Box 869, Kamloops V2C 5M8, tel. 604/578–7222) has 47 runs. The failing of this resort is that the only on-mountain lodging facility is a B&B that accommodates up to 32 people. **Mt. Mackenzie** (Box 1000, Revelstoke V0E 2S0, tel. 604/837–5268) has 20 runs and offers deep-powder skiing. Revelstoke, located 5 kilometers (3 miles) from the base, has a wide selection of lodging.

Whistler The vertical drops and elevation at **Blackcomb** and **Whistler** mountains are, perhaps, the most impressive features to skiers. Blackcomb has a 5,280-foot vertical drop (North America's longest); Whistler has a 5,020-foot drop. The top elevation is 7,494 feet on Blackcomb and 7,160 on Whistler.

Also enticing is that these mountains have the most advanced ski-lift technology, with lift capacity on Blackcomb being 23,850 skiers per hour; on Whistler, it is 20,395 per hour. Other reasons to ski here are the 85 marked trails on Blackcomb and 96 on Whistler; both mountains have an average of 450 inches of snow per year; and Blackcomb is open June–August for summer glacier skiing.

Heli- and Heli-skiing operators are often located at well-established re-
Snowcat Skiing sorts, taking clients into otherwise inaccessible deep-powder regions of the mountains. Others operate as independents and offer accommodations, dining, and recreational facilities in their deluxe lodges. Some companies offer Snowcat skiing, in which an enclosed all-terrain vehicle takes you into the wilderness areas.

In Kootenay Country, try **Kootenay Helicopter Skiing** (Box 717, Nakusp V0G 1R0, tel. 604/265–3121; in Alberta and the U.S., 800/663–0100). With accommodations at Nakusp Lodge, they run seven-day packages to and from Kelowna, Spokane, and Castlegar. **Selkirk Wilderness Skiing** (General Delivery,

Meadow Creek V0G 1N0, tel. 604/366–4424) offers five-day packages (including remote lodging) to and from Nelson.

In the High Country, **Cat Powder Skiing** (Box 1479, Revelstoke V0E 2S0, tel. 604/837–9489) organizes two-, three-, and five-day packages that run into the Selkirks and on the upper slopes of Mt. MacKenzie in Revelstoke.

In Whistler, **Canada Heli-Sports** (tel. 604/932–2070), **Tyax Heli-Skiing** (tel. 604/932–7007), and **Whistler Heli-Skiing** (tel. 604/932–4105) have day trips with up to four glacier runs or, 12,000 vertical feet of skiing for experienced skiers; the cost is about $300.

Dining and Lodging

Dining

Throughout British Columbia you'll find a variety of cuisines, from Victoria's numerous French and Continental restaurants (*see* Chapter 6) and Vancouver Island's seafood places to interior British Columbia's wild game-oriented menus. Prices vary from location to location, but ratings reflect the categories listed on the dining chart.

Category	Cost*
Very Expensive	over $35
Expensive	$25–$35
Moderate	$15–$25
Inexpensive	under $15

per person, excluding drinks, service, and GST tax (7%), in Canadian dollars

Highly recommended restaurants are indicated by a star ★.

Lodging

The lodging possibilities across the region are as diverse as the restaurant menus. Accommodations range from bed-and-breakfast inns and rustic cabins to deluxe chain hotels. In the cities, especially, there is an abundance of accommodations, but once you get off the beaten track, guest rooms are often a rare commodity and may require advance booking.

Prices below are quoted in Canadian dollars.

Category	Cost*
Very Expensive	over $125
Expensive	$90–$125
Moderate	$50–$90
Inexpensive	under $50

All prices are for a standard double room; excluding 7% GST tax. Prices are in Canadian dollars.

Highly recommended lodgings are indicated by a star ★.

North of Vancouver Island

Prince Rupert
Dining

Smile's Seafood Café. If you don't mind walking among the fish-processing plants by the railway, you'll find this place a real change of pace. It has been a mainstay of Prince Rupert since 1935 and has succeeded because it provides small-town friendly service along with its seafood menu. Favorites include the halibut cheeks and the fisherman's platter. *113 George Hills Way, tel. 604/624–3072. No reservations. Dress: casual. MC, V. Moderate.*

Lodging

The Highliner Inn. A modern highrise near the waterfront, this facility, located in the heart of the downtown shopping district and one block away from the airline terminal building, has a view of the harbor from some of the rooms' private balconies. *815 1st Ave. W., V8J 1B3, tel. 604/624–9060. 126 rooms; handicapped rooms available. Facilities: restaurant, lounge, convention facilities, beauty salon, laundromat. AE, DC, MC, V. Moderate.*

Dining and Lodging
★

Crest Motor Hotel. It may surprise you to find a four-diamond AAA hotel in this small community, but this warm, modern hotel is probably the finest in the north. It's one block away from the two shopping centers, but is situated on a bluff overlooking the harbor. The pleasantly decorated Crest restaurant has brass rails, beam ceilings, and a waterfront view, and specializes in seafood; particularly outstanding are the salmon dishes. *222 1st Ave. W, V8J 3P6, tel. 604/624–6771 or in B.C. and Alberta, 800/663–8150; fax 604/627–7666. 103 rooms. Facilities: restaurant, lounge, coffee shop, convention-banquet facilities, cable TV, nightly entertainment. Reservations required for restaurant. Dress: casual but neat. AE, DC, MC, V. Moderate.*

Queen Charlotte Islands
Dining and Lodging

Tlell River House. The smell of fresh-cut wood welcomes you into this new secluded lodge overlooking the Tlell River. From the property in the middle of the woods, it's only a few kilometers to the beach (and the shipwreck of the *Pezuta*). The rooms feature all-wood panelling, floral curtains, and thick down comforters; many have views of the river. The restaurant serves excellent seafood and a variety of deliciously rich cheese cakes. *Beitush Rd., just south of the Tlell River Bridge on Hwy. 16, Tlell V0T 1Y0, tel. 604/557–4221. 10 rooms. Facilities: restaurant, lounge, meeting room, laundromat, boat rentals. MC, V. Moderate.*

Lodging

Alaska View Lodge. On a clear day, you can step onto your porch at this bed-and-breakfast and see the mountains of Alaska in the distance. The lodge is bordered by a long stretch of sandy beach on one side and by woods on the other. Eliane and Charly Feller, both European by origin, offer simple beachhouse rooms with few of the amenities you're likely to find in a Hilton; but the private balconies more than compensate. For an additional cost, Eliane makes a three-course dinner, using classical recipes based on Queen Charlotte fare, such as venison, scallops, and Dungeness crab. *Tow Hill Rd., Box 227, Massett V0T 1M0, tel. 604/626–3333. 3 rooms. No credit cards. Inexpensive–Moderate.*

Spruce Point Lodge. This cedar-sided building, encircled by a balcony, attracts families and couples because of its inexpensive rates and down-home feel. Like most Queen Charlotte accommodations, this one is more rustic than luxurious and features locally made pine furnishings that go with the northern-woods motif. For the money you get a Continental breakfast and an occasional seafood barbecue, with a menu that depends on the daily catch. Kayakers and hikers on a budget should ask about the bunk rooms, usually available at a low nightly rate. *609 6th Ave., Queen Charlotte City V0T 1S0, tel. 604/559–8234. 7 rooms. DC, MC, V. Inexpensive.*

Okanagan Valley

Kamloops
Lodging
★

Lac le Jeune Resort. This is the property that locals use when they want to combine the outdoors and sophisticated, modern surroundings. With 160 kilometers (99 miles) of cross-country skiing, a lake stocked with trout, and a restaurant that serves robust helpings, this is a good choice for an accommodation. The rustic, self-sufficient cabins are perfect for families because of their ample size and amenities, and pets are permitted. *Off Coquihala Hwy., 29 km (18 mi) southwest of Kamloops, Box 3215, Kamloops V2C 6B8, tel. 604/372–2722. 42 rooms. Facilities: restaurant, lounge, meeting room, gift shop, indoor whirlpool, sauna, boat rentals. AE, MC, V. Moderate.*

Kelowna
Dining

Papillon. This contemporarily furnished restaurant features a Continental menu that offers pasta, seafood, and steak. While seafood is not necessarily the specialty here, the colonial salmon with curry sauce is superb and highly recommended. The wine list includes a wide selection of imported and local wines that work nicely with the meals. *375 Leon Ave., tel. 604/763–3833. Reservations advised. Dress: casual. AE, MC, V. Closed weekend lunch. Moderate.*

Dining and Lodging

Hotel Eldorado. In 1989, the owners bought the old Eldorado Arms, built in 1926, and floated it by barge to its present location. Shortly thereafter, the old property burned down, but a new Eldorado has been built in its place, with much of the old-style charm intact. Rooms tend to be small and cozy, with light greens, floral patterns, and antique furnishings; many have balconies affording superb views of Okanagan Lake. The restaurant has earned a fine reputation, serving fresh rack of lamb and seafood dishes. Ask for a seat on the waterfront patio. *500 Cook Rd., Kelowna V1Y 4VV; tel. 604/763–7500. 20 rooms. Facilities: restaurant, lounge, conference room, marina, Jacuzzi suite. Dress: casual but neat. AE, MC, V. Expensive.*

Lodging
★

Lake Okanagan Resort. This Five-Star Resorts and Hotels property is a popular, self-contained destination on the west side of Okanagan Lake. All rooms have either kitchens or kitchenettes and range in size from one-room suites in the main hotel to spacious three-room chalets situated around the 300 acres. The resort shows some signs of age, particularly in the worn floors; but functional, earth-tone furnishings, wood-burning fireplaces, and perfect views of the lake make this a good choice of accommodations. *Westside Rd., Box 1321, Station A, 17 km (10.5 mi) north of Kelowna, V1Y 7V8; tel. 604/769–3511 or 800/663–3273. 170 rooms. Facilities: restaurant, café, poolside lounge, 3 pools, par-3 9-hole golf course, 7 tennis courts, horse stables, full-service marina. AE, DC, MC, V. Expensive.*

★ **Gables Country Inn and Tea House.** Make reservations early for this B&B, but it'll be worth the time spent planning ahead. Across the road from Indian lands, surrounded by vineyards, and the sparkling waters of Lake Okanagan, the inn is only 10 minutes from downtown. The 19th-century Heritage house promises a garden-, mountain-, or lake view from every room; ask for the one with a private balcony overlooking the water. Breakfasts include homemade scones; fresh fruits; and cherry, plum, and peach jams made from fruit trees on the property. *2405 Bering Rd., Box 1153, V1Y 7P8; tel. 604/768–4468. Adults preferred. 3 rooms. Facilities: garden, pool. No credit cards. Inexpensive.*

Merritt
Dining and Lodging
★

Corbett Lake Country Inn. The locals want to keep this one a secret, but not owner Peter McVey, a French-trained chef. His restaurant offers a different, fixed menu every night, but it will probably feature some sort of fish fresh from Lake Corbett. For a hefty fee, you can fish McVey's two privately stocked lakes, with no limit on trout, but any more than one becomes part of that night's menu. The six single cabins (with extra beds) and two duplexes are comfortable, but not plush. Small pets are allowed. *Off Hwy. 5A, 11 km (6.8 mi) south of Merritt, Box 327, V0K 2B0, tel. 604/378–4334. 8 cabins. Facilities: 2 stocked lakes; boat rentals; groomed, cross-country ski trails open all winter. Reservations required for restaurant. Dress: casual. No credit cards. Closed Mar.–Apr., Oct. 15–Dec. 23. Moderate.*

Penticton
Dining
★

Granny Bogner's. The decor in this mostly Continental restaurant is a bit contrived, with flowing lace curtains, Oriental rugs, wood chairs, cloth-covered tables, and waitresses adorned in long paisley skirts, conveying that this is a "homey" place. But the food is par excellence, with each order prepared meticulously to order. The poached halibut and roasted duck have contributed to the widely held belief that this is the best restaurant in the Okanagan. *302 Eckhardt Ave. W, tel. 604/493–2711. Reservations advised. Dress: casual. AE, MC, V. Closed lunch; Sun. and Mon.; Jan. Moderate–Expensive.*

Lodging

Coast Lakeside Resort. On the shore of Okanagan Lake, the inn is both a peaceful retreat and right in the center of the action. For relaxation the waterfront offers reprieve, and the nearby Penticon Golf and Country Club invites a competitive round of golf. Vancouver businesspeople love this place because it provides comfort and convention facilities. The newly renovated rooms are bright and airy, and many of them have lake views. *21 Lakeshore Dr. W, V2A 7M5, tel. 604/493–8221 or 800/663–9400; fax 604/493–0607. 204 rooms. Facilities: 2 restaurants, lounge, beauty salon, 2 tennis courts, volleyball, windsurfing, sailing, waterskiing, indoor pool, health club, sauna, Jacuzzi, game room. AE, DC, MC, V. Expensive.*

For bed-and-breakfast information contact **Okanagan Bed and Breakfast** (Box 5135, Kelowna V1Y 8T9, tel. 604/868–2700).

Vernon
Dining

Intermezzo. This intimate Italian restaurant combines dim lighting, high-backed chairs, olive green wall panelling, and a lounge with a fireplace. The effect is formal and old European, although the service is anything but stiff. Owner Jean DeLisle offers standard veal, fish, and pasta dishes, and an excellent selection of wines, as displayed in the wood cabinet of the main dining room. *3206–34th Ave., Box 22, Vernon V1T 6M1; tel.*

604/542–3853. Reservations accepted. Dress: casual but neat. AE, MC, V. Inexpensive.

Lodging **Village Green Inn.** This hotel offers access to 4 golf courses and to the Silver Star Ski Resort, just 22 kilometers (14 miles) away. The bright, pleasant decor makes this reasonably priced hotel a good alternative to the other hotels that line Highway 97. The rooms are spacious and the service is personal and friendly. *4801 27th St., V1T 4Z1, tel. 604/542–3321; fax 604/549–4252. 138 rooms. Facilities: restaurant, coffee shop, lounge, night club, tennis courts, volleyball, indoor and outdoor pools, sauna, Jacuzzi. AE, DC, MC, V. Moderate.*

Vancouver Island

Campbell River **Royal Coachman Inn.** This is another of those informal, black-
Dining board-menu restaurants that dot the landscape of the island. The menu is surprisingly daring for what is essentially a high-end pub, and the inn draws crowds nightly, especially on Tuesday and Saturday (prime rib nights). The menu, however, changes daily, so if ribs aren't your favorite try one of the other specials. Come early for both lunch and dinner to beat the crowds. *84 Dogwood St., tel. 604/286–0231. No reservations. Dress: casual. AE, MC, V. Inexpensive–Moderate.*

Lodging **Painter's Lodge.** In business for more than 50 years, this is one
★ of the region's major resorts. The wood-frame lodge was rebuilt in 1985, and is decorated with wood furnishings and old photos of award-winning catches. Most packages include guided fishing, but this resort, overlooking Discovery Passage, is appealing even to those who don't fish. *1625 MacDonald Rd., V9W 5C1, tel. 604/286–1102 or 800/663–7090. 80 rooms. Facilities: restaurant, lounge, pub, pool, Jacuzzis, gift shops, 2 golf courses in area, boats, fishing guides. Open late-Mar.–Oct. AE, MC, V. Moderate–Expensive.*

Comox/Courtenay **The Old House Restaurant.** This split-character restaurant of-
Dining fers both formal and casual dining, in a restored 1938 home with large cedar beams and a stone fireplace. Upstairs, among linen and fresh flowers, you select from an innovative Continental menu, with a delightful pepper steak leading as the house specialty. Downstairs, where it is decidedly more informal, you can get sandwiches, pastas, and salads. *1760 Riverside La., Courtenay, tel. 604/338–5406. Reservations advised upstairs; no reservations downstairs. Dress: casual but neat upstairs; casual downstairs. AE, DC, MC, V. Moderate.*

Lodging **The Kingfisher Inn.** Situated among trees and set off the high-
★ way overlooking the Straight of Georgia, this hotel is five minutes south of Courtenay. The inn's solid furnishings, clean white-stucco walls, bright lobby with lots of greenery, and rooms with mountain- and ocean views offer a nice change from the majority of plain accommodations lining the main drag. *Site 672, RR 6, Courtenay V9N 8H9, tel. 604/338–1323. 30 units. Facilities: restaurant, lounge, 2 tennis courts, outdoor pool, sauna, whirlpool. AE, DC, MC, V. Inexpensive–Moderate.*

★ **The Greystone Manor.** This nonsmoking B&B, set in a 70-year-old house with period furnishings, looks right out on Comox Harbor. The antiques, wood stove, and wood paneling add to the hospitable, cozy feel of this inn. Breakfast, which includes fresh fruit, muffins, fruit pancakes, or quiche, is enough to keep you filled most of the day. *4014 Haas Rd., Courtenay V9N*

8H9, tel. 604/338–1422. 4 rooms. Facilities: garden, walking trails. No credit cards. Inexpensive.

Nanaimo
Dining
★

Old Mahle House. This casually elegant place serves innovative Northwest cuisine, such as braised rabbit with Dijon mustard and red wine sauce. Twelve items adorn the regular menu, including a succulent carrot and ginger soup, and a catch of the day. Care to detail, an intimate setting, and a new addition to the three country-style rooms make this one of the finest dining experiences in the region. *Cedar and Heemer Rds., tel. 604/ 722–3621. Reservations advised. Dress: casual but neat. MC, V. Closed lunch and Mon.–Tues. Moderate.*

The Grotto. A perennial favorite, The Grotto is a Nanaimo institution that specializes in a variety of seafood. The restaurant is set against a waterfront background, and dining here is relaxed and casual. Try the prime rib or the seafood platter— zum-zum—that's big enough for two. *1511 Stewart Ave., tel. 604/753–3303. Reservations accepted. Dress: casual. AE, MC, V. Closed lunch and Sun. Inexpensive–Moderate.*

Dining and Lodging
★

Yellow Point Lodge. Yellow Point is a spit of land south of Nanaimo, east of Ladysmith, that has a series of luxurious rustic lodges of which this is the finest example. Rebuilt in 1985 after a fire destroyed the original, the lodge lost almost nothing in ambience and gained a great deal: Larger rooms have better facilities (all have private baths). Situated on a rocky knoll overlooking the Stuart Channel, the hotel has nine lodge rooms (open year-round) and beach cabins, field cabins, a range of different size cottages, and beach barracks (closed mid-October to mid-April) for the hardy. Beach cabins can be private and include tree-trunk beds and wood-burning stoves; beach barracks are not as sound, and noises carry from unit to unit, but the location along the shore makes them popular. One hundred thirty-two acres of land for strolling make the lodge an estate experience. Three full meals and snacks are included in the tariff. *Yellow Point Rd., RR 3, Ladysmith, V0R 2E0, tel. 604/245– 7422. 50 rooms. Facilities: restaurant (for guests only), 2 tennis courts, seawater pool, hot tub, sauna, canoes, mountain bikes. MC, V. Expensive.*

Lodging

La Coast Bastion Inn. This hotel is conveniently located in the middle of the downtown area, and is appealing to travelers because of its proximity to the ferry terminal. All rooms with balconies have views of the old Hudson's Bay fort and the ocean and are modernly furnished. The three eating/entertainment establishments located within the hotel make this a self-sufficient accommodation. *11 Bastion St., V9R 2Z9, tel. 604/753– 6601 or 800/663–1144. 179 rooms. Facilities: restaurant, lounge, Irish deli/pub, gift shop, boutique, convention facilities, sauna, hot tub. AE, DC, MC, V. Moderate–Expensive.*

Dorchester Hotel. Don't let the dull blue exterior fool you. Once the Nanaimo Opera House, this elegant hotel overlooking the harbor has a distinctive character, with gold knockers on each of the doors, winding hallways, and a spacious library. The rooms are small, but exceptionally comfortable, and many have views of the harbor. *70 Church St., V9R 5H4, tel. 604/754– 6835; fax 604/754–2638. 70 rooms. Facilities: restaurant, meeting rooms, library, rooftop patio. AE, DC, MC, V. Moderate.*

Parksville
Dining

The Judge's Manor. The interior of this former judge's manor home reflects his love for fine antiques and warm surroundings. Today, the family-run restaurant (with a glorious ocean view)

still conveys kindness, from the service to the carefully prepared dishes. Local and organic produce, venison, rabbit, and
other game highlight the eclectic menu. Other tasty choices include loin-of-lamb medallions. *193 Memorial Ave., tel. 604/
248–2544. Reservations advised. Dress: casual but neat. AE,
MC, V. Closed weekend lunch and Mon. during summer;
closed weekend lunch, Mon., Tues., and Wed. during winter.
Moderate.*

Lodging   **Beach Acres Resort Hotel.** For a family vacation, this collection
of cottages set in the woods facing the Georgia Strait is both
charming and practical. Each unit is a home away from home,
with one or two bedrooms, living room, kitchen, and storage
areas. In July and August, only stays for a minimum of a week
are reserved. *1015 E. Island Hwy., V0R 2S0, tel. 604/248–
3424; fax 604/248–6145. 60 cottages. Facilities: restaurant, indoor pool, sauna, whirlpool, playground, 3 tennis courts,
health club. AE, DC, MC, V. Expensive.*

The Roadhouse Inn. This Swiss chalet is set on three acres, and
is central to four of the region's golf courses. There are only a
limited number of rooms, but all are comfortable. *1223
Smithers Rd., V9P 2C1, tel. 604/248–2912. 6 rooms. Facilities:
restaurant. MC, V. Inexpensive.*

Port Hardy   **Glen Lyon Inn.** All of the rooms have a full ocean view of Hardy
Lodging   Bay and, like most area motels, have clean, modern amenities.
Eagles are often on the premises, eying the water for fish to
prey on. It's a short ride from the inn to the ferry terminal.
*6345 Hardy Bay Rd., Box 103, V0N 2P0, tel. 608/949–7115;
fax, 604/949–7415. 29 rooms. Facilities: restaurant, lounge,
nearby marina, boat launch. AE, DC, MC, V. Moderate.*

Sooke   **Sooke Harbour House.** This original 1931 clapboard farmhouse
Dining and Lodging   turned inn presents three suites, a 10-room addition, and a din-
★   ing room—all of which exude elegance. One of the finest restaurants in British Columbia, it is well worth the trip to Sooke,
from Victoria. The fish is just-caught fresh, and the herbs,
picked from some 200 varieties, are grown on the property.
Four chefs sharing the kitchen guarantees an abundance of creative dishes. On a nice summer evening you may want to sit on
the terrace, where you can catch a glimpse of the sea mammals
that play by the spit of land in front of the restaurant. Equally
exquisite are the romantic guest rooms, with natural-wood and
white finishes adding to each unit's unique theme. Rooms
range from the Herb Garden Room—decorated in shades of
mint, with French doors opening onto a private patio—to the
Longhouse Room, complete with Native American furnishings. All units, with fireplaces and either ocean- or mountain
views, come with fresh flowers, a decanter of port, and wet
bars that include herbal teas and cookies. Breakfast and lunch
are included in your room rate. Hosts Frederica and Sinclair
Philip have been paying attention to details here since 1979.
*1528 Wiffen Spit Rd., RR 4, V0S 1N0, tel. 604/642–3421. 13
rooms. Facilities: restaurant. Reservations strongly advised
for restaurant. Closed lunch except for hotel guests. Dress: casual. AE, MC, V. Restaurant: Expensive–Very Expensive.
Hotel: Very Expensive.*

Ucluelet/Tofino   **Whale's Tale.** This is a no-frills, dark but warmly decorated
Dining   place where mama's seafood cooking comes straight from the
kitchen. The view isn't much but the building, set on pilings,
shakes with a good gust of wind. The menu is highlighted by

prime rib and a variety of local seafood. *1861 Peninsula Rd., Ucluelet, tel. 604/726–4621. Reservations accepted. Dress: casual. MC, V. Closed lunch and Nov.–Jan. Moderate.*

★ **The Wickaninnish Restaurant.** Before the Canadian government acquired this wonderful, wood building for its interpretive center, it was indeed a wonderful lodge. The beach setting, combined with the restaurant's glass exterior and a stone-and-beam interior—accented by a stone fireplace—cannot be matched anywhere else in the area. It is run by the same people who make Painter's Lodge in Campbell River (*see* above) such a delight. Seafood is the primary experience here—especially the West Coast chowder—but if you take the chicken-and-prawn stir-fry, you won't be disappointed. *On Long Beach, 16 km (11 mi) north of Ucluelet, tel. 604/726–7706. Reservations advised for parties of 7 or more. Dress: casual. AE, MC, V. Closed mid-Oct.–mid-Mar. Moderate.*

Lodging **Chesterman's Beach Bed and Breakfast.** This is one of several
★ small, romantic B&Bs located on the beach, but the front yard—which is the rolling ocean surf—makes this one unique. You can while away the hours just walking the beach, searching the tidal pools, or—during the right time of year—watching whales migrating by the front door. The self-contained suite in the main house and the separate Lookout Suite are romantic, cozy, and unique; both have comfortable beds and a view of the beach. The self-sufficient one-bedroom garden cottage offers no ocean view but accommodates up to four; it's a good option for a family vacation. Owner Joan Dublank makes hot muffins every morning. *1345 Chesterman's Beach Rd., Tofino V0R 2Z0, tel. 604/725–3726. 3 suites. Facilities: bikes, surfboards, beach. V. Moderate–Expensive.*

Pacific Sands Beach Resort. Just a mile north of Pacific Rim National Park is this rustic resort with motel suites and individual two-bedroom cottages. The motel rooms are basic with modern furnishings, but fireplaces make them seem cozier. Pacific Sands is close to Long Beach golf course and is on the ocean. *1421 Pacific Rim Hwy., Box 237, Tofino V0R 2Z0, tel. 604/725–3322. 58 rooms. AE, MC, V. Moderate–Expensive.*

Canadian Princess Fishing Resort. If old ships are to your liking, this converted survey ship has 30 comfortable, but hardly opulent, cabins. Each offers one to six berths, and all share washrooms; for something a bit more spacious, request the captain's cabin; or roomier than the ship rooms and complete with more contemporary furnishings are shoreside rooms. Promising an unusual experience, this spartan resort provides the bare necessities—mostly to scuba divers and fishermen, who flock here during the summer. *The Boat Basin, Box 939, Ucluelet V0R 3A0, tel. 604/726–7771 or 800/663–7090; fax 604/726–7121. 76 sleeping units. Facilities: 10 charter boats. AE, MC, V. Inexpensive–Moderate.*

Whistler

Dining **Il Caminetto Di Umberto, Trattoria di Umberto, The Grill.** Umberto Menghi is Vancouver's best-known restaurateur because of his fabulously successful Italian restaurants. Now there are three in Whistler. Il Caminetto and the Trattoria are in the village and The Grill is in Whistler Creek, a couple of miles south. Umberto offers home-style Italian cooking and specializes in pasta dishes like crab-stuffed cannelloni or a four-cheese lasa-

gna, that mix well with the relaxed atmosphere. The Trattoria
has a Tuscan-style rotisserie, featuring a pasta dish served
with a tray of chopped tomatoes, hot pepper, basil, olive oil, anchovies, and Parmesan so that you can mix it as spicy and flavorful as you like. The Grill's specialty is lean grilled beef and
chicken, and Il Caminetto, perhaps the best restaurant in the
Whistler area, is known for its veal, osso buco, and zabaglione.
*Il Caminetto: 4242 Village Stroll, tel. 604/932–4442; Trattoria:
Mountainside Lodge, tel. 604/932–5858; The Grill: Whistler
Creek Lodge, tel. 604/932–3000. Reservations advised for dinner. Dress: neat but casual. AE, DC, MC, V. Expensive.*

The Wildflower Cafe. Although this is the main dining room of
the Chateau Whistler, it's an informal, comfortable restaurant.
Huge picture windows overlook the ski slopes and let in the
bright sun reflected off the snow. The rustic look of the Chateau Whistler lobby continues in the Wildflower—more than
100 old wood birdhouses decorate the room, and chairs and tables have that farmhouse look. Although there is an à la carte
menu that focuses on Pacific Northwest cuisine, the restaurant
features a terrific breakfast, lunch, and dinner buffets that
may include sweet potato-and-parsnip soup, barbecued salmon, smoked halibut, artichoke-and-mushroom salad, pepper
salad, seafood pâté, pasta in a spicy tomato sauce, and cold
meats. *Chateau Whistler Hotel, tel. 604/938–8000. Reservations advised for dinner. Dress: neat but casual. AE, DC, MC,
V. Expensive.*

Lodging Any accommodations, including pensions, can be booked
through the Whistler Resort Association (tel. 604/932–4222).
All pensions are outside the village, so if you don't have a car,
pick one within walking distance.

Chateau Whistler. Whistler's most extravagant hotel is a large
and friendly looking fortress, just outside the village. The hotel, built and run by Canadian Pacific Railway, is the same style
as the Banff Springs Hotel and the Jasper Park Lodge. The
marvelous lobby is filled with rustic Canadiana, handmade
Mennonite rugs, enormous fireplaces, and enticing overstuffed
sofas. Floor-to-ceiling windows in the lounge, the health club,
and the Wildflower Cafe overlook the base of Blackcomb Mountain. Skiers can ski from there right into the basement of the
hotel. The standard rooms are called premier and are fairly
small, but the suites are fit for royalty, with specially commissioned quilts and artwork, and are complemented by antique
furnishings. Both the Wildflower Cafe (*see* Dining, above) and
La Fiesta, a tapas bar, are very good choices for a meal. Look
for summer rates that drop by 50%. *4599 Chateau Blvd., Box
100, V0N 1B0, tel. 604/938–8000, fax 604/938–2020. 303 doubles, 40 suites, handicapped rooms. Facilities: 2 restaurants,
bar, indoor-outdoor pool, indoor and outdoor Jacuzzis, morning stretch classes for skiers, 3 covered tennis courts. AE, DC,
MC, V. Very Expensive.*

Pension Edelweiss. The Edelweiss is one of seven charming and
very European bed-and-breakfasts around Whistler, and is
within walking distance of Whistler Village. Rooms have balconies and fireplaces and that crisp, northern European spic-
and-span feel, in keeping with the Bavarian chalet style of the
house. Each morning a different breakfast (included in room
rate) is served: Scandinavian, American, French, German. For
dinner, proprietor Ursula Morel serves fondue or raclette.

Minimum stay in high season is three nights. *7162 Nancy Greene Way, Box 850, tel. 604/932–3641, fax 604/932–3776. 7 rooms, all with private bath. Facilities: sauna, transportation to lifts. MC, V. Moderate.*

9 Southeast Alaska

By Mike Miller

Updated by
Barbara Hodgin

Southeast, as Alaskans call the region, stretches below the state like the tail of a kite. It is a world of massive glaciers, fjords, and snowcapped peaks. Thousands of islands are blanketed with lush stands of spruce, hemlock, and cedar. Bays, coves, lakes of all sizes, and swift, icy rivers provide some of the continent's best fishing grounds—and scenery as majestic and unspoiled as any in North America.

Like anywhere else, the region has its drawbacks. For one thing, it rains a lot. If you plan to spend a week or more here, you can count on showers during at least a few of those days. Loyal Southeasterners simply throw on a light slicker and shrug off the rain. Their attitude is philosophical: without the rain, there would be no forests, no lakes, and no streams running with world-class salmon and trout, no healthy populations of brown and black bear, moose, deer, mountain goat, and wolves.

Another disadvantage—or advantage, depending on your point of view—is an almost total lack of connecting roads between the area's communities. To fill this void, Alaskans created the Marine Highway System of fast, frequent passenger and vehicle ferries. The ships, complete with staterooms, observation decks, cocktail lounges, and heated, glass-enclosed solariums, connect Seattle and Prince Rupert, B.C., with Southeast's Ketchikan, Wrangell, Petersburg, Sitka, Juneau, Haines, and Skagway. Smaller Bush Route vessels connect more remote towns and villages.

Beyond the ferries, there are the big cruise ships that ply Southeast waters, about 20 or so of them during the height of the summer. Regular jet service also provides access from the lower 48 states and from mainland Alaska to the north. Closer to the lower 48 states than any other Alaskan region, Southeast is therefore the least costly to reach.

The native peoples you'll meet in the Southeast coastal region are Tlingit, Haida, and Tsimshian (pronounced KLIN-git, HY-da, and SIM-see-EN) Indians. These peoples, like their coastal neighbors in British Columbia, continue a culture rich in totemic art forms, including deeply carved poles, masks, baskets, and ceremonial objects.

There are, by the way, only a few Alaskan Eskimos in the region, and those who do live here are relative newcomers, as are other immigrants of European, Filipino, and African descent.

Southeast Alaska is a busy and bustling region; it's a place of commercial fishermen, loggers, pulp-mill workers, government civil servants, modern-day miners, merchants, and white-collar professionals. It's a region vastly different from South Central or Interior Alaska, just as those regions differ dramatically from Alaska's Arctic or Canada's Yukon.

Because of its location, you might find Southeast a logical place to begin your Alaskan odyssey.

Essential Information

Getting Around

By Plane   **Alaska Airlines** (tel. 800/426–0333) operates several flights daily from Seattle and dozens of other Pacific Coast and southwestern cities to Ketchikan, Wrangell, Petersburg, Sitka, Glacier Bay, and Juneau. The carrier connects Juneau to the north with Yakutat, Cordova, Anchorage, Fairbanks, Nome, Kotzebue, and Prudhoe Bay. **Delta Airlines** (tel. 800/241–4141) has at least one flight daily from Seattle to Juneau and from Juneau to Fairbanks.

By Car   Only Skagway and Haines, in the northern Panhandle, and tiny little Hyder, just across the border from Stewart, B.C., are accessible by conventional highway. To reach Skagway or Haines, take the Alaska Highway to the Canadian Yukon's Whitehorse or Haines Junction, respectively, then drive the Klondike Highway or Haines Highway southwest to the Alaska Panhandle. You can reach Hyder on British Columbia's Cassiar Highway, which can be reached, in turn, from Highway 16 just north of Prince Rupert.

By Ferry   From the south, the **Alaska Marine Highway System** (tel. 800/642–0066) operates stateroom-equipped vehicle and passenger ferries from Bellingham, WA, and from Prince Rupert, B.C. The vessels call at Ketchikan, Wrangell, Petersburg, Juneau, Haines, and Skagway, and they connect with smaller vessels serving Bush communities. One of the smaller ferries also operates between Hyder and Ketchikan. In the summer, staterooms on the ferries are always sold out before sailing time; reserve months in advance. Early reservations are also highly recommended for vehicle space.

BC Ferries (1112 Fort St., Victoria, B.C., Canada V8V 4V2, tel. 604/669–1211) operates similar passenger and vehicle ferries from Vancouver Island, B.C., to Prince Rupert.

By Train   At present, Southeast Alaska's only railroad, the **White Pass and Yukon Route** (tel. 800/343–7373), operates round-trip summer sightseeing excursions between Skagway and the White Pass summit and Fraser, B.C., a mountain-climbing, cliffhanging route of 28 miles each way. Bus connections are available at Fraser to Whitehorse, Yukon.

By Bus   Year-round service between Whitehorse and Anchorage (including Fairbanks) is available from **Alaska Direct Bus Lines** (Box 501, Anchorage, 99510, tel. 907/277–6652 or 800/328–9730). Service to and from Minneapolis is also available most of the year. For Minneapolis information call 612/228–1009 or 800/328–9730. **Gray Line of Alaska** (tel. 800/544–2206) offers summertime connections from these same cities to Anchorage, Fairbanks, and other stops en route. **Alaska-Yukon Motorcoaches** (tel. 800/637–3334) offers similar seasonal service between Haines and Anchorage. Though it's a long ride, you can travel **Canadian Greyhound** (tel. 604/662–3222) from Vancouver or Edmonton to Whitehorse and make connections there with Gray Line buses to Southeast Alaska.

By Cruise Ship   Southeast waters attract cruise ships varying in size from 65 feet, with capacity for a few dozen passengers, to nearly 800 feet, with beds for more than a thousand.

Scenic Drives   The descent (or ascent, depending on which direction you're traveling) from the high, craggy Canadian mountain country to the Southeast Alaska coast makes both the **Klondike Highway** into Skagway or the **Haines Highway** to Haines especially memorable traveling. At the top of the respective passes, vegetation is sparse and pockets of snow are often present, even in summertime. The scenery is stark, with mountains and major features silhouetted sharply against frequently blue skies. As you near the saltwater coast of the Panhandle, the forest cover becomes tall, thick, and evergreen. Both drives are worth an excursion, even if you don't intend to drive any farther than the Canadian border and return. (*See* Car Rentals in Chapter 1 if you need to rent a vehicle.)

Every city, town, and village in Southeast Alaska has one or more waterfront drives that take in hustling, bustling dock scenes and tranquil bays and beaches, and they also offer the possibility of seeing wildlife. Inquire at local information centers.

Guided Tours

Alaska Sightseeing Tours (tel. 800/367–3334) and **Bendixen Yacht Cruises** (tel. 206/285–5999) offer cruises through the Panhandle in vessels small enough to visit secluded coves and bays such as the iceberg-clogged waters of LeConte Bay near Petersburg.

Yacht charters—for sightseeing, fishing, (limited) whale watching, and simply cruising—are available in every community in Southeast Alaska for trips that range from a half-day around one community to more than a week around the whole Panhandle. Only a few are listed below. Contact visitor information offices for additional names, addresses, and phone numbers.

Haines   **Alaska Nature Tours** (907/766–2876) conducts bird-watching and natural history tours to the Bald Eagle Preserve.
Alaska Rafting and Wildlife Tours (tel. 907/766–3195) packages float trips through the Chilkat Bald Eagle Preserve, home of the largest concentration of bald eagles in the world. Tours include viewing of brown bears, wolves, and other wildlife.
Alaska Sightseeing Tours (tel. 907/766–2435 or 800/637–3334). Visitors travel by motor coach to historic Fort Seward, the Alaska Indian Arts Center, Sheldon Museum, and the bald eagle viewing grounds.
Haines Street Car Company (tel. 907/766–2819) offers city tours of Haines, Fort Seward, Chilkoot and Chilkat state parks, and the Chilkat Bald Eagle Preserve. It also provides bus service between the state ferry terminal and town.

Juneau   **Alaska Discovery Tours** (tel. 907/586–1911) offers guided Southeast Alaska wilderness trips by kayak or canoe in Glacier Bay, Yakutat, and Admiralty Island.
Alaska Rainforest Treks (tel. 907/463–3466) schedules daily, escorted hikes on trails around Juneau. Terrain includes mountains, glaciers, forests, and ocean shores. Food and rain gear provided.
Alaska Travel Adventures (tel. 907/789–0052) packages a half-day guided raft trip (there's *almost* white water) down the Mendenhall River; includes mid-trip snack of Alaska smoked

salmon, reindeer sausage, cheeses, apple cider, and an alcoholic brew called Mendenhall Madness.

Alaska Sightseeing Tours (tel. 907/586–6300 or 800/637–3334) and **Gray Line of Alaska** (tel. 907/586–3773 or 800/544–2206) both offer motor-coach sightseeing tours of Juneau, Mendenhall Glacier, and other points of interest.

Alaska Up Close (tel. 907/789–9544) provides custom sightseeing tours in small vans, specializing in natural history and fine art.

Juneau Carriage Company (tel. 907/586–2121) offers Southeast Alaska's newest horse-drawn carriage tour, 45 minutes through and around downtown Juneau's historic district.

Phillips Cruises & Tours (tel. 907/276–8023 or 800/544–0529) schedules daily six-hour cruises from Juneau to the twin glaciers at Tracy Arm fjord. Also offers nightly dinner cruise in waters around Alaska's capital city.

Ptarmigan Ptransport and Ptours (tel. 907/789–5179) has sightseeing tours to Juneau, neighboring Douglas, and Mendenhall Glacier in a bright red double-decker bus.

Temsco Helicopters (tel. 907/789–9501) pioneered helicopter sightseeing over Mendenhall Glacier with an actual touchdown and a chance to romp on the glacier. **Era Helicopters** (tel. 907/586–2030) offers a similar quality experience.

Ketchikan   **Alaska Sightseeing Tours** (tel. 907/225–2740 or 800/637–3334) offers sightseeing motor coach tours of downtown Ketchikan, Totem Bight State Historical Park, and Totem Heritage Center. Boat tours of Misty Fjords and the Inside Passage are also available.

Gray Line of Alaska (tel. 907/225–5930 or 800/544–2206) offers a city tour comparable to the above, plus a day tour to nearby Annette Island and the Tsimshian Indian community of Metlakatla.

Captain Ted Pratt (Bar Harbor, Box 9419, Ketchikan 99901, tel. 907/225–0055) schedules tours throughout the Panhandle aboard the 70-foot *Midnight Sun,* surely one of the most luxurious cruise yachts in Southeast Alaska. (Would you believe a *wood-burning fireplace* in the main lounge?)

Outdoor Alaska (tel. 907/225–6044) provides cruise or cruise-fly day-long excursions from downtown Ketchikan to Misty Fjords National Monument, a wilderness of steep-walled fjords, mountains, and islands. Harbor cruises of the Ketchikan waterfront are also available.

Petersburg   **LeConte Cruises** (Box 913, Petersburg, 99833, tel. 907/772–4790) offers yacht tours for sightseeing, photography, and fishing.

Pacific Wing, Inc. (tel. 907/772–9258) gets high marks from locals for its flightseeing tours over LeConte Glacier.

Sitka   **Alaska Travel Adventures** (tel. 907/789–0052) operates boat and motorized Zodiac raft excursions to a seal rookery and bird refuge; en route, see porpoises, sea lions, and (if you're lucky) whales.

Baidarka Boats (tel. 907/747–8996) rents sea kayaks and offers guided custom trips in the island-dotted waters around Sitka.

Prewitt Enterprises (tel. 907/747–8443) meets state ferries and provides short city tours while vessels are in port; stops at Sitka National Historical Park, Sheldon Jackson Museum, and downtown shopping area. Also offers more inclusive three-hour sightseeing tours that visit St. Michael's Cathedral, Old Sitka, Castle Hill, and old Russian cemetery.

Skagway **Alaska Sightseeing Tours** (tel. 907/983–2828 or 800/637–3334) and **Gray Line of Alaska** (tel. 907/983–2241 or 800/544–2206) provide motor-coach tours through Skagway's historic district, Gold-rush Cemetery (where frontier "bad guy" Soapy Smith lies buried), and the trailhead of the Chilkoot Trail to the Yukon gold fields.

Gold Rush Tours (tel. 907/983–2289) provides a spectacular drive across the Canadian border to a picnic in the world's smallest desert. This is no joke—there really is a tiny desert a few miles north of Carcross, Yukon.

Skagway Hack (tel. 907/983–2472) offers horse-drawn transportation through the historic district of Klondike National Historical Park, also trailhead or waterfront tours.

Wrangell **Aqua Sports** (tel. 907/874–3811) specializes in waterborne glacier tours, river running, photo excursions, and fishing.

TH Charters (tel. 907/874–3455) provides a fast-pace jet-boat ride into the Stikine River wilderness country to Shakes Glacier, Shakes Hot Springs, and other historic and natural attractions.

Important Addresses and Numbers

Tourist Information **Southeast Alaska Tourism Council** (Box 710, Juneau 99802, tel. 907/586–4777).

Gustavus Visitors Association (Box 167, Gustavus 99826, tel. 907/697–2358).

Glacier Bay National Park and Preserve (Gustavus 99826, tel. 907/697–2230).

Haines/Fort Seward Visitor Information Center (2nd Ave. near Willard St., tel. 907/766–2202). Open June–August, 8 AM–8 PM daily; winter hours posted.

Juneau Convention and Visitors Bureau (76 Egan Dr., Suite 140, Juneau 99801, tel. 907/586–1737) and **Davis Log Cabin Information Center** (134 3rd Ave., tel. 907/586–2201). Information also available at the kiosk on the cruise ship dock, downtown at Marine Park.

Ketchikan Visitors Bureau (131 Front St., Ketchikan 99901, tel. 907/225–6166). Open daily May 15–September 30, 8–5; weekdays in winter 8–5.

Petersburg Chamber of Commerce Visitor Center (221 Harbor Way, Box 649, Petersburg 99833, tel. 907/772–3646). Located downtown in the Harbormaster building overlooking the boat harbor.

Sitka Convention and Visitors Bureau (Box 1226, Sitka 99835, tel. 907/747–5940). Open weekdays 8–5 and when cruise ships are in port. **The Greater Sitka Chamber of Commerce** (Box 638, Sitka 99835, tel. 907/747–7816). Open weekdays 9–5. Both are located in the Centennial Building on Harbor Drive downtown.

Skagway Convention and Visitors Bureau (City Hall, 7th Ave. and Spring St., Box 415, Skagway 99840, tel. 907/983–2854). Open 8:30–noon and 1–5.

The Klondike Gold Rush National Historical Park visitor center (2nd Ave. and Broadway, Skagway 99840, tel. 907/983–2921)—which has lots of information on the city as well—is housed in the old White Pass and Yukon Route railroad terminal downtown. Open 8:30–noon, 1–5.

Wrangell Convention and Visitors Bureau (Box 1078, Wrangell 99929, tel. 907/874–3800). Located at the Wrangell Museum, 122 2nd Street, a block and a half up the hill from the ferry terminal. Open May 15–September 15, Monday–Saturday, 1–4 and for an hour whenever a cruise ship or ferry is in port; in winter, open Tuesday evenings 7–9, and Wednesday 1:30–4. **Chamber of Commerce Visitors Center** (Box 49, Wrangell 99929, tel. 907/874–3901) in the A-frame on the waterfront next to City Hall. Open when cruise ships or ferries are in port, and at other posted times during the summer.

Emergencies
Police and Ambulance In Haines/Fort Seward, Juneau, Ketchikan, Petersburg and Sitka, dial 911. Gustavus EMS (tel. 907/697–2222). Skagway: Police (tel. 907/983–2301), Ambulance (tel. 907/983–2300). Wrangell: Police (tel. 907/874–3304), Ambulance, Fire Department (tel. 907/874–2000).

Doctor and Dentist **Haines/Fort Seward Health Clinic,** next to the Visitors Information Center, tel. 907/766–2521. Pharmacy needs also cared for.
Juneau: Bartlett Memorial Hospital, 3260 Hospital Drive, located just off the Egan Expressway, about four miles north of downtown, tel. 907/586–2611.
Ketchikan General Hospital, 3100 Tongass Avenue, in the north end of the city business district, tel. 907/225–5171.
Petersburg General Hospital, located downtown at 1st Street and Fram Street, tel. 907/772–4291.
Sitka Community Hospital, 209 Moller Drive, north of downtown, tel. 907/747–3241.
Skagway Health Clinic, on 11th Avenue between State Street and Broadway, tel. 907/983–2225.
Wrangell Hospital, on the airport road, next to the elementary school, tel. 907/874–3356.

Pharmacy **Juneau: Juneau Drug Co.,** 202 Front Street, downtown, across from McDonald's, tel. 907/586–1233. **Ron's Apothecary,** 9101 Mendenhall Mall Road, located about 10 miles north of downtown in Mendenhall Valley, next to the Super Bear market, tel. 907/789–0458; after-hours emergencies, 907/789–9522.
Ketchikan: Race Pharmacy/Downtown, 300 Front Street, tel. 907/225–5171. **Race Pharmacy,** 2300 Tongass Avenue, across from the Plaza Portwest shopping mall, tel. 907/225–4151. After hours, call the hospital.
Petersburg: Rexall Drugs (tel. 907/772–3265). After hours, call the hospital.
Sitka: White's Pharmacy, 705 Halibut Point Road, tel. 907/747–5755. **Harry Race Drug,** 106 Lincoln Street, tel. 907/747–8666.
Wrangell: Wrangell Drug, Front Street, tel. 907/874–3422.

Exploring Southeast Alaska

Orientation

The Southeast Panhandle stretches some 500 miles from Yakutat at its northernmost to Ketchikan and Metlakatla at the southern end. At its widest the region measures only some 140 miles, and in the upper Panhandle just south of Yakutat it's a

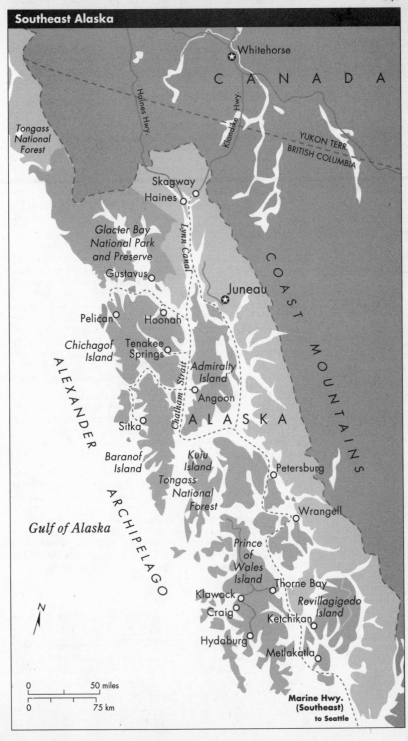

Southeast Alaska

Whitehorse

C A N A D A

Haines Hwy.

Klondike Hwy.

YUKON TERR
BRITISH COLUMBIA

Tongass
National
Forest

Skagway
Haines

Lynn Canal

Glacier Bay
National Park
and Preserve

Gustavus

Juneau

Pelican

Hoonah

Chichagof
Island

Tenakee
Springs

C
O
A
S
T

Chatham Strait

Admiralty
Island

Angoon

A L A S K A

M
O
U
N
T
A
I
N
S

Sitka

A
L
E
X
A
N
D
E
R

Baranof
Island

Kuiu
Island

Petersburg

Tongass
National
Forest

Gulf of Alaska

A
R
C
H
I
P
E
L
A
G
O

Wrangell

Prince
of
Wales
Island

Thorne Bay

Revillagigedo
Island

N

Klawock

Craig

Ketchikan

Hydaburg

Metlakatla

0   50 miles

0   75 km

**Marine Hwy.
(Southeast)
to Seattle**

skinny 30 miles across. Most of the Panhandle consists of a sliver of mainland buffered by offshore islands.

There are, in fact, more than a thousand islands up and down the Panhandle coast—most of them mountainous with lush covers of timber. Collectively they constitute the Alexander Archipelago. On the mainland to the east of the U.S.–Canadian border lies British Columbia.

You can get to and around the area by ship or by plane, but forget the highway. The roadways that exist in these parts run at most a few dozen miles out from towns and villages, then they dead-end.

Not surprisingly, most of the communities of the region are located on islands rather than on the mainland. The principal exceptions are Juneau, Haines, Skagway, and the Indian village of Klukwan. Island outposts include Ketchikan, Wrangell, Petersburg, Sitka, Metlakatla, and a number of other towns, Indian villages, and logging camps.

If shipboard sightseeing is your pleasure, more than two dozen cruise ships and state ferries await your booking. The usual (though not the only) pattern is for cruising visitors to board ship at Vancouver, B.C., or San Francisco, then to set sail on an itinerary that typically includes Ketchikan, Juneau, Skagway, and Sitka. Other itineraries go to Glacier Bay as well. Cruise ship travel includes a mix of sailing and port visits, which can vary from a few hours to a full day. The state ferries (southern ports of origin: Bellingham, WA or Prince Rupert, B.C.) rarely spend much time in the cities where they call, but you can get off one ship, spend a day or more ashore, then catch another vessel heading north or south to your next destination.

Don't overlook the region's alternative means of travel. Small float planes, some carrying five or fewer passengers, and yachts sleeping a half dozen or so ply the routes from the larger population centers to tiny settlements and even more remote sites where there are no permanent residents at all (unless you count bears).

If you're interested in fishing you have a number of options to choose from (or mix). There are saltwater salmon charter boats, salmon fishing lodges (some near the larger communities, others remote and accessible by float plane), fly-in mountain lake lodges where the fishing is for trout and char, and—bargain hunters take special note—more than 150 remote but weather-tight cabins operated by the U.S. Forest Service. The USFS rents these units for the absurdly reasonable rate of $15 per night per group (*see* Off the Beaten Track, below).

Ketchikan

Numbers in the margin correspond to points of interest on the Ketchikan map.

Alaskans call Ketchikan "the First City," not because of size or population, but because in the days before air travel it was always the first Alaskan port of call for northbound steamship passengers. For many travelers today—arriving by air, cruise ship, or ferry—the tradition continues.

Ketchikan is perched on a large mountainous island underneath 3,000-foot Deer Mountain. The island's name is a jaw breaker, Revillagigedo (Alaskans just say "Revilla"), named by English mariner George Vancouver, who was exploring the Inside Passage in 1793. He often named things for his crew and friends; in this case it was named after the viceroy of Mexico.

The site at the mouth of Ketchikan Creek was a summer fish camp for the Tlingit Indians until white miners and fishermen came to settle in the town in 1885. Gold discoveries just before the turn of the century brought more immigrants, and valuable timber and commercial fishing resources spurred new industries. By the 1930s the town bragged it was the "Salmon Canning Capital of the World."

Today Ketchikan ranks fourth among Alaskan cities in size (7,600 residents in the city proper, 5,000 in the borough, or county). Fishing and timber are still the mainstays of Ketchikan's economy, although tourism is certainly helping out.

It's an easy town to sightsee in and enjoy. **Alaska Sightseeing Tours** (tel. 907/225–2740) and **Gray Line of Alaska** (tel. 907/225–5930) offer city tours by motor coach that take in points of interest, including totem parks both within the city and out in the borough. **Royal Hyway Tours** offers similar excursions, but only for passengers aboard ships of their parent company, Princess Cruises.

There's a lot to be seen in downtown Ketchikan on foot. The

❶ best place to begin is at the **Ketchikan Visitors Bureau** on the dock, where you can pick up a free historic walking tour map. From there head up Mission Street, past the Sub–Post Office located in the Trading Post (the main post office is inconveniently located several miles south, near the ferry terminal), to

❷ Bawden Street and **St. John's Church and Seaman's Center.** The 1903 church structure is the oldest remaining house of worship in Ketchikan, its interior formed from red cedar cut in the native-operated sawmill in nearby Saxman. The Seaman's Center, next door to the church, was built in 1904 as a hospital. It later housed the *Alaska Sportsman Magazine* (now *Alaska Magazine*), which began publication in Ketchikan in 1936.

❸ At Dock St., your tour passes the *Ketchikan Daily News* build-
❹ ing, then jogs east to the **Tongass Historical Museum and Totem Pole.** Plan to spend a half hour or so here browsing among Indian artifacts and pioneer relics of the early mining and fishing era. Among exhibits: a big and brilliantly polished lens out of Tree Point Lighthouse, the bullet-riddled skull of a notorious and fearsome old brown bear called Old Groaner, Indian ceremonial objects, and a Chilkat blanket. There's even a 14-foot model of a typical Alaskan salmon fishing seine vessel. *Museum admission: $1.50 Mon.–Sat.; free on Sun. Open Mon.–Sat. 8–5, Sun. 9–4.*

❺ Continuing north, then east on Park Street, you can see **Grant Street Trestle,** constructed in 1908. At one time virtually all of Ketchikan's walkways and streets were wooden trestles. This is the last remaining example of the city's early road system.
❻ Get out your camera and set it for fast speed at the **Salmon Falls, Fish Ladder,** and **Salmon Carving** just off Park Street. When the salmon start running in mid-summer and later, thousands will literally leap the falls (or take the easier ladder

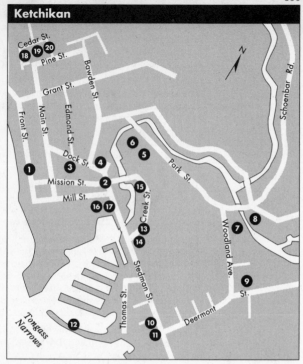

Ketchikan

route) to spawn in Ketchikan Creek's waters farther upstream.

7 Many can be seen in the creek feeding the falls. At **City Park** you can see small ponds that were once holding areas for the first hatchery that operated in the area, from 1923 to 1928. The

8 modern **Deer Mountain Hatchery** now disperses tens of thousands of salmon annually into local waters, much to the satisfaction of local sport and commercial fishermen. Also at the park is

9 the **Totem Heritage Center and Nature Path.** Definitely plan to spend some time in the center viewing authentic ancient examples of the carver's art. *Admission: $1.50. Open Mon.–Sat. 8–5, Sun. 9–4.*

Continuing south to Deermount Street and then west on

10 Stedman Street, you pass the **Ketchikan Indian Corporation** site of a former Bureau of Indian Affairs school, and a colorful

11 wall mural called *Return of the Eagle.* It was created by 21 native artists on the walls of the Robertson Building of the Ketchikan campus, University of Alaska–Southeast.

12 Next comes **Thomas Street** and **Thomas Basin.** The street was constructed in 1913 to be part of New England Fish Company's cannery here; Thomas Basin is a major, and picture-worthy, harbor. One of four harbors in Ketchikan, it is "home port" to a wide variety of pleasure and work boats.

13 Now your tour takes you to **Creek Street.** Formerly this was Ketchikan's infamous red-light district; today its small, quaint houses, built on stilts over the creek waters, have been restored as trendy shops. The street's most famous brothel,

14 **Dolly's House,** has been preserved as a museum, complete with furnishings, beds, and a short history of the life and times of Ketchikan's best-known madam. *Admission: $2. Open when cruise ships are in port.*

Farther up Creek Street, there's more good salmon viewing in season at the **Creek Street Footbridge.** Head south to Mill Street ⑮ and see the **Federal Building/U.S. Forest Service and historic** ⑯ **Knox Bros. Clock,** a large outdoor timepiece. It's one of three ⑰ that once served the city's downtown business district.

If you're into steep street climbing, head up Main Street past ⑱ the Ketchikan Fire Department to the **Kyan Totem Pole,** a replica of a 1913 original that once stood near St. John's Church. Local legend says "Rub its tummy, you'll surely have money" ⑲ within 24 hours. Nearby is the **Monrean House,** a 1904 struc- ⑳ ture on the National Register of Historic Places, and a **scenic lookout** that looks down on City Float and the waters of Tongass Narrows.

Ketchikan's two most famous totem parks (there are more totems in Ketchikan than anywhere else in the world) are, respectively, **Totem Bight State Historical Park,** 10 miles north on North Tongass Highway, and the park at **Saxman Indian Village,** two miles south on South Tongass Highway. The poles at both parks are, for the most part, half-century-old authentic replicas of even older totems brought in from outlying villages as part of a federal government works/cultural project during the 1930s.

Totem Bight, with its many totems and hand-hewn Indian tribal house, sits on a particularly scenic spit of land facing the waters of Tongass Narrows.

Most cruises include a tour of Saxman Village (named for a missionary who helped Indians settle there before 1900), which has recently added new totems to their collection, as well as a new, large tribal house believed to be the largest in the world. There's also a carver's shed nearby where new totems and totemic art objects are created, and a stand-up theater where a multimedia presentation tells the story of Southeast Alaska's Indian peoples. Finally, there's a gift shop at the park. Ask the sales clerk to differentiate for you the authentic handcrafted items on sale there and the mass-produced, but cheaper, curios and souvenirs.

Out the highway in either direction, you won't go far before you run out of road. The North Tongass Highway ends about 18 miles from downtown, at Settler's Cove Campground. The South Tongass Highway terminates at a power plant. Side roads soon terminate at campgrounds and trailheads, viewpoints, lakes, boat-launching ramps, or private property.

If you're a tough hiker, the three-mile trail from downtown to the top of **Deer Mountain** will repay your effort with a spectacular panorama of the city below (facing the water), and the wilderness behind. **Ward Cove Recreation Area,** about six miles north of town, offers easier hiking beside lakes and streams and beneath towering spruce and hemlock trees.

Wrangell

Numbers in the margin correspond to points of interest on the Wrangell map.

Next up the line is Wrangell, located on an island near the mouth of the fast-flowing Stikine River. A small, unassuming timber and fishing community, the town has had three flags flown over it since the arrival of the Russian traders. Known as Redoubt St. Dionysius as part of Russian America, the town was renamed Fort Stikine after the British took it over. The name was changed to Wrangell when the Americans bought it.

Tourism is much less structured in Wrangell than in the larger cities of the Panhandle—a plus in the minds of many visitors. This is a do-it-yourself touring town. There are no motor-coach excursions. To get the most out of a visit here you should mingle with the locals at cafes, bars, and shops.

The big tourist ships don't come here, but the town welcomes state ferries, the cruise yacht *Sheltered Seas*, and numerous other small craft that pull into port to sample the city's "real Alaskan hospitality."

You can see a lot in Wrangell on foot, and a good place to start
❶ your tour is the A-frame **Chamber of Commerce Visitor Information Center** close to the docks at Front Street and Outer
❷ Drive. It's near **City Hall** and its very tall totem pole. The visitor center is open when cruise ships and the ferries are in port and at other times throughout the summer (tel. 907/874–3901). If you need information and the A-frame is closed, drop by the City Museum (122 2nd St.). The Wrangell Convention and Visitors Bureau is located there. *Bureau open summer, Mon.–Sat. 1–4 PM, and whenever cruise ships or ferries are in port.*

❸ **KikSadi Indian Park,** a "pocket park" of Alaska greenery and impressive totem poles at St. Michael's and Front Street, is a pleasant place to stroll through.

On your way to Wrangell's number one attraction—Chief
❹ Shakes Island—stop at **Chief Shakes gravesite,** uphill from Hansen's Boat Shop on Case Avenue. Buried here is Shakes V, one of a number of local chiefs to bear that name. He led the local Tlingits during the first half of the 19th century. Two killer-whale totems mark the chief's burial place.

❺ On **Shakes Island,** reached by a footbridge off the harbor dock, you can see some of the finest totem poles in Alaska, as well as a tribal house constructed in the 1930s as a replica of the original, which housed many of the various Shakes and their peoples. The interior, which contains six house totems, two of them more than 100 years old, is unfortunately not open very often. It is scheduled for viewing when ships are in port or by appointment. *Tel. 907/874–3503 or 907/874–3747. A donation of $1 is requested.*

After your visit to the island, wander out to the end of the dock
❻ ❼ for the view and picture taking at the **seaplane float** and **boat harbor.**

❽ North and west from the A-frame info center are the **cruise ship**
❾ **dock;** the **public library,** with its small collection of ancient petroglyphs (more about these curious rock carvings later), and
❿ the **Wrangell City Museum** (2nd St. and Bevier St., tel. 907/874–3770). Since its construction in 1906, the museum building has served as a library, a morgue, a doctor's office, and city hall. Now it contains a historical collection that varies from totem fragments, petroglyphs, and other Indian artifacts to

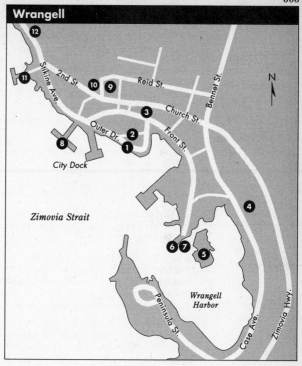

a bootlegger's still and even a vintage 1800's linotype and presses.

⑪
⑫ Beyond the **state ferry terminal** lies another museum, called **"Our Collections"** by its owners, Bolly and Elva Bigelow. It's located in a barnlike building on the water side of Evergreen Avenue. To some, the gathering that comprises the collection is less a museum and more a garage sale waiting to happen. Still, large numbers of viewers seem quite taken by the literally thousands of unrelated collectibles (clocks, animal traps, waffle irons, tools, etc.) that the Bigelows have gathered in half a century of Alaska living. *Tel. 907/847–3646. Call before setting out to visit.*

A five-minute walk beyond the Bigelows' brings you (at low tides only) to **Petroglyph Beach,** one of the more curious sights in Southeast Alaska. Here, scattered among other rocks, are three dozen or more large stones bearing designs and pictures chiseled by unknown, ancient artists. No one knows why the rocks were etched the way they are. Perhaps they were boundary markers or messages; possibly they were just primitive doodling. Study them and draw your own conclusions.

If you want a unique souvenir of your Wrangell visit, go to **Norris Gifts** on Front Street and buy rice paper and crayon-rubbing supplies. The staff or the people at the city museum will demonstrate the proper rubbing technique for recording your own copy of the petroglyph designs. Do not, of course, attempt to move any of the petroglyph stones.

There are other stones in Wrangell that you can take with you. These are natural garnets, gathered at Garnet Ledge, facing the Stikine River. The semiprecious gems are sold on the streets for 50¢ or a dollar.

A lot of recreation, for both locals and visitors, centers around boating on the Stikine River. (*See* Guided Tours, above, for the names of operators that offer trips by speedy jet boat and other craft through the Stikine wilderness.)

Petersburg

Numbers in the margin correspond to points of interest on the Petersburg map.

Getting to Petersburg is an experience, whether you take the "high road" by air or the "low road" by sea.

Alaska Airlines claims the shortest jet flight in the world from takeoff at Wrangell to landing at Petersburg. The schedule calls for 20 minutes of flying, but it's usually more like 10.

At sea level, ferries and smaller cruisers squeak through Wrangell Narrows with the aid of more than 50 buoys and range markers along the 22-mile crossing. At times the water channel seems too incredibly narrow for ships to pass through, making for a breathtaking—though safe—trip.

At first sight of Petersburg you may think you're in the old country. Neat, white, Scandinavian-style homes and storefronts with steep roofs and bright-colored swirls of leaf and flower designs (called "rosemaling") and row upon row of sturdy fishing vessels in the harbor invoke the spirit of Norway. No wonder. This prosperous fishing community was founded by Norwegian Peter Buschmann in 1897.

You may occasionally even hear some Norwegian spoken, especially during the Little Norway Festival held here each year on the weekend closest to May 17. If you're in town during the festival, be sure to partake in one of the fish feeds that highlight the Norwegian Independence Day celebration. You won't find better beer-batter halibut and folk dancing without going to Norway itself.

Petersburg, like Wrangell, is a destination for travelers who prefer not to be hand-held, or spoon-fed information by a tour guide. On your own, sample the brew at **Kito's Kave** bar on Sing Lee Alley (in the afternoon if you don't like your music in the high-decibel range) and examine the outrageous wall decor there, which varies from Mexican painting on black velvet to mounted Alaska king salmon and two stuffed sailfish from a tropical fishing expedition. Wander, at high tide, to **Hammer Slough** for one of Southeast's most popular picture-taking opportunities—houses and buildings on high stilts reflected perfectly in still slough waters. Or simply wander down Nordic Drive, the city's main shopping street, and window-shop the imported Norwegian wool sweaters or metal Viking helmets, complete with horns.

One of the most pleasant things to do in Petersburg is to simply wander among the fishing vessels tied up at dockside. This is one of Alaska's busiest, most prosperous fishing communities and the variety of seacraft is enormous. You'll see small trollers, big halibut vessels, and no small number of sleek pleasure craft as well. Wander, too, around the fish processing structures. There are no tours inside these facilities but even from the outside, watching shrimp, salmon, or halibut coming ashore, you'll get a real appreciation for this vibrant industry and the hardworking people who engage in it.

① From the **visitor center** overlooking the city harbor there are great viewing and picture-taking vantage points. Out Nordic **②** Drive to **Sandy Beach** where there's frequently good eagle viewing and access to one of Petersburg's favorite picnic and recreation locales.

③ Heading north up the hill brings you to the **Clausen Museum** and the bronze "Fisk" (Norwegian for "fish") sculpture at Second and Fram streets. The monument, featuring literally scores of separately sculpted salmon, halibut, and herring, celebrates the bounty of the sea. It was created in 1967 as part of Petersburg's celebration of the 100th anniversary of the Alaska Purchase from Russia.

The museum—not surprisingly in this busiest of Southeast Alaska's commercial fishing ports—devotes a lot of its space to fishing and processing. There's an old "iron chink" used in the early days for gutting and cleaning fish, as well as displays that illustrate how the several types of fishing boats do their thing. A 126.5-pound king salmon, the largest ever caught when it came out of a fish trap on Prince of Wales Island in 1939, is on exhibit, as is the world's largest chum salmon—a 36-pounder. Indian history and artifacts are included, as is an old Indian canoe.

④ ⑤ ⑥ Three pioneer churches—**Catholic, Lutheran,** and **Presbyterian**—are located nearby at Dolphin and 3rd streets, Excel and 5th streets., and on Haugen Street between 2nd and 3rd streets, respectively. Of the three, the half-century-old Lutheran edifice is the oldest. It is said that young boys wheelbarrowed fill from elsewhere in the city for landscaping around the foundation. Their compensation? Ice cream cones. The enticement was so successful that after three years of ice cream rewards, it was necessary to bring in a bulldozer to scrape off the excess dirt.

The large, white, barnlike structure on stilts that stands in **⑦** Hammer Slough off Indian Street is the **Sons of Norway Hall,** an organization devoted to keeping alive the traditions and culture of the old country. North of the hall, from the Nordic Drive **⑧** bridge, is the high-tide **Hammer Slough** reflecting pool so favored by local and visiting photographers.

Petersburg's other attractions are located south of the city along the Mitkof Highway, where you pass seafood processing plants and the state ferry terminal (at Mile .8) en route to the **⑨** **Frank Heintzleman Nursery** at Mile 8.6 (named for a much-loved former territorial governor); the **Fall's Creek fish ladder** at Mile 10.8, where coho and pink salmon migrate upstream in late summer and fall; and the **Crystal Lake State Hatchery/ Blind Slough Recreation Area** at Mile 17.5, where more than 60,000 pounds of salmon and trout are produced each year.

Petersburg's biggest attraction lies about 25 miles east of town but is accessible only by water or air. **LeConte Glacier** is the continent's southernmost tidewater glacier and one of its most

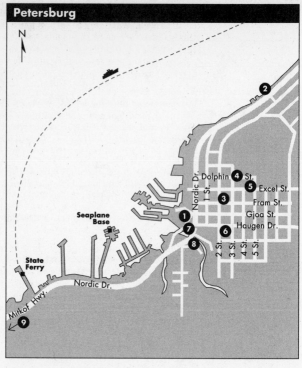

Petersburg

active, often calving off so many icebergs that the lake at its face is carpeted wall-to-wall with floating bergs. Ferries and cruise ships pass it at a distance. Sightseeing yachts, charter vessels, and flightseeing tours are available. For a list of operators, contact the Visitors Bureau.

Sitka

Numbers in the margin correspond to points of interest on the Sitka map.

For centuries before the Russians came at the end of the 18th century, Sitka was the ancestral home of the Tlingit Indian nation. Unfortunately for the Tlingits, Russian Territorial Governor Alexander Baranov (often spelled Baranof, as the island is now spelled) came to covet the Sitka site for its beauty, mild climate, and economic potential. In the island's massive timbered forests he saw raw materials for shipbuilding; its location offered trading routes as far east as Hawaii and the Orient, and as far south as California.

In 1799 Baranof negotiated with the local chief to build a wooden fort and trading post some six miles north of the present town. He called the outpost St. Archangel Michael and shortly after moved a large number of his Russian and Aleut fur hunters there from their former base on Kodiak Island.

The Indians soon took exception to the ambitions of their new neighbors, and in 1802 they attacked Baranov's people, burned his buildings, and assumed they were done with the trouble-some outsiders.

Fortunately for Baranov, he was away at Kodiak at the time. He returned in 1804 with a formidable force including ship-board cannons, attacked the Indians at their fort near Indian River (site of the present-day 105-acre **Sitka National Histori-cal Park**), and drove them to the other side of the island.

Under Baranov and succeeding managers, the Russian-Ameri-can Company and the town prospered until, in the middle of the 19th century, it could be called "the Paris of the Pacific." Be-sides the fur trade, the community contained a major shipbuild-ing and repair facility, boasted saw mills and forges, had a salmon saltery, and even initiated an ice industry. The Rus-sians shipped blocks of ice from nearby Swan Lake to the boom-ing San Francisco market. Baranov shifted the capital of Russian America to Sitka from Kodiak.

Amenities of the town included schools, a library, a hospital, and the crown jewel of the Russian Orthodox Church in Russian America—St. Michael's Cathedral.

❶ A good place to begin a tour of modern-day Sitka is at the Sitka Visitors Bureau headquarters, located in the **Centennial Build-ing** on Harbor Drive. A big Tlingit Indian war canoe rests near-by, while inside the building you'll find a museum, auditorium, art gallery, and lots of advice on what to see and how to see it. The staff will know if the colorfully costumed New Archangel Russian Dancers are performing, whether concerts or recitals are on tap for the annual Sitka Summer Music Festival, or if log-ging competitions or the community's annual salmon derby is scheduled soon.

In the Centennial Building there's also an accurate model of New Archangel, as the Russians called their colony. It shows where the Russians built boats, milled their flour, and cut ice for shipment to gold-rush–booming San Francisco bars.

❷ For photo taking, atmosphere, and outdoor orientation, you would do well to stop at **Castle Hill.** It overlooks Crescent Bay, the John O'Connel Bridge to Japonski Island, and no small number of other islands, isles, and rocks in the nearby waters. A path and steps beside the post office will take you to the top. For years after Sitka's founding, a succession of residences for Russian managers was located on this lofty promontory. The last one—called Baranof's Castle, though he never lived there—burned in 1894.

Atop the hill now are venerable Russian cannons and the flag-pole where, on October 18, 1867, the czarist Russian standard was lowered and the Stars and Stripes of the United States raised. Each Alaska Day (October 18), citizens of Sitka in peri-od costumes reenact the ceremony with the same pomp and cer-emony that signified the official transfer of Alaska to the United States.

At this same site, on January 3, 1959, jubilant Alaskans raised the first 49-star American flag, signifying Alaskan statehood.

❸ The large four-level red-roof structure with the imposing 14-foot statue in front is the **Sitka State Pioneers' Home,** built in 1934 and the first of several state-run retirement homes and medical-care facilities for Alaska's senior citizens. The statue,

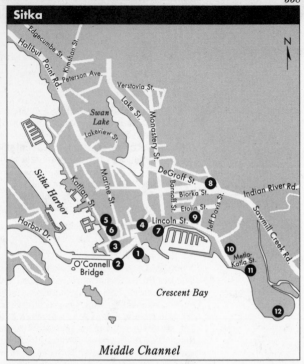

symbolizing Alaska's frontier sourdough spirit, was modeled by an authentic pioneer, William "Skagway Bill" Fonda. It portrays a determined prospector with pack, pick, rifle, and supplies on his back headed for the gold country.

Across the street in **Totem Square** you'll find three old anchors discovered in local waters and believed to be 19th-century British in origin. Look on the totem pole in the park for the double-headed eagle of czarist Russia carved into the cedar.

❹ **St. Michael's Cathedral,** in the middle of Lincoln Street, had its origins in a log-built, frame-covered structure erected between 1844 and 1848. In 1966 the church was totally destroyed in a fire that swept through the downtown business district. As the fire engulfed the building, local townspeople risked their lives and rushed inside to rescue the cathedral's precious icons, religious objects, vestments, and other treasures brought to the church from Russia.

Using original measurements and blueprints, an almost exact replica of onion-domed St. Michael's was built and dedicated in 1976. Today, visitors can see numerous icons, among them the much-prized Our Lady of Sitka (also known as the Sitka Madonna) and the Christ Pantocrator (Christ the Judge) on either side of the doors of the interior altar screen. Among other objects to be viewed: ornate gospel books, chalices, crucifixes, much-used silver-gilt wedding crowns dating back to 1866, and an altar cloth said to have been worked by Princess Maksoutoff, who lies buried in the Russian cemetery nearby. This is an active church, so visitors should respect the services and privacy of worshipers. *A $1 donation is requested. Open June 1–Sept. 30, daily 11–3.*

5 North of the Pioneer Home on the west edge of town are the **Russian blockhouse** and the **Russian cemetery** where Princess Maksoutoff, wife of Alaska's last Russian governor and others are buried. The old headstones and crosses of the Russian Orthodox faith make this a striking sight.

7 The **Russian Bishop's House** also stands on Lincoln Street, constructed by the Russian-American Company for Bishop Innocent Veniaminov in 1842. Now restored by the National Park Service as a unit of Sitka National Historical Park, the structure is one of the few remaining Russian log structures in Alaska. *Admission free. Open daily 8–5.*

8 Farther north and east is the **Sitka National Cemetery** on Sawmill Creek Road, where America's dead from the Civil War and the Aleutian Campaign of World War II are buried along with many notable Alaskans.

9
10 Southeast on Lincoln Street lies the campus of **Sheldon Jackson College,** founded in 1878, and the **Sheldon Jackson Museum.** The octagonal museum, built in 1895 and now under the jurisdiction of the Alaska State Division of Museums, contains priceless Indian, Aleut, and Eskimo items collected by Dr. Sheldon Jackson in the remote regions of Alaska he traveled as an educator and missionary. Carved masks, Chilkat Indian blankets, dogsleds, kayaks—even the helmet worn by Chief Katlean during the 1804 battle between the Sitka Indians and the Russians—are on display here. Budget at least an hour at the museum. *Admission: $1 adults, free for students. Open daily 8–5.*

11 **Sitka National Historical Park's** Visitor Center and totem park is located at the end of Metlakatla Street, about a half mile from town. Audiovisual programs and exhibits at the site, plus Indian and Russian artifacts, give an overview of Southeast Alaska Indian culture, both old and new. Often, contemporary Indian artists and craftsmen are on hand to demonstrate and interpret the traditional crafts of the Tlingit people.

12 A self-guiding trail through the park to the actual site of the **Tlingit Fort** passes by some of the most skillfully carved totems in the state. Some of the poles are quite old, dating back more than eight decades. Others are replicas, copies of originals lost to time and a damp climate. *Admission free. Open June–Sept. daily 8–5; Oct.–May weekdays 8–5.*

Juneau

Numbers in the margin correspond to points of interest on the Juneau map.

Juneau, like Haines and Skagway to the north, is located on the North American mainland. Unlike Haines and Skagway, you can't drive there by conventional highway from the rest of the United States and Canada. No matter. There are lots of easy ways to reach Alaska's capital and third-largest city. For one, there's the Alaska Marine Highway ferry system, which provides near daily arrivals and departures in the summer. For another, virtually every cruise ship plying Southeast waters calls at Juneau. And two jet airlines—Alaska and Delta—provide several flights daily into Juneau International Airport from other points in Alaska and the other U.S. states.

Juneau owes its origins to two colorful sourdoughs, Joe Juneau and Dick Harris, and to a Tlingit chief named Kowee. The chief led the two white men to rich reserves of gold, both in the out-wash of the stream that now runs through the middle of town and in quartz rock formations back in the gulches and valleys.

That was 1880, and shortly after the discovery a modest stam-pede resulted in the formation of first a camp, then a town, then finally the movement of the Alaska district government (such as it was) to the area in 1906. Thus Juneau became the capital of Alaska, a title the community still retains.

For 60 years or so after Juneau's founding, gold remained the mainstay of the local economy. In its heyday, the AJ (for Alaska Juneau) gold mine was the biggest low-grade ore mine in the world. It was not until World War II, when the government de-cided it needed Juneau's manpower for the war effort, that the AJ and other mines in the area ceased operations.

After the war, mining failed to start up again, and govern-ment—first territorial, then state—became the city's princi-pal employer.

These days, government (state, federal, and local) remains Juneau's number one employer. Tourism, transportation, and trading—even a belated mining revival—provide the other ma-jor components of the city's economic picture.

A good place to start a walking tour is the visitor kiosk at
❶ Marine Park on the dock where the cruise ships tie up. The park itself is a little gem of benches, shade trees, and shelter, a great place to enjoy an outdoor meal purchased from any of Juneau's several street vendors. The kiosk is staffed from 9 AM to 6PM
❷ daily in the summer months. The **Log Cabin Visitor Center** up Seward Street at 3rd Street operates weekdays 8:30–5 and weekends 10–5. The cabin is a replica of a 19th-century struc-ture that served first as a Presbyterian Church, then as a brew-ery.

Head east a block from Marine Park to S. Franklin Street. Buildings here and on Front Street are among the older and most interesting structures in the city. Many reflect the archi-tecture of the 1920s and '30s, and some are even older.

The smallish (40 rooms) **Alaskan Hotel** at 167 S. Franklin Street was called "a pocket edition of any of the best hotels on the Pa-cific Coast" when it opened in 1913. Owners Mike and Bettye Adams have restored the building with period trappings, and it's worth a visit even if you're not looking for lodging. The bar-room's massive mirrored oakwood back bar, accented by Tiffa-ny lights and panels, is a particular delight.

Also on S. Franklin Street: **The Alaska Steam Laundry Build-ing,** a 1901 structure with a windowed turret that now houses a coffee house, a film processor, and other stores. Across the street, the equally venerable **Senate Building mall** contains one of the two Juneau Christmas Stores, a children's shop, and a place to buy Russian icons.

Close by are numerous other curio and crafts shops, snack shops, two salmon shops, and the tourist-filled **Red Dog Saloon,**

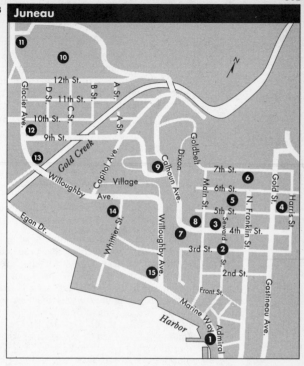

Juneau

a decades-old institution now housed in new but still frontierish quarters at 159 S. Franklin Street.

After a S. Franklin Street foray, head one block toward the water, then uphill on Seward Street past the Log Cabin Visitor Center. You'll come across 4th Street to an older, obviously governmental building fronted by huge marble pillars. The pillars are of native Southeast Alaska marble, and the building is the **Alaska State Capitol,** constructed in 1930 to serve the city as federal building, governor's office, post office, and meeting place for the biennial sessions of the Alaska Territorial Legislature. Today the structure still houses the governor's offices and other state agencies, and the state legislature meets there four months each year. *Tel. 907/465–4565. Tours in summer, daily 8:30–5.*

Uphill one block and two blocks to the east stands quaint little **St. Nicholas Russian Orthodox Church,** constructed in 1894— the oldest original Russian church in Alaska. *326 5th St. A donation is requested. Check the visitor center for hours.*

Directly uphill behind the Capitol Building, between 5th and 6th streets, stands the **five-story totem,** one of Juneau's finer totems, and at the top of the hill on 7th Street stands **Wickersham House,** the former residence of pioneer judge and delegate to Congress, James Wickersham. The home, constructed in 1899, is now a part of the Alaska state park system. Summer tours operate Sunday–Friday, 10–5. Memorabilia from the judge's travels throughout Alaska range from rare native basketry and ivory carvings to historic photos, 47 faithful diaries (maintained even on treks through snow and blizzards), and a Chickering grand piano that came "round the horn" to Alaska while the Russians yet ruled in these parts. Admission is free.

7 Back down the hill on 4th Street, you'll pass "the S.O.B."—or **State Office Building.** There on Fridays at noon you can pack a lunch like the state workers do and listen in the four-story atrium to organ music played on a grand old theater pipe organ, a veteran of the silent-movie era.

Head west from the front of the Capitol Building, then north on **8** Calhoun Avenue past the **City Museum** (with old mining equipment, historic photos, and pioneer artifacts) and another pho**9** to-worthy totem, you come shortly to the **Governor's House,** a three-level colonial style home completed in 1912. There are no tours through the house, but it's okay to take pictures of the totem pole on the entrance side of the building—surely the only one of its kind to grace the walls of a U.S. governor's mansion.

If you're still game for walking, head down Calhoun Avenue, pass the Gold Creek bridge, and keep going until you come to **10** **Evergreen Cemetery.** A meandering gravel road leads through the graveyard where many Juneau pioneers (among them Joe Juneau and Dick Harris) lay buried. At the end of the lane **11** you'll come to a monument commemorating the **cremation spot 12** **of Chief Kowee.** Turn left here, walk past the **Federal Building 13** **and Post Office** at 9th and Glacier, pass the **Juneau–Harris Monument** near Gold Creek, then walk on to Whittier Street, **14** where a right turn will take you to the **Alaska State Museum.** *319 Whittier St., Juneau, tel. 907/465-2901. Open May 15– Sept. 15, weekdays 9–6, weekends 10–6; Sept. 16–May 14, Tues.–Fri. 10–6. Admission: $1 adults, children and students free.*

This is one of Alaska's top museums. Plan no less than an hour here, longer if you can spare the time. Whether your tastes run to natural history exhibits (stuffed brown bears, a replica of a two-story-high eagle nesting tree), native Alaskan exhibits (a 40-foot walrus hide oomiak whaling boat constructed by Eskimos from St. Laurence Island and a re-created interior of a Tlingit tribal house), mining exhibits, or contemporary art, the museum is almost certain to please.

Finally, on Willoughby Avenue at Egan Drive, there's Ju**15** neau's **Centennial Hall**—the meeting place for large conventions in the capital city and the site of an excellent information center operated by the U.S. Forest Service and the U.S. Park Service. Movies, slide shows, and information about recreation in the surrounding Tongass National Forest or in nearby Glacier Bay National Park and Preserve are available here. *Open daily in summer 9–6; 8–5 weekdays the rest of the year.*

Haines

Numbers in the margin correspond to points of interest on the Haines map.

Missionary S. Hall Young and John Muir, the famous naturalist, picked the site for this town in 1879 as a place to bring Christianity and education to the native Indians. They could hardly have picked a more beautiful spot. The town sits on a heavily wooded peninsula with magnificent views of Portage Cove and the Coastal Mountain Range. It lies 80 miles north of Juneau via fjordlike Lynn Canal and 13 water miles south of Skagway.

Unlike most cities in Southeast Alaska, you can reach Haines by road (the 152-mile Haines Highway connects at Haines Junction with the Alaska Highway). It's accessible as well by state ferry and by scheduled light-plane service from Juneau.

The town has two distinct personalities. On the northern side of the Haines Highway is the portion of Haines founded by Hall and Muir. After its missionary beginnings the town served as the trailhead for the Jack Dalton Trail to the Yukon during the 1897 gold rush to the Klondike. The following year, when gold was discovered in nearby Porcupine (now deserted), the booming community served as a supply center and jumping-off place for those gold fields as well. Today things are quieter; the town's streets are orderly, its homes are well kept, and for the most part it looks a great deal like any other Alaska seacoast community.

South of the highway, the town looks like a military post, which is what it was for nearly half a century.

In 1903 the U.S. Army established a post—**Fort William Henry Seward**—at Portage Cove just south of town. For 17 years (1922–1939) the post (renamed Chilkoot Barracks to avoid confusion with the South Central Alaska city of Seward) was the only military base in the territory. That changed with World War II. Following the war the post closed down.

Right after the war a group of veterans purchased the property from the government. They changed its name to Port Chilkoot and created residences, businesses, and an Indian arts center out of the officers' houses and military buildings that surrounded the old fort's parade ground. Eventually Port Chilkoot merged with the city of Haines. Although the two areas are now officially one municipality, the old military post with its still-existing grass parade grounds is referred to as Fort Seward.

The Haines–Fort Seward community today is recognized for the enormously successful Indian dance and culture center at Fort Seward, as well as for the superb fishing, camping, and outdoor recreation to be found at Chilkoot Lake, Portage Cove, Mosquito Lake, and Chilkat State Park on the shores of Chilkat Inlet. The latter locale, one of the small treasures of the Alaska state park system, features quality views of the Davidson and Rainbow glaciers across the water.

➊ To sightsee the community you can pick up walking-tour maps of both Haines and Fort Seward at the **Visitor Center** on 2nd Avenue. The easiest place to start your tour, however, is at the
➋ **Sheldon Museum and Cultural Center** near the foot of Main Street. This is another Alaskana collection, home grown with personal care by an Alaskan family. Steve Sheldon began assembling Indian artifacts, Russian items, and gold-rush memorabilia, such as Jack Dalton's sawed-off shotgun, in 1924. His daughter, Elisabeth Hakkinen, carries on and is usually on hand to serve Russian tea, to recall the stories behind many of the items on display, and to reminisce about growing up in

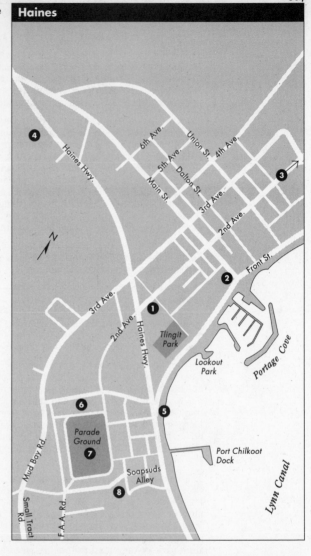

Haines

Haines before World War II. *25 Main St., tel. 907/766–2366.
Small admission fee.*

❸ One of the most rewarding hikes in the area is to the north summit of **Mt. Ripinsky,** the prominent peak that rises to 3,610 feet behind the town. Be forewarned: It's a strenuous trek and requires a full day. The **trailhead** lies at the top of Young Street, along a pipeline right-of-way. For other hikes, pick up a copy of "Haines is for Hikers" at the Information Center.

❹ The **Southeast Alaska State Fairgrounds** is probably worth a drive-through if you're a fair buff or interested in things agricultural. If you happen to be in Haines during the annual fair held each August, plan to spend several hours. It's one of several official regional fall blowouts staged around the state, and in its homegrown, homespun way it's a real winner.

In addition to the usual collection of barnyard animals (chickens, goats, horses, etc.), the fair offers the finest examples of local culinary arts and the chance to see Indian dances, displays of Indian totemic crafts, lots of hobby crafts, and some surprisingly fine art and photography.

⑤ As noted, the Haines Highway roughly divides Haines/Fort Seward. At the base of the highway is **Mile 0,** the starting point of the 152-mile road to the Alaska Highway and the Canadian Yukon. Whether you plan to travel all the way or not, you should spend at least a bit of time on the scenic highway. At about Mile 6 there's a delightful picnic spot near the Chilkat River and an inflowing clear creek; at Mile 9.5 the view of the Takhinsha Mountains across the river is magnificent; and around Mile 19 there is good viewing of the **Alaska Chilkat Bald Eagle Preserve,** where, especially in late fall and early winter, as many as 4,000 of the great birds have been known to assemble. The United States–Canada border lies at Mile 40. If you're traveling on to Canada, stop at Canadian customs and be sure to set your clock ahead one hour, noon in Alaska being 1 PM in this part of Canada. (If you're headed south *from* Canada, check in with U.S. Customs, and of course set your timepiece back an hour.)

The Haines Highway is completely paved on the American side of the border and, except for a few remaining stretches, almost entirely paved in Canada.

Back in town, head for Fort Seward, and don't budget too little time for this unique community. Pull out your Fort Seward walking tour map and wander past the huge, stately, white-columned former commanding officer's home, now a part of the **⑥** **Halsingland Hotel.** Circle the flat but sloping parade grounds, **⑦** with its **Indian tribal house** and sourdough log cabin. In the eve- **⑧** ning, visit the **Chilkat Center for the Arts.** This building once was the army post's recreation hall, but now it's the scene of Chilkat Indian dancing (Mon. and Sat. evenings) or the outrageous "Lust for Dust" historical melodrama (Sun. performances may be at the tribal house; check posted notices.) *Both shows start at 8:30 PM and charge $5.*

Between the Chilkat Center for the Arts and the parade grounds stands the former fort hospital, now being used as a workshop for the craftsmen of **Alaska Indian Arts,** a nonprofit organization dedicated to the revival of Tlingit Indian art forms. You'll see Indian carvers making totems here, metalsmiths working in silver, even weavers making blankets. *Admission free. Open weekdays 9–noon and 1–5.*

The Haines ferry terminal is located 4½ miles northwest of downtown.

Skagway

Numbers in the margin correspond to points of interest on the Skagway map.

Skagway lies 13 miles north of Haines by ferry on the Alaska Marine Highway. If you drive by conventional highway the distance is 359 miles, as it's necessary to cover first the Haines

Highway to Haines Junction, Yukon, then a hundred miles of
Alaska Highway south to Whitehorse, and then a final hundred
south to Skagway on the Klondike Highway. North country
folk call this the Golden Horseshoe or Golden Circle tour, because it takes in a lot of gold-rush country in addition to lake,
forest, and mountain scenery.

However you get to Skagway, you'll find the town an amazingly
preserved living artifact from one of North America's biggest,
most storied gold rushes. Most of the downtown district is part
of the Klondike Gold Rush National Historical Park, a unit of
the national park system dedicated to preserving and inter-
preting the frenzied stampede that extended to Dawson City in
Canada's Yukon. Old false-fronted stores, saloons, and brothels—built to separate gold-rush prospectors from their grub-
stakes going north or their gold pokes heading south—have
been restored, repainted, and refurnished by the federal government and Skagway's people. When you walk down Broadway today, the scene is not appreciably different from what the
prospectors saw in the days of 1898, except that the dust (or
mud) of Broadway has been covered with pavement to make
your meandering easier.

Actually, there are several units to the National Historical
Park. The most southern is at Pioneer Square in Seattle, near
the Alaska ferry departure docks. It's an ideal place to look
over displays and exhibits and get an advance orientation of
what you'll see when you get to Alaska. A closer unit covers the
Chilkoot Trail leading from nearby Dyea ("Die-EE") over the
Chilkoot Pass to Lake Lindeman.

Skagway had only a single cabin, still standing, when the
Yukon gold rush began. At first the argonauts, as they liked to
be called, swarmed to Dyea and the Chilkoot Trail, nine miles
to the west of Skagway. Skagway and its White Pass trail didn't
seem as attractive until a dock was built in town. With that,
Skagway mushroomed overnight into the major gateway to the
Klondike, supporting a wild mixture of legitimate businessmen, con artists (among the most cunning, Jefferson "Soapy"
Smith), stampeders, and curiosity seekers.

Three months after the first boat landed in July 1897, Skagway
numbered perhaps 20,000 persons and had well-laid-out
streets, hotels, stores, saloons, gambling houses, and dance
halls. By spring of 1898, the superintendent of the Northwest
Royal Mounted Police in neighboring Canada would label the
town "little better than a hell on earth."

A lot of the "hell" ended with a real-life shootout one pleasant
July evening in 1898. Good-guy Frank Reid (the surveyor who
laid out Skagway's streets so wide and well) faced down bad-
guy Soapy Smith on Juneau dock downtown near the present
ferry terminal. After a classic exchange of gunfire, Smith lay
dead and Reid lay dying. The town built a huge monument at
Reid's grave. You can see it in Gold Rush Cemetery and read
the inscription on it today: "He gave his life for the honor of
Skagway." For Smith, whose tombstone was continually chiseled and stolen by vandals and souvenir seekers, today's grave
marker is a simple wooden plank.

One of Soapy Smith's saloons still stands. It's located on 2nd
Avenue, and it's open from time to time for tourist visits. No

longer, however, are "suckers" invited out back to "see an eagle," then bopped on their heads and rolled for their pokes.

To begin a visit to this storied town, head first to **City Hall** on
7th Avenue. There, on the first floor of a large granite structure built in 1899 to house McCabe Methodist College, the
Skagway Convention and Visitors Bureau will give you maps
and lots of suggestions for seeing their town. Your first stop
should be right upstairs in the City Hall building, where the
❶ **Trail of '98 Museum** is located.

Frank Reid's will is preserved under glass there, as are papers
disposing of Soapy Smith's estate. Gambling paraphernalia
from the old Board of Trade Saloon is on display along with native artifacts, gold scales, a red-and-black sleigh (one-horse variety), a small organ, and a curious blanket made from the skin
of duck necks and fortified by pepper bags sewn behind the skin
for moth protection.

After you've browsed the museum, wander back to Broadway
❷ and 6th Avenue to the **Eagles Hall.** Mentally mark this locale
and plan to return for the show the locals perform daily called
"Skagway in the Days of '98." You'll see cancan dancers, learn a
little local history, and watch desperado Soapy Smith sent to
his reward. *Posted show hours depend on ship arrivals and departures. Performances are usually at 10 AM and 8 PM.*

❸ Farther south on Broadway you come to **Arctic Brotherhood
Hall,** the likes of which you'll not see anywhere else in Alaska.
The Arctic Brotherhood was a fraternal organization of Alaskan and Yukon pioneers. To decorate the exterior false front of
their Skagway lodge building, local members created a mosaic
covering out of 20,000 pieces of driftwood and flotsam gathered
from local beaches.

❹ **Soapy's Parlor** is located on 2nd Avenue just west of Broadway,
❺ while the former **White Pass and Yukon Route rail depot** is located on the east side of the main thoroughfare. This building,
now headquarters and information center for the **Klondike
Gold Rush National Historical Park,** contains exhibits, photos,
and artifacts from the White Pass and Chilkoot trails. This is
of special interest if you plan to take a White Pass train ride,
drive the nearby Klondike Highway, or hike the Chilkoot
Trail.

Lots of other stops along Broadway and its side streets merit
inspection. For children, the **Sweet Tooth Saloon** with its ice
cream and sodas is a special favorite. For adults, the 19th-cen-
tury **Red Onion Saloon** (with its former brothel upstairs) is an
interesting and thirst-quenching stop. The **Golden North Hotel,** constructed in 1898 and Alaska's oldest hotel, has been lovingly restored to its gold-rush era milieu. It's worth a stroll
through the lobby even if you're not staying there. Curio shops
abound, and among the oldest—probably *the* oldest—in all of
Alaska is **Kirmse's** (pronounced "KIRM-zees") on Broadway.
Visit the shop and see the world's largest, heaviest, and most
valuable gold nugget watch chain. On display as well is a companion chain made of the world's tiniest, daintiest little nuggets.

❻ At the foot of State Street is the starting place of the **Klondike
Highway.** The Klondike often parallels the older White Pass
railway route as it travels northwest to Carcross and White-

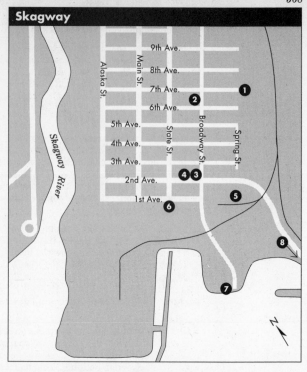

horse in the Canadian Yukon. It merges just south of White-horse for a short distance with the Alaska Highway, then it heads its own again to its end at Dawson City on the shores of the Klondike River. From start to finish, it covers 435 miles.

Along the way the road climbs steeply through forested coastal mountains with jagged, snow-covered peaks. It passes by big, deep, fish-filled lakes and streams in the Canadian high country, where travelers have at least a chance of seeing mountain goat, moose, black bear, or grizzly.

If you're driving the Klondike Highway north from Skagway you must stop at **Canadian Customs,** Mile 22. If you're traveling south to Skagway, check in at **U.S. Customs,** Mile 6. And remember to change your clock setting at the border. When it's 1 PM in Canada at the border, it's noon in Skagway.

Just south of Broadway lies the **ferry dock,** a pleasant half-mile walk from town, and somewhat farther south is the **cruise-ship dock** where the big ships land. The mountainside cliff behind the cruise-ship dock, incidentally, is rather incredible, with its scores of advertisements and ships' names brightly painted on the exposed granite face. Most photographed of all the "murals" at the site is a large skull-like rock formation that has been painted white, given appropriate cavities, and named Soapy's Skull.

Two more excursions from Skagway are notable. The first is the previously mentioned **Chilkoot Trail** from Dyea to Lake Lindeman, a trek of 33 miles that includes a climb up Chilkoot Pass at the United States–Canada border. The National Park

Service maintains the American side of the pass as part of the Klondike Gold Rush National Historical Park. The trail is good; the forest, mountain, and lake scenery is both scenic and richly historic, and campsites are located strategically along the way to make the several overnights as comfortable as possible.

The Chilkoot is not, however, an easy walk. There are lots of ups and downs before you cross the pass and reach the Canadian high country and rain is a distinct possibility. To return to Skagway, hikers have three choices. They can end their trek at Lake Bennett where a rail motorcar will transport them to Fraser and further rail connections to Skagway, or they can walk a cutoff to Log Cabin on the Klondike Highway. There they can either hitchhike back to town or flag down Gray Line of Alaska's Alaskon Express motor coach heading south to Skagway from Whitehorse. *Tel. 907/983–2241 or 800/544–2206. Fare: $16.*

For the thousands that complete the hike each year, it is the highlight of a trip to the North country. For details, maps, and references contact the National Park Service information center at 2nd Avenue and Broadway.

If you're not a hiker, there's an easier way to follow the second, a prospector's trail to the gold-rush country. You can take the **White Pass and Yukon Route** (WP&YR) narrow-gauge railroad over the "Trail of '98."

This is a premier railroading experience, rated world-class by countless railroad buffs and travelers. The line ceased operations in '82, and many feared the historic gold-rush railroad—which had its start in 1898—would never operate again. Happily, the line's diesel locomotives are once again chugging and towing vintage viewing cars up the steep inclines of the route, hugging the walls of precipitous cliff sides, and exposing thousands of travelers to the view of craggy peaks, plummeting waterfalls, lakes, and forests. It's a summertime operation only.

Two options are available. Twice daily the WP&YR leaves Skagway for a 3-hour round-trip excursion to the White Pass summit. Sights along the way include Bridal Veil Falls, Inspiration Point, and Dead Horse Gulch. The fare is $69. Through service to Whitehorse, Yukon, is offered daily as well—in the form of a train trip to Fraser where motor coach connections are available on to Whitehorse. The one-way fare to Whitehorse is $89. For information call 907/983–2217 or 800/343–7373.

Glacier Bay/Gustavus

Nearly 200 years ago, Captain George Vancouver sailed by Glacier Bay and didn't even know it. The bay at that time, 1794, was hidden behind and beneath a vast glacial wall of ice. The glacier was more than 20 miles across its face and, in places, more than 4,000 feet in depth. It extended more than 100 miles to the St. Elias Mountain Range. Over the next hundred years, due to warming weather and other factors not fully understood even now, the face of the glacial ice has melted and retreated back with amazing speed, exposing nearly 50 miles of fjords, islands, and inlets.

In 1879, about a century after Vancouver's sail-by, one of the earliest white visitors to what is now **Glacier Bay National Park and Preserve** came calling. He was naturalist John Muir, drawn by the flora and fauna that had followed in the wake of glacial withdrawals and fascinated by the vast ice rivers that descended from the mountains to tidewater. Today, the naturalist's namesake glacier, like others in the park, continues to retreat dramatically. Its terminus is now scores of miles farther up bay from the small cabin he built at its face during his time there. (For more on the park, *see* Southeast Alaska in Chapter 4.)

The waterways provide access to no fewer than 16 tidewater glaciers, a dozen of which actively calve icebergs into the bay. The show can be mind-boggling. With a noise that sounds like cannons firing, bergs the size of 10-story office buildings sometimes come crashing from the "snout" of a glacier. The crash sends tons of water and spray skyward, and it propels mini-tidal waves outward from the point of impact. Johns Hopkins Glacier calves so often and with such volume that even the large cruise ships can seldom approach its face closer than two miles.

Companies that offer big-ship visits include Holland America Lines, Princess Cruises, Royal Viking Line, and World Explorer Cruises. During the several hours that the ships are in the bay, National Park Service naturalists come aboard to explain the comings and goings of the great glaciers, to point out features of the forests and islands and mountains, and to help spot black bears, brown bears, mountain goats, whales, porpoises, and the countless species of birds that call the area home.

Smaller, more intimate, and probably more informative is the day boat *Gold Rush*, which operates daily from the dock at Bartlett Cove, near Glacier Bay Lodge (tel. 800/622–2042). Uniformed Park Service naturalists sail aboard these excursions, too.

At Bartlett Cove, where the glaciers stood and then receded more than two centuries ago, the shore is covered with stands of high-towering spruce and hemlock. This is a climax forest, thick and lush and abounding with the wildlife of Southeast Alaska. As you sail farther into the great bay, the conifers become noticeably smaller, and they are finally replaced by alders and other leafy species, which took root and began growing only a few decades ago. Finally, deep into the bay where the glaciers have withdrawn in very recent years, the shorelines contain only plants and primitive lichens. Given enough time, however, these lands, too, will be covered with the same towering forests which you see at the bay's entrance.

The most adventurous way to see and explore Glacier Bay is up close. Real up close—as in paddling your own kayak through the bay's icy waters and inlets. You can book one of **Alaska Discovery's** (369 S. Franklin St., Juneau 99801, tel. 907/586–1911) four- or seven-day guided expeditions. Unless you really know what you're doing, you're better off signing on with the guided tours. Alaska Discovery provides safe, seaworthy kayaks, and tents, gear, and food. Their guides are tough, knowledgeable Alaskans, and they've spent enough time in Glacier Bay's wild country to know what's safe and what's not.

Within Glacier Bay Park and Preserve there's only one over-night facility, Glacier Bay Lodge. If it's booked, or too pricey for your budget, don't worry. About a half hour's drive via the 10-mile road that leads out of the park is Gustavus, where additional lodges, inns, and bed-and-breakfast inns abound (*see* Lodging, below).

Gustavus calls itself "the way to Glacier Bay," and for airborne visitors the community is indeed the gateway to the park. The long, paved jet airport, built as a refueling strip during World War II, is one of the best and longest in Southeast Alaska, all the more impressive because facilities at the field are so limited.

Alaska Airlines, which serves Gustavus daily in the summer, has a large, rustic terminal at the site, and from a free telephone on the front porch of the terminal you can call any of the local hostelries for courtesy pickup. Smaller light-aircraft companies that serve the community out of Juneau also have on-site shelters. But aside from these facilities, there's only a small gift shop (the "Puffin Mall," with colorful art offerings and other curios) and a little A-frame where you can sample and purchase tenderly smoked salmon from the Salmon River Smokehouse.

With little in the way of industry or activity at the airport, Gustavus also boasts no "downtown." In fact, Gustavus is not a town. The 150 or so year-round residents there are most emphatic on this point; they regularly vote down incorporation as a city. Instead, Gustavus is a scattering of homes, farmsteads, arts and crafts studios, fishing and guiding charters, and other tiny enterprises peopled by hospitable individualists. It is, in many ways, exemplary of today's version of the frontier spirit in Alaska. For a listing of the 33 firms that make up the Gustavus Visitors Association, write to Box 167, Gustavus 99826.

What to See and Do with Children

Canoe rides in the modern equivalent of an Indian war canoe provide fun and exercise for young people and old at a woodsy lake near Ketchikan. *Alaska Travel Adventures, tel. 907/225–2840. Cost: $49 adults, $30 children.*

Fishing is popular among youngsters from toddlers on up, and no fishing license is required in Alaska for kids under 16. For the best saltwater shoreline, lake, or stream fishing, call the local Alaska Department of Fish and Game office in the city you're visiting. Ask where the hot spots of the moment are to be found. For little children, fishing off one of the region's many docks (life jackets are a must!) can be fun and productive.

Gold panning is fun and sometimes children actually uncover a few flecks of the precious metal in the bottom of their pans. You can buy a pan at almost any Alaska hardware or sporting goods store, or you can look for gold-panning excursions at visitor information centers.

Indian dancing will dazzle the younger set. Masked performers wearing bearskins and brightly designed dance blankets act out the stories of great hunts, fierce battles, and other legends.

Among the best known dance groups is the Chilkat Indian Dancers of Fort Seward in Haines. *Performances Mon. and Sat. at 8:30* PM. Admission: $5.

There are **totem pole parks**—featuring the sometimes fearsome countenances of bears, killer whales, great birds, and legendary hunters—at Ketchikan, Wrangell, Sitka, Juneau, and Haines/Fort Seward *(see* Exploring Southeast Alaska, above). Other fine examples of the carver's art can be seen at the Indian villages of Kake, Angoon, and Hoonah *(see* Off the Beaten Track, below). At Kake, you can see a 132.5-foot totem that, when it was carved for the 1970 world's fair in Osaka, Japan, was the tallest in the world.

Kayaking in front of Mendenhall Glacier is sure to create vivid memories for youngsters as well as active adults *(see* Guided Tours, above, for tour operators and outfitters).

Summer sports are a passion in Southeast Alaska, and at Petersburg both young and old visitors are welcome to join in recreational softball or volleyball games. Call the Parks and Recreation Department for details (tel. 907/72–3392).

Off the Beaten Track

Surely one of the world's great travel bargains is the network of 150 or so **wilderness cabins** operated by the U.S. Forest Service alongside remote lakes and streams in the Tongass National Forest of Southeast Alaska. These cabins are weathertight A- frames and Panabodes equipped with bunks for six to eight occupants, tables, stoves, and outdoor privies. The cost: only $15 per night per party. Most are fly-in units, accessible by pontoon-equipped aircraft from virtually any community in the Panhandle. You provide your own sleeping bag, food, and cooking utensils. Don't be surprised if the Forest Service recommends you carry along a 30.06 or larger caliber rifle, in the unlikely event of a bear problem.

If you're a hot-springs or hot-tub enthusiast, **White Sulphur Springs** cabins, out of Sitka, or **Shakes Slough** cabins, accessible from Wrangell or Petersburg, boast these amenities. There's also a hot-springs pool of sorts, big enough for two or three to lounge in, at Bailey Bay, just north of Ketchikan's Revilla Island on the mainland. A 10-minute hike from a landing in a nearby lake or a two-mile trek on an unmaintained but negotiable trail from salt water will bring you to the site. Have your pilot fly over to show you your foot route before you land. Shelter here is a three-sided Adirondack shelter built as a public project during the Depression. *Details and reservation information from the USFS office in each community or call or write: U.S. Forest Service, Box 1628, Juneau 99802, tel. 907/ 586–8806.*

Offbeat, but boasting the ultimate in catered comfort, is the **Waterfall Resort** (Box 6440, Ketchikan, tel. 907/225–9461 or 800/544–5125) on Prince of Wales Island near Ketchikan. At this former commercial salmon cannery you sleep in Cape Cod–style cottages (former cannery workers' cabins, but *they* never had it so good); eat bountiful meals of salmon, halibut steak, and all the trimmings; and fish from your own private cabin cruiser under the tender loving care of your own private fish guide. Pricey, but worth it.

Farther north, **Baranof Wilderness Lodge** (Box 21022, Auke Bay 99824, tel. 907/586–8110) is one of the Panhandle's newer lodge facilities, located at Warm Springs Bay on Baranof Island. Kayaking, canoeing, hiking, and exploring are all options at this facility, as well as fresh- and saltwater fishing. Most popular activity of all is probably hot tubbing, in waters supplied by the warm springs.

One of Southeast Alaska's pioneer lodges is **Thayer Lake Lodge** (in summer, Box 211614, Auke Bay 99821, tel. 907/789–5646; in winter, Box 5416, Ketchikan 99901, tel. 907/789–0944), on Admiralty Island near Juneau. This is a rustic lodge-and-cabins operation that has been satisfying Juneau folk and Alaskan visitors for decades. Bob and Edith Nelson built this resort after World War II on one of the high country lakes in the Admiralty Island wilderness. They did it mostly with their own labor, using native timber for their buildings. Lake fishing is unexcelled for cutthroat and Dolly Varden trout (though they're not overly large). There's also canoeing, hiking, and wildlife photography.

Tenakee Springs is a tiny little fishing, vacation, and retirement community that clings to (in fact hangs out over) the shores of Chichagof Island. The town is accessible from Juneau by air or by the smaller Alaska ferry *LeConte* on an eight-hour run. You certainly won't find any Hiltons here, but there is a cozy Victorian-style lodge on the beachfront, or the local general store can rent you a cabin. With either type of accommodation comes the privilege of partaking in the town's principal pastime—bathing. Tenakee Springs' **bathhouse** is the centerpiece of the community's lifestyle. There is no coed time. Use the baths twice in two days and you'll likely meet three-fourths of the city's population who are of your gender. Use it three times and you'll meet the rest. Between baths you can fish for salmon, halibut, or crab; hike; pick berries; and visit with some of the friendliest townsfolk in the state. For cabin rentals, write Snyder Mercantile (Box 505, Tenakee Springs 99841, tel. 907/736–8001).

Tenakee Inn offers a cozy, beachfront Victorian-style lodge with kitchenettes, private bath, and family-style meals. Also provided are kayaks, bicycles, and skiff. *In summer, Box 54, Tenakee Springs 99841, tel. 907/736–9238; in winter, 167 S. Franklin St., Juneau 99801, tel. 907/586–1000.*

In Sitka, Burgess Bauder rents out his hand-built **Rockwell Lighthouse** (Box 277, Sitka 99835, tel. 907/747-3056) across the sound for $125 a day for a family. The price includes the use of a motorboat to get there.

Finally, if you hanker to know how the Indian village peoples of Southeast Alaska live today, you can fly or take the state ferry *LeConte* to **Kake, Angoon,** or **Hoonah.** You won't find much organized touring in any of these communities, but small, clean hotel accommodations are available (advance reservations strongly suggested), and fishing trips can be arranged by asking around. *In Kake: contact the New Town Inn, Box 222, Kake 99830, tel. 907/785–3472. In Angoon: write or call Kootznahoo Inlet Lodge, Box 134, Angoon 99820, tel. 907/788–3501; or Whalers Cove Lodge, Box 101, Angoon 99820, tel. 788–3123. In*

Hoonah: contact Totem Lodge, Box 320, Hoonah 99829, tel. 907/945–3636.

Shopping

Art Galleries   Along with the usual array of touristy work by talented but un-spectacular artists, Southeast Alaska shops and galleries carry some impressive Alaskan paintings, lithographs, and draw-ings. Among the best: **Scanlon Gallery,** with locations down-town in Ketchikan (310 Mission St., tel. 907/225–4730) and in the Plaza PortWest, a couple of miles north of downtown. They not only handle major Alaska artists (Byron Birdsall, Rie Munoz, John Fahringer, Nancy Stonington) and local talent (E-lizabeth Rose and Dick Miller) but also traditional and contem-porary native art, soapstone, bronze, and ivory. In Juneau, knowledgeable locals frequent the **Rie Munoz Gallery** (210 Ferry Way, tel. 907/586–2112) near the cruiseship lightering dock downtown. Ms. Munoz is one of Alaska's favorite artists, creator of a stylized, simple, but colorful design technique that is much-copied but rarely equaled. Other artists' work is also on sale at the Munoz Gallery, including wood-block prints by nationally recognized artist Dale DeArmond. Various books il-lustrated by Rie Munoz and written by Alaskan children's au-thor Jean Rogers are also available.

Gift Ideas   Totem poles, a few inches high to several feet tall, are among the popular Indian-made items available in the Southeast Alas-ka Panhandle. Other handicrafts from the Tlingit and Haida In-dians include wall masks, paddles, dance rattles, baskets, and tapestries with Southeast Alaska Indian designs. You'll find these items at gift shops up and down the coast. If you want to be sure of native Alaskan authenticity, buy items tagged with the state-approved "Authentic Native Handcraft From Alas-ka" label.

Gold-nugget rings, bracelets, necklaces, and watchbands, though costly, are popular among Alaskans and Alaska visi-tors. One Juneau dealer, the **Nugget Shop** on Front Street, will even sell you plain gold nuggets if you've missed finding any in the streams around the region.

Salmon—smoked, canned, or packaged otherwise—is another popular take-home item, for your own consumption or for friends who had to stay behind. Virtually every community has at least one canning and/or smoking operation that packs and ships local seafood. Throughout the region in food stores and gift shops, you'll likely run into **Silver Lining Seafoods** prod-ucts, a Ketchikan-based company with a consistently high-quality product in attractive packaging.

Another gourmet delicacy is a product Southeasterners refer to as Petersburg shrimp. Small (they're seldom larger than half your pinky finger), tender, and succulent, they're much treas-ured by Alaskans and often sent "outside" by them as thank-you gifts. You'll find the little critters fresh in meat depart-ments and canned in gift sections, at food stores throughout the Panhandle. You can buy canned Petersburg shrimp in Peters-burg at the Greens and Grains Deli, downtown on First St. or mail order them from Box 5, Petersburg 99833 (tel. 907/772–3392).

A new item in recent years is salmon skin leather—made into wallets, belts, keyholders, purses, and other items. A Juneau firm, **Alas Skins, Inc.** (on S. Franklin St. opposite the cruise ship terminal, tel. 907/780–6900), has pioneered this new industry. See their wares in local shops or visit their showroom.

You can't take it with you because of limited shelf life, but when you're "shopping" the bars and watering holes of Southeast Alaska, ask for Chinook Beer, an amber beer brewed and bottled in Juneau. Alaskans rate Chinook highly—and so did the judges at 1988's national Great American Beer Festival competition in Denver. Against 160 other beers, Chinook brought home a gold medal in the Alt-style category and was elected the people's choice among the 4,500 people attending the festival. Visitors are welcome to visit the mini-brewery's plant and sample the product during the bottling operation on Tuesday and Thursday 11–4. *5429 Shaune Dr., Juneau, tel. 907/780–5866.*

Up the stairs in the restored old Senate Building on S. Franklin Street in Juneau is the **Russian Shop** (tel. 907/586–2778), a depository of icons, samovars, lacquered boxes, nesting dolls, and other items that reflect Alaska's 18th- and 19th-century Russian heritage. One side of the shop is similarly, and surprisingly, devoted to Norwegian wares, including traditional Norwegian wool sweaters.

Participant Sports

Bicycling
In spite of sometimes wet weather, bicycling is very popular in Southeast Alaska communities. There are plenty of flat roads to ride (and some killer hills, too, if you're game) and the cycling can be glorious beside saltwater bays or within great towering forests. Unfortunately, bike rentals in the region seem to cycle in and out of business faster than you can shift derailers. Best bet if you don't bring your own in the back of a car or camper is to call bike shops or the parks and recreation departments in the towns you're visiting. Ask who in town is supplying rentals at the moment. Lodgings at Tenakee and Gustavus have bikes on hand for the use of their guests.

Canoeing/Kayaking
Paddling has been a pleasant way for visitors to see Southeast Alaska since the first Russians arrived on the scene in 1741 and watched the Indians do it. In Ketchikan, contact **Alaska Travel Adventures** (tel. 907/225–2840) for an Indian canoe excursion on Connel Lake north of town; smoked fish and other Indian delights are part of the experience. The **Ketchikan Parks and Recreation Department** (tel. 907/225–3111) rents kayaks. At Sitka, **Baidarka Boats** (tel. 907/747–8996) offers seakayak rentals and custom guided trips. In Juneau, **Alaska Discovery** (tel. 907/586–1811) is the company to see for escorted boat excursions in Glacier Bay National Park and Preserve or Admiralty Island, or for kayaking in the lake in front of Mendenhall Glacier.

Kayak rentals for unescorted Glacier Bay exploring and camping can be arranged through **Glacier Bay Sea Kayaks** (Box 26, Gustavus 99826, tel. 907/697–2257). Twice a day, at 9 AM and 6 PM, their experienced kayakers give orientations on handling the craft plus camping and routing suggestions. The company will also make reservations aboard the regular sightseeing day boat to drop kayakers off and pick them up in the most scenic country.

Fishing The prospect of bringing a lunker king salmon or a leaping, diving, fighting rainbow trout to net is the reason many visitors choose an Alaska vacation. Local give-away guidebooks and the State of Alaska's *Official Vacation Planner* contain the names of scores of reputable charter boats and boat rental agencies in every community along the Panhandle coast. Your best bet for catching salmon in salt water is from a boat. Similarly, the very finest angling for freshwater species (rainbows, cutthroat, lake trout) is to be found at fly-in lakes and resorts. Still, there's more than adequate fishing right from saltwater shores or in lakes and streams accessible by roads. To learn where the fish are biting at any given time, call the local office of the Alaska Department of Fish and Game in the community you're visiting, or contact the ADFG's main office (Box 3-2000, Juneau 998023, tel. 907/465–4112).

Golf Juneau's par-three nine-hole **Mendenhall Golf course** (2101 Industrial Blvd., tel. 907/789–7323) is pretty modest. Still, its location on saltwater wetlands beside the waters of Gastineau Channel makes it one-of-a-kind. You probably won't haul your clubs all the way to Alaska to sample these fairways and roughs, but rentals are available.

Hiking and Backpacking Trekking woods, mountains, and beaches is Southeast Alaska's unofficial regional sport. Toddlers, teens, young adults, and oldsters can be seen along Southeast's trails and paths. Many of the trails are old, abandoned mining roads. Others are natural routes—in some sections, even game trails—meandering over ridges, through forests, and alongside streams and glaciers. A few, like the backpacking Chilkoot Trail out of Skagway, rate five stars for historical significance, scenery, and hiker aids en route. There's not a community in Southeast Alaska that doesn't have easy access to at least some hiking or backpacking. For more information, contact the visitor bureau or parks and recreation department in the community you're visiting. The Alaska Division of Parks Southeast regional office (400 Willoughby Ave., tel. 907/465–4563) will send you a list of state-maintained trails and parks in the Panhandle. Parks and Recreation/Juneau (tel. 907/586–5226) sponsors a group hike each Wednesday morning for locals and visitors.

Motor Scooters and Mopeds Two-wheeled travel has suddenly sprung upon the Ketchikan and Juneau scenes. **Scooter Rentals, Inc.,** of Ketchikan operates from downtown on the wooden cruise-ship dock. If no one is around, call the number on the door, and someone will rush right down to help you. Only available in good weather.

Running and Jogging The national running craze is alive and well along Southeast streets, roads, and trails. Hotel clerks and visitor information offices will be glad to make route suggestions if you need them. If you plan to run, bring along a light sweatsuit and running rain gear as well as shorts and a T-shirt. The weather can be hot and sweaty one day, chilly and wet the next. If you plan to be in Juneau early in July, call the Parks and Recreation Department (tel. 907/586–5226) and check the date of the annual **Governor's Cup Fun Run.** Hundreds of Juneau racers, runners, joggers, race walkers, and mosey-alongers take part in this three-mile event. Other marathons, half marathons, 5Ks, or similar events take place in various communities throughout the summer. The most grueling race in these parts is the annual fall **Klondike Trail of '98 Road Relay** event, spanning 110 miles between Skagway and Whitehorse on the Klondike and Alaska highways. For details: Carol Clark, Tourism Industry Association of the Yukon (102–302 Steele St., Whitehorse, Yukon, Canada Y1A 2C5, tel. 403/668–3331).

Scuba Considering that the visibility is not very good in most Southeast waters, there's a lot of scuba and skin-diving activity throughout the region. Quarter-inch wet suits are a must. So is a buddy; stay close together. Local dive shops can steer you to the best places to dive for abalone, scallops, and crabs, and advise you on the delights and dangers of underwater wrecks. Shops that rent tanks and equipment to qualified divers include **Mac's Dive Shop** (2214 Muir, Juneau, tel. 907/789–5115), **Scuba Crafts, Inc.** (4485 N. Douglas Hwy., Juneau, tel. 907/586–2341), **Alaska Diving Service** (1601 Tongass Ave., Ketchikan, tel. 907/225–4667), and **Southeast Diving & Sports** (203 Lincoln Ave., Sitka, tel. 907/747–8279).

Skiing Nordic skiing is a favorite winter pastime for outdoor enthusi-
Cross-country asts, especially in the northern half of the Panhandle. Although promoted mostly by and for the locals, visitors are always welcome. In Petersburg, the favorite locale for Nordic types is the end of **Three Lakes Loop.** Old logging roads and trails are popular, as well. If you arrive without your boards, call the Chamber of Commerce Visitor Center (tel. 907/772–3646). They'll try to line up some loaners for you.

In Juneau, ski rentals are available along with many suggestions for touring the trails and ridges around town from **Foggy Mountain Shop** (134 S. Franklin St., tel. 907/586–6780).

From Haines, **Alaska Nature Tours** (Box 491, Haines 99827, tel. 907/766–2876) operates a winter Nordic shuttle bus to flat-tracking in the Chilkat Bald Eagle Preserve and across the Canadian border atop Chilkat Pass in British Columbia.

Downhill **Eaglecrest** (155 Seward St., Juneau 99801, tel. 907/586–5284) on Douglas Island, just 30 minutes from downtown Juneau, offers late November to mid-April skiing on a well-groomed mountain with two double-chair lifts, a beginner's platter-pull, cross-country trails, ski school (including downhill, Nordic, and telemark), ski rental shop, cafeteria, and trilevel day lodge. Because this is Southeast Alaska, knowledgeable skiers pack rain slickers along with parkas, hats, gloves, and other gear. Weekends and holidays there are bus pickups at hotels and motels.

Tennis You won't find the likes of Wimbledon in Southeast Alaska, but you will find courts in Ketchikan, Wrangell, Petersburg, Juneau, and Skagway. The **Juneau Racquet Club,** about 10 miles north of downtown, adjacent to Mendenhall Mall, will accommodate out-of-towners at their first-class indoor tennis and racquetball courts. Facilities include sauna, Jacuzzi, exercise equipment, snack bar, massage tables, and sports shop. *Tel. 907/789–2181. 1-day fee for nonmembers: $5 until 4 PM, $8 until 8:30 PM, $5 8:30–10 PM.*

Spectator Sports

With the possible exception of basketball, Southeast Alaska's spectator sports probably don't offer much visitor excitement. High school sports (basketball, wrestling, track, limited football, skiing, and swimming) and Little League baseball in the summertime attract large numbers of locals, but not very many fans from outside the region. There are no semi-pro or professional baseball teams in the Panhandle. The devotion of large numbers of Southeast adults to summer softball, however, borders on outright addiction.

Basketball Watching two teams of five trying to shoot balls in hoops is Southeast Alaska's major spectator sport. Each January in Juneau, the local Lions Clubs' Golden North tournament attracts teams from all over the Panhandle and even nearby Canada. And the University of Alaska–Southeast Whales and Lady Whales teams likewise are often in town to offer respectable court action. For schedules, contact University of Alaska–Southeast (11120 Glacier Hwy., Juneau 99801, tel. 907/789-4400).

Dining and Lodging

Highly recommended hotels and restaurants are indicated with a star ★ .

Major credit cards are usually accepted, but there are exceptions. It's best to inquire in advance.

Dining Portions are almost universally generous and the variety of offerings ranges from standard American steak and potatoes to Italian, Mexican, Tex-Mex, Chinese, Japanese, and, in recent years, Vietnamese. Seafood, not surprisingly, comprises a large share of most restaurant menus. In summertime the king salmon, halibut, king crab, cod, or prawns are likely to be fresh from the sea. By late fall through to spring, they may have been frozen—and frankly not as tasty—so it pays to ask if its fresh.

Restaurants and cafes in the Panhandle are uniformly informal. Gentlemen in coats and ties and ladies in dresses will always feel comfortable in the nicer places, but so will diners in more casual slacks, sweaters, and sport shirts. Clean jeans and windbreakers are fine in most places. Restaurant hours vary seasonally. It is best to call ahead before you start out.

Restaurants are listed in the following price categories:

Category	Cost*
Expensive	$40–$60
Moderate	$20–$40
Inexpensive	under $20

per person without tax, service, or drinks

Lodging Hotels, motels, lodges, and inns run the gamut in Southeast Alaska from very traditional urban hostelries—the kind you'll find almost anywhere—to charming small-town inns and rustic cabins in the boondocks.

The most rooms, and the most choices, are to be found in Ketchikan and Juneau. Accommodations in any of the Panhandle communities, however, are usually not hard to come by even in the summer, except when festivals, fishing derbies, fairs, and other special events are underway. To be on the safe side and get your first choice, you should make reservations as early as possible. With the exception of bed-and-breakfasts (B&Bs), most hotels accept the major credit cards. Hotels and lodging places are listed under the following categories:

Category	Cost*
Very Expensive	over $120
Expensive	$90–$120
Moderate	$50–$90
Inexpensive	under $50

double room without tax or service

Glacier Bay/ Gustavus Dining

★ **Glacier Bay Country Inn.** Another inn where the emphasis is on gourmet dining, with foods fresh from the sea and the inn's own garden. The inn is a large rambling log structure of marvelous cupolas, dormers, gables, and porches. Among guests' favorites: halibut with fresh sorrel sauce, homemade fettuccine, and rhubarb custard pie. Dinner guests not staying at the inn must make reservations in advance. *On the main road halfway between the airport and Bartlett Cove, tel. 907/697–2288. No credit cards, but personal checks accepted. Moderate.*

★ **Gustavus Inn.** The family-style meals at this former homestead are legendary. Hosts David and Jo Ann Lesh—carrying on a tradition established decades ago by David's parents—heap bountiful servings of seafood and fresh vegetable dishes on the plates of overnight guests and walk-ins who reserve in advance. *On the main road, tel. 907/697–2254. MC, V accepted, but cash or personal or traveler's checks preferred. Moderate.*

Glacier Bay Lodge. If it swims or crawls in the sea hereabouts, you'll find it on the menu in the dining room at this, the only lodge actually in Glacier Bay National Park and Preserve. Steaks and other selections are available as well. Located on the main floor of the massive, timbered lodge, the dining room looks out on the chill waters of Bartlett Cove. *Tel. 907/697–2225. AE, MC, V, DC. Inexpensive–Moderate.*

Open Gate Cafe. Nothing fancy here, just good wholesome cooking that the locals seem to like—fresh baked breads, pastries, deli sandwiches. Monday night is pizza night; Saturdays feature prime ribs. *On the dock road, tel. 907/697–2227. No credit cards, but personal checks accepted. Inexpensive.*

Lodging

★ **Gustavus Inn.** Established in 1965 on a pioneer Gustavus homestead, the Gustavus Inn continues a tradition of gracious Alaska rural living and vacationing. In the original homestead building and in a new structure completed in 1988, there are rooms with full private bath and a few that share facilities. Glacier trips, fishing expeditions, bicycle rides around the community, or berry picking in season are things-to-do options. The option of choice for many guests is simply to do nothing but enjoy the quiet, tranquillity, and notable food the inn has to offer. *On main road (mailing address: Box 60, Gustavus 99826), tel. 907/697–2254. Courtesy-car pickup at the airport. MC, V ac-*

cepted, *but cash or personal or traveler's checks preferred. Very Expensive.*

★ **Glacier Bay Country Inn.** This is the "new kid on the block" among inns in Gustavus. It opened in 1986 with accommodations for 14 guests in a picturesque but fully modern structure built from local hand-logged timbers. Innkeepers Al and Annie Unrein outfitted the inn with cozy comforters, warm flannel sheets, and fluffy towels in each room for a homelike feeling. The Unreins will arrange sightseeing and flightseeing tours. They also operate charter-boat trips into Glacier Bay and nearby waters aboard their elegant *M/V Pacific*, a 42-foot yacht with teak woodwork, two staterooms (sleeping four to six) and two bathrooms. *On main road halfway between the airport and Bartlett Cove (mailing address: Box 5, Gustavus 99826), tel. 907/697–2288; fax 907/697–2289. No credit cards, but personal checks accepted. Expensive.*

Glacier Bay Lodge. The only hotel accommodations actually within Glacier Bay National Park and Preserve. The lodge is constructed of massive timbers, and in spite of its substantial size it blends well into the thick rain forest that surrounds it on three sides. Room accommodations—fully modern—are accessible by boardwalk ramps from the main lodge. From the Bartlett Cove dock out front, visitors venture on day boats or overnight cruises up bay into the glacier country. *Located at Bartlett Cove (mailing address: Box 108, Gustavus 99826 or 523 Pine St., Seattle, WA 98101), tel. 907/697–2225 or 800/622–2042. Facilities: lounge, gift shop, flightseeing reservations desk. AE, MC, V, DC. Expensive.*

The Puffin Bed & Breakfast. These are attractive cabins located in a wooded homestead. Bath and shower are in a separate building. Bikes are available for guests' use. Full breakfast is included. The owners also operate Puffin Travel, for fishing and sightseeing charters, and Puffin Arts and Crafts Shop at the airport. *In central Gustavus (mailing address: Box 3, Gustavus 99826); tel. 907/697–2260 in summer, 907/789–9787 in winter. AE, MC, V. Inexpensive.*

Haines **The Lighthouse Restaurant.** Located at the foot of Main Street
Dining next to the boat harbor, the Lighthouse offers a great view of Lynn Canal, boats, and boaters, along with its fine barbecued ribs, steaks, and seafoods. Its Harbor Bar is a popular watering hole for commercial fishermen. It's colorful but can get a little loud as the night wears on. *Front St. on the harbor, tel. 907/766–2442. AE, MC, V. Moderate.*

The Bamboo Room, Popular for sandwiches, burgers, fried chicken, and seafood. *2nd Ave. near Main St., tel. 907/766–9109. Inexpensive.*

The Catalyst. Serves up seafood, fine pastries, and a generous salad bar in a European atmosphere. *Main St. and 3rd Ave., tel. 907/766–2670. Closed Sun. Inexpensive.*

Chilkat Restaurant and Bakery. Offers family-style cooking in a homelike setting. *5th Ave. near Main St., tel. 907/766–2920. Closed Sun. Inexpensive.*

Commander's Room Restaurant and Lounge. Located in the large white rambling home that served as the former commanding officer's quarters at old Fort Seward, this is the dining room for the Halsingland Hotel. It has been satisfying hotel guests and Haines folk for decades. Seafood is the specialty here and halibut is a consistent pleaser. The restaurant has a full salad bar and full "potato bar" of baked potatoes, boiled red potatoes, rice pilaf, and vegetables with varied toppings (cheese, chili, etc.). Nearby, at the Indian Tribal House on the parade grounds, the Halsingland also prepares a nightly salmon bake called the Port Chilkoot Potlatch, priced at $17.50 for all you can eat. *At Ft. Seward, tel. 907/766–2000. AE, DC, MC, V. Inexpensive.*

Lodging
★ **Captain's Choice Motel.** A conventional motel, located in downtown Haines and featuring amenities such as cable TV, phones, and rooms with bath and toilet facilities. Ask for a room looking out over the waters of Portage Cove. *2nd St. and Dalton St. (mailing address: Box 392, Haines 99827), tel. 800/478–2345 within Alaska or 800/247–7153 outside Alaska. 40 rooms, including 3 deluxe suites: AE, MC, V. Moderate–Expensive.*

Halsingland Hotel. The officers of old Fort Seward once lived in the big, white structures that today comprise the 60-room Halsingland Hotel. Most of the rooms have private baths, a few do not. All are fully carpeted and have wildlife photos on the walls. *On the parade grounds, Ft. Seward (mailing address: Box 1589, Haines 99827), tel. 907/766–2000 or 800/542–6363 outside Alaska. AE, MC, V. Inexpensive–Moderate.*

There are several B&Bs in Haines, and one youth hostel. For more information call the visitor information center (2nd Ave. near Willard St., tel. 907/766–2202).

Juneau
Dining
★ **The Summit.** Unlikely as it may seem, this small, intimate, candle-lit restaurant in the Inn at the Waterfront is the city's most prestigious dining place. Of 30 entrees on the menu, 20 are seafood—including abalone sautéed in butter and almonds, scallops, prawns, halibut, and a tender salmon offering called Salmon Gastineau. If you like steak, their New York La Bleu features New York strip steak with blue cheese. *455 S. Franklin St., tel. 907/586–2050. Reservations strongly recommended. AE, DC, MC, V. No lunch. Moderate–Expensive.*

Mike's. For decades Mike's, in the former mining community of Douglas across the bridge from Juneau, has been serving up seafood, steaks, and pastas. Their treatment of tiny Petersburg shrimp is particularly noteworthy. Rivaling the food, however, is the view from the picture windows at the rear of the restaurant. Mike's looks over the waters of Gastineau Channel to Juneau and the ruins of the old AJ mine. *1102 2nd St. in Douglas, tel. 907/364–3271. AE, DC, MC, V. No lunch weekends. Moderate.*

★ **The Fiddlehead.** This is probably Juneau's favorite restaurant, a delightful place of light woods, gently patterned wallpaper, stained glass, hanging plants, and historic photos on the wall. The food is healthy, generously served, and, well, *different.* Would you believe, for instance, a light dinner of black beans and rice? Or pasta Greta Garbo, which is locally smoked salmon tossed with fettuccine in cream sauce? Or chicken and eggplant Szechuan, consisting of chicken and eggplant sautéed with bean paste and served over rice? Homemade bread from their bakery is likewise laudable. *429 Willoughby Ave., tel. 907/586–3150. No smoking. Reservations recommended. MC, V. Inexpensive–Moderate.*

The Silverbow Inn. Here's another place so popular with locals that you should reserve ahead for meals during normal dining hours. The decor is "early Juneau," with settings, chairs, and tables (no two are alike) of the kind you might have found in someone's parlor during the city's gold-mining era. The main structure, for years one of the town's major bakeries, was built in 1912. The wine list is limited but selective; dinner entrées change daily and might include halibut with almonds, salmon Florentine, stir-fry prawns, or red snapper. *120 2nd Ave., tel. 907/586-4146. AE, DC, MC, V. Hours vary Oct.-April. Inexpensive-Moderate.*

El Sombrero. It's tiny and a trifle crowded, but the fare in this north-of-the-border Mexican restaurant would make Poncho Villa homesick. If you eat here at noon you get more food for your dollar than if you dine in the evening. A dinner favorite combines a meat or chicken taco, cheese enchilada, plus rice or beans. Order the same meal at noon, and for the same price you get rice *and* beans. *157 S. Franklin, tel. 907/586-6770. AE, DC, MC, V. Closed Sun. Sept.-April. Inexpensive-Moderate.*

★ **Gold Creek Salmon Bake.** The decor here is the Alaska outdoors. You eat under a roofed shelter on comfortable benches and tables, but all around you are trees, mountains, and the rushing water of Gold Creek (where gold was discovered in 1880). The salmon bake itself is thought to be Alaska's oldest such outdoor offering. Fresh caught salmon (supplemented sometimes by halibut as well) is cooked over an alder-smoke fire until it's tender but done. A simple but succulent sauce of brown sugar, margarine, and lemon juice adds the final appetizing touch. Along with the salmon comes hot baked beans, salad, Jello, sourdough or wheat bread, and a can of beer, soft drink, or coffee. (Fixed price, $17.) After dinner you can pan for gold in the stream (pans are available for your use, no charge, keep all the gold you find) or wander up the hill to the remains of AJ gold-mine buildings. *End of Basin Rd., tel. 907/586-1424. Free bus ride from in front of the Baranof Hotel in downtown Juneau. No credit cards. Closed mid-Sept.-April. Inexpensive.*

Lodging **The Baranof Hotel.** For half a century the Baranof has been—for commercial travelers, legislators, lobbyists, and tourists—the city's prestige address. That designation has been challenged in recent years by the Westmark (like the Baranof, a unit of the Westmark chain), but the nine-story hostelry probably remains the hotel of choice for most visitors to the capital city. The lobby and most rooms have been extensively refurbished in recent years in tasteful woods and a lighting style reminiscent of 1939, when the hotel first opened. Facilities include the Capital City Cafe for coffee and light snacks, the Bubble Room lounge and piano bar, and the Gold Room for fine dining. Also on site: a travel agency and Alaska Airlines ticket office. *127 N. Franklin St., tel. 907/586-2660 or 800/344-0970. 200 rooms. AE, MC, V. Very Expensive.*

Westmark Juneau. A high rise (by Juneau standards), the seven-story Westmark is situated across Main Street from Juneau's Centennial Hall convention center and across Egan Drive from the docks. Rooms are basically modern in decor, and the lobby is distinguished by a massive carved eagle figure. Extensive additional wood-mural carvings may be seen on the wall of the Woodcarver Dining Room. *51 W. Egan Dr., tel. 907/586-6900 or 800/544-0970. 105 rooms. AE, MC, V. Very Expensive.*

★ **The Prospector.** A short walk west of downtown and right next door to the State Museum, this smaller but fully modern hotel is what many business travelers and a number of legislators like to call home while they're in Juneau. You'll find very large rooms here, and in The Diggings dining room and lounge you can enjoy what some consider to be the finest prime rib in Southeast Alaska. Steaks and seafood are also popular. *375 Whittier Ave., tel. 907/586–3737 or 800/331–2711. 60 rooms. AE, MC, V. Expensive.*

Airport TraveLodge. The rooms and furnishings are pretty standard fare. The structure, matching Fernando's Restaurant inside, is Mexican in design and decor. The motel is one of only two in the community with an indoor swimming pool—a plus if you want to unwind after a day of touring. *9200 Glacier Hwy., tel. 907/789–9700. 86 rooms. AE, MC, V. Moderate.*

Country Lane Inn. Another motel with a pool and a Jacuzzi, the Country Lane Inn is a Best Western. Baskets of multicolored flowers hang along the entrance walk to rooms, a pleasant welcome indeed. The lobby, though quite small, seems like a country home parlor, with comfortable chairs, pillowed couch and library books available. The coffee is on all the time. *9300 Glacier Hwy., tel. 907/789–5005 or 800/334–9401. 50 rooms. AE, MC, V. Moderate.*

Travelers who enjoy staying in restored historic hotels have three to choose from in downtown Juneau: the **Silverbow Inn,** in the old bakery building dating from the late 1890s (120 2nd St., tel. 907/586–4146. 6 rooms. Moderate); the **Alaskan Hotel,** a 1913 structure (167 S. Franklin St., tel. 907/586–1000. 40 rooms. Inexpensive/Moderate); and the 1898 **Inn at the Waterfront** (455 S. Franklin St., tel. 907/586–2050. 29 rooms. Inexpensive–Moderate).

Ketchikan **Salmon Falls Resort.** This is Ketchikan's newest (and many say
Dining nicest) eating place. It's a half-hour drive from town, but the
★ seafood and steaks served up in the huge, octagonal restaurant make the drive more than worthwhile. The chef especially recommends seafood caught fresh from adjacent waters. Locals give high marks to the halibut and shellfish stew. The restaurant is built of pine logs, and at the center of the dining room, supporting the roof, rises a 40-foot section of 48-inch pipe manufactured to be part of the Alaska pipeline. The dining area overlooks the waters of Clover Passage, where sunsets can be vivid red and remarkable. *Mile 17, North Tongass Hwy., tel. 907/225–2752 or 800/247–9059. Reservations recommended. AE, DC, MC, V. Moderate.*

Charley's. Located in the Ingersoll Hotel, Charley's is a favorite breakfast/luncheon spot for Ketchikan business types. It's a popular family place, too, offering dinners that don't devastate the pocketbook. Decor is sort of nostalgic, with brass railings, deep-maroon trim on chairs and tables, and an etched-glass window. Seafood is a specialty here—salmon, halibut, or whatever is fresh. For breakfast, try reindeer sausage with your eggs. For dinner, the lobster is first rate, even though it's not from these waters. Bar service available; music in the evenings. *208 Front St., tel. 907/225–5090. AE, DC, MC, V. Inexpensive–Moderate.*

Gilmore Gardens. Eating or sipping a drink here is another stroll down memory lane. Deep burgundy patterns in the carpets, lace place mats under each china table setting, padded old-fashioned chairs, and hanging lights combine to revive the 1930s and '40s. It's also the city's only cappuccino and espresso bar. Among notable international menu items is the prawns amaretto, prepared with amaretto liqueur, a touch of white wine, cream, and just a hint of orange. Prawns, in fact are a specialty, and the menu also includes prawns scampi and sweet-and-sour prawns. For breakfast try their eggs Alaska, which some may confuse with eggs Benedict, except it's prepared with Alaska smoked salmon, not ham. For dessert, locals recommend the peanut butter pie. *326 Front St., tel. 907/225–9423. AE, DC, MC, V. Inexpensive–Moderate.*

Other better-than-adequate eating places in the community include the **Clover Pass Resort** (Mile 15, North Tongass Hwy., tel. 907/247–2234. Inexpensive–Moderate) for excellent seafood and a view of sport fishermen coming, going, and bringing home their catches; **Grandeli's** (in the Plaza Portwest Mall, tel. 907/225–1414. Inexpensive); and **Kay's Kitchen** (2813 Tongass Ave., tel. 907/225–5860. Inexpensive) for homemade soups and generous sandwiches.

Lodging   **Royal Executive Suites.** Nothing in the plain, square exterior of this hotel building or in its Spartan lobby reflects the deluxe accommodations waiting within. Some of the 14 units are split level with circular stairways; all are carpeted in steel grays or other light colors with pastel shaded furniture and natural wood trims. Many of the units have full kitchens and Jacuzzis, and all guests have access to an exercise room with treadmill, hot tub, and sauna. Windows are large and look out on the busy water and air traffic in Tongass Narrows. There is no restaurant on site, but meals can be brought to your room. Located between downtown and the ferry terminal. *1471 Tongass Ave. (mailing address: Box 8331, Ketchikan 99901), tel. 907/225–1900. AE, DC, MC, V. Expensive–Very Expensive.*

★   **Ingersoll Hotel.** Old-fashioned patterned wallpaper, wood wainscoting around the walls, and etched-glass windows on the oak registration desk set a 1930s mood for this three-story downtown hotel (actually built in the mid-'20s). Furnishings are standard, with bright Alaskan art on the walls. Some rooms have a view of the cruise dock and the waters of Tongass Narrows. *303 Mission St. (mailing address: Box 6440, Ketchikan 99901), tel. 907/225–2124. 60 rooms. Charley's restaurant on site. AE, DC, MC, V. Moderate.*

The Landing. The sign outside still says "Hilltop Motel," but the new name is "The Landing," in recognition of the ferry landing site in the waters of Tongass Narrows across the street. The hotel is modern, and the 46 rooms are nicely furnished in typical American motel decor. *3434 Tongass Ave., tel. 907/225–5166. Cafe, lounge on site. AE, DC, D, MC, V. Moderate.*

The Gilmore Hotel. Like the Ingersoll down the street, the Gilmore's narrow lobby sets the mood of the place with 1930s-style wine-colored carpeting, hanging lights, and a comfortable little sitting area (on a landing up the stairs) with easy chairs, table, and a stained-glass window. Rooms are plain but clean, with bright bedspreads of floral and leaf patterns. Standard furnishings include a desk, chairs, chest of drawers, and TV. A few of the hotel's 42 rooms share toilet facilities down the hall. *326 Front St., tel. 907/225–9423. No elevator. AE, MC, V. Inexpensive.*

Petersburg   **The Beachcomber Inn.** Seafood, with a distinctly Norwegian
Dining   flair, is the specialty in this restored cannery building on the
★   shores of Wrangell Narrows. If you're there on a smorgasbord night you may sample red-snapper fish cakes, salmon loaf, Nor-

wegian (emphatically *not* Swedish) meat balls, creamed potatoes, and sugary desserts such as *sandbakkelse*, *lefsa*, or
krumkakke cones. Petersburg's famed beer-batter halibut is
also served here, as are salmon steaks and other traditional
seafoods. *Mile 4, Mitkof Hwy., tel. 907/772–3888. AE, MC, V.
Inexpensive.*

Helse. Natural foods, including enormous vegetable-laden
sandwiches, are a specialty here. Also soups, chowders, home-
baked breads, and salads. *Sing Lee Alley and Harbor Way, tel.
907/772–3444. No credit cards. Inexpensive.*

The Homestead. Nothing fancy here, just basic American
steaks, local prawns and halibut, salad bar, and especially generous breakfasts. A popular place with the locals. *217 Main St.,
tel. 907/772–3900. DC, MC, V. Inexpensive.*

Pellerito's Pizza. You'll get authentic pizzas with homemade
sausages here. Or try the pizza with local shrimp. *Across from
the ferry terminal. Tel. 907/772–3727. No credit cards. Inexpensive.*

One of the most hospitable eateries in town is **Greens and
Grains** for deli selections to go or sit-down meals at the restaurant. Try the Petersburg shrimp. *Nordic Dr. and Excel St., tel.
907/772–4433. Inexpensive.*

Lodging
★
Tides Inn. This is the largest hotel in town, a block uphill from
Petersburg's main thoroughfare. It has 46 rooms, all fully modern, with standard furnishings and full baths, showers, and toilet facilities. There's always coffee on in the small, informal
lobby, and in the morning you're welcome to complimentary
juices, cereals, and pastries. Some units are equipped with
kitchens. Ask for a room in the new wing; these units have a
view of the boat harbor. *1st and Dolphin Sts. (mailing address:
Box 1048, Petersburg 99833), tel. 907/772–4288. AE, DC, MC,
V. Moderate.*

Scandia House. Very old country Norwegian, this 24-unit hotel
on Petersburg's main street has been a local fixture since 1910.
Here, too, the coffee is always on in a small lobby accented by
etched-glass windows on the entrance doors and large oil paintings on the wall showing local old-timers in colorful Norwegian
garb. "American" units have full toilet facilities; "European"
rooms have showers and toilets down the hall. At least one unit
has kitchenette facilities, and all rooms are squeaky clean, with
standard furnishings including TV. Norwegian rosemaling designs on the exterior make this a frequent camera subject. *110
Nordic Dr. (mailing address: Box 689, Petersburg 99833), tel.
907/772–4281. AE, DC, MC, V. Inexpensive–Moderate.*

*Sitka
Dining*
★
Channel Club. This is Sitka's number one gourmet eating establishment—the winner on five different occasions of the Silver Spoon award from the Gourmet Club of America. It's a
toss-up whether to order steak or seafood here, but whatever
you choose will be good. Halibut cheeks are a consistent favorite; if you order steak, don't ask the chef for his steak seasoning
recipe—it's a secret. Decor is ship-oriented, with glass fishing
balls, whale baleen, and Alaska pictures on the wall. *Mile 3.5,
Halibut Point Rd., tel. 907/747–9916. AE, DC, MC, V. Moderate–Expensive.*

Raven Room. Located in the Westmark Shee Atika Hotel, the
Raven Room offers seafood, pasta, and steaks in a setting rich
in Southeastern Alaska native decor. Dancing in the evening in

the Kadataan Lounge. *330 Seward St., tel. 907/747–6241. AE, DC, MC, V. Moderate.*

Also recommended: **Marina Restaurant,** for Mexican or Italian fare (205 Harbor Dr., tel. 907/747–8840. Inexpensive); and **Staton's Steak House** for (you guessed it) steak and seafood (Harbor Dr. and Maksutoff St., tel. 907/747–3396. Inexpensive).

Lodging **Westmark Shee Atika.** If you stay here for a night or two, you
★ will surely come away with an increased appreciation for Southeast Alaska Indian art and culture. Displays throughout the hotel—full wall murals in the lobby and additional artwork in the rooms—tell of the history, legends, and exploits of the Tlingit people. Many of the hotel's nearly 100 rooms overlook Crescent Harbor and the islands in the waters beyond; others have mountain and forest views. *330 Seward St. (mailing address: Box 78, Sitka 99835), tel. 907/747–6241 or 800/544–0970. AE, DC, MC, V. Very Expensive.*

A number of B&Bs have sprung up in Sitka in recent years; ask the visitor center for a referral or write to the **Sitka Convention and Visitors Bureau** (Box 1226, Sitka 99835).

Skagway **Chilkoot Dining Room.** If it's not packed with tourists the Chil-
Dining koot offers some of Skagway's most gracious dining. Try, therefore, to avoid the 6:30 PM rush hour. Decor here is gold rush, but a lot grander and more plush than anything the stampeders ever experienced. If it's on the menu, try the family-style crab dinner. *3rd Ave., east of Broadway, tel. 907/983–2291. AE, DC, MC, V. Moderate.*
Golden North Restaurant. This is the dining room in the Golden North Hotel, and to eat here is to return to the days of gold rush con man Soapy Smith, heroic Frank Reid, and scores of pioneers, stampeders, and dance hall girls. The decor is *authentically* Days of '98—because the hotel was actually built that year and has been tastefully restored to the era. Popular choices include sourdough pancakes for breakfasts; soups, salad bar selections, and sandwiches for lunch; salmon or other seafood for dinner. If you're not staying at the Golden North, mosey through the lobby after eating. It's almost like a visit to a historical museum. *3rd Ave. and Broadway, tel. 907/983–2294. AE, DC, MC, V. Inexpensive–Moderate.*
Prospector's Sourdough Restaurant. You'll meet as many Skagway folk here as you will visitors, particularly at breakfast time when the sourdough hotcakes or snow-crab omelets are on the griddle. Salmon steak is a popular favorite in the evening. Decor features the colorful works of local artists on the walls. *4th Ave. and Broadway, tel. 907/983–2865. AE, DC, MC, V. Inexpensive.*

Two other worthy cafés in the inexpensive category are the **Kountry Kitchen** at 4th and State and the **Northern Lights Café** at 4th and Broadway.

Lodging **Westmark Inn.** Formerly called the Klondike Hotel, this is Skagway's largest inn (210 rooms). In keeping with the locale, the decor is gold-rush elegant, with rich red carpeting, matching wallpapers, and brass trim. You'll find historical pictures throughout. Room furnishings are first class. Ask for a room in the main structure rather than the annex on the south side of Third Street. The rooms are larger and you don't have to leave the building to visit the restaurant or lounge. *3rd St., east of Broadway, tel. 907/983–2291. Reservations necessary. Facilities: dining room, lounge. Open summer only. AE, DC, MC, V. Very Expensive.*

★ **Golden North Hotel.** No question about it, this is Alaska's most historic hotel. It was built in 1898 in the heyday of the gold rush—golden dome and all—and has been tenderly, lovingly restored to reflect that period. Pioneer Skagway families have contributed gold-rush furnishings from their homes to each of the hotel's 32 rooms, and the stories of those families are printed and posted on the walls of each unit. *3rd Ave. and Broadway (mailing address: Box 343, Skagway 99840), tel. 907/983–2451 or 983–2294. Facilities: dining room, lounge. AE, MC, V. Moderate.*

★ **Skagway Inn Bed & Breakfast.** "More like a home than a hotel" is the way the owner advertises this 12-room inn, with each room bearing the name of a gold-rush gal. The building was constructed in 1897 and is thus one of Skagway's oldest. Rooms are private, but baths are shared. Guests are welcome to lounge and socialize in the home-style living room. Tea is served each afternoon in Miss Suzanne's Tea Room, and dinners (by reservation only) are available each evening. *Between 6th Ave. and 7th Ave. on Broadway (mailing address: Box 13, Skagway 99840), tel. 907/983–2289. AE, MC, V. Moderate.*

Wind Valley Lodge. Located a long walk or a short drive from downtown, the Wind Valley Lodge is one of Skagway's newer hotels. All 30 rooms are modern and there is a free shuttle to downtown. *22nd Ave. and State St. (mailing address: Box 354, Skagway 99840), tel. 907/983–2236. MC, V. Moderate.*

Wrangell
Dining

Dock Side Restaurant. This is the coffee shop and dining room for the Stikine Inn, located right on the dock and offering good views of the harbor. Seafood and steaks are staples here. *One block from ferry terminal, tel. 907/874–3388. AE, DC, MC, V. Inexpensive–Moderate.*

Roadhouse Lodge. The walls here carry practically a museum of early Alaskana. The food is wholesome, tasty, and ample. Specialties include local prawns (sautéed, deep-fried, and boiled in the shell) and deep-fried Indian frybread. A courtesy van will pick you up in town. *Mile 4, Zimovia Hwy., tel. 907/874–2335. AE, DC, MC, V. Inexpensive–Moderate.*

Lodging

Stikine Inn. This is Wrangell's largest hotel—34 rooms with tasteful, modern furniture. Located on the dock in the main part of town, the inn offers great views of Wrangell's harbor. The Dock Side Restaurant is on site, as is the Stikine Bar, which can get pretty loud at night. (Unless you're going to be among the late-night party crowd, ask the registration clerk to assign you a room away from the bar.) There's no extra charge for kids under 12. *Box 990, Wrangell 99929, tel. 907/874–3388. AE, DC, MC, V. Facilities: travel agency, beauty salon. Moderate–Expensive.*

Harding's Old Sourdough Lodge. This lodge is located on the docks, in a beautifully converted construction camp. The Harding family welcomes guests in the big open dining/living room with home-baked sourdough breads and local seafood. The 16 guest rooms are paneled—the building's exterior with cedar hand-milled by Lloyd Harding. *Box 1062, Wrangell 99929, tel. 907/874–3613. AE, MC, V. Facilities: conference room, charter boats. Inexpensive–Moderate.*

Roadhouse Lodge. This is not a large facility (10 rooms and 1 suite), but it's fully modern and offers a variety of services including bar, restaurant, car rentals, courtesy car, laundry facilities, and gift shop. The lodge will also arrange fishing and sightseeing charters. *Mile 4, Zimovia Hwy. (mailing address: Box 1199, Wrangell 99929), tel. 907/874–2335. AE, DC, MC, V. Inexpensive–Moderate.*

Clarke Bed & Breakfast. Marlene Clarke offers B&B housing in her comfortable A-frame facing the harbor. Breakfasts include sourdough waffles, freshly ground coffee, and juice. *732 Case Ave. (mailing address: Box 1020, Wrangell 99929), tel. 907/ 874–2125 or 874–3863. No credit cards. Inexpensive.*

Southeast Region Lodging   **Alaska Bed & Breakfast Association** (Box 21890, Juneau 99802, tel. 907/586–2959. Inexpensive–Moderate). Contact this association for B&B accommodations in Juneau, Sitka, Skagway, Petersburg, Haines, Angoon, and Gustavus.

The Arts

Theater   Southeast Alaska's only professional theater company, **Perseverance Theater of Juneau** (914 3rd St., tel. 907/364–2421), covers everything from Broadway plays to Shakespeare to locally written material throughout the fall-winter-spring season.

Haines hosts a statewide drama competition called ACTFEST in April every other year. The festival is held at the Chilkat Center for the Arts at Fort Seward, with entries from community theaters both large and small. For details: City of Haines Tourism Office (Box 576, Haines 99827).

It may be stretching the word "theater" beyond its logical limits, but several communities stage summer musicals or melodramas for the entertainment of visitors. In Haines it's called "The Lust for Dust"; in Juneau, "The Lady Lou Revue"; in Ketchikan, "The Fish Pirate's Daughter"; and in Skagway, the "Days of '98 Show."

More cultural are the Chilkat Indian Dancers, who demonstrate Tlingit dancing twice weekly in Haines, and the New Archangel Dancers of Sitka, who perform authentic Russian Cossack–type dances whenever cruise ships are in port.

Call local information centers for times and dates.

Music Festivals   At least three music festivals are worthy of attention. The annual week-long **Alaska Folk Festival** (Box 21748, Juneau 99802) is staged each April in Juneau, drawing singers, musical storytellers, banjo masters, fiddlers, and even cloggers from all over the state and Yukon Territory.

Early in the summer Juneau is the scene of yet another musical gathering, this one called **Juneau Jazz 'n Classics** (Box 22152, Juneau 99802). As the name implies, it celebrates things musical from Brubeck (the trio having been guests during the 1988 gathering) to Bach.

Southeast Alaska's major classical music festival is the annual **Sitka Summer Music Festival** (Box 3333, Sitka 99835), a three-week June celebration of workshops, recitals, and concerts. Held in the Centennial Building, downtown.

Nightlife

Bars and Nightclubs

Socializing at a bar or "saloon" is an old Alaska custom, and the towns and cities of the Southeast Panhandle offer no exception. Following are some of the favorite gathering places in these parts:

Haines/Fort Seward

The Harbor Bar (Front St. at the Harbor, tel. 907/766–2442). Commerical fisherfolk gather here nightly at this old (1907) bar and restaurant. Sometimes live music.

Juneau

Alaskan Hotel Bar (167 S. Franklin St., tel. 907/586–1000). Equally popular with locals and distinctly less touristy. If live music isn't playing, an old-fashioned player piano usually is.

Bubble Room (127 N. Franklin St., tel. 907/586–2660). This comfortable lounge off the lobby in the Baranof Hotel is quiet—and the site (so it is said) of more legislative lobbying and decision making than in the nearby state capitol building. The chairs are soft, and so is the music from the piano bar.

The Red Dog Saloon (159 S. Franklin St., tel. 907/463–3777). Unquestionably the state's best-known frontier watering hole, it's in a new location but carries on in a tradition of sawdust on the floor, mounted bear and other game animals on the walls, and lots of historic photos. Live music and lively crowds when the cruise ships are in port.

Ketchikan

Charley's (208 Front St., tel. 907/225–5090). Located in the Ingersoll Hotel, and sort of '40s in character, Charley's is popular for sipping as well as for suppering. There's usually live music.

Frontier Saloon (127 Main St., tel. 907/225–9950). Don't expect gold-rush music or even country-western here. It's rock 'n' roll all the way.

Pioneer Bar (122 Front St., tel. 907/225–3210). This is the place for country-western, a popular spot for Ketchikan folk who like to listen well into the wee hours.

Petersburg

The Harbor Bar (Nordic Dr. near Dolphin St., tel. 907/775–4526). The name suggests the decor here, a place of ship's wheels, ship pictures, and a mounted 50-pound red snapper.

Kito's Kave (Sing Lee Alley, tel. 907/772–3207). Pretty loud as the night wears on, but most tourists seem to want to at least peek inside. Walls are covered with a variety of items, from Mexican paintings on velvet to stuffed fish and sports pennants. There are also pool tables and dart boards.

Sitka

Kadataan Lounge (330 Seward Ave., tel. 907/747–6241). Live soft rock music plays here in the lounge of the Westmark Shee Atika Hotel.

Skagway

Moe's Frontier Bar (Broadway between 4th and 5th Sts., tel. 907/983–2238). A long-time fixture on the Skagway scene, Moe's is likewise a bar much frequented by the local folk.

The Red Onion (Broadway at 2nd St., tel. 907/983–2222). You'll meet at least as many Skagway people here as you will visitors. Madame Jan, the proprietress of the establishment, will tell you all about the Red Onion's colorful past. (The upstairs was a gold-rush brothel.)

Wrangell   **The Stikine Bar** (107 Front St., tel. 907/874–3388). This can be a louder-as-the-night-gets-later bar when a rock band is playing, but it's a friendly place to meet the locals.

Index

Personal Itinerary

Departure *Date*

            Time

Transportation

Arrival *Date*   *Time*

Departure *Date*   *Time*

Transportation

Accommodations

Arrival *Date*   *Time*

Departure *Date*   *Time*

Transportation

Accommodations

Arrival *Date*   *Time*

Departure *Date*   *Time*

Transportation

Accommodations

Personal Itinerary

Arrival *Date*   *Time*

Departure *Date*   *Time*

Transportation

Accommodations

Arrival *Date*   *Time*

Departure *Date*   *Time*

Transportation

Accommodations

Arrival *Date*   *Time*

Departure *Date*   *Time*

Transportation

Accommodations

Arrival *Date*   *Time*

Departure *Date*   *Time*

Transportation

Accommodations

Personal Itinerary

Arrival *Date*   *Time*

Departure *Date*   *Time*

Transportation

Accommodations

Arrival *Date*   *Time*

Departure *Date*   *Time*

Transportation

Accommodations

Arrival *Date*   *Time*

Departure *Date*   *Time*

Transportation

Accommodations

Arrival *Date*   *Time*

Departure *Date*   *Time*

Transportation

Accommodations

Personal Itinerary

Arrival	*Date*	*Time*
Departure	*Date*	*Time*
Transportation		
Accommodations		

Arrival	*Date*	*Time*
Departure	*Date*	*Time*
Transportation		
Accommodations		

Arrival	*Date*	*Time*
Departure	*Date*	*Time*
Transportation		
Accommodations		

Arrival	*Date*	*Time*
Departure	*Date*	*Time*
Transportation		
Accommodations		

Personal Itinerary

Arrival *Date*   *Time*

Departure *Date*   *Time*

Transportation

Accommodations

Arrival *Date*   *Time*

Departure *Date*   *Time*

Transportation

Accommodations

Arrival *Date*   *Time*

Departure *Date*   *Time*

Transportation

Accommodations

Arrival *Date*   *Time*

Departure *Date*   *Time*

Transportation

Accommodations

Personal Itinerary

Arrival *Date*   *Time*

Departure *Date*   *Time*

Transportation

_____

_____

_____

Accommodations

_____

_____

_____

Arrival *Date*   *Time*

Departure *Date*   *Time*

Transportation

_____

_____

_____

Accommodations

_____

_____

_____

Arrival *Date*   *Time*

Departure *Date*   *Time*

Transportation

_____

_____

_____

Accommodations

_____

_____

_____

Arrival *Date*   *Time*

Departure *Date*   *Time*

Transportation

_____

_____

_____

Accommodations

_____

_____

_____

Addresses

Name	*Name*
Address	*Address*
Telephone	*Telephone*
Name	*Name*
Address	*Address*
Telephone	*Telephone*
Name	*Name*
Address	*Address*
Telephone	*Telephone*
Name	*Name*
Address	*Address*
Telephone	*Telephone*
Name	*Name*
Address	*Address*
Telephone	*Telephone*
Name	*Name*
Address	*Address*
Telephone	*Telephone*
Name	*Name*
Address	*Address*
Telephone	*Telephone*
Name	*Name*
Address	*Address*
Telephone	*Telephone*

Addresses

Name	*Name*
Address	*Address*
Telephone	*Telephone*
Name	*Name*
Address	*Address*
Telephone	*Telephone*
Name	*Name*
Address	*Address*
Telephone	*Telephone*
Name	*Name*
Address	*Address*
Telephone	*Telephone*
Name	*Name*
Address	*Address*
Telephone	*Telephone*
Name	*Name*
Address	*Address*
Telephone	*Telephone*
Name	*Name*
Address	*Address*
Telephone	*Telephone*
Name	*Name*
Address	*Address*
Telephone	*Telephone*

Fodor's Travel Guides

U.S. Guides

Alaska
Arizona
Boston
California
Cape Cod, Martha's
  Vineyard, Nantucket
The Carolinas & the
  Georgia Coast
The Chesapeake
  Region
Chicago
Colorado
Disney World & the
  Orlando Area
Florida
Hawaii

Las Vegas, Reno,
  Tahoe
Los Angeles
Maine,Vermont,
  New Hampshire
Maui
Miami & the
  Keys
National Parks
  of the West
New England
New Mexico
New Orleans
New York City
New York City
  (Pocket Guide)

Pacific North Coast
Philadelphia & the
  Pennsylvania
  Dutch Country
Puerto Rico
  (Pocket Guide)
The Rockies
San Diego
San Francisco
San Francisco
  (Pocket Guide)
The South
Santa Fe, Taos,
  Albuquerque
Seattle &
  Vancouver

Texas
USA
The U. S. & British
  Virgin Islands
The Upper Great
  Lakes Region
Vacations in
  New York State
Vacations on the
  Jersey Shore
Virginia & Maryland
Waikiki
Washington, D.C.
Washington, D.C.
  (Pocket Guide)

Foreign Guides

Acapulco
Amsterdam
Australia
Austria
The Bahamas
The Bahamas
  (Pocket Guide)
Baja & Mexico's Pacific
  Coast Resorts
Barbados
Barcelona, Madrid,
  Seville
Belgium &
  Luxembourg
Berlin
Bermuda
Brazil
Budapest
Budget Europe
Canada
Canada's Atlantic
  Provinces

Cancun, Cozumel,
  Yucatan Peninsula
Caribbean
Central America
China
Czechoslovakia
Eastern Europe
Egypt
Europe
Europe's Great Cities
France
Germany
Great Britain
Greece
The Himalayan
  Countries
Holland
Hong Kong
India
Ireland
Israel
Italy

Italy 's Great Cities
Jamaica
Japan
Kenya, Tanzania,
  Seychelles
Korea
London
London
  (Pocket Guide)
London Companion
Mexico
Mexico City
Montreal &
  Quebec City
Morocco
New Zealand
Norway
Nova Scotia,
  New Brunswick,
  Prince Edward
  Island
Paris

Paris (Pocket Guide)
Portugal
Rome
Scandinavia
Scandinavian Cities
Scotland
Singapore
South America
South Pacific
Southeast Asia
Soviet Union
Spain
Sweden
Switzerland
Sydney
Thailand
Tokyo
Toronto
Turkey
Vienna & the Danube
  Valley
Yugoslavia

Wall Street Journal Guides to Business Travel

Europe
International Cities
Pacific Rim
USA & Canada

Special-Interest Guides

Bed & Breakfast and
  Country Inn Guides:
  Mid-Atlantic Region
  New England
  The South
  The West

Cruises and Ports
  of Call
Healthy Escapes
Fodor's Flashmaps
  New York

Fodor's Flashmaps
  Washington, D.C.
Shopping in Europe
Skiing in the USA &
  Canada

Smart Shopper's
  Guide to London
Sunday in New York
Touring Europe
Touring USA